Nations and Nationalism:
A Global Historical Overview

VOLUME 4

1989 to Present

Nations and Nationalism: A Global Historical Overview

VOLUME 4

1989 to Present

GUNTRAM H. HERB

DAVID H. KAPLAN

Editors

ABC CLIO

SANTA BARBARA, CALIFORNIA   DENVER, COLORADO   OXFORD, ENGLAND

Copyright 2008 by ABC-CLIO, Inc.

Library of Congress Cataloging-in-Publication Data

Nations and nationalism : a global historical overview / Guntram H. Herb and
David H. Kaplan, editors.
   p. cm.
 Includes bibliographical references and index.
 ISBN 978-1-85109-907-8 (alk. paper)
1. History, Modern—18th century. 2. History, Modern—19th century. 3. History,
Modern—20th century. 4. Nationalism—History. I. Herb, Guntram Henrik, 1959–
II. Kaplan, David H., 1960–

 D299.N37 2008
 320.54—dc22

                                    2008004478

12 11 10 09 08   1 2 3 4 5 6 7 8 9 10

This book is also available on the World Wide Web as an ebook. Visit abc-clio.com for details.

ABC-CLIO, Inc.
130 Cremona Drive, P.O. Box 1911
Santa Barbara, California 93116-1911

Senior Production Editor Cami Cacciatore
Production Editor Kristine Swift
Production Manager Don Schmidt
Media Manager Caroline Price
Media Editor Katherine Jackson
File Management Coordinator Paula Gerard

This book is printed on acid-free paper ∞

Manufactured in the United States of America

Nations and Nationalism: A Global Historical Overview

VOLUME 4

1989 to Present

Contents

List of Contributors

Marco Adria
University of Alberta

Christopher A. Airriess
Ball State University

Mohammed Hassen Ali
Georgia State University

Stephen Alomes
Deakin University

Celia Applegate
University of Rochester

Christopher P. Atwood
Indiana University

Ghania Azzout
University of Algiers

Alan Bairner
Loughborough University

Frederic Barberà
Lancaster University

Joshua Barker
University of Toronto

Roderick J. Barman
University of British Columbia

Patrick Barr-Melej
Ohio University

Berch Berberoglu
University of Nevada, Reno

Stefan Berger
University of Manchester

Chris Bierwirth
Murray State University

Brett Bowden
University of New South Wales at
   the Australian Defence Force Academy

David Brandenberger
University of Richmond

David Brown
Murdoch University

Linda Bryder
University of Auckland

Melanie E. L. Bush
Adelphi University

Roderick D. Bush
St. John's University

Juan Manuel Carrión
University of Puerto Rico

Sun-Ki Chai
University of Hawaii

Colin M. Coates
York University

Saul B. Cohen
Queens College CUNY

Jerry Cooney
Louisville University (emeritus professor)

Stella Coram
Independent Scholar

Stéphane Corcuff
University of Lyon

Jeffrey J. Cormier
University of Western Ontario

Ralph Coury
Fairfield University

Philippe Couton
University of Ottawa

Kathryn Crameri
University of Sydney

Ben Curtis
Seattle College

Patrice M. Dabrowski
Harvard University

Dev Raj Dahal
Friedrich-Ebert-Stiftung Nepal

Gertjan Dijkink
University of Amsterdam

Jason Dittmer
University College London

Chris Dixon
University of Queensland

Christine Doran
Charles Darwin University

Maria Dowling
St. Mary's College

Stéphane Dufoix
Universite Paris X–Nanterre

Kevin C. Dunn
Hobart and William Smith Colleges

Jordana Dym
Skidmore College

Jonathan Eastwood
Washington and Lee University

Aygen Erdentug
Bilkent University

Kyle T. Evered
Michigan State University

Søren Forchhammer
University of Copenhagen

Will Fowler
University of St. Andrews

Michael E. Geisler
Middlebury College

Paul Gilbert
University of Hull

Eagle Glassheim
University of British Columbia

Arnon Golan
Haifa University

Liah Greenfeld
Boston University

Jouni Häkli
University of Tampere

Seyoum Hameso
University of East London

Paul Hamilton
Brock University

Samira Hanifi
University of Algiers

Dennis Hart
Kent State University

David Allen Harvey
New College of Florida

Stephen Heathorn
McMaster University

Ulf Hedetoft
Aalborg University

Jennifer Heuer
University of Massachusetts, Amherst

Vernon Hewitt
University of Bristol

Helen Hintjens
Institute of Social Studies, The Netherlands

Yaroslav Hrytsak
Central European University

Hugh Hudson
Georgia State University

Bonny Ibhawoh
McMaster University

Grigory Ioffe
Radford University

Zachary Irwin
Penn State University–Erie,
    The Behrend College

Tareq Y. Ismael
University of Calgary

Nils Jacobsen
University of Illinois–Urbana-Champaign

Laura Dudley Jenkins
University of Cincinnati

William Jenkins
York University

Steve Jobbitt
University of Toronto

Lonnie R. Johnson
Austrian-American Educational Commission
    (Fulbright Commission), Vienna

Rhys Jones
University of Wales, Aberystwyth

Cynthia Joseph
Monash University

John E. Joseph
University of Edinburgh

Gregory Jusdanis
The Ohio State University

Aristotle A. Kallis
Lancaster University

Antoni Kapcia
Nottingham University

Martha Kaplan
Vassar College

Sharon Kelly
University of Toronto

James Kennedy
University of Edinburgh

Robert Kerr
University of Central Oklahoma

P. Christiaan Klieger
Oakland Museum of California

David B. Knight
University of Guelph

Hans Knippenberg
University of Amsterdam

Taras Kuzio
George Washington University

Albert Lau
National University of Singapore

Orion Lewis
University of Colorado, Boulder

Hong-Ming Liang
The College of St. Scholastica

Catherine Lloyd
University of Oxford

Ouassila Loudjani
University of Algiers

Norrie MacQueen
University of Dundee

Paul Maddrell
Aberystwyth University

Fouad Makki
Cornell University

Virginie Mamadouh
University of Amsterdam

Christopher Marsh
Baylor University

Warren Mason
Miami University, Ohio

John Maynard
University of Newcastle, Australia

John M. McCardell Jr.
Middlebury College

John McLane
Northwestern University

Kim McMullen
Kenyon College

Neil McWilliam
Duke University

Nenad Miscevic
Central European University

Graeme Morton
University of Guelph

Joane Nagel
University of Kansas

Byron Nordstrom
Gustavus Adolphus College

Kevin C. O'Connor
Gonzaga University

Shannon O'Lear
University of Kansas

Steven Oluic
United States Military Academy

Kenneth R. Olwig
Swedish University of Agricultural Sciences

Brian S. Osborne
Queen's University

Cynthia Paces
The College of New Jersey

Razmik Panossian
International Centre for Human Rights and
    Democratic Development

Christopher Paulin
Manchester Community College

Hooman Peimani
Bradford University

Nicola Pizzolato
Queen Mary University of London

Linda Racioppi
Michigan State University

Pauliina Raento
University of Helsinki

Jane M. Rausch
University of Massachusetts–Amherst

Elizabeth Rechniewski
University of Sydney

Angelo Restivo
Georgia State University

Elisa Roller
European Commission

Luis Roniger
Wake Forest University

Marianne Rostgaard
Aalborg University

Victor Roudometof
University of Cyprus

Mona Russell
East Carolina University

Jörg Schendel
Independent Scholar

Conrad Schetter
University of Bonn

Klaus Schleicher
University of Hamburg

Katherine O'Sullivan See
Michigan State University

Nanda R. Shrestha
Florida A&M University

Daniel Speich
ETH Zurich

Alberto Spektorowski
Tel Aviv University

Daniel Stone
University of Winnipeg

Christine Straehle
University of Quebec at Montreal

Laszlo Strausz
Georgia State University

William H. Swatos Jr.
Association for the Sociology of Religion

Ray Taras
University of Colorado

Jessica Teets
University of Colorado, Boulder

Anne Marie Todd
San Jose State University

Anna Triandafyllidou
Hellenic Foundation for European and
    Foreign Policy

Toon van Meijl
University of Nijmegen

Neil Waters
Middlebury College

Peter J. Weber
University of Applied Languages (SDI),
    Munich

Ben Wellings
The Australian National University

George W. White
Frostburg State University

Joseph M. Whitmeyer
University of North Carolina, Charlotte

Peter Wien
University of Maryland

Michael Wood
Dawson College

Kathleen Woodhouse
Rutgers University

David N. Yaghoubian
California State University, San Bernardino

Takashi Yamazaki
Osaka City University

Antonina Zhelyazkova
International Center for Minority Studies and
    Intercultural Relations, Sofia, Bulgaria

Research Assistants
Gruia Badescu
Zachary Hecht-Leavitt
Jonathan Hsu
Kathleen Woodhouse

Cartography
Conor J. Stinson
Jonathan Hsu

Preface

What is a nation? What is nationalism? What does it mean to examine them in global perspective? We conceive of a nation or national identity as a form of loyalty. People have a multitude of loyalties: to family, friends, places, clubs, institutions, regions, countries, even to their place of work or brands of products. What distinguishes loyalty to a nation is the primacy it holds on people's allegiance. It is so powerful that people are willing to give their lives to ensure the continued existence of the group members and territory that make up their nation. By extension, we call nationalism the process that defines, creates, and expresses this essential loyalty to the nation. We view the term nationalism in a neutral sense. While this process can take extreme forms and lead to violent aggression and the extermination of others, nationalism can also be benign and form the basis for peaceful coexistence.

Nations and nationalism have found a bewildering range of expressions across the world and through time, and it is this geographic and temporal variation that we seek to address in a systematic fashion. Given the sheer number of nations that exist or have existed historically—some scholars argue that there are as many as 4,000–5,000 in just the contemporary era—our global perspective does not attempt to be comprehensive. Instead we have chosen to follow cross-sections through time and space. We identify major historical eras in the development of nations and nationalism to examine characteristic themes and representative cases from all major regions of the world.

Our emphasis is on depth rather than breadth. The 146 entries in this encyclopedia are full-length articles that go in depth to cover major debates and issues instead of brief descriptions of general features. They are authored by reputable scholars and try to provide accessible introductions to topics that are ambiguous, complex, and frequently misunderstood. Because literature on nations and nationalism arguably ranks among the most diverse and convoluted, our goal is to provide students, nonspecialists, and even junior scholars with concise information on this subject. In deciding what cases and themes to use, we take representative examples from each world region. These run the gamut from large powerful nations such as China and Russia to smaller nations that do not enjoy any form of sovereignty, like Tibet and Wales. We try to cover both prosperous nations of the developed world along with ex-colonial nations in the less-developed world. Similarly, some nations only appear during one time period, and others do not appear at all, because the most important consideration for us was that at least one representative example from all major regions of the world was included, even if scholarship has sorely neglected or sidelined that area, such as in Africa.

The selection of specific themes and cases that are treated intensively means that our coverage will have some unavoidable gaps. For example, there are no thematic chapters that treat race independently. This omission is not because we consider the issue to be of little significance, but because we feel that race is so elemental to discussions of nations and nationalism that it cannot be separated out. Similarly, it was not always possible to stick to the neat historical categorization into the four time periods. Some of our entries bridge several volumes to provide the most effective treatment of individual cases and themes.

This encyclopedia is arranged chronologically in four volumes. The first volume traces the origins and formative processes of nations and nationalism from 1770 to 1880. The second volume covers the aggressive intensification of nationalism during the age of imperialism, from 1880 to 1945. The third volume deals with the decline of nationalism in the aftermath of the Second World War, from 1945 to 1989. The final volume outlines the transformations of nationalism since the end of the Cold War in 1989.

All 104 country essays have the same format, and each is approximately 4,000 words. Each includes a chronology to position the reader in time; a discursive essay on main features; illustrations to help the reader visualize specific issues, situations, or persons; and a brief bibliography to guide additional inquiries. The case study essays also contain sidebars that highlight unique events, persons, or institutions. The main essays all contain five sections that help structure the inquiry and provide a universal key to access the information: (1) "Situating the Nation" places the national case in a historical, political, social, and geographic context; (2) "Instituting the Nation" examines key actors and institutions as well as philosophical foundations; (3) "Defining the Nation" discusses the role of ethno-cultural, civilizational, and geographic markers in creating the us–them distinction that is at the heart of national identity; (4) "Narrating the Nation" addresses particular events, stories, and myths that are used to create a community of belonging; and (5) "Mobilizing and Building the Nation" focuses on actions and strategies that help legitimize the national idea.

Our 42 thematic essays address the interplay between national identity, politics, culture, and society and are generally 6,000 words long. They focus on geopolitical contexts and economic conditions, such as postcolonialism and globalization; social relations, such as gender and class; dominant philosophies and ideologies, such as fascism and fundamentalism; and nationalist cultural creations and expressions, such as art, literature, music, or sports. Though specific themes vary in each of the four volumes, each of the thematic essays include bibliographies and illustrations, and touch on the following questions: (1) How were the issues/phenomena under discussion important? (2) What is the background and what are the origins? (3) What are major dimensions and impacts on different groups, societal conditions, and ideas? (4) What are the consequences and ramifications of this issue for the character and future development of nations and nationalism?

We feel that our encyclopedia makes an important addition to the current reference literature on nations and nationalism. Existing encyclopedias in the field generally contain only very brief entries (Spira 1999, 2002; Leoussi 2001); are dated (Snyder 1990); neglect such civic nations as the United States or Switzerland (Minahan 2002); or are uneven because they combine a few excessively long survey articles with several extremely short entries (Motyl 2001). A universal and significant shortcoming is the lack of maps and illustrations. Except for a limited number of general maps and select illustrations in Minahan, the other works do not have a single map, figure, or image. We believe that an encyclopedia on nationalism must contain visual information for it to effectively convey the contexts within which nationalist movements arose and to depict the important symbology that was used to galvanize national sentiment.

Our encyclopedia also offers a unique and novel way to access information on nations and nationalisms. The thematic entries give insights into the larger contexts for the country essays and illustrate linkages among them in regard to general topics such as national education. The individual country entries allow readers to compare and contrast developments in different places and to examine trends in major regions of the world during different time periods. Finally, since some of the places and themes appear in all four volumes, it is possible to trace developments and identify linkages not only among places, but also through time.

We hope that this encyclopedia helps to further an understanding of perhaps the most influential set of identities and ideologies in the world today. We also hope that this collection of cases and themes selected across space and time sheds some light on the different ways in which these loyalties are manifested. While this encyclopedia constitutes a very large body of work, it can only scratch the surface of all of the different varieties inherent in a study of nations and nationalism. We encourage the reader to follow up on some of the selected readings that are listed at the end of each entry and to further explore some of the various cases and themes that have not been explicitly addressed.

References

Leoussi, Athena S. 2001. *Encyclopedia of Nationalism*. New Brunswick, NJ: Transaction.

Minahan, James. 2002. *Encyclopedia of Stateless Nations: Ethnic and National Groups around the World*. Westport, CT: Greenwood Press.

Motyl, Alexander J. 2001. *Encyclopedia of Nationalism*. San Diego: Academic Press.

Snyder, Louis. 1990. *Encyclopedia of Nationalism*. New York: Paragon House.

Spira, Thomas. 1999 (vol. 1), 2002 (vol. 2). *Nationalism and Ethnicity Terminologies: An Encyclopedic Dictionary and Research Guide*. Gulf Breeze, FL: Academic International Press.

Acknowledgments

An enormous undertaking such as this four-volume work could not be accomplished without the help of several individuals. Of course we would like to thank all of our contributors, who were wonderful about following formatting guidelines, making revisions, and cheerfully supplying additional material as the need arose. We are very saddened that one of our contributors, Jeffrey Cormier, did not live to see the publication of this work. We would also like to pay special thanks to the people at ABC-CLIO, among them Ron Boehm, Wendy Roseth, Kristin Gibson, and especially Alex Mikaberidze. The efforts of ABC-CLIO's publication team have allowed us to complete this project in a sustained and timely manner.

Above all we wish to extend our gratitude to those people who have worked tirelessly in assisting us in this endeavor. Their efforts are reflected throughout these four volumes. Kathleen Woodhouse from Kent State University was instrumental in helping to conceive of this project, in identifying and lining up the contributors, and in evaluating and editing each and every entry in Volumes 3 and 4. She also played a major part in the development of three of the essays. She has been an enormous asset and has worked tirelessly to see this project from start to finish.

Gruia Badescu, Zachary Hecht-Leavitt, Jonathan Hsu, and Conor Stinson provided invaluable assistance in Middlebury, Vermont. Their contributions would not have been possible without the generous support of Middlebury College, which is deeply appreciated. Zach and Gruia aided in identifying contributors, selecting illustrations, and managing numerous administrative tasks. Zach's excellent writing and editorial skills ensured that many of the entries authored by non-native English speakers were transformed into stylistically polished pieces. Gruia's remarkable linguistic skills and knowledge of the scholarship of nationalism allowed him to contribute deep insights to the review process as well as to the drafting of two introductory essays.

Jonathan Hsu and Conor Stinson are to be credited for the beautiful cartographic design. Producing maps for these volumes proved to be a challenging and enormous project. The maps needed to vary greatly in scale—from small areas, such as Estonia, to giant regions, such as Russia—but at the same time needed to allow for easy comparisons. The historical maps were particularly difficult given the numerous border changes that took place and the lack of good reference sources, but Jonathan mastered this hurdle with ease. He is not only a gifted cartographer but an excellent researcher.

Putting on the finishing touches to turn the massive manuscript and numerous images and maps into a coherent and beautiful set of volumes was also an enormous challenge, and we were fortunate to have the able assistance of Cami Cacciatore, Kristine Swift, and Kerry Jackson at ABC-CLIO and of Samuel Lazarus, Caitlin Sargent, and Mithra Harivandi at Middlebury College. Finally, we would like to thank our families for the unwavering support they gave us throughout this giant undertaking. We dedicate this work to the memory of David Woodward.

Introduction

Volume 4: 1989 to Present

This fourth and last volume covers the period roughly from 1989 until the present day. The year 1989 commenced with events that profoundly influenced the nature of national identity, which led to the development of new states and altered prevailing views of nationalism. Most obviously, this year witnessed the dismantlement of the Soviet Bloc and the Soviet Union itself. Several new states emerged as a result. But we can also view this modern era as a time in which nationalism reasserted itself. Before 1989, the world was locked in an ideological struggle between communism and capitalism. This struggle, conveniently placed within a political economy rubric, defined the global order and influenced how each nation envisioned itself. After 1989, communism was in demise. With the exception of some holdouts—China adheres on its face to the communist ideology (while rapidly building a market-driven economy), Cuba continues as an officially communist country (while eagerly courting Western tourism), and North Korea retains an intensely weird brand of totalitarianism—communism as an ideology no longer shapes the world order.

We can consider four changes as being of fundamental importance during this era. The first and most significant was the disintegration of the Soviet Bloc, culminating in the collapse of the Soviet Union itself and its replacement by 15 separate countries. The second would be the accelerated impact of globalization as the world became ever more connected in ways both good and bad. Third would be the growth of religious/nationalist movements that shook the world in ways unseen for several decades. The fourth and last change involves the new economic dynamism that has allowed some countries, particularly those that have hitherto been a part of the so-called Third World, to assert themselves through economic growth and development.

The consequences of the collapse of the Soviet Bloc have been so far-reaching that we have yet to experience all the ramifications. The most obvious consequence of this change—beginning with the people's revolutions in several Eastern European countries and ending with the collapse of the Soviet Union itself—was the end of the Cold War. The United States consequently emerged as the sole superpower in the world, what some would describe as a hyperpower without equal. These developments may have given American politicians and other countries an enhanced sense of the U.S. ability to shape global events and could have led to an overestimation of how much influence and power the United States truly had. It also appeared to signal an ideological shift as well. Frances Fukuyama's book, *The End of History*, called the collapse of the Soviet Bloc a victory for "Western" values and the triumph of economic and political liberalism.

This change also led to the creation of several new states and the resurgence of nationalism, particularly within Yugoslavia and the Soviet Union. The 1990s saw the bloody disintegration of Yugoslavia into its constituent republics. Accusations of genocide and ethnic cleansing followed the breakup of Yugoslavia into Slovenia, Croatia, Macedonia, and, most notably, Bosnia Herzegovina. Other countries began to split apart as well. Czechoslovakia quietly divided into the Czech Republic and Slovakia. Eritrea became independent from Ethiopia. The Soviet Union finally dissolved into 15 separate countries. And Russia itself was beset by a series of separatist movements. Notably, this period also saw the reintegration of Germany, which had been divided between its Eastern and Western halves for so long. The emergence of new states happened fitfully as new countries sought to align their newly founded political sovereignty with a national mission. Issues as in how to accommodate minority groups became very important. The political composition of these new states diverged. Some became true democracies, while others took on new forms of dictatorship and repression. Economic fortunes varied as well. Several of these newly independent states joined the ranks of the developed West and joined an expanded European Union. In other places, economic development was illusory.

The second major change that occurred during this modern era was continued globalization. Globalization has resulted from a shrinking world where people have the ability to interact with others across the world, an ability accentuated to levels unimagined just a few decades ago. The expansion of telecommunications networks allows for a virtually seamless outsourcing of a variety of services. Brands have become globally omnipresent as more and more trade is interconnected. One defining feature of globalization lies in the growth of the World Wide Web and Internet access that allows everywhere to be part of a virtual community. The era began with the Chinese uprising in Tiananmen Square in 1989, broadcast largely by fax machines. News of later insurgencies—notably the Zapatista movement in the Mexican state of Chiapas—were posted on the Web. Immigration, which has been a feature of society since the very beginning of the nationalist era, has changed its complexion as it has become more possible for people to keep in touch with one another and retain ties to their national communities. Transnationalism among the wealthy and others is far more common. In fact, the era has been marked by an increased "hybridity," where identities are less discrete and may straddle two or more cultures—the era of "Spanglish."

There is a dark side to this development, however, as globalization threatens local control and community interests. Transnational corporations are able to conduct business everywhere, and many fear that they feel no allegiance to anywhere. Corporations both large and small run roughshod over cultural sensibilities and the interests of nations. A bland "McWorld" typified by ubiquitous golden arches and Mickey Mouse represents a loss of economic autonomy and local identity.

The growth of new social movements during this era is thus based on a desire to fight back against the faceless transnational corporations and regain some local control. Labor, too, was hit by the increased flexibility of capital and its ability to obtain the cheapest labor anywhere in the world. The demonstrations against the World Trade Organization in Seattle brought voice to these frustrations.

The third major change involves the growth of religious movements, often fused with new nationalist movements. Of course, religious identity is nothing new, but it began to take on an added level of urgency as several countries adopted a stridently religious form of government and recast their national identity along fundamentalist lines. The Iranian revolution of 1979 heralded this shift, later joined by a series of nationalist religious movements based in the Middle East and elsewhere. Such movements are not confined to states or governments. Radical Islamic movements, most prominently Al Qaeda and Hezbollah, attempt to achieve through violent means what they believe cannot be accomplished otherwise.

The events of September 11, 2001, demonstrated that terrorism rooted in a fundamentalist religious ideology could strike anybody at any time. This event restructured how Americans and many in the West view their own identity and also modified the politics and cultural values of some existing states. To some it also crystallized inherent conflicts among different religio-national ideologies. Samuel Huntington's book, *The Clash of Civilizations*, vividly describes some of the tensions between Christian and Muslim and other religious realms. While Huntington's overall thesis has been denigrated by many, notably Edward Said who criticized his use of simplistic abstractions, the argument seemed to gain traction in public policy circles. The so-called War on Terror was initiated to root out terrorist cells and those countries that provide safe havens for them. Most notably, the war in Iraq was cast as an attempt to eliminate the terrorists over there before they could come over here.

This new religious fundamentalism challenged some of the forces of globalization, especially the saturation of Western values, Western commercialism, and Western corporate interests. Samuel Barber's book, *Jihad versus McWorld*, characterized the tension between these two forces of religious fundamentalism and globalization.

The fourth major change taking place within the last two decades has been the rapid economic growth in some countries that were previously impoverished. While the economy in much of the developed world stagnated, and while much of sub-Saharan Africa continued to be mired in extreme levels of poverty, several national economies expanded quite rapidly. The rise of the so-called Asian Tigers has been particularly notable. Countries such as South Korea, Taiwan, Hong Kong, and Singapore moved from a source of cheap labor to major centers of capital investments. Their prosperity began to rival the West. Other countries, particularly within east and southeast Asia, acted to develop their economies in fundamental ways. There have been other successes as well. Latin American countries such as

Brazil have begun to flex their economic muscles. Chile, during the 1970s and 1980s under the thumb of a military dictatorship, has made some spectacular advances.

One interesting facet of the economic resurgence along the Asian Pacific Rim has been the idea—promulgated particularly by Singapore's premier—that Asian countries do not necessarily have to follow the Western political model to advance economically. In particular, the two demographic giants China and India have begun to experience rapid economic growth. Both of these countries are very different from the United States and countries within Europe. They have different views of nationalism and different ways in which they project their identities. Yet they both seem to be on the verge of overtaking several of the older, richer economies, and the expectation is that both countries will become the world's largest economies by century's end.

Thomas Friedman's book, *The World Is Flat*, discusses how recent technological and social changes have rapidly expanded access and opportunity to places once isolated and deprived. The necessity for members of nations throughout the world to participate in an increasingly seamless economy will even the playing field and alter the global balance of economic power. While an optimist might view this development as a deterrent to future conflict, the past shows us that growing wealth quite often seeks greater political sway and an assertion of national goals. National identity and nationalist ideology will likely retain their potency for years to come.

DAVID H. KAPLAN

Cinema and National Identity

Angelo Restivo and Laszlo Strausz

The problem of cinema's relationship to national identity is a complex one. On the one hand, film history has traditionally been written as the histories of various national cinemas (French cinema, Iranian cinema, etc.), and indeed the national origin of a film continues to be a major classification device for film festivals. On the other hand, certain national cinemas—particularly Hollywood, and more recently Bollywood, the prolific Indian film industry centered in Bombay—reach global audiences and in many nations reach a larger audience than do indigenous national film. Thus, the extent to which any national cinema can be said to reflect or to express a particular national culture is complicated by uneven exchanges in the global flow of images. To further complicate matters, in its short history of barely over a century, the cinema has passed through four major phases of development: early cinema (from 1895 to the mid-1910s); a "classical" period (mid-1910s to 1960); a period of modernization and "new waves" (from the mid-1950s to the 1980s, but continuing to the present); and currently a period of media convergence, in which cinema is situated within a much larger digital image environment (television, home video, video games, and the Internet). Each of these four phases is characterized by a distinct mode of production, as well as by different forms of distribution, different reception environments, and even different audience demographics.

Origins

Industrial Art and the Mass Audience

The invention of moving pictures in 1895 came at the end of a century that had seen the emergence of great modern nation-states in Europe and North America. While the earliest films—the *actualités* of Lumière, the Neapolitan city films of Elvira Notari—recorded everyday events and were grounded in the local, by 1913 the standard-length feature film emerged, along with narrative conventions that allowed filmmakers to tell more complex stories in images. At the same time, the cinema, which in the first years of its life was more an attraction than a respectable mode of entertainment like the theater, broadened its audience to include the middle classes. Thus, as the cinema-going public became more and more a cross section of the nation, it is not surprising that some of the most important films of the post-1913 period were ones that attempted to tell the national story.

In the United States, for example, David Wark Griffith made the controversial *The Birth of a Nation* in 1914, and Abel Gance made the epic film *Napoleon* in 1927, both of which were seen by millions. Both of these films were set in critical historic moments in the national history and allowed a mass audience to collectively share a vision of the nation's imagined origin and destiny, regardless of their inaccurate or exclusionary vision.

Griffith's vision of America in *The Birth of a Nation* proved incendiary. While President Wilson, a former historian, described the film as "history written with lightning," liberal intellectuals and politicians condemned the work for its racist portrayal of African Americans; the film sparked riots in several cities. In *Birth*, Griffith tells the story of a northern and a southern family during the Civil War. At the very beginning of the film, he spends considerable time establishing the audience's sympathies with the southern slaveowners by portraying them as well-meaning, sympathetic gentlemen. As the film propels forward, however, the director switches back and forth between the two families, using an omniscient storytelling technique that allows the viewer to witness the hardships of the war on both sides. While *Birth* clearly depicts the southern plantation life as idyllic and superior, the sacrifices of the opponent, the North, are also dramatized by Griffith as part of a national effort.

The film romanticizes the idea of a nation that does not change. Griffin's adaptation of Thomas Dixon's novel *The Clansman* offers a xenophobic historical vision, which is as much a document of American social history as of film history. Both in the book and the film, social unrest begins with the mixing of the races. The liberated African American slaves are depicted not only as unable to assimilate into a nation envisioned by Griffith but also as brutes that represent a threat to society. According to the film, the "real nation" consists of the North and the South, uniting to heal the wounds of the Civil War and Reconstruction. However, African Americans are excluded from this image of the nation by being portrayed as rapists, drunks, and criminals. In addition, this exclusion is manifested in the film's actual production by the fact that the roles of the black characters in the film are played by white actors with their faces painted black.

The problematic nature of Griffith's film stems from the fact that his racist views were presented via techniques that revolutionized film form. The director frequently relies on the power of closer framings to show the emotional state of his characters and so create audience identification. *Birth* also makes use of point-of-view shots, which put the spectator in the visual position of select characters. Both of these techniques are used in the film to show the viewer the threat of miscegenation for innocent white characters. It was especially Griffith's use of parallel editing (two different lines of action happening at different places but at the same time), however, that showed how an effective storytelling technique can create powerful emotional responses in the audiences.

Critically, Griffith and his work have posed a problem for film studies because, even though he was a pioneer in film form, thematically his work was reactionary.

Members of the National Association for the Advancement of Colored People picket under the marquee of the Republic movie theater against race discrimination featured in the movie *The Birth of a Nation* in New York, 1947. They carry signs asking for a ban on hate films. (Corbis)

Probably the best answer to this conundrum has been offered by Soviet filmmaker and theorist Sergei Eisenstein, who made the case that parallel editing echoes a basic Manichean aspect of American social life. According to this argument, parallel editing is a formal expression of the need to divide the world into black and white categories. Thus, Eisenstein outlined an early and structural explanation for how cinema might display the deeper characteristics of a national culture.

For the Soviet filmmakers during the early 1920s, whose aesthetic also centered on editing and montage but in a different way than in U.S. filmmaking, cinema proved a very effective way to project an image of the nation, which emanated from the collectivist communist ideology. In a country where large parts of the population were illiterate, motion pictures represented a highly efficient way of depicting a collective and classless national identity while agitating for an egalitarian economy. This view of the centrality of the cinema to the revolutionary efforts of the nation was expressed by Lenin, who is often quoted as saying, "for us, cinema is the most influential art form." In 1919, the former Russian film industry was nationalized. This allowed the Communist Party to use film to communicate its political views to the masses that were scattered across a vast country.

Formally, the editing-centered style of the Montage School could express abstract political concepts in a nonverbal form. The aim was to create an international language of the image, which would transcend cultures and help export the revolutionary ideology of the Soviets to other countries. In Eisenstein's 1925 film *Battleship Potemkin*, the crew of the vessel revolts against their oppressive leaders after being systematically abused. The ship and the entire conflict serve as a microcosm of the nation and, more broadly, the struggle of all working classes. In *Battleship Potemkin*, first the sailors unite to stand up against the captain, then the shipyard workers of Odessa unite, and finally the entire fleet joins the revolt. The allegory of the ship, which serves as a source for spreading the communist ideology, was strengthened by Eisenstein's idea of the intellectual montage in which editing was used to create connections between a statue of an awakening lion and the rising working classes. Another of the Soviet montage directors, Dziga Vertov, in *Man with a Movie Camera* (1928) took a different route to express the revolutionary character of the new nation. In the film, the director combined documentary footage with political commitment and ideological statement. By following one day in the life of a modern city and its working-class inhabitants, Vertov depicts the everyday as spectacular and extraordinary. The viewers can recognize themselves as characters in the film and thus as equal members of the body of the nation.

In one of the earliest studies on motion pictures and national culture, Siegfried Kracauer analyzed German Weimar cinema (of the 1910s and 1920s) and its connections to national identity. *From Caligari to Hitler* (1947) examines the connections between a particular form of cinematic expression and the collective imagination of a nation. According to Kracauer, predominant psychological dispositions of post–World War I Germany can be exposed by analyzing German films produced between 1918 and 1933. He argues that the connections between cinema and national culture are complex, but more direct than that of other artistic media, for two reasons: films are not the products of individuals but of collectives, and they address the widest possible audiences. Therefore, cinema sheds light on what is not said, or, on what is hidden in the "underground" of the social psyche. The motion picture camera records normally unperceived behavior, what he called "visual hieroglyphs," automatically.

Kracauer's main argument is as follows. As a result of the humiliation of Germany after World War I, German citizens fled into the fictional world of films that offered two general trends: diverse anti-authoritarian tendencies without a positive perspective, and the image of the war hero, a charismatic leader, who leads the nation out of its chaotic state. Films such as *The Cabinet of Dr Caligari* (Robert Wiene, 1919), *The Golem* (Paul Wegener, 1920), *The Last Laugh* (F. W. Murnau, 1924), and *Metropolis* (Fritz Lang, 1925) revolve around characters who are haunted by their historical or cultural milieus and find ways out of this situation by escapist strategies. The disturbed souls of Weimar cinema cannot be cured by any concrete social action; rebels of these films finally submit to the authorities they revolt against, and their recurring doubles, or doppelgangers, remind the viewer of their split personalities.

Kracauer concludes that Weimar cinema offers a precise portrayal of the German mentality, and later events confirm its validity. The rise of the Nazi Party and Hitler was an answer to the psychological disposition of the nation, which looked at itself as a defeated community without a historical perspective. The Expressionist films show that the historical events in Germany after 1933 had their roots in the collective unconscious of a nation, and this disposition is mirrored in the films produced during that period. Kracauer's argument has been criticized as simplistic, partly because he is charged with writing history "teleologically," that is, with the conclusion already predetermining the interpretation of the causes. Nevertheless, his work recognized that films are essential documents for understanding how each national culture represents itself and further made the point that the idea of the nation is only perceived against the background of a particular historical trauma, which the cinema can reveal in an encoded form.

Relevance

Realism as International Style

Whereas silent cinema was an international art form that made it easy to cross national borders (since language barriers were easily overcome via changing the intertitles), the diffusion of synchronous sound made "the talkies" less exportable. The need to translate and dub films for foreign markets not only increased production costs but also resulted in protectionist strategies as nations tried to defend their film markets from overseas products. Several European countries started to adopt protectionist rules to reduce the economic impact of Hollywood films. As the national film markets started to withdraw into themselves, the cinematic projection of the nation changed as well.

In the Soviet Union, cinema became a contested space between Socialist Realism and the Constructivism of the montage filmmakers. Behind the theoretical differences lay various political views about the role of art. Should art realistically mirror existing social settings and character interaction, or should it portray more abstract scenarios, social forces, and movements? After the early 1930s, the Stalinist state started to exert power over a cinema dominated by the Montage School filmmakers, who did not uncritically support the party. In the subsequent years of Socialist Realist cinema, films became straightforward celebrations of the existing order without critical or artistic challenges. The "production films," which focused on the joys of collective work and mechanization, and the "partisan films," which focused on the heroic army's resistance to fascism, all depicted heroes designed to serve as role models for the Soviet people and to exhibit loyalty to the party. The pluralism of the montage filmmakers gave way to a monolithic Stalinist cinema and put an end to diverse and conceptual depictions of the nation. These were replaced with a one-dimensional propagandistic style that, ironically, closely resembled the classical Hollywood style.

The fascist countries in 1930s' Europe also realized the importance of cinema and used the medium either to compete with the Hollywood product as a sign of nationalistic pride (Italy) or to mobilize the audiovisual power of film in the orchestration of political spectacles (Germany). Certainly it is true that more than 50 percent of the films in Nazi Germany were light comedies and musicals, and the Third Reich created its own image by commissioning a broad range of films beyond the political spectacle. However, the most well-known example of Nazi cinema remains Leni Riefenstahl's pseudo-documentary *Triumph of the Will* (1935), which records a rally of the Nazi Party that became a modern media event staged for the motion picture cameras. Besides the monumental sets, the Führer is depicted as a deity who gives shape to the needs of the nation and its people.

Goebbels, the Nazi minister of propaganda, remarked that German films should learn from the enemy, especially in their ability to intoxicate mass audiences. The enemy, of course, was Hollywood. In Hollywood, the 1930s brought about the golden age of classical style and genre perfection. In terms of projecting images of the nation for mass consumption, two interesting and opposing genres to look at are the Western and film noir. Both create a dualistic world where social experiences are depicted through the prism of genre iconography. Scholars of genre theory agree that the recurring narrative types of the genres epitomize problems that society revisits in a symbolic form. In the case of the Western, this problem revolves around the whole issue of American "exceptionalism," the idea that, because of the uniqueness of the American experience and the existence of the frontier, America always afforded individuals the opportunity to escape the class hierarchies of Europe and engage in a process of self-invention in the un-developed West. However, in this genre film, a conflict unfolds between the forces of development and the lack of institutional and legal structures that will allow personal development to flourish. The setting for this clash is the wild frontier that literally and metaphorically represents a dividing line between the two sides and where the status quo is most often embodied by the outlaw or the Native American Indians. Character agency plays a key role in the world of the Western. For example, the law of the community is best protected by the actions of a lone, heroic individual, usually unattached to any established community. Thus, the character of the Western hero serves to represent the very contradiction in America's conception of itself insofar as he is necessary for the establishment of law and order, while, at the same time, he feels the need to constantly escape its confines.

Whereas the setting for Western films is the small town on the frontier, gang-ster films of the 1940s (film noir) look at the coexistence of the criminal under-world and the world we know in the urban spaces of large cities. The numerous connections between the two spheres do not allow for a clear separation, and thus the film noir protagonists interiorize this split. The prospects for individual agency are portrayed much more cynically here than in the Western. The estab-lished world and the underworld cannot be separated in the lives of the film noir protagonists, and the Freudian conflict of consciousness and the unconscious often ends with the demise of the hero. The Western and film noir, despite their differences, both project an image of the nation that is structured around the dualistic struggle of opposing forces. Using a style that scholars describe as clas-sicism, the two genres allow the audiences to identify with specific characters, thus positioning themselves on either side of the film's conflict, though of course identifying with the official hero by the film's end.

Dimensions

Popular Fronts, Resistance, Decolonization

The emergence of Italian neorealism in 1943 represents a decisive break from the various realisms of the major national cinemas of the 1930s. Neorealism became extremely influential worldwide as a "counter-style" to the dominant language of the commercial national cinemas. The early neorealist films (1943–1948) devel-oped in a period of great instability in the Italian nation. In 1943 Mussolini was ousted from power, Italy switched sides in the war, and partisan forces mounted resistance to both German and Italian fascists. Indeed, this resistance to fascism and Italy's liberation by the Allied powers provided important subjects for neo-realist films. Rossellini's *Open City* (1945), for example, dramatized everyday life in Rome under the German occupation, whereas his later *Paisa* (1946)—whose title in Italian has the double meaning of "home town" and "nation"—told a chronological story of Italy's liberation in six vignettes that moved from Sicily up through the peninsula.

But it was the style in which these stories were told that made neorealism such a revolution in film language. Neorealist films preferred the actual location to the studio set, nonprofessional actors to professionals, and scripts that, although fictional, were based on real historical incidents as remembered by the people. In other words, neorealist films were not interested in telling the official history of the nation but rather in telling the national story by way of "counter-memories," which were often excluded from the official history books. The power of *Open City*, for example, comes partly from the shock of recognition that Italians had upon seeing such incidents as the looting of a bread shop by hungry citizens. At the premiere of Visconti's 1943 film *Ossessione*, an incensed Vittorio Mussolini, son of il Duce and head of the Italian film studios, was reported to have exclaimed, "This is not Italy!" It certainly wasn't the Italy of grand hotels and posh Riviera parties that had characterized much of the commercial cinema in Italy during the fascist period. The urgency and the unfinished quality that characterizes neorealist films reflect a nation that was in the difficult process of redefining itself. But more than this, there is an ethical dimension to neorealism that is probably the most important factor in its influence worldwide; cinema's power was its power to bear witness to the lives of those—especially the poor—who were left out of the official national narrative.

A moment in Vittorio DeSica's *Bicycle Thieves* (1948), the most beloved of the neorealist classics, can illustrate this ethical aspect. The story is simple: in a devastated postwar Rome where jobs and money are scarce, a young father finds that he can get a job, but only if he has a bicycle. Since his bicycle had already been pawned so that the family could survive, he and his wife decide to pawn the only thing of value they have left, their linens, to retrieve the bicycle. When they hand their linens over to the clerk, the camera follows the clerk across a large room until he arrives at a ladder. When the camera pans up, we see stacks upon stacks of other people's linen, all pawned out of desperation. In one quick stroke, the film makes us understand how this story of one man is only one of thousands.

In a sense, neorealism showed that it was possible for a national cinema to challenge the myths of national unity often promulgated in commercial national cinemas by showing audiences what was repressed in those mass-market features. Less a formula than an attitude, neorealist style has often been taken up in other national contexts, especially in the face of pressing national problems that official governments do not want the world to see. To give only one of hundreds of possible examples, Brazilian director Hector Babenco, in the film *Pixote* (1981), wanted to expose the problems of impoverished youth living in the *favelas* or makeshift shantytowns surrounding Rio and São Paulo, many of whom were forced by poverty and homelessness into lives of crime and who even became the target of police death squads. To tell the story, Babenco adopted a textbook neo-realist style, shooting on location in the *favelas*, casting nonprofessional teenag-ers in the film's lead roles, and developing storylines that came from the actual events the young boys experienced in their lives. The rawness and authenticity Babenco achieved in presenting his brutal and shocking material made the film an international sensation.

Of all of neorealism's many afterlives, perhaps the most significant is the way it helped shape filmmaking in the Third World context. In the 1950s, many young aspiring filmmakers from Latin America enrolled as students in Italy's national film school, the Centro Sperimentale di Cinematografia in Rome. Upon returning to their home countries, they developed a filmmaking practice—initially called "imperfect cinema" and later "Third Cinema"—that, while indebted to the urgency and immediacy of the neorealist program, pushed the aesthetic in important new directions. This approach was necessary because the very concept of a national cinema was quite different in Latin America than in the developed world for three reasons: (1) many of the Latin American nations were "client states" whose central governments could hardly be thought of as representing the people; (2) in terms of infrastructure and annual film output, the national cinemas of Latin America were relatively underdeveloped; and (3) foreign images, usually from Hollywood, circulated widely. The problem in this context was to decide what an Argentine cin-ema or a Chilean cinema would resemble and whether filmmakers could get be-yond the clichés of the gaucho films or the other populist genres in Latin America.

Cuba, because of its successful socialist revolution in 1959, took the lead by developing a vibrant new film culture that was able to express both the utopian aspirations and the recalcitrant problems faced by the new nation without falling into the trap of "socialist realism." In Argentina between 1966 and 1968, the col-lective Grupo Cine Liberación shot the epic, four-and-a-half-hour film *Hour of the Furnaces* (1968), a landmark of the new Latin American cinema. The film literally rewrites the history of Argentina, showing the relationships between the lives of the rich colonial elites and the exploited living conditions of the common people. Two of the filmmakers involved in the project, Fernando Solanas and Octavio Get-tino, followed up with a manifesto titled "Towards a Third Cinema," which served as a program for remaking national cinemas in the postcolonial nations. Third Cinema, they argued, should not strive for the technical perfection of First (i.e., Hollywood) and Second (i.e., European) cinemas but instead should exploit for political effect the limitations imposed by underdevelopment. This goal meant no beautiful images but instead images fraught with immediacy and truth. For-mally, their argument thus suggests connections both to "imperfect cinema" and, further back, to Italian neorealism. The manifesto goes further by arguing that, in the Third World, filmmakers must also rethink the systems of production and distribution of films. Thus, *Hour of the Furnaces* was produced collectively, with factory workers and students involved in the production, and shown directly to workers outside of the cinemas.

Modernization and New Waves

The economic booms of the 1950s in the United States and Western Europe, the rise of a new consumer culture, and the widespread diffusion of television, had a profound impact on the cinema. On the one hand, mainstream cinema attendance dropped as television provided in-home dissemination of popular entertainment, news, and product information. On the other hand, many young directors rebelled against the constraints of classical cinema and created vibrant "new waves," which reflected the energy, optimism, and exuberance of the youth cultures sweeping the West. In the case of France (which gave us the first self-proclaimed "new wave"), a group of young film critics at the journal *Cahiers du cinéma* programmatically attacked what they saw as an outmoded "tradition of quality" in French mainstream cinema, which they sarcastically dubbed the *cinéma du papa* ("cinema of the old man"). A typical "tradition of quality" film might be a reverent, middle-brow adaptation of a classic French story; but, according to the new wave critics, such films presented a view of Frenchness and French national culture that was more like a sanitized museum piece than a living expression of contemporary culture. Thus, when these critics began to make films in 1959, they created a picture of France unlike anything seen before. Their two main influences seemed paradoxical opposites: Italian neorealism and Hollywood genre filmmaking. From neorealism they borrowed location shooting and a focus on the immediacy of everyday experience. They took from Hollywood genre filmmaking its visual energy, perhaps because they sensed that the United States was less burdened by the weight of heritage.

Taken together, the French new wave films paint the most loving portrait of Paris ever put on celluloid, and they did this not by focusing on the clichéd national symbols of Paris such as the Eiffel Tower or the Champs-Elysées but rather by long scenes set in out-of-the-way cafes and bistros, with pinball machines tucked in the corners and Parisian traffic visible outside the plate-glass windows. Equally important, the directors' improvisatory style put onscreen entirely new social types inhabiting the modern consumerist metropolis; the director Jean-Luc Godard called them "the generation of Marx and Coca-Cola." Among these unforgettable social types are the heroine of Godard's *My Life to Live* (1962), a young, aspiring film actress who works in a record store and casually slips into a life of prostitution, and the young people populating *Masculine-Feminine* (1966), Godard's incisive portrait of his "generation of Marx and Coca-Cola." This new wave reflected the attitudes of a younger generation for whom the older national stories seemed out of date.

With the French new wave, a critical question emerges regarding the cinema's role in constructing a picture of the nation, for the new wave attacked the notion of heritage. They took exception to the fact that heritage is often organized and curated by official, middle-class institutions to maintain a shared sense of national identity. Of course, the existence of some kind of national heritage is inevitable. What irked the new wave directors was the elitist and aesthetically uninteresting management of this heritage. This argument against an overly exclusionary heritage was to move beyond the borders of France in the 1960s, and the conflict between "heritage filmmaking" and "new cinemas" was to play out in many surprising ways in different national cinema traditions. In Britain, for example, the Angry Young Man movement in the 1960s made the exploited working-class bloke —in such films as *This Sporting Life* (1963)—a central figure, with filmmakers adopting a kitchen-sink realism derived in part from neorealism. In the mid-1960s, with the rise of the working-class rock group The Beatles, director Richard Lester freely borrowed techniques from the French new wave in his films, *A Hard Day's Night* (1964) and *Help!* (1965), to construct an image of Britain that was hip and youthful, in contrast to the staid, class-bound view of the nation that heritage films presented.

In the United States, where Hollywood had arguably been less tied to a rigidly class-based establishment, the new cinema of the 1960s focused on critiquing the monolithic national mythologies that the classical Hollywood genres tended to promote. Nowhere is this focus more evident than in the revisionist Western. In classical Hollywood, the Western was the genre specifically charged with setting forth a vision of the idea of America as a place of infinite possibilities for self-invention. By the late 1950s, however, even the veteran Western director John Ford began to see the limited vision of the classic Western; in *The Searchers* (1956), he began to show the dark side of the cultural clash between settlers and the native Indian population, and in *The Man Who Shot Liberty Valence* (1962), the film's clever flashback structure allows it to expose the way newspapers promulgate ideological myths at the expense of reality. Perhaps the most elegiac of the new Westerns was Sam Peckinpah's beautiful but underrated *Pat Garrett and Billy the Kid* (1973). In Peckinpah's version of the story, the American West is no longer a place to escape from the confining class hierarchies of the East as it is already being bought up by rich capitalist barons and developers. The idealized bandit Billy the Kid thus becomes the charmed but ultimately doomed representative of the promise of the American West.

Since the 1960s and continuing to the present day, new waves have occurred in many national cinemas across the globe, from Czechoslovakia, Japan, and Spain to Iran, Hong Kong, Taiwan, and Korea. In all cases, these new waves can be seen as connected to processes of modernization. Space does not permit a discussion of all these national cinema developments; however, Taiwan provides an interesting recent example. Because of its history of brutal foreign occupations, Taiwan is more akin to a postcolonial country than to an indigenous nation. In this context, the entire issue of heritage and national identity is configured very differently, because colonial occupation tends to devalue indigenous traditions and replace them with the heritage derived from the mother country. Thus, the Taiwanese "New Cinema Movement," which emerged in the early 1980s, was initially connected to a nativist movement in Taiwanese literary culture that attempted to assert indigenous language and cultural forms as a way for Taiwan to define itself.

The key director in the early phase of the Taiwanese new wave was Hou Hsaio-hsien. His early autobiographical films broke from the commercial martial-arts/melodrama tradition with their adoption of a low-key, neorealist-influenced exploration of the everyday lives of ordinary Taiwanese in urbanized environments. Then, in 1989, after the government lifted the ban on any public discussion of the infamous massacres of February 28, 1947, Hou released *City of Sadness* (1989). This film, which won awards at major festivals around the world, broke the silence surrounding the February 28, 1947, incident and is one of the great national historical epics ever filmed. In the film, Hou does not abandon his attention to the nuances and rhythms of everyday life but rather uses this aesthetic to sublime advantage; the February incident is never explicitly shown onscreen but rather haunts the film all around its edges, suggesting that the nation never really faced or came to terms with this major trauma in its history. Of the directors who followed Hou in the development of Taiwanese New Cinema, Edward Yang and Tsai Ming-liang are particularly important. More clearly at home in the intensely urbanized and economically booming Taipei of the 1990s, these younger directors masterfully explore the interrelationship between new urban spaces and the modernized young Taiwanese who attempt, with more or less success, to accommodate themselves to them. In this way, they remind us of Godard's portraits of a modernizing France but with an original and powerful cinematic language that makes the Taiwanese new wave one of the most important national cinemas of recent times.

Consequences

New Technologies, Globalization, and National Image Cultures

Since the emergence of national television networks in the 1950s and 1960s, new technologies of image diffusion have challenged the primacy of the cinema as the principal site of national image culture. However, since the 1980s, the impact of new technology on national image culture has become more and more pronounced with the advent of, first, new video technologies such as the VCR and lightweight, easy-to-use video cameras, second, the personal computer and the World Wide Web, and, third, the ever-increasing digitization of images. These new technologies are themselves part of an overall globalization in the organization of capitalism that has challenged traditional notions of national boundaries and distinct national cultures. In an age characterized by global flows of capital, populations, and media images, it is not surprising that the very idea of the "national cinema" is currently being rethought, although, at this point, film and media scholars have not arrived at any theoretical consensus about the relationship of global image culture to national cinemas.

A few things should be noted at the outset, however. The cinema still exists. As noted earlier, the various cinematic "new waves" now occurring in the developing nations still work to articulate a sense of national identity, and the Holly-wood blockbuster still attracts a vast international audience while, at the same time, expressing a uniquely American vision. However, the relative cheapness and availability of digital video cameras and image-editing computer programs, along with the possibilities for distribution of streaming video via the Internet, is beginning to complicate our picture of national "mediascapes." In mainland China, for example, there is a national film school that trains directors to make films to comprise the "official" national cinema; however, there is now also a lively, and partly "underground," flow of digital videos made mostly by young people and exhibited in venues like clubs and cafes that present an image of China that is decidedly different from the official national cinema.

Another factor complicating any model of contemporary national cinemas is the changing role of television. From its initial diffusion in the 1950s until rela-tively recently, national television systems were organized around a few large net-works. One could argue that, in the age of the older large networks, television took over from cinema the main tasks of defining the national project. We can now see how it functioned to assimilate various working-class ethnic groups into the "melting pot" of American culture, how it promoted consumerism and dis-seminated information intended to normalize and regulate the practices of every-day life. The emergence of cable, satellite, and digital television, with their endless channels and choices, tends to fragment the national audience into niche mar-kets while linking the niches of one nation to those of other nations having the same interests. This phenomenon of a transnational community defined around specific common interests is even more pronounced in Internet culture. For ex-ample, technocrats in Dublin or Milan might find that they have more in com-mon with members of the technocratic elites in Mumbai or Buenos Aires than with some of their own fellow citizens, as the Internet makes establishing global interconnections easy. No doubt this technology will have significant future ef-fects on the notions of national identity and national culture, affecting even the cinema. Theoretically, the concept of "hybridity" has gained ground as a possible way to understand these new global cultures, yet the extent to which hybridity manifests itself in particular national cinemas remains relatively unexplored.

Perhaps the best way to end this overview is by way of a dramatic example of how new media technologies are forcing us to reconsider fundamental national questions. When Los Angeles police officers stopped Rodney King for a minor traffic violation and ended up brutally beating him, a witness with a store-bought camera managed to capture the incident on videotape. The images of the beating were quickly disseminated via television across the nation and, indeed, the world. What ensued was a vigorous national debate about the persistence of structural racism in the United States and the precarious social status of the young black male in America—issues that had been largely ignored in the official national media culture by both cinema and television. What is most instructive for film and media scholars, however, is that, although the amateur video might have had the quality of immediacy and urgency that characterized the neorealist cinema of resistance, it nevertheless failed to "speak for itself." Whereas African Americans saw the videotape as reflecting a lamentable everyday fact of life, for many other viewers the videotape mobilized already existing racist fantasies surrounding black youth in the ghettoes of America.

In contemporary cinema, the relevance of nation and national identity are seemingly undergoing significant changes. With Hollywood products dominating the screens internationally, localized national cinematic voices are more difficult to discern. At the same time, the "look" of commercial films produced worldwide is more homogenous than ever. In adapting to the logic of a globalizing world, the screen industry is expanding horizontally by entering new markets worldwide and vertically by outsourcing productions, working with independent producers, and forming partnerships with foreign investors to spread risks and increase capitalization. In addition, the cinematic image itself has fundamentally changed with the emergence of CGI, or computer-generated images, which have become standard elements of contemporary filmmaking practice. Not only does the computer-generated image allow for outsourcing—for example, making the shots with the movie stars in Los Angeles, then shipping them to lower-cost studios across the globe for the addition of backgrounds and effects—but it also severs the image from its grounding in a particular "location," which was so important to the cinematic traditions of neorealism and the new waves. These simultaneous processes challenge the traditional notions of cinematic national identity. Thus, as the production, circulation, and reception of images undergo a transformation across the world, the need for film and media scholars to develop models for understanding the workings of this international flow of images is more pressing than ever.

Selected Bibliography

Armes, Roy. 1971. *Patterns of Realism*. South Brunswick, NJ: A. S. Barnes.

Gunning, Tom. 1991. *D. W. Griffith and the Origins of American Narrative Film: The Early Years at Biograph*. Urbana: University of Illinois Press.

Hansen, Miriam. 1999. "The Mass Production of the Senses: Classical Cinema as Vernacular Modernism." *Modernism/Modernity* 6, no. 2 (April): 59–77.

Kracauer, Siegfried. 2004. *From Caligari to Hitler: A Psychological History of the German Film*. Princeton, NJ: Princeton University Press.

Lu, Feii, ed. 2005. *Island on the Edge: Taiwan New Cinema and After*. Hong Kong, China: Hong Kong University Press.

Marie, Michel. 2003. *The French New Wave: An Artistic School*. Malden, MA: Blackwell Publishers.

Miller, Toby. 2001. *Global Hollywood*. London: British Film Institute.

Nichols, Bill. 1994. "The Trials and Tribulations of Rodney King." In *Blurred Boundaries: Questions of Meaning in Contemporary Culture*, edited by Bill Nichols. Bloomington: Indiana University Press.

Nowell-Smith, Geoffrey, ed. 1996. *The Oxford History of World Cinema*. New York: Oxford University Press.

Restivo, Angelo. 2002. *Cinema of Economic Miracles: Visuality and Modernization in the Italian Art Film.* Durham, NC: Duke University Press.

Rosen, Philip. 1984. "History, Textuality, Nation: Kracauer, Burch and Some Problems in the Study of National Cinemas." *Iris* 2, no. 2: 60–83.

Solanas, Fernando, and Octavio Getino. 1976. "Towards a Third Cinema." In *Movies and Methods*, edited by Bill Nichols, 44–64. Berkeley: University of California Press.

Wang, Yiman. 2005. "The Amateur's Lightning Rod: DV Documentary in Postsocialist China." *Film Quarterly* 58, no. 4: 16–26.

Constructions of National Symbolic Spaces and Places: The State of Place in Identity

Brian S. Osborne

Political independence, the implementation of centralized systems of power, the development of a military capability, and the consolidation of territory all contribute to the functional organization of people in a state. But the formation of a state nationalism requires the evocation of the ideas, myths, and dreams that comprise the nonrational core of national identity. That is, old nations and modern states alike cannot exist or function without symbolic underpinnings.

Relevance

In the 19th century, young nation-states and older polities both attempted to mobilize public identification with a nationalistic mission by nurturing what Benedict Anderson has called an "imagined community." Railways, the telegraph, and national postal systems overcame the obstacles of time and space. However, the political myopia of local geographical and historical identities required other strategies to ensure loyalty to the new structure, the nation-state. Capital-capitol complexes, imposing state architecture, inspirational monuments, and patriotic theatrics all heroically chronicled the emergence of state power. Indeed, for much of the 19th and early 20th centuries, these nationalizing states deployed several devices intended to propagate memory-making and identity formation.

The second half of the 20th century witnessed several trends that weakened the power of traditional national identities. These included the optimistic internationalism that followed the defeat of nationalist fascisms; the technological and economic assertions of a globalized world society, together with its cultural equivalent, cosmopolitanism; and the emergence of transnational loyalties that reflected the impact of migrations and international connections. Nevertheless, many nationalizing states still construct monolithic identities in both old established nation-states and newly constructed nation-states. To this end, connections with symbolic landscapes, reverence for impressive monuments, and extravaganzas of performed identity are still sponsored by national bureaucracies dedicated to the perpetuation of heroic, albeit often mythic, narratives.

But there are signs of reaction. This is particularly true of plural societies that enjoy liberal democracies and open transnational connections. Here, the symbols of identity have changed because the reception and expectations are more complex. Traditional narratives are being challenged by discourses of race, class, and gender. The formality of bronze and marble memorials is being countered by new imaginations and practices. These need to be better understood in the ideological landscape of nationalism in the 21st century.

Origins

Storied Places

The principal initiative of nationalizing states lies in the construction of a shared collective memory. The imagery of collective memory focuses on particular people, events, and their spatial reference points: places of recollection. These are reinforced in the collective memory by acts of commemoration that structure our time and space in a mental geography.

Two seminal thinkers have highlighted this: Maurice Halbwachs and Pierre Nora. For Halbwachs, storied places provide spatial and temporal coordinates for remembering. In a similar vein, Nora seeks out the roots of French cultural identity by analyzing the events, places, and concepts that crystallized collective heritage and collective memory. For both Halbwachs and Nora, geography is more than the stage for the acting out of history: the two are intertwined throughout.

Identities are constantly being reconstituted according to the needs of the present, through selective appropriation, manipulation, and even imaginative invention. The past is socially constructed through archives, museums, school curricula, monuments, and public displays. All of these propagate national solidarity, encourage people's pride in citizenship, and promote their full participation in economic, social, and political life.

Accordingly, most nationalizing states renegotiate history, memory, and identity in terms of foundation myths, sacred places, and the personification of assumed national qualities. National histories chronicle how communities and individuals want to be perceived by themselves and others. Always spatially grounded, they are associated with specific locales that become imbued with historically produced cultural meanings that can transcend into Mircea Eliade's *genius loci*, or spirit of place.

In particular, people's identification with particular places is essential for the cultivation of national identity. Places become loaded with material forms that are powerful prompts for shared narratives, values, and putative hopes and fears for the future. Carefully selected because of their emotive power, they become iconic and are empowered by the careful cultivation of mythologies. In this way, the familiar material world becomes transformed into symbolically charged sites and events—as well as silences—that provide social continuity, contribute to the collective memory, and provide spatial and temporal reference points for society.

Dimensions

Patriotic Topographies

Nationalizing states have always been aware of persons' strong bonds to place and have deployed them through landscape. Initially considered as the material expression of human impact on the land and evidence of societies' various ways of life and cultural history, landscape has increasingly been deconstructed as a repository of symbolic meaning. In particular, it is transformed from an external phenomenon to be engaged visually to a psychic terrain of internalized symbolic meaning. In this way, particular landscapes have been appropriated as visual representations of the essence of homelands, motherlands, and fatherlands. Indeed, the German term *heimat* is the most nuanced expression of that profound link between identity, land, and place. The mental image of particular patriotic landscapes becomes coded with reference to golden ages, heroic deeds, and national stories that transcend the prosaic realities of geology and topography, and land and water, and become intimately tied to nationality, nationhood, and national destiny. As the dominant expressions of symbolic space and time, story-laden landscapes came to play an instrumental role in the formation of national identities.

Symbolic landscapes can be challenged. Consider the case of Canada's long-preferred national iconography of "The North." No mere identification with nature and wilderness, it has been charged that there were strong ideological forces behind the imagery of Nordicity. That is, Canada turned its back on the St. Lawrence–Great Lakes front that united, yet divided, American and Canadian geopolitics. It rejected the shared experience of urbanism, industry, and pluralism and espoused the symbolism of the north and wilderness. Canada searched for national distinctiveness by shunning continentalism and cosmopolitanism in favor of a pristine nativism imbued with heavy doses of chauvinism, environmental determinism, and even racialism. Some contemporary Canadian artists have reacted by deterritorializing the landscape and refer to outside influences and internal differences as new tokens of Canadian identity. Similar ideologically loaded patriotic geographies may be associated with the English countryside, the American frontier, and Australia's outback. These viewpoints are often most evocatively rendered in such patriotic songs and anthems as "Land of My Fathers," "America the Beautiful," "Ma Vlast," and "Waltzing Matilda."

Artistic conventions of the picturesque and the sublime have also been appropriated to represent preferred nationalist and imperialist self-images. But there are often "dark sides" to the landscape that have to be dealt with. In some cases, places of past violence and tragedy are permanently expunged from the landscape in an attempt at preventing the collective remembering of things that nation-states wish to avoid. Nevertheless, a litany of sites of war, mass murders, political assassinations, violent labor and race riots persist as sites of remembering. It is in this vein that the world's engagement with the mind-numbing immensity of the horror of the Holocaust is ensured through the preservation of the death camps and the erection of evocative markers.

Figuring Out Place

Didactic sites were purposefully introduced into landscapes that have evolved organically over time. Monuments served as material signifiers for collective remembering and identity of great victories, beloved monarchs, or revered political leaders. National images were to be found in past heroes, geniuses, and messiah-saviors, who were rooted in homelands and golden ages and were advanced as surrogates for the nation's innate virtues, past achievements, and future destiny. In particular, portrait-sculpture personalized the nationalizing state, scripted mythic histories in an allegorical visual text, and legitimized authority by consensual acceptance of an official historical metanarrative. Royalty, political leaders, military heroes, and mythic figures were presented in standard poses with an array of such predictable accoutrements as swords or crosses or books or horses or lions. The female image was particularly manipulated as an allegory of virtue, motherhood, and home. Often located in heroic pantheons in national capitals, these symbols were also symbolically placed: the Statue of Liberty in New York, Vercingétorix at Alesia, King Alfred in Winchester, Queen Boadicea at London's Westminster, Bismark in Berlin, the Magyar chiefs in Budapest's Heroes' Square. In this way, portrait-sculpture joined flags, anthems, national chronicles, currency, and coins in building a sense of community, identity, and nationalism.

War has had a particular role in this process. World War I stimulated a more populist and ubiquitous mode of monumental public statuary: war monuments. In fact, nation-states everywhere incorporated war into the national project by centrally coordinated programs of memorialization, commemoration, and ritualized performance. However, the very human face of suffering in the name of nationalism had much to do with the demise of monumental patriotism.

But after the Great War, the elaborate visual language of monumental symbolism and allegory became incomprehensible for most people. Monumental statuary was favored only by dictatorships that manipulated pomp, gigantism, and poor taste into symbolic statements of power. Even war memorials were less popular as, after World War II, returning troops often preferred that their service and sacrifices be commemorated by "memorial" hospitals, schools, and recreation centers. To be sure, the heroic flag-raising on Iwo Jima has become iconic for both the U.S. Marine Corps and the nation, but the dramatically somber statement of Washington's Vietnam monument is an evocative reflection of other reactions to wartime suffering.

Recently, attention has been directed to commemorating the services and sacrifices of workers and public servants in everyday society. Thus, in Canada, the "Day of Mourning Act" received Royal Assent in 1991. Since that date, April 28 has come to be recognized worldwide as the day for commemorating loss and suffering in the workplace. For others, the materialization of abstract ideas has transformed the quality of life in liberal societies. Canada recognizes such important initiatives as "Peace Keeping," the Constitution, multiculturalism, gender rights, and immigration reform. Two initiatives stand out: the invasion of the monumental pantheon on Parliament Hill, Ottawa, by the "Alberta Five," five courageous women activists who fought for women's rights in Canada; and Toronto's now highly acclaimed and internationally duplicated monument to "Multiculturalism" with its message of global links and sensitivities. These moves are echoed in the United States and elsewhere. A fine example is the role of presidential libraries as part of the civil religion of American patriotism. Critical attention has also been directed at the symbolism of "standing soldiers and kneeling slaves" as well as the discourses running through such revered icons as the flag, the Statue of Liberty, Mount Rushmore, the Lincoln Memorial, and, of course, post-9/11 memorial initiatives.

While monuments are intended to foster social cohesion, they may also provoke a public redefinition of identity. This is especially true when monuments

Monument to Multiculturalism and Canadian Charter of Rights and Freedoms, erected in Toronto on July 1, 1985. (Rudy Sulgan/Corbis)

last too long. Memorials freeze ideas in space and time as the dated messages of bronze, iron, marble, and granite structures survive into uncomprehending futures. As their original purpose is redefined, they can be sites of conflict, dissent, or—perhaps even worse—indifference. And always, iconoclasm is the handmaiden of shifting ideologies. With the fall of the Berlin Wall and the "Second Springtime of Freedom," monuments of Karl Marx and Friedrich Engels, and Joseph Stalin and Vyacheslav Molotov went the way of an imperialist Queen Victoria before and a dictatorial Saddam Hussein later.

Performing Place

While some monuments are trivialized by disinterest or neglect, ritualized remembrance ensures the continued relevance of others. Such planned spectacles have always required an architecture of people that has long been part of Western political culture going back to Greece, Rome, and the Papacy. Indeed, nation-states have nurtured patriotism akin to a state religion. Formerly associated with the processionals and icons of religious ceremony, nationalizing states established a civic calendar of publicly performed ceremonials that shifted public attention from theology to patriotism. State ceremonies were orchestrated to ensure that the collective memory focused on particular events and places. They drilled into the collective memory a national ideological agenda that was reinforced by performance, mass participation, and repetitive reenactment intended to encourage collective remembering, propagate consensual values, and overcome social differences.

The gross theatrics of Hitler and Mussolini have a more benign equivalent in the regal displays of British royalty and the ever-expanding trappings of the American presidency. A particularly egregious demonstration of the theatrics of power was President George W. Bush's choreographed declaration of victory in the Iraq War in May 2003 on the deck of the USS *Lincoln*. Consider the script and set design: the arrival by fighter jet, the costume of a fighter pilot, the prop—a banner proclaiming "Mission Accomplished," a supporting cast of enthusiastic military personnel, and a multimillion media audience in cyberspace. Such powerful exercises in controlled spectacle are intended to reinforce ideologies, create mythic histories, and through the involvement of large numbers of people, attempt to generate a sense of common identity and purpose.

At the other extreme is the informal performance of identity, often in the context of tragedy and trauma. Be it the death of Princess Diana, the mass murders of children at schools, such as Columbine, or communities' grief in reaction to the loss of local military in combat, spontaneous commemorations have come to have their own repertoire of rituals and material signifiers of loss. Within hours of the horror of 9/11 at the World Trade Center in New York, rescue workers and the public at large created informal memorials and sites of remembrance. In a similar vein, the recent unveiling of the Tomb to the Unknown Soldier in Ottawa was accompanied by predictable pomp and ceremony. What followed was unplanned and completely spontaneous: an unknown mourner deposited a red poppy on the grave; others followed and took their own poppies from their lapels and deposited them there. Soon, a mound of red blanketed the bronze sarcophagus. It is now an annual event following the formal state service on November 11, Remembrance Day.

Consequences

The Need for New Strategies and Tools

Clearly, identity and sense of belonging are complex concepts affected by plural connections. Class, gender, religion, and ethnicity compete with local, regional, and national associations, as well as globalization and migration. In particular, transnational identities are challenging the liberal, nation-bound concept of citizenship and sovereignty. It follows, therefore, that the representation of national identity embraces the challenge posed by people's nested sets of identities in a multinational and cosmopolitan world. Obviously, the preferred model for most modern democratic states is a civil nationalism based upon a rational adherence to liberal principles, rather than an ethnic nationalism characterized by emotional links to "blood and soil." And yet, while national identity is best defined in terms of a rational assessment of rights and obligations, it must also be accompanied by a modicum of symbolic attachment to the idea for which any particular nation stands.

Shared histories of difference may sometimes be antagonistic and irreconcilable and create their own counternarrative that critiques the dominant culture and the structures underpinning it. Consequently, there is a need to carefully consider future strategies for history-making, monumentalism, and commemoration in forward-looking nation-states in the 21st-century world. The idea of looking back on previous forms of national narratives and revisiting commemorative texts aids us in understanding these landscapes. Change within society also breeds new types of expression through Web-based information. As the world becomes more connected, we must also remember that nations should seek to nurture a national culture that celebrates their distinctiveness while also respecting global patterns of diversity.

Selected Bibliography

Anderson, B. 1991/1983. *Imagined Communities.* London: Verso.

Appiah, K. A. 2006. *Cosmopolitanism: Ethics in a World of Strangers.* New York: W. W. Norton.

Boime, A. 1998. *The Unveiling of National Icons: A Plea for Patriotic Iconoclasm in a Nationalistic Era.* Cambridge: Cambridge University Press.

Brooks, D., and P. N. Limerick. 1995. *Sweet Medicine: Sites of Indian Massacres, Battlefields, and Treaties.* Albuquerque: University of New Mexico Press.

Daniels, S. 1993. *Fields of Vision: Landscape Imagery and National Identity in England and the United States.* Princeton, NJ: Princeton University Press.

Eliade, M. 1959. *The Sacred and the Profane: The Nature of Religion.* Translated by Willard R. Trask. New York: Harcourt, Brace.

Foote, K. E. 1997. *Shadowed Ground: America's Landscapes of Violence and Tragedy.* Austin: University of Texas Press.

Gillis, J. 1994. *Commemorations: The Politics of National Identity.* Princeton, NJ: Princeton University Press.

Halbwachs, M. 1980. *The Collective Memory.* Translated by F. Ditter and V. Y. Ditter. New York: Harper and Row. (Orig. pub. 1950.)

Hobsbawm, E., and T. Ranger. 1983. *The Invention of Tradition.* Cambridge: Cambridge University Press.

Hufbauer, B. 2005. *Presidential Temples: How Memorial and Temples Shape Public Memory.* Lawrence: University Press of Kansas.

Loewen, J. W. 1999. *Lies across America: What Our Historic Sites Get Wrong.* New York: The New Press.

Manning, E. 2003. *Ephemeral Territories.* Minneapolis: University of Minnesota Press.

Neal, A. 1998. *National Trauma and Collective Memory: Major Events in the American Century.* Armonk, NY: M. E. Sharpe.

Nora, P. 1996. *Realms of Memory: Rethinking the French Past.* Translated by Arthur Goldhammer. New York: Columbia University Press.

Osborne, B. 2001. "Landscapes, Memory, Monuments, and Commemoration: Putting Identity in Its Place." *Canadian Ethnic Studies* 33, no. 3: 39–77.

Osborne, B. 2006. "From Patriotic Pines to Diasporic Geese: Emplacing Culture, Setting Our Sights, Locating Identity in a Transnational Canada." *Canadian Journal of Communications* 31:147–175.

Savage, K. 1997. *Standing Soldiers, Kneeling Slaves: Race, War, and Monument in Nineteenth-Century America.* Princeton, NJ: Princeton University Press.

Schwartz, B. 2000. *Abraham Lincoln and the Forge of National Memory.* Chicago: University of Chicago Press.

Spillman, L. 1997. *Nation and Commemoration: Creating National Identities in the United States and Australia.* Cambridge: Cambridge University Press.

Vale, J. 1992. *Architecture, Power, and National Identity.* New Haven, CT: Yale University Press.

Verdery, K. 1999. *The Political Lives of Dead Bodies: Reburial and Postsocialist Change.* New York: Columbia University Press.

Walkowitz, D. J., and M. Knauer, eds. 2004. *Memory and the Impact of Political Transformation in Public Space.* Durham, NC: Duke University Press.

Cosmopolitanism and Nationalism in Liberal Political Theory

Christine Straehle

Albert Einstein once described nationalism as "the measles of the human race," a disease of infancy translated onto the state. This disdain for everything nationalistic has been reflected by liberal political theory that for the longest time promoted the ideal of cosmopolitanism as the only viable way to reflect liberal values, like individual liberty and autonomy. However, nationalist movements have not died out, as cosmopolitans may have hoped, but instead are alive and well in many parts of the world. They take different forms, from national minority movements as in Canada, Belgium, Spain, and the United Kingdom, to movements for national self-determination, as in the Czech Republic, to national movements that are motivated by principles of democratic accountability, as in the Ukraine. Are all supporters of national movements infantile or at least illiberal? To answer this question, both cosmopolitanism and its supposed converse, nationalism, will have to be examined more closely. What are the basic principles of cosmopolitanism and how is it tied to liberal thought? Why are both supposedly at odds with nationalism? Or can we conceive of a version of nationalism that encompasses liberal values?

Origins

What Is Cosmopolitanism?

Cosmopolitanism can be defined as that school of thought whose proponents regret the privileging of national identities in political life. Instead, cosmopolitans subscribe to the idea that we should consider ourselves as citizens of the world, rather than of particular nation-states. According to cosmopolitans, we should be concerned with the well-being of all people, not only that of our compatriots. And we should promote the idea of individual liberty through democratic government, globally, not only in the boundaries of our nation-state. These cosmopolitan convictions arise from the context in which cosmopolitan thoughts emerged, namely the Enlightenment. The Enlightenment is that period in the history of ideas that initiated the slow embrace of what we now consider to be the core liberal ideas about how to decide on the shape of our lives: the freedom to reason and deliberate what life we want to lead based on our own needs and experiences, not on traditional identities and fixed social roles. Instead of being locked into a religion, social class, or other identificatory group by birth, individuals were supposed to be set free from such constraints. They were to determine for themselves what identity they were to embrace, through rational deliberation. This was the great achievement of the Enlightenment.

Today, not many people would be as hopeful about the prospects for a peaceful global state as, for example, the Marquis de Condorcet who believed in the ultimate establishment of a world state. However, political theorists and philosophers still take on cosmopolitan stances when making their arguments. What role does cosmopolitanism play in political theory? To answer this question, we need to set cosmopolitanism in context with its opposite, nationalism.

Relevance

What Is Nationalism?

Nationalism implies that belonging to a nation and sharing in its national identity carry special significance for us that other ties don't. The meaning of the terms "national identity" or "shared nationality," which are used interchangeably in the literature, is heavily debated. But most authors today share a core definition that can serve as the basis for this discussion. Nationality, most agree, is a way of expressing our place in the world that works like all other identities, as a framework of references within which we can define ourselves. Nationality describes a community of people bound together by history, language, culture, and, usually, territory. Nationality is thus often tied to ethnicity and a shared cultural background. We recognize each other easily among compatriots; we identify with each other and share a sense of belonging together.

Moreover we identify with our common history as a nation and are conscious of being involved in the ongoing national project to the point that we would potentially die for our nation. Sharing in a national identity allows us to partake meaningfully in a larger history than that of our individual lives or immediate community. Our nationhood provides us with a collective political subject. And finally, national identity promotes the solidarity and trust among compatriots needed to sustain the institutions of the democratic welfare state, such as redistributive taxation and democratic civility. This function of national identity has been described as a stimulus or "battery" for the nation-state.

How Cosmopolitanism and Nationalism Disagree

To the cosmopolitan, however, any favoring of the national community over that of humanity more generally is morally arbitrary. Why, asks the cosmopolitan, should we privilege the belonging to our nation over any other kind of belonging when thinking about how we want to lead our lives? And why should we owe special obligations to conationals that we don't owe to others? Cosmopolitans don't deny that we owe duties to others, but they deny that such obligations end at the nation's borders. Our obligations to others hold true regardless of where we live and whether or not we share a nationality or identity or a state. This version of cosmopolitanism is related to another Enlightenment thinker, Immanuel Kant, and his idea of universal principles that we should apply when thinking about how to lead our lives. Kant articulated this belief in his "categorical imperative," which stated that we should live according to principles that could serve as foundations for universal law. Cosmopolitans hold on to the belief that we share a common humanity. And they think that because of our shared humanity we have some obligations toward people wherever they live. Some authors defend, for example, our obligation to promote and realize international justice by fighting for a fairer system of international trade or a more global approach to social justice. So the first cosmopolitan critique of nationalism is that nationalists make claims based on national identity, which privileges compatriots, when thinking about our mutual obligations—at the expense of those obligations we have toward other humans.

A second problem with nationalism, from the cosmopolitan perspective, is that the promotion of nationalism stands in opposition to ideas of individual emancipation and personal liberty. Nationalism's critics describe it as an irrational and illiberal form of attachment, an identity ascribed to us that provides the national community with more power over the individual than it ought to have. This is a criticism worth exploring. Let's take the example of the ultimate allegiance to our nation, the idea that we should give our lives for the welfare of our country, the call—to put it in more patriotic terms—"*pro patria mori*," as the Romans rallied. What comes with this call to patriotic duty on the battlefield is the idea that, whatever our individual stance toward specific governmental policies, if need be we should be willing to die for our nation. "My country right or wrong" seems thus to go hand in hand with the duty we owe our nation. Consider a young Israeli recruit who refuses to serve in the West Bank. Some Israeli "refuseniks," as they have been called, refuse military service because they believe that Israeli military policy goes beyond what is necessary to sustain and protect the well-being of the nation, even though the Israeli state may defend its actions as being necessary for its survival. The refusenik is faced with a conflict between individual belief and the call to defend the nation. Should she follow her own assessment of her duty and of the interests of the nation? Or should she suppress her misgivings and demonstrate her loyalty by doing military service despite her disapproval of the policy and skepticism as to its necessity?

A "chauvinist" nationalism, as it has been called, allows for no such conflict. The nation is conceived of as an independent entity with a life and destiny of its own. It is not the sum or the collective will of its individual members. The nation is an organic whole, an elemental force that drives human action without those involved having much influence on it. This understanding of nationalism dates back to German Romanticism, which viewed societies as organic entities that had their natural territory and their distinct culture. According to this view, individuals are born into a nation and hence share certain personal characteristics with their conationals. Our national identity plays an important part in our personal identity, and moreover, we cannot escape our ties to our national identity. To come back to the example of the Israeli recruit, the welfare of the national community, in a strict application of this kind of nationalist doctrine, will and should take precedence over individual welfare or belief. What's more, there can be no ethical limits to the pursuits of the nation if these pursuits are justified by the national interest—even to the detriment of interests of other people and peoples. This kind of nationalism is both an illiberal and belligerent doctrine—the potentially terrible expanse of which was illustrated by Nazi Germany with its territorial policy of "the homeland," its racial and social policies, and the subjugation of individual interests to that of the Reich. But is this all there is to nationalism?

Dimensions

Forms of Nationalism

Some authors have suggested distinctions between different kinds of nationalisms. Some believe, for example, that we should distinguish "western," rational nationalism, which encompasses individual rights and is profoundly liberal in its concern with individual liberty and autonomy, and "eastern" nationalism, which is seen as mystical and primordial, founded on quasi-tribal bases for the nation that would count as illiberal. Most importantly, "western" nationalism would allow for individuals to disagree with nationalist doctrines because this kind of nationalism would embrace freedom of conscience as a fundamental human right—a right, in fact, that was invoked by many of the Israeli refuseniks in their campaign against military action in the West Bank.

The distinction between "western," rational nationalism and its "eastern," primitive counterpart has survived and has been ushered into political theory in the distinction between "civic-territorial nationalism" in the West and its "eastern ethnic-genealogical" counterpart. And in fact, some assume that this distinction helps to clarify and answer the challenge to nationalism by cosmopolitanism. If indeed civic-territorial nationalism encourages individual liberties, then surely it is helping rather than hindering individual autonomy, the goal of Enlightenment thinking? This conclusion might hold true and might answer some of the qualms cosmopolitans have with nationalist doctrines, but only if the distinction between "ethnic" and "civic" nationalism can be shown to stand up against closer scrutiny. First, let's look at what the distinction implies. It suggests that we can differentiate between two fundamentally different *types* of nationalisms. The civic type promotes an understanding of what it means to belong to a nation based on civil rights: all members have democratic citizenship rights and enjoy an equal range of individual liberties, for example, freedom of expression or freedom of conscience and assembly. A nation thus understood, we are led to believe, is founded on a set of consciously chosen and shared principles. The example most often invoked for a civic-territorial nation is, of course, the United States.

The ethnic type, on the other hand, is supposedly distinguished by its reliance on ethno-cultural traits, like customs and language, for the foundation of the nation. In such a nation, one can only belong by showing the right "bloodline" or ancestry, one that can be traced back to early days. To illustrate, the ethnic type of reference is often made to the German interpretation of national identity. Indeed, until 1998, citizenship in Germany was automatically conferred to children born to German parents, regardless of where they lived, while it proved to be all but impossible to naturalize children who had been born and bred in Germany but who were descended from Turkish immigrants, for example. On the other hand, German governments would accept ethnic Germans whose families had resided for generations in Russia as German citizens—even though they might lack any knowledge of German or of what life was actually about in Germany.

Nationalism since the 1980s

With the differences between "civic" and "ethnic" nationalism spelled out, we can ask if this distinction helps us make sense of national movements today. Many have criticized both concepts, and for different reasons. Can we really say that the civic version is entirely "civic" and not imbued with cultural traits? Can we neglect the relevance of language, to take an obvious cultural denominator, in choosing and determining to which principles we as a nation ought to subscribe? More often than not, some authors argue, the distinction comes down to the "good" nationalists in the West, who promote liberal citizenship and individual rights, and the "bad" nationalisms in the East, who impose an ethno-cultural yoke on their members.

Moreover, a division between "east" and "west" doesn't help us understand national movements today. Regardless of antinationalist expectations long held by liberal theorists, we have witnessed ever-new nationalist movements around the globe. Some of the eastern European movements have been linked to the demise of the Soviet Union, for example, in the Czech Republic, the Baltic states, Georgia, and most recently in the Ukraine. As many cases of nationalist movements—in Québec in Canada, the Basque country and Catalonia in Spain, in Indonesia, the Kurds in Turkey, and the Kashmiri in India and Pakistan—show, however, new nationalist movements are not restricted to that region. Many contemporary national movements tie national self-determination to the principles of democratic government structures and principles of accountability and transparency. Thus, beyond traditional claims, referring to the ethno-cultural heritage and traditions, they also make a case for national self-determination. By making both sets of claims, however, they transcend the division between civic and territorial nationalism. We therefore need to wonder if we can conceive—theoretically—of nationalism other than in the dichotomy of civic versus ethnic, that is, in a way that takes the cultural identity basis of these nationalisms into account *alongside* their goals that reflect democratic principles like self-determination and citizenship rights.

Liberal Nationalism

The theoretical challenge was taken up in the early 1990s when some liberal theorists turned their attention to questions of nationality and nationhood. Shedding previous disdain, they asked if we can conceive of a national community that would respect both the principles of individual liberty and autonomy, on the one hand, and the ethno-cultural requirements for the national community to flourish, on the other. These "liberal nationalists," as they have been called, have advanced a case to rethink our position toward nationalism. Many political theorists now think that those who fight for national independence want to protect their national culture, their language, and their heritage through political independence because they believe that a flourishing national culture makes life meaningful for them.

Let's look at the issue of language—clearly still a strong cultural denominator in today's world and one that is tied to our individual well-being. Just think of our daily dealings with authorities, but also of those with our immediate neighbors and the people we cross in our daily lives that require our use of language. Only if we can relate to them in a meaningful way can we actually make sense of the world and position ourselves in it. To be sure, many people will be able to learn a second or third language over the course of their lives. However, for most people, their native language will remain the one in which they will feel most comfortable. Especially when it comes to deliberating about more complicated issues, like politics, people prefer to express themselves in their native language—only then do they have a sense of good comprehension and understanding of the issues at stake. Except for an elite, most people prefer to conduct politics in their vernacular.

In Catalonia and Québec, to take two examples of the Western liberal democratic world that illustrate the dynamics of many national liberation movements, people are proud of Catalán and Québécois, respectively, and would want the language to survive. It carries meaning, links them to their heritage and culture, their ancestors, the land and the history of their national culture. In short, their language represents what it means for them to be Catalán or Québécois; it expresses their national identity. This is, of course, one reason why it is vital for members of either group to be able to take pride in their language. Until recently, however, both Cataláns and Québécois had to be able to speak Spanish and English, respectively, to be economically successful. These were the languages of public life, the markets, businesses, and so on. If the Catalán or Québécois government hadn't made strong efforts to support their languages, chances are that they would have been on a not so slow demise—with extinction being a likely outcome. Moreover, only because these regional governments made efforts to turn these formerly private languages into the language of vibrant emerging economies can Catalán and Québécois serve as a vehicle of individual pride and achievement today. The reason why Cataláns and Québécois value their languages, however, has nothing to do with chauvinist or "bad ethnic" nationalism, but rather with the fact that it forms a vital part of their identity. It is a social good that they are proud of and that they want to be able to teach to their children.

John Stuart Mill, in the cosmopolitan vein, famously wrote that it would be far better for a Breton (and other minority groups in 19th-century France) to blend into the French nation and to participate in the progress that it would bring than to insist on his cultural heritage and the use of his traditional language. What we can learn from the example of language and the role language plays in the life of individuals, however, is that it does not necessarily help the freedom and autonomy of minority-language speakers to only have one viable language available. Looked at from this angle, then, a sense of nationality and what it is tied to could actually foster the cosmopolitan ideals of individual liberty and autonomy—rather than hinder their realization. To be able to protect these languages meaningfully, on the other hand, Québécois and Catalán had to have strong provincial governments to make their case and implement the necessary measures in the bigger framework of the Canadian and Spanish states, respectively. The cultural identity issue of language, thus, called for a certain degree of national political self-determination.

But how does this address allegations made by cosmopolitans that what Québécois and Catalán (or Kurds or the Welsh) are concerned with is "purity" of the national culture at the expense of other values, for example, cultural diversity and intercultural dialogue? Asked otherwise, how is language protection as an aim for national politics different from chauvinist nationalism? The difference, some argue, is in the motivational drive: national minorities don't want to protect their cultures because they think it is the best one around; they want to protect the cultural background that is important for their well-being. So the first lesson liberal nationalism seems to teach cosmopolitan critics is that having and sustaining strong national cultures does not prohibit individual emancipation from ascribed identities. Rather, liberal nationalist authors argue, strong national cultures are vital for individual emancipation, if we understand emancipation to imply that we have a range of options available to us along which we can make choices about our lives.

What can we make of the second claim cosmopolitans make? How does liberal nationalism address the fact that nationalism in whatever form seems to privilege members of our national community when thinking about our moral obligations rather than advocating the obligations we have toward all human beings? Some liberal nationalist authors have tackled this question head on and have proposed that we should not consider cosmopolitan ethics and the "ethics of nationality" as mutually exclusive. Rather, we should consider the nation and its political expression, the institutions of the nation-state, as the best opportunity to fulfill our obligations toward others, without, however, neglecting any international obligations we may have. Others invite us to consider cosmopolitanism not as a call to tend to all the needy around the world, which would be too big and abstract a task to attempt. Instead, we should take the world we live in, our neighborhood, school or religious community, or our national community as the playing field for our moral obligations. What we should distinguish is what motivates our acts, the reasons why we act in a certain way, which can be—and from a cosmopolitan perspective, should be—universal in nature, and the realm in which we act on these reasons, which can be local or national. For example, we may try to help out at our local soup kitchen as often as we can fit it into our schedule, not because we think that our fellow nationals should not go hungry, but because we think that nobody should be hungry—but our local soup kitchen is where we feel we can make the biggest contribution. This does not prevent us from making donations to aid organizations that help people in faraway countries, of course, but neither should our monetary contributions buy us out of the obligations we have to the homeless on our street. Liberal nationalism can then be understood, in other words, to be able to assuage at least some of the cosmopolitan concerns. How does liberal nationalism fare in its other tasks? Most importantly, can liberal nationalist authors explain national self-determination movements over the last two decades?

Consequences

Problems

Unfortunately, the world is more complicated than liberal theorists (and maybe some others) would like it to be—and it gets particularly messy once we look at the ethno-cultural makeup of modern states. Most states today, to point to the biggest problem first, are not homogenous nation-states but are made up of different national groups, including national minorities. National minorities are now understood to be ethno-national groups that relate to a specific territory as their ancestral home and share a language and culture, but who are by now outnumbered or surrounded by a larger majority nation. Examples of national minorities are the Québécois and aboriginal nations in Canada, the Basques and Cataláns in Spain, and the Maori in New Zealand. For these groups to have a sense of security and viability, cultural minority rights may be needed to provide minority nations with safeguards against the majority. Among those favoring such rights are those who claim that we ought to provide national minorities with language rights—which, as we have seen, is an important cultural component of national identities—and other cultural self-protection rights like self-government arrangements that may be couched in federal administrative setups, like in Canada or Belgium. However, what ought we to do if a country has a multinational population without these groups necessarily being territorially concentrated, as in the case of Canada and Belgium? Dispersion of minority members makes institutional accommodation of the national group problematic, of course, including any territorial federal arrangements. One prominent example of a multinational territory without clearly demarcated territorial boundaries was Bosnia-Herzegovina before attempts by all ethnic groups were made to establish such dividing lines between the different ethno-cultural groups. And in fact, as the conflict in the Balkans illustrated well, multinational countries often also exhibit a multinational citizenry, with children born to parents of different ethno-national ancestry. If we accept, as liberal nationalist authors would like us to, that national identity is a crucial part of our personal identity, it seems that we would have to identify with one national identity rather than feel comfortable in this mélange of identities that multinationality brings with it. This begs the question: Can liberal nationalism take multinational and multiethnic identities into account?

Liberal nationalists don't advocate ethnic purity or anything like it. Instead, they promote shared public cultures and public spheres in which different ethnic groups making up society can come together and create a national identity with which all can identify, to which all can subscribe. A *liberal* nationality, then, is supposed to constitute itself from, on the one hand, our cultural heritage and traditions—its "ethnic" components, so to speak—and, on the other hand, from the shared principles and values we can all agree on—its "civic" components. How would this work? As we have seen above, the idea that we can draw lines between the two, between our ethnic heritage and our civic principles and values, is debated. So the first lesson we can draw from applying liberal nationalist theory to the world around us is that it leaves certain questions concerning the implementation of liberal nationalism unanswered.

A second criticism stems from a more inquisitive look at the potential consequences of liberal national policies. Imagine that we provide ethno-cultural minorities in our midst with chances to contribute to and shape the nature of our national identity. To what extent, we may ask, does the emerging identity still have strong ties to *our* national identity—which is, according to the liberal nationalist view, why we attribute value to our nationality—as an expression of our shared cultural background? To illustrate this, let's look at the example of immigrant minorities, a prominent case study when discussing ethnic diversity as part of a liberal national identity. Assume that it is inoffensive and even enjoyable for most of us to taste foreign foods and appreciate cultural artifacts other than those produced on our home turf over the last centuries. How far can our acceptance go before, indeed, we end up having a "cosmopolitan"-tasting national identity? The criticism that we, in fact, all watch American TV, love pizza, and enjoy a bottle of French wine—in short, that we all already lead cosmopolitan lives rather than the ones prescribed by our national identity—has been leveled against those who propose to put so much value on national identity. A "reality check" based on the mandate to integrate immigrants in a public culture seems to suggest that, if we apply the idea of a diverse public culture to nationality, it may indeed change the nature of our national identity by integrating multiethnic components. This may be a welcome development, but to what extent does the newly forged national identity still fit into the liberal national framework?

Now, let's look at the challenges posed by national minorities to liberal nationalism. Assume we provide national minorities with cultural self-determination rights, like jurisdiction over education, language policy, and immigration policies, as in the case of Québec. To what extent do we pave the way for minority secession justified by the ethno-national character of the minority in question—a development that was exemplified by the violent demise of the Yugoslav federation? Are we not—somewhat secretly—advocating national purity and nation-states again if the basis of rights is the national culture of a group, rather than its democratic tradition, say, or its societal project? Put differently, to what extent does the application of liberal nationalist principles let ideas of "ethnic" nationalism back into the argumentative ring?

These problems have led some authors to argue that any attempts to address the complexities of today's world with 19th-century solutions, that is, attempts to update our take on the nation-state, are doomed to failure. Instead, they argue for a broader framework of governance, as provided, for example, by the European Union, since minorities would feel more comfortable and secure in a transnational institutional framework. Should we refurbish the cosmopolitan model then?

Global Governance

Some authors have indeed advocated that we should start thinking about cosmopolitan governance in a more principled manner. Apart from the obvious shortcomings with the nation-state model outlined above, these authors base their recommendations on a close inspection of today's world. The first argument comes from the sphere of economics. Politics today is dictated by the economy and, more specifically, by needs arising from the globalization of markets, media, and communication. According to some, market forces are so overpowering that the idea that we could hold on to national governments as providers of the institutional security—the things, in fact, that liberal nationalist authors praise the nation-state for, like social integration, recognition, channels of democratic decision-making processes, and so on—is outdated. All national economies participate in international trade regimes (like the North American Free Trade Agreement) or are subject to monitoring organizations like the World Trade Organization or the International Monetary Fund, to name just a few. Furthermore, nation-states are integrated into international regimes like the North Atlantic Treaty Organization, the European Union, or the United Nations (UN). So instead of insisting on the continued role of the nation-state in such a context, some authors advocate a model of cosmopolitan governance, bringing Condorcet's ideal into the 21st century.

Are such calls plausible? Some argue that institutions of international trade coupled with the institutions of the United Nations and its bodies and charters, and the many nongovernmental organizations (NGOs), which now work on an international level (making them into INGOs), provide us with instances of a global or world government that would make the cosmopolitan ideal a realistic option for the first time in human history. However, if we subscribe to the cosmopolitan ideals of individual emancipation and autonomy (rather than simply accept the cosmopolitan fact of our lives), should we really embrace the global sphere, as we know it? Can we really hold that we can lead self-determined lives in such a global sphere?

For liberals, self-determination is intimately tied to the political makeup in which we lead our lives, namely to the democratic nature of the polity. Democracy implies that we can actually influence the political decisions that affect our lives—and it is debated in the literature to what extent we actually can achieve this on the level of international institutions. Most international organizations are built on the nation-state model—it is national governments that agree on and ratify international treaties and resolutions. For individual citizens to actually have a voice in these deliberations is rare—particularly considering that international topics hardly ever make it onto electoral platforms of political parties, leaving citizens in the dark about their candidate's position on international topics. So how can we have democratic input?

Some believe that the existence of NGOs, like Amnesty International or Greenpeace, points to an emerging cosmopolitan civil society through which

The increasing presence of UN soldiers—such as these two patrolling the Green line in Cyprus—is an example of a developing sense of global governance. (Corel)

citizens can achieve democratic self-determination. But to really make a differ-ence as a member of an NGO, their representational clout would have to be sig-nificantly increased because today the organizational structure of international bodies is based, as we know, on the representation of the nation-state. To tackle this, proposals have been made to the effect that we should actually install a second chamber at the United Nations in which, for example, NGOs, INGOs, and ethno-cultural minorities could be represented. Until any such changes occur, however, the sphere of international organizations will remain dominated by nation-states and their governments.

But what about the main claim? Is it true, as liberal nationalists hold, that the relevance of national identity lies in the fact that it promotes solidarity and trust among our compatriots, both feelings we need to be able to enjoy the fruits of the democratic welfare state? Do we have a cosmopolitan sense of identity, and if so, does it perform the same role as national identity? There are today, of course, genuine transnational identities that are detached from national (e.g., French) or regional (e.g., European) units but grounded in the individual sense of belonging to the global community—people who identify with global concerns like human rights and the protection of the global environment. If members of Greenpeace protest against resource exploitation in the Arctic, they don't perceive themselves as particular nationals, but rather as members of an international movement tak-ing issue with the destruction of our global environment. And to be sure, we can think of other issue-specific transnational identities. Even if we agree, however, that such identities exist, and as much as we would wish for more international thinking along these lines, the question remains to what extent can these identi-ties replace the vital role played by national identity? Can we really assume that issue-specific international identities can forge a collective political subject that will enable us to sustain collective action over long periods of time? This seems to be the main challenge to cosmopolitanism. As we have seen, liberal nationalists make arguments for liberal nations based on their concern with individual iden-tity and autonomy. This identity, so the argument goes, derives some of its value from its ties to the national project: in sharing in a national identity, we share in something bigger and potentially more worthwhile than our individual lives can achieve. In that sense, national identity provides us with the opportunity to tran-scend our limited personal lives. And since national identity has such a strong pull on us, we are willing to do things for our nation that we would not necessar-ily do for others. Put otherwise, we feel a sense of belonging to our national com-munity that is not equaled by any other community membership we may have. Therefore, we are willing enough to pay taxes to keep the overall infrastructure of the nation intact, but furthermore, we also agree to pay taxes to support those less well-off in our midst. We show a sense of social cohesion, trust, and solidarity with our compatriots. Could we achieve this in a cosmopolitan world? The emer-gence of issue-specific transnational identities may explain why Greenpeace members are willing to make sacrifices for the environment around the world, but it doesn't explain why Greenpeace members should be willing to make sacrifices for, say, ethno-cultural minorities around the world, particularly those, like the Inuit in Canada, who demand the right to engage in practices potentially harmful to the environment. To put this simply, why should members of Greenpeace stand up for the Inuit if they engage in whale hunting? Democracy, however, demands that we work out solutions to our conflicting interests and so works best when there is some sort of common identity, which transcends these conflicting interests.

This point is highlighted if we take debates surrounding immigration as an indicator of what we feel we ought to give to our compatriots, compared to what we feel we owe to others. While most countries make distinctions between refugees and immigrants, there is a clear sense that what we owe to "our own" (in social support, healthcare, education, etc.) is different from what we ought to give to the rest of the world. This may be very much to the dismay of cosmopolitans in that it privileges those living in the national boundaries compared with those somewhere else. And nothing postulates that this is how it will remain forever. However, neglecting the realities of life in thinking about the world would be just another instance of theoretical blindness toward the facts of the world.

In conclusion, nationalism has certainly led to many historical ills, which is why Einstein so clairvoyantly condemned it as a disease. However, to neglect the drive toward a communal identity entirely and to advocate instead a cosmopolitan creed seems to put us on par with Condorcet's high-minded yet endearingly naive ideas. Instead of engaging in wishful thinking, some liberal political theorists have therefore engaged in a project to design a framework of "liberal nationalism." Their proposals are challenged by those who, both from a normative and empirical perspective, argue that the idea of the nation and its state as the organizing principles of our world is obsolete. Both claims certainly have their merits, but both also have serious shortcomings. It remains a task for political theory, therefore, to fine-tune its analytical tools to be in a position to appropriately grasp the state of our world, with both its national and cosmopolitan forces.

Selected Bibliography

Archibugi, D., and D. Held. 1995. *Cosmopolitan Democracy—An Agenda for a New World Order.* London: Polity Press.

Canovan, M. 1996. *Nationhood and Political Theory.* Cheltenham, UK: Edward Elgar.

Held, D. 1995. *Democracy and the Global Order: From the Modern State to Cosmopolitan Governance.* Stanford, CA: Stanford University Press.

Ignatieff, M. 1994. *Blood and Belonging: Journeys into the New Nationalism.* London: Vintage.

Kohn, H. 1944. *The Idea of Nationalism.* New York: Macmillan.

Kymlicka, W. 1995. *Multicultural Citizenship.* Oxford: Oxford University Press.

Kymlicka, W., and C. Straehle. 1999. "Cosmopolitanism, Nation-States and Minority Nationalism." *European Journal of Philosophy* 7, no. 1: 65–88.

Lu, C. 2000. "The One and Many Faces of Cosmopolitanism." *Journal of Political Philosophy* 8, no. 2: 244–267.

Mill, J. S. 1991. *On Liberty and Other Essays.* Edited by John Gray. Oxford: Oxford University Press.

Miller, D. 1995. *On Nationality.* Oxford: Oxford University Press.

Nussbaum, M. 2000. "Patriotism and Cosmopolitanism." In *For Love of Country?* edited by J. Cohen. Boston: Beacon Press.

Plamenatz, J. P. 1976. "Two Types of Nationalism." In *Nationalism: The Nature and Evolution of an Idea*, edited by E. Kamenka. London: Edward Arnold.

Smith, A. 1986. *The Ethnic Origins of Nations.* Oxford: Blackwell.

Tamir, Y. 1993. *Liberal Nationalism.* Princeton, NJ: Princeton University Press.

Tan, K.-C. 2004. *Justice without Borders—Cosmopolitanism, Nationalism, and Patriotism.* New York: Cambridge University Press.

Waldron, J. 2000. "What Is Cosmopolitan?" *Journal of Political Philosophy* 8, no. 2: 227–243.

Diaspora and Nationalism

Stéphane Dufoix

Relevance

Talking about nationalism implies drawing a line between Us and Them, the nation being a commonly shared circle of land, people, and history surrounded by a periphery composed of all the other lands, peoples, and histories. The nation is inscribed within strict boundaries separating it from the rest of the world. The inside is national; the outside is not. The more homogeneous the inside, the more united and the more true the nation. In this respect, the coincidence between the land and the people functions as an indicator of the limits of the nation. Though an ideal one, this view was fundamental in the age of nation-building: once the nation-state was established, it contained the right population on the right portion of land, with the exception of possible irredentist claims. Everything that contradicted this vision was treated as an anomaly, be it the presence of nationals abroad or the presence of foreigners within. As it could already be read in Plato's *Laws*, going abroad is as dangerous to the purity of the city as letting foreigners in. In either case, any relationship with the exterior had to be seriously monitored, if not strictly forbidden, for contact with foreign people or foreign lands was seen as a kind of pollution. But there was one important exception: this contact would be favored if it could benefit the nation, for instance, by adding new territories to it.

Therefore, displacement toward other lands and the presence abroad of "national" populations historically belonged to two completely different experiences: colonization on the one hand, in which the link to the metropolis was organized around the idea of empire and of domination by the state of those distant lands, as well as of the indigenous populations living there; and individual or collective emigration, on the other hand, for which the upholding of a link with the metropolis was, most of the time, subordinated to the existence of a "spirit of return" to the homeland, as though physical and temporal distance from the home territory was tantamount to affective distance from the nation itself and to the probable weakening of the allegiance to the state. In the first case, the nation expands. In the second, it loses subjects. In 19th-century German states, if a citizen emigrated and did not return before 10 years, he was considered as having renounced his citizenship and was deprived of it.

This latter example was not an isolated case at the time, and we can still see traces of this national reluctance concerning distance. Most democratic countries established differences among their own citizens, depending on whether they resided on national territory or abroad. Even the countries of emigration that strived to maintain a formal link with their emigrants—generally through the implementation of a strong right of blood (*jus sanguinis*), which almost prevented any possibility of renouncing one's citizenship once and for all—at the same time denied those emigrants the capacity to accomplish from abroad such important duties of citizenship as the right to vote, thus making them second-rank citizens due to their spatial distance from the homeland. Historical evidence shows that the opportunity for expatriate citizens to vote from abroad was offered rather late in some Western democracies, such as France, the United Kingdom, and the United States.

For a long time, distance and dispersion from the homeland, materialized in the form of a state or not, were incompatible with the normal existence of a nation; the scattering of a whole people was a terrible curse, while dispersed life was seen as a provisory situation until return to the land could occur. This view has only recently changed. Nowadays, expatriate populations are more and more integrated into the national landscape.

Two forms of a link between the inside and the outside may be elaborated: a struggle from outside to make the land the territory of a nation or of the real nation, and actions by the authorities and/or by "national" communities living abroad to construct, transform, or maintain a link keeping together all parts of the nation. If one wants to study the relationship between the definition of the nation and the physical distance from the land considered as being precisely the crucible of the nation, one has to draw a difference between two types of situations.

In the first case, the definition of the nation is at stake in a conflictual context linked to a war of independence, a war against the occupation of the land by a foreign power, or the claim by groups living outside the boundaries that the home regime is illegitimate. In those cases, as long as no significant opposition is able to develop in the country, the truth of the nation is abroad. The fight for the expected result (i.e., acceding to independence, regaining self-determination, or overthrowing the illegitimate regime) is mostly in the hands of politically active people living in foreign countries. Usually, this situation is known as exile, and we have recently described as exile polities the trans-state national political fields formed by the collaboration and also sometimes concurrence between these groups. Anti-Franco Spaniards, anticommunist East European exiles, anti-Castroist Cubans, Tibetans struggling for a return to independence, Kurds, Tamils, and Palestinians advocating for the creation of a new state for a stateless people: the list could be long of all those populations for which the true spirit of the nation was living abroad for some time before it could eventually find a place, or find it again, with the establishment or reestablishment of an independent state, or a political change. True Poland, real Cuba, Tibet, or Palestine only have a political existence in the hearts and in the actions of people living far away from their national land.

In the second case, there is no challenge to the political legitimacy to the regime: the expatriates are not exiles fighting from abroad for self-determination, the liberation of the country, or a political change. They are mere migrants, or sons and daughters of migrants, who, despite their distance to the national territory, want to be integrated into a broader definition of the nation or become objects of such a redefinition within the framework of a state policy directed toward nationals abroad.

Some recent evolutions tend to show that a de-territorialized logic is increasingly being added to the previous territorial logic of the nation. Transformations of dual nationality and dual citizenship laws, of external voting, of political representation of citizens living abroad, and more generally, of public policies directed toward national populations abroad correspond to a large process in which home states, host states, but also trans-state mobilizations by migrants are involved. Examples of such policies through which states attempt to organize their relationship to the scattered parts of the nation and to breathe life into this link are numerous all around the world: Ireland, Estonia, Latvia, Lithuania, Russia, India, Italy, Greece, Eritrea, Australia, Kenya, Mexico, Armenia, Nigeria, and Colombia, to cite but a few.

If not always contradictory, these two forms may seem to stand at opposite ends of the spectrum. Yet, the evolution of the word "diaspora" for a few decades has encompassed them, as though they were identical. "Diaspora" is now used to describe exile polities as well as any national group away from the homeland. In a sense, this shift is logical because both phenomena ask a single question: what are the spatial limits of the nation? Yet, merging both situations may result in confusion of the issues. It is therefore compulsory to understand why "diaspora" has come to such a crucial role in the vision of a nation that is no longer confined to territorial limits.

Origins

If thinking about "diaspora and nationalism" is in fact thinking about "distance and nationalism," the word "diaspora" cannot just be cast away as though it were not important. On the contrary, the evolutions of its uses are fundamental to anyone trying to understand changes in nationalism issues since the 1960s.

Diaspora is an ancient Greek word that was first used in the Greek translation (known as the Septuagint) of the Hebrew Bible in the third century BC, in which it described the divine punishment Jews would endure (i.e., their dispersion throughout the world) if they would not respect the law of God. Until the 1960s, this old word was mostly limited to the religious realm. It was most often applied to Jews, but also to Catholics and Protestants with the meaning of "religious minority." Moreover, as it stemmed from the Jewish experience, it carried the weight of a negative reputation: "diaspora" meant exile and persecution.

From the 1960s onward, new developments have occurred and the word has acquired a much more positive meaning without yet replacing the negative one.

As compared with its earlier uses marked by religious (Jewish, Catholic, and Protestant) history, it has undergone a progressive secularization, with more and more nonreligious uses becoming acceptable in the social sciences. Another intellectual factor favored this transformation. On the one hand, scholarly works began addressing the issue of the "survival" or of the "upholding" of African cultures in the New World, thus giving the opportunity for populations who were often discriminated against because of the color of their skin to see themselves as having a history and to build bridges with Africa. Another factor in the making of a more positive vision of "diaspora" came from the evolution of the link between the state of Israel and world Jewry. Of course, the creation of the state of Israel in 1948 resulted from the Zionist refusal of a Jewish existence dispersed among the nations. Yet, the fact that a million Jews refused to migrate to Israel despite the Law of Return, while at the same time claiming their "particular attachment" to the fate of this country, gave credit to the opinion that the boundaries of a nation were not necessarily the territorial boundaries. "Diaspora" became a positive notion.

This possibility of an ethno-national link between a territorial center and dispersed communities combines with the increasing theoretical and empirical recognition of potentially plural ethnic or cultural identities to generate a split in the meaning of "diaspora." From the end of the 1960s, it could be used in reference to very different phenomena. It could mean the dispersion of a people without a state (the Armenian or the Palestinian diaspora), a community of people sharing the same origin though not being citizens of the state they feel close to (the Jewish diaspora), or a broad cultural community sharing the belief in a common origin without any relationship to a center at all (the black or African diaspora).

From the early 1960s onward, the original cultural identity of migrants was no longer considered something that was bound to disappear. This important change in the interpretation of identity gave rise to multicultural programs and policies in some Western states (United States, United Kingdom, Australia, Canada) and fostered new, plural theories of ethnicity, taking into account the fact that living in a territory did not necessarily mean keeping a one-and-only relationship to its culture. Moreover, in parallel, some philosophical, anthropological, and sociological theories (post-structuralism, postmodernism, cultural studies, etc.) emerged from the late 1960s. They were characterized by the ambition to deconstruct the notions of unity and oneness to concentrate on multiplicity and to condemn the notion of center to concentrate on the periphery. By doing this, they granted a particular importance to the ideas of space and spatialization, thus making it possible for dispersion to be a different rather than a pathological mode of being in the world. This new vision quickly fitted with the discovery in the 1980s that the world was becoming increasingly global. Taking into account new opportunities to connect people and groups beyond state boundaries, the network became the key notion to understanding the contemporary world. This trend was confirmed by the irruption of new technologies for information and communication (fax machines, mobile phones, and especially, the Internet). In this context, "diaspora" happened to be the right word at the right time. This new insistence on space, on link, and on the potential multiplicity of identities quite naturally met the word and made it a fundamental entry into the new world. But the process of globalization is far from being uniform in its consequences. As the political scientist James Rosenau and the sociologist Zygmunt Bauman have separately demonstrated, instead of favoring homogenization, globalization rather tends to juxtapose two opposite dimensions: a state dimension and a nonstate dimension, the dimension of travel and the dimension of origin, or to put it in the words of the anthropologist James Clifford, the juxtaposition of "routes" and "roots." As we saw earlier, the acquired polysemy of "diaspora" authorized it to describe centered as well as centerless relationships. "Diaspora" thus became a word capable of describing the world of the past as well as the contemporary world, the state as well as the network, what is out of date as well as what is forthcoming.

Finally, the affinity between the word "diaspora," with all its stratified meanings, and the multifaceted transformations of the worlds of identity and space and their interpretation in the social sciences made it possible for the word to go beyond a mere conceptual use. Imported from the social sciences by community leaders, civil servants, journalists, and Web masters, this practical use resulted in its increasing capacity to embrace more and more populations and situations. Now having become a "global word" that fits the "global world," it may be used without any precaution or definition. Its conceptualization made it available for politicians and statesmen; its use even became institutionalized within the framework of state policies, "diaspora" being increasingly used as the very name of national populations or populations of national origin living abroad. Whereas the notion of "ethnic group" can define the common particularities of a population living in one territory, the notion of "diaspora" made it possible to define a community all over the world.

If we concentrate more precisely on the link between "diaspora" and "nationalism" in the social sciences, we can notice that it was hardly mentioned before the second half of the 20th century. If C. A. Macartney, in his *National States and National Minorities* (1934), described the Gypsies as a people "which, however, unlike all the others, has never attempted to found a state of its own, but has been content, it appears, to live in an eternal diaspora," he was an isolated case before Arnold Toynbee granted a greater importance to diaspora peoples in his *Study of History* (1934). The study of the relationship between diaspora and nationalism really took shape in the second half of the 1970s and early 1980s.

In an article titled "Mobilized and Proletarian Diasporas," published in the *American Political Science Review* in 1976, John Armstrong was certainly one of the first scholars to seriously examine the role of diaspora, which he defined as "any ethnic collectivity that lacks a territorial base within a given polity, i.e., is a relatively small minority throughout all portion of the polity." One year later, Hugh Seton-Watson, in his *Nations and States*, wrote a section devoted to "diaspora nations." Experts in nationalism studies, such as Anthony Smith or Benedict Anderson, often referred to Jewish, Armenian, and Greek attempts at building a state of their own in terms of "diaspora nationalism."

As a sign that distance was not contradictory with nationalism any more, the historian Benedict Anderson coined in the mid-1990s the phrase "long-distance nationalism" to signal the current acceleration of an older phenomenon: identification to a nation arising from confrontation with others and from the risk of seeing one's particularity diluted. In this respect, nationalism would in some way be born out of exile. Transnationalization linked to the development of post-industrial capitalism not only favors migrations but also the organization by migrants and their descendants of some kind of relationship to their country of origin, sometimes even influencing homeland policies so that the latter may take into account their presence abroad.

Dimensions

Considering the distinction that we established at the beginning between exile communities and communities living abroad, it may seem at first glance that their experiences are completely opposite from one another. Yet, the major axes of their link to the homeland belong to the same broad categories. We can identify two of them, for which we'll show the differences for the two aforementioned subgroups: the importance of time and space, and the question of the political legitimacy of the populations abroad.

Physical distance from the homeland logically implies a specific relationship to space, but, as the sociologist Norbert Elias demonstrated, space cannot be dissociated from time. Being away in space also means being away in time. In this respect, exiled polities and expatriate communities resemble each other. Away from the land, they also live in a different time, since their host countries or countries of residence possess their own national time. There is nevertheless a great difference between exile and expatriate communities as far as this relationship to time and space is concerned. Whereas expatriate communities generally have the possibility of keeping contact with both the space and time of the homeland, the exile cannot afford this contact and most often refuses it because he considers any physical contact with the territory they are fighting for to represent the recognition of the present situation. For instance, people who have fled their country for fear of persecution because of their political opinions and who have been granted refugee status must accept that they cannot go back to the homeland. If they do, they will officially not be recognized as refugees any more. That dimension of exile is fundamental. Exile polities can only develop if they organize a symbolic suspension of time and space, as though neither were linked to the homeland any more. By doing this, exiles justify a struggle that is bound to last until they return to the homeland. They also run the risk of totally disconnecting themselves from the homeland, since going back will expunge that vital aspect of their political identity.

In his book *Imagined Communities* (1983), Benedict Anderson insisted on the role that the invention of printing played in the diffusion of nationalism: identical words could then be read by different people in distinct places, thus building a bridge between them and potentially synchronizing their spirits in a single realm. The development of nation-states resulted in the formation of national temporalities binding people together: time and space coincided. During the modern period, every distance in space was therefore a distance in time, that is, a distance to the nation. The period that witnessed the rise of electronics and information science has been labeled "late modernity," "second modernity," or "hypermodernity" precisely because space has progressively become more and more independent of time. The consequences of such a revolution are obvious as far as the upholding of a link to the nation is concerned. It has now become possible for distant people to communicate almost instantaneously via e-mails, mobile phones, chat rooms, portals, etc. The so-called new technologies of information and communication allow migrants not to live their situation merely as a "double absence," neither here nor there, as the French sociologist Abdelmalek Sayad put it a decade ago, but rather as a potential "double presence," here and there, because even these words have lost part of their meaning.

The Internet is obviously the most important medium for this development of potential ubiquity. Governmental sites giving expatriates as much information as possible about their rights or about the internal evolution of the country, or ethno-national portals designed by migrants or their descendents, instill continuity and instantaneity into the relationship established among state representatives and "diaspora" representatives. The creation of an Internet site devoted to this purpose is now of the very first claims by expatriates. As a matter of fact, the recent creation (2002) by the Eritrean government of a specific institution in charge of contact with Eritreans abroad was immediately accompanied by a Web site project as well as the construction of a database. Such core sites established by states like India, Armenia, Greece, Italy, and so on, cohabit with other Web sites, the purpose of which is to connect the various poles of the periphery. Similarly, exile polities, too, take advantage of the lobbying, diffusion, and connection opportunities offered by the Internet. In 1996, a Burmese militant from the University of Wisconsin campaigned for democracy in Burma on his Free Burma Coalition site, which led the U.S. Congress to put the issue of economic sanctions against the Rangoon regime on the agenda. Most exile organizations, be they Sikh, Kurdish, Tamil, or others, make these sites powerful political platforms and even, sometimes, the very place of their political alternative. Some years ago, one could read the following on the first page of the Sikh site (www.khalistan.com): "Welcome to the sovereign cyberspace of Khalistan!"

Besides the relationship between time and space, the issue of legitimacy is the second important axis. Earlier, we saw that, from a traditional vision, people were considered weaker and less reliable the farther they were from the land. If the legitimacy of distance is ever recognized, in the case of political struggle from abroad, for instance, it seldom survives the contact between the nation and the land again. The role of exile in the birth or in the return of the nation is often forgotten, if not denied. Algerian nationalism was born in France among Algerian immigrants during the interwar period, and France remained the crucible of nationalism even during the Algerian War. Yet, after independence in 1962, that fact was obliterated, whereas the national soil and the struggle of Algerians in Algeria was highlighted. It took almost 20 years before the real history started to be told.

When the definition of the real nation was not at stake, national populations living outside the frontiers would not be considered deserving of much attention for a long time. In the 19th century, the national territory was the container of the nation, citizenship as such was only taking shape as a matter of international law, and emigrants used to be seen by the home state as lost citizens. The recognition that diplomatic protection of citizens residing abroad was part of the duties of the state only started at the end of the 19th century, but it seldom gave birth to actual positive policies directed toward them. There was a shift from indifference or abstention to the implementation of a policy of attention toward expatriates from the 1960s to the 1970s onward.

Three domains are affected by these policies: dual nationality, external voting, and political representation, each one representing a further step in the recognition of expatriates' importance for the nation. If we first look at citizenship, we can notice that a major change occurred around the 1960s, driving more and more countries to at least tolerate dual nationality. In 2001, 92 countries in the world allowed, implicitly or explicitly, some form of multiple citizenship. To take an example, only 2 out of the 19 Latin American—Spanish- and Portuguese-speaking—countries recognized dual nationality before the 1980s: Uruguay (1919) and Panama (1972). Throughout the last 30 years, 8 others voted for provisions in this domain, 6 of them during the 1990s (Brazil, Colombia, Costa Rica, the Dominican Republic, Ecuador, Mexico). The same acceleration process took place on all continents, often following waves of access to independence. Out of the 14 non-Spanish- and non-Portuguese-speaking countries of Central and South America, 9 of them recognize dual nationality, and out of those 9, 8 of them recognized it just after their independence (from the early 1960s until the end of the 1980s). Many of the countries that allowed their citizens to retain their nationality in the last 30 years had earlier been part of empires, and significant portions of their population had migrated to and settled in the metropolis or in other regions of the empire. Such nationality policy was therefore crucial in the national project.

Contrary to a commonly held view, dual nationality and dual citizenship are different things. The latter implies full access to political rights, including voting from abroad, which is not the case with the former. Often neglected, this issue is crucial. At the end of the 20th century, only about 60 states had legal provisions allowing external voting (i.e., gave their citizens residing abroad the possibility to vote without going back to their home country). Interestingly, the most ancient democracies refused this possibility until recently: Australia admitted it in 1901, France just after World War II, the United States in 1975, the United Kingdom in 1985, and Canada in 1993! It seems that there is now an increasing trend, but the introduction of external voting can be explained by national peculiarities rather than by the waves of democratization of the 20th century.

Finally, a few countries went so far as to allow citizens abroad to vote for their own representatives. Only three European countries have chosen to do so: France, Portugal, and, recently, Italy. The latter case is particularly interesting. The Berlusconi government formed in June 2001 included a ministry for Italians abroad. It was headed by Mirko Tremaglia who had parliament adopt the law allowing Italians to vote from abroad and notably to elect 12 deputies and 6 senators. In one of history's frequent ironies, it was precisely the Italian vote from abroad that sealed Berlusconi and Tremaglia's defeat in the April 2006 general elections by electing 4 pro-Prodi senators and thus giving the Unione Party a majority in the senate.

"Diaspora" has certainly become the most common name used in political discourses to encompass all national, or of national origin, populations living abroad. Contrary to what is usually considered the definition of nationalism, diaspora helps to identify a group without—and not within—its boundaries. The emotional dimension implied by the opportunity to be in direct connection, more or less formally, with the homeland makes "diaspora policies" rather popular, inside and outside the country. "Diaspora" is much more inclusive than such former denominations as "citizens abroad" or "nationals abroad" for it keeps the idea alive that the nation is a family and that distance does not really matter. Giving a specific name—and especially diaspora—to populations abroad shows the particularity to create the group in question rather than only describing it. The philosopher John Austin decades ago insisted on the performative dimensions of speech: language sometimes does what it says. When we say "I swear," we indeed do it through speech. I want here to insist on another potential dimension of speech, what I call its formative dimension. When a politician or the leader of an organization says "our diaspora numbers 2 million people," he does not only count dispersed people but he makes them a single group; he contributes to forming the group he only pretends to describe.

That dimension insisting on primordial ties is symbolically important to the general framework of nationalism, but it sometimes hides other interests, most often economic ones, as can be seen in the cases of China and India. In the 1970s, both countries shifted from a policy of abstention (even encouraging their expatriates to integrate abroad) to a policy of attention favoring financial investment from abroad to accelerate the modernization of the country. This policy has proven to be successful in China, since it is estimated that 70 percent of the foreign direct investment (FDI) in this country comes from overseas Chinese. It represented a total $26.8 billion between 1979 and 1991 (Thorpe 2002, 8–9). It reached around $40–45 billion per year between 1997 and 2001, and even rose to $72 billion in 2005, thus making China the first country in the world in terms of FDI received (UNCTAD 2006, 51).

The beginnings of the Indian policy follow the same path. In the late 1970s, the government created the category Non Resident Indians (NRIs) and offered facilities for investing and setting up businesses in India. The relative failure of this policy, the fact that expatriates claimed a stronger link to the homeland, and the coming to power of the nationalist Hindu party, the Bharatiya Janata Party (BJP), all account for the launching of a broader policy in the late 1990s. In 1999, this policy created the PIO (Person of Indian Origin) scheme, giving the possibility even to former Indian citizens to return without a visa. In 2001, an official report drew the lines of that new policy, insisting on an ethnic definition of the nation and on the economic importance of expatriates at the same time. However, success is not certain because the Indian population, inside or outside the country, is fragmented along four lines that still remain predominant: religion, language, region of origin, and caste.

Today we see evidence of more and more nation-states trying to include expatriates and people of national origin into the definition of the nation. Also, an

Indian government ministers assemble during the fifth Pravasi Bharatiya Divas (Overseas Indian Conference) in New Delhi, January 8, 2007. During the annual gathering of Non Resident Indians (NRI), the government seeks to tap the Indian diaspora's expertise, experience, and capital for balanced economic development of the country. (Raveendran/AFP/Getty Images)

increasing number of ethnic organizations abroad claim the creation of better links with the homeland. Yet, this trend also gives way to a few backlashes. The greatest one is the accusation of disloyalty aimed at expatriates on the grounds that they live away from the homeland. Nowadays, disloyalty is often replaced by lack of confidence. It is often estimated that expatriates would be better citizens if they lived in the country rather than abroad. So, Ireland and Greece do not have any provision on external voting, even though their rates of citizens residing abroad are certainly the highest among the countries of the European Union, precisely because they fear domestic politics could be influenced by people not living in the country.

The second backlash is the risk of exaggerated primordialism. The development of policies of return that allow any returnee of national origin to recover his/her citizenship often coincides with a noninclusive nationality law in the country, thus preventing foreigners and minorities from ever being part of the national community. Such is the case in Israel, Greece, Italy, Estonia, and Germany. The primordial tie is seen as the base of the nation; "diaspora" may then be part not of a national but of a nationalist framework proclaiming the idea of a closed—as pure as possible—national identity. Logically, however, such policies may be strongly resented in countries where great numbers of dual nationals live. As a matter of fact, their loyalty to the host country may be suspected in times of military crisis (during both world wars for instance) or in times of identity crisis, an example of the latter being Samuel Huntington's reflections on the dilution of American identity due to the rise of dual nationality.

Consequences

Globalization is very often interpreted as the end of the nation-state because state boundaries cannot function as walls of the national container any more. The emergence of many flows, financial, economic, informational, and human, has made them porous. But this porosity is not necessarily to the detriment of the state, for trans-state phenomena are not necessarily nonstate phenomena. Evidence shows that states also go through a "trans-statization" of themselves. If the globalization process is an open spatialization of economic, political, cultural, and social relations, it also encompasses state capacities to go beyond their borders. The evolutions that have taken place in some countries for the last 30 years certainly point out that the relation of the state, as a historical political form, to space and distance is changing; being "out of sight" is not tantamount to being "out of mind" any more. The nation extends its limits beyond state borders, and the very definitions of nation and nationality are being transformed since not only citizens abroad, but also former citizens or descendents of former citizens, still belong to the nation. Arjun Appadurai called these new entities "trans-nations," but this term does not show that many nations live beyond state borders; I would rather call them "trans-state nations." This new paradigm has certainly never been more clearly presented than by Mexican president Ponce de Leon in a discourse before the Mexican Federal Congress in May 1995: "The Mexican nation *goes beyond the territory contained by its borders.* Therefore an essential element of the 'Mexican national program' will be *to promote the constitutional and legal amendments designed for Mexicans to retain their nationality*" (quoted in Vargas 1996, 3–4; italics added for emphasis).

One might think, considering the examples given so far, that the insistence on national "diasporas" is the prerogative of nonindustrialized and non-Western countries. That was certainly true until recently. There is recent evidence of evolution in this respect. For instance, an official Summit of European Diasporas that gathered the representatives of 24 European states was held in June 2003 in Thessalonica at the initiative of the Greek foreign ministry. Its aim was to raise awareness on this issue and "to focus attention on the importance of Europe's diasporas, the role they can play in EU policy development, and to begin a process that will lead to stronger EU-diaspora ties" (Summit of European Diasporas 2003, 2). Moreover, the 2004 comparative study report issued by the European Confederation called "Europeans throughout the World," sponsored by the European Commission, called for the inclusion by any European Union (EU) member state of legal provisions concerning national election voting rights for any citizen living abroad:

> There is a need for the Member States and the EU institutions to formally recognise in all appropriate instruments, the solidarity with expatriate European citizens, wherever they are found in the world and to fully recognise the resource: economic, cultural, educational, social, linguistic . . . which the expatriates represent for the countries and for Europe. (European Confederation 2004, 39)

For their part, Australian authorities, too, have engaged in exploring opportunities of building stronger bridges with their "diaspora," thus slightly changing the definition of the country itself, making it not only a country of immigration but also a country of emigration.

This recognition of the place expatriates occupy in the frame of the nation can even go further when people of national origin come to be included in the definition of the "diaspora." Besides the Indian case with the PIO scheme and the enforcement of an Overseas Citizenship of India since December 2, 2005, the Irish and Armenian cases are emblematic of this trend. Mary Robinson, president of the Republic of Ireland from 1990 to 1997, played a prominent role in this acknowledgment of the "Irish diaspora," most notably in her "Cherishing the Irish Diaspora" discourse of February 3, 1995, before the two chambers of the Parliament:

> Four years ago I promised to dedicate my abilities to the service and welfare of the people of Ireland. Even then I was acutely aware of how broad that term the

people of Ireland is and how it resisted any fixed or narrow definition. One of my purposes here today is to suggest that, far from seeking to categorize or define it, we widen it still further to make it as broad and inclusive as possible. (Robinson 1995)

The current Article 2 of the Irish Constitution, modified by referendum in May 1998, specifically states that "the Irish nation cherishes its special affinity with people of Irish ancestry living abroad who share its cultural identity and heritage."

The Armenian case is an interesting example of a shift from exile polity, as long as the Republic of Armenia was a Soviet Republic, to an expatriate community from the Armenian independence in 1991 onward. The most important feature of the diaspora policy of the Armenian Republic is the organization of Armenia-Diaspora conferences that gather representatives of the state and of the Armenian communities in the world. Three of them actually took place in 1999, 2002, and 2006. Their findings did not result in the immediate acceptance of dual citizenship, since the constitutional ban on dual citizenship was not removed before a referendum held on November 27, 2005. Yet, these conferences actually drew the spatial trans-state limits of the Armenian nation, as it is clear from the final decision of the first conference in 1999:

> All the components of our national entity—the Republic of Armenia, Artsakh and the Diaspora—are interdependent. . . . The Republic of Armenia and its state institutions must necessarily readdress their role in support of the Diaspora's needs and aspirations. Armenians are Armenian everywhere, and there is no difference as to where they are. They cannot be "odars" [foreigners] in their homeland, and the Republic undertakes to overcome the Constitutional exclusion of dual citizenship, and to allow each and every Armenian to establish a full presence in his or her homeland. (Armenia-Diaspora Conference 1999)

This short excerpt, as well as the other examples cited above, shows well how globalization and technology have transformed the relationship between those who live inside and those who live outside. The opportunity to create or restore links without taking spatial distance into account allows for original forms of community. Dispersion may not be considered a curse any longer, for the creation of trans-state networks—including states—might well be the form of being together that best fits the world we now, and certainly tomorrow will, live in.

About 200 years after the development of classical nationalism that was centered on the exclusive notions of territory, peoplehood, and nationality, an alternative framework and definition of the nation emerged. In this new definition, the inside—the national territory—is intimately connected to the outside—the diaspora—thus giving birth to possible unbound, trans-state nations. This does not mean that the nation-state as such has disappeared or is bound to disappear. Recent technological and intellectual transformations have made it possible to dissociate the nation-state from its "natural" territorial borders and to include kin populations living abroad. The scope of the nation and of nationalism has thus been extended, and "diasporas" are less and less considered social aberrations and have become actors and targets of national policies.

Selected Bibliography

Anderson, B. 1983. *Imagined Communities: Reflections on the Origin and Spread of Nationalism.* London: Verso.

Appadurai, A. 1996. *Modernity at Large: Cultural Dimensions of Globalization.* Minneapolis: University of Minnesota Press.

Armenia-Diaspora Conference. 1999. *Final Declaration of the First Armenia-Diaspora Conference.* September 22–23. Yerevan. (Retrieved June 14, 2007), http://www.armeniadiaspora. com/conference99/text1.html.

Armstrong, J. A. 1976. "Mobilized and Proletarian Diasporas." *American Political Science Review* 70, no. 2 (June): 393–408.

Austin, J. 1962. *How to Do Things with Words.* Oxford: Clarendon.

Basch, L., N. Glick Schiller, and C. Blanc-Szanton. 1994. *Nations Unbound: Transnational Projects, Postcolonial Predicaments, and Deterritorialised Nation-States.* Basel, Switzerland: Gordon & Breach.

Bauman, Z. 1998. *Globalization. The Human Consequences.* London: Polity Press.

Clifford, J. 1997. *Routes: Travel and Translation in the Late Twentieth Century.* Cambridge, MA: Harvard University Press.

Cohen, R. 1997. *Global Diasporas: An Introduction.* London: UCL Press.

Curtin, P. D. 1984. *Cross-Cultural Trade in World History.* Cambridge: Cambridge University Press.

Dufoix, S. 2003. *Les diasporas.* Paris: Presses Universitaires de France [to be published in English by the University of California Press in March 2008].

European Confederation. 2004. *Democratic Rights of European Expatriates.* Comparative Study Report. "The Europeans throughout the World," 1–56. (Retrieved June 15, 2007), http:// www.viw.be/PDF/ettw%20voting%20rights.pdf.

Gellner, E. 1983. *Nations and Nationalism.* Oxford: Basil Blackwell.

Huntington, S. 2004. *Who Are We? The Challenges to America's National Identity.* New York: Simon & Schuster.

Jones-Correa, M. 2001. "Under Two Flags: Dual Nationality in Latin America and Its Consequences for the United States." *International Migration Review* 35, no. 4 (Winter): 997–1029.

Macartney, C. A. 1934. *National States and National Minorities.* London: Oxford University Press.

Robinson, M. 1995. "Cherishing the Irish Diaspora." Address to the Houses of the Oireachtas, February 2. (Retrieved June 14, 2007), http://www.emigrant.ie/emigrant/historic/ diaspora.htm.

Rosenau, J. 1990. *Turbulence in World Politics: A Theory of Change and Continuity.* Princeton, NJ: Princeton University Press.

Sayad, A. 1999. *La double absence. Des illusions de l'émigré aux souffrances de l'immigré.* Paris: Seuil.

Seton-Watson, H. 1977. *Nations and States.* Boulder, CO: Westview.

Shain, Y. 1999. *Marketing the American Creed Abroad: Diasporas in the U.S. and Their Homelands.* Cambridge: Cambridge University Press.

Sheffer, G. 2003. *Diaspora Politics: At Home Abroad.* Cambridge: Cambridge University Press.

Summit of European Diasporas. 2003. *Summary Report & Recommendations.* June 30: 1–9.

Thorpe, M. 2002. "Inward Foreign Investment and the Chinese Economy." Paper presented at the New Zealand Conference of Economists Annual Conference, Wellington, June 26–28. (Retrieved March 12, 2007), http://www.nzae.org.nz/files/%2346-THORPE.PDF.

UNCTAD. 2006. *FDI from Developing and Transition Economies: Implications for Development.* World Investment Report. New York: United Nations.

Vargas, J. A. 1996. "Dual Nationality for Mexicans?" *Chicano-Latino Law Review* 18, no. 1: 1–58.

Education and National Diversity

Cynthia Joseph and Stella Coram

"Everyone has the right to education"
—Universal Declaration of Human Rights

Relevance

This chapter examines the interplay between education and nationalism in the 20th and 21st centuries. The modern educational system emerged at the same time as the creation of the modern nation-state. The goals of the education system are to educate and socialize individuals into society and to create productive and responsible citizens. The educational system is an important social and political institution in the teaching of knowledge and the development of faithful and loyal citizens. The educational system is also a mediator in the organizing and preparation of citizens for their entry into society. During the process, citizenship can be uniform and assumed to be a unitary category as aspects of social differences in relation to class, gender, race, ethnicity, culture, and language can be overlooked in terms of educational policy and practice.

In understanding the link between education and nationalism, it is necessary to consider that not all peoples within a nation-state have equal access to social, cultural, and economic resources. There is a tension between the roles of the education system as a mediator of nationalism and the dominant cultural group, on the one hand, and of democracy and cultural differences, on the other. This is an important distinction to make because it highlights the broadness and scope of expectations in education. Multicultural societies such as Britain, Australia, Canada, Singapore, South Africa, Malaysia, and other nations teach diversity and tolerance in education yet educational values are generally linked to one cultural group. For example, educational values in the Australian setting are characteristically British due to the historical context. An English-based education system can exclude citizens socialized to different linguistic and cultural values. In this way, a nationalist program may not always function as a system of unification, especially where there are different cultural and ethnic groups.

Education within a nation-state must also be understood within the broader social, economic, and political forces. Significant technological changes and globalization have increased the capacity to obtain, share, or be exposed to different knowledge. Economic and social differences between and within nations also have to be considered in exploring the relationship between education and nationalism. Although there are overlapping issues in the educational policies of nations, the ways in which these policies are put into practice and their outcomes are dependent on the economic and political wealth and strength of the nation both at the nation-state, regional, and global levels.

Globalization plays a vital role in understanding education and nationalism in contemporary times. Globalization is generally understood as the global flows of people and goods, ideas, images, and messages, and capital and technologies. Within the contexts of global migration and capital, expanding knowledge and technological developments, the role of education with young people becomes increasingly important. Moreover, such recent events as the London bombings, the Spanish bombings, the Bali bombings, and other post-9/11 events place increasing importance on the role of the nation-state in ensuring an education system that is inclusive of people who identify as culturally different.

The goal of education has been to produce disciplined, reliable, and productive citizens who contribute to the economic growth of the nation. In present globalizing times, nation-states formulate education policies and practices within the frameworks of liberalism and capitalism in addition to nationalism. The global market also plays a crucial role in shaping education particularly within Western nation-states. Education becomes associated with social and economic capital. The knowledge worker is now a goal of most nations. The knowledge-based economy, in which educational outcomes based on the knowledgeable worker are emphasized, represents the agenda of transnational agencies or corporations and OECD (Organisation for Economic Co-operation and Development) countries. New modes of learning, such as E learning or electronic learning that are emphasized within current education systems match the goals of lifelong learning and the development of the knowledge worker.

The knowledge worker is someone who is creative, efficient, analytical, and immersed in lifelong learning. A knowledge worker is also ICT (Information and Communication Technology) savvy. Human capital is now an essential aspect of the education objectives of such transnational and global agencies as the OECD. Individualism and consumerism are also important within such an approach. Education as advocated by the OECD now operates within the global economic framework. Performance indicators are used to assess the success of an education system and that of the individual in the production of a flexible, compliant, and global workforce.

At the core is lifelong learning. Workers can expect to change jobs, and to do that, they need to be technically proficient in a number of capacities. This is reflected in the employee flexibility now valued over employee loyalty in the competitive market environment. The national agenda in effect trains workers to compete in putting their skills on the global market. This is directly related to primary education, as education is now about teaching compliance in the preparation of the national and now global workforce. In terms of global market (capital) forces, education plays a central role in the creation of the high-performing professional who is attuned to market forces either as an employee or consumer of technologically advanced products. A uniform approach to education is seen as crucial to this process.

In examining education and nationalism, it is necessary to understand the role of education nationally. The business of education in schools, colleges, and universities is to pass knowledge on to the next generation. As a major public asset, education policies tend to emphasize social justice, balance, and harmony. While education and official policies might promote such values, the ways in which education works in relation to access and success in education can be contradictory. As discussed earlier, there are tensions within education, in particular the creation of the productive and global citizen, that differ from education based on an inquiring citizen.

Education systems aim to address social inequalities that exist within the nation-state so as to ensure that all citizens contribute through meaningful and creative ways that are beneficial to the individual, community, and nation. Education addresses not only national and global imperatives but also the needs of the people of a nation-state. Nationalism in education also increases in importance in the need for unification, particularly after the creation of an independent nation-state such as East Timor. A key starting point in the rebuilding of a society in the wake of political upheaval or a newly created democratic government is education infrastructure. National education systems must also emphasize ethnic or religious differences.

Origins and Dimensions

Values and Practices of Education and Nationalism

The values and practices of education and nationalism are very much dependent on such factors as the development of the nation, the economic and political stability of a nation, and the global standing of the nation. Global players, such as the United States, Britain, and other European nations, differ significantly in educational policies, priorities, and achievements compared with that of war and conflict-ridden nations, such as Iraq and Afghanistan, and developing nations, such as Pakistan, Indonesia, and the newly independent eastern European nations and other nations.

There has been a rise of neoliberalism in educational policies in such Western nations as the United States and Britain. These nations are two of the main players in the global economic competition. Education, in such nations, is used as a social and political tool in the development and maintenance of a highly qualified and flexible workforce to ensure the Western nations' position in the competitive global marketplace. Education policies and practices within these nations are focused on educational credentialism with an emphasis on academic testing and standards. Schools and educational institutions are seen as market places, with parents and students being customers or clients. The educational institutions in these countries are also managed along the lines of commercial enterprises. Standardized curriculum and tests, school choices, and privatization of education provision are some of the characteristics of this new capitalist and competitive-market approach to education.

There is also an increased level of bureaucracy that includes surveillance and monitoring with this market model of education. The main focus of education within these nations then becomes the development of skills that are required by students and young people to become economically productive members of the nation. The idea of a well-rounded liberally educated person is no longer significant within such education systems. Individuals are now responsible for their own educational and vocational choices, and the idea of a shared community is no longer important. These markets systems and the competitive examination systems result in inequalities among and within educational institutions. Governments in these Western nations argue that markets, competition, and choices are necessary to prepare students for the global economy. While these nations are the main players within the global education scenario, there are also increasing issues concerning social and economic inequalities within such a market model of education. Not all parents and students have equal access to educational opportunities and pathways. The economic and cultural capital of individuals, families, and communities become the determining factor for educational success. These powerful nations also need to address these issues of inequality amid the competitiveness of the global environment.

Australia and New Zealand are Western nations located within the Asia-Pacific region. In Australia, the dominant population are descendants of European, namely British and Irish, settlers. Australia is a nation of migrants originally from Europe but now more recently from Asia and Africa, including the Sudan and the Horn of Africa. Of the 20 million people living in Australia, approximately 2 percent of the population are Aboriginals or Torres Strait Islanders—the indigenous peoples of Australia. Some of the challenges of the Australian education system in present times include marketing education, the public and private divide in the schooling system, tertiary education as an entrepreneurial activity, the professionalism of the teaching force, success and access to education for indigenous peoples, and multicultural education. There is tension here because Australian educational practice is founded on diversity and multiculturalism. The philosophy of multiculturalism is reflected in the 1997 Multicultural Policy for Victorian Schools. The role of education in the implementation of multicultural policy is to ensure that racism and prejudice do not hinder individual participation and that all students are assisted to develop skills that will enable them to achieve their full potential.

However, multiculturalism has been reduced to celebrations of cultural difference, which serves to strengthen the authority of the dominant culture. Multiculturalism must go beyond mere celebrations of cultural diversity and food festivals, and it must consider how education is used to produce and reproduce social inequalities (Jakubowicz 2002).

There is a wide gap between indigenous Australians and mainstream Anglo-Celtic Australians in education, health, and employment. Indigenous learners favor what is referred to as two-ways learning based on a combination of indigenous and English education. This learning approach emphasizes culturally relevant educational practice. To assimilate into the dominant education system for many indigenous peoples means to displace their values and beliefs. However, to not obtain a (white) mainstream education then limits the opportunities for indigenous people in the main economy.

The Australian government and communities have developed various programs and policies to address these social issues of the indigenous communities. Some examples are the Parent School Partnerships Initiatives, focused on early childhood education, improving indigenous outcomes, and enhancing indigenous culture and knowledge in Australian higher education; the Indigenous Youth Mobility Programme; the Sporting Chance Programme (school-based sports academies); and the Indigenous Youth Leadership Programme.

The need for culturally relevant educational practices for indigenous peoples is an ongoing challenge for community leaders, policy makers, and politicians. The New Zealand experience provides an example of this. Maori education was segregated. However, Maori schools were closed in 1956 with the beginning of a period of assimilation for consecutive decades where Maori were taught English curriculum. The learning of Maori was not encouraged. New Zealand is home to Pakehas (Europeans), the dominant ethnic group, Maori (the indigenous peoples) who constitute approximately 10 percent of the population, and other ethnic groups, including Indian, Chinese, Tongan, Samoan, Fijian, and more recently, refugees from the Middle East. New Zealand is a bicultural nation, which means that Maori is now an "official" language with the writing of legal documents in English and Maori.

The last 20 years has seen significant change, with the integration of Maori language and learning into mainstream schooling. This is seen in the establishment of education initiatives undertaken by Maori such as Maori language nests or preschool (*Kohanga Reo*), Maori immersion elementary schools (*Kura Kaupapa*), Maori secondary schools (*Kura Tuarua*), and Maori tertiary institutions (*Whare Wananga*). The return of Maori schooling may be significant for a national approach to education in New Zealand. Although it is crucial that Maori continue to be immersed in Maori learning, there are implications for non-English-speaking migrants such that they and their children must learn English and Maori language and culture. The context of nationalism in New Zealand is specific in that it is represented through bicultural values in education. The discussion so far indicates that the cultural and historical contexts of the citizens are important aspects of nationalism and education within each nation-state.

Canada is a multicultural Western nation. In Canada, education is the responsibility of each province and territory. Canada's education system plays a

major role in the balancing required to maintain healthy roots for the two official linguistic cultures in Canada. In 1999, the Council for Ministers of Education
in Canada developed a statement in the Victoria Declaration that summarizes
the scope and impact of education in Canada as a lifelong learning process. As
with other nations, nationalism and the responsible, creative, and productive
citizen are represented in official and education policies. However, the Canadian government places much importance on cultural diversity. Various policies
and reports on ethnic groups, such as migrant youth, aboriginal education, as
well as education for African Canadians, take into account the importance of
cultural diversity in educational practices. There is also the Canadian Council for
Multi-Intercultural Education that works on increasing the multicultural dialogue throughout Canada.

Education policies and practices in multiethnic Western nations are located
within multiple cultural contexts. On the one hand, education is a social and political tool of integration in the development of the responsible, loyal, and productive citizen. Yet there are also challenges in addressing cultural diversity within
the education institutions.

Nations in the Southeast Asian region have different cultural and historical
environments. These nations also vary in their economic and cultural positioning
in the global order. Singapore is seen as a globalized nation within this region.
Singapore is a multiethnic nation with heterogenous ethnic composition, 76.8 percent Chinese, 13.9 percent Malays, 7.9 percent Indians, and 1.4 percent "Others."
The Singapore education system is a mix of the historical colonial British examination structure and curricula and a contemporary curriculum that focuses on
the Singaporean national and cultural identity. The desired outcomes of education
in Singapore are an educated citizen who is responsible to his family, community,
and country. An important part of this is the Singapore Ministry of Education's
vision of "Thinking Schools, Learning Nation" that was first announced by the
then prime minister Goh Chok Tong in 1997. This vision describes a nation of
thinking and committed citizens capable of meeting the challenges of the future,
and an education system geared to the needs of the 21st century. The Singapore
government uses various educational policies and strategies (such as the Thinking Schools, Learning Nation; National Education) in the shaping of a national
identity and the management of ethnic diversity.

Political and economic wealth is generally within the Chinese collective in
Singapore. Success and access to educational opportunities and futures vary
along ethnic and class dimensions. Having stated this, there are specific programs within the Education Ministry that address ethnic underachievement.
The Malays have generally been "underperforming" in educational institutions.
The majority of the Malays in the labor force were concentrated in the low-
income occupations. Yayasan MENDAKI is a self-help group dedicated to the
empowerment of the disadvantaged through excellence in education. This council was set up in the 1980s to involve Malay political leaders and the Malay/

Muslim community in partnership with the government to devise and implement solutions to assist in uplifting the social, economic, and educational status of this ethnic collective.

The partnership between the Singapore Ministry of Education and the political and community leaders of the Malay community has resulted in an increase in the percentage of Malays entering tertiary institutions and in the proportion of Malays holding higher-level and skilled jobs. The proportion of Malay workers holding blue-collar jobs in production and in cleaning and laborer jobs has also declined with this education initiative. While the Singapore government ensures the dominance of the Chinese ethnic collective, there are efforts to ensure that other ethnic groups like the Malays are not disadvantaged to the detriment of the nation's progress and global standing.

Singapore's neighbor, Malaysia, is also a multiethnic nation with 65 percent Malays, 24.5 percent Chinese, and 7.2 percent Indians. The Malays monopolize the public and government sectors, and the Chinese monopolize the business and corporate sectors. The Indians as an ethnic collective lag behind economically, educationally, and socially compared with the Malays and the Chinese.

The Malaysian education system aims to give education to the masses, as is noted in the National Philosophy of Education of Malaysia. However, there is a Malay bias of bureaucracy within the Education Ministry as in all other government sectors due to policies implemented since independence in 1957. The Malaysian government also takes into account the educational needs of the other ethnic groups by ensuring that the dominance of the Malay ethnic collective within the state's machineries and politics is never threatened.

Social and educational inequalities have been created through the vernacular education system comprising government-aided Chinese and Tamil primary schools, community-funded Chinese secondary schools, the national primary and secondary schools, as well as the residential science schools and junior science colleges and the other types of Malaysian schools. These inequalities are further exacerbated at the postsecondary and tertiary education levels.

The Chinese ethnic schools are thriving with the economic and cultural backing of the Chinese community. These schools are seen as a great success story both in relation to the Chinese ethnic community and nationally as well. The Tamil ethnic schools are an example of an ethnic education that is a social and educational handicap to the Indian ethnic minority group. The social and political marginalization of the Indian community does not help in the deplorable state of these schools. The small group of 1 percent of the indigenous people continues to be disadvantaged on many levels within the education system. There are also other groups, such as the non-Malay groups of Bumiputeras and the non-citizen migrant workers that are disadvantaged. The residential science schools and junior science colleges for the Malays not only create an ethnic divide but also an intra-ethnic divide, as the Malays who benefit from these well-resourced and funded schools are generally not the Malay poor. Students in these different schools do not have equal opportunities in the acquisition of education and skills needed for social and economic mobility within the Malaysian society. There are also inequalities in terms of physical infrastructures and resources in these different schools. These social injustices within the current education and schooling system are further exacerbated in terms of access and future pathways at the postsecondary and tertiary education levels.

Singapore and Malaysia are postcolonial multiethnic nations. The history of colonialism is evident in some of the education practices. However, these countries have successfully developed a national identity that is based on unique cultural and ethnic values and identities. There are dominant ethnic groups in these countries, and it is the agendas of these groups that are embedded within various educational policies and reforms. Minority ethnic groups are considered, but the power is still with the dominant groups. These nation-states also consider both global and national imperatives in their education policies and practices.

South Africa is a relatively new independent nation in the global order. South Africa comprises 79.3 percent black Africans, 9.5 percent whites, 8.8 percent coloreds, and the rest Indians or Asians (Gilmour et al. 2006). The education system was used as a political and cultural tool for the propagation of the apartheid South African government between 1948 and 1994. This government's ideology was that African people and other people of color had no rights or entitlements in the world of white people. There was and still are significant differences, social inequalities, and injustices that run along race, class, culture, and religious lines.

One of the major educational goals when the new government came into power in 1994 was to formulate a national education policy. The new government's priorities were the following: reconstruction of the bureaucracy, governance, and management; the integration of education and training; restructuring of school education; curriculum reforms; early childhood care, adult basic education, and special education; teacher training and education; restructuring higher education; and restoring buildings and physical resources.

Education in South Africa is shaped by two major priorities: a postapartheid education providing equal citizenship to all on the basis of national liberation, and a global, macroeconomic agenda of market-led development. Education restructuring in South Africa aims to remove racial discrimination as well as emphasize the development of the skilled and global citizen.

The postapartheid education system has been successful in creating elitist, capitalist, and professional groups of black South Africans through its various educational reforms. There are now more South Africans having access to educational resources and future pathways. But South Africa is also at a crossroads, with an increase in the crime rate, unemployment rate, poverty, and HIV/AIDS over these past years. In this respect, the education system has not been successful in dealing with these social inequalities and issues.

China has the largest education system in the world. In 2003, there were over 240 million students and 12 million full-time teachers. The Ministry of Education in its 2003–2007 Action Plan for Invigorating Education aims to use education to turn China's huge population into an abundant human resource for fostering domestic development and international competition in the knowledge economy. Ninety-two percent of Chinese are Hans, and the rest comprise 55 minority nationalities. Ethnic minorities in China form a population of about a million. The State Council of the People's Republic of China in 1999 stated in its policy that all members of ethnic groups are expected to share the common goals of the nation: unity, modernization, and the construction of socialism with Chinese characteristics.

Access and participation to education between these groups also vary. The white paper, *National Minorities Policy and Its Practice in China* (1999), provides insight into the Chinese government's approach to social, economic, political, and educational issues related to ethnic minorities at the turn of the century. Education in the Chinese context is seen as a vital vehicle in reproducing a national Chinese culture. There are still disparities in terms of social and educational indicators in China that run along lines of ethnicity, socioeconomic status, and regions.

China is a nation with a rapidly expanding market economy. The various challenges that Chinese policy makers and educationalists face in present-day China include the need for proficiency in information technology (IT) and English language, the overemphasis of examinations, and heavy student loads within the schooling system. Other challenges include education for migrant children, and the "brain drain" and "brain gain" of Chinese academics. As with other nations, China also considers national and global imperatives in the interplay between nationalism and education, and it must also consider the needs of the minority groups.

The Middle Eastern region of Israel and Palestine provide a different picture of the interplay of education and nationalism. Palestine has been occupied for hundreds of years. The religious culture of Palestine is largely Islamic. The Palestinian education system is located within two conflicting nations, Israel and Palestine. Education in Palestine is seen by its peoples and political leaders as being vital for nation-building and achieving a genuine and sustainable peace. Palestinians are very committed to education even though the education system has been affected by the Israeli occupation. The challenges that the Palestine Ministry of Education and Higher Education face in present-day Palestine, as indicated on the ministry's official Web site, includes the unification of the two systems of education in Gaza and the West Bank, the expansion of school buildings to meet the enormous demand on education, the equipping of schools with needed labs and equipment, the training of teachers, and the development of special programs to meet the different needs of the population. Various educational initiatives have been developed and implemented over the years, such as the curriculum, information and communication technology, special education programs, and teachers training programs.

The Israeli education system includes Jewish education (comprising state-secular, state-religious, and ultra-orthodox schools) and non-Jewish education (Arab and Druze schools). The objectives of Israeli schools are to instill national pride in Jewish boys and girls and to integrate these students into the wider society. There are also the Arab schools for mainly Arab students. These different types of schools tend to separate Jewish and Arab societies rather than being agents of social cohesion and inclusion. Some of the challenges facing the Israeli education system as discussed by Israeli educationalists include the gaps between levels of enfranchisement for different groups in Israeli society, the struggle between national unity and pluralism, and teacher training. Educationalist writings on these challenges also highlight the budgetary constraints that are due to the internal and external conflicts from the Arab world.

In discussing education and nationalism in the Middle Eastern region, especially in relation to Palestine and Israel, it is necessary to consider the sociohistorical and the political aspects of this region. Different political and cultural stances results in different constructions of the educational systems.

Conflict-ridden countries such as Afghanistan and Iraq are currently in war zones. The education systems in these countries are in a deplorable condition due to the lack of physical infrastructure and human resources to support a viable schooling and education system. At one time, education in Afghanistan was highly regarded and attracted students from Asia and the Middle East. However, this

Girls at Samangan School in Afghanistan. (USAID)

changed with the Taliban regime and various global and internal conflicts that led to the demise of the country's social, political, cultural, and educational institutions. Reconstruction of the Afghan educational system is far from complete. Issues to do with financial funding, access in rural areas, girls' education, and the aftermath of these war conflicts continue to pose a great challenge in the nation's efforts. The U.S.-led occupations, UN sanctions, and internal conflicts have badly affected education in Iraq. Nations located within conflict and war zones have a tremendous task in reconstructing their education and schooling system. Education priorities in such countries would focus on providing basic literacy and numeracy skills to their younger population. Education policies and practices would also focus on developing a viable working force for the nation to progress forward economically and culturally.

Consequences

The discussions in the previous sections indicate that there are tensions between official values and practices of education in relation to nationalism. Education has always been a vital tool in the construction of nation and nationalism. Within this framework, it is appropriate to consider whose interests may be served and which groups may be privileged or marginalized in the shaping of a national agenda and, furthermore, the outcomes of education. These are significant issues that have to be considered in the interplay of nationalism and education.

Different rates of development must be taken into account in addressing these issues. Western and advanced capitalist nations, such as the United States, the United Kingdom, and Australia, clearly differ from developed nations in the East Asian and Southeast Asian regions, such as Singapore and Korea. China and India are now considered important players in the global context. Developing nations located within the African continent and eastern Europe, for example, must also be considered. The challenge to nationalism for nation-states must vary significantly, particularly for nations shaped by colonialism and by global forces, including mass migration.

It is also important to consider shifting contexts in understanding nationalism. Hypernationalism refers to the increased awareness of national identity following catastrophic events, including such global events as 9/11 and such post-9/11 events as the Bali and London bombings. These events have also intensified ethnic, racial, and religious politics regionally and globally. These events are seen as threats (based on terror) to Western civilization and are linked to national security. The increased fear and insecurity that has resulted from these events have had an impact on nationalism. Corporate globalization is now part of the national objective for economic growth within Western countries and advanced capitalist states, such as the United States, the United Kingdom, and Australia.

Patriotism, nationalism, and protection of national borders are now important aspects of the U.S. response to 9/11. This form of hypernationalism has the effect of exacerbating fear of cultural and religious diversity. Education is now used as a political tool to reinforce nationalism and hypernationalism.

Educational institutions provide a powerful means to maintain the status quo within and beyond nation-states. National values, interests, and knowledge are embedded in education. In turn, educational policies, structures, and processes affect nationalism. Nationalism can serve where unity is needed, yet it can also be oppressive where differences are denied.

Selected Bibliography

Council of Ministers of Education, Canada. 2003. *Framework for the Future*. http://www.cmec.ca/publications/CMECReview.en.pdf.

Department of Education and Training (DEST), State Government of Victoria. 2005. *Multicultural Education–Multicultural Policy: Legislation and Policy for Schools*. (Retrieved January 16, 2006), http://www.sofweb.vic.edu.au/lem/multi/mpol.htm.

Department of Education, Training and Youth Affairs (DETYA) and the South Australian Department of Education, Training and Employment (DETE). 2001. *The Development of Education: National Report of Australia*. http://www.dest.gov.au.

Dukmak, S. J. 2006. "Palestine's Education System: Challenges, Trends and Issues." In *Schooling around the World: Debates, Challenges and Practices*, edited by K. Mazurek and M. A. Winzer. Boston: Allyn and Bacon.

Gilmour, D., C. Soudien, and D. Donald. 2006. "Post-Apartheid Policy and Practice: Education Reform in South Africa." In *Schooling around the World: Debates, Challenges and Practices*, edited by K. Mazurek and M. A. Winzer. Boston: Allyn and Bacon.

Gumpel, T. P., and A. E. Nir. 2006. "The Israeli Education System: Blending Dreams with Constraints." In *Schooling around the World: Debates, Challenges and Practices*, edited by K. Mazurek and M. A. Winzer. Boston: Allyn and Bacon.

Henry, M., B. Lingard, F. Rizvi, and S. Taylor. 2001. *The OECD, Globalisation and Education Policy*. Oxford: Pergamon.

Hursh, D. 2005. "Neo-Liberalism, Markets and Accountability: Transforming Education and Undermining Democracy in the United States and England." *Policy Futures in Education* 3, no. 1: 3–15.

Jakubowicz, A. 2002. "White Noise: Australia's Struggle with Multiculturalism." In *Working through Whiteness: International Perspectives*, edited by C. Levine-Rasky, 107–125. Albany: State University of New York Press.

Joseph, C. 2006. "The Politics of Educational Research in Contemporary Postcolonial Malaysia: Discourses of Globalization, Nationalism and Education." In *World Yearbook of Education 2006: Education Research and Policy*, edited by J. Ozga, T. Popkewitz, and T. Seddon. London: Routledge.

Koh, A. 2004. "The Singapore Education System: Postcolonial Encounter of the Singaporean Kind." In *Disrupting Preconceptions: Postcolonialism and Education*, edited by A. Hickling-Hudson, J. Matthews, and A. Woods. Flaxton, Australia: Post Pressed.

Law, W. 2006. "Education Reforms for National Competitiveness in a Global Age: The Experience and Struggle of China." In *Schooling around the World: Debates, Challenges and Practices*, edited by K. Mazurek and M. A. Winzer. Boston: Allyn and Bacon.

Lee, B. 2003. "Education and National Identity." *Policy Futures in Education* 1, no. 2: 332–341.

Ministry of Education, Singapore. (Retrieved March 21, 2006), http://www.moe.gov.sg.

Smith, G. 2003. "Kaupapa Maori Theory: Theorizing Indigenous Transformation of Education and Schooling." Paper presented at the Kaupapa Maori Symposium, NZARE/AARE Joint Conference, Auckland, New Zealand. (Retrieved September 13, 2006), http://www.kaupapamaori.com.

State Council of the People's Republic of China, Information Office. 1999. *National Minorities Policy and Its Practice in China*, white paper. (Retrieved May 15, 2006), http://english.peopledaily.com.cn/whitepaper.

Religious Fundamentalism

William H. Swatos Jr.

Relevance

If we are to understand the current relationship between the seemingly conflicting dynamics of globalization and fundamentalism, we need to examine the culture of modernity itself. World-system theorist John Meyer notes, "Modern world culture is more than a simple set of ideals or values diffusing and operating separately in individual sentiments in each society." Its power "lies in the fact that it is a shared and binding set of rules exogenous to any given society, and located not only in individual sentiments, but also in many world institutions." These institutions, such as the United Nations and the World Court as well as world financial institutions that make a world economy work (embodied, for example, in the World Trade Center), involve an element of faith; that is, they rest on a belief that what they do is both right and natural (these two conditions are bound together, for example, in the phrase "human rights"). This worldview has not characterized human history taken as a whole, even into our own day.

Globalization particularly flies in the face of the belief in absolute nation-state sovereignty—what Frank Lechner terms "institutionalized societalism" —which, ironically, reached its apex as the very capstone of the globalization process that now threatens its undoing. On the one hand, the globe appears as a union of sovereign states, recognized by world institutions as having transcendent integrity. On the other hand, the sovereignty of these states as political actors is circumscribed by a set of principles—a "higher law"—that in fact rests on beliefs generated by specific world orientations that are themselves metaphysical; that is, the principles of global society are generated by accepting some kinds of faith propositions and not others. In general, these propositions reflect Anglo-American utilitarian-pragmatic philosophy, which lacks absolutes and is thus subject to contradiction as circumstances change.

Globalization breaks across cultural barriers through finance, media, and transport. Anglo-America is the preeminent global societal actor. English is the language of air traffic control and the Internet. The dollar, mediated by European bourses, is the measure of world economic value. These technical systems, however, do not speak to the "soul"; that is, the human personality seems to have, at some times and for some people more strongly than others, something generally called a "spiritual" dimension. This dynamic is not, however, purely psychological; spirituality involves an element of power. Although each of the Abrahamic faith traditions—Judaism, Christianity, and Islam—contextualizes divine power differently, none fails to assert that the presence of God is the presence of power.

(Although there are also fundamentalist movements within contemporary Hinduism, these are responses to Islamic fundamentalism, which is one of the Abrahamic traditions.) In the global setting specifically, the nature of Abrahamic monotheism coupled with the hegemonic position of Anglo-American "know-how" provides a potential resource for confrontation both within our own society and among societies.

Origins

Strictly speaking, the word *fundamentalism* refers to a specific theological movement that originated in American Protestantism at the beginning of the 20th century. A group of Protestant leaders, concerned about what they considered to be a process of modernism—initially in regard to evolution—that was shaking the foundations of the Christian religion, set forth five "fundamentals" that they considered essential to the Christian faith. People who subscribed to these were subsequently termed—first by their detractors and later by themselves—fundamentalists.

When the worldwide religious resurgence of the 1970s gained attention, however, the term fundamentalist was applied in a more extensive fashion. It was now extended to all contemporary religious movements that display what Eugen Schoenfeld has demarcated "exclusive militancy." In a definition that rivals Roland Robertson's definition of globalization as "seeing the world as a single place" for simplicity, T. K. Oommen has similarly defined fundamentalism as "text without context." What this means is that religious texts (or scriptures) that were originally written in a specific historical context, hence social setting, are decontextualized and held to be applicable without regard to local circumstances. At the same time, however, all other competing texts are rejected as having any corresponding claim to truth.

It is important to recognize that all fundamentalisms as they are advanced around the globe today are specifically modern products and heterodox faith traditions. This claim is never made by fundamentalists themselves, but it is easily documented by historical surveys of the faith traditions they claim to represent. The majority of those who claim to be Christians do not belong to fundamentalist churches—and never have. The majority of Muslims do not belong to fundamentalist sects of that faith—and never have. The historic creeds to which the majority of those who call themselves Christians do assent are not held by most fundamentalists; the central concerns of fundamentalist Muslims are not the essential "Five Pillars" of Islam. Ultra-orthodox Jews are more orthodox than the Orthodox, which is in fact a contradiction in terms. All religious fundamentalisms as we know them today were constructed during our own time as responses to the modern world-system, which had its beginnings in the 16th century but has come to fruition in the global project that has progressed with increasing certainty since World War II.

Dimensions

We will examine three encounters between "the globe" and fundamentalist agendas, none of which can be separated from the joint issues of messiahship and the state of Israel. Although the specifics are different in each case, note that in each there is a significant commonality in the direction of hostilities, whether rhetorical or corporeal, against national political leaders who favor global peace on the basis of a universal value of human worth. Such hostilities originate with people within their own countries who demand acknowledgment of a particularist view of human action based on transcendent realities. In other words, current religiopolitical crises are not so much based on different ideas about God as they are on different claims about how God expects human beings to behave.

The American Religious Right

"Mixing politics and religion" is not new in the United States or other nations influenced by American thinking. Not only the civil rights and antiwar movements of the recent past but also prohibitionism and abolitionism mixed heady doses of politics and religion. One of the differences between some earlier religiopolitical alliances in the United States and the contemporary Religious Right, however, is the global dimension of our experience. Exactly when this began may be debated for generations to come by historians, but we might profitably start with the 1950s and the "Communist Menace."

At the center of this religious historiography was the newly founded (or refounded) state of Israel. Marxism was laid over against the restoration of Israel as a nation-state as part of a grand theological plan to herald the end of time (the Millennium), the return of Christ, and the judgment of the world. Elaborate explanations, often with increasingly technologically sophisticated visual representations, were constructed to herald a religious end of history. Atomic and hydrogen weaponry only enhanced the cataclysmic drama that would attend Armageddon, the great final battle. Did every Christian American believe this? Certainly not. People did hear enough of the great weapons race of the superpowers, the launching of satellites, and espionage and counterespionage, however, not to dismiss all of it as pure craziness.

The 1967 attack on Israel by a coalition of Muslim Arab states further enhanced the fundamentalist argument. Whether true or not, the Arabs were perceived as working with Soviet backing—both philosophically and materially. The Israeli triumph was enthusiastically received throughout the United States. A sudden alliance of good feeling and mutuality came to prevail among liberals, moderates, and fundamentalists. The victory in Israel was taken as an American victory. It justified American principles and served to give a tentative point of unity to a nation otherwise divided over civil rights issues at home and the Vietnam War abroad. As the years passed, this picture changed. Further military conflict in 1973 and Palestinian problems, the dragging on of a settlement, the rise of militant Islam in Iran, battles in Lebanon, and so on, increasingly tried American patience. The fall of the Soviet empire in 1989 without any apparent resolution of the situation in the Holy Land began to make fundamentalist biblical exegesis of prophetic texts less gripping. A new American religious coalition was building over "family values," and a new missionary thrust to the formerly communist countries had more immediate success.

What is often called the Religious Right or (New) Christian Right today emerged in its present form in response to an appeal made by Richard Nixon during his presidency to America's "silent majority." Amid the protests of the Vietnam era, Nixon was sure that a silent majority of Americans (sometimes called the "silent generation") agreed with him and his handling of the situation. Before too many years had passed, a Virginia Independent Baptist pastor with a simply formatted television worship service, Jerry Falwell, had formed a political action group, the Moral Majority, that attempted to move the silent generation at least to send money to allow him to lead the nation to righteousness. The formation of Falwell's group coincided fairly closely with the election of the nation's first bona fide "born again" or evangelical president, Southern Baptist Jimmy Carter, but in fact, Falwell's vision was quite different from Carter's. The Moral Majority would support tangentially Christian Ronald Reagan, not Carter, in the 1980 presidential election.

Ironically, the Religious Right nevertheless gained very little of its specifically religious agenda during the administrations of favored sons Ronald Reagan and the elder George Bush. Although both presidents talked the right language on abortion and school prayer, neither was able to effect any significant changes. The fall of the "evil" Soviet empire may have been hastened by the Reagan-Bush line, but it was so entirely unanticipated in the West that this can hardly have been a major factor. Wise investors used these years to internationalize the American economy even further, rather than the reverse, and China first became a significant economic player in American markets. Reagan and Bush proved virtually powerless to resolve Holy Land crises—indeed, the worst single loss of American lives in the Holy Land, the bombing of the Marine barracks in Lebanon, occurred during the Reagan years. Also, the nation was plunged ever further into debt.

At the same time, other religious groups, most notably Reform Jews and the religiously unaffiliated, advanced ahead of the Christian fundamentalists into the political-economic elites. Hence, evangelical-fundamentalist Protestants, traditionalist Catholics, and Orthodox Jews formed a loose political alliance that attempted to assert citizen control over local issues. The aim of the "stealth" candidates of the Christian Coalition in the early 1990s, for example, was to place religious conservatives on local boards of education, city councils, and county commissions. And it is certainly the case that George W. Bush's embrace of "faith-based" programs and "charitable choice" are especially directed toward this constituency rather than the historical Protestant or Catholic mainstream. All post-2004 election evidence indicates that Bush's second-term election was squarely set upon the foundation of religious conservatism.

Islamization

Many Muslims would prefer, because of the historically Christian associations of the word fundamentalist, that the movement often termed "Islamic fundamentalism" be termed "Islamization" and its adherents "Islamicists." The movement's roots are varied, but they can probably be traced to reactions to the British colonial presence in Egypt and in that part of India now known as Pakistan. Until the Six Day War of 1967, however, these movements had little effect. Although for different reasons, they were largely sidelined, as were the U.S. Christian fundamentalists. The failure of the Arab alliance to succeed in defeating the Israelis, however, began to give new urgency to Islamic conservatives.

The attack on Israel was the dream of Egyptian (later, United Arab Republic) president Gamal Abdel Nasser, largely a secularist, who enticed other secular Arab leaders to join his plan. When it failed, this began to allow an opening for conservative Muslim preachers to claim that the basis for the defeat was not Jewish military superiority but rather the failure of Muslims to immerse themselves adequately in Islam. Human pride rather than submission to Allah was at the heart of the Arab defeat.

The momentum for Islamization built slowly because most secular Arab leaders were reluctant to allow the mullahs opportunities to promulgate their critiques. Economic pressures often intervened. Again, an increasing disparity between those largely secular Arabs who benefited from the oil trade and the rest of the population sent the disenfranchised looking for alternative explanations for their plight. University students, small-business people, craftsmen, and some members of the old middle class (not least those who provided men with vocations to Muslim ministry) provided fertile soil for the seeds of Islamization. Palestinians who were termed "terrorists" in the West were made heroes in the Muslim world. Nevertheless, such activities remained relatively marginal to the world-system until 1978 and 1979, with the rise of the Ayatollah Khomeini in Iran.

Perhaps no more perfect case of both the interaction of and confrontation between globalization and local intransigence could be imagined than Iran; indeed, in some ways, it stretched the imaginations of many social scientists, who gave inadequate weight to the religious dimension when they attempted to predict Iranian outcomes. Mohammad Reza Shah Pahlavi, Iran's ruler for almost four decades prior to the Iranian revolution, who ascended the throne at age 22, was a dedicated modernist. He rejoiced in U.S. political and economic support and enjoyed the Western lifestyle. He saw his vocation as bringing Iran into the forefront of global geopolitics. He claimed that "Iran could be the showcase for all of Asia. America cannot spread its assistance in every country everywhere. Here is the place with the best prospect for a great transformation."

Perhaps the Shah was correct in his analysis, but in hindsight, we can see that he made at least three mistakes in implementation: (1) economically, he placed too much emphasis on oil and did not demand sufficient diversification of U.S. assistance to share the benefits of Iran's oil resources and geopolitical setting adequately throughout the population; (2) socioculturally, he demanded changes that exceeded the prerequisites of the project of modernization (such as not permitting the wearing of the veil by women attending universities, reducing support for the mosques, and implementing policies to displace small shopkeepers); and (3) politically, he created a secret police force (SAVAK) that used extreme cruelty to attack those who disagreed with his policies.

By the late 1970s, spiraling inflation, population pressures in the cities, and a crisis on the world oil market clearly put the Shah in trouble. That was not too much of a surprise to U.S. social scientists savvy in Middle Eastern studies. What was a surprise was the role that came to be played by the Islamicist Ayatollah Ruholla Khomeini in the foundation of the Islamic Republic of Iran. Why? Preeminently because secular social science had totally overlooked the persistence of the religious dimension as a possible trajectory for the demonstration of human resentment against oppression—this despite the fact that practically every foundational social theorist, including Karl Marx, had recognized the religious dimension as integrally connected to deprivation, although not merely a reflection of deprivation.

For the Ayatollah, it was not enough that the Shah was a professing Muslim. What the Ayatollah demanded was a life-world level affirmation of stability, a continuation of things the way they always *ought* to have been. The word *ought* is important to understanding the fundamentalist dynamic, because what fundamentalism protests against as much as anything in the internationalist vision of globalization is the relativization of cultural values that seems to be part and parcel of impersonal market "forces" that drive high-technology multinationalist capitalism. Only the most naive fundamentalist would claim that in some past time, "everyone" was religious or moral or both. What the fundamentalist would claim was that in the past there was a religioethical core within sociocultural systems that was generally acknowledged: sin was sin, and truth was truth.

The world of the historic nation-state, whether in the Arab world or in Christian Europe, provided a buffering device that established cultural prerogatives. The Reformation principle of *cuius regio, eius religio* and Muslim principles surrounding the caliphate had a commonsense reality for everyday activity, particularly when language separated major cultural groups. People who "talked different" were different. Every culture knew it was right and others were wrong. Common language and common religion went hand in hand.

Globalization changed this simple worldview: accommodation and compromise became the order of the day. When we look at Islamization efforts, for example, we see that with few exceptions they are directly proportional to involvement by a Muslim leader in the ethic (ethos) of globalization; that is, in that "shared and binding set of rules exogenous to any given society" of which John Meyer speaks.

The murder of Egyptian president Anwar Sadat in 1981 is an excellent but not the sole example. Sadat's case was similar to the set of values to which the Shah of Iran was at least giving lip service, and it is the basis on which a female leader, such as Benazir Bhutto of Pakistan, ultimately attempted to sustain her claim to legitimacy and was also assassinated. Although Americans often see specific acts of Islamicist terrorism directed against them, the bigger picture clearly shows the primary targets to be Muslim leaders themselves. It is not "the American way of life" itself that is under attack by Islamicists but rather attempts to harmonize Islam with that way of life. Unlike the New Christian Right, most Islamicists are quite willing to let the United States go to hell if it wants to. What they resist are attempts by the global system of states, of which they see the United States as the principal economic and cultural actor, to alter their lifeworld.

Nowhere do the contradictions between the global system of states and the Islamic life world become more pronounced than in the place given to the state of Israel, particularly by the United States. The state of Israel is an "offense" to Muslims, not merely because the Jews are people of a different religion—because Islam has generally been tolerant toward Jews, indeed in many cases far more so than Christianity. Rather, the state of Israel places into juxtaposition irrational and rational political policies, which themselves result from a unique religious configuration in the United States between Jews and the Christian Right. The creation of the state of Israel caused an undermining of the secular ideology of the nation-state in the Muslim world because, in a Western betrayal of its own commitments to the secular-state norm of modern political theory, a religious ideology was used to justify the creation of Israel. The establishment of the state of Israel was clearly a response to the Holocaust, but it was also intimately related to fundamentalist Protestant understandings of the necessity for the reunion of the Jewish peoples at Jerusalem prior to some form of millennial return and reign of Jesus Christ. Inseparable from this is the demographic fact that from World War II until 2006, the United States had the largest Jewish population in the world, and the fact that Israeli citizens may hold unique joint citizenship in the United States and Israel, a condition virtually unknown elsewhere in the entire global system.

Muslims, thus, see a moral fissure in the ethic of globalization along these lines: The state of Israel has been established in the center of the historic Islamic world as an outpost for a new campaign to blot out the Islamic way of life. Like the crusades of old, this effort seeks to impede the practice of Islam through other standards of behavior, to which Muslims will be forced to conform or else by which they will be excluded from the benefits of global citizenship. From the Muslim point of view, by contrast, Islam itself provides a set of principles for universal world government. Here, then, is the center of the conflict between Islamization and globalization: as preeminently a system of rules, not beliefs, Islam offers an alternative to the dominant model of secular high-technology multinational capitalism that forms the basis for the global system of states in late modernity. Islamization proposes the universalization of the particular and, by contrast, it views the Western system as doing nothing but the same. That is, Islamicists see the Western system of globalization not as the implementation of "universal" human values but rather of specifically Western values.

This observation highlights one of the central propositions of globalization theory, particularly as articulated in the work of Roland Robertson and colleagues; namely, the role of ethics (ethoses) in constructing systems of interaction. Derived from the work of both Weber and Parsons, this point of view suggests that systems of valuing, whether or not they originate in material conditions, have an influence, perhaps a determinative influence, on subsequent political and economic relationships. Peoples whose worldview continues to be shaped by Islam, which is founded on a warrior ethic, will be essentially at variance with the core values of globalization. Failure to recognize the depth to which these cultural components structure political organization leads Westerners to think that the assumptions of modern rationalism can provide a basis for "reasonable" compromise, when in fact they cannot.

Instead, the warrior ethic sees standoff as a transcendent scenario in which different "strong men" contend for power. This view "came home" to Americans most dramatically in the events of September 11, 2001, with the Al Qaeda attacks on the World Trade Center—perhaps no more dramatic symbol of international capitalism could have been chosen for a Star Wars–esque scenario wherein the hub of globalization was attacked by the forces of an almost mythical strong man domiciled in one of the most remote parts of the world, governed by the most religiously reactionary regimes. It is true that, unlike the Ayatollah Khomeini, who was manifestly a religious leader, Osama bin-Laden is an entirely secular figure; bin-Laden constructs the self-image of a war lord, and as such, sees himself as much as Khomeini as restoring the rights of Islam and pursuing the international vocation of Islam as a world faith.

A fascinating Weberian study of religion and political democracy by James Duke and Barry Johnson takes up a variant of Weber's Protestant ethic thesis to demonstrate that, using four different indicators of democracy, Islamic nations appear at the bottom of five major religious groups on two of the four indicators and next to the bottom (higher only than tribal religions) on the other two. This is intensified by the fact that in the poorest nations (per capita gross national product [GNP] of less than $399) democracy is weak across the board, but states with tribal religions drop out of the picture at the uppermost end of the GNP spectrum, whereas Islamic nations do not. In addition, the undemocratic nature of Islamic regimes is unrelated to whether or not a previous colonial regime was of a more or less democratically oriented religion (e.g., English Protestantism or French Catholicism).

We might turn this around and say that, from the Islamicist viewpoint, Muslim leaders who adopt the ethic of globalization as Meyer summarizes it have already betrayed the faith; that is, the warrior ethic mediates between "upstream" doctrine and day-to-day practice. This dynamic runs through the bulk of Islamic history, although the specific terms have differed across time. Ironically for the

West, movements toward democratic pluralism on the global level have actually allowed Islamicist activities to grow in their degree of both local and international influence because the same means of communication, transport, and exchange that provide the infrastructure to globalization can be employed for the deployment of Islamicist values (much the same way, for example, as Christian televangelists in the United States use the very media of which they are hypercritical as the means for propagating their own views). The Ayatollah Khomeini himself sent audiotape cassettes to Iran while he was a refugee in France, just as bin-Laden continued to provoke his adversaries and encourage his followers through videotapes. Those societies of Muslim heritage that have most intentionally embraced Western democratic models have created the conditions for the growth of Islamicist parties, which in their extremism simply reinforce the tendencies that are already latent in the warrior ethic.

Ultra-Orthodoxy

For more than a quarter century, Americans have come to anticipate various forms of Palestinian-Islamicist terrorism in and adjacent to the territory now occupied by the state of Israel. Bus bombings, airplane hijackings, suicide attacks, and so on, are recurrent copy for television and newspaper headlines. Thus, it was with no small surprise that Americans learned that the assassin of Israeli prime minister and Nobel Peace Prize–winner Yitzhak Rabin in 1994 was not a Muslim, or even a Palestinian sympathizer, but a Jew who proclaimed "I did this to stop the peace process. . . . We need to be cold-hearted. . . . When you kill in war, it is an act that is allowed."

As the story developed, it became clear that there was an intimate connection between the inspiration of assassin Yigal Amir and Orthodox Jewry in New York City. Specifically, New York rabbi Abraham Hecht, leader of Brooklyn's largest Syrian synagogue, had publicly ruled the previous June that Rabin and his colleague, Shimon Peres, were in a state of *mosher*, of someone who surrenders his people. As such, Hecht said, the two had committed a sin worthy of death. Hecht even credited the greatest of all Jewish philosophers, Maimonides, to the effect that someone who kills a *mosher* has done a good deed.

This most prominent murder among the thousands who have lost their lives in the 20th-century battle for the Holy Land uniquely highlights the intersecting dynamics of globalization and fundamentalism: a local congregational pastor in one part of the world, thousands of miles from a law student elsewhere, inspires the death of a major figure not only in the Middle Eastern "peace process" but also potentially in the entire global system—thanks to media of communication and transport that brought his remarks into one of the crucial value expressions of globalization, a free press. Indeed, so much was this the case that Israelis immediately after the assassination attempted to formalize laws that would actually restrict the publication of such "opinions" as those of Hecht (who was, in fact, fired by his New York congregation shortly after Rabin's murder).

Pallbearers carry the coffin of Yitzhak Rabin, Prime Minister of Israel, after his 1995 assassination by right-wing radical Yigal Amir. (David Turnley/Corbis)

In the assassination of Yitzhak Rabin, the global norms of freedom of religion and freedom of the press, written, for example, into a whole series of world institutional documents, yielded antiglobal results, enabled by the very technologies that advance the globalization to which, for example, Islamicists object. Indeed, one might argue that from an Islamicist viewpoint, the assassination of Rabin could be taken as evidence that globalization will be its own grave digger.

There is a counterargument, however—namely, that the creation of the state of Israel as it was effected by the allies following World War II, and especially by the United States, was in conflict with, and contrary to, the norms of globalization; hence, we should anticipate ongoing actual conflict over this sociopolitical fact. The United States will be especially immediately involved in this conflict because of its violation of the principles of nation-state citizenship rules—because of the unique citizenship privileges that pertain between Israeli citizens of American origin. In other words, the world systemic conflict in and about the state of Israel is the "exception that proves the rule" of globalization theory precisely because the foundation of the state of Israel essentially violates the "value-neutral" or "secular" politics that is the norm of global society.

From the restriction of the papal empire within the walls of the Vatican to the transformation of the Ottoman Empire into modern Turkey, the de-deification of the emperor of Japan, and the disestablishment of one state church after another, the entire trend of globalization has been away from the particularizing of politics by intrasocietal cultural norms associated with the historical religions. How could the state of Israel possibly be founded in contradistinction to this trend? The answer is multiplex.

First, the psychodynamics of guilt over the Holocaust must be acknowledged. Although specific numbers may be debated until time immemorial, the genocide inflicted on European Jews by the Nazi regime while the majority of "liberal" politicians of all Western democracies stood largely deaf, dumb, and blind yielded in due time its legitimate emotional remorse. The state of Israel was a global irrational response to an even more overwhelming irrational system of oppression. It flew in the face of the rational politics of the world system, but those political principles were themselves still in the stage of formal institutionalization in such bodies as the United Nations. Not to be forgotten is the fact that the first attempt toward operationalizing these principles in the League of Nations failed, and perhaps one reason that it failed was the lack of membership of the United States, which as a result of the Holocaust had become the nation with the largest Jewish population in the world by 1945.

Second, the Jewish people themselves were disarrayed by the Holocaust; many of the proponents of the idea of a "Jewish homeland" (i.e., the modern state of Israel) articulated the concept in secular terms. In other words, when the state-of-Israel concept was discussed in political circles, it was advanced not as a religious cause but rather as an efficient political solution to a world political problem of refugee peoples and a resolution to colonial control of a portion of the Middle East. In apparent ignorance of the actual population of Palestine, many Western politicians saw the creation of the state of Israel as an act of political self-determination consistent with world societal principles. The British were keen to withdraw from the region and saw American support for the state of Israel as the ideal avenue for their own exit.

Third, the same infrastructural developments that have allowed the Christian Religious Right and Islamism to move from life-world conditions to system actors have allowed the development of a Jewish religious form—ultra-orthodoxy—that has been heretofore unknown in Judaism. Whereas ultraist forms of Judaism have previously been privatizations of the spiritual dynamic, the "open market" of globalization has allowed the conditions for the appearance of a public spirituality making political demands. Among the Jews especially, who have traditionally been what Max Weber terms a "pariah people," only the free conditions of globalization have allowed the politicization of action that could result in the assassination of a world political leader. The great Maimonides may well have said that killing a *mosher* would be doing a good deed and meant it, but that Maimonides ever thought he was saying that killing the prime minister of Israel for participating in the global peace process was a good deed is quite inconceivable. Maimonides was speaking to a global situation in which Jews were a pariah people and not actors in the world system of states.

This final observation brings us to the heart of globalization theory as an explanation and demonstrates its value in understanding the "resurgence of religion" in our time. It is to be found in the simple definition of fundamentalism introduced at the outset: "text without context." What happened between Maimonides and Yigal Amir was that the context changed. Maimonides said what he said and meant what he said. In addition, in the context in which he was writing—namely, that of Jews as a pariah people—he could well be considered morally right. By contrast, Rabbi Hecht was absolutely wrong in his application of the text; he was wrong because he chose to discount context, which from a contemporary social-scientific standpoint is morally unjustifiable. The words of Maimonides are sociocultural products. This does not mean that they are not true. It does mean that all truth is mediated by context. To say this is not the same thing as saying that "everything is relative" but rather to assert that sociocultural context is integral to the truthfulness of any proposition about social relations. This is most succinctly epitomized in sociology in the phrase "definition of the situation," coined by W. I. Thomas. Situations by their very nature have always been historically particular, hence the universalizing dynamic of globalization creates an inherently perilous setting for misinterpretation when the particular is universalized (i.e., text is taken out of context). This is precisely what led to the death of Yitzhak Rabin, and this is also what makes religious fundamentalism within the context of globalization so powerful a force for nationalisms. By appealing to religious texts from previous historical epochs as if they are of immediate contemporary applicability, nationalist partisans create contexts for political violence on a global scale.

Consequences

Globalization has created a new publicization of religion (the "resurgence" of religion) that is at variance with the dominant chord of secularization theories. At the same time, however, the resurgent forms of at least the Abrahamic traditions that are at the core of nationalist conflicts centering on religious fundamentalisms throughout the world are also at the same time *new forms* of these religions that are discontinuous with the dominant forms of these traditions, which have actually adapted over time to changing sociohistorical conditions.

The global resurgence of religious traditions in new forms is evidence for both the truth of the relation of context to religion, which is inherent to the participation of human beings in religion, and the essential error of the secularization concept as it was once advanced in Western social science. On the one hand, all religion is secular because all religion exists in relation to both system and life world; how specific religions orient and reorient themselves to system and life world will vary as systems and life worlds change. At the same time, however, systems and life worlds will include religious considerations in the total matrix of experience and interpretation that leads to specific action and hence to changes in patterns of action. The very processes that created the sociocultural contexts in and through which globalization has occurred also have created the contexts for the resurgent religious forms that we tend to characterize as fundamentalisms. This dialectic between material and ideal culture is inherent in all sociocultural processes, hence a complete globalization theory should anticipate countersystem tendencies by the very nature of the dynamics that create the system itself. Such a theory will explain both why the systems of religion that are rising are rising and why those that are falling are falling. It should also explain why those forms that are rising are probably unlikely to achieve their ultimate goals, and why those that may appear to be falling may not experience the "withering" that either their critics or mourners expect.

Selected Bibliography

Beyer, P. 1992. *Religion and Globalization.* London: Sage.

Duke, J. T., and B. L. Johnson. 1989. "Protestantism and the Spirit of Democracy." In *Religious Politics in Global and Comparative Perspective*, edited by W. H. Swatos Jr., 131–146. New York: Greenwood.

Froese, P. 2005. "'I Am an Atheist and a Muslim': Islam, Communism, and Ideological Competition." *Journal of Church and State* 47:472–501.

Juergensmeyer, M. 2001. *Terror in the Mind of God: The Global Rise of Religious Violence.* Berkeley: University of California Press.

Lechner, F. 1985. "Modernity and Its Discontents." In *Neofunctionalism*, edited by J. Alexander, 157–176. Beverly Hills, CA: Sage.

Lechner, F. 1989. "Cultural Aspects of the Modern World System." In *Religious Politics in Global and Comparative Perspective*, edited by W. H. Swatos Jr., 11–27. New York: Greenwood.

Meyer, J. 1980. "The World Polity and the Authority of the Nation State." In *Studies of the Modern World-System*, edited by A. Bergesen, 109–137. New York: Academic Press.

Oommen, T. K. 1994. "Religious Nationalism and Democratic Polity." *Sociology of Religion* 55:455–472.

Parsons, T. 1964. "Christianity and Modern Industrial Society." In *Religion, Culture, and Society*, edited by L. Schneider, 273–298. New York: John Wiley.

Robertson, R. 1992. *Globalization.* London: Sage.

Robertson, R., and J. Chirico. 1985. "Humanity, Globalization, and Worldwide Religious Resurgence." *Sociological Analysis* 46:219–242.

Schoenfeld, E. 1987. "Militant Religion." In *Religious Sociology*, edited by W. H. Swatos Jr., 125–137. New York: Greenwood.

Swatos, W. H., Jr. 1992. "The Problem of Religious Politics and Its Impact on World Society." In *Waves, Formations and Values in the World System*, edited by V. Bornschier and P. Lengyel, 283–304. New Brunswick, NJ: Transaction.

Swatos, W. H., Jr. 1995. "Islam and Capitalism: A Weberian Perspective on Resurgence." In *Religion and the Transformations of Capitalism*, edited by R. H. Roberts, 47–62. London: Routledge.

Weber, M. 1930. *The Protestant Ethic and the Spirit of Capitalism.* New York: Scribners.

Nationalism and Globalization

Victor Roudometof

Origins

The conventional wisdom among the scholarly community is that nations and nationalism are forces closely tied with our heritage, culture, ethnicity, and the legacy of our forefathers. Of course, scholars of nationalism still discuss whether nations are solely a force coming out from our distant past or whether they are in large part a product of 19th-century modernization. Some scholars view nations as features of our distant past with a history stretching several centuries, while others view them as having a history of no more than a few centuries. Irrespective of this disagreement, this mainstream view of nations as creatures of either our recent or distant past will be our starting point for the discussion in this chapter.

In contrast to this view of nations, many, perhaps most, scholars of nationalism view globalization as something relatively recent. Many scholars and journalists think of globalization in terms of the Internet, cell phones, cable or satellite TV, ethnic restaurants bringing us exotic foods, economic restructuring of manufacturing plants, and so on. For the purposes of our discussion in this chapter, then, globalization is defined as those social processes responsible for the gradual interconnection of different places of the globe into a whole. This interconnectivity is achieved through a variety of means, such as mass media, electronic communication, economic exchanges, trade, the growth of international treaties and nongovernmental organizations, and many others. In fact, there are too many of them to provide an exhaustive list. Many scholars also accept that this interconnectivity often promotes or at the very least contributes to making the world a single place—that is, integrating the entire globe into a single network or polity or culture.

To sum up the above, then, nations are creatures of our past while globalization is a force that has only recently come about. If we accept these definitions, globalization is the harbinger of two distinct outcomes. The first outcome of globalization is the end of the self-reliance or independence of the nation-state. More and more, nation-states are made dependent upon larger economic, cultural, and social interactions with the world beyond their borders. For example, most states around the globe are now signatories to international agreements for the protection of the environment, nuclear nonproliferation, extradition of criminals, removal of mines from their territories, and so on. They have to take concrete steps to honor such agreements, and they are held accountable to international organizations and other states if they fail to do so. This means that states do not enjoy complete *sovereignty* over their actions. Sovereignty is one of the basic terms in the study of the state: it refers to the fact that, traditionally, a state's actions within its boundaries were not subject to any external regulation. This meant that the state exercised unrestrained control over its own territory, and this is the classical definition of sovereignty. But, today, this is no longer true; sovereignty is being eroded on a regular basis, and states can no longer pursue their own national interests without taking into account how this will impact people and organizations that extend beyond their borders.

Globalization brings global social integration as it tears down the walls that states have erected to protect their population. States have traditionally justified their efforts to protect their own people on the basis of serving the national interest. Serving the national interest is an expression of nationalism. Nationalism is a force that divides up the world into unique cultural units that we call nations. By tearing down the walls that protect our nations, globalization is eroding the very foundations of nations, our very sense of being different from other people who live beyond our borders. Some scholars have even suggested that in the future, the world will become united under a single world government or in the form of a global federation among nations. Such visions are clearly contrary to a key idea behind national movements, the idea that each nation should have its own, self-reliant and completely independent state.

The process of Europeanization, for example, is set against the reality of modern European nations: turning French, Germans, Italians, and others into Europeans is working against the various European states' national interests for it undermines the people's attachment to their respective nations. Those scholars who think along these lines have suggested that, ultimately, humanity's future lies in moving into a post-national world, a world where nations will no longer be the major reference point for individuals and communities around the world. There are numerous variations of this perspective, but all of them agree that our future trajectory is that of post-nationalism. So, the first interpretation that will be considered in this chapter is that globalization is a force that inhibits the power of nationalism worldwide.

In contrast, the second interpretation suggests exactly the opposite trend: in this line of thinking, globalization can contribute to the reassertion of nationalism. In a world dominated by cultural homogenization and economic integration, people might cling to their roots in an effort to protect their communities from the negative consequences of getting too close with outsiders. As a matter of fact, most scholars—and laymen—would agree that the idea of the nation has not been superseded as a source of loyalty by other transnational ties (such as gender, class, or religion). In this respect, the increases in global communication and the ability of people to move around the globe faster and in greater numbers than ever before is an important factor for the revitalization of ethnic ties. When we look at the world from this perspective, the connections inscribed by globalization strengthen suppressed or hitherto marginalized constituencies within existing nation-states. Globalization enables them to mobilize effectively to question or challenge the authority of their respective nation-state. Globalization offers to such communities the ability to speak to a global audience, thereby bypassing national channels and bringing their concerns into global institutions—such as the International Court of Human Rights, the United Nations (UN), and others. Moreover, global interconnectedness can contribute to the expression of nationalist mobilization among new immigrant communities, giving birth to long-distance or transnational nationalism.

These two different interpretations are not mutually exclusive. We do not need to see them as an "either/or" choice. Rather, they are different aspects of the world as it is today. They stand for different trends that point to opposite directions. It is possible to find empirical support for both trends in the record of the post-1980 period. The following two sections briefly consider each trend and present some examples that lend support to each of the two theses. This chapter's discussion cannot possibly be comprehensive, nor is there an attempt to present in great detail every possible case. Such tasks are better left to specialists. Instead, in the following, emphasis is placed on the analytical side, on what are the different tracks upon which each trend has been proceeding. In the chapter's final section, an attempt is made to synthesize these trends and move conceptually beyond the dominant view on the relationship between nationalism and globalization.

Relevance

Will Globalization Bring the End of the Nation-State?

The growth of transnational institutions, the construction of a world culture, the voluminous international treaties, and the proliferation of major economic alliances—such as the North American Free Trade Agreement (NAFTA) and the European Union (EU)—have provided the backdrop for the argument that the era of the nation-state is now over. We are being told that today the growth of interregional trade among Asia, Europe, and North America has led to the de-nationalization of formerly national economies. Even economically powerful states, like the United States or Germany, do not have the ability to control their economic fortunes; their economies are being de-nationalized. As more and more foreign capital runs through them, many foreign investors are in control of key sectors in their economies leaving no room for state intervention. This de-nationalization is typically used as the best evidence for arguing that the nation-state no longer controls economic activities that have become increasingly transnational or regional in nature.

Upon close inspection, however, we find that this argument is rather weak in the case of the economy—and specifically, when it comes to economic policy. For example, former U.S. secretary of labor Robert Reich has argued that U.S. policy in an era of globalized capitalism has to promote a new economic nationalism that would allow the U.S. population to be the beneficiary of the most lucrative and highly paid jobs in the new global economy, leaving behind the rest of the world to compete against each other. This argument makes abundantly clear that the new global economy by no means brings an end to economic nationalism. Rather, public policy moves into a different terrain: its role now is to structure the rules of the international competition in ways that benefit specific countries. The above is not an abstract academic thesis: as a secretary of labor in the Clinton administration, Robert Reich himself was part of a broader policy team that emphasized the necessity for high-tech innovation and for moving into the Information Age. Former U.S. president Clinton repeatedly stressed this particular developmental model and promoted it both at home and abroad.

In Europe, Ireland has provided a similar model. While in past decades Ireland was a poor country and the Irish often migrated abroad to find a better future, in the post-1980 period, Ireland's economic fortune changed as the country successfully exploited its geopolitical position as a bridgehead between the United States and Europe. Many international companies chose it as their base of operation, and in the process, Ireland became one of the fastest growing European economies. In the course of the 1990s, it became a case carefully studied by teams of other European economic policy experts seeking to duplicate its economic miracle across Europe. Hence, while the nation-state might no longer be in a position to isolate and effectively manipulate the national economy, the end result is not the disappearance of nationalism but rather the application of the national interest into the field of economic policy.

A second but more viable variation of the same line of argument pertains to the emergence of a post-national model of social relations. This argument is based on several post–World War II international trends. These trends include the erosion of state sovereignty through the multiplication of international treaties and the emergence of an international post–World War II regime of international law, rules, and related conventions. As a result, significant constraints are now in place with regard to the ability of states to do as they please. New international or global policy regimes are put into place in diverse fields, ranging from the protection of the environment to the treatment of minorities and to nuclear proliferation. States are bound by these new globally inscribed regulations and are held accountable if they fail to comply with them. Several scholars have viewed this development in a positive light, suggesting that this new cosmopolitan internationalism can improve people's lives around the globe by making governments more accountable with respect to an entire range of social problems from AIDS to gender equality or ethnic tolerance.

From this point of view, the age-old principle of state sovereignty is but a remnant of the past that is no longer useful in the post-1989 New World Order. The 1990–1991 Iraqi war and, later on, the international interventions in the former Yugoslavia offered good examples of international coalitions and UN-sponsored interventions that coerced states to do what they did not want to. In the Iraqi case, a UN-sponsored international coalition drove the Iraqi forces out of Kuwait, while in Yugoslavia, the U.S.-led international intervention led to the 1995 Dayton Accord that terminated the bloody civil war in Bosnia-Herzegovina. Four years later, the international community intervened militarily once again, forcing the Serb forces to stop their campaign against Albanian insurgents in Kosovo. The Serb forces withdrew from Kosovo and an international peace force assumed control of the province. These examples have provided good test cases to plausibly argue that the world was now operating under a very different set of rules than in the pre–World War II era. It was along these lines that even a change in the North Atlantic Treaty Organization (NATO) rules was contemplated that would make it possible for NATO to intervene in violations that took place within nation-states that failed to comply with international norms. It was not accidental that the proposal was made in the aftermath of the 1999 NATO intervention in Kosovo. The Kosovo Crisis provided a paradigmatic case of international intervention to circumscribe the effects of Serb nationalism. The decision to forcefully alter Serb policy in the area and to create an international protectorate under UN control owed much to the strength of the U.S.-sponsored globalist thinking of the 1990s. In many respects, it provided a tangible application of U.S. debates about nationalism (and internationalism or cosmopolitanism) in the mid-1990s. The theme already explored in the mid-1990s concerned the degree to which a new form of cosmopolitan society was now emerging and which, if any, was the place of nationalism (or patriotism) in the New World Order.

These debates have not been confined to the United States. On the other side of the Atlantic, a similar agenda was pursued in the 1990s: in the aftermath of the Amsterdam (1999) and Maastricht (1992) treaties and the evolution of the European Community (EC) into the EU, it looked as if a future united European state would be a tangible project that could supersede local European nationalisms. The EU logo "unity in diversity" was therefore tilted more toward the first of the two components. Signs that indicated the limited participation of immigrants into the local governance of the European states were hailed as signs of a move toward post-nationalism. That is, immigrants who were hitherto excluded from the benefits of formal citizenship could find informal or semiformalized ways to participate in the national or local politics of their host countries, thereby eroding the exclusive nature of citizenship. Since the late 1990s, scholars have been contemplating the possibility of cosmopolitanism as a perspective that would free people from the boundaries of their national attachments. Many view cosmopolitanism as an expression of an emerging European worldview that will transcend local European nationalisms in favor of a larger European identity. Others view cosmopolitanism as little else than the ideology of a small elite, and they suggest that the cosmopolitan worldview might be nothing more than the class consciousness of frequent travelers, business leaders, managers, and other professionals for whom local ties no longer count that much.

Flag of the European Union (EU). Formed by twelve nations in 1991, the EU is a powerful economic and political bloc promoting European unity. Entering into the EU involves meeting rigorous economic and political conditions. By 2007, the list of member states had grown to 27. (European Commission)

All of the above represent trends popular in the post-1980 period among the academic community but also in discussions in the press and the public in several countries. The tenor of such debates did not always coincide with contemporary developments. In general, over the pre-9/11 period, many academics and journalists viewed post-nationalism positively and were willing to pay less attention to trends challenging this scenario. For example, when the Austrian ultra-right-wing conservatives won the 1999 national elections, the general European and American reaction was that of surprise: great effort was put into explaining why Austria was an exception to European standards. In addition, the EU reacted by enforcing an effective and persistent embargo against the new government, and that embargo quickly led to a different coalition government in Austria.

If in 1999 Austria could be explained away as a somewhat anomalous case, the post-9/11 shifts in the cultural and political landscapes of North America and western Europe cast grave doubts upon the possibility of treating nationalism as a remnant of the past. In the United States, the 9/11 tragedy was quickly nationalized and the war on terrorism soon assumed the characteristics of a national crusade to vindicate American patriotism. In the EU, popular opinion also shifted toward localism amid the terrorist attacks in London and Madrid and fears of additional acts of terrorism. Such fears further accelerated and legitimized xenophobic sentiments that had been on the rise throughout the 1990s. The post-9/11 Europeans' shift toward nationalism led to the rejection of the EU Constitution in France and the Netherlands, and this was a blow to visions of a united Europe. Following its 2004 enlargement, the EU became a community of 25 (and by 2007, a group of 27) countries, and the inclusion of so many eastern European countries caused skepticism about the EU's ability to continue to operate effectively. Fear that the national interests of smaller countries would be lost in a larger EU contributed to growing skepticism about the necessity of a politically unified Europe. At the same time, the prospect of Turkey joining the EU came to the forefront of the public debate. Needless to say, resentment toward immigrants, fear of terrorist attacks, and the growing skepticism toward the EU have all combined to produce a persistent fear of a future Turkish membership in the EU. While many European governments are open to such an eventuality, many polls across Europe have suggested that the majority of the European public is opposed to such a membership. But this issue is not really just about Turkish membership to the EU. Rather, this issue has served as a good template upon which to register resentment against immigration or mere xenophobia.

It remains to be seen whether the sea change that took place in the political and cultural landscapes of North America and Europe in the wake of 9/11 will be an enduring feature of 21st-century public life. Suffice it to say that, in the first decade of the 21st century, it is clear that post-nationalism no longer captures the public's imagination. On the contrary, new forms of localism have been revived, and among them, various local nationalisms have been instrumental in providing justification for numerous shifts in public policy and attitude. In the long run, however, things might be different. Therefore, although post-nationalism remains the least likely in the short run, it is important to stress that global post-national trends could be revived.

Dimensions

The Ethnic Revival and Long-Distance Nationalism

The scholarly community never uniformly accepted the post-national idea. Dissenters argued that international migration and multiculturalism do not bring about the de-nationalization of national politics, but rather they contribute to the re-nationalization of the political body by strengthening xenophobia, racism, and ethnocentrism. Others pointed out that increased cross-cultural communication is not necessarily going to bring about the erosion of the nation, and that the global culture of our times, powerful as it is, might not be in a position to upset local national traditions and their embedded mechanisms responsible for maintaining and reproducing national memory. Both in Europe and the United States, there is plenty of evidence to suggest that immigration and multiculturalism—both of them excellent examples of contemporary globalization—have contributed to a backlash against people who are culturally different than the national mainstream. Such a backlash is often clothed in the costume of nationalism or patriotism. One is reminded of a slogan familiar to U.S. ears: "America, love it or leave it." In the 1990s, persistent U.S. efforts were undertaken to curb illegal immigration, and after 9/11, new restrictions were applied in an effort to keep potential terrorists away from U.S. soil. In many European countries (France, Italy, Austria) ultra-right-wing political parties combined nationalist sentiments with xenophobic attitudes. Both in North America and Europe, populist reactions to globalization often turn to nationalism as a force that can be used to rally the people against globalization.

Since the early 1980s, scholars of nationalism argued that an ethnic revival could be observed around the globe. This ethnic revival took distinct forms in different regions of the globe. In African, Asian, and Latin American countries, ethnicity was evoked as a rallying cry for the national mobilization of minorities. In global surveys of the field, the majority of post-1945 ethnic conflicts around the world are attributed to minority issues. In the post–World War II period, the protection of minorities from state-sponsored policies of cultural homogenization and economic oppression found a new, global audience thanks to the new electronic media (CNN, BBC, etc.), nongovernmental organizations (Amnesty International, Human Rights Watch, International Crisis Group), international agencies (such as the UN High Commission on Refugees), and the creation of a global public. The Zapatista movement in Mexico is perhaps the most widely cited example of such an indigenous movement that was quickly catapulted into the global arena. Initially, the Zapatista rebellion was staged locally but was broadcasted globally, turning what otherwise would have been a purely local event into a global symbol of revolt against NAFTA and the Mexican state's agricultural policies. Elsewhere, armed minority movements—from Sri Lanka to Sudan and Somalia, Eritrea, or Namibia—captured both the imagination of a global audience and the attention of UN-sponsored processes of peacekeeping and/or conflict resolution.

While certainly a popular theme for journalists, the nationalist mobilization of minorities has not been a feature exclusively affiliated with Third World states. On the contrary, even within the heart of Europe, peripheral nationalisms have expressed their strength by challenging the authority of the centralized state and—ironically—using the EU as a supranational agent that could legitimize their aspirations. Such movements are observed in Italy (through the creation of the Northern League), in Spain (through the Basque and Catalan movements), in France, and of course, in the United Kingdom (through the Welsh and Scottish national movements). The EU has often sought to capitalize on such developments by fostering the construction of a "Europe of the Regions," thereby explicitly suggesting that such subnational units like Catalonia or Northern Italy or Scotland could find a convenient shelter in a united Europe. Partly, the EU has promoted itself as an institution that would allow greater autonomy to such movements from their respective national centers. This has been a very clever attempt to use the substate nationalisms of European nation-states as agents that would promote the EU's own post-national institution building. Through this coalition of local substate nationalisms and post-national European bureaucrats, it became possible to speak of several European "nations without states"—such as the cases of Catalonia or Scotland. In these instances, regional governance has been strengthen to such an extent that it can act as a canopy protecting and spearheading the construction and reproduction of national difference, albeit without full access to the resources of a national state.

With the 1999 collapse of communism in Eastern Europe, many of the formerly communist eastern European nations without states were no longer content to stay within their former state or federal boundaries. On the contrary, populist nationalist activists and politicians viewed the collapse of communism as an opportunity to formalize their status as separate nations by seeking recognition as independent, sovereign states. In formerly communist Eastern Europe, three multiethnic or multinational units (the Union of Soviet Socialist Republics, Yugoslavia, and Czechoslovakia) disappeared from the map as a result of such nationalist mobilization. While in the Union of Soviet Socialist Republics and in Czechoslovakia local statesmen were able to find amicable ways for their breakup, in Yugoslavia, this type of nationalist mobilization paved the way for the bloody warfare in Croatia and Bosnia. Of course, the nationalist mobilizations in several East European nations made ample use of preexisting territorial components. That is, the communist regimes had already provided a territorial reference point for these nations (such as Ukraine, Croatia, Slovenia, etc.) by creating state structures that existed within the context of larger federal units (such the Union of Soviet Socialist Republics and Yugoslavia). Technically, these states were in a position akin to the United States: they were states that formed part of larger federal structures. Initially, these states were meant to remain under the control of the Communist Party. In such a manner, their right to succession would remain purely theoretical. When the communist regimes collapsed, this abstract, theoretical statehood was quickly used as a means for obtaining their formal recognition as sovereign, independent states. The challenge involved in this transformation pertained to the artificiality of their borders. The borders of Ukraine or Serbia or Croatia were originally meant to be internal borders within the context of a larger federation. They were not drawn as external, international borders among truly sovereign states. The logic followed by the communists in constructing them served purposes completely different from circumscribing the boundaries of a nation-state: the inclusion of the Crimea within the People's Republic of Ukraine is an apt example of past communist practices. It was quite predictable, then, that border disputes and national rivalries would emerge in a forceful manner.

However, catastrophic outcomes—such as the Yugoslav wars of the 1990s—are typically born out of a more complicated situation. Such outcomes are the result of an institutional interplay among the simultaneous actions of three agents. First, there are nationalizing states set on assimilating minorities into their mainstream. Second, there are national minorities that identify with nation-states other than the ones in which they are located. Third, there exist external national homelands that these national minorities come to view as their desired or natural places of belonging. In the 1990s, the ethnic rivalries between Romania and Hungary (and Romania and Moldova) provided another similar case; yet, these states were able to deal with the situation more constructively than the former Yugoslavia.

Finally, in addition to this resurrection of nationalism in the heart of Europe, contemporary globalization has brought the possibility of strengthening nationalism as a condition or a consequence of the new reality of cross-cultural and international communication and the movement of peoples across the globe. Feelings of nostalgia for the homeland and the experience of living in the midst of a culturally alien milieu can provide the context for the resurgence of national feelings. This form of long-distance nationalism, of course, is not a novelty of the contemporary era. In earlier historical periods, Polish, Scottish, Greek, and Irish immigrants to the United States all harbored dreams of liberty for their homelands. But, what sets apart contemporary trends is the massive character of population movements and routine communication between home and abroad.

In this respect, it was research on immigrant communities that, somewhat unexpectedly, stressed global interconnectedness as a means for national mobilization. Research on international migration has stressed the degree to which transnational communities act as a constituency deeply involved in home society politics and as a force that is responsible for changing the political trajectory of the home country. These new transnational communities of the contemporary period are different from past immigrant communities exactly on the basis of maintaining their ties to the home country. As they are no longer forced to acculturate into the host culture and are empowered by new media of instant communication, the post–World War II immigrants have been enabled to inhabit both the world of the home country and that of the host country. In the 1990s, the example of Haiti, where expatriate communities facilitated the return of President Aristide to power, has provided an almost paradigmatic application for such long-distance nationalism. The involvement of U.S.-based Mexican immigrants in Mexican domestic politics has provided another powerful and enduring example of the same tendency. Many Mexican politicians did not hesitate to cross borders and campaign in immigrant communities that reside in the United States.

From the early 1990s forward, then, researchers in other social and cultural contexts and within several disciplines have been busy researching the influence of diasporic communities in the nation-formation processes of their home countries. Examples abound, with the Irish, Palestinians, Armenians, Lebanese,

Indian, and Chinese communities providing some additional cases beyond the classic Latin American examples of the Haitians, Cubans, Mexicans, Dominicans, and others. This is a major area of contemporary research, where increasingly these two fields of inquiry (the field of nationalism and that of international migration), fields that hitherto had little to do with each other, grow increasingly interconnected.

Let me refer here to one particular example of such transnational nationalism. During the post-1945 period, immigrants from the region of Macedonia in the central Balkans settled in Australia and Canada. In due course of time, these immigrants developed ethnic or national identities that mirrored the development of national identities in that region. Specifically, they adopted Bulgarian or Greek or (ethnic) Macedonian identities, while simultaneously holding to or acquiring their Canadian or Australian citizenships. These links and their interpretations of the past were cultivated through the creation of ethnic churches and communities affiliated with each immigrant subgroup as well as the proliferation of modern media (books, newspapers, talks, festivals, Internet chat rooms, etc.) that contributed to ethnic revival. However, these immigrant groups were not simply content with celebrating their own status but also fiercely claimed the Macedonian heritage for their own group, refusing to accept the claims of others and contesting even the appellation "Macedonian" as a legitimate label for the other groups. In the 1980s and 1990s, the result was a nationalist battlefield, albeit one situated mostly within immigrant communities that lived far and away from their original homeland. Such a seemingly paradoxical situation shows how it is possible in a globalized world to have nationalist disputes that are no longer contained within specific borders but operate in a de-territorialized fashion.

Consequences

Understanding Nationalism in a Global Age

On the basis of the cases mentioned and the arguments described in this chapter, it is fair to conclude that globalization has had a multifaceted influence upon the trajectory of various nationalisms around the world in the post-1980 period. This influence can be summed up as follows: First, the construction of larger, supranational units has provided the impetus for using nationalism to rally the public against the real or imagined negative consequences of the EU, NAFTA, and so on. In this regard, the appeal to nationalism is strongly colored by regionalism, xenophobia, and anti-immigrant sentiment. In this instance, nationalism becomes a new form of localism. Second, the construction of supranational entities has significantly strengthened subnational units and enabled them to claim a national status even without the formal requirement of independent statehood. The cases of Scotland and Catalonia provide paradigmatic examples of this trend. Third, globality has contributed to an ethnic revival in several countries around the world by allowing substate nationalisms to state their claims to a global audience. Fourth, global communication and mass migration have also contributed to long-distance nationalism, whereby immigrants are able to influence developments in their home countries, albeit without having a physical presence in their country of origin.

The picture that emerges from the above is that nationalism might be a vocal, grumpy companion to globalization instead of being its deadly adversary. Such a conclusion makes it necessary to rethink the conventional wisdom that these two concepts should be sharply juxtaposed. Looking upon globalization as a force inherently antithetical to nationalism is clearly a methodological strategy unsuited to account for the complex relations between the two. Rather, the multi-faceted trends reviewed in this chapter suggest that globalization does not necessarily entail the displacement of the nation as a key agent in global politics and as a reference point for the cultural life of communities. While state sovereignty might be limited as a result of the regulatory power of transnational and supranational institutions, such a trend only reinforces an awareness of the problematic link between nation and state. Unlike earlier eras, the connection between nation and state can no longer be taken as a given. In turn, this means that the relationship between nationalism and globalization is one of mutual interdependence. Nationalism gains newfound strength from the use of the global media and transnational trends, while globalization reshapes national identities and makes them mobile and free of the cage of territoriality.

In fact, the de-territorialization of national identities is a feature that has become quite pronounced in the post–World War II era. This trend has highlighted the dividing line between territory and belonging. Belonging is a culturally constructed property and in a globalized world it often sheds off its ties to a specific geographic setting—albeit not its connection to a symbolically constructed place. As a result, nationalisms can now become de-territorialized, as physical presence in a specific locale is no longer a necessity for having feelings for the soil and acting for a national cause. Today, many people live outside their homelands' borders; but this does not necessarily diminish their feelings of attachment and loyalty to their nation. In this regard, examining the interplay between nation and globality provides a good illustration of the ways that the processes of globalization involve the construction or reconfiguration of already existing places of belonging.

By far the most likely outcome for the 21st century is that we are going to witness the emergence or reemergence of various local nationalisms on a global scale. Most often, such nationalisms will be only minimally or symbolically connected to an ancestral land; instead, they will be felt across national boundaries and into a variety of different national contexts. Their carrier groups will be transnational communities of immigrants, refugees, diasporas, and expatriates who become considerably more empowered by the media, communication technologies, and the sheer ability of maintaining national attachments in a variety of locales. Simultaneously, new groups will be formed within existing nation-states to claim or reclaim the status of a nation from their respective governments. Such groups will often form alliances with transnationals who live outside state borders. In this complex web of transnational relations, globality and nationality will coexist side by side—one force uniting the world, while the other seeks passionately to divide it into unique cultures.

Selected Bibliography

Anderson, B. 1993. "The New World Disorder." *New Left Review* 193 (May-June): 3–14.

Basch, L., N. Glick Schiller, and C. S. Blanc. 1994. *Nations Unbound: Transnational Projects, Postcolonial Predicaments, and Deterritorialized Nation-States.* New York: Gordon and Breach.

Beck, U. 1999. *World Risk Society.* Malden, MA: Polity Press.

Brubarker, R. 1996. *Nationalism Reframed.* Cambridge: Cambridge University Press.

Cohen, L. K. 1993. *Broken Bonds: The Disintegration of Yugoslavia.* Boulder, CO: Westview Press.

Glick Schiller, N., and G. Fourton. 2001. *George Woke Up Laughing: Long Distance Nationalism and the Search for Home.* Durham, NC: Duke University Press.

Guibernau, M. M. 1999. *Nations without States: Political Communities in a Global Age.* Oxford: Basil Blackwell.

Gurr, T. R. 1993. "Why Minorities Rebel: A Global Analysis of Communal Mobilization and Conflict since 1945." *International Political Science Review* 14:161–201.

Hayden, R. 1999. *Blueprints for a House Divided: The Constitutional Logic of the Yugoslav Conflicts.* Ann Arbor: University of Michigan Press.

Held, D., A. McGrew, D. Goldblatt, and J. Perraton. 1999. *Global Transformations: Politics, Economics and Culture.* Stanford, CA: Stanford University Press.

Nairn, T. 1997. *The Break Up of Britain.* London: New Left Books.

Ohmae, K. 1995. *The End of the Nation-State: The Rise of Regional Economies.* New York: Free Press.

Reich, R. 1991. *The Work of Nations: Preparing Ourselves for 21st Century Capitalism.* New York: A. A. Knopf.

Roudometof, V. 2002. *Collective Memory, National Identity and Ethnic Conflict: Greece, Bulgaria and the Macedonian Question.* Westport, CT: Praeger.

Sassen, S. 1996. *Losing Control? Sovereignty in an Age of Globalization.* New York: Columbia University Press.

Smith, A. D. 1981. *The Ethnic Revival in the Modern World.* Cambridge: Cambridge University Press.

Smith, A. D. 1995. *Nations and Nationalism in a Global Era.* London: Polity Press.

Soysal, Y. N. 1994. *The Limits of Citizenship: Migrants and Post-National Membership in Europe.* Chicago: University of Chicago Press.

National Identity and Immigration

Anna Triandafyllidou

Relevance

National Identity and the Challenge of Immigration

During the summer months of 2006, European television channels and the press were increasingly obsessed with the arrival of undocumented migrants on the southern coasts of Italy and Spain. Old-fashioned dinghies, the famous *pateras* or *cayucos* (in Spanish), transported African immigrants from Morocco across the Strait of Gibraltar to southern Spain or from Mauritania to the Canary Islands that form part of the Spanish state. Similar boats transported North and sub-Saharan African immigrants from Libya to the tiny islands of Lampedusa and Pantelleria in the south of Italy. Although migrants arrived usually in the tens and not in the thousands, the media hype created an impression of European countries being flooded by economic immigrants from Asia and Africa. They were seen to threaten the public order, the public health, and the overall prosperity of developed countries.

Only half a year earlier, during the last months of 2005, European media had been again overwhelmed, this time not by pictures of young sub-Saharan Africans on small boats at sea but by images of burning cars and violent street riots that took place in Paris and other major French cities. These riots were the culmination of growing social unrest among French citizens of immigrant origin. The rioters included, to a significant extent, young people of North African origin that had abandoned school early, were unemployed, and felt unwelcome and discriminated against in their own country, France.

These media stories exemplify the two main challenges posed by migration for contemporary nations. The first challenge is the one related to entry: is immigration desirable for a nation? And if yes, how should immigration flows be managed to the best interest of the receiving nation? The second challenge concerns the question of immigrant integration in the host society. How can immigrants be accepted as equal members of the nation? Can they ever become truly part of the national in-group, or will they always be stigmatized as "newcomers," "foreigners," "strangers?"

UN reports tell us that, during the last two decades, there have been a growing number of people—asylum-seekers or economic immigrants—who legally or sometimes illegally cross national borders and settle in a country different than their own. European countries and North America emerge as major destinations for immigrants and refugees from developing countries. Indeed, the United States accepts about 1 million new immigrants every year, Canada welcomes nearly

200,000 per year, while major European countries like France, Britain, and Germany have also accepted about 100,000 newcomers each annually in the period between 1994 and 2004.

Immigration receiving countries are thus faced with the necessity of dealing with these "Others within" whose presence defies the national order. By definition, immigration involves members of one nation emigrating to a country of which they are not nationals. Abdelmalek Sayad, a French sociologist, has called this the "paradox of migration." The phenomenon of emigration-immigration involves an absence-presence that is against the national order: the immigrant is absent from the country of which s/he is a national, while s/he is present in a different country in which s/he does not belong.

In the modern world, where political organization has mainly taken the form of nations and nation-states, this absence from the country of origin and presence in a foreign land leads to the exclusion of the immigrant from both societies.

When considering migration, governments and public opinion tend to forget that migration is a feature of human history that is related to the very nature of human societies. It used to be a marginal and unregulated phenomenon within empires but has increasingly become a matter of concern for nation-states during the modern era. Migration is framed as a problem in the modern world mainly because it challenges the national order, the idea that ethnic and cultural boundaries between communities should coincide with borders between states.

However, the notion of the foreigner is inherent in the definition of the nation. National identity performs a double role. It brings the members of the in-group together and at the same time it differentiates them from members of other nations or minority groups. Each nation develops its distinctive identity by valorizing its special traits: a national language, a common territory—the nation's homeland—a belief in common ancestry, shared customs and traditions, a common political culture, a set of national symbols, myths, and heroes, shared collective memories, and a sense of common destiny. These features also become the markers of difference from other nations or minority groups and serve to emphasize the in-group's unity and uniqueness.

Origins

The Historical Context and Nature of the Challenge

Immigration policy and, more particularly, the issue of acceptance and integration of immigrants into the host society are legally and conceptually related to citizenship. The immigrant is an outsider, a foreigner. S/he is not a citizen of the host country. The notion of citizenship regards the rights conferred by a state to the individuals who live in the territory over which the state exerts its sovereign control. Citizenship is closely linked to nationality—sometimes the two are synonymous. This is mainly because citizenship has found its modern expression in the democratic nation-state. The role of national identity in the constitution of citizenship has been primarily functional. It has helped to define the political identity of the citizen. However, citizenship needs not to be tied to national origin.

Immigrants are allowed to become part of the nation, that is, to become citizens of the country of settlement, but they have first to prove that they *fit* culturally, socially, and economically into it. Some countries have very stringent citizenship laws requiring a long period of settlement in the country (10 or 12 years for instance) to allow for naturalization and also require that the applicant is fluent in the national language and acquainted with the national culture and political system (e.g., Germany, Switzerland, Poland, and Greece). These are nation-states in which citizenship is defined mainly through genealogical descent, putting the emphasis on blood and cultural ties. Other countries (e.g., the United States, Canada, Britain, Sweden, and France), notably immigrant nations but also countries with a long experience in receiving migrants, have rather open citizenship policies that allow for immigrants to apply for naturalization after a five-year legal stay, with loose requirements about the level of the applicants' knowledge of the national language and culture. In these countries, national identity has primarily a territorial and civic character, while parental lineage plays a lesser role. Most nation-states combine both territorial and ethnic elements in their definition of national identity and citizenship.

Most European countries and many states around the world, like Japan, China, and Russia for instance, conceive of themselves as national states, where the state is the political expression of the dominant nation. This idea implies that the culture and ethnic composition of the nation are homogenous and unique. Their presumed purity and authenticity has to be protected from the intrusion of immigrants, who are seen as alien, not belonging *here*, not part of *us*.

In some countries, though, immigrant communities are integrated into the national history. The historical, cultural, territorial, or civic links between these populations and the nation are officially recognized. Thus, as happens in France, the Netherlands, and Britain, the links between the mother country and its former colonies are deemed to justify, under certain conditions, the conferral of citizenship on people of immigrant origin. Nonetheless, often the status of citizenship does not suffice to guarantee the social integration of these people. In fact, it is not unusual for individuals of immigrant origin, who have acquired by birth or residence the citizenship of the country of settlement, to be discriminated against in practice. The riots of October 2005 in France or those of the summer of 2001 in northern England are but an indication of the sometimes uneasy cohabitation between national majority and ethnic minorities.

The situation is different in immigrant nations like Canada, the United States, and Australia, where immigration and settlement forms an integral part of the national narrative. Nonetheless, in these countries, too, immigration poses a challenge to the cohesion and self-definition of the nation. Such a challenge is, for instance, the dominance of Hispanic migration to the United States in recent decades and the related changing balance in terms of language use in public places and services. Something similar happens in Australia where the dominant national narrative of Anglo-Saxon white origins is challenged by increasing immigration from neighboring Asia, Indonesia, and the Pacific.

According to the State of the World Population report published by the United Nations in 2006, international population movements have increased in the post–World War II era, partly as a result of the development of transport and communication infrastructure and because of growing disparities between the global North and the global South. Currently 191 million people live outside their country of birth, but they account for less than 3 percent of the total world population. About 41 million people have moved during the period between 1980 and 1995, whereas only 36 million have moved during the last 15 years (1990–2005). However, three-quarters of all movements have developed countries as their destination, notably North America and Europe. One out of every four immigrants lives in North America, and one out of every three lives in Europe.

These general data provide for an overview of the size of the immigration challenge for national identity nowadays. Indeed, both immigrant nations (such as Canada, Australia, and the United States) and historical nation-states (such as

Girls play together at Melcombe Primary School, an inner-city school in London, where many of the students come from diverse backgrounds such as non-native English-speaking homes or hold refugee status. (Gideon Mendel/Corbis)

most European countries) are under pressure from international immigration, which brings with it substantial cultural, ethnic, and religious diversity. This diversity challenges the self-understanding of the nation.

However, when considering the impact of immigration on national identities, it is necessary to distinguish between *postwar* and *new* types of migration. Post–World War II migrations involved organized, legal, long-term population movements that often followed the signature of bilateral agreements between sending and receiving countries or direct recruitment schemes of large corporations (e.g., the London Underground recruited employees abroad in the 1950s and 1960s). This took place during the period of reconstruction and industrial development of the 1950s until the 1970s. Migrants worked usually in large factories in the primary sector (in heavy industries, like coal mines, the steel industry, or car manufacturing for instance) and were covered by collective trade union–employer agreements and welfare contributions. The main countries involved in these population movements were southern European countries (e.g., Italy, Greece, Spain, or Portugal, also Yugoslavia to a certain extent) that sent workers to northern and Western Europe as well as to Canada, Australia, and the United States. Also, northern African and Middle Eastern countries (Morocco, Algeria, and also Turkey) and countries from the Indian subcontinent, the Caribbean, and to a lesser extent, from sub-Saharan Africa were involved in this process by sending immigrant workers to Britain, France, Germany, or the Netherlands. Workers from Africa (e.g., Ghana or Ethiopia), Latin America (Mexico, but also Brazil, Venezuela, Colombia, or Peru, for instance) and Asia (China, Malaysia, Indonesia, or India, for instance) migrated to North American countries (the United States and Canada).

The term "new migrations" refers to international population movements that have been taking place since the late 1980s and are typical of the last two decades. New migrations are short-term, often illegal movements and involve multiple destinations or frequent returns to the country of origin. Some migrants engage in forms of mobility that involve several repeated short-term stays, which have been called "shuttle" or "commuting" migration. These new immigrants find employment in secondary job markets, such as construction, domestic care, cleaning and catering services, or agriculture. They are usually employed in the so-called three D jobs (dirty, dangerous, and demanding), often without proper contracts or welfare contributions. These migrations are not part of a phase of economic growth but rather are attracted by structural disparities in the economies of developed countries. Contemporary immigrants take advantage of the improved means of communication and transport but are also easy prey to the economic and social forces of globalization.

The challenges of *postwar* migration for national identity became apparent when immigrant populations began to settle in their destination countries and demanded the recognition and accommodation of their cultural, linguistic, or religious identities. Moreover, they started bringing in their families and formed larger immigrant communities and even ethnic neighborhoods in metropolitan cities, with distinctive cultural and religious features. They thus challenged the vision of the nation as a unitary, homogenous, and stable entity.

New migrations pose less of an identity and cultural challenge to the nation because immigrants rarely establish themselves in one place to voice demands for integration. Moreover, many among the new immigrants live and work undocumented and hence are deprived of the possibility of raising any claims to the receiving state or society. They are employed in the shadow economy and live at the margins of society. Nonetheless, as time passes and the second generation comes of age, new immigrants also become settled and pose an identity challenge to the receiving country.

In postwar migrations, immigrants posed a challenge through their presence, settlement, and participation in the economic and social life of the receiving countries. They were thus constructed as the outsider within in relation to their racial, cultural, or religious difference from the native population. New forms of migration are constructed as "Others" mainly because they are "invisible" in their societies of settlement. The lack of knowledge about them and their undocumented status make them easy targets for stigmatization. Media and political debates often represent them as criminal or culturally inferior, thus unfit to become part of the nation.

Dimensions

Immigrant Exclusion and Ethnic Prejudice

Although different countries experience in different ways and in different degrees the challenge of immigration, there is one common element in their national identity discourses: immigrants are viewed as outsiders, and often deemed threatening. However, not every immigrant is perceived as threatening or inferior by members of the nation. In Europe and North America, citizens from other developed countries may be considered foreigners but are not part of the negative stereotype usually associated with immigration. Discrimination, if experienced, is minor and certainly not the rule but rather the exception to it.

The common feature that characterizes those immigrants that are constructed as the nation's threatening Others is their *subordinate* position in society and the existence of ethnic, cultural, religious, or racial "markers" that distinguish them from the dominant group. Such markers are not the reason for which these groups are perceived as threatening out-groups. There is nothing intrinsically problematic in being a Muslim or being of eastern European or Asian origin. Difference acquires a negative connotation because of the context in which it is placed. Thus, anti-Muslim sentiment in Britain, France, or Germany points to religion as an important and indeed negative marker of difference for Muslim immigrants. In a similar vein, negative stereotypes for Albanians make nationality an important marker of difference between Greek natives and Albanian immigrants. In some cases, ethnic and religious categorizations are intertwined to mitigate or enhance the sense of difference: Thus Bulgarian or Russian immigrants in Greece, who are Christian Orthodox, are seen as less threatening than Muslim Albanians or Turkish Muslims. On the other hand, sub-Saharan African immigrants of Christian faith in Italy may experience stronger discrimination and racism than Ukrainian Catholics.

This selective discrimination against specific groups has less to do with the features of these groups (racial, ethnic, or religious) and more with the identity of the receiving nation. Prejudice and discrimination against specific immigrant groups serves the interests and identity of the dominant nation. Immigrants become the negative Other in contrast to whom a positive in-group identity can be constructed and reinforced. Moreover, they provide for a flexible and cheap labor force that can be relatively easily dispensed with because they are not nationals. The construction of the immigrant's image as inferior, negative, or threatening serves to legitimize the immigrant's exploitation and marginalization.

The relationship between power or privilege and racism or cultural prejudice has been explored from different perspectives—economic, sociological, linguistic, and ideological—by a large number of scholars. It has been shown that racial or ethnic prejudice and discriminatory discourse or behavior are related to the power structure of society and serve to maintain the privilege of one group over another.

Discriminatory behavior or practices are related to race, namely skin complexion and phenotypic characteristics, culture, or a combination of both. Muslim women wearing a headscarf or black African people are thus often the victims of racist behavior and cultural prejudice. As one German African citizen put it in a research interview: "people spitting in your head to see if it sticks well in that kind of hair" (interview 63, POLITIS project, http://www.uni-oldenburg.de/politis-europe/index.html, interviewee anonymity is protected). European media often portray young Muslim women that wear a headscarf as backward, oppressed, and unable to decide for themselves. Black African youth in Portugal were stereotyped as delinquents after the media erroneously reported about a group of youngsters who rushed through a crowded beach in the south of the country robbing people of their belongings. North Africans in France are stereotyped as lazy and uneducated; people that you cannot trust. Latinos in the United States are often labeled as illegal immigrants, while black Africans in Ireland are seen as bogus asylum seekers. In these cases, stereotyping takes place on the basis of their appearance rather than of any deeper knowledge of their nationality, origin, and reason for coming to the host country.

Racism or ethnic prejudice can take two forms. One is that of overt biological racism claiming that the human race is divided into different "races" and that these are characterized by specific biological and intellectual traits. This racist ideology argues that the white "race" is superior to the other "races." This type of ideology has found its most infamous expressions in the African slave trade between the 16th and 19th centuries and in the Holocaust genocide of the Jews. Biological racism has since been discredited not only in the positive and social sciences but also in public opinion. Most citizens in Western democracies find unacceptable the use of overtly racist language. This, however, does not mean that discrimination or racism has disappeared.

A second type of stereotyping and prejudice refers to cultural characteristics. This type of discourse presents differences between certain cultures as irreducible. Thus, immigrants from certain countries or ethnic groups or of specific religious faiths are said to be *unable* to integrate into the host society. This type of discourse has been particularly pronounced during the last few years with regard to Muslim immigrants in both North America and Europe, irrespective of their country of origin. They are represented as people who voice unreasonable demands upon their receiving societies. They are stereotypically portrayed as dangerous—potential terrorists because supposedly that is what their religion commands.

The notion of race includes a variety of features, such as parental lineage, phenotype (skin color, stature, and genetic traits), as well as the combination of physical attributes with cultural features (e.g., a specific dress code, a mode of behavior, the observance of specific religious practices, customs, and mores related to family life and kinship relations). Racism is not necessarily linked to ethnicity or nationalism. What is common to the various definitions of the concept is that it is associated with *natural* difference: it implies that people belonging to a given race share some biological or cultural features that cannot be chosen or shed. This does not mean that racial difference is indeed natural but rather that it has been socially constructed as such. It is perceived as irreducible and, hence, threatening for the nation.

Clearly, one should not equate a sociopolitical situation that allows for the perpetuation of latent racism with one in which the perpetration of racist behaviors, the organization of racist movements, and the acceptance of institutionalized racism are integrated into the system. This, however, does not mean that *subtle* or *symbolic* racism is harmless. It still treats difference as permanent because it is natural, and inherently threatening.

The discourse of cultural difference has some similarity with that of biological racism because it links culture to nature. Cultural difference is seen as irreducible, because it is dependent upon ethnic descent, a presumed psychological predisposition, environmental factors, or a specific genetic makeup. Thus, immigrants are constructed as alien, unfamiliar, and less developed. In fact, nationalism brings with it the seed of discrimination against minorities. The notion of "authenticity" of the national culture, language, or traditions implies that cultural difference within the nation is undesirable.

Arguments that present cultural difference as irreducible and somehow natural are racist, even if they do not refer directly to race. Of course, cultural difference provides scope for fluidity and change in people's behavior and allegiances: members of minority groups may make conscious decisions to abandon some, but hold on to other, attributes of their minority culture as they see it. Young Muslim girls in Britain or the United States, for instance, may adopt a modern way of dressing, may study, and may have a career but, at the same time, wear a headscarf to denote their religious identity. Minority groups may themselves strive to maintain cultural distinctiveness by emphasizing certain aspects of their tradition (like specific festivities, dress codes, or dietary habits) alongside full social and political integration in the society of settlement. Race, in contrast, cuts across a population without the possibility of creating nuances or changing one's skin color.

The key to understanding the importance of race and culture and their role in the relationship between the nation and the immigrant is the fact that they can both be defined as transcendental notions, linked to *nature* rather than *nurture* and, hence, irreducible. Thus, they justify the exclusion of the immigrant from the national in-group and the assertion of the national identity as supposedly *authentic* and *pure* from foreign influences.

Consequences

Beyond the Nation? Transnational Immigrant Identities

The previous sections of this chapter concentrate on the exclusion of immigrants from the nation and on the ways in which specific cultural or ethnic differences are used to marginalize immigrants and reinforce the national identity. This section considers how the national identity of immigrant minorities is transformed through their interaction with the receiving society.

Immigrant communities usually have close symbolic and material ties with their nations of origin. "Diaspora nationalism theories" emphasize the importance of these ties for both the immigrant populations and those left behind, in the country of origin. They see the relationship between immigrants and the receiving country as one of limited integration, if not alienation. In the diaspora nationalism perspective, immigrants and natives are forced to live together mainly for economic reasons. They are both assumed to be longing for national and cultural *authenticity* and *purity* that could be achieved only through the return of the minority to the home country.

Links between the country of origin and the immigrant population are important for the lives of immigrants, especially the first generation. These links help explain why sometimes immigrant communities and native populations live separate from one another and even form segregated neighborhoods. These links, however, cannot explain the process of identity transformation that takes place among second- and third-generation migrants. Diaspora nationalism approaches place too strong an emphasis on the presumed alienation (or lack of integration) of the minority into the receiving society while neglecting the importance of the migration process as a human experience. They tend to overlook how immigrants change through their experiences of life and work in the country of settlement, their contact with natives, and their getting accustomed to new customs and habits, and a new language.

Contemporary migrations are characterized by complex relationships between hosts, migrants, and their communities of origin within which national and ethnic affiliations are molded and redefined. Such processes give rise to such transnational political and economic activities as the twinning of Mexican and North American towns initiated by Mexican immigrants in the United States or the political activism of Iraqi or Kurdish Turks across Europe.

It would be misleading to analyze such processes through the lens of national identities understood as stable and cohesive. For instance, recent studies on returning Greek Americans have highlighted the dual nature of national identity among immigrant diasporas. Young second- or third-generation Greek Americans who *return* to Greece realize that they belong fully neither here nor there. They experience the United States as their actual *home*, while Greece, which was imagined as *home*, too, is to a certain extent experienced as an alien culture and place. These dual or multiple identifications of immigrants of second or third generations reveal the complexity of the migrant's situation that cannot be understood through classical definitions of national identity as stable and cohesive.

Transnational identities among immigrant populations are part of the new context of intensive communications and socioeconomic globalization. It is cosmopolitan theories that have paid more attention to these issues, notably to the overall processes of social transformation in the late 20th and early 21st centuries. They emphasize the features of postindustrial societies, such as highly improved communications across the globe, better, quicker, and cheaper means of long-distance transports, media that select and cover events worldwide, all of which result in the compression of time and space. Today people may live and work in Germany, watch TV news and soap operas from Turkey, phone their relatives in Britain or Canada, and chat on the Internet with friends across the globe in an instant. Moreover, traveling between the country of origin and the place of settlement takes only several hours, less than a day, while the distance between the two places may be several thousand miles. Thus, immigrants become able to maintain frequent and intense ties with their countries of origin.

In making sense of these new virtual realities of compressed time and space, sociologists have argued that individuals are today free and able to create their own individualized and flexible identities. They may be understood as free floating agents picking and choosing from different cultures and traditions the features that best suit them. Sociologists have thus argued that immigrants live in a mobile world of culturally open societies and may therefore adapt to different cultures and habits, without having any longer a sense of primary national identity. They rather negotiate choices among available options.

The cosmopolitan perspective is a useful tool in analyzing how migrants adapt their national and ethnic identity to the host society environment, negotiating emotive and cultural attachments that are both *here* and *there*. However, it neglects the fact that the use of new technologies may also lead to polarization. People may imitate consumption patterns or youth subcultures and at the same time hold on to traditional behaviors that emphasize their belonging to a given nation or ethnic group. New technologies, such as satellite TV or the Internet, may enable the preservation of immigrant identities and cultures as closed containers with direct ties between the country/region of origin and that of settlement.

One important question that is also open to investigation is the extent to which new technologies have fostered new attitudes or practices among immigrant populations, or whether new technologies have simply intensified and widened the realities that existed before. Mexican or Puerto Rican immigrants in the United States for instance have led transnational lives even before the advent of new technologies. They moved regularly between the United States and Mexico or Puerto Rico, took up work in the United States, but sent remittances back home, had personal and family networks in both places, and sometimes even engaged in long-distance politics in their hometowns while residing in Texas, California, or New York City.

Also, there is another facet to this that can work against cosmopolitan practices among migrants. Children born out of immigrant parents (the second generation) are sometimes ghettoized by the very policies and social attitudes in their countries of settlement. While they may feel they belong to the country in which they were born, they may be categorized by other citizens as aliens because their parents were immigrants. Thus, they are trapped in the label "immigrant," "Latino," "*Maghrebin*" (person from a North African country), "Chinese," "Albanian," or "Russian," even if they personally do not identify with the national origins of their parents. Their wish for leading a cosmopolitan lifestyle can thus be hampered by the attitudes of others toward them.

Socioeconomic factors should not be neglected either. Not all migrants have equal access to new technologies and cosmopolitan lives. Unavoidably, migrants with more economic resources, a higher education, and better social skills will have more access to the necessary infrastructure, thus becoming potentially more cosmopolitan than their poorer fellow nationals. Moreover, there may be a generation effect: younger immigrants are more likely to be literate in new technologies than their parents or generally middle-aged or older immigrants.

Immigrants may develop multiple identities, combining their roots in the country and culture of origin and their day-to-day experiences in the country of settlement. Their mixed identities cannot be understood within a narrow conception of national identity as a static set of features that all the members of a nation share in equal terms. Transnational immigration experiences and transcultural modes of expression are a reality, and especially so in metropolitan cities like London, Paris, New York, Singapore, and Sydney. Nonetheless, in smaller places and also in the context of a neighborhood or small town, immigrants are part of kinship and ethnic networks that continue to affirm the significance of national identity and homeland connections. They thus reinforce a sense of difference between the national majority and the immigrant community.

In conclusion, national identity and nationalism still retain a strong command over people's sense of who they are and to whom they are related. At the same time, the power of individuals to negotiate personal identities, national cultures, and globalized economic realities is not to be neglected.

Selected Bibliography

Aksoy, A. 2006. "The Challenge of Migrants for a New Take on Europe." In *Transcultural Europe: Cultural Policy in a Changing Europe*, edited by U. H. Meinhof and A. Triandafyllidou, 181–199. Basingstoke, UK: Palgrave Macmillan.

Anthias, F., and N. Yuval Davis. 1992. *Racialised Boundaries*. London: Routledge.

Barth, F. 1981. "Ethnic Groups and Boundaries." In *Process and Form in Social Life: Selected Essays of Fredrik Barth*, vol. 1, 198–231. London: Routledge and Kegan Paul.

Bogdanor, V., ed. 1987. *Blackwell Encyclopaedia of Political Institutions*. Oxford: Blackwell.

Cesarani, D., and Fulbrook, M., eds. 1996. *Citizenship, Nationality and Migration in Europe*. London: Routledge.

Habermas, J. 1994. "Citizenship and National Identity." In *The Condition of Citizenship*, edited by P. van Steenbergen, 20–35. London: Sage.

King, R. 2002. "Towards a New Map of European Migration." *International Journal of Population Geography* 8:89–106.

Modood, T., A. Triandafyllidou, and R. Zapata Barrero. 2006. *Multiculturalism, Muslims and Citizenship. A European Approach*. London: Routledge.

Riggins, S., ed. 1997. *The Language and Politics of Exclusion. Others in Discourse*. London: Sage.

Sayad, A. 2006. *The Suffering of the Immigrant*. Cambridge: Polity Press.

Spohn, W., and A. Triandafyllidou. 2003. *Europeanisation, National Identities and Migration: Changes in Boundary Constructions between Western and Eastern Europe*. London: Routledge.

Triandafyllidou, A. 2001. *Immigrants and National Identity in Europe*. London: Routledge.

United Nations Population Fund (UNFPA). 2006. *The State of World Population. A Passage to Hope. Women and Migration*. October. http://www.unfpa.org/publications.

Vertovec, S. 2003. "Migration and Other Modes of Transnationalism: Towards Conceptual Cross-Fertilization." *International Migration Review* 37, no. 3: 641–666.

Vertovec, S. 2004. "Migrant Transnationalism and Modes of Transformation." *International Migration Review* 38, no. 3: 970–1001.

Nationalism and Music

David B. Knight

Relevance

Music that speaks to the hearts and minds of a particular people who accept themselves as a nation can be a powerful expression of their nationalism. Military music has long been used to lift soldiers' spirits before and after battle, and it also speaks more generally to nationalists. Such music may remember campaigns and triumphantly recall battle successes achieved in the name of the nation. Above all, military music celebrates a sense of nationalistic pride. Some music written to accompany movies is nationalistic and, with the message of the movie, stirs the emotions of audiences. In addition, national anthems express a variety of sentiments related to the nation and inherently are expressions of nationalism. Some popular music, as expressions of "resistance," has recently developed nationally based characteristics that reflect on the nation and state from the perspective of youthful minorities.

Other music, written for orchestras and performed mostly in concert halls, can be profoundly nationalistic. This music incorporates or reflects any of the following: (1) national traditions, myths, and legends; (2) folk, popular, and military music; (3) major events—whether glorious, triumphant, or sorrowful—of significance to the nation and its people; and (4) national songs that proclaim the importance of the nation. Some of the orchestral music to be discussed was composed when the nations in question were under the control of an outside power. The composers sometimes knew they were creating music that would speak to the soul of emerging nationalism. They expressed an identification with the nation in ways that spoke powerfully to the adherents of nationalism. In time, much of this music came to have universal (i.e., extra-national) acceptance, but when composed, the music had—and generally still has—special meaning for the specific nations in question.

Music that ultimately speaks to a nation takes on special meaning for listeners who identify closely with the nation. The music is held to have special value, whether to cultural elites, politicians, or the general public. Each person may have a slightly different perspective on the music's contrasting elements, but to all who belong to a nation, the music is celebrated because it gives voice to aspects of the nation and its nationalism.

Origins

Some military music is profoundly nationalistic. The origin of military music is ancient, starting perhaps with just a ram's horn. Trumpets and drums later were used to give battle signals and to help soldiers keep a good pace as they marched. Turkish military drums (precursors of the modern timpani, or kettle drums), cymbals, and triangles were added to European military and orchestral music in the early 18th century.

National anthems have also been around for a long time. Britain's is the oldest, having been in use since 1744. It predated other clear expressions of nationhood, thus it was centered on the ruling monarch. Verses added at later times widened its scope. National anthems elsewhere generally incorporated the idea of a people (the nation) within its special territory (the state), and referred to history and/or the future.

Following on from the Romantic revolution in literature, which began in the late 18th century, a similar revolution in orchestral music emerged, led principally by Ludwig van Beethoven, Hector Berlioz, Felix Mendelssohn, and others. Their early 19th-century compositions began the process whereby clear expression of emotions, including passion, and the telling of stories was possible in music. They thereby broke the constraints of the earlier classical forms of musical composition.

Some early 19th-century composers spoke to a growing sense of Germanness, including Carl Maria von Weber in his opera *Der Freischütz* (1821). The work thrilled German audiences, including a young Richard Wagner. He was astounded by the work, for its music and for the expression of love for Germany. From about 1840 until 1882, Wagner created numerous towering compositions that drew upon mythic stories, including the vast four-part cycle of operas known as *The Ring of the Nibelung*, or *The Ring Cycle*. *Die Walküre* (1870), the second opera, includes the famous *Ride of the Valkyries*. Wagner's many masterful musical dramas represented the grand flowering of German cultural nationalism. Sadly, in the 1930s and 1940s, Hitler and the Nazis "adopted" Wagner's music as their own, using it to promote their racist agenda and thus spoiled the music ever thereafter for many listeners.

During much of the 19th century, Germanic forms of musical composition were dominant throughout most of Europe, Russia, and the Americas. Toward the close of the century, some composers developed styles of music that were different and that challenged this dominance. Their music was quickly recognized as being regionally distinctive in style, being unlike music found elsewhere in Europe. Further, however, their music reflected something of their people's specific identity, love of land, stories and myths, and nationalistic dreams, whether or not they lived in their own independent state. These new forms of nationalistic expression in music became stronger as the century progressed and continued into the 20th century. Much of the music of this nature originated in eastern Europe, though nationalistic music also developed elsewhere, including Finland, Norway, the British Isles, and the Americas.

Dimensions

War-Related Music

Some nationalistic music is war based. Resistance to Napoleon's aggressiveness provoked many composers. Franz Joseph Haydn's *Lord Nelson Mass*, or *Mass in the Time of Peril* (1798), first expresses (in the *Kyrie*) Austrians' despair as Napoleon's armies swept across Europe and then (in the *Benedictus*) represents the defeat of Napoleon's fleet in the Battle of the Nile by the British admiral Lord Nelson. Written in the classic style, its references to these events is not clear to all listeners. In contrast, Beethoven's *Wellington's Victory* (1813) is direct. Based on the 1813 Battle of Vitoria (in northern Spain), it opens with the British and French armies challenging each other before charging into battle. Rifle shots (ratchets) and cannons (bass drums) are written into the score. The blocks of soldiers advance and, with a constant rhythm played at increasing tempos, the two sets of cavalry charge. Beethoven then triumphantly signals the British victory by quoting *God Save the King*, to the delight of British audiences. The music also quotes the British tune *Rule Britannia* and the French tune *Malbrouck s'en va t'en guerre*. The work is thought of as either exciting or trite. There is no expression of hurt or sorrow. In another work on *The Battle and Defeat of Napoleon*, part of the *Háry János Suite* (1927), Hungarian composer Zoltán Kodály expresses in music the French emperor's army falling over like toy soldiers. Russian composer Piotr Tchaikovsky's famous *1812 Overture* (1880) celebrates the defeat of Napoleon's forces (*La Marseillaise*) by the Russians (*God Preserve the People*). In this patriotically joyous music, Tchaikovsky includes Moscow's many church bells (orchestral bells) and Russian army cannons (bass drums or, on occasion, actual cannons). Today, the work is enjoyed around the world.

Some war music celebrates the advance of soldiers, as in Franz Liszt's *Hungarian Attack March* (1875). It is flashy, and surely still delights Hungarian audiences. In contrast, *Mars, the Bringer of War*, the powerful first movement of English composer Gustav Holst's *The Planets*, is aggressive. *The Planets* is an immensely popular work in Britain, perhaps as much for later sections on, for example, *Venus, the Bringer of Peace* and *Jupiter: the Bringer of Jollity*, but it is the first movement that hits hardest. *Mars* is menacing and disturbing. The message is clear: war is evil, be aware, and be prepared. Written in 1914, the work seemed to be a warning of what was to come. Though thought-provoking, Holst's music lacks the direct human impact of some music by Russian Dmitri Shostakovich.

Shostakovich, who lived in Russia when Stalin's totalitarian regime ruled with an iron fist, walked a fine line between self-expression and meeting the state's demand for conformity. He was in Leningrad (now St. Petersburg) in 1941 when Hitler's troops attacked Russia. The German army surrounded Leningrad, but the Russians heroically held them off, though at a terrible cost. About 1 million people (one-third of the population) died from months of attacks, lack of food, and disease. Shostakovich started to write his *Symphony No. 7* (called by others the *Leningrad Symphony*) while he was in the city, where he served as a fireman. He was evacuated to Kuybyshev (named the temporary capital of the Soviet Union due to the German army's march on Moscow), and he completed the work there.

The first movement, which he originally called *War*, is a haunting, increasingly angry, and very powerful expression of the relentless march of the German army toward Leningrad, and of the terror (for one hears the screams) being experienced by those in the path of the advancing troops. In later sections, the music reflects on memories—on Leningrad's quiet streets and the bank of the River Neva at sunset—and on the moral victory of the Russian people. The 900-day German siege of Leningrad was still ongoing when the music was performed in Leningrad before a large and wearily appreciative audience. The composition still speaks powerfully to the Russian people. Shostakovich wrote another war-based work, his *Symphony No. 8* (1943). The possibility exists that it (unlike the *Leningrad*) refers not to the external war with the Germans but to the deadly ongoing Stalinist "war" on the Russian people. Some national governments do not condone dissent. Shostakovich and other Russian composers suffered from the dictates of the state, as did Chinese composers during the Cultural Revolution in the 1960s and 1970s. Shostakovich said in music what he couldn't say in words.

Other music related to World War II is appreciated by British audiences. It tends to be jauntily heroic, celebrating victory. For example, a concert piece was excerpted from William Walton's music written for the movie *The First of the Few* (1942). Called *Spitfire: Prelude and Fugue*, it celebrates the famous World War II British fighter plane and its pilots during the Battle of Britain. Eric Coates took from his musical score for the movie *The Dam Busters* (1954) a still-popular march by the same name.

Music that speaks particularly to U.S. audiences was composed by American Richard Rodgers and arranged by Robert Russell Bennett for the 26 episodes in the television series called *Victory at Sea* (1952–1953). The films were taken during World War II action in the Atlantic, Europe, and especially, the Pacific. The dramatic music (but without the searing pain of Shostakovich's work) plays a major part of the storyline. Bennett later arranged the music into two orchestral suites, each called *Victory at Sea*. The shorter version is a "pops" concert favorite in the United States. Ultimately, Rodgers's music is heroic, perhaps because of the desire to show the American population that their armed forces had overcome terrible odds.

In the late 1940s and 1950s, many American and British movies were made about World War II–based stories concerning soldiers, flying crews, naval crews on ships and in submarines, and spies and code breakers. As boosters of nationalism, they had a powerful impact on young audiences. Not so incidentally, the music scores accompanying the movies were equally dramatic. A similar situation applied to a heroic and very nationalistic movie that celebrated allegiance to king and country, namely, *Scott of the Antarctic* (1949). It was about the 1913 British Antarctic expedition's attempt to reach the South Pole under the leadership of Captain Robert Scott. Englishman Ralph Vaughan Williams's accompanying music was later developed into *Symphony No. 7, Sinfonia Antartica* (1953). The musical exploration of the Antarctic environment is fascinating. The resulting sound pictures illustrate how music can deal with a daring feat in a landscape of extremes. Ultimately, in an eerie manner, the music conveys the defeat of the humans' valiant effort to conquer nature.

Still other music written during and after World War II gave expression to the widespread horror of what can happen when nationalisms run rampant. Many composers reacted to fascism; to the bombing and destruction of cities in Britain, the European continent, and Japan; and to the horrors of the Holocaust, when the Nazis and their cohorts imprisoned and slaughtered millions of Jews, Roma, and others. The powerful music of protest includes Frenchman Olivier Messiaen's *Quartet for the End of Time* (1941), composed and first performed while he was imprisoned by the Germans, Austrian-American Arnold Schoenberg's *A Survivor from Warsaw* (1947), Polish Krzysztof Penderecki's *Threnody: To the Victims of Hiroshima* (1960), Englishman Benjamin Britten's *War Requiem* (1962), and Canadian Robert Evans's *For the Children: No Silence of the Soul* (1997). The latter work uses poems written in Terezin (a Nazi concentration camp) by Jewish children aged 8 to 15, almost all of whom were later gassed. These several composers sought to transcend nations and nationalisms. Their music mourns, surely in the hope that a better world can replace nationalistic violence.

A distinctive form of war-related music that speaks to specific nations was developed by armies for their respective bands (including those of The Black Watch and Grenadier Guards in Britain, and of the armed services in the United States) and choirs (the most famous being the Russian Red Army Choir). Some of their music remembers battles fought by the armies, or regiments within them.

Nationalistic Music

The notion of "My Country" above all others is inherent in all nationalisms. The love for country can be expressed in epic poems, national anthems, and, too, instrumental music. This love can lead to some people getting lumps in their throats when their national anthem or some other tune special to their nation is performed.

Frédéric Chopin was an early 19th-century composer who wrote nationalistic music that was inspired by folk sources. His brilliant and uniquely Polish mazurkas and polonaises for piano led composers elsewhere to recognize that they, too, could write music based on national folk music.

One of the earliest instances of music causing audience nationalistic arousal occurred in Budapest in 1846 when the French composer Hector Berlioz (1803–1869) conducted the premiere performance in Hungary of his *Rakoczy March*. Hungary, part of the Austro-Hungarian empire, was dominated by the German language and culture. Berlioz's extensive use of woodwinds and brass and punctuating percussion, including drum beats (like distant cannons) and cymbal clashes, not only enlivened the work but set an example for other Romantic composers to follow. What mattered to the Hungarians of the day, however, was the tune itself, and what Berlioz had done with it. The *Rakoczy* tune, Berlioz knew, would speak to the powerful patriotic feeling that Hungarians felt for themselves as a distinct people; however, its reception surprised him. As they listened, the audience first got agitated and then so excited as the work proceeded that as it neared its conclusion their cheers drowned out the music. Berlioz immediately repeated the work, and the same audience reaction occurred. Such can be the power of nationalism in music. Hungarian Franz Liszt later captured a distinctly Hungarian sound in *Hungarian Rhapsodies* (1850s/1880s) and *Hungarian Fantasia* (1852). Early in the 20th century, Hungarian composers Béla Bartók (e.g., *Hungarian Sketches* [1931]) and Zoltán Kodály (e.g., *Galánta Dances* [1933] and *Peacock Variations* [1938–1939]) each drew from folk songs they had gathered in the countryside, and so fed a desire among the people for music that was distinctly Hungarian.

Bohemia (now the Czech Republic) was another part of the Austro-Hungarian empire where music gave voice to a growing sense of national identity (then still subnational, within the empire). Bedřich Smetana, born in 1824, was 19 when he moved to Praha (Prague), the leading city, where, as in most of Europe at that time, nationalistic ferment reigned. He became a famous composer. His music is recognized for its stunning representation of Czech national color and musical rhythms. He wrote several operas, including *The Brandenburgers in Bohemia* (it was enjoyed by patriotic Czechs but it upset the German-oriented critics) and *The Bartered Bride*. The latter includes well-known Czech dances.

Smetana also composed the major orchestral statement on Czech nationalism; it is the most important extended example of nationalistic music. *Má Vlast* (composed during 1872–1879), which consisted of six symphonic poems, considers Bohemian life, the countryside, history, and legends. The first symphonic poem, *Vyšehrad*, refers to the imposing high rock that guards the point at which the country's principal river, the Vltava, enters Prague. It was the site of a legendary royal fortress. The music refers to a person singing about the castle's ancient splendor, its events such as tournaments and battles, and its eventual decline and ruination.

In the second symphonic poem, *Vltava* (or *Moldau*, its German name), the river starts its flow at two springs (represented by two flutes) in southern Bohemia. The music sparkles. The sense of evolving joy is captivating. The streams soon merge and become a river of growing consequence. As the work proceeds, following the river in its course, the music represents the lovely Bohemian countryside and the river flowing past a moonlit field. A hunter's horn sounds and a joyous wedding is celebrated on the river's bank before the river continues with a strong and steady flow, a reminder of Czech nationalism's core strength. But then, to remind Czechs of some difficult times, the orchestra vividly depicts turbulence as the river rushes through rapids. The musical outburst soon subsides, and with a majestic restatement of the main theme, the river flows past the high castle of Vyšehrad at Praha and flows off into the distance. (*Vltava* is often played separately in concert programs.) *Šárka* follows, representing a famous Czech legend about a maiden getting revenge for her lover's infidelity. Next, in *From Bohemia's Woods and Meadows*, Smetana uses expansive melodies and a lively polka theme to describe dimly lit woods and bright open fields. *Tábor* represents a critically important time in Czech history: the 15th-century Hussite wars. Smetana quotes a Hussite hymn, "Ye Who Are Warriors of God." The concluding symphonic poem, *Blaník*, first develops the same Hussite tune before representing the warriors retreating to the hollow Mount Blaník. There they will remain asleep until they can awaken to triumphantly ride out to save their fatherland—in Czech, *Má Vlast*. The work ends with the Hussite chorale linked to a joyous rendition of the first poem's opening theme. One might imagine that *Má Vlast* would speak only to Czechs, for it is a powerful expression of their nationalism, but it also has great universal appeal.

Antonín Dvořák, another Czech, wrote *Hussite Overture* (1883), 16 *Slavonic Dances* (1878/1887), and many tone poems and nine symphonies that also spoke directly and profoundly to Bohemian audiences. Dvořák and Smetana drew from the dominant Germanic style of composition, but each developed a distinctly Czech style by incorporating folk elements, history, and legends within their own respective styles of music.

In the late 19th century, Russian imperialism had a firm grip on Finland. Moved by the spirit of Finnish resistance to the Russians, Jean Sibelius wrote several symphonies and tone poems based on Finnish legends and folklore that were distinctly different from anything composed by Russians. His major works include *Kullervo Symphony* (1891), *En Saga* (1892), and the four-part *Lemminkänen* cycle, which includes the hauntingly beautiful *The Swan of Tuonela* (1893). But it was *Finlandia* (1899) that most captured people's attention. However, the music so stirred the raw emotions of Finnish nationalism that the Russians banned the work. As a statement in music of a people and their land, it clearly was powerfully meaningful to Finns. It is still played today, in Finland and elsewhere.

A quieter form of nationalism in music was expressed by Edvard Grieg (1843–1907). Unlike Sibelius, who drew inspiration from Finnish folklore, Grieg used Norwegian folk music and dances as the basis for much of his work, though he, too, was fully inventive in his own manner. His music became known as distinctly Norwegian, and it nourished the awakening nationalism of a people then under

Swedish control. His most famous orchestral work, *Peer Gynt* (1875), in two parts, is a significant musical drama in a Romantic style. The work relates the story of a wandering Norwegian who, in time, returns to Norway. Grieg loved western Norway's rural countryside and composed in a cabin located on a fjord, with a glacier opposite. Like Sibelius, Grieg was strongly influenced by a love of nature. *Peer Gynt* is filled with lovely melodies and incorporates birdsong and a shepherd's horn at sunrise. The delightfully expressive work spoke subtly but distinctly to Norwegians. It was not deemed by the Swedish government to be threatening so, in contrast to the experience of Sibelius, Grieg's nationalistic music was performed without interference.

Composers elsewhere also sought to create their national music, not least in Russia. Mikhail Glinka's opera, *A Life for the Tsar* (1836), was an early expression of a Russian style. In his next opera, *Ruslan and Lyudmila* (1842), based on work by Russian poet Aleksandr Pushkin, Glinka explicitly founded a national style. Tchaikovsky, though famous and the composer of wonderful tunes, was criticized by some for not having the compositional skills of German composers Beethoven and Brahms. A group of composers (known as The Russian Five or "the mighty handful": Mili Balakirev, Aleksandr Borodin, Cesar Cui, Modest Mussorgsky, and Nikolai Rimsky-Korsakov) sought to compose distinctively Russian music, freed of German influences. Tchaikovsky was not invited to join the group. The strongest nationalistic statements appear in Mussorgsky's powerful opera *Boris Godunov* (1869), Mussorgsky's diabolical *Night on Bald Mountain* (1867), Borodin's *Polovtsian Dances* (1875), and Rimsky-Korsakov's *Russian Easter Festival Overture* (1888). Rimsky-Korsakov, Tchaikovsky, and others used, or were inspired by, Russian Orthodox Church melodies and folk tunes. Some composers used "exotic" musical influences: Borodin included Russian and Oriental influences in his *In the Steppes of Central Asia* (1880), while Rimsky-Korsakov wrote a wonderful (and strongly Russian) *Capriccio español* (1887) based on Spanish influences.

French composers also were interested in Spanish music, with its distinctive rhythmic and melodic idioms, and they composed their versions of Spanish music, including Emmanuel Chabrier's *España* (1883) and Maurice Ravel's *Rapsodie espagnole* (1907). Spanish composers were developing their own national voice. Their works include Isaac Albéniz's *Rapsodia españole* (1887), *Catalonia* (1899), and *Iberia* (1905–1908); Enrique Granados's *Spanish Dances* (1888–1890) and *Goyescas* (1914), the latter inspired by the work of Francisco de Goya; Joaquín Turina's *Danzas fantásticas* (1920) and *Sinfonia Sevillana* (1920); Joaquín Rodrigo's *Concierto de Aranjuez* (1939); and Manuel de Falla's many compositions, including the opera *La vida breve* (1905) and the engaging ballet *El Amor Brujo* (1915), from which his brilliant and hugely popular *Ritual Fire Dance* has been extracted.

Nationalism in music was profoundly expressed in Italy. For most of the 1800s, Italy consisted of many kingdoms; the unification process took many decades. Giuseppe Verdi was born near Busseto in 1813 and lived until 1901. He thus witnessed the struggle to unite the country. He believed strongly that each nation

should create its own distinctive music. In his opera *Nabucco* (1842), set in ancient Egypt, a chorus of Hebrew slaves sing "Va, pensiero," giving voice to a people
being freed from domination. "Their" song was quickly adopted as the song of liberation by Italians seeking the end of Austria's rule of Lombardy. Indeed, Verdi's
chorus became like an underground "national hymn" for those patriots. Verdi,
staunchly pro-Italian, was a figurehead for Italy's unification movement. In 1861,
following the second Italian War of Independence, he was elected to Italy's first
national parliament. However, it was his music for which he is remembered, not
his political role. He gave the ever-increasing sense of a truly Italian national
identity a boost in the opera *Aida* (1871). It was more triumphant—some would
say overbearing—than *Nabucco* in its nationalistic expression, though in both
works strong patriotic undercurrents are evident. In *Aida*, Verdi sets a love story
against a plot of Ethiopia invading Egypt. Though "exotic" in theme to Italian audiences, the music spoke directly to Italian nationalism, with a highlight being
the famous "Triumphal March," in which trumpets blare. The work clearly celebrates Italianness, and nothing Egyptian.

Also late in the 19th century, several British composers set out to create
"their" music, led by Welshman Joseph Parry (*Blodwen* [1878]); Scotland's Hamish
MacCunn (whose distinctly Scottish *Land of the Mountain and the Flood* [1887]
remains popular) and Alexander Mackenzie (*Highland Ballad* [1893] and *Scottish
Concerto* [1897]); and Ireland's Charles Villiers Stanford (including *Irish Symphony*
[1886]). Each showed in their work something of the character of their respective
countries. Several British compositions stand out as statements in music that
revel in national and imperial pride, including Edward Elgar's five *Pomp and Circumstance* marches, especially the first, titled "Land of Hope and Glory" (1901);
Hubert Parry's patriotic hymn, "Jerusalem" (1916); William Walton's two coronation tunes, "Crown Imperial" (1937) and "Orb and Septre" (1953); and Henry Wood's
Fantasia on British Sea Songs (1905), which concludes with a rousing rendition
of "Rule Britannia" (the latter a poem by James Thomson, set to music by Thomas
Arne around 1740). These works were immediately adopted by the general British listener, not just by sophisticated audiences. They are still played regularly
during nationalistic celebrations, such as the Last Night at the Proms, held each
summer at London's Royal Albert Hall, when the audience enthusiastically joins
in while the orchestra performs. The music feeds the sentimental attachment to
a national past that is deemed still to be of value.

In the United States, composers were initially strongly influenced by German
music. Few composers used local influences, though Louis Moreau Gottschalk,
born in New Orleans in 1829, drew upon African American and Creole influences
for some of his compositions. In the 1880s, Antonín Dvořák suggested to Americans that Negro (African American) and Indian (Native American) music could
form the basis of a distinctly American music. Some composers took up his recommendations. Some drew upon Indian material; for example, Edward Mac-
Dowell's *Suite No. 2, Indian* (1897) quotes Iroquois and Kiowa melodies. Later,

George Gershwin used jazz idioms in *Rhapsody in Blue* (1924) and various African American idioms in his often-performed opera, *Porgy and Bess* (1935). Other composers, including Ferde Grofé in the *Grand Canyon Suite* (1931), drew inspiration from the American landscape.

Charles Ives, born in Danbury, Connecticut, the son of the local bandmaster, sought to develop a distinctly American music. His music is either lovely, with flowing melodies, or jaggedly discordant. *Central Park in the Dark* (1906) describes a scene in New York he knew well. It includes a raucous middle section, representing the hustle and bustle of the street scene beyond the otherwise quiet park. *Three Places in New England* (ca. 1912–1921) celebrates a Civil War battle that is remembered on a monument in Boston; a Revolutionary War story in Redding, Connecticut; and a walk Ives took with his wife one Sunday morning near Stockbridge, Connecticut. These and others of his works are uniquely American in style.

New Yorker Aaron Copland was the first American composer to be recognized outside the United States for his distinctly personal, and national, style. He used western themes in *Billy the Kid* (1938), which includes a dramatic gunfight, and *Rodeo* (1942). In *Lincoln Portrait* (1942), a speaker reads excerpts from President Abraham Lincoln's speeches. *Fanfare for the Common Man* (1942) is performed widely. His most famous extended work, *Appalachian Spring* (1944), makes exquisite use of the Shaker hymn "'Tis the Gift to be Simple." It is often performed at concerts celebrating American nationalism, such as Independence Day (July 4th). Copland's friend Leonard Bernstein was a later composer to write in a particularly American style, though his is restrictively New York. The finger-snapping pulse of his *West Side Story* (originally a Broadway musical [1957], later an orchestral suite [1960]) has, however, not reached the level of public acceptance as a nationalistic epic in the manner achieved by Copland's *Appalachian Spring*.

Composers in many other parts of the world have intentionally created their national music. For example, Mexican Carlos Chávez, who wrote in a Mexican nationalist style, including *Suite de Caballos de Vapor* (1927) and *Sinfonia India* (1935), was influenced by indigenous "Indian" music, but he rarely quoted it directly. Brazilian composer Heitor Villa-Lobos sought to provoke nationalistic pride by using in his music rich Brazilian colors and rhythms, as in *Descrobimento di Brasil* (1936–1937, 1942). Argentinian Alberto Ginestera drew from the gaucho guitarists and their folk dances while developing a distinctively Argentinian nationalistic style for his *Panambi* (1937) and *Estancia* (1941).

Composers elsewhere include Peter Sculthorpe in Australia (e.g., *The 5th Continent* [1963] and *Kakadu* [1988]) and Douglas Lilburn in New Zealand (*Aotearoa Overture* [1940]). Sculthorpe and others have used references to Aborigines in their music, and some New Zealand compositions use Maori references, including Christopher Blake's *The Coming of Tane Mahuta* (1987), Maria Grenfell's *Stealing Tutunui* (2000), and Maori composer Gillian Whitehead's *O Matenga* (1984). Other contemporary composers who have written music that is distinctly reflective of their nations include Japanese composer Tōru Takemitsu who, for example, has composed remarkable compositions inspired by specific Japanese landscapes, as in *Green* (1968) and *Tree Line* (1988). His younger contemporary, Toshio Hosokawa, has composed *Memory of the Sea* (2000), about the recovered city of Hiroshima after its destruction by the atomic bomb.

Some Chinese composers mix the Western orchestra with traditional Chinese instruments, as in Vanessa-Mae's *Happy Valley* (1997), which is about the takeover of Hong Kong by China. Another contemporary Chinese composer, Tan Dun, is notable for his distinctively Chinese compositions mixed with Western idioms and Western instrumentation. However, he is forging something new in orchestral music; his compositions often clearly transcend China rather than referring to a Chinese nationalism. In contrast, some works by other Chinese composers are explicitly centered in China. Whereas Smetana, Sibelius, and Grieg reacted to *external* political control of their homelands, many Chinese composers—indeed most intellectuals, and also countless others from all walks of life—experienced immense hardship from a source *within* the state during the so-called Cultural Revolution (1966–1976). Wang Xilin's music relentlessly represents the persecution and censorship experienced by him and others during the Revolution. Like Shostakovich in Russia, Wang has sought to give voice in his music to criticism of the authorities while suffering from a lack of freedom of thought and action. Another Chinese composer, Sheng Bright, composed *H'un [Lacerations]: In memoriam 1966–76* (1988), a mournful, dissonant, orchestral evocation of the suffering of the Chinese people during that Cultural Revolution. And following the remarkable display of defiance by students and others in Beijing's Tiananmen Square in 1989, Chou Wen-chung composed *Windswept Peaks* (1990) to represent the people who stood tall against the military might and thought-controlling dictates of the state. These several composers in China, as with composers elsewhere in other times and other places, have demonstrated in their music that it is possible to challenge the state and, thus, the nation, to think afresh.

Traditional Music, New Music, and Resistance

African, Middle Eastern, and Asian cultures are renowned for drumming. Styles vary from one region to another, but musical traditions of independence and virtuosity exist that speak to each region's national traditions and celebrations. In addition, hand clapping, singing and associated dancing, and the use of other instruments are employed. Instruments vary, but include the *zeze* (a flat-bar zither) in the Congo; the *valimba* (gourd-resonated xylophones) in southern Malawi; the "penny whistle" in South Africa; the *tanbur* (flute) and the 14-stringed Herati *dutar* in Afghanistan; the plucked *sehtar* and mallet-struck *santur* in South Asia (specifically India); and many instruments in Southeast Asia, including the Balinese *gamelan* (comprising gongs, metallophones, xylophones, cymbals, flutes, and fiddles). Some instruments are used in widely separated locations, including versions of the lyre in Crete and Kenya. These and other culturally significant instruments are used to perform music that is appreciated locally and regionally and sometimes is understood to represent national music, and, thus, it speaks to specific nationalisms.

Fascinatingly, with recent migrations—for example, to France from various African territories and the Middle East, to Germany from Turkey, to Britain from southern Asia and the Caribbean—musical styles and instruments have been transferred and, in the new settings, have been merged with other traditions to create new styles of music. Much of this new music no longer speaks to specific nationalisms, however, and it is now generally categorized as "world music."

Some musical styles have been adopted far from the countries of origin and developed afresh. Such has been the case with rap music. Although modeled on their U.S. counterparts who originated the genre, Cuban rappers, for example, have developed *rap Cubano* in terms of their own style and content, content that speaks to being Cuban. Similarly, in France (notably recent immigrant minorities), Italy, Zimbabwe, South Africa, and New Zealand, vernacular forms of rap have developed that are different from one another and from the U.S. hip-hop mainstream. These "resistance vernaculars" express the desires of particular populations, mainly youths, who are seeking to preserve the "local," which is nationally based.

Music by Bands

Brass, concert, and military bands can speak powerfully to nationalisms. After the French Revolution, the band of the Garde Républicaine in Paris established a pattern that was thereafter largely followed by bands in other European countries. Rather than just using brass instruments (trumpets, trombones, euphoniums, and drums and cymbals), they incorporated wind instruments (including clarinets and oboes). The bands played for parades and concerts. Since the second half of the 19th century, military and civilian band parades have been visible and enjoyed spectacles in all European countries and elsewhere. For example, in Japan, bands playing European-styled military marches date from when the late-19th-century Meiji government began modernizing the Japanese armed forces. Elsewhere, tunes specific to the countries are still performed, including Russia ("Slavonic Farewell March" from World War I), New Zealand ("Invercargill" [1900]), and Canada ("The Maple Leaf Forever March" [1867]). Ties to days of empire remain, thus bands using European instruments perform in such former colonial countries as India, Kenya, and Fiji.

The combination of the players' uniforms, precision marching, brightly shining instruments, twirling sticks, and, of course, stirring patriotic music can be special. Some such music is quietly patriotic, as with Czech composer Julius Fucik's marches, including "Entry of the Gladiators" (1900) and "Florentine March" (1910), whereas other music is more strident. The latter includes such toe-tapping marches by the American John Philip Sousa as "Semper Fidelis" (1888), "Washington Post" (1889), "The Thunderer" (1889), "The Liberty Bell" (1893), and the U.S. official march, "Stars and Stripes Forever" (1896). These and similar works are played throughout

Elmira Cornet Band, 33rd Regiment of the New York State Volunteers, July 1861. (Library of Congress)

the United States at various national patriotic events, sports games, and during summer concerts in parks. For the British, nothing is better than the rousing marches by Kenneth J. Alford, including "Colonel Bogey" (1913), "The Voice of the Guns" (1917), "The Thin Red Line" (1925), "Army of the Nile" (1941), and "By Land and Sea" (1941). These works are often played at national events, such as the queen's birthday celebrations and the trooping of the colors in London. They speak directly to British patriotism or at least to those who are enlivened by such music. For Scots, bagpipe music has a quickly recognizable sound (no matter what tune is being played). It spurred Scots into battle and was feared by opposing armies. Many tunes are nationally significant, including "Scotland the Brave."

National Anthems

All states have a national song or tune—in English, referred to as a national anthem —that is performed on official occasions (e.g., the opening of parliament or a national service remembering war dead) or at certain times (including, in some countries, at sports events, in movie theaters, or to open and close a day's TV or radio broadcast). It is also used at international events, such as at the Olympics and when two countries play against each other in, for example, rugby or hockey. Such a tune, like the national flag, is part of a state's iconography that helps bind together the people of the nation. While important to the people of the state, the tune itself may not be memorable in terms of musical importance. Some national anthems are march-like (e.g., France's "La Marseillaise"), others are hymns (e.g., the United Kingdom's "God Save the Queen/King"), several are in 19th-century opera mode (e.g., El Salvador), a few are brief fanfare-like tunes without words (e.g., United Arab Emirates), and some are based on folk music (e.g., Japan and Sri Lanka).

The longest serving national anthem is that of the United Kingdom, "God Save the King" (or Queen). Derived from 17th-century material, it was first used in 1744. It was played around the British empire during the 18th to 20th centuries, and it is still used in most Commonwealth countries, especially when Queen Elizabeth II is present. Interestingly, the tune was adopted by many European countries during the 19th century, using different words. It is still used by Liechtenstein. At various times following the Declaration of Independence, Americans used the tune for "God Save America," "God Save George Washington," and even "God Save the Thirteen States." It is now used in the United States for "America," with the patriotic words "My Country, 'Tis of Thee."

The oldest anthem is "Wilhelmus van Nassouwe" (words, ca. 1570; music 1626) but only in terms of origin, for it was not used until Wilhelmina became queen of the Netherlands in 1898, when it gradually replaced the earlier "Wien Neêrlandsche bloed door d'adren vloeit" (adopted in 1816 following the creation of the Kingdom of the Netherlands). Other old anthems include those in Argentina (1813), Denmark (1819), Bolivia (1845), and Finland (1848).

France's national anthem has had a conflicted history. Written in 1792 as a military marching song, it was published as "Chant de guerre pour l'armée du Rhin." Shortly afterward, it was sung by a battalion of volunteers from Marseillaise during a march into Paris. It was thereafter called "La Marseillaise," and as such, it was formally accepted as the French national anthem in a decree passed July 14, 1795. However, Napoleon banned it due to its revolutionary associations. Upon the restoration of the Crown in 1815, it was also banned by Louis XVIII. It was re-accepted following the July Revolution of 1830, but then banned yet again by Napoleon III. Only in 1879 was it finally reinstated. Now clearly the national song of France, for a time the tune was also used for "The Internationale," the international revolutionary movement's song. In 1888 the latter song was given its presently used tune. The tune for "La Marseillaise" has been quoted in numerous orchestral works, including Tchaikovsky's *1812 Overture* and Debussy's *Feux d'artifice*.

The words for the U.S. national anthem, "The Star-Spangled Banner," written in 1814 by Francis Scott Key, were set to a popular British drinking song. In time, it became an American patriotic song, but it was not until 1931 that it was officially accepted as the U.S. national anthem.

Numerous anthems were written in Europe after World War I and in Africa, Asia, and the Pacific during the decolonization period after World War II. Many states officially accepted their national anthems upon, or shortly after, achieving political independence. For example, Israel adopted its national anthem in 1948, India in 1950, Ghana in 1957, Botswana in 1966, and Kiribati in 1979.

The words of national anthems varyingly celebrate the "homeland" (as the place of the nation, including its physical characteristics), the nation (its people, its values, its qualities, and its future), historical events (struggles, battles, and victories), and leaders (king/queen and soldiers as heroes). A national anthem is meaningful to members of a nation, though not necessarily to anyone else.

Consequences

The music that has been discussed here is regionally distinctive. The music expresses sentiments special to particular peoples who, as nations, belong, or claim to belong, to particular political territories (whether or not their particular territory was politically independent when the music was composed). Most of the composers identified above set out to create music that was distinct from the dominant (notably German) musical traditions in Europe. This occurred in two ways: (1) composers, when writing their music, drew from and sometimes directly quoted local folktales and myths, traditions, and folk music; (2) composers created their own distinctive styles of music by sometimes breaking traditional rules of form, harmony, melodies, rhythm, and tone colors. The composers' inventiveness thus gave expression to musical "localisms" that were readily understood and appreciated by their local audiences (as in Finland and in Bohemia, for example). Some of this music clearly expressed something of the growing nationalistic sentiments of the respective nations and so helped enhance the people's sense of nationalism. The music in question touched people's hearts and may have impacted their souls, for it expressed something essential about the spirit of the nation. This impact continues.

Nationalistic music makes the most sense to those of the nation who identify with the composer's statements; the composer's music becomes their music. Interestingly, some such music can also have universally accepted qualities, so it can serve as a sort of musical ambassador in other countries. Even so, the music can be appreciated most fully by referring to the national origins of the pertinent composer—to his or her local influences—and by becoming aware of the distinctiveness of the particular national styles of music. Much military music and all national anthems are quintessential expressions of nationalism in music.

As identified, some of the older expressions of nationalism in music were defiant, some were suppressed, and some were quietly distinct and did not threaten then-dominant political authorities. Threats by the state still evoke reactions in orchestral music, as in China in recent times where composers have used a mix of European and traditional Chinese instruments. Some popular forms of music also express resistance and is often defiant. A number of disenchanted groups today, in various countries, have adopted rap to express their thoughts and hopes. Rather than blindly mimic U.S. styles, they have created distinctive nationally centered voices. Such music may thus be the latest expression of nationalism in music.

Selected Bibliography

Bierley, P. E. 1973. *John Philip Souza: American Phenomenon.* Englewood Cliffs, NJ: Prentice Hall.

Boyd, M. 2001. "National Anthems." In *The New Grove Dictionary of Music and Musicians*, vol. 17, 2nd ed. Edited by S. Sadie, 654–687. New York: Macmillan.

Csepeli, G., and A. Örkény. 1997. "The Imagery of National Anthems in Europe." *Canadian Review of Studies in Nationalism* 34:33–41.

Hazen, M. H., and R. M. Hazen. 1987. *The Music Men: An Illustrated History of Brass Bands in America, 1800–1920.* Washington DC: Smithsonian Institution Press.

Knight, D. B. 2006. *Landscapes in Music: Space, Place, and Time in the World's Great Music.* Lanham, MD: Rowman & Littlefield.

Murray, D. 1994. *Music of the Scottish Regiments.* Edinburgh, UK: Pentland.

Taruskin, R. 2001. "Nationalism." In *The New Grove Dictionary of Music and Musicians*, vol. 17, 2nd ed. Edited by S. Sadie, 689–706. New York: Macmillan.

Turner, G., and A. Turner. 1994–1997. *The History of British Military Bands*, vols. 1–3. Staplehurst, UK: Spellmount.

Vaughan Williams, R. 1996. *National Music and Other Essays.* 2nd ed. New York: Clarendon.

Whiteley, S., A. Bennett, and S. Hawkins, eds. 2004. *Music, Space and Place: Popular Music and Cultural Identity.* Burlington, VT: Ashgate.

Zikmund, J. 1969. "National Anthems as Political Symbols." *Australian Journal of Politics and History* 15, no. 3: 73–80.

New Social and Environmental Movements in Relation to Nationalism

Joseph M. Whitmeyer

Relevance

"New social movements" is a term coined by Western European social theorists—
Alain Touraine, Albert Melucci, and John Keane are commonly mentioned—to
refer to certain types of collective action that became prominent beginning in
the 1960s in Western Europe. These movements appeared to be different from
the types of movements that were common earlier in the 20th century or before,
in both the objectives of the movements and the social position of the majority
of the participants, hence the qualifier, "new." Theorists most frequently clarified
what constituted a new social movement (henceforth NSM) by what it was not: it
was not oriented to social class; it was not made up primarily of the lower classes,
such as peasants or the industrial working class, contrasting with labor movements, in particular; it was not a regional or religious movement. Jan Willem
Duyvendak (1994, 62–63) gives an explicit definition: "A 'new' movement must
consist of a majority of middle-class individuals believing in post-materialist values. Other elements such as the pursuit of identity objectives, or strong universalist inclinations constitute practical aid in the identification of a new movement."
Common examples of NSMs are movements for peace, for social solidarity or
against racism, for the environment, against nuclear power, for feminist causes,
for gay and lesbian rights, and against free trade.

It should be clear from the above that the "new" in "new social movements" is
part of the label rather than a defining adjective. Some NSMs, such as feminist
movements or environmental movements, existed in the late 19th or early 20th
centuries and are not new; and some new movements, such as the antiabortion-
ists, skinheads, or Islamic terrorists, would be excluded from NSMs by most theorists who use the term. Theorists of NSMs also plainly understand their political
location to be on the left. The essential element of "post-materialist values" in the
definition above is intended to make this clear: NSMs are hostile or, at a minimum, indifferent to the market economy and objectives of participants in the
market economy. Yet, some fairly recent social movements fit almost all of the
criteria for NSMs, except that ideologically they are on the right rather than the
left. In the United States, these include the antiabortion movement and various
conservative political and social movements, from the Moral Majority on. Rather
than quibble over labels and definitions, or what constitutes a "post-materialist
value," this essay excludes right-wing movements on the grounds that most schol-

ars would do so and accepts Duyvendak's definition of NSMs as being a representative characterization, and more specific than most.

It seems clear, then, that NSMs, as defined, will not include nationalist movements. We could anticipate, in fact, that NSMs will be likely to be antagonistic to nationalist movements, which frequently are right-wing. In affluent countries, for example, the recent conservative movements mentioned above typically are in sympathy with majority nationalism, in contrast with NSMs. When we look outside the affluent countries, however, we see that the relationship between NSMs and nationalism is more complicated. Before we delve into it, it will be helpful to clarify "nationalism."

A standard definition of nationalism has it as an ideology, such that those who hold it believe that their people, typically some sort of ethnic, regional, or language group, should be coterminous with the state. A nationalist movement then is collective action with this as its goal. This article takes "pro-nation" sentiment to be the crucial characteristic and extends the concept to cover a broader range of phenomena. Thus, it also includes anti-immigrant movements, such as Jean-Marie Le Pen's in France, and pro-ethnic movements, such as ones that seek not necessarily a state but perhaps regional autonomy or more rights or privileges for a minority. Moreover, it even includes patriotism, especially as it is directed against other nations or countries. Both this and anti-immigrant movements fall under the label of "majority nationalism." Without these extensions, we would have to exclude most affluent countries, with the exception of Ireland and the Basque region of Spain, from consideration.

Origins

With these definitions under our belt, we now observe that the relationship between NSMs and nationalism varies greatly by country, or more precisely, by region of the world. This means we must turn next to looking at this relationship in different national contexts.

NSMs are most easily understood in their original context, Western Europe, and more broadly, in affluent, advanced industrial societies. In that setting, the relationship between NSMs and majority nationalism ranges from indifference to antagonism. Prototypical NSMs tend to have a transnational ideology: they are for women's rights, gay rights, peace, an improved natural environment, and so forth, *everywhere*. Where this conflicts with nationalistic goals in these affluent societies—which, for example, may include economic development and accompanying environmental degradation, or the advance of national interests that involves the risk or reality of war—NSMs must be antinationalist.

One can think here of the support for the Kyoto treaty on greenhouse gas reduction by environmental groups, or the peace movement that galvanized Europe, particularly West Germany, and the United States during the early 1980s. In these cases, the NSMs were opposing positions that were plainly nationalist: the Bush administration's resistance to a treaty that it took to be bad for the American economy, and the Reagan administration's antagonism toward the Soviet Union as the "evil empire." In France during the period we are considering, the most prominent of the NSMs was the surge of collective action against racism after 1983, especially in 1985 in response to the popularity and electoral success of Le Pen's anti-immigrant Front National. Even the anti-free-trade movement that disrupted the World Trade Organization (WTO) meeting in Seattle in 1999 was much less nationalist than old-time opposition to free trade, which was protectionist, ostensibly in the interests of the country, rather than antibusiness.

The exception to the lack of sympathy of affluent country NSMs for nationalism within their borders is minority nationalism. For example, in the United States, Greenpeace and other NSMs have come to the aid and support of Native American groups seeking to preserve or obtain territorial rights and autonomy. Similarly, NSMs in Australia have been supportive of Aboriginal groups and rights. Often this support for minority indigenous groups dovetails with other objectives of the NSMs, such as environmental causes.

Outside of the affluent countries, NSMs generally are weaker and their relationship to nationalism is different. Consider three groupings: the former Soviet Union and Eastern Europe, Latin America, and other places.

Riot police confront protesters during the 1999 World Trade Organization (WTO) conference in Seattle. (Christopher J. Morris/Corbis)

In Eastern Europe and the former Soviet Union, the pattern is broadly as follows. In the 1980s in many regions there was large growth in NSMs, especially environmental movements, and in popular support for them. These NSMs were more or less explicitly nationalistic, except in Russia. In the 1990s, the association between the NSMs and nationalism ended. Nationalist and nationalism-linked movements generally continued to receive popular backing, while NSMs saw their support collapse and became appendages of international NSMs, that is, NSMs based in affluent countries.

As this synopsis suggests, the time line here is crucial: in 1989, largely peaceful revolutions ended Soviet control over Eastern European countries; in 1991, the Soviet Union broke up and states formerly incorporated into the Soviet Union, including the Ukraine and the Baltic countries, became independent. Thus, in the 1980s, we see NSMs that were either overtly or latently nationalist. In some places, these NSMs were clear surrogates for nationalist movements that could not manifest themselves as such. In others, they created social and social organizational potential that nationalist entrepreneurs and a nationalist populace could use when the moment became propitious for nationalist action.

In the Ukraine, and other components of the Soviet Union, the NSM that mattered was the antinuclear-power movement, which arose in response to the Chernobyl disaster. This movement was at least implicitly against domination by central government, which was, of course, Russian in nationality. Therefore, outside of Russia, the movement was at least latently nationalist. In the 1990s, once the Soviet Union broke up, this became obvious, and, in fact, it became apparent that the nationalism was more fundamental than the environmental and safety concerns, for these movements disappeared completely, or nearly so, once nationalist movements could appear openly at various points in the 1990s. The antinuclear and associated movements could be strong and influential when overt nationalist movements were politically impossible, and they were important in catalyzing the nationalist movements that subsequently appeared, but as mass phenomena, the nationalist movements completely superseded them.

We see a similar phenomenon in satellites of the Soviet Union and in the nations that comprised Yugoslavia. In East Germany in the 1980s, there was a strong upsurge in popular interest in environmental issues, especially following the Chernobyl disaster. Environmental movements were not linked explicitly to nationalism, but they were antigovernment, anti-regime, and played an important role in the peaceful revolution of 1989. The 1990s, however, saw an almost complete eclipse of popular support and interest in environmental causes. Croatia, likewise, had women's groups and a strong environmental movement prior to the 1990s, but they lost much of their support during the war in 1991–1992.

Generally, across Eastern Europe, environmental movements directed against the industrial and building policies pursued by the communist governments obtained much popular support by the end of the 1980s. Yet, for example, following these countries' acquisition of independence and democracy, none has exhibited a green party with any electoral success. Although they never had the popularity that environmental movements did, women's movements show the same trajectory. Paul Stubbs tells the revealing story of how, in Slovenia, the trial of a journalist transformed a pro-peace women's movement struggle to end compulsory female service in the Yugoslav army into a Slovenian nationalist movement.

The continued existence of NSMs in places like the Ukraine, Russia, Slovenia, and Croatia, has depended on near total support by international, that is to say, outside groups. The same is true for environmental movements in the eastern portion of Germany from the 1990s, which is dependent on outside financing and support from organizations in the western portion. Across the region of eastern Europe, environmental and other NSMs have little grassroots support. They have become small, professionalized pressure groups that depend on financial support from western Europe. Accordingly, they typically are concerned more with issues of foreign elites than with those of the domestic population. In contrast, nationalist movements in this region frequently are much stronger, and often have considerable popular support.

In Latin America in the period under consideration, NSMs and their relationship to nationalism display yet another pattern. This stems from the economic, political, and social conditions prevailing, albeit with great variation, in Latin America. Economically, while the Latin American countries manifest considerable differences in prosperity and production, none approaches the affluence of western Europe. Politically, these countries have not been consumed by a single dominant issue like the struggle to cope with and then break free of Soviet or Serbian domination. Socially, relevant to nationalism, for most countries in this region, ethnicity or race is an important and frequently contentious dimension of society.

These characteristics of Latin American countries have produced a situation in which identification of NSMs is less straightforward and more controversial. This problem is not particularly surprising, given that the NSM concept was coined in response to the situation and events in Europe and not elsewhere. As for the relationship of Latin American NSMs—or pseudo-NSMs—to nationalism, it is more complicated and murkier. Frequently, these movements mingle typical NSM goals with older-style goals, such as land reform and land rights. There also may be a divergence between the concerns and goals of the elites who organize the movements and those of the rank and file. A movement also may appeal to international NSMs and so emphasize NSM-type goals publicly, to its global audience, even though those are not the primary focus of the membership. Moreover, here the appeal is not generally for financial support but rather for political support.

Some scholars and others looking at this region have found NSMs tied to varieties of nationalism, or nationalistic movements that they see as NSMs. Wade (1997, 95–96), for example, explicitly claims strength and expansion in the 1980s and 1990s for NSMs, for which he includes "squatters' associations, Christian Base Communities, animal rights groups, workers' cooperatives, indigenous land rights organizations, and ecological groups." These may be considered NSMs because they do not emphasize modernization and revolution as earlier movements did; instead, they aim more at making a place for themselves in society and are more concerned with identity.

Yet Latin American social movements typically have old-style objectives as well. At their core, most of the strong movements in Latin America have been about land rights, which is one of the oldest concerns of social movements, pre-dating, for example, the labor disputes that industrialization brings. The land conflicts frequently are connected with issues of indigenous identity and rights, yet identity and post-materialist values may not be significant motivations for many of the participants in these movements. Here there may be a divergence be-tween the goals of the leadership, more oriented toward NSM-type goals, and those of much of the membership, more oriented toward material goals, such as obtaining land. In addition, the leadership may emphasize the indigenous aspect of conflicts publicly in order to garner international sympathy and support.

Similarly, some Latin American indigenous groups have taken a pro-ecology, conservationist stance as a tactic in the struggle for land rights. These move-ments proclaim an espousal of environmental values and pursuit of environmen-talist ends, at least in part to attract support from the society around them and perhaps foreign support that otherwise might overlook them. Yet, especially when a primary goal of a movement's membership is land rights, specifically concern-ing use of land for agricultural purposes, there is likely to be considerable incon-sistency between what the group members do and the environmentalist values the groups announce. Moreover, rich-country observers and even the movements themselves may be tempted to shade their public portrayals of the movements for political purposes.

The Zapatista rebellion launched in Chiapas, Mexico, on January 1, 1994, shows many of these characteristics. This uprising captured the imagination of many intellectuals in affluent countries who found its combination of indigenism and opposition to free trade (in the form of the North American Free Trade Agree-ment [NAFTA]) appealing. They also liked its postmodern style as displayed through the pronouncements and self-presentation of its leader, the Subcoman-dante Marcos. It seems a genuine conjunction of a new social movement and in-digenist nationalism.

The truth, however, is more complicated. The leaders of the Zapatistas were not indigenous; they were Marxist revolutionaries whose ultimate objective was to overthrow the Mexican government. The ordinary members seem to have been primarily motivated by the age-old goal of peasant movements: land they could farm as their own. The free-trade issue was of little importance to them, and they were not particularly nationalist. The issue of indigenous rights emerged only subsequent to the initial confrontation as part of negotiations with the Mexican government and only in response to pressure from supporters, such as the local Catholic bishop. Another complication is that, like many land-rights movements in poor countries, the Zapatistas were in direct conflict with environmental objectives: a substantial proportion of the territory they wanted to farm was restricted from agricultural use because the federal government had designated it for ecological preservation.

In short, the Zapatista rebellion is something of a hybrid. For its members, the struggle was mostly for land they could farm, but their landlessness was closely related to their ethnicity and social class, and the survival of their movement depended on its appeal to the post-materialist sensibilities of affluent country observers. Thus the movement evinces a nationalist dimension and some of the characteristics of NSMs, but at core is far more old-fashioned.

Finally, we turn to other less affluent countries. As a populous, large, and therefore complicated country, India displays many of the same interpretive difficulties as Latin America, for similar reasons. Some Indian movements do reflect post-materialist values and, therefore, might be called NSMs—they are concerned, for example, with women's rights, ecology, health, and civil liberties. They have little mass support, however, compared with class-oriented movements. Movements with wider appeal include farmers' and anti-caste movements, which, being mass movements, also have attracted the support of politicians. Widespread, also, are nationality movements, which seek autonomy to a greater or lesser extent. These often protest against environmental destruction and, moreover, seek decentralization as many NSMs, including environmental groups, do.

The nationality movements, however, comprise mostly farmers, and although ethnicity or nationality is important to them, an even stronger motivation tends to be land-rights issues. Moreover, while, as elsewhere, the tactical strategies of nationality movements can dovetail with the objectives of NSMs, in particular, environmental groups, this does not make them NSMs, and the alliance is likely to be temporary. In short, neither the nationality movements nor the farmers' and anti-caste movements are manifestations of post-materialist values; they are not NSMs as defined by the theorists of NSMs.

In the less affluent countries, because there is little domestic audience for its post-materialist positions, an NSM may make nationalistic appeals to nationalism to increase its support at home. This is especially likely when NSMs cannot link with foreign-based NSM organizations and therefore lack financial and organizational backing from outside. In Algeria, for example, a women's movement arose in the 1980s that linked itself to women who participated in the struggle against the French decades earlier. In the occupied territories of Palestine, also, there has been some coincidence of a women's movement with nationalism. As one might expect from the weakness of NSMs in less affluent places, however, the women's movement has had a lower priority than the Palestinian cause.

A century ago, in much of Asia as well as places like Turkey, Egypt, Iran, and Afghanistan, there was mutual support between feminism and nationalism, which in that era was directed against colonial powers. In general, this is no longer the case. In these places, nationalist movements are in the position of strength.

When nationalist movements declare that women are primarily responsible for the reproduction of the group, they make it difficult for feminist movements to ally with them.

The preceding overview of countries makes the relationship between NSMs and nationalism fairly clear. We can identify three patterns: (1) In affluent countries in which people can and do pursue post-materialist values collectively, NSMs are indifferent or even hostile to majority nationalism. They may be sympathetic to minority nationalism, although the minority nationalist movement itself is not an NSM. (2) In countries in which nationalism is effectively repressed, NSMs offer a concealed, or perhaps even latent, means of expressing or pursuing nationalistic ends. Moreover, these NSMs facilitate the quick eruption of full-blown nationalism should the repression lapse. (3) In countries that are not affluent but do not repress majority or minority nationalism, NSMs have very weak local support. Where possible, their organizations are outposts of foreign-based, that is, affluent country–based, NSMs; they are supported by those foreign-based NSMs and answer to them. Thus, they are essentially irrelevant to their society and to any nationalisms in it.

An important aspect of politically oriented collective action, such as both new social movements and nationalist movements, is their relationship to elites and leaders. In the affluent countries, NSMs and nationalist themes generally play to different audiences, sometimes in disregard of each other, sometimes in opposition to each other. Politicians who have made nationalist appeals—mainstream leaders like Thatcher in the United Kingdom with the Falklands War and Reagan and George W. Bush in the United States, and more radical individuals, such as Le Pen in France and Pim Fortuyn in the Netherlands—generally have not drawn much support from members of NSMs or their sympathizers. Indeed, in some countries such nationalist movements have catalyzed the appearance of NSMs in opposition—in France and Germany, for example. Moreover, in the affluent countries, there often is a substantial political constituency for NSM objectives. This can be seen in the success of Green parties in some western European countries, notably Germany.

Outside of the affluent countries, there is little political constituency for the objectives of NSMs and consequently not much in the way of ties between NSMs and political or cultural leaders. Nationalist goals and movements, in contrast, often have a substantial political presence and ties to prominent politicians and leaders. Some observers have seen the indifference or antagonism of NSMs to nationalism in these countries as a missed opportunity. In eastern Europe, for example, the international organizations on which NSMs are dependent have compelled the NSMs to be antinationalist. This has ruled out the possibility of substantial popular support. One particular instance is a proposal for a union of Croatian nongovernmental organizations (NGO), which would have increased efficacy of these NGOs in their dealings with the Croatian government. International NGOs, however, refused to allow the union.

Dimensions

At this point, it should be clear that it is important to consider affluent countries and less affluent countries separately. This can be summed up in the most important subtheme: in affluent countries, NSMs are stronger and generally antagonistic to (majority) nationalism; in less affluent counties, NSMs are weaker and more likely to accommodate nationalism.

We can specify this further. In affluent countries, we find enduring NSMs with mass support, and they are composed mostly of the somewhat affluent, the middle class, and the upper middle class. We are more likely to find majority nationalism, in contrast, in the lower middle and working classes. Thus, there are class and corresponding ideological differences between NSMs and majority nationalism that leaves them antagonistic.

In less affluent societies, NSMs generally have little popular support. Frequently, they depend, for both resources and recognition, on foreign-based NSMs. Alternatively, they may try to piggyback onto nationalist movements or appeal to nationalist sentiments. They can be mass movements only when the government suppresses overt political opposition. The NSMs then can be surrogates for political opposition movements, and are often nationalist.

One way to make sense of these themes is in terms of the post-materialist values that are the hallmark of NSMs. To have post-materialist values means to attach importance to qualities to which material production is indifferent or even hostile, such as the environment, more favorable treatment of women and minority groups, peace, and gay and lesbian rights. Only affluent countries have large numbers of people who are materially comfortable and secure enough to be able to afford post-materialist values, namely, their middle classes. People in these affluent classes in these affluent countries also are unlikely to see foreigners and immigrants as competitors for material goods or their jobs. Hence, the mass NSMs in affluent countries are not nationalistic. In affluent countries, majority nationalism exists in the less affluent classes, who are less secure in their material existence and do see other countries and peoples as a potential threat.

Less affluent countries do not have a sizable portion of the population that can afford post-materialist values. Hence, what we might call the "natural state" of these countries is to have weak or nonexistent NSMs. Repression of nationalist or other social movements, such as pro-democracy ones, may divert people into mass collective action that manifests itself as an NSM, often an environmental movement. When the repression terminates, the mass support shifts away from the NSM. Thus, in the absence of repression, there are only two ways for an NSM to survive in a less affluent country. It must depend on lifelines from affluent country–based organizations, or it must compromise and take a nationalistic flavor to maintain domestic viability.

It should be noted that NSMs and nationalist movements after 1980 tend to share some features simply because they are all social movements and exist at the same time. This is aside from ideologies, which, as described above, may be compatible in some circumstances and antagonistic in others. The fact that both NSMs and nationalist movements are forms of collective action directed toward changing the state or state policies inclines them toward some similarities of form and tactics.

One particular area of commonality is that of communication. Both NSMs and nationalist movements have taken advantage of the considerable improvements over the past few decades in the technology of media and communication. Like NSMs, contemporary nationalism is likely to spread its message via electronic media: television, videos, and increasingly, the World Wide Web. This also facilitates linkages between people in different countries and even continents. Far-reaching, transnational networks are a typical feature of contemporary NSMs, but they have been seen also in new nationalist movements in eastern Europe, which have drawn on financial and conceptual support from the ethnic diaspora in such places as Canada.

Backlashes

One interesting question is whether NSMs are a unifying or fragmenting force. Within affluent countries, NSMs are a fragmenting force. This stands in contrast to nationalism, which usually embraces and correspondingly unifies the vast majority of the population. The advocacy of some NSMs for stigmatized groups in society, and their opposition to production and its agents more generally, sets them at odds with large swathes of the population.

Transnationally, however, across countries rather than within them, NSMs tend to create positive ties. Unlike nationalism, which almost by definition tends to foster suspicion if not hostility toward foreign countries, NSMs have no ideological opposition to transnational bonds. Nationalist considerations are not likely to inhibit NSMs from forming such bonds, at least in affluent countries, because these NSMs are opposed to nationalism. Indeed, NSMs welcome the increase in size, reach, and power that transnational ties promise. Links of communication and coordination facilitate opposition to multinational corporations, for example, as well as to states. Technological advances make these ties ever easier.

A related question is how people in power frame the relationship between NSMs and nationalism. In fact, given that people in power are a fairly pragmatic bunch, whether by circumstance or selection, their take on NSMs versus nationalism tends to be straightforward and logical. In affluent countries, they generally appeal to one or the other, to NSMs or to nationalist sentiments, but not to both. In less affluent countries, except where they are surrogates for nationalist movements, NSMs are not important enough for politicians to pay attention to them.

Finally, we might ask to what extent NSMs are used to undermine authority. Social movements are by definition oppositional. Frequently, they oppose the state or at least state policies, although they are also cooperative and even supportive in the sense that typically they seek to influence and redirect the state rather than overthrow it. They also may oppose powerful actors in society or even widespread cultural patterns. This all is true of NSMs. As described above, they oppose the state when they are surrogates for nationalist movements in less affluent countries, but in affluent countries primarily, they tend to fight production and its chief agent, big business. Indeed, NSMs often tend to work to bolster the power of central governments, for at least pragmatic reasons. For it is primarily through the state that they can and do get what they want, whether it be rights and privileges for some group, alterations of behavior that benefit the environment, restrictions on corporate practices, or other changes.

For the same reasons, NSMs frequently support international authority. This is not true when the international organization and activity is pro-production; the opposition to the WTO and its work is an obvious example. But we can point to, in contrast, international pressure in such matters as women's rights, human rights, and peace, exerted through the United Nations and other multistate groups, which NSMs back. Likewise they advocate international accords by governments on such matters as environmental improvement, for example, the Kyoto treaty.

Consequences

Theorists of NSMs, such as Touraine, have contrasted them to older class-oriented social movements and certainly have seen them as the antithesis of nationalist movements. For example, Keane (1996) gives the enterprise of "the protagonists of civil society"—namely, NSMs—as "a continuous struggle against the simplification of the world," and that of the nationalists as "a continuous struggle to undo complexity." This essay, however, takes a less abstract view of the relationship, and in particular considers also NSMs' struggle to survive and flourish. In other words, NSMs have dual motivations: to embody given post-materialist values, but also to endure and, usually, to obtain mass support.

These twin motivations of NSMs are responsible for the themes concerning NSMs above and yield predictions for the future; namely, until countries become affluent, NSMs will be very small and likely look outside to foreign countries for support and recognition. If and when countries become more affluent they will begin to develop NSMs as a mass social phenomenon of the middle classes. At that point, NSMs will be opposed to nationalism, at least of the majority group. Nationalism will coexist with the NSMs, however, at least in the working classes.

So if we ask how NSMs advance the cause of nationalism, we can refer back to the subthemes presented earlier. In countries in which overt nationalism and nationalist movements are suppressed, NSMs can be surrogates for them. This pattern was seen in Eastern Europe under communist governments. While the pattern has disappeared along with the communist regimes, it could reappear there or elsewhere. All it would take is a conjunction between strong nationalist yearnings and strivings and governments able and willing to repress overt nationalism but less able or willing to stifle NSMs easily.

A secondary story is the support NSMs in affluent countries offer for small minority nationalisms. For these minority movements, this constitutes backing along with possible organizational benefits, such as publicity and even mobilization within the majority population. Because of the weakness of small minorities in majoritarian democracies, such support from NSMs is helpful and may even be critical to achieving any nationalist aims.

Finally—and this is a venture into sheer speculation—it is possible that an international environmental incident or disaster could occur that would drive NSMs and nationalist movements together. One could imagine nationalist antagonism for one or more countries toward another that is held responsible for some environmental problem, such as a nuclear event, water catastrophe, or even climate change, which therefore would dovetail with environmental movements and may even be stimulated by information and publicity by those movements. This has not happened yet, although international anger at the Soviet Union over the Chernobyl disaster and against the United States for refusing to sign the Kyoto treaty clearly has nationalist tinges.

A similar coincidence of nonenvironmental NSMs and nationalist movements or sentiments is harder to imagine. For example, the Taliban government in Afghanistan was recognized widely as seriously repressive of women, and the improvement of women's status was considered an important benefit of the removal of that government. Yet the oppression of women provoked no nationalist outrage or actions and, thus, no conjunction of women's movements and nationalism. It took the September 11, 2001, attack on the World Trade Center to produce the nationalist reaction, particularly in the United States, that removed the Taliban regime, and the treatment of women was largely irrelevant to that reaction.

Finally, let us consider how NSMs affect different groups. They affect nationalist movements and nationalist groups differently depending on the external circumstances. Within affluent countries, we can distinguish between majority and minority nationalisms. Through their support, NSMs may encourage minority nationalism. Minority nationalist groups also may try to deepen and extend the natural affinity of NSMs for minority nationalisms by avowing commitment to the causes and values of NSMs, such as protection of the environment and peace. The frequent mutual antagonism between NSMs and majority nationalism may stimulate activism on either side or both. A case in point is the sudden surge of the antiracist movement in France in response to the electoral success of Le Pen's stridently nationalist Front National. In less affluent countries, on the other hand, any impact is likely to be reinforcing. If nationalist movements are suppressed, NSMs can provide a temporary surrogate. In addition, they establish an organization, a structure of contacts, coordination, and communication, which a newly possible nationalist movement may use and thus achieve a high level of effectiveness very quickly.

This returns us to perhaps the most obvious question on this topic: whether NSMs weaken nationalism. The above remarks suggest that the answer is no, and perhaps often the contrary. That is, in less affluent countries, NSMs may facilitate nationalism, while in affluent countries they may support minority nationalisms and may stimulate majority nationalisms through their opposition to majority nationalist causes.

We also can consider how NSMs might weaken nationalism. In less affluent countries, NSMs simply are too weak by themselves to exert much negative effect. In affluent countries, on an individual level, NSMs may attract people who might otherwise join nationalist causes. This seems unlikely, given the difference in motivations for joining the different types of movements (see the discussion of the subthemes, above). On a societal level, NSMs may be able to weaken majority nationalism to the extent that they gain enough power to influence policy enough to stop or slow nationalist movements and causes. There is some sign of this in western Europe where, for example, Green parties have achieved some electoral success and obtained executive positions in some governments.

Selected Bibliography

Abdo, N. 1994. "Nationalism and Feminism: Palestinian Women and the *Intifada*—No Going Back?" In *Gender and National Identity: Women and Politics in Muslim Societies*, edited by V. M. Moghadam, 148–170. London: Zed Books.

Burgmann, V. 2003. *Power, Profit and Protest: Australian Social Movements and Globalisation.* Crows Nest, Australia: Allen & Unwin.

Dawson, J. I. 1996. *Eco-Nationalism: Anti-Nuclear Activism and National Identity in Russia, Lithuania, and Ukraine.* Durham, NC: Duke University Press.

Duyvendak, J. W. 1994. *The Power of Politics: New Social Movements in France.* Boulder, CO: Westview.

Jayawardena, K. 1986. *Feminism and Nationalism in the Third World.* London: Zed Books.

Kaldor, M. 1996. "Cosmopolitanism versus Nationalism: The New Divide?" In *Europe's New Nationalism: States and Minorities in Conflict*, edited by R. Caplan and J. Feffer, 42–58. New York: Oxford University Press.

Keane, J. 1996. *Reflections on Violence.* London: Verso.

Kopecký, P. 2003. "Civil Society, Uncivil Society and Contentious Politics in Post-Communist Europe." In *Uncivil Society? Contentious Politics in Post-Communist Europe*, edited by P. Kopecký and C. Mudde, 1–18. London: Routledge.

Melucci, A. 1985. "The Symbolic Challenge of Contemporary Movements." *Social Research* 52:789–816.

Moghadam, V. M. 1994. "Introduction and Overview: Gender Dynamics of Nationalism, Revolution and Islamization." In *Gender and National Identity: Women and Politics in Muslim Societies*, edited by V. M. Moghadam, 1–17. London: Zed Books.

Omvedt, G. 1993. *Reinventing Revolution: New Social Movements and the Socialist Tradition in India.* Armonk, NY: M. E. Sharpe.

Rink, D. 2002. "Environmental Policy and the Environmental Movement in East Germany." *Socialism–Nature–Capitalism* 51:73–91.

Stubbs, P. 1996. "Nationalisms, Globalization and Civil Society in Croatia and Slovenia." *Research in Social Movements, Conflicts and Change* 19:1–26.

Touraine, A. 1981. *The Voice and the Eye*. New York: Cambridge University Press.

Wade, P. 1997. *Race and Ethnicity in Latin America*. London: Pluto Press.

Nationalism and Separatism

Sun-Ki Chai

The historical era following World War II is often referred to as the era of decolonization, the time when the former European powers, as well as America and Japan, gave up their overseas empires and dozens of new sovereign countries came into being. However, it could just as easily be called the era of nationalist separatism, as the sheer number of ethnic and pan-ethnic movements seeking independence from the political status quo multiplied greatly.

Relevance

The relevance of these movements is clear, since they fundamentally altered the shape of the world's geopolitical map. They brought into being dozens of new countries and changed the boundaries of dozens of existing ones. They also altered the world balance of power by creating an "unaligned bloc" of independent countries who were not willing to stand under the shadow of the United States or its great Cold War adversary, the Soviet Union. Finally, they set the stage for the most recent period of post–Cold War history, in which ethnicity-based nationalism plays a major, or even dominant, role in international conflict.

Origins

While there were many reasons for the origins of these various types of nationalisms, they can be attributed to two major causes: The first related to the events leading up to and following the dismantling of the colonization system, which raised numerous questions about what the basis ought to be for the resulting newly independent countries. The other major cause was the rise of cultural sentiments (particularly in Western countries) that placed a great deal of importance on cultural identity. This in turn strengthened the impetus for nationalist movements even in well-established, modern countries.

Dimensions

The separatisms and regionalisms that occurred were so varied that it is difficult to make generalizations regarding their effects on different groups. However, admittedly with some simplification, it is possible to divide them into three different major categories: the anticolonial, the postcolonial, and the modern industrialized versions. Even in each category, there are numerous dimensions of variation that cannot be completely covered in a single chapter. Moreover, because of the huge number of movements that arose and changed shape during this period, we will have to focus on discussing large cases and major trends rather than encompassing the entire picture.

Decolonization

While the process called "decolonization" is conveniently dated as beginning immediately after the surrender of the Axis forces in 1945, the dismantling of colonies itself started earlier and has been a long and drawn-out process. Even if we exclude Spain and Portugal's loss of their Latin American colonies in the 19th century, there had been some earlier attrition in the Western colonial project, most notably with the nominal independence of Arab, post-Ottoman, League of Nations Mandates occurring in the 1930s and during the war itself. Mandates were territories that were given special status under Article 22 of the League's covenant, which promised most Mandates eventual independence. And while the single largest ex-colony, India and Pakistan, gained independence in 1947, most African colonies did not do so until the 1960s or later. Even today, Western powers retain vestiges of their overseas possessions in the Pacific and Caribbean, so the process is not complete.

Because of the protracted dying throes of colonialism, much of the separatist nationalism of the postwar era was originally directed against those colonial powers that remained in place, or was aimed at shaping the political configuration and boundaries of postindependence states.

In British India, the focus by 1945 was on the latter. The devastation of the British economy in the aftermath of World War II led to a quickly moving consensus within Britain that the maintenance of its huge colonial possessions in South Asia, encompassing many times the population of the British Isles themselves, was unsustainable and an impediment to postwar reconstruction. The defeat of Winston Churchill by Clement Atlee's Labour Party in the election of 1945 removed the main impediment to this divestment of what was increasingly seen as an onerous responsibility by the British public.

In this atmosphere, Indian domestic politics turned into a jockeying for influence over the disposition of independent India. Most notable there was the conflict between the Congress Party, led by Jawaharlal Nehru, and the Muslim League, led by Muhammad Ali Jinnah, over Jinnah's "two-nation" theory through which he sought to promulgate the idea of a separate independent Muslim state, Pakistan. The origins of the Congress–Muslim League conflict were long-seated and complex, but what is important to note is that, despite the religion-based nature of their conflict, both parties were led primarily not by religious extremists but by men of quite pragmatic, and if we may say so, secular, outlooks. Nonetheless, by the last preindependence elections of 1946, there was little room for compromise, as the Congress Party was committed to governing alone and the Muslim League was equally committed to the idea that Muslims would be oppressed in an undivided India.

The communal slaughter that followed the partition into independent India and Pakistan in 1947 was one of the great human tragedies of the 20th century. Whether or not the human cost of maintaining an undivided India in an atmosphere of incessant religious strife would have been greater or lesser than the cost of partition is a question that is very difficult to answer, though this has not stopped many from trying. Moreover, the debate over the "two-nation" versus unified vision of the subcontinent continues to be a boulder in the way of improving relations between the two countries, manifested in the way that each side frames the status of Kashmir (a situation that is discussed in the next section).

The decolonization process in Northeast Asia, though smaller in scale than that of South Asia, was equally seen as inevitable as World War II reached its conclusion. The defeat of Japan meant that the maintenance of its colonies in Korea, Taiwan, and Manchuria was out of the question. Furthermore, due to the much more constricted room for indigenous party politics that the Japanese colonial powers had allowed, there was greater uncertainty over the outcome of contestation among local politicians regarding the post-Japanese political system.

The main question in the case of Taiwan, and to a lesser extent, Manchuria, was whether possession would revert to whichever Chinese government would be able to take power in the aftermath of the Japanese withdrawal. Taiwan was a peripheral domain that had only been officially incorporated into Chinese territory in the 19th century, while Manchuria, being the ancestral home of the deposed Ching Dynasty, had long maintained a separate identity from the ethnic Chinese (Han) core, despite Manchuria and China being politically unified for centuries. However, at the time, there was no movement for Taiwanese or Manchurian separatism strong enough to seriously challenge the notion held by both the Communists and Nationalists that both territories were "naturally" a part of China. Korea, on the other hand, was a historically unified state with a strong sense of common identity, hence division of the peninsula as a viable ideology was never seriously raised. This in turn made the partition into North and South that occurred upon Japanese withdrawal much more traumatic for Koreans than the division between Taiwan and the Chinese mainland that occurred a few years later.

In Southeast Asia, the situation in the Philippines was the closest to that of South and Northeast Asia, with independence promised by an American government that was retreating into immediate postwar isolationism prior to the chill of the Cold War. The Dutch and British East Indies were a different situation, as various events conspired against immediate independence.

The Indonesian nationalist movement for independence from the Dutch was perhaps the strongest and most sustained in the colonized world next to that of India, yet it was internally divided and faced a colonial power that was far less willing to give up power than were the British. The active collaboration of many Indonesian nationalist leaders, including Sukarno and Hatta, with the Japanese was an additional factor that reduced international pressure for Dutch withdrawal in the postwar era. Hence, although the Japanese passed power over to Indonesian nationalists as their own authority slipped away, the Dutch immediately sought to reassert their control over their erstwhile possessions. It was only after four years of protracted warfare that the Dutch were forced to withdraw and independence was achieved.

In the British East Indies, the colonial power had promised independence by 1949, yet another eight years were required before that actually occurred. This was not due to the lack of any nationalist political activity within the country, but rather due in part to two factors. The first was the resistance among some ethnic Malay leaders to the idea that postwar Malaysia would be a multiethnic, secular state, with similar treatment given to Malays and to minorities of China and Indian ancestry, who had been brought in as immigrants through earlier British policies. This conflict was exacerbated by the extended revolt by the Chinese-led Malayan Communist Party (MCP), which threatened the stability of any post-independence government. It is important to note, however, that the MCP was not a separatist organization. After all, it would have been difficult to separate the Chinese population from the rest, since they were distributed throughout the Straits Settlements. Moreover, the flag-bearer of Malay ethnic nationalism, the United Malays National Organization, soon formed an alliance with Chinese and Indian political parties, illustrating the complexities of the political situation as Malaysia gained independence in 1957.

In French Indochina (Vietnam, Cambodia, and Laos), the Vietnamese communist nationalist faction (Viet Minh) never allied itself with the Japanese occupation. However, it benefited from the undermining of established French authority, enabling the faction to assert its control over much of urban Vietnam soon after the end of the war. This control was only temporary, and efforts to negotiate with the French broke down over the French desire to retain its position in southern Vietnam (Cochinchina) while ceding authority to much of the North. A war of independence followed, reaching its conclusion in the famous battle of Dien Bien Phu in 1954, followed by the Geneva Agreement that left the country free from French rule, but divided between the Viet Minh government in the North and the regime in the South led by the charismatic leader Ngo Dinh Diem. This division, however, did not reflect separatist sentiments in each region but, rather, was the outcome of external forces on two competing regimes, both purporting to represent the entire Vietnamese nation. Cambodia and Laos obtained independence at about the same time, but remained internally divided as the inheritor regimes to whom the French handed over power were opposed on multiple fronts by domestic opposition forces.

The toll exacted on French military and political resources by the Indochina war created an opportunity for independence movements in a major group of its colonies in a very different part of the world, North Africa. These colonies included Tunisia, Morocco, and Algeria. After banning the Tunisian nationalist Neo-Destourian Party and imprisoning their leader, Habib Bourguiba, in 1952, the colonial government two years later freed Bourguiba, unbanned the party, and granted autonomy, effectively setting Tunisia on a clear path to independence. Likewise, they allowed the nationalist sultan Muhammad V to return to power in Morocco in 1956, setting off a similar pattern of events. In both cases the French government made major concessions to nationalist movements, choosing to avoid once again expending itself fighting a sustained insurgency. The situation was quite different in Algeria, which had a much larger European-descended population and which France had long considered an integral part of its territory. The brutal Algerian War of Independence lasted from 1954 until 1962, during which French and world popular opinion turned increasingly against the violent tactics used by both sides against civilian populations. Even independence and the ascendancy of the Front de Libération Nationale to power did not bring about peace, as a massive exodus of Europeans and reprisals against alleged collaborators followed soon after.

In contrast to events in the various regions of Asia and northern Africa, independence in sub-Saharan Africa came relatively late. The first country to gain independence, Ghana, did not achieve this until 1957, while the Portuguese colonies of Angola and Mozambique had to wait until 1976 to gain their independence. There are a number of reasons for this, including the fact that, with a few exceptions (e.g., Nkrumah's Convention People's Party), nationalist parties in the region were of relatively recent vintage and had not consolidated demands for independence during World War II in the way that parties in other parts of the world had. Furthermore, many of the newer parties were organized around ethnic lines, which made it more difficult for them to claim legitimacy for a takeover from imperial rule. This latter fact, which would come back to haunt postindependence Africa, was itself due in part to the largely arbitrary boundaries that the colonial powers had drawn around their possessions. Finally, another reason can be found in the presence of colonial powers, such as Belgium and Portugal, who had deliberately prevented the rise of an educated indigenous class that could take over the reigns of government. Hence decolonization here was a protracted process, despite the fact that both the British and French governments had by the mid-1950s publicly committed themselves to expediting decolonization in sub-Saharan Africa.

The history of separatism and regionalism during the dying days of Western colonialism is a complex one, since in many cases political parties were simultaneously fighting to gain independence for their nations while jockeying for influence over the postindependence dispensation. Overarching these struggles were a few larger ideological forces that drove much of the process forward. Not the least of these was the very idea of nationalism itself, which was by now quite familiar to the educated indigenous elites. Nationalism was an organizing principle empowered the rhetoric of anticolonial leaders and allowed them to place their aspirations in a framework that legitimized them according to universal norms familiar to the publics of the Western powers. Nor was nationalist ideology simply a pragmatic tool for gaining external support; it was a powerful force for unifying large and often disparate groups of people under a single banner (though this would serve as a double-edged sword in the postcolonial era). Hence it was an appropriate ideology for anticolonial struggles in a way that more parochial ideas, on the one hand, and sweeping class analysis, on the other, were not.

Regionalism

The "birth of the new states" after decolonization presented a variety of conundrums for intellectuals and policy makers, but perhaps the greatest concern to both, after economic development, was that of how these often artificially created artifacts of colonial policies would resist political fragmentation without the coercive hand of the Western powers holding them together. This concern was multiplied (at least in the West) by the advent of the Cold War, and the fact that each of these new states was seen as a potential ally, enemy, or even battleground in the battle for world supremacy. In relation to this, there was a widespread belief that political chaos would leave these new states "ripe for Communism."

Because of this, "nation-building" became the mantra of much of the political development studies, with this term referring to the replacement of parochial ties and loyalties with broader ties to larger political entities, particularly the state. Visionary political leaders sought to "activate" their populations from becoming passive subjects to becoming participants in their country's program of transformation.

Almost immediately, however, the complexities and contradictions of the nation-building exercise became clear. Once the process of national identity creation was set in place through education, media campaigns, and urbanization, there was no way to contain it within a single set of entities corresponding to existing state units. The ideas and emotions of nationalism could just as easily, and in many cases more easily, be harnessed to attract allegiance to racial, religious, linguistic, and regional identities that were larger than the traditional parochial ones, yet still incongruent with the aim of creating citizens of a unitary state. Often these various types of ethnic identities were at a level below the state, but just as often they cross-cut state boundaries, bringing into motion regional and international conflicts that themselves threatened state integrity.

In South Asia, the partition of India and Pakistan did not bring an end to separatist sentiments, and indeed, it triggered a series of events that threatened the territorial integrity of both countries. The most immediate source of such threats was the accession of Jammu and Kashmir, a Muslim-majority territory, to India, as a result of the acquiescence of its traditional ruling leader, Maharajah Hari Singh. This accession fundamentally went against Pakistan's own self-proclaimed role as defender of South Asia's Muslim populations, as well as the apparent sentiments of the majority population in Kashmir itself. Because of its Muslim majority, the disposition of Kashmir has often been viewed as a crucial case for the one-nation/two-nation ideological battle between the two countries, and has led to war between the countries on three different occasions, the most recent being the 1998 Kargil conflict.

Pakistan suffered from an even greater threat to its boundaries in the form of East Pakistan, the Bengali-speaking portion of the country, separated from the West by India. Despite containing over half the population of the entire country, East Pakistanis were marginalized in the halls of power, which were dominated by Punjabis and Mohajirs (refugees from Urdu/Hindi-speaking areas of North India). This sense of repression came to a head when the Bengali Awami League under the leadership of Sheik Mujibur Rahman won a National Assembly majority in the 1970 election under the banner of autonomy for the East. This led to the imposition of martial law and a bloody crackdown against Bengali nationalist interests by the Pakistani Army. The intervention of India, however, shifted the war decisively against Pakistan and led to the creation of an independent Bangladesh by the end of 1971. It is important to note, however, that while Bangladesh to a great extent was a creation of Bengali nationalist impulses, this was more in the context of the division of power within the Muslim-majority areas of the subcontinent rather than the expression of pan-Bengali sentiment. Indeed, the merger of India's Hindu-majority Bengali-speaking West Bengal into a greater Bangladesh was never a notion put forward by actors on either side of the border.

The late 1970s saw the rise of another independence movement in India, the movement for an independent Sikh homeland, Khalistan, in the Punjab. The origins of Sikh separatism were complex, but historical causes include a combination of memories of the grand Sikh-Punjabi kingdom of Ranjit Singh in the early 19th century, anger over the division of Punjab between India and Pakistan, and discontent over the partition of Indian Punjab into multiple states. Proximate causes included an economic downturn in the 1980s, as well as the emergence of the radical Sikh separatist militant Jarnail Singh Bhindranwale, whose followers occupied the seat of the Sikh religion, the Golden Temple in Amritsar. Operation Blue Star, the attack in June 1984 by Indian troops on Bhindranwale's followers, succeeded in defeating them but also set off a Sikh radical backlash culminating in the assassination of Indira Gandhi a few months later. Insurgency continued on for a few years, but eventually died down due to a combination of policies, including a violent crackdown against Khalistani supporters and a simultaneous effort by the Indian government to co-opt moderate nationalists from the Akali Dal party.

Sri Lanka (then Ceylon) had always held a separate political status as a Crown colony under British rule and attained independence separately in 1947. Almost immediately, however, tension grew between the Sinhalese population, predominantly Buddhist, which held majority power in the new state, and minority Tamils, predominantly Hindu, who had enjoyed disproportionate status under British rule. Under the leadership of Sinhalese nationalist leaders such as Nathan Ban-daranaike a series of laws were passed enshrining the Sinhalese language and the Buddhist religion within the Sri Lankan state. Tamil political parties responded by asserting a right to autonomy for Tamil-majority areas in the north and east of the country. The most radical of these Tamil parties espoused separatism and the creation of an independent Tamil state, or Eelam. This viewpoint was soon domi-nated by the Liberation Tigers of Tamil Eelam (LTTE) who launched a string of increasingly successful military attacks against Sri Lankan armed forces and Tamil interests who questioned their vision of Tamil nationalism. The Indo-Sri Lankan accords brought Indian troops into the country in 1987, but they were forced to withdraw after the Sri Lankan government revoked its support. A num-ber of uneasy cease-fires have held since the early part of the current century, but the conflict remains far from settled.

In Northeast Asia, the strength of separatist activity in the postcolonial era has been far weaker than in South Asia for a variety of reasons. Both Japan and Korea have long viewed themselves as relatively homogenous states with only tiny minority populations. And while Korea is divided between North and South, this is, like the former division between North and South Vietnam, not the result of separatist politics but of a stalemate between two sides that each purport to represent the entire country. Likewise, as long as the Guomindang Party retained

Women fighters of the Liberation Tigers of Tamil Eelam (LTTE) march in October 2002. (AFP/ Getty Images)

single-party power in Taiwan, the government there viewed itself as the legitimate ruler of all China, hence did not express its opposition to the mainland Communist regime in separatist terms. And while the mainland itself was ethnically quite plural, the coercive power of the Communist state effectively squelched all but the mildest forms of Tibetan and Uygur nationalism until the end of the 1980s.

Southeast Asia, on the other hand, faced a variety of separatist movements, most occurring on the peripheries of its large multiethnic peninsula and island states. Perhaps the worst hit was Indonesia, with its wide expanse of islands and almost incalculable diversity. Almost from its very outset, it faced a powerful and well-armed separatist movement in Aceh, one that had been going on continuously against the previous Dutch occupiers since the beginning of the 20th century. Active insurgency began with the rise of the Free Aceh Movement (GAM) in the mid-1970s, and continued without much letup until movement toward a peace agreement began in the wake of the devastating tsunami of late 2004. Another insurgency arose from Indonesia's forcible annexation of East Timor following the sudden withdrawal of its Portuguese colonial rulers in 1977. An extended fight against the FRETILIN (Frente Revolucionária de Timor-Leste Independente) separatist group resulted eventually in the granting of independence to East Timor in 2002. In West Papua (Irian Jaya), short-lived independent status was followed by occupation and attempts by the Indonesian government to bind its predominantly Melanesian population to the state through a much-condemned so-called Act of Free Choice and a policy of transmigration. This has led to a low-level guerilla war by the forces of the West Papuan Liberation Movement (OPM) since the mid-1960s.

In the Philippines, the postindependence government faced opposition from the Muslim populations of Southern Mindanao, which culturally had more in common with its neighbors to the south in Malaysia and Indonesia than to the predominately Catholic mainstream Philippine culture. A 1996 agreement between the government and the largest Moro nationalist group, the Moro Nationalist Liberation Front (MNLF), failed to halt the conflict, as other groups continued to reject that basis for the agreement. In Thailand, a superficially similar situation exists in the south, which contains a large Malay-speaking Muslim population in a predominately Buddhist society. Yet large-scale Muslim nationalist insurgency did not start there until the mid-1990s.

In North Africa, the major ethnic divide has long been seen as the one between Arab and Berber populations. Nonetheless, despite frequently expressed grievances by Berber political parties throughout the region against Arabization policies, this has rarely been expressed in separatist terms or as armed rebellion. Indeed, the longest-running separatist conflict in North Africa is outside of the Arab-Berber divide, occurring continuously in the Western Sahara since the 1960s, and since the 1970s under the leadership of the Polisario Front against Moroccan occupation of this former Spanish colony. Another long-running separatist conflict, that between the primarily Nilotic groups of southern Sudan and the

Arab north, has recently been the subject of a much-awaited peace agreement. Eritrean separatism from Ethiopia, ultimately successful, was in many ways a by-product of the joint struggle of Eritrean, Amhara, and Tigrean forces against the Marxist government of Mengistu Haile Mariam.

In sub-Saharan Africa, the ubiquity of ethnically based political parties within political boundaries set by Western imperialists had made rampant separatism seem like an inevitability. Yet while separatist movements have not been unknown, most of the conflict between ethnic groups, though often quite violent, has taken place within a larger acceptance of existing colonially drawn boundaries, as arbitrary as those boundaries may seem. The most notable exception to this rule was the attempt by Igbo nationalists to split away from the Nigerian state to form the independent state of Biafra, leading to the bloody civil war of 1967–1970. The earlier attempt by Katanga province, under Moise Tshombe, to secede from Zaire was defeated over the course of 1960–1963 with the aid of United Nations (UN) forces. Different as they were, one factor that these two cases had in common was the relative wealth of the ethnic groups in whose names separatist movements functioned. The expressed desire of the leaders of these groups was to withdraw from what they viewed as the chaos of a multiethnic state where other groups were poorer, less educated, and yet, in the majority.

It can be argued with some justification that the process of decolonization, given the way that it was carried out, left behind conditions under which separatist activity was inevitable in the new states. Boundaries had been drawn in a way that reflected administrative convenience and did not reflect the geographical patterns of ethnic identities. The boundaries themselves had often been in flux during the colonial period, and their final location was often the result of last-minute compromise. Within those boundaries were left new governments that were internally divided and often lacked personnel with administrative experience. The very newness of postindependence political institutions brought in another element of instability. Hence, many postindependence governments had difficulty enforcing their authority and were often subject to frequent challenges both from within and without. Given these problems, it might seem a miracle that separatism was not even more common in the postcolonial era.

Yet, in some ways, it could also be argued that the problems faced by postcolonial governments, at their most extreme, tended to limit separatist violence, though often by substituting other forms of conflict. Where governments were extremely weak and unstable, there was little incentive for opposition groups to aim for control over a portion of the country's territory when the entire territory might be ripe for picking. Furthermore, even if a government agreed to autonomy or independence for a portion of its territory, its ability to enforce and maintain this agreement over time would be limited. The complexity of ethnic divisions also tended to mitigate somewhat against separatism. The intertwining of residence patterns among different ethnic groups made it difficult to clearly demarcate the homeland of one group from that of another. Furthermore, the sheer number of possible ways in which ethnicity could be mobilized sometimes meant that it was difficult for political groups to enunciate a clearly understood demand for a political homeland, one that would not be challenged by alternative, equally appealing calls to identity among the same group of people.

Separatism and Regionalism in Modern, Industrialized States

Neither the preponderance of anticolonial separatist activity nor the continuation of nationalist movements within new states was a great surprise to social theorists studying ethnicity, conflict, and development. Nationalism, after all, was largely seen as a product of the "transitional stages" between tradition and modernity, as mediated by the stresses and strains caused by the passing of the old and introduction of the new. The extent of violence had perhaps been more than was generally expected or hoped for, but it nonetheless did not require a fundamental reworking of the findings of social theory.

However, beginning from approximately the late 1960s and early 1970s, there took place a resurgence in nationalist separatist activity in the region of the world where it was least expected, the industrialized West, often in the very home countries of the former colonial powers. True, the West was conventionally viewed as the birthplace of nationalism and had gone through massive nationalist ferment beginning from the period of the Napoleonic wars until World War I. However, the feeling had been that, with the advent of modernity, the era of nationalism had passed, with World War II and the Cold War being the harbingers of more sweeping global ideologies, such as capitalism, communism, fascism, and socialism.

The upsurge of nationalist violence in Northern Ireland, the growth of Basque separatism in Spain, and the movement for Québec independence were only some of the strong and often violent movements that arose during the 1960s and 1970s. Numerous theories have been put forward for why this occurred, ranging from those who saw no significant differences between the forces causing separatist nationalism in the industrialized world and in developing countries to those who saw these movements as a manifestation of a postmodern condition of "identity politics" found predominantly in the West. In a way, however, each of the major separatist movements in Western countries has its own dynamics, and they resist being placed within a single social change paradigm, whether it be modern or postmodern.

The separatist movement by Catholic radicals in Northern Ireland is perhaps the best known case of this kind of resurgent nationalist revolt. The height of this movement, usually referred to as "The Troubles," began during the 1960s and continued up until the mid-1990s, being brought (at least formally) to a close by the Good Friday Agreement in 1998. It is hard to characterize the original causes of this conflict as postmodern, since violent disputes over the partition of Ireland date to the creation of the Free State in 1920. However, the upsurge in violence can be traced to a chain of causation, beginning with the rise of the Catholic civil rights movement and its suppression by the government, which moved to violent clashes between Protestant and Catholic activists, leading to the direct introduction of British military forces. Disagreement among republicans over tactics led to the formation of the Provisional Irish Republican Army (IRA) in 1970, whose support base was greatly increased by the "Bloody Sunday" shooting deaths of 13 civilians by British soldiers during a protest march.

Besides the IRA, the best-known violent separatist movement in the industrialized West is ETA (Basque Nation and Freedom), active in the Basque region of Spain and to a lesser extent France. The cause of Basque nationalism, like Irish nationalism, dates prior to the 20th century, but like the rise of the Provisional IRA, the rise of ETA was linked to social and cultural changes occurring in Western Europe, as well as in the atmosphere of repression under the postwar Francisco Franco regime in Spain. ETA began as a radical offshoot of the mainstream nationalist movement, and it gained popularity during the 1960s, as its policy of targeted violence against figures of Franco's regime was regarded as legitimate by large segments of the Western European public. This support has dropped greatly, however, in the aftermath of democratization in 1977 and the split of ETA itself into two factions.

Other major separatist and regionalist movements in the West during the post–World War II period have been generally nonviolent in nature. Perhaps the most prominent among these has been the Québec sovereignty movement, which became an active voice in Canadian politics with the birth of the Parti Québécois in 1968. The separatist message of the Parti Québécois gained the support of nearly half the province's electorate during referendums on independence in 1980 and 1994.

There is no doubt that these "new" separatisms were affected in some fashion by the political upheavals and challenges to the status quo that took place across Western Europe and North America during the 1960s. However, it is difficult to argue for a simple causal relationship between the two, since the nationalist movements in question also drew upon longer-running grievances as well as support groups that were quite different from those who supported the American antiwar movement or the European radical uprisings of 1968. Perhaps the most plausible argument that can be made is that the events of the 1960s legitimized the rights of minorities to self-determination as well as the notion of "direct action" against established authorities, and hence contributed to, even if they were not completely responsible for, the new wave of nationalisms in the West.

Consequences

As can be seen, despite the clear upsurge in separatist activity that occurred during the period under our review, it is difficult to attribute this upsurge to a simple set of causes.

It is intuitive that any force that destabilizes the existing political status quo will tend to bring to the surface conflicting demands for recognition, which would include ethnic identities based upon race, religion, language, and region. Needless to say, there were a number of events in the latter half of the 20th century that tended to lead to such destabilization. It is tempting to group the many factors that have been discussed under the broader rubrics of "modernization" or "post-modernization," but this simply begs the question of identifying the nature of such larger processes.

What is true without question is that events from the 1950s on set into motion a period of the most widespread sustained nationalist and separatist political activity in world history, one that continues to shape international politics to the present day.

Selected Bibliography

Ahmida, A. A., ed. 2000. *Beyond Colonialism and Nationalism in the Maghreb. History, Culture and Politics.* New York: Palgrave.

Anderson, B. 1983. *Imagined Communities: Reflections on the Origin and Spread of Nationalism.* London: Verso.

Brubaker, R. 1996. *Nationalism Reframed: Nationhood and the National Question in the New Europe.* Cambridge: Cambridge University Press.

Connor, W. 1994. *Ethnonationalism: A Quest for Understanding.* Princeton, NJ: Princeton University Press.

Furnivall, J. S. 1956. *Colonial Policy and Practice: A Comparative Study of Burma and Netherlands India.* New York: New York University Press.

Geertz, C., ed. 1663. *Old Societies and New States.* New York: Free Press.

Hasan, M., ed. 2000. *Inventing Boundaries: Gender, Politics and the Partition of India.* New Delhi: Oxford University Press.

Hewitt, C., and T. Cheetham. 2000. *Encyclopedia of Modern Separatist Movements.* Santa Barbara, CA: ABC-CLIO.

Hodson, H. V. 1997. *The Great Divide: Britain-India-Pakistan.* Karachi, Pakistan: Oxford University Press.

Horowitz, D. L. 1985. *Ethnic Groups in Conflict.* Berkeley: University of California Press.

Kedourie, E. 1970. *Nationalism in Asia and Africa.* New York: World Publishing.

Khalidi, R., L. Anderson, M. Muslih, and R. Simon, eds. 1993. *The Origins of Arab Nationalism.* New York: Columbia University Press.

Nairn, T. 1977. *The Break-up of Britain: Crisis and Neo-Nationalism.* 2nd ed. London: New Left Books.

Reid, A. J. S. 1974. *Indonesian National Revolution, 1945–58.* London: Longman.

Roff, W. R. 1967. *The Origins on Malay Nationalism.* New Haven, CT: Yale University Press.

Tiryakian, E. A., and R. Rogowski, eds. 1985. *New Nationalisms of the Developed West: Towards Explanation.* Boston: Allen and Unwin.

Wallerstein, I. 1961. *Africa: The Politics of Independence.* New York: Vintage Books.

Young, C. 1976. *The Politics of Cultural Pluralism.* Madison: University of Wisconsin Press.

Technology and Nationalism

Marco Adria

Relevance

Technology is either central or adjunct to many current theories of nationalism. It is emphasized particularly in those accounts in which nationalism is regarded as a modern phenomenon. Histories of nationalist movements seek to explain the establishment and maintenance of the modern state in conjunction with a national community. Modern states are the product of technologically mediated communication and often use technological innovation to highlight their status and influence in relation to other states.

Although nationalism is not in itself an ideology, or system of ideas, its aims are carried forward through ideology. As the sociologist Alvin Gouldner has pointed out, the alternating historical process of first generating ideas, and then deploying technology in support of those ideas, requires the continuous production and circulation of symbols using communications technologies. Ideologies give life to such large-scale social movements as nationalist projects. This is possible only through the use of the technology of mass media. For many nationalist projects, the newspaper has been the medium by which nationalist ideas have gained wide circulation.

The uses of technology in relationship to nationalism may be regarded as belonging to either or both of two primary categories: demonstrational and mediating. The demonstrational use of technology involves obtaining, developing, or using technology in support of a nationalist cause. An example would be military technology, such as aircraft, tanks, and firearms, which may be used to enforce either a national unification or separation. The technology used by armed forces has always been central to the maintenance and extension of nationalist programs. Commonly used definitions of the state highlight the importance of technology in relation to nationalism. These definitions distinguish the state from other organizations or entities by pointing to the state's monopoly on the use of violence that is approved by law. The state deploys the technology of warfare outside its borders and of criminal justice within.

The mediating use of a technology involves publicly justifying state action within the national community, while transmitting messages in support of the nationalist project. In many countries, including the United Kingdom, Australia, Canada, and Sweden, a national broadcasting agency with public funding has been established for such a purpose. The legislation establishing such agencies requires that the national character is to be reflected in and promoted by the national broadcaster. In broadcasting enterprises of all kinds, technology is a carrier of cultural information in the form of television shows, radio broadcasts, and so on. It is also a structuring influence in regional, national, and international economies, because it can help to create and change patterns of trade and development. Culture and power therefore exist historically in a mutual relationship of development. As the Canadian historian Harold Adams Innis (1951, 133) noted, a state's ability to engage in "intense cultural activity during a short period of time and to mobilize intellectual resources over a vast territory assumes to an important extent the development of armed force to a high state of efficiency."

The use of technology may be *both* demonstrational and mediating. Radio, for example, has been used as a mediating technology in the development of national identities in many regions of the world. Radio has supported nationalist projects by promoting cultural and political events in which the glory of the national culture is celebrated. It has helped to revive folk musical traditions and lore, as well as local dialects and linguistic variants. It has also been used to demonstrate the socially progressive character of a national identity. By providing universal access to radio signals as a public benefit available to members of the nation, the national identity is enhanced and made more attractive to the population. By embracing communications technologies, the character of the national identity is promoted as being modern, along with the promise of economic and social advances. Radio's social uses in such instances would therefore be both demonstrational and mediating in support of nationalism.

Origins

The relationship between technology and nationalism has become an active area of inquiry for scholars of nationalism only relatively recently. The main reason for the slow appearance of technology in theories of nationalism may be related to the unconscious effects of technology—the fact that we use technology in many contexts without being fully aware of its influence and ultimate outcomes. The roots of the study of the relationship between technology and nationalism lie in the mediating use of technology.

In the 1950s and 1960s, the U.S. sociologist Karl Deutsch argued that communications technologies (the printing press, newspaper, telegraph, radio, television) supported the establishment of nationalist movements by allowing for the convenient and frequent exchange of ideas within a region. Technology and nationalism in this view were brought together primarily through culture. Before the invention of the printing press and subsequent media innovations, cultural sharing occurred only in small groups. The oral traditions of speaking, singing, and, for people with basic education, writing and reading, were used to pass culture from one generation to the next. With the invention of such technologies as books, newspaper, radio, and television, the enduring preferences, values, and habits of culture were circulated more intensively within an emerging nation. Deutsch's cultural argument for the varying consequences for societies of different media was built on the earlier economic work of Innis, which drew historical conclusions from the "bias" of a communication medium to either space or time. The conception of space and time as a phenomenon mediated by technology has profound implications for the genesis and extension of nationalist projects.

Deutsch sought evidence for his argument in three ways. First, he used social-psychological indicators that would measure the degree to which one medium functioned in tandem with another in a complementary fashion to allow for the gathering and passing on of values, preferences, and memories. Second, he measured the rate by which minority groups blended in with the mainstream culture, hypothesizing that this rate depended on information about experiences exchanged within elite groups and then disseminated to the larger population. Third, he established rates of social mobility by measuring shifts from rural to urban occupations. Deutsch suggested that in some cases, the use of communications technologies led to diverging cultural preferences and separate national cultures.

Scholars have continued to bring social and historical perspectives to the varying influence of particular media on the development of nationalist projects. To consider one example, Mexican radio throughout the middle of the 20th century has been examined to reveal the effects of its modern form and its antimodern orientation. Radio is characterized by the intense modern characteristic of "flow." Radio programming is continuous and irreversible, suggesting something of the rapidly changing nature of modern life. It is also a medium by which antimodern oral communication predominates. Ancient techniques, such as mnemonics (using acronyms as memory aids, for example) and formulaic phrases, are combined with modern techniques for maximizing the economic returns for owners of the broadcasting enterprise.

For Ernest Gellner, the British historian, nationalism's roots are to be found in the profound changes in society that occurred during industrialization during the 18th and 19th centuries. During this time, manufacturing, mechanization, and international commerce developed from a revolution in social communications and the universalization of standardized education. Technology has been at the heart of this revolution, allowing for the rapid exchange of ideas and for the archiving and preservation of texts. Benedict Anderson (1991) has argued that the technology of the printing press in particular allowed for the development of "imagined communities." These communities are larger and more diverse than those that existed before the printing press. Before the printing press, communities were bound by the face-to-face transmission of narratives and other forms of cultural knowledge. An individual's memory limited the scale of a community. Thereafter, community memory could be committed to books and other printed artifacts and disseminated to a larger population. With a common language, one which replaced a wider number of dialects and language variants, the newspaper helped to create an imagined community and also a public venue for the exchange of opinions and ideas about the status and future of the nation. The number of members, land base, and diversity of the national community could grow quickly.

Dimensions

Cause and Effect in the Study of Technology and Nationalism

Technology for some historians and sociologists is a cause or antecedent of nationalism, but for others it is an effect or outcome. The "technology as cause" approach suggests that by creating conditions that favor the development of a recognizable national identity, technology enables nationalism to take root. For example, the standardization of a national language following the use of the printing press, and in particular the medium of the newspaper, enabled communities to consolidate their national identity. Using the common language and forum created by the newspaper, a larger, national community could coordinate economic activities that then supported and helped extend nationalist projects. Technology in this way can be a necessary antecedent of nationalism.

For other scholars, technology is an outcome or effect of a nationalist movement. Technological innovation is deployed and exploited in order to show what social and economic benefits may flow from the nationalist project. The "technology as effect" approach is based on the assumption that nationalist sentiments and energies already exist within societies. They thrive and spread, in part by exploiting technology and fostering technological advances. This approach has been central to recent studies of Asian nationalist movements. The development of the Indonesian aircraft industry from 1976 until 1997, for example, was made possible by the nationalist rhetoric employed by influential bureaucrats, politicians, technologists, and engineers in that country. This rhetoric provided legitimacy to a policy of intensive research and development and the production of sophisticated aircraft. For example, it involved the public discussion of the influential idea of "technology leapfrogging." This is the idea that a national community can pass over intermediary stages of industrial development by investing heavily in a new, technologically advanced area of research, development, and production.

Causal explanations of how national identity is established, developed, and disseminated must increasingly take account of social and psychological changes introduced by the widespread use of the Internet. Many people now experience what the historian Mark Poster (1999) has called a "profound bond with machines." This bond obscures the cause-effect relationship between technology and social movements, such as nationalism. The continuous and intensive exchange of ideas has created a new environment in which technology may be considered both a cause *and* an effect of nationalism.

The Demonstration Effect

The term "demonstration effect" in nationalism studies refers to a social event, such as a coup d'état, or popular overthrow of a government. It may be defined as a revolutionary event in one location that stimulates or influences a revolutionary event elsewhere. Although the term is often used to refer to *social* events, its theoretical roots lie in the theory of the diffusion of innovations, which is concerned with how and at what rate *technological* adaption occurs within a population. The theory of the diffusion of innovations has developed increasingly complex models of the adaptation of technologies and other innovations, including social innovations. The basic principle of the theory is that the messages of mass media alone cannot account for the adoption of a technological or social innovation. Instead, potential adopters seek interpersonal sources, such as friends and family members, as sources of expertise and experience. Diffusion of innovations therefore posits a two-step flow of, first, message receipt through a media channel, and, second, validation of the message through interpersonal communication.

Following the two-step flow of diffusion of innovations theory, the demonstration effect suggests that technology "teaches" by becoming an exemplar of the benefits of nationalism. Technological innovation may be used as a means of publicly illustrating the material and social advantages that a nationalist project offers individuals and groups. By creating "news" about the innovations inherent in a nationalist project, the demonstration effect stimulates face-to-face conversations about the project. The demonstration effect is mediated through technology, and its subject is technology.

The demonstration effect may in some instances be rooted in a distant part of the world. A consequence of such an event is that a nationalist movement is provided with a view of what is possible in its own part of the world. Alternatively, the demonstration effect may be found in the homeland of the nationalist project. An example of the latter is provided by a university created in an oil-rich province of Canada in 1970 (Adria 2000). The university's mandate was organized around technology and anchored in the historical aspirations of farmers and small-business owners and, later, white-collar workers to improve their economic opportunities within the region by changing the way significant institutions operated. The new university was given a radical mandate to apply information and communications technologies intensively with the purpose of serving students by distance education. The new university contributed to the mobilization of popular sentiment for a consumerist model of education, which in turn supported a shift in state economic priorities. Before 1970, education had been a favored beneficiary of spending by an "allocation" state, that is, a state that carried out the role of redistributing economic benefits. From 1971 to 1975, a dramatic decrease occurred in the proportion of state funds directed to public education. The "production" state that emerged was associated with new state priorities to develop the domestic economy by such techniques as adding value to natural resources before export, by deploying technology throughout the region:

> Begun in 1971, the production state . . . represented an attempt to diversify the economy through industrialization, primarily through the forward linkages (adding value to the primary resource) of petroleum refining and processing. Refineries were built, for example, in an effort to "sow the oil" (use oil revenues to create new sources of economic activity) and export value-added products. (Adria 2000, 586)

The demonstration effect occurred with the establishment of this new educational institution because it illustrated the social and economic benefits that would be available through the new project of regional identity and economic development.

Technological Nationalism

A special analysis of the relationship between technology and nationalism is inherent in "technological nationalism," which refers to the rhetorical use of technology for the purpose of developing a nationalist project. Technological nationalism involves the explicit use of technology as the subject of a nationalist project's communication strategies. For example, technological nationalism in Canada has historically developed as a set of arguments and stories referring to a national culture arising out of social process, rather than product. A popular Canadian television program in the 1980s depicted an aboriginal confronted by a steam locomotive. The image of the railroad had become associated with the historical "national dream" of social unity to be accomplished through technological achievement. Such an achievement would be accomplished particularly through the development of communications technologies, like a transnational telegraph/railroad in the 19th century, a national radio and television service in the 1930s and 1940s, satellite communications in the 1970s, and, most recently, broadband Internet service for remote communities.

Technological nationalism combines the ideology of technological progress with the sentiments and goals of nationalism. The state seeks legitimacy for its actions by creating, through rhetoric, a nation that mirrors its own objectives. Technological nationalism is a view of nationalism that examines the rhetorical devices and techniques within nationalist projects.

Impact on Different Groups

A single technology may be interpreted differently by various groups. The influence of technology on the development of nationalism has been of particular interest in the context of European-colonized communities. Rather than using military force and the deployment of a large part of its population to warfare, the European conquest of many parts of the world in the 18th and 19th centuries relied on the technology of trade and industry. Colonized peoples were conquered through the new economic and cultural technologies of train and telegraph, rather than the older methods of fortress and firepower. The adoption and deployment of technology in colonial countries was followed by unintended social consequences that included the collapse of colonial empires themselves. Colonized countries were lost to their respective empires throughout the 20th century, but principally between 1905 and 1960. Technology was interpreted and used by colonizers to display their advanced capacity to administer and organize the colonized lands for the purpose of enhanced trade. It was also used to support and protect imperial culture, maintaining the native culture as a museum specimen. For colonized peoples, technology was interpreted as a means of improving living standards and reviving native ways of life, which supported independence movements.

In the late colonial landscape of Dutch Indonesia, leading up to the invasion by Japan in 1942 and the subsequent independence of the country, radio had a conspicuous role in both encouraging an indigenous culture for the native population and in connecting the colonists to home. Differing metaphors for radio broadcasting were adopted by the native Indonesians on the one hand and by the colonial Dutch on the other. For the native community, radio provided a means of developing a regional musical identity, as it did in the form of the *kroncong*, a popular genre of Hawaiian-like song. The *kroncong* was favored by not only the native Indonesians but by other surrounding native cultures, including the Chinese. The medium represented casual entertainment, popular cultural development, and diversion for the native Indonesians. For the colonists, by contrast, radio was an unseen telephone cable from the colonized country to the homeland of the Netherlands. It was a means of maintaining Dutch cultural isolation within Indonesia. Radio featured news from the homeland, expressions of musical and literary tradition, and cultural uplift.

A historical view of other technologies in the colony, including roads, buildings, optical technologies, and media, allows an understanding of Indonesian nationalism as a shared enterprise between the native Indonesians and the Dutch. Together, the two groups created a national identity for the country that was more modern, oriented to technological progress, and outward-looking. Asphalt roads were built following an increase in Dutch concerns about intermingling with the native population. An influential Dutch pharmacist warned against infection, which the technology of asphalt would lift drivers away from:

> Natives . . . were speaking and writing flesh and blood, or simply mud. Wherever the natives went, and especially as they dared to approach a modern road, they were read and pronounced as carrying that soft stuff on themselves, on their tongues, on their feet, and on their wheels. (Mrázek 2002, 27)

Technology was to provide a buffer between native and colonizer in Indonesia. Neither group recognized the essentially modernizing effect of the road, which once established became understood by both as a movement toward modernity and, by extension, an emerging national identity. The technologies of radio and road were developed as part of the industrial and cultural infrastructure by which the colony was governed. Eventually, with the emergence of regional cultural forms such as the *kroncong*, technology in Indonesia was to become a cultural wedge between colonized and colonist, thereby indirectly encouraging the development of a distinct nationalist native-Indonesian culture.

Technology as a Unifying or Fragmentary Force

Technology supports and extends nationalisms in some contexts but separates national groups in others. The historical differentiation of the Dutch people from the North Germans, for example, was supported by the special importance of dikes and low-lying tracts of land in Holland during the Middle Ages. The dikes kept water out of the agricultural plots but required systems of pumping and maintenance. Family farms and communities were arranged around these systems. The technological innovation of the dike therefore helped to maintain a separate way of life for the Dutch, because it required patterns of work and social life that had at their center the maintenance of distinctive agricultural methods.

Technology may bolster and support the authority of elites in the promotion of nationalism, as aeronautical technology did for the Indonesian nationalist government of the 1970s and 1980s. Technology may also undermine the authority of political elites. In the European colonies, technology was at once the means by which the colony was established and the pathway to its dismantling. The advances of transportation, communication, and production that colonizing powers introduced into Latin America, the East Indies, Africa, and other regions allowed for the effective harnessing of local natural resources and human energies. The diffusion of even the most sophisticated of technologies leads to adoption, exploitation, and improvement by local populations. Native populations in colonies were employed to operate the factories, trains, and radio and telegraph transmitters. The authority of colonizing political elites was reduced as it became clear that a monopoly over the use of technology could not be maintained indefinitely.

Consequences

Technology will continue to figure prominently in those historical and sociological accounts in which nationalism is regarded as a feature of modernity and in which industrialization is considered to be a key explanatory factor for the emergence and spread of nationalism. The wide circulation of new ideas about national identity within a society gives life to a nationalist project. Indeed, the spread of nationalism has relied on the increasingly mediated character of modern communications. Modern political messages are never exchanged directly between politician and the polis but between politician and mass audience, as mediated by communications technologies. Because the mass media are subject to control by individuals and small groups, the spread of nationalism, too, is subject to hegemonic control. It is for this reason that Habermas points out that nationalism is "by definition susceptible to manipulative misuse by political elites" (1995, 564). The cultural context in which appeals for nationalist sentiment are made will therefore continue to be of central interest to scholars of technology and nationalism.

Studies of nationalism may use both qualitative and quantitative inquiry, poetry and statistics, and firsthand accounts and theoretical reflections to demonstrate the complexity and richness of the increasingly mediated social world of emerging nationalist projects. Interdisciplinary accounts in particular help to show when and in what circumstances members of political and social elites find it possible to mobilize popular sentiment in support of nationalism and when and in what circumstances the nationalist strategy is likely actually to succeed.

The most promising approaches to technology and nationalism are not likely to deal directly with the question of whether technology is primarily a cause or effect of nationalism. In social and historical research in which large-scale movements of people and ideas occur, there are too many variables that are liable to confound such an enterprise. In the case of the many nation-states established in the 19th century, there is the added barrier of using archives and sources that, even where they are accurate and reliable, must be reinterpreted by the historian. Accounts that seek to describe and explain the social construction of particular technological formations in relation to particular nationalist projects have the potential to extend our understanding of how the dialectic of ideology and technology unfolds in nationalist movements.

The Internet is the most recent media innovation in history within which the relationship of technology to nationalism must be assessed. Four issues are worthy of examination in connection to this new medium.

First, it should be noted that digital technologies are changing the way that individuals participate in the development of a national identity. The Internet is itself becoming a kind of national culture, and the global and the local become entwined for many people using the Internet. While analog media (LP records and tape recordings, for example) gave some priority and privilege to the original cultural object, digital media allow for endless reproduction of cultural texts at almost no cost, and with little direct controls available to monitor this reproduction. The power of the nation-state has been curtailed to the extent that digital culture has escaped the power to control it fully. If the state's defining feature is that of the prerogative to use force legitimated by law, some part of that force has been mitigated or removed.

Second, the convergent nature of the Internet has yet to be understood fully in relationship to the development and promulgation of nationalist programs. Historical media that have had a formative influence on nationalism, such as the printing press, radio, and television, are all reproduced on the Internet. Text, sound, and moving images are presented within the same communications channel.

Tibetan monks surf the net at an Internet cafe in Lhasa of the Tibet Autonomous Region, China, in 2006.

Since each converging medium is quite different in terms both of how it is interpreted by audiences as a medium and how its messages influence users, the proportionate use of various media on the Internet may determine the rate and means by which nationalist projects develop.

Third, the relative impermeability, or resistance to outside influence, of distributed networks means that the Internet may potentially become less a force for global understanding, as its more optimistic proponents claim, than for incremental resistance to openness. Local and regional groups that are small, robust, resilient, and relatively closed are likely to continue to form. The Internet may in this way discourage the brokering and coordination of subnational cultures that in the past have been the precursors of an emergent nationalism.

Finally, global diaspora communities, made up of emigrants from a home nation, are making use of the Internet in ways that are likely to change how national identity is developed and expressed. The creation of virtual communities by diaspora communities is occurring at a rapid rate. The Internet is used variously by prospective immigrants and new arrivals in many countries and has a function as well in assimilating new citizens. The increased ethnic churn in Western industrial democracies in the context of the creation of a large number of virtual communities with relatively impermeable cultural boundaries is likely to be of interest to scholars and students of technology and nationalism in the coming years.

Selected Bibliography

Adria, M. 2000. "Institutions of Higher Education and the Nationalist State." *British Journal of Sociology of Education* 21, no. 4: 573–588.

Adria, M. 2003. "Arms to Communications: Idealist and Pragmatist Strains of Canadian Thought on Technology and Nationalism." *Canadian Journal of Communication* 28:167–184.

Amir, S. 2004. "The Regime and the Airplane: High Technology and Nationalism." *Indonesia Bulletin of Science, Technology & Society* 24, no. 2: 107–114.

Anderson, B. 1991. *Imagined Communities: Reflections on the Origins and Spread of Nationalism.* Rev. ed. London: Verso.

Charland, M. 1986. "Technological Nationalism." *Canadian Journal of Political and Social Theory* 10, nos. 1–2: 196–220.

Deutsch, K. W. 1966. *Nationalism and Social Communication: An Inquiry into the Foundations of Nationality.* 2nd ed. Cambridge, MA: MIT Press.

Giddens, A. 1985. *The Nation-State and Violence.* Cambridge: Polity Press.

Habermas, J. 1995. "The European Nation-State—Its Achievements and Limits." In *Mapping the Nation*, edited by G. Balakrishnan. London: Verso.

Hayes, J. E. 2000. *Radio Nation: Communication, Popular Culture, and Nationalism.* Tucson: University of Arizona Press.

Innis, H. A. 1951. *The Bias of Communication.* Toronto: University of Toronto Press.

McLuhan, M. 1963. *Understanding Media: The Extensions of Man.* New York: Signet.

Mrázek, R. 2002. *Engineers of Happy Land: Technology and Nationalism in a Colony.* Princeton, NJ: Princeton University Press.

Poster, M. 1999. "National Identities and Communications Technologies." *The Information Society* 15:235–240.

Rogers, E. 1995. *Diffusion of Innovations.* New York: Free Press.

Terrorism and Nationalism

Virginie Mamadouh

Relevance

Since September 11, 2001, terrorism has been represented as intrinsically connected to the Islamic fundamentalism of Al Qaeda and similar jihadist movements; prior to that, it was more often associated with such nationalist movements as the Irish Republican Army (IRA) in Northern Ireland, the Basque nationalists of Euskadi Ta Askatasuna (ETA) in the Basque country, the Tamil Tigers in Sri Lanka, and diverse Palestinian organizations. This article deals with terrorism and its links with nationalism. Terrorism is only one of the instruments nationalist movements can use to advance their cause. Likewise, nationalism is only one of the possible ideologies used by terrorists to justify their acts. It is the overlap between the two that is the focus of this article.

The review begins with conceptual issues about terrorism and nationalism. It then addresses the historic origins of terrorism and its development in modern times. The Memorial Institute for the Prevention of Terrorism (MIPT) Terrorism Knowledge Base is used to discuss the dimensions and impact of terrorism since 1980 to show that nationalist demands remain predominant motivations among terrorist movements and to show the distribution of terrorist attacks among world regions. Finally, consequences and ramifications are addressed in terms of the direct costs of the destruction and the indirect consequences in the targeted communities.

Defining Terrorism and Other Forms of Violence: Terrorist or Freedom Fighter?

Although it is widely understood that terrorism implies the use of physical violence (or the threat to use it), it is open to discussion when political violence is or is not terrorism. Definitions coined by policy makers, legislators, intelligence services and counterterrorist agencies, analysts, scholars, or opinion makers differ. Analyzing 109 definitions of terrorism, Alex Schmid identified 22 categories of expressions used to characterize terrorism. The most frequently named element is by far "violence" (84 percent of the definitions), followed by "political" and "fear" (see Table 1). Most definitions of terrorism share some basic elements: the political use of violence against indiscriminate targets (for example, a crowd at a station) with the aim of creating fear among the population as a way of gaining leverage on decision makers. The latter means that in terrorist campaigns, the targets of the demands (governments, media) differ from the targets of the acts themselves (often random, innocent victims).

Table 1 Frequencies of the Top 12 Definitional Elements in 109 Definitions of Terrorism (occurring in 20 percent or more of the collected definitions)*

Element	Rank	Frequency, %
Violence, force	1	83.5
Political	2	65.0
Fear, terror emphasized	3	51.0
Threat	4	47.0
(Psychological) effects and (anticipated) reactions	5	41.5
Victim-target differentiation	6	37.5
Purposive, planned, systematic, organized action	7	32.0
Method of combat, strategy, tactic	8	30.5
Extra-normality, in breach of accepted rules, without humanitarian constraints	9	30.0
Coercion, extortion, induction of compliance	10	28.0
Publicity aspect	11	21.5
Arbitrariness; impersonal, random character, indiscrimination	12	21.0

*Source: Schmid and Jongman 1988, 5–6.

Besides this common ground, several areas of contention and discussion emerge. Is the assassination of a politician terrorism? Is terrorism always the work of illegal movements, or can states also be accused of terrorism? Is armed resistance against an illegitimate regime terrorism? Is an act of violence that is not claimed publicly by an organization with articulated demands terrorism or just crime? Can an isolated individual acting alone be considered a terrorist? Let's consider these five issues in turn.

The first question concerns the destabilizing effect of murder. While a political assassination does destabilize state and society, it generally does not generate the same feelings of insecurity as "blind" attacks on crowds of civilians. Nevertheless the distinction between the two is not easy to draw: some groups will attack soldiers or policemen because the group sees them as representatives of the state agency, even if they obviously do not have a position of power in that agency; other groups will even attack any citizens of the state that they are fighting against, because they are seen as representatives of that state.

The second question is key to the distinction between political violence by state agencies and by nonstate actors. Some prefer to limit the use of the word "terrorism" to nonstate actors as rebellious movements, while others underline that terrorist activities can be sponsored by states and even carried on by state agencies. The difference between regular violent activities of the state, such as war and terrorism, is their legality. State terrorism consists of uses of violence that do not respect the national and international legal frameworks that regulate the activities of police and army forces—including rules of war. Think, for example, of the bombing of residential neighborhoods, the use of torture, or the assassination of political opponents. Although it is important to include state terrorism and state-sponsored terrorism in a discussion of the relations between terrorism and nationalism, it is imperative to distinguish these two types of terrorism: terrorism from below (i.e., grassroots terrorism) and terrorism from above (i.e., state terrorism).

The third question refers to the often-quoted paradox that someone's terrorist might be someone else's freedom fighter. Although some people reject any use of violence by principle, most people accept the use of violence for legitimate objectives, for example, to police the public space, to protect the national territory, and, possibly, to eliminate threats to national sovereignty. In that case, political violence can be legitimate, depending on the objectives of the perpetrators. Protagonists and their activities are therefore viewed differently. While from the one side, the acts of a group might be seen as terrorist attacks on a legitimate regime, from the other side, they might appear as legitimate acts of resistance against an abusive regime. Still, in academic writings, it is generally agreed that the targeting of noncombatants qualifies the use of force as terrorism, whatever the motives of the action are.

The fourth question concerns the distinction between terrorism and crime. Limits between crime and terrorism are blurred. Terrorist groups often carry out criminal activities (bank robberies, racketeering, arms trade, drugs trade, kidnapping, trafficking, and so on) to finance their movements, and political rhetoric about self-determination might be used to cover up criminal activities, for example, to keep state agencies out of a region of drugs production or a crucial route for an illegal trade. In the absence of political motives and of the publication of these motives and demands by a terrorist organization, it is difficult to label an act of violence as terrorism. Obviously, such an act of blind violence generates fear among the population and has an effect quite similar to terrorism, but the fact that no political rationalization is offered, that violence is not an instrument to achieve political goals but an end in itself should keep us from putting it in the same category as terrorist acts. On the other hand, a political organization might choose not to claim a terrorist act to create confusion and fear among the population, while sometimes several competing groups claim responsibility for the same attack. The anthrax letters sent through the mail in the United States after 9/11 that killed five people are generally seen as a terrorist campaign, despite the fact that no information is available about the origin of these letters and the purpose of the perpetrators.

The fifth and last question pertains to the idea that terrorism is an organized collective action. Single, isolated individuals (so-called lone wolves) are generally not included in accounts of terrorism, although it depends on the context. Compare the perception of the two political murders in the Netherlands, a western European country where politics has long been very boring and peaceful. Politician Pim Fortuyn was killed in May 2002 by an animal rights' activist who was perceived as a lone wolf, and the murder was not seen as an act of terrorism. However, one and a half years later, when film director Theo van Gogh was killed in November 2004 by an Islamist fundamentalist, this was perceived as an element in an international terrorist threat, even if there was no reason to believe that any transnational terrorist network commissioned it. The label terrorism reflects in both cases the perception that this individual was inspired by, and connected in some way with, broader movements justifying terrorism.

Nationalism as Motivation for Terrorism

As definitions, typologies of terrorism are very diverse, depending on the characteristics chosen to classify terrorist incidents: the actors, the victims, the tactics, the targets, the motivations, and so on (see Schmid and Jongman 1988, 40ff). Different types of terrorism are generally distinguished according to the political background of the perpetrators. Political arguments have several functions: they are used to analyze the situation, to name and represent problems, to present and promote specific solutions to these problems, to legitimate demands, to legitimate tactics and the use of violence in particular, and to remember to motivate combatants, to mobilize support for combatants, and to essentialize differences between opposed camps.

Nationalism is only one of the many discourses that can motivate the use of terrorism. It is possible to identify terrorist activities, linked to virtually any political ideology—left or right—except those founded on pacifism. Religious justifications of terrorism have been articulated in most religions, although nowadays Islamic terrorism is the most publicized. Frequently, the distinction between nationalism and other motivations is blurred: for example, in leftist nationalist movements and when national identities are religiously defined.

Nationalism comes in many guises, ranging from national emancipation movements to nation-building imposed from above by the state. Nationalist movements can use terrorism among other forms of political activism. Alternative tactics include all kinds of legal collective actions, ranging from demonstrations to petitions, from strikes to boycotts, from elections to court cases, depending on the political opportunity structure of the political arena they are operating in. Terrorism is not likely to be used when there are plenty of legal ways to organize and mobilize a national group. On the other hand, it is an unlikely tactic when repression is very harsh. Apart from local opportunities, tactical decisions are also influenced by foreign actors who might provide logistical help and moral support, and who might encourage or discourage local groups to use political violence.

Liberation wars against foreign occupation or colonial rule generally involve terrorist episodes in which nationalist movements act in the name of a state that is not yet sovereign. In that case, one rather talks about a national liberation front or a national liberation army. Similarly, state revolutionaries can invoke nationalism against the state and claim to act in the name of the people against a regime that is usurping national sovereignty.

Alternatively, nationalism can be invoked by the political elite to outlaw political challengers, to prevent a popular movement from access to power, and to exclude, expel, or even annihilate a minority group framed as a threat to national security or the territorial integrity of the state.

State terrorism is also only one among various tactics available to state agencies to mobilize and control the population of the state territory. State terrorism is incompatible with liberal democracy based on the rule of law, political and civic rights, and free elections. A democratic state will try to assimilate a minority or persuade it to leave the territory, through financial incentives for emigrating or for adopting a new language, culture, or way of life, rather than eliminating it physically. States can also be involved in terrorist activities on foreign soil, supporting terrorist organizations abroad, as part of their foreign policies, for example, to destabilize a regime they would prefer to see replaced. State-supported terrorism is not compatible with international law. Accusations of sponsoring terrorism are frequently made against Iran and Pakistan but also against the United Kingdom and the United States. The Taliban regime's support of Al Qaeda was used as the justification for the bombing and invasion of Afghanistan by a U.S.-led coalition in retaliation for the Al Qaeda attacks on September 11, 2001.

The state-centered thinking that characterizes nationalism is not foreign to analysts: they distinguish between domestic and international terrorism. Domestic terrorism refers to incidents by local nationals against a domestic target. International terrorism involves the crossing of state borders. When it comes to the terrorists themselves and their organizations, crossing international borders has always been important: a neighboring country can be a safe haven for domestic terrorists—where they can recover and regroup, train and organize between terrorist strikes in their own country. Diasporas have been instrumental to many nationalist terrorist groups, supporting them with money, assistance, and new recruits. International terrorism refers instead to groups that target national targets abroad (for example, diplomats, embassies, representative businesses, or even nationals); groups that target foreign representatives in the country (for example, foreign diplomats, foreign embassies, foreign branches, or even foreign citizens); or groups whose acts or objectives are transnational (for example, hijacking a plane during an international flight or articulating grievances about an international agreement).

All in all, terrorism has an outspoken negative connotation. Labeling a group "terrorist" is a way of discrediting its political objectives. The protagonists will rather call themselves militants, activists, revolutionaries, paramilitaries, soldiers, or people's freedom fighters. This labeling is not only a matter of choosing sides; the general assessment can change over time. Once widely labeled as terrorists by the international community, Menachem Begin (*Irgun* against British rule in Palestine), Yasir Arafat (Fatah against Israeli occupation), and Nelson Mandela (African National Congress against the apartheid regime in South Africa) were ultimately granted Nobel Peace Prizes for their efforts to defend the interests of their nations: Menachem Begin with Mohamed Anwar Al-Sadat in 1978, Yasir Arafat with Shimon Peres and Yitzhak Rabin in 1994, and Nelson Mandela with

Frederik Willem de Klerk in 1993. They are now widely recognized as major "freedom fighters" of the Israeli nation, the Palestinian nation, and the South African nation, respectively.

Origins

Despite the impression that the numerous commentators might give on the tragic events of September 11, 2001, terrorism is not a recent phenomenon. Historical accounts of terrorism commonly acknowledge the existence of terrorist movements like the *sicarri*—a religious sect in the Zealot struggle in Palestine against Roman rule (AD 66–73)—and the Hashshashin (or Assassins)—an Islamic sect, killing officials (prefects, governors, caliphs) of the Abbasid Caliphate from the 11th to the 13th centuries. According to the American historian Walter Laqueur (1977, 11) systematic terrorism began in the second half of the 19th century in Europe, after the French Revolution (and its regicide) and the rise of nationalism throughout Europe.

The terms "terror" and "terrorism" are modern terms, associated with the French Revolution and, more specifically, with two periods: the establishment of an exception court and massacres in prisons in Paris and other cities during August–September 1792, and the period from June 1793 to July 1794. This later period, under the leadership of the most radical faction of the Jacobins, is known as the Reign of Terror. This revolutionary government used violence to combat the "enemies of the people" at the borders and inside the national territory. The Jacobins used the word *terreur* in a positive sense and justified the use of it: "*La terreur n'est autre chose que la justice prompte, sévère, inflexible*" ("Terror is nothing other than prompt, severe, inflexible justice"), as goes the famous quote by Robespierre, the leader of the Jacobins at the Convention in February 1793, or "*Tous les moyens sont légitimes pour lutter contre les tyrans*" ("All means are legitimate against tyrants") by Babeuf in 1792. Revolutionary courts condemned thousands to the guillotine, which became the symbol of the age (although, strictly speaking, the former King Louis XVI was executed before the start of the Reign of Terror). The period June–July 1794 is even called The Great Terror; it started with the removal of the advocate at revolutionary courts and ended with the execution of Robespierre himself on July 28, 1794. After that episode, the negative connotation of the word became widespread, as in Burke's famous phrase about the French Revolution, written in 1795, "thousands of those hell hounds called terrorists."

Later, the word "terror" was widely used during revolutionary periods to characterize systematic political violence by either side of the revolution, such as the Red Terror and White Terror during the Russian Civil War that followed the 1917 Revolution.

Late-19th- and Early-20th-Century Terrorism

By the end of the 19th century, terrorism was a widespread tactic used among revolutionaries, anarchists, and nationalists: Russian revolutionaries, Irish nationalists, Indian groups in Bengal, Macedonians, Serbs or Armenians, Polish socialists, and anarchists and their "propaganda by deed" in France, Italy, Spain, and the United States. Earlier in the United States, the Ku Klux Klan used terrorism to advocate white supremacy in southern states during the Reconstruction period (1866–1870) after the U.S. Civil War. The second Ku Klux Klan (1915–1944), inspired by *The Birth of a Nation*, a controversial film released in 1915, followed suit with a similar ideology and violent attacks. Finally, individual Klan groups reappeared against civil rights movements from the beginning of the 1950s onward.

The assassination of Franz Ferdinand, the heir of the Austro-Hungarian empire, on June 28, 1914, in Sarajevo by a Serbian nationalist, was the famous direct cause of World War I. Paradoxically, antiwar activists also used terrorism, such as the Preparedness Day bombing in San Francisco on July 22, 1916, of a parade that was held in anticipation of the entry of the United States into that war.

After the Great War, nationalism became an even more important motivation for terrorism. Next to separatist movements in Ireland and Bretagne, right-wing terrorism increased during the 1920s in many European countries. In colonized countries, terrorism was also an option for movements claiming independence, especially in the British empire: the Muslim Brotherhood and Young Egypt in British Egypt, and *Irgun* and LEHI (Fighters for the Freedom of Israel, also known as the Stern Gang) in British Palestine. During World War II, nationalism inspired resistance movements to fascist regimes and German occupation.

Terrorism after World War II

After 1945, liberation movements in colonized countries often used terrorism, a noticeable example being the Algerian War of Independence (1954–1962).

In the 1960s and 1970s, terrorism was used by nationalist/separatist and leftist movements and movements combining both orientations. The symbolic landmark of political and social mobilization across the Western world—1968—was also a watershed for the radicalization of many small leftist revolutionary groups all over the world. The most famous exponent of that movement was probably the *Rote Armee Fraktion* (the Red Army Faction, also known as the Baader-Meinhof Group) in West Germany. In the United States, there were the Weathermen, the Black Liberation Army, and the Symbionese Liberation Army.

Nationalist/separatist movements using terrorism in that period were numerous in Western Europe, especially in Northern Ireland (IRA, Provisional IRA, and their opponents the Ulster Defense Association [UDA], and the Ulster Volunteers Force [UVF]), in the Basque country (ETA), and to a lesser extent in Catalonia, Corsica, Bretagne, South Tyrol, and the like. In North America, similar nationalist movements included the "Front de libération du Québec" (Québec Liberation

Front) in the 1960s and the Puerto Rican Fuerzas Armadas de Liberación Nacional (Armed Forces of National Liberation [FALN]) in the 1970s and 1980s. In South Africa, the African National Congress (ANC) turned in 1961 to political violence to defend the rights of the black population against the apartheid regime.

Nationalist/separatist movements in former colonies, generally unsatisfied with the territorial arrangements agreed on at independence, used terrorism against the new state. Of these many occurrences, most conflicts, up to this day, have not been solved, and terrorist campaigns are still going on: Kurdish organizations, especially the Kurdistan Workers Party (PPK, also known as KADEK and *KongraGel*) against the Turkish state, Palestinian organizations (Fatah, the Popular Front for the Liberation of Palestine [PFLP], PDFLP, Hamas, and many others since) against the Israeli state and against Israeli occupation of the Palestinian territories, the Liberation Tigers of Tamil Eelam (LTTE) in Sri Lanka, and so on. Sometimes claims were addressed to the former colonial state, as with the terrorist campaign of the South Moluccan Suicide Commando group and other Moluccan secessionist groups in the Netherlands in 1975 and 1978, demanding independence from Indonesia.

The 1970s also saw the emergence of international terrorism: terrorist groups of different countries working closely together and terrorist attacks being organized in different countries at the same time. From 1968 onward, airline hijacking increased dramatically, culminating in September 1970 when the PFLP simultaneously hijacked four planes to land them on Dawson's Field in Jordan. In September 1972, the Palestinian group Black September took hostages and murdered Israeli athletes during the Olympic Games in Munich, Germany. The Japanese Red Army is another example of a group operating internationally.

Right-wing terrorist activities should not be forgotten, especially in Latin America and in western Europe, as they are also inspired by nationalist ideologies to resist leftist movements. In Italy, Ordine Nuovo (New Order) bombed Piazza Fontana in Milan (1969), the Rome-Messia train (1970), an anti-fascist demonstration in Brescia (1974), and Central Station in Bologna (1980).

Terrorism since 1980

Since 1980, leftist radical movements seem to have vanished in the West and increased in the global South, for example, the Communista del Peru Sendero Luminoso (Shining Path) in Peru from 1980 onward and, later, Ejército Zapatista de Liberación Nacional (EZLN, the Zapatista Army of National Liberation) in Mexico.

Nationalist/separatist movements and right-wing nationalist movements remained important terrorist groups, but obviously the dynamics of conflict changed. For example, in the Basque country, ETA unexpectedly continued its terrorist campaign against the Spanish state after the democratization and decentralization of the state that gave the Basque country as a region comprehensive competencies. Where conflict resolution progressed, the splintering of the separatist groups could fuel new terrorist campaigns (for example, the bombing in Omagh in Northern Ireland on August 15, 1988, by the Real IRA after the Good Friday Agreement). In the case of the Palestinian cause, objectives and grievances changed with the official recognition of Israel and the establishment of the Palestinian Authority and the emergence of new—religiously inspired—organizations alongside the traditionally left-wing and secular organizations united in the Palestine Liberation Organization (PLO).

Tactics also changed. The major "innovation" of the late 20th century was the deployment of suicide bombers. Suicide attacks by combatants were not new in war situations but were less common as terrorist tactics, until the beginning of the 1980s when embassies and U.S. and French army barracks were bombed in Beirut during the Lebanese Civil War. It has since been extensively used, mainly by the Tamil Tigers in Sri Lanka (including the assassination of the former Indian prime minister Rajiv Gandhi in 1991 near Chennai, India) and by Islamic terrorists in the Arab and Muslim world, especially in Palestine/Israel, Lebanon, and more recently, Iraq, and around the world.

Newcomers on the terrorist scene include new separatist movements, which appeared with the disintegration of federations formerly held together by a centralist and monopolistic party (Union of Soviet Socialist Republics, Yugoslavia), with the enduring conflict in and around Chechnya being the most dramatic instance. In the United States, the most deadly attack before 2001 was the Oklahoma City bombing on the Alfred P. Murrah Federal Building on April 19, 1995, which killed almost 170 people, including 19 children. The two men convicted of the bombing, Timothy McVeigh and Terry Nichols, were related to the militia movement and claimed that this attack on a federal agency was a revenge for the siege of a Davidian ranch in Waco, Texas, by a federal agency (the Bureau of Alcohol, Tobacco, and Firearms) that ended with a fire on April 19, 1993, killing over 70 followers, including many children. Acting in the name of the people against the state is also a form of nationalist terrorism.

Finally, the most important change in the terrorist landscape of the past decade has been the expansion of Islamic terrorism across the world, and especially its global networks, such as Al Qaeda, the organization claiming responsibility for the attacks on New York City and Washington on September 11, 2001. Originating in the jihad against communist rule in Afghanistan, supported at the time by the U.S. administration as a pawn in the U.S. containment policy toward the Soviet Union, the objectives of this network developed into a holy war against U.S. intervention in the Middle East, especially against the presence of U.S. troops in Saudi Arabia. Islamic groups using terrorism generally aimed at changing state institutions into an Islamic state might also have separatist ambitions for territories inhabited by a Muslim population confronted with a secular state or a state associated with another religion, or supranational ambitions to federate Muslim populations in a new, larger supranational Islamic state.

On September 11, 2001, Al Qaeda terrorists crashed two commercial passenger airplanes into the twin towers of the World Trade Center in New York City. Although religious groups have supplanted them in terms of injuries and fatalities, nationalist groups remain responsible for the largest number of terrorist incidents across the world. (AP/Wide World Photos)

Dimensions

To sketch the dimensions and the impact of terrorism, we can rely on existing databases registering terrorist incidents. In this section, I use the Terrorism Knowledge Base (TKB, available at www.tkb.org). The TKB is an American initiative supported by the Memorial Institute for the Prevention of Terrorism (MIPT), the Department of Homeland Security (DHS), DFI International, RAND Corporation, and the American Terrorism Study. It is important to remain aware of the limitations of such sources. The TKB is based on the RAND Terrorism Chronology 1968–1997 and RAND-MIPT Terrorism Incident Database (1998–present). Both are limited to terrorism incidents by nonstate actors and are based on open source materials, such as newspapers, not on secret intelligence collected by state agencies. The first source was limited to international terrorism incidents; the second also included domestic terrorism. Despite these limitations, the database provides an insightful overview of the phenomenon, registering incidents, injuries, and fatalities. It will be used here to assess the importance of nationalism as a motivation of terrorist acts, compared with other claims, and to assess the impact of terrorism in different regions of the world. Similar data on state terrorism are not available, but reports and estimations published about the civilian victims in Chechnya, Palestine, Afghanistan, and, foremost, Iraq suggest much higher figures.

To differentiate among the main dimensions of terrorism, we can look at the perpetrators. The TKB distinguishes 11 types of terrorist movements: anarchist, antiglobalization, communist/socialist, environmental, leftist, nationalist/separatist, other, racist, religious, right-wing conservative, and right-wing reactionary. It is unclear how the coding went for groups with mixed motives, for example, communist and nationalist, anarchist and environmentalist, religious and right-wing conservative, right-wing reactionary and nationalist.

During the period 1980–2005, nationalist/separatist religious groups accounted for almost a third of terrorist incidents (30 percent) followed by leftist groups (26 percent) and religious groups (24 percent). Looking at casualties, religious motivations ranked first with 54 percent of the injuries and 52 percent of fatalities, far above nationalist motives (36 percent each), while the numerous leftist and communist/socialist terrorist incidents caused far less human suffering. Over time, nationalist terrorism lost its predominance, while religious terrorism grew starkly, especially after 1990 (see Table 2).

As for the overall impact of terrorism, the Middle East is by any account the region most affected by terrorism, with 35 percent of the incidents, 34 percent of the injuries, and 40 percent of the fatalities located there (Table 3). Western Europe ranks second in terms of incidents (20 percent), but only fifth for injuries and seventh for fatalities. South Asia ranks third in terms of incidents but is the second most affected region in terms of injuries and fatalities, while North America, the least affected region in terms of incidents, ranks third in terms of fatalities due to the unusual scope of the attacks of September 11, 2001, with almost 3,000 fatalities for one single incident.

Table 2   The Declining Importance of Nationalist/Separatist Groups*

	1968–1969		1970–1979		1980–1989		1990–1999		2000–2005	
	n	%	n	%	n	%	n	%	n	%
Incidents										
Nationalist/separatist	32	43.8	416	45.1	883	39.3	668	33.0	2,204	38.7
Religious		0	61	6.6	206	9.2	305	15.1	1,534	27.0
Injuries										
Nationalist/separatist	163	74.4	1,488	60.5	4,078	57.2	5,825	25.8	13,471	38.5
Religious		0	65	2.6	843	11.8	15,924	70.4	18,098	51.7
Fatalities										
Nationalist/separatist	25	71.4	635	59.6	1,715	60.0	1,272	34.2	5,414	32.5
Religious		0	24	2.3	735	25.7	1,854	49.8	9,427	56.6

*Source: MIPT Terrorism Knowledge Base (accessed October 24, 2006).

Table 3 Terrorist Incidents (Nonstate Terrorism) by Region, 1980–2005*

	Incidents		Injuries		Fatalities	
	n	%	n	%	n	%
Africa	890	3.8	8,462	10.1	3,256	9.8
East & Central Asia	215	0.9	5,324	6.4	223	0.7
Southeast Asia & Oceania	690	3.0	3,752	4.5	1,143	3.4
South Asia	4,134	17.8	19,649	23.5	6,791	20.4
Middle East/Persian Gulf	8,126	35.1	28,668	34.3	13,266	39.8
Eastern Europe	1,312	5.7	5,010	6.0	1,933	5.8
Western Europe	4,623	20.0	5,096	6.1	1,157	3.5
North America	281	1.2	4,054	4.9	3,533	10.6
Latin America & the Caribbean	2,890	12.5	3,566	4.3	1,991	6.0
Total	23,161	100	83,581	100	33,293	100

*Source: MIPT Terrorism Knowledge Base (accessed October 24, 2006).

Unfortunately, it is not possible to generate cross-tabulations that would show whether nationalist terrorist groups cluster in certain world regions, but it is likely that the typical European pattern (relatively less casualties for relatively more incidents) is the likely result of the predominance of nationalist/separatist terrorism in that part of the world.

Moreover, we can look at the most devastating terrorist attacks of the past five years, those with more than 100 casualties:

- The attacks on New York and Washington (with about 3,000 casualties), September 11, 2001
- Mumbai's train bombing (with about 200 casualties), July 11, 2006
- Bali's holiday resort bombing (with about 200 casualties), October 12, 2002
- Madrid's train bombing (with about 200 casualties), March 11, 2004
- Manila's ferry bombing (with about 120 casualties), February 27, 2004

To this list, one should add two hostage crises where high numbers of people were killed during the raid of Russian forces that ended these sieges:

- The Beslan school siege (with about 350 civilian casualties), September 1–3, 2004
- The Moscow theater hostage crisis (with about 130 casualties among the hostages), October 23–26, 2002

All these attacks were perpetrated by Islamic organizations. All attacks took place in localities where Muslims were a minority, but in very different parts of the world: North America, Western Europe, South Asia, Southeast Asia, and Russia. Many of these organizations were transnational and primarily religious, but some of them can also be characterized as nationalist/separatist: the Abu Sayyaf Group in the Philippines (Mindanao) and the Chechen separatists in the Russian federation.

Consequences

The effects of terrorism are manifold. The most obvious consequences are the direct costs of the destruction inflicted by terrorists. It includes the loss of lives and the physical injuries mentioned above, but also psychological disorders, the destruction of infrastructure (sometimes complete cities), and the lasting disruption of everyday life and economic life. Economic costs increase when a campaign lasts, because tourists and foreign investors stay away and wealthier, educated, and dynamic people leave for better places. In the case of New York City, numerous studies addressed the physical, economical, and social consequences of the destruction of September 11, 2001. But these consequences are rather limited compared to the impact of state terrorism on cities: think of the systematic destruction of British, German, and Japanese cities during World War II, or more recently, the fate of cities like Grozny, Jenin, Ramallah, Gaza, Baghdad, and Kabul.

Beyond these direct costs are many indirect costs, such as the disruption of public order and the destruction of trust in society, plus the costs of counterterrorism policies and attempts to prevent further terrorist incidents.

Reactions to terrorism often trigger political violence from state and nonstate actors, including the violent repressive policies of a state trying to isolate terrorist groups from their grassroots and violent action groups that decide to rescue the state against terrorism by using the same methods. This vicious circle frequently leads to civil war. In the Algerian War of Independence, the Front de libération nationale (FLN) was countered by state terrorism (including the widespread use of torture) and, in 1961–1962, by the grassroots terrorism against independence of the Organisation de l'armée secrète (OAS), while in the Basque country, the ETA had to face the Grupos Antiterroristas de Liberación (GAL, Antiterrorist Liberation Groups) in the 1980s. Similarly, terrorism from above often generated violent resistance, as shown in the rise of bottom-up terrorism in territories under military occupation (Israel/Palestine Territories, Iraq, Afghanistan, Chechnya).

Another type of consequence consists of changes in the built environment to prevent terrorism and protect possible targets from it. Think of the hardening of potential targets to attempt to protect individuals, buildings, neighborhoods, or even complete regions. In Belfast, urban restructuring to defend the inner city against bombing attacks by the IRA took the form of a "ring of steel" in the 1980s, with security gates and sealed streets. The ring of steel in London, designed to protect the city against the IRA, also included a circulation plan, banning cars from the inner city, and regulating access to the city, and was completed after September 11, 2001, and the attacks of July 2005 to protect the city from homegrown Islamic terrorism. Another famous example is the security fence built by Israel "to keep Palestinian suicide bombers out of Israel," locking Palestinian communities in enclaves surrounded by the wall and greatly impeding the personal mobility of Palestinians and the viability of the Palestinian economy.

Changes in policing also involved the militarization of everyday life with the increased presence of security guards on the streets, at the entrances of buildings, in stations, and on public transportation, including identity checks in public space, closed-circuit television surveillance (CCTV), registration of activities, such as library borrowings, listening to phone calls, scanning emails, and other preventive interventions that severely impinged on the civil rights and privacy of citizens. The hidden costs of such reduction of personal freedom and institutionalized fear are high, if not always directly visible. The same instruments could easily have been used to enhance state control over citizens for other purposes. Control procedures at airports, ports, and border crossings have greatly increased costs—in time and money—for millions of travelers and for freight traffic.

In the United States, dramatic reforms in this field were introduced by the USA PATRIOT Act (in full, the Uniting and Strengthening America by Providing Appropriate Tools Required to Intercept and Obstruct Terrorism Act) of 2001 and the creation of the Department of Homeland Security in November 2002.

Counterterrorism involves different levels of government besides national agencies, as well as private actors such as security firms at offices, factories, schools, and gated communities. Numerous international (and regional multilateral) conventions deal with acts of terrorism, to begin with, the 1963 Tokyo convention regarding air safety. The hijacking of planes has long been the primary concern of international cooperation regarding terrorism. More recently, states have cooperated to prevent and counteract the financing of terrorist organizations and their activities. There are several lists of terrorist organizations, the national ones and those compiled by supranational organizations like the United Nations and the European Union. The lists are used to impose travel limitations and financial penalties on individuals connected to these organizations identified as terrorist.

International terrorism has been widely acknowledged as a specific security threat of great importance. Approaches differ, however; American policies focus on rogue states, states that are suspected to support and promote terrorism (see the National Security Strategy 2002 and 2006), whereas European policies focus on failed states that are not functioning properly, that is, not controlling their territory so that it can be used as a safe haven by terrorism networks (see the European Security Strategy adopted by the European Council in 2003). Policy consequences of these different approaches are great. The U.S. targets a few rogue states and favors preemptive military interventions to deal with them, while most European states and the European Union are concerned with numerous failed states and try to promote security through development aid and good governance.

Since 9/11, the United States has led an international campaign against international terrorism known as the War on Terror (also known as the Global War on Terrorism, GWOT). The United States could count on the support of many states, including other liberal democracies, at the time of the invasion of Afghanistan in 2001, but far fewer for the invasion of Iraq in 2003. Criticisms, inside and outside the United States, of the War on Terror are numerous and rising, they pertain to the notion of preemptive war, U.S. unilateralism, the justification of the invasion of Iraq, the costs of the war, abuses on the scene, and foremost, the consequences for civil liberties.

Last but not least, terrorism has a serious impact on the nationalist ideologies that it is supposed to serve or oppose. It can foster solidarity in both camps, especially in the camp of the targets. Think of the U.S. response to the 9/11 attacks and the many expressions of solidarity with New Yorkers from all over the country, and other parts of the world as well (remember the "We are all Americans" heading on the front page of *Le Monde* on September 13, 2001). On the other hand, terrorism is often divisive because different nationalist factions generally have different opinions about the need and the effectiveness of violent tactics. This can weaken a nationalist movement, erode its support in the population, and paralyze and jeopardize its ability to negotiate with the opposite side, because the methods—terrorist tactics—discredit the goals of the whole movement. Moreover, terrorism polarizes conflicts, as its horrendous consequences generally deepen the divide between contenders. It is not easy to make a political compromise with terrorists acceptable.

A final question is whether terrorism is a successful tactic. The American historian Walter Laqueur, who wrote many influential books on terrorists over the past three decades, claims it is not, with the noticeable exception of nationalist terrorism. Still, in these cases, terrorist groups are generally only one of the components of much broader nationalist movements, and then the question remains whether terrorism has been successful as a strategy, or whether the nationalist demands have been heard *despite* the use of terrorism. It is therefore not possible to claim that terrorism itself produced a new territorial arrangement, when in such a case, autonomy or independence is eventually granted.

In conclusion, nationalism and terrorism are not necessarily allies, but they often are associated with each other. In the recent past, many occurrences of terrorism from below and from above have been justified with nationalist ideologies of various kinds. Still, in the past decades, religious groups have supplanted nationalist groups as the major perpetrators of terrorist incidents. Nevertheless, it is important to remember that nationalist grievances are often high on the agenda of these religiously motivated terrorists, be it in Chechnya, Palestine, Afghanistan, or Iraq. In these many cases, religious arguments supplement nationalist demands rather than supplant them. Policies that take these nationalist demands seriously might therefore be more helpful than theological discussions to avert terrorism and reduce its appeal among the discontented.

Selected Bibliography

Coaffee, J. 2003. *Terrorism, Risk and the City: The Making of a Contemporary Urban Landscape.* Aldershot, UK: Ashgate.

European Council. 2003. *European Security Strategy: A Secure Europe in a Better World.* Brussels. http://ue.eu.int/uedocs/cmsUpload/78367.pdf.

Flint, C., ed. 2004. *The Geography of War and Peace: From Death Camps to Diplomats.* New York: Oxford University Press.

Graham, S., ed. 2004. *Cities, War and Terrorism: Towards an Urban Geopolitics.* Malden, MA: Blackwell.

Hewitt, K. 1983. "Place Annihilation: Area Bombing and the Fate of Urban Places." *Annals of the Association of American Geographers* 73, no. 2: 257–284.

Laqueur, W. 1977. *Terrorism.* Boston: Little, Brown and Company.

Laqueur, W. 2003. *No End to War: Terrorism in the Twenty-First Century.* New York: Continuum.

Laqueur, W., ed. 2004. *Voices of Terror: Manifestos, Writings and Manuals of Al Qaeda, Hamas, and Other Terrorists from around the World and throughout the Ages.* New York: Reed Press.

The National Security Strategy of the United States of America. 2002. President of the United States of America. Washington DC. www.whitehouse.gov/nsc/nss.html.

The National Security Strategy of the United States of America. 2006. President of the United States of America. Washington DC. www.whitehouse.gov/nsc/nss/2006.

Newman, D. 2003. "Barriers or Bridges? On Borders, Fences and Walls." *Tikkun Magazine* 18, no. 6: 54–58.

Schmid, A. P., and A. J. Jongman. 1988. *Political Terrorism: A New Guide to Actors, Authors, Concepts, Data Bases, Theories and Literature.* New Brunswick, NJ: Transaction Books.

Sorkin, M., and S. Zukin, eds. 2002. *After the World Trade Center: Rethinking New York City.* New York: Routledge.

Sparke, M. 1998. "Outsides Inside Patriotism: the Oklahoma Bombing and the Displacement of Heartland Geopolitics." In *Rethinking Geopolitics,* edited by G. Ó Tuathail and S. Dalby, 198–223. New York: Routledge.

Updike, J. 2006. *Terrorist.* New York: Alfred A. Knopf.

Alsace

David Allen Harvey

Chronology

1648	Most of Alsace is annexed to France following the Thirty Years' War.
1681	Strasbourg is incorporated into France.
1789	The French Revolution begins; Alsace is divided into Bas-Rhin (north) and Haut-Rhin (south).
1792	The French declare war against Austria and Prussia.
1798	Mulhouse is incorporated into France.
1806	Beginnings of the Continental System.
1815	Napoleon is defeated.
1848	Revolutions in France and Germany.
1870	The Franco-Prussian War begins.
1871	The Treaty of Frankfurt recognizes German annexation of Alsace and part of Lorraine.
1914	World War I begins; there is a brief French foray into the Haut-Rhin.
1918	Armistice ends World War I; Alsace is annexed to France.
1919	Triage Commissions determine the nationality of Alsatian residents.
1926	Formation of autonomist *Heimatbund*.
1939	War is declared between France and Germany; civilians are evacuated from border zones to the French interior.
1940	Germany is victorious and occupies northern France; Alsace is annexed to the Reich.
1944–1945	Alsace is liberated; Alsace is annexed to France.
1949	Schuman Note proposes Franco-German economic cooperation.
1953	Alsatian Waffen-SS members are tried in Bordeaux.
1957	The Treaty of Rome establishes a European Economic Community.
1968	Foundation of cultural autonomist Cercle René Schickelé.
1979	European Parliament is established in Strasbourg.
1997	Front National holds a national congress in Strasbourg.

Situating the Nation

Alsace's status as a frontier region is defined, first and foremost, by its geography. A narrow territory hemmed in between the Rhine to its east and the Vosges Mountains to its west, Alsace forms part of a broader region, running along the Rhine Valley from the Alps to the North Sea, which has historically been both a commercial and cultural crossroads and a contested frontier. Alsace was part of the ninth-century kingdom of Lotharingia, the middle state carved out of Charlemagne's empire, caught between the other Carolingian successor states, which were to serve as the historical cores for the emergence of the French and German nations. Later, Alsace, along with the Rhineland to its north, constituted the far western edge of the Holy Roman Empire. A patchwork of free imperial cities, tiny ecclesiastical and noble estates, and corners of larger fiefdoms extending beyond the region, Alsace was further divided by the Reformation, which left behind a mixed population of Catholics, Lutherans, and Calvinists, as well as a small Jewish minority.

Alsace has historically been linked by cultural and commercial ties to the other regions of the Rhine Valley, and its dialect is a form of German. Nevertheless, it was not until the French conquest of Alsace in the 17th century that this extremely heterogeneous region became politically unified as a province under a single ruler. The kingdom of France was able to annex much of the region following the Thirty Years' War in 1648, although Strasbourg was not incorporated into France until 1681 (and Mulhouse not until 1798). From the 17th century until the present, the political destinies of Alsace have been determined not by its inhabitants but by the broader European processes of state-building, revolution, and war.

Instituting the Nation

The 19th-century historian Fustel de Coulanges declared that "what made Alsace French was not Louis XIV; it was our Revolution. Since that moment, Alsace has followed all of our destinies, she has taken part in our life" (Harvey 2001, 12). The French Revolution opened an age of popular nationalism in which sovereignty derived from cohesive, self-aware communities of citizens rather than from dynastic monarchs with claims to divine right. The French Revolution ended the exceptional status that Alsace had enjoyed under the Old Regime (it had stood outside France's tariff frontiers, was exempt from the *gabelle* or salt tax, and Alsatian Protestants were not subject to the discriminatory measures applied to their counterparts elsewhere in France following the 1685 revocation of the Edict of Nantes), divided the province into the new departments of Bas-Rhin and Haut-Rhin, and introduced a new and deeply divisive revolutionary political culture. Alsace constituted the front line of the revolutionary regime's war against the dynastic powers of Europe, and the French national anthem, originally entitled the "War Song of the Rhine Army," was composed not in Marseilles but in Strasbourg. Alsatian textile industries, already expanding in the late 18th century, received a decisive boost from the incorporation of the Swiss canton of Mulhouse in 1798 and the exclusion of British goods from European markets under Napoleon's Continental System after 1806.

Following the defeat of Napoleon in 1815, Alsace remained an integral part of the French state, its politics and economic life dominated to a large degree by a small number of French-speaking, Protestant families whose fortunes had been made through industry and commerce. The majority of the inhabitants of the two

Rhine departments continued to speak a Germanic dialect, but few of them questioned their status as members of the French nation, and the waves of German nationalism that swept through central Europe during the Restoration era found little echo in Alsace. Nineteenth-century Alsace was not free of social conflict, but most tensions developed along class or religious lines rather than those of language use or nationality. Until the coming of the Franco-Prussian War, few Alsatians imagined that their province would become one of the most hotly contested territories in all of Europe.

Defining the Nation

One of the central paradoxes in what was known to generations of diplomats as the "Alsace-Lorraine" question is that Alsace can legitimately be seen, depending upon one's criteria, as essentially either French or German. Being French, under the Old Regime, meant primarily being a subject of the Bourbon monarchs; it did not necessarily imply sharing a common language or culture. Under the French Revolution, it came to mean sharing in the radical restructuring of the political community, ultimately making nationality, in Renan's famous formulation, "a daily plebiscite" (Harvey 2001, 9). Being German, at least prior to the proclamation of the Second Reich in 1871, was a matter of belonging to a shared language and cultural tradition; Ernst Moritz Arndt famously declared that the German fatherland was "wherever the German tongue is heard" (Schulze 1991, 54). Later in the 19th century, as issues of race became more central to Western social thought, German identity came to acquire an ethnic/biological component as well, and one that increasingly came to include *Volksdeutsche* (ethnic Germans) throughout central and eastern Europe, and to exclude minorities, such as Jews, even when these formed part of a shared cultural community.

Alsace posed a dilemma from the standpoint of 19th-century risorgimento nationalism, which sought to redraw the map of Europe along lines of nationality. Alsace had been an integral part of the French state for two centuries, and most Alsatians who gave such matters any thought considered themselves citizens of France. Only a small minority of Alsatians spoke French as their primary language, however, primarily among the upper classes and in a few enclaves in the Vosges Mountains; the majority of Alsatians spoke a Germanic dialect. French patriots, stressing historical continuity, state structures, and voluntarism, could plausibly claim that Alsace formed part of the French nation, while their German counterparts, for whom blood ran thicker than water, could just as plausibly demand the liberation of their brethren from "foreign" rule.

Narrating the Nation

Historical narratives and appeals to a wide range of national pasts have long been used to invoke concepts of collective identity in Alsace. Alsatians were well represented among the military leaders of the revolution and empire, most famously François Kellerman, who turned back an invading army under the Duke of Brunswick at the Battle of Valmy in 1792; Jean-Baptiste Kléber, who led revolutionary forces against the Vendée rebels; and Jean Rapp, who served in Napoleonic campaigns and rallied to the emperor in the Hundred Days. This shared legacy of struggle and glory was often cited by partisans of a French Alsace and was reflected in the region's urban topography: the main public square in Strasbourg has been known as Place Kléber for most of the modern era (but was renamed Karl Roos Platz under the Nazi occupation, in honor of a pro-Nazi Alsatian activist executed by the French). Those who sought to recover Alsace's German heritage looked back to the more distant period before the French conquest, in which Alsace had formed part of the medieval German Reich. The medieval castle of Haut-Koenigsberg, perched upon a mountaintop towering over the valley below, was restored at the wishes of Kaiser Wilhelm II, as a visual memorial to link a German imperial past to the new German empire.

Reichsland

From 1871 until 1918, Alsace and annexed Lorraine (the current department of the Moselle), were administered as a single territorial unit, the "imperial territory" or *Reichsland Elsaß-Lothringen*. The Reichsland was governed by a German official, called the *Statthalter*, appointed by the Kaiser and answerable only to him, as well as an indirectly elected regional parliament, the *Landesausschuß*, with limited powers. This institutional arrangement was unsatisfactory to many Alsatians, who felt that Alsace-Lorraine had not been granted equal status to other German federal states, or *Länder*. A new provincial constitution, issued in 1911, created a new parliament, the *Landtag*, with an elected lower house, but still maintained imperial oversight over Alsatian affairs.

Mobilizing and Building the Nation

Since the annexation of Alsace and part of Lorraine in 1871 by the newly proclaimed German Second Reich, a variety of state actors and institutions have sought, with varying success, to mobilize the population of Alsace into the broader national community, whether French or German. The most radical means that the modern nation-state possesses to mobilize the nation is its authority to extend or deny the rights of citizenship, which forms a legal as well as a conceptual boundary between those who are accepted as part of the national community and those who are excluded from it. In response to Alsatian protests against the German annexation, Bismarck allowed Alsatians who wished to remain French citizens to do so by making a public declaration of their intent. Pro-French Alsatians used this declaration, the "option," as a means of expressing their opposition to the annexation; however, the German state required Alsatians who wished to retain French citizenship to emigrate by October 1872; those who remained were simply naturalized en masse.

Each subsequent change of rule in Alsace brought with it new official policies regarding national citizenship, which provoked mass movement of affected populations. In the aftermath of World War I, the victorious French established "triage commissions" to examine the legal status and national origins of the residents of Alsace, issuing identity cards identifying them as French citizens, foreigners from neutral nations, or enemy aliens (German or Austrian citizens). Just over 1 million residents of the province were classified as "French Alsatians" by the triage commissions, while about 500,000 were classified as "enemy aliens" and nearly 200,000 as "mixed" heritage, an indicator of the high degree of migration and integration of Alsace into Germany between 1871 and 1918. Those Alsatians identified as enemy aliens were subject to a variety of forms of discrimination, and many of them were deported to Germany, while others chose to leave of their own accord. Approximately 150,000 people left Alsace for Germany in the aftermath of World War I.

A 1918 poster depicts a girl in Alsatian costume with a French flag draped around her (presumably the personification of Alsace). The poster reads: "March 1, 1871 to March 1, 1918. In liberated Alsace young girls willingly make sacrifices to hasten the liberation of the part of Alsace still annexed [to Germany]. Follow their example." (Library of Congress)

Commissions de triage

The *commissions de triage* or "triage commissions" were established by French occupation authorities following the recovery of Alsace after the end of World War I in 1918. Alsace had formed part of the German Second Reich for nearly half a century, and hundreds of thousands of Germans had crossed the Rhine to settle in the province. While some Alsatians would later claim that Alsatians and "Alt-Deutsche" lived hermetically separate lives during this period, demographic statistics tell another story, as intermarriage was common, and opposition to German rule faded after 1890. These commissions, staffed by French army officers (often of émigré Alsatian heritage themselves) made summary classification of the entire population of the province based on national origins, and also heard tens of thousands of appeals from residents who felt they had been unfairly classified. A total of 1,082,650 A-cards (indicating Alsatian-French origins), 183,500 B-cards (mixed heritage), 55,050 C-cards (foreign nationals), and 513,800 D-cards (German or Austrian citizens) were issued. About 150,000 residents of Alsace left the province for Germany, whether voluntarily or involuntarily, in the aftermath of the war.

During the "phony war" of October 1939 to May 1940, several hundred thousand residents of Alsace were evacuated to the interior of France in anticipation of a German attack on the province, and many later complained of being labeled *boches* (a derogatory term for Germans) by their new neighbors. Following the collapse of the French Third Republic, Alsace was reannexed to Germany, and German officials organized the repatriation of Alsatians who wanted to return home, while at the same time expelling nearly a hundred thousand undesirables (Jews, political radicals, and French newcomers) from the province. German officials actively promoted the re-Germanization of the province, symbolized by the slogan "*Hinaus mit dem welschen Plunder!*" ("Out with the French garbage!"), and forbade obvious symbols of Frenchness (such as the beret, not part of traditional Alsatian attire, but popular during this period as a badge of French allegiance). From 1940 to 1945, Alsace formed part of the Third Reich, and young Alsatian men were subject to conscription to the German Wehrmacht (the army of the Third Reich). These *incorporés de force*, as they were called by their fellow Alsatians to emphasize the unwilling nature of their service, served on multiple fronts in World War II.

The residents of Alsace were not, of course, simply the passive recipients of official nation-building efforts emanating from Paris or Berlin. Local institutions, actors, and political parties struggled to mobilize their constituencies and defend their interests in this rapidly changing environment. Perhaps the strongest bulwark of Alsatian particularism against both Lutheran Prussia and the militantly secular Third Republic was the Catholic Church, to which a majority of the province's residents belonged. For 20 years after the annexation of Alsace to Germany, a broad anti-annexationist movement called the "protestation" dominated Alsatian politics, sweeping all Reichstag elections in the territory prior to 1890.

Malgré-nous or incorporés de force

Following the German victory over France in 1940, Alsace and Lorraine were once again annexed to the German Reich. The Nazi *Gauleiter* (provincial leader) for Alsace, Robert Wagner, demanded that Alsatians be incorporated into the Reich's war effort on the same terms as other Germans, but German military commanders' doubts as to the reliability of Alsatian conscripts delayed the implementation of conscription until August 24, 1942. About 160,000 Alsatians were drafted into the German army and served primarily on the Eastern Front, where around 50,000 perished. Many others were taken prisoner and found that their Soviet captors did not recognize their claims to French citizenship or their status as unwilling combatants. Around 40,000 Alsatians either avoided the draft or deserted once in uniform. The most controversial of these *malgré-nous* ("against our will") or *incorporés de force* ("forcibly incorporated") were those who served in occupied France. Twelve Alsatians formed part of the notorious Waffen-SS unit that committed the massacre of French civilians at Oradour-sur-Glane on June 10, 1944. They were tried and convicted by a French court for war crimes in 1953, but, as their former commander remained in impunity in West Germany, they were subsequently pardoned.

The protestation of the 1870s and 1880s was coordinated to a great degree by the church, and many activist clergy, such as Abbé Wetterlé, were elected as deputies to the Reichstag. In the 1920s, Catholic activists again played a prominent role in Alsatian autonomism, with another priest, Abbé Xavier Haegy, serving as the spiritual leader of the *Heimatbund* (homeland federation) movement. Socialism, which emerged in Alsace under the auspices of the German Social Democratic Party (SPD) in the 1890s and beyond, offered another alternative to Alsatians who could accept neither German nationalism nor political Catholicism. In addition to mobilizing the province's rapidly growing industrial proletariat, the SPD also absorbed much of the anti-Prussian protest vote that had previously gone to the autonomist movement.

The autonomist movements of the 1870s and 1920s, as the term suggests, generally sought political and cultural autonomy for Alsace within the existing

---

Protestation

The protestation, the Alsatian protest movement against annexation to the German Second Reich, began with the appeal of the deputies of Alsace and Lorraine to the French National Assembly on February 17, 1871. From 1874—the first Reichstag elections in which Alsace and Lorraine took part—until 1890, elections in Alsace were swept by candidates who rejected the incorporation of their province into Germany. The protestation was a broad, cross-class political movement in which pro-French Catholic clergy, notably Abbé Emile Wetterlé, played a leading role. Beginning in 1890, with the realization that the annexation of Alsace was not likely to be reversed in the short term, the unity of the protestation gave way to political divisions along class and religious lines.

German or French states, well aware that national boundaries would not be redrawn without a major war that could devastate the province, and that Alsace, a small territory with just over a million inhabitants, could not hope for independence in an age of warfare between the great powers of Europe. For these reasons, there has rarely, if ever, been an "Alsatian nationalist" movement, and Alsace has seldom been imagined as a "nation" in its own right but rather has been imagined as part of the larger French or German nations. The more radical branch of interwar autonomism, which might be seen as an exception to this pattern, took an increasingly national-separatist stance in the 1930s, but this was generally no more than a cover for *völkisch* (racialist) German nationalist sentiments, as the wartime collaboration of many erstwhile autonomists, such as Joseph Rossé, Charles Hueber, and Jean-Pierre Mourer, demonstrate.

In the years since 1945, the "Alsace-Lorraine" question has largely been forgotten, as the Federal Republic of Germany has abandoned claims to the region, which has become more thoroughly integrated into the French nation. The expansion of mass media—print newspapers, and especially radio and television—has, along with the expanded education system, made French the dominant language in Alsace for the first time in the region's history. The role of the mass media in producing a standardized national culture has been particularly pronounced in Alsace, as nearly all programming is in the French language and is broadcast nationwide. One of the public television networks airs some local programming, including a few programs in Alsatian dialect, but the shift in language usage has been striking, as the once-dominant dialect has been almost completely displaced and is now used only by a dwindling number of elderly speakers.

The political culture of postwar France has also changed significantly from that of the Third Republic, allowing Alsace to blend more comfortably into the French mainstream. The militant anticlericalism of the Third Republic, which alienated many pious Alsatian Catholics during the 1920s and 1930s, has largely faded, and "Jacobin centralization" has given way to at least limited efforts at regionalization. Similarly, the rise of a moderate, pro-republican right, in the form of the Catholic MRP (Mouvement Républicain Populaire) during the Fourth Republic and the Gaullist RPR (Rassemblement pour la République) during the Fifth has not only stabilized democratic institutions in France but also provided a political home for many socially conservative Alsatians, who were never integrated into the culture of French republicanism during the interwar period.

Perhaps the greatest factor in the resolution of the "Alsace-Lorraine" question, however, has been the end of the Franco-German antagonism and the rise of cooperation between the two former enemies, which have instead become the anchors of a new, transnational European order. It was the Lorraine-born French foreign minister Robert Schuman who first proposed Franco-German cooperation for industrial reconstruction following World War II, leading to the creation first of the European Coal and Steel Commission, and later, following the 1957 Treaty of Rome, to the creation of the six-member European Economic Community, the forerunner of today's 25-member European Union. With the establishment of the European Parliament in Strasbourg, Alsace's largest city became a European capital, second only to Brussels in importance. The formerly disputed province thus became a keystone of a federalized European order.

In this new international climate, Alsatian autonomism, let alone separatism, has all but disappeared as a political movement. In 1981, a handful of middle-aged Alsatian veterans of the German Wehrmacht, calling themselves the "Black Wolves" (*Schwarze Wölfe*), bombed a Croix de Lorraine monument in the Vosges Mountains, but this gesture drew nearly universal condemnation in the province and produced no lasting consequences. Cultural autonomists remain somewhat more active, as such groups as the Cercle René Schickelé, founded in 1968 to promote bilingual education in Alsace, have focused on the preservation of Alsatian dialect and folk culture. During the 1970s, cultural autonomists in Strasbourg sponsored a folk festival called the *Musauer Wacke*, or "fools of the Musau" (river), which used carnivalesque imagery, marionettes, and masquerades to celebrate Alsatian popular culture and the local dialect. Such groups do not seek to redress the political allegiance of the province but rather can best be seen in the context of nationwide efforts to promote decentralization and the revitalization of the historic regions of France.

Demographic changes have also impacted the ways in which Alsatians define themselves and their neighbors. As an early industrial region, with a substantial textile and machine construction industrial base in the early 19th century, Alsace has long been a magnet for immigrant labor, drawing first peasants from the Alsatian countryside, later Swiss and German seasonal migrants, and, by the start of the 20th century, Italian and Polish immigrants as well. During the postwar period, however, Alsace, like the rest of France, has increasingly attracted immigrants from the former French empire, particularly North African Muslims. Immigration has erased older cultural markers while creating new ones, as Alsatians today define themselves less against Germans or the "French of the interior" but in opposition to a non-European Other.

Alsatian political culture at the dawn of the 21st century thus presents two contradictory faces. One of these is the modern, cosmopolitan, and progressive European orientation of the province, perhaps best symbolized by former Strasbourg mayor Catherine Trautmann, who went on to serve as minister of culture in the government of Lionel Jospin in the late 1990s. The other face of Alsatian political culture, however, is far less attractive, as the province has given the far-right Front National and its leader, Jean-Marie Le Pen, some of their highest vote totals anywhere in France, in recognition of which the party held its annual convention in Strasbourg in 1997. Alsace, like much of Europe, thus finds itself on the brink between the progressive cosmopolitanism of the European Union and the resurgence of racism and exclusivist nationalism that is embodied by such groups as the Front National.

Selected Bibliography

Baechler, C. 1982. *Le parti catholique alsacien, 1890–1939: Du Reichsland à la république jacobine.* Paris: Ophrys.

Brubaker, R. 1992. *Citizenship and Nationhood in France and Germany.* Cambridge, MA: Harvard University Press.

Caron, V. 1988. *Between France and Germany: The Jews of Alsace-Lorraine, 1871–1918.* Stanford, CA: Stanford University Press.

Dreyfus, F. 1969. *La vie politique en Alsace, 1919–1936.* Paris: Armand Colin.

Ellis, G. 1981. *Napoleon's Continental Blockade: The Case of Alsace.* Oxford: Clarendon Press.

Fischbach, B., and R. Oberlé. 1990. *Les loups noirs: Autonomisme et terrorisme en Alsace.* Mulhouse, France: Alsatia Union.

Ford, F. 1958. *Strasbourg in Transition, 1648–1789.* New York: Norton.

Goodfellow, S. 1999. *Between the Swastika and the Cross of Lorraine: Fascisms in Interwar Alsace.* De Kalb: Northern Illinois University Press.

Harp, S. 1998. *Learning to Be Loyal: Primary Schooling as Nation Building in Alsace and Lorraine, 1850–1940.* De Kalb: Northern Illinois University Press.

Harvey, D. A. 2001. *Constructing Class and Nationality in Alsace, 1830–1945.* De Kalb: Northern Illinois University Press.

Hau, M. 1987. *L'industrialisation de l'Alsace, 1803–1939.* Strasbourg, France: Association des Publications près les Universités de Strasbourg.

Igersheim, F. 1981. *L'Alsace des notables: la bourgeoisie et le peuple alsacien, 1870–1914.* Strasbourg, France: Nouvel Alsacien.

Ketternacker, L. 1973. *Nationalsozialistische Volkstumspolitik im Elsass.* Stuttgart, Germany: Deutsche Verlags Anstalt.

Levy, P. 1929. *Histoire linguistique d'Alsace et de la Lorraine.* Paris: Société des Editions les Belles Lettres.

Rothenberger, K.-H. 1976. *Die elsass-lothringische Heimat- und Autonomiebewegung zwischen den beiden Weltkriegen.* Frankfurt-am-Main, Germany: Peter Lang.

Schulze, H. 1991. *The Course of German Nationalism.* Translated by Sarah Hanbury-Tenison. Cambridge: Cambridge University Press.

Silverman, D. 1972. *Reluctant Union: Alsace Lorraine and Imperial Germany, 1871–1918.* University Park: Pennsylvania State University Press.

Vassberg, L. 1993. *Alsatian Acts of Identity: Language Use and Language Attitudes in Alsace.* Clevedon, UK: Multilingual Matters.

Wahl, A., and J.-C. Richez. 1993. *La vie quotidienne en Alsace: Entre France et Allemagne, 1850–1950.* Paris: Hachette.

Basque Country

Pauliina Raento

Chronology

1876	The Basques lose their historical rights and privileges (*fueros*) in Spain.
1895	The first Basque nationalist party, Partido Nacionalista Vasco/Eusko Alderdi Jeltzalea (PNV/EAJ), is founded in Bilbao, a center of trade, industry, and immigration.
1930	The radical nationalist party Acción Nacionalista Vasca/Eusko Abertzale Ekintza (ANV/EAE) is founded in Bilbao, following internal disagreements among Basque nationalists.
1936	The Civil War begins in Spain between the republican government (Left) and Spanish nationalist coalition (Right) led by General Francisco Franco.
1936–1937	First Basque autonomy in Spain.
1937	Aerial bombardment of the "sacred" Basque town, Guernica. Picasso protests by painting *Guernica*. The republican and Basque nationalist troops are defeated in Bilbao; the Basque autonomous government is exiled in Paris.
1939	General Franco's dictatorship and promotion of "one Spanish nation" begins in Spain.
1959	The separatist, clandestine Basque resistance organization Euskadi Ta Askatasuna (ETA) is founded.
1968	ETA kills for the first time. The conflict between the Spanish central government and Basque nationalists escalates. Basque nationalists face new internal ideological divisions.
1975	General Franco dies. Spain begins political transition toward representative democracy.
1978	Spain's new constitution recognizes the country's ethno-linguistic minorities and divides the state into 17 autonomous communities.
1979	The Basque Autonomous Community is created in Spain.
1980	The first parliamentary elections in the Basque Autonomous Community establish nationalist rule.
1982	The Foral Community of Navarra is created in Spain.
1986	Spain joins the European Community (European Union).
1995	The first formal transfrontier agreement is signed between Spain and France.
2002	The radical Basque nationalist party Batasuna and its predecessors are banned in Spain.
2006	Peace talks attempted between ETA and the Spanish central government.

Situating the Nation

The Basque Country is a mountainous borderland in Spain and France. For centuries, Basques have maintained their own language (*Euskara*) and cultural traditions in their seven historical provinces (see map and sidebar on Multiple Territories, Names, and Boundaries). These provinces became parts of the emerging Spanish and French states at different times and through various means. For example, Álava (in Basque, *Araba*), Guipúzcoa (*Gipuzkoa*), and Vizcaya (*Bizkaia*) were subjected to the Crown of Castile by the 13th century, whereas the Kingdom of Navarra (*Nafarroa*) was defeated and annexed in 1512. All these regions kept certain economic privileges, their own legal-political practices (codified in charters known as the *fueros*), and distinct identities. The drawing of the international boundary between Spain and France (beginning in the 17th century) and the French Revolution (1789) tied the three Basque provinces in France to the orbit of Paris. The Basque-speaking minority population in the distant borderland provinces of Labourd (*Lapurdi*), Bassenavarre (*Benafarroa*), and Soule (*Zuberoa*) thus became subjects of the French revolutionary leaders' promotion of an ethno-culturally uniform state.

In Spain, the Basques' expertise as seafarers, shipbuilders, and clergymen earned them a prominent role in the Crown's imperial endeavors in the Americas. This participation increased the power of Basque financial elites in Spanish national affairs and the wealth of Basque cities. Emigration supported traditional Basque lifestyle by alleviating population pressure, because the Basque farmstead (*baserri*) was passed on between generations as an undivided whole: while the oldest child continued farming, the siblings had to look elsewhere. These global opportunities expanded individual horizons and dispersed wealth through interpersonal networks. Not only the well educated but also shepherds and maids could make independent decisions about their lives and careers.

Multiple Territories, Names, and Boundaries

The Basqueness of the seven historical Basque provinces, together known as *Euskal Herria*, is based on ethno-linguistic characteristics. This generally agreed definition becomes highly contested when it is equated with *Euzkadi* (the name given to the independent Basque country of seven provinces by 19th-century nationalists) or *Euskadi* (the new spelling of the same ideal, adopted by the radical nationalist youth in the 1950s). Currently, *Euskadi* usually refers to the three-province Basque Autonomous Community. Navarra, a historical Spanish Basque province known for its distinct identity, forms its own autonomous community, the Foral Community of Navarra. In the (radical) Basque nationalist view, *Euskal Herria* and *Euskadi* should be synonymous names of an independent state.

The division of the seven provinces into two states, Spain and France, adds to this politico-administrative and identity-political complexity. The three Basque provinces in France belong to the Department of Pyrénées Atlantiques and the Region of Aquitaine, without a separate status of their own. For (radical) Basque nationalists, the international boundary and the usage of Spanish- and French-language place names represent oppression. This is challenged by a pointed usage of geographical Basque-language names *Hegoalde* (Southside) and *Iparralde* (Northside) for the Spanish and the French Basque Country or by talking about *beste aldea* (the other side), depending on the speaker's location. Spain's membership in the European Community (now the European Union) has eased exchanges across the international boundary, but politico-administrative complexity has increased.

The Basque Autonomous Community has 2.13 million and the Foral Community of Navarra has 600,000 residents (2006). Together they account for roughly 90 percent of the population in *Euskal Herria*. Metropolitan Bilbao is the largest city in the area.

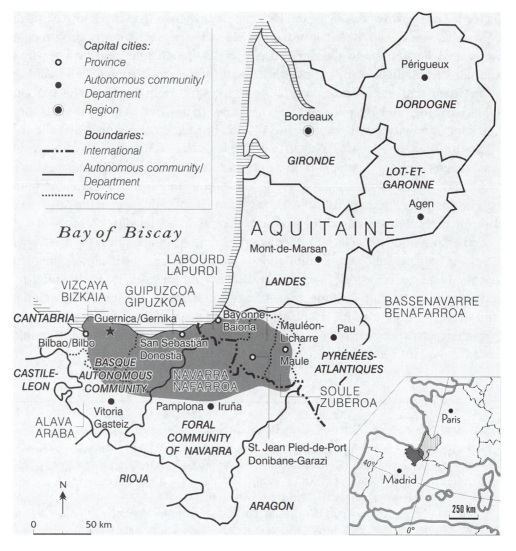

The boundaries and administrative status of the seven historical Basque provinces in Spain and France. The grey shade indicates the core area of Euskara, the Basque language. Spanish and French place names precede their Basque counterparts because those two languages are better known among English speakers. (Map by Pauliina Raento and Kirsti Lehto)

The consolidation of Spain and France and their boundaries in the 19th century increased the economic and political distance between the four Spanish Basque and the three French Basque provinces. The latter remained peripheral and rural, with an aging population and high rates of out-migration. The Spanish side featured major urban settlements, a lucrative shipbuilding industry, powerful financial institutions, upscale tourism in such cities as San Sebastián (*Donostia*), and active international connections. Natural resources further supported the onset of rapid heavy-industrial development in the late 19th century. The mills in Bilbao (*Bilbo*) and its surroundings attracted workers from the country-side and from the rest of Spain, increasing and diversifying the urban population on the Basque coast. A dramatic economic and sociocultural change, and the loss of the *fueros* in 1876 after the so-called Second Carlist War in Spain, provoked a defense reaction among the native middle classes and created the Basque nationalist movement in the context of rising nationalist sentiments across Europe. However, these ideals failed to take root in the French Basque provinces because of their very different societal and economic conditions. These differences within the historic Basque territory illustrate how different state policies, economic structures, and politico-administrative boundaries steer regional and local developments. These differing histories also help one understand some later developments, internal diversity, and practices of Basque nationalism.

Instituting the Nation

The Basque Nationalist Party (PNV/EAJ, Partido Nacionalista Vasco/Eusko Alderdi Jeltzalea), was founded in Bilbao in 1895 under the ideological leadership of Sabino Arana (1865–1903). In his writings, he portrayed Basques as racially superior to Spaniards, romanticized traditional Basque culture and rural lifestyle, and called for the restoration of the *fueros* and for *Euzkadi*, a sovereign Basque homeland of seven provinces (see map and sidebar on Multiple Territories, Names, and Boundaries). To Arana, Spanish immigrant workers and Basque financial elites embodied the enemies of the Basque nation.

The PNV/EAJ was not only class specific, but also local, focusing on the interests of Bilbao and Vizcaya rather than the entire territory it claimed. Some of the critics of this *bizkaitarrismo* favored a more action-oriented approach, which led to countercurrents within the movement. The division of Basque politics into moderate Basque nationalists, radical Basque nationalists, and non-nationalists (Spain- or France-affiliated groups) was already in place in the early 20th century. Among the most influential radical Basque nationalist groups was the Basque Nationalist Action (ANV/EAE, Acción Nacionalista Vasca/Eusko Abertzale Ekintza).

Basque nationalists achieved a short-lived autonomy during the Spanish Republic, after the breakout of the Spanish Civil War in 1936. The aerial bombardment of the town of Guernica (*Gernika*) in 1937, and the defeat of republican Bilbao soon afterward, marked the victory of General Francisco Franco's troops in the Basque Country. His final victory against the republican government in 1939 established a Spanish nationalist dictatorship in Spain and led many Basques to political exile, mostly to France and Latin America. The first president (*lehendakari*) of the Basque autonomy, José Antonio Aguirre (1904–1960), and his government received a diplomatic status in Paris. After the fall of France to Nazi Germany in 1940, however, some property of the Basque government was confiscated and Aguirre fled to Latin America. He returned to France in the early 1950s.

Franco's ideal of one Spanish nation and the oppression of minority cultures radicalized Basque nationalists. Especially the nationalist youth was dissatisfied with the cautious resistance strategies of the PNV/EAJ and the exiles. This radi-

Autonomous Communities and Political Representation in the Spanish Basque Country

The Basque Autonomous Community was created in 1979 as the first of those 17 autonomous communities outlined in the Spanish constitution of 1978. The autonomy, as defined in the so-called Statute of Guernica, gives the three constituting provinces their own parliament, government, and president with broad legislative powers over the autonomous territory. The Foral Community of Navarra, created in 1982, has similar self-governing structures, which reflect the cultural distinctiveness and history of self-government in these territories.

The Basque Autonomous Community and Navarra are exceptional among Spain's autonomous communities, for they have a right to collect their own taxes. The Basque Autonomous Community also has its own autonomous police force, the *Ertzaintza*. The Basque language is an official language in the Basque Autonomous Community, but legally secondary to Spanish in the wording of the Spanish Constitution. Public institutions, such as the University of the Basque Country (Universidad del País Vasco/Euskal Herriko Unibertsitatea, UPV/EHU), are bilingual, but the possibilities of using the minority language vary according to location and local language environment within the Basque Autonomous Community. Fluent Basque-speakers (one-third of the population in the three provinces; see sidebar on Multiple Territories, Names, and Boundaries) concentrate on the coast, especially in Guipúzcoa, whereas many who communicate in Basque with some difficulty live in Álava and the major cities. In Navarra, the legal status of the Basque language is conditioned by region due to considerable cultural differences within the Foral Community. In the northernmost third of the province, daily life proceeds in Basque.

In the autonomous parliament in Vitoria, the moderate Basque nationalist coalition (PNV/EAJ and EA [Eusko Alkartasuna, Basque Solidarity]) is the largest group with 39 percent of the votes cast and 29 of the 75 available seats (election in 2005). The second-largest party is the Spanish socialist PSE-EE/PSOE (Socialistas Vascos Euskal Sozialistak de Euskadi or Spanish Socialist Workers' Party), with 23 percent of the vote and 18 seats. In Navarra's parliament in Pamplona, the largest party is the regionalist UPN (Navarrese People's Union), with 42 percent of the vote and 23 of the 50 seats (election in 2003). The PSOE holds 11 seats with 22 percent of the vote as the second-largest party. The Basque nationalist groups have a total of 8 seats (16 percent of the vote) in Navarra. In both autonomous communities, almost one-third of the voters abstained in these parliamentary elections, some in protest against the current practice of "Basque national self-determination." The ban on the leading radical Basque nationalist party in Spain in 2002 left 10–25 percent of the voters without representation at the polls in the Basque Autonomous Community.

Official information about the two autonomous communities is available at www.euskadi.net and www.navarra.es.

calization coincided with another phase of industrialization and immigration, which now reached the rural inland and small towns. A new radical nationalist organization, ETA (Euskadi Ta Askatasuna, Basque Homeland and Liberty), was created in 1959. It promoted an independent, Basque-speaking, and socialist Basque Country of seven provinces through active resistance strategies (such as sabotage against infrastructure and, later, through political assassinations), which raised some sympathy in France. From the 1960s to the 1980s, the French Basque provinces served ETA and other Basque nationalist activists as an operative base and a political refuge, with the help of Basque seamen's expertise in contraband. The marginal status of the three provinces in France, ideological disagreements between the French and Spanish central governments, the Basque language, and old social and cultural contacts across the international boundary supported these exchanges.

The death of General Franco in 1975 launched Spain's political transition process toward representative democracy and brought Spain and France politically closer to one another. The Spanish constitution of 1978 recognized the rights of the country's ethno-cultural minorities and sketched a new state structure based on autonomous communities. The first regional parliamentary elections in the Basque Autonomous Community (see sidebar on Autonomous Communities and Political Representation in the Spanish Basque Country) in 1980 established the rule of Basque nationalists in this region. However, the desire of Navarra to form its own autonomous community disappointed the Basque nationalist ideal of unity. The Basque Autonomous Community and the Foral Community of Navarra were brought under the umbrella of European cooperation with Spain's membership in the European Community (European Union) in 1986.

Defining the Nation

The creation of these two autonomous communities reflects the long history of difference and disagreement within the historical Basque territory. Under dispute are the definitions of Basque identity and territory, and the acceptable goals and methods of their promotion. For example: Can the goal of "Basque national self-determination" be satisfied with a degree of autonomy or only with independence? What and who are acceptable forms and partners of cooperation? Is political violence acceptable? How useful are referenda in solving these matters? Should the search for answers to these questions involve three, four, or seven provinces, and who should have the right to decide this?

Territorial-ideological views and loyalties override the conventional ideological division into Left and Right in Basque politics. Radical nationalists have typically detested the engagement of moderate nationalists in political dialogue and cooperation with nonnationalists and the central governments. In this view, the seven provinces form an indivisible whole, similar to the traditional farmstead. "Basque national self-determination" thus means separation from Spain and France and full independence, but this does not imply that all radical nationalists accept the use of political violence. Moderate nationalists generally accept autonomy and the current boundaries as political realities (despite their at times fierce rhetoric and resistance) and condemn violence. In the view of nonnationalist Basques and regionalist parties within the contested territory, the Basque provinces are culturally distinctive but integral parts of Spain and France, and ETA cannot be tolerated under any circumstances. In sum, what exactly constitutes "the Basque Country," what it should be called, and how it should be managed are strongly contested matters.

Fractures within organizations characterize Basque nationalism. One extreme example of operative-strategic and cultural-political fragmentation is ETA, an offspring of the PNV/EAJ's youth organization. Some of ETA's numerous splinter groups have moved toward party-political or civic-organizational activities, whereas others have adopted increasingly harsh methods to promote separatism. Another rupture in the PNV/EAJ created an ideologically "mediating" nationalist party, EA (Eusko Alkartasuna, Basque Solidarity), in 1986, due to ideological, interpersonal, and regional tensions. Over the years, several radical Basque nationalist groups have appeared on, and disappeared off, the Basque political scene. To prevent reincarnations, the Spanish central government's ban on the leading radical nationalist party Batasuna (Unity) in 2002, for the party's alleged connections to ETA, included a ban on its two predecessors, Herri Batasuna and Euskal Herritarrok (see sidebar on Autonomous Communities and Political Representation in the Spanish Basque Country).

The contested Basque territory forms a complex map of ideological centers, peripheries, and transitional zones. San Sebastián has been a radical nationalist stronghold compared to PNV/EAJ-dominated Bilbao or to prominently nonnationalist Vitoria (*Gasteiz*) and Pamplona (*Iruña*). These two capital cities are also known for their regionalist parties, which ride on the historically and culturally distinct identity of the surrounding provinces. This is nothing new, for Spanish Basque cities and provinces have historically competed with one another and have often differed in their ideological preferences and territorial loyalties. In Spain, the densely populated, urban-industrial, prominently nationalist, and fluently Basque-speaking coastal provinces stand apart from the less populous, rural, nonnationalist, and Spanish-speaking inland provinces with more recent industrialization. Álava and Navarra are further divided internally, for their northern areas are firmly in the orbit of Basque-speaking culture and nationalist politics. These areas thus form an internal cultural and political borderland within the historical Basque territory and within the two autonomous communities. The Basque provinces in France remain predominantly rural and largely Basque-speaking (despite some decline in its usage), although tourism and specialized industrial production have developed on the coast. The modest support for Basque nationalism in France continues to favor radical nationalism.

The outcome is a fragmented and highly conflictive (at times, lethal) political culture. The political atmosphere is particularly tense in areas where several ideological viewpoints and interest groups compete. Since the political transition in Spain, the conflict has focused on Basque society itself rather than on the confrontation between Basque nationalists and the Spanish and French central governments, although protests against the ban on Batasuna and the peace talks between the Spanish central government and ETA (in 2006) somewhat redirected this emphasis.

Narrating the Nation

The "Basque nation" is the core of Basque nationalist loyalties despite the disagreements. The foundations of Basque nationalist identity, history, and culture come together in the symbolic power of the town of Guernica in Vizcaya. In the Middle Ages, this centrally located, thriving commercial center became a political center, where local and regional representatives gathered to manage the *fueros* and make political decisions. These were confirmed under an oak tree, the remains of which are preserved next to a historical Basque Assembly House. The visits by the Kings of Castile to Guernica to confirm and respect the Basque privileges under their rule enhanced the town's symbolic value and distinct Basque identity, especially in the 16th and 17th centuries.

Since the 19th century, Guernica has signified war, conflict, and resistance due to repeated conflicts with the central government. Especially, the conflictive end to the *fueros* and the Spanish Civil War associated Guernica with outside oppression against the Basque nation and identity. Guernica also reminds Basque nationalists of the ideological and regional conflicts within the Basque Country —those of Basque nationalists and Spanish republicans (coast) against Spanish nationalists and nonnationalist Basques (inland). Because of these conflicts, Guernica stands for resistance and heroism. This was evident in the naming of Basque nationalist military units in the Civil War after the sacred town. Through the bombardment of Guernica, through his military victory, and through cultural and political oppression during his rule, General Franco thus hit the heart of Basque nationalist identity, making Guernica a symbol of sacrifice, tragedy, and genocide.

Pablo Picasso's war-protesting painting *Guernica* (1937) gave global recognition to the town's name. Numerous commercial and civic establishments across the Americas had already been named after the town and its oak in celebration of ethno-cultural origins, but now the name represented a wish for peace on Earth. All these meanings come together in the frequent usage of the name "Guernica" (or Gernika) and related symbolism in the Basque Country, where at least two

An old oak, the Tree of Guernica, is among the most important symbols of Basque national identity and history. The entire town of Guernica, with its multiple identity-political references, qualifies as "sacred ground" for Basque nationalists. (Pauliina Raento)

nationalist political organizations, a pacifist group, and the Basque autonomous police force use them in their names or emblems. Guernica is the site for numerous nationalist rituals and monuments. For example, each new Basque autonomous parliament swears its oath at the Tree of Guernica. Few electoral or other political campaigns of Basque nationalists bypass Guernica. The Basque "national anthem," other important identity-political songs, the Basque national(ist) flag (the red, white, and green *ikurriña*), the Basque language, and Basque folklore are prominent in these rituals.

Mobilizing and Building the Nation

Basque nationalists are notably active and aggressive in their efforts to maintain and attract support. The highly politicized and competitive environment, the legacy of oppression, and the ban on radical nationalist parties have steered the methods of nationalist mobilization. Information passes forward by word of mouth through private and informal spaces and networks, which involve the street, the mountains, homes, cooking clubs, taverns, and churches. In addition, each political group has more formal channels of information (such as party-affiliated newspapers and Web sites) and organizational infrastructure (such as labor unions, women's groups, and youth organizations). Mass power is typically exhibited in street demonstrations, for or against a particular issue or event. The contents, methods, and style of political mobilization vary according to campaign organizer, subject matter, intended audience, and location.

Particularly varied—and the loudest—approach to political mobilization is that of radical Basque nationalists. Their strategies vary from persuasive celebration and promotion of Basque culture to openly propagandist political messaging, commemoration, and confrontation. Examples of the former approach include street festivals, concerts, and sports events in support of Basque language and traditions. The latter features (clandestine) painting of graffiti and murals in public spaces; commemorative and welcoming ceremonies for the fallen, imprisoned, or freed Basque nationalist "freedom fighters"; mass gatherings (which occasionally have included such acts as the burning of the Spanish flag); and acts of violence against infrastructure and political opponents.

In the predominantly Spanish-speaking, nonnationalist southern borderland, persuasive tones and cultural emphases are favored over political confrontation and violence. The style is more aggressive and varied in the nationalist core areas, where the radical nationalist message needs to challenge moderate nationalist and nonnationalist views and to confirm and celebrate the identity of those who already support the promoted ideology. Sensitive to the heterogeneity of the contested territory, the emphasis of mobilization adjusts to local issues, in Basque, Spanish, or French. The preferences of age groups are considered as well:

contemporary Basque radical nationalist rock music, old political protest songs, and traditional poetry improvisation contests may be performed at the same festival to attract a broad audience and to show that generations unite behind "the cause." That location, visibility, and active participation matter is well exemplified by the clandestine radical nationalist campaign of street-sign painting in centers of ideological contest—in Guernica and its surroundings, at the international border between Spain and France, and in Álava and Navarra in the transitional zones between Basque- and Spanish-language majority cultures. The Spanish (or French) spellings are erased in black paint from the signage so that only the Basque place names are left visible (or added) to promote a monolingual, Basque-speaking Basque Country and to challenge the presence of the "oppressor states" in the claimed territory.

However, most of the daily nation-building proceeds quietly in administrative offices and meeting rooms despite the conflictive atmosphere, public protests, and heated political debate. The political transition and consolidation of autonomies in Spain (see sidebar on Autonomous Communities and Political Representation in the Spanish Basque Country) have contributed to the institutionalization of Basque political, administrative, cultural, and economic practices. For example, the status of *Euskara* in public settings has been enhanced, and education is now available in Basque from kindergarten to university. From the crafting of basic autonomous infrastructure, the attention has shifted toward broadening its scope and functions, and toward economic development and regional cooperation across politico-administrative boundaries. With the help of funding and regional policies from the European Union, the historical Basque territory has acquired characteristics of a functional borderland region. Money, people, and businesses move increasingly fluently between the two states and the two autonomous communities in Spain. The ambitious expansion and promotion of the historically important port of Bilbao, now the second-most important port in Spain, and related logistical distribution services at the international border zone have promoted the Basque coast as an international transportation hub, revitalizing many of its past global connections. Projects related to high technology, energy and the environment, the media, and tourism are among the foci of regional cross-border development and financial support from supranational and national sources. Successes have improved the Basque economy by diversifying employment options, lowering unemployment, and attracting new investments. All this has supported the transition from dramatically declined heavy-industrial production toward specialized centers of high technology and innovation. Old sociocultural contacts across the boundaries support this development and the diversification of Basque cultural expression, bringing the Spanish and French Basque regions closer to one another.

Basque, Spanish, and French political histories complicate these local and regional achievements in multiple ways. One source of continuous friction between the Basque autonomous government and the Spanish central government is the incomplete transfer of power from Madrid to Vitoria. Suspicion, competition, and some legal limitations complicate cooperation between the Basque Autonomous Community and the Foral Community of Navarra. Cooperation has been slow between Madrid and Paris as well, for their first formal transfrontier agreement was reached in 1995. By this time, it was evident that the now open boundary between the two countries had strongly differentiated the Basque provinces in many practical matters (such as administrative procedures) despite the shared cultural and social heritage. Cross-border development projects have suffered from incompatible maps and statistics. The number of involved parties and interests has grown and represents a range of actors, from supranational (European Union) to local levels (cities and towns). Paradoxically, the current situation in the historical Basque territory both supports and complicates the process of Basque nation-building—however that is defined.

Conflicts between political groups in Basque society, between cities and provinces, and between Basque nationalists and the central governments in Madrid and Paris are parts of daily life in the historical Basque territory. Each interest group in the Basque Country continues its nation-building work according to its own historically informed territorial-ideological vision. The historical Basque territory continues to be divided into multiple politico-administrative units and into distinct subregions with different profiles and interests regarding language, culture, economy, political ideology, and population development. The Basque economy as a whole continues to diversify and does relatively well in the context of integrating Europe, but especially projects that involve local, regional, national, and international actors sometimes proceed slowly. The political atmosphere in the Basque Country remains tense and sensitive to bad memories despite new forms of cooperation and signs of a peace process in Spain.

Selected Bibliography

Clark, R. P. 1984. *The Basque Insurgents*. Madison: University of Wisconsin Press.

Conversi, D. 1997. *The Basques, the Catalans, and Spain*. London: Hurst & Company.

Corcuera Atienza, J. 1979. *Orígenes, ideología y organización del nacionalismo vasco 1876–1904*. Madrid: Siglo XXI.

del Valle, T. 1994. *Korrika*. Reno: University of Nevada Press.

Douglass, W. A., ed. 1989. *Essays in the Basque Social Anthropology and History*. Reno: Basque Studies Program, University of Nevada.

Douglass, W. A., and J. Bilbao. 1975. *Amerikanuak*. Reno: University of Nevada Press.

Douglass, W. A., C. Urza, L. White, and J. Zulaika, eds. 1999. *Basque Politics and Nationalism on the Eve of the Millennium*. Reno: Basque Studies Program, University of Nevada.

Jacob, J. 1994. *Hills of Conflict*. Reno: University of Nevada Press.

Nordberg, I. 2007. *Regionalism, Capitalism and Populism*. Helsinki: Finnish Academy of Science and Letters.

Raento, P. 1997. "Political Mobilization and Place-Specificity: Radical Nationalist Street Campaigning in the Spanish Basque Country." *Space & Polity* 1, no. 2: 191–204.

Raento, P. 1999. "The Geography of Spanish Basque Nationalism." In *Nested Identities*, edited by G. H. Herb and D. H. Kaplan, 219–235. Lanham, MD: Rowman & Littlefield.

Raento, P. 2002. "Integration and Division in the Basque Borderland." In *Boundaries and Place*, edited by D. H. Kaplan and J. Häkli, 93–115. Lanham, MD: Rowman & Littlefield.

Raento, P., and C. J. Watson. 2000. "Gernika, Guernica, *Guernica*? Contested Meanings of a Basque Place." *Political Geography* 19, no. 6: 707–736.

Zulaika, J. 1988. *Basque Violence.* Reno: University of Nevada Press.

Bosnia and Herzegovina

Steven Oluic

Chronology

12th century   Bosnia's existence begins as a series of medieval kingdoms situated between more powerful neighbors; Hungary to the north and Serbia in the east. Prior to Ottoman conquest, the majority of the population was divided among the Bosnian, Catholic, and Orthodox churches.

1463   The majority of Bosnia falls to Ottoman Turkish invaders. The Ottomans would not exert control of entire Bosnia and Herzegovina until 1527.

1878   Treaty of Berlin; Austro-Hungarian empire occupies and administers Bosnia, although it ostensibly remains part of the Ottoman Empire. Ottoman state influence in Bosnia is all but extinguished.

1908   Austria-Hungary annexes Bosnia. Sarajevo, Bosnia's largest town, serves as the administrative center and capital of Austria's new province.

1918   Bosnia and Herzegovina become part of the kingdom of Serbs, Croats, and Slovenes. The Serbian *Karageorgević* royal dynasty becomes the ruling monarchs of the new state. To many, the kingdom is a greater Serbia.

1929   The Kingdom of Yugoslavia is established in reaction to political unrest and resistance to Serb hegemony in the state.

1941   Yugoslavia is invaded by German, Italian, and Bulgarian forces in April 1941. Shortly thereafter, Croatia is established as an independent fascist state that incorporates most of Bosnia.

1945   Liberation of Yugoslavia and establishment of a communist federal state under Marshal Josip Broz Tito.

1968   Muslims become an officially recognized nation in Yugoslavia.

1980   Marshal Josip Broz Tito dies, and a republic-based annually rotating presidency is instituted.

1991   Yugoslavia descends into chaos as Slovenia and Croatia declare independence.

1992   Bosnia declares independence in April, and civil war ensues, lasting until 1995.

1995   The Dayton Peace Accords are signed, ending the war and establishing Bosnia and Herzegovina as a state composed of two entities.

2005   The 10th anniversary of the Dayton Peace Accords is celebrated.

Situating the Nation

The notion of a Bosnian nation is a relatively new phenomenon. Following the 15th century and prior to Bosnia and Herzegovina's recognition as a state in 1992, Bosnia had always existed as part of other states or empires. Being a Bosnian, or *Bosanac*, was a regional and not national designation, the term nationality being inextricably linked to one's religion.

For most of the 45 years following World War II, Bosnia was a secular society. The casual religious characteristics of the population coupled with the
antireligious stance of the Communist Party leadership meant that religion
played little to no role in Bosnia. The *muezzin*'s call to prayer from the local Bosnian mosque was not a common occurrence and rarely, if ever, heeded in large
towns and cities. Intermarriage was widespread; roughly 40 percent of urban
marriages were mixed, and over 20 percent of urban Bosnians declared themselves "Yugoslav" or "other" in the years before civil war.

A certain harmony existed between all ethnic groups, primarily within urban
settings. Bosnia's five largest towns—Sarajevo, Banja Luka, Tuzla, Zenica, and
Mostar—accounted for barely one-quarter of Bosnia's 4.4 million citizens in 1991.
Three-quarters of the population were in rural or small town settings where attitudes were remarkably different from those in the cities. This points to a dis-
connection in the identities of urban and rural communities—one that would
dramatically impact Bosnia and Yugoslavia in the early 1990s.

The Bosnian rural folk and villagers tended to be much more conservative in
behavior and in matters of religion and national identity. Urban Bosnians saw
themselves as European, if not cosmopolitan, while the villagers kept up their religious practices. Islamic values and practices clashed with the urbanites' secular
views on life. Moreover, the urban Muslim had more in common with the urban
Serb or Croat as opposed to the Muslim villager. In many, if not most, cases, entire

villages were made up of single ethnic communities. The true secularism of the urban centers simply did not exist in the smaller towns, villages, and countryside. This situation was endemic within all of the prewar Yugoslav republics, whether Muslim or Christian.

As Yugoslavia descended into chaos, the forces of virulent nationalism radicalized all elements of Bosnian society, admittedly much less so in the urban centers. The influx of nationalists from Croatia and Serbia polarized the communities further until actual fighting began in April 1992. Religious affiliation determined on which side one would find himself.

Bosnia still suffers from the ravages of the civil war that would come to epitomize the violent breakup of the former Yugoslavia. Although the Dayton Peace Accords ended the violence in December 1995, Bosnia suffers from a weak central government, as the primary political power resides in two entities, the Republika Srpska (RS) dominated by the Bosnian Serbs and the Federation dominated by the Bosnian Muslims, or Bosniaks, with the Bosnian Croats being the junior member. The future of the Bosnian state is far from certain as it consists of Bosniaks, Croats, and Serbs—not Bosnians.

Instituting the Nation

Post-Dayton Debacle

The post-Tito rise of nationalism, onset of war, and exceptionally brutal aspects of the Bosnian Civil War radicalized all elements of Bosnia's people. The Bosnian Muslims were especially victimized by Croat and Serb aggression, leading to the growth and cohesion of a Bosniak nation. The internationally recognized leader of the newly independent Bosnia, Alija Izetbegović, a Bosniak, came to represent primarily Muslim interests and less so the Croats who would become junior partners of the Bosniaks later in the war. As each national group fought for its own political and territorial goals, the notion of a truly Bosnian national identity representing all the people of Bosnia was lost.

The end of the Bosnian Civil War, as part of the overall disintegration of Yugoslavia, brought with it international guarantees of sovereignty and external oversight. The 1995 Dayton Peace Accords established two political entities within Bosnia: the Republika Srpska (RS), dominated by the Bosnian Serbs, and the Federation, overwhelmingly Bosniak with the Bosnian Croats being the junior member. The Federation itself is further divided into 10 cantons, which for the most part are politically dominated by either the Bosniaks or Croats. The Dayton Peace Accords intentionally left the Bosnian state politically weak to bring an end to the fighting and address national groups' concerns.

The entities are separated by a 1,200-km-long Inter-Entity Boundary Line (IEBL) that in most areas reflects the former lines of confrontation. The RS is administratively divided into municipalities that mirror the prewar municipality structure, except in cases where the boundaries are truncated by the IEBL.

The Federation is a bit more complex, divided into 10 cantons that are further divided into municipalities. As with the RS, these municipalities reflect prewar administrative organization. Bosnia has gone from 110 municipal districts to about 145, due to the winding route of the IEBL. In some cases, like Mostar, which went from 1 to 6, these new municipalities were created to accommodate the tensions between the Croat and Muslim communities, allowing them to live in their own mono-ethnic municipalities.

Each entity possesses its own constitution and entity institutions, such as a judiciary, police force, health care, postal, and telecommunications systems. In the Federation, this political complexity increases with the further devolvement of institutions to the canton level. Of the 10 cantons, 5 are predominantly Bosniak, 3 Croat, and the last 2 mixed. Each canton possesses the responsibility for its police forces, education policy, social welfare administration, and so on.

Partitioning of Bosnia into two entities poses great problems for state-building and the exercise of authority. Although common state structures do exist, such as the Tri-Partite Presidency (which rotates between the three national groups), a Council of Ministers, which is the executive branch, and legislative and judicial branches, their authority is limited. In fact, the state-level institutions are threadbare and wanting of any real power. The intent is to hopefully ensure that no partisan behavior by any one national group occurs in such critical positions. A common state-level Ministry of Defense was established in 2005, and the international community celebrated this institution as a clear sign of success in a bitterly fractured state. But upon closer scrutiny, the Bosnian military is still organized along national lines as each of the army's three brigades are mono-ethnic, there being a Croat, Muslim, and Serb brigade stationed in its respective national territory. For all intents and purposes, the central government's authority is limited to the conduct of foreign affairs, international commerce, and fiscal policy—all of it under the purview and control of the High Representative and the European Union (EU).

Defining the Nation

Religion and Identity

Bosnia and Herzegovina were settled by Slavs, beginning in the sixth century. Although the Bosnia of today is still chiefly populated by Slavs, differences exist not of race but of religion. The three primary faiths of Bosnia: Eastern Orthodox of the Serbs, Islam of the Bosniaks, and Roman Catholicism of the Croats are the critical components of national identity.

Language, normally a key element of nationhood, is not a significant factor in Bosnia's notions of nationhood. Although language dialects exist in Bosnia, religion is the source of inter-ethnic tension. While Serbs do use the Cyrillic alphabet in addition to the Latin script of the Bosniaks and Croats, it again is not a major component of antagonism between them.

The notion of an "ethnicity" arrived in Bosnia during the 19th century when Bosnian Christians began to acquire ethnic and national ideas arriving from Serbia and Croatia. Some argue that this was the first time Serbs, as Orthodox Christians, and Croats, as Catholics, came to understand themselves as separate nations within Bosnia. However, the treatment of Christians as second-class citizens under Ottoman rule contributed to the development of Croat and Serb identity before the advent of modern nationalism in the late 18th century.

The corrupt and failing Ottoman Empire faced significant unrest in Bosnia during the 19th century. In 1875, a major revolt by the Serbs of Herzegovina broke out, threatening to cause a major war among the Great Powers of Austria-Hungary, Britain, and Russia. The revolt ended in failure, and the overall Balkan situation was resolved and stabilized with the 1878 Treaty of Berlin, in which Bosnia was transferred to Austro-Hungarian administration although ostensibly still part of the Ottoman Empire.

The transfer to Austro-Hungarian control occurred with much consternation on the part of Bosnia's three religious groups. The Austrians imported a secular school system that found the Muslims worried that they would be compelled to convert to Catholicism—the religion of the Habsburg Empire. The Austrian administrator, Benjamin von Kallay, attempted to weaken predatory Croat and Serb nationalist ideologies by advocating that all Bosnian communities embrace the notion of *bošnjastvo*, or Bosniakdom. It was a failure among Bosnia's Christian population because they looked outside of Bosnia for their identity, but it did lay the seeds of a Bosniak identity among the Muslim population.

The "loose fit" or more liberally practiced Islam of Bosnia was seen as a problem by educated Muslims. The lack of a sophisticated Islam coupled with retained Christian traditions and the power of the Austrian state led many to worry about conversions. The Muslim elite involved themselves in the affairs of the villages in an attempt to stave off threats to the Muslim religion. This moderate resurgence strained the relations with Bosnia's Christian population, which had always viewed the Muslims skeptically because of the power and privilege the Muslims possessed due to the Ottoman legacy.

The 1908 annexation of Bosnia by Austria-Hungary was followed by a period in which the Catholics received a favored position and the Muslims would, in many instances, also be in the emperor's grace. The Orthodox Serbs, the majority of whom lived in the rural areas, were still in the position of second-class citizens.

The position of the Serbs of Bosnia would change with the end of World War I in 1918. Bosnia became part of the Kingdom of Serbs, Croats, and Slovenes that would later become the Kingdom of Yugoslavia in 1929. The Serbian *Karageorgević* royal dynasty became the ruling monarchs of the new state, which saw favored status transferred to the Serbs.

The short-lived independent Yugoslavia was quickly overrun by the Axis forces in April 1941. Shortly thereafter, Croatia was established as an independent fascist state with new boundaries incorporating most of Bosnia. As Bosnia only had a 20 percent Croat population, the new Croatian fascist leadership of the *Ustaša* (term used to denote Croatian fascists) actively sought Muslim support in its plan to eradicate the Serbs, Jews, and Roma. Croatia's plan was to kill, convert, or expel the Serbs. It was during World War II that the ethnic element of Bosnia assumed a clearly religious dimension, creating intractable hatreds that linger to this day and have been used as grounds for national revenge.

The end of World War II brought the Yugoslav Communists to power under the charismatic leadership of Josip Broz Tito. In 1945, Yugoslavia was a Communist-dominated state, divided into six republics, each based on a dominant ethnic group. The only exception was Bosnia, which included Serb, Muslim, and Croat nationalities. Tito recognized that nationalism posed a constant threat to the new state. He also realized that strong adherence to one's religion correlated to a strong tie to one's national community, which could lead to separatist nationalism. Religion was anathema to communism and Tito's credo of "Brotherhood and Unity," and he therefore strove through rhetoric and the secret police to eliminate these nationalist threats.

Yugoslavia did progress as a country, by some accounts phenomenally well, but a policy of decentralization over the years left increasing power in the hands of the separate Yugoslav republics. By 1968, the Muslims, after realizing that they did not fit in as "Muslim Croats" or "Muslim Serbs," became an officially recognized nation in Yugoslavia. Their label, "Muslim" (*Musliman*), possessed a double meaning. Similar to the Jewish community, the new, officially declared Muslim was a member of a religious community and also an ethnic group.

Some scholars consider that Bosnia does qualify for nationhood and that the multiethnic character of today's Bosnia will fuse into being a Bosnian one. Moreover, some assert that the Bosnian nation derives its being more from territory than from any other cultural characteristic. Territories are what frame national identities, and given the common history, shared place, and past commonalities, Bosnia will become "Bosnian"—not Bosnian Croat, Bosnian Serb, or Bosniak.

An argument can be made that the mechanisms asserted as critical in forming a Bosnian identity are missing. The state structure was overtly left weak and unwieldy at the Dayton Peace Accords to satisfy Bosnian Croat and Serb demands addressing national survival. This, coupled with the radicalization of the recent war, inhibited the development of a true Bosnian identity as conceived in current ethnic and national identity scholarship. The state of Bosnia and the identity of "Bosnian" are perceived as the desire of the Muslims and now as a detriment to Croat and Serb identity.

Narrating the Nation

The Bosniaks, Croats, and Serbs cherish their national heroes, traditions, history, and symbols. Tito's legacy and the Yugoslav peoples' national struggle against fascism in World War II no longer serve as a uniting force. Moreover, there is a well-coordinated effort in Bosnia, especially in Croat-dominated areas, to eradicate the Communist legacy.

The recent civil war created new histories and symbolic sites, especially for the Bosniak community. The siege of Sarajevo and the massacres of Bosniaks by Serbs and Croats at such places as Srebrenica and Ahmići have come to define the Bosniak's sense of self in terms of a national struggle against powerful neighbors. It can be said that the civil war created the Bosniak nation. However, Bosnia's Croats and Serbs, through the course of the war, strengthened their identity and linkage with neighboring Croatia and Serbia.

Within Bosnia, these national identities are manifested at different political levels: the state level for the Bosniaks, to which they believe they are entitled as victims of aggression, the entity level of the RS for the Serbs, and the cantonal level within the Federation entity for the Croats. There does not appear to be any near-term accommodation among Bosnia's three national groups in adjusting their notions of a truly "Bosnian" national identity and territory. In fact, the current status quo is greatly under threat as the Muslim nationalist Party of Democratic Action (Stranka Demokratske Akcije, or SDA) aggressively pushes for the revision of the Dayton Peace Accords (DPA) and abolition of the RS.

The bond between place and nation is a phenomenon that strengthens over time. Given that there are active processes conflating territory with national identity, separate national territorial spaces are developing in Bosnia. The marking and renaming of places in Bosnia is an overt manifestation of this that lends permanency to Bosniak, Croat, and Serb claims to territory in Bosnia. Coupled with ethnic cleansing and the removal of the historical trace of another ethnic group's dominance, the supremacy of each national group within their respective spaces is assured.

The renaming of place has become commonplace in all regions of the former Yugoslavia. In the capital city of Sarajevo, all place names that once bore the name of Serb heroes and historical events were changed to typically Ottoman-era historical figures and events. Each group is guilty of this activity. The role of religion and nationality is manifested across the countryside, as each group uses religious structures to mark territory. The Serbs have built new Orthodox churches in places that had prewar Bosniak majorities. There is a duality to this process: the first is the marking of one's territory, but second, and more sinister, is the use of such symbols to prevent the return of prewar populations. In Croat-controlled areas, it is common to see war memorials and graffiti that exhibit symbols associated with the World War II Croat fascist *Ustaša*.

Recreating the Bosnian Cultural & Political Landscape

Ethnic Cleansing in Bosnia

The 1991–1995 Bosnian Civil War was noted for an extreme savagery not witnessed in Europe since World War II. Ethnic cleansing, a phrase coined by the media during the war, referred to military actions that expelled enemy national groups. In many instances, both military and civilians were massacred, and all traces of their former historical presence removed. Towns and villages were severely damaged, and many homes and religious sites eradicated. The Srebrenica massacre is the most famous example in which Bosnian Serb forces overran the UN safe haven of Srebrenica, executing several thousand Bosniak males.

Claiming of National Space

The Bosnian Civil War left Bosniaks, Croats, and Serbs segregated in the newly constructed political administrative units of entities and cantons. Each group is actively remaking its territory into a mono-ethnic place. While traveling through these regions, one cannot help but notice the construction of exclusive national edifices, whether churches, mosques, or monuments. They are meant not only as markers but as signs to inhibit the return of refugees in postwar Bosnia.

The Serbs have been overt in their dismissal of assuming "Bosnian" as part of prewar place names in the RS through the renaming of place, such as renaming Bosanski Brod to Srpski Brod and the town of Foča to Srbinje. All references to Bosniak, Croat, and Turkish names and historical events in the street names of Serb Banja Luka have been replaced with the names of Serb national heroes and historical events. Even the color of signs manifests a national scope; in several Bosniak-dominated areas, green is the color of choice as background for municipal signs. Green is traditionally associated with Islam. The manifestation of uniquely national symbols contradicts the longed-for notion of a Bosnian identity and unified Bosnia, illuminating the still ongoing struggle, albeit nonmilitary, among Bosnia's Bosniaks, Croats, and Serbs.

Mobilizing and Building the Nation

Two institutions—the nationalist political parties and organizations and the national religious leaders—were and continue to be the primary mechanisms for mobilizing the Bosniaks, Croats, and Serbs. As Yugoslavia disintegrated following Marshal Tito's death, nationalist political parties filled the power vacuum left by Tito and the faltering Communist Party. Each of Bosnia's main national groups established strong and adversarial nationalist parties and political platforms.

Outside the Bosnian state and its two-entity, pseudo-state arrangement, the United Nations (UN) and North Atlantic Treaty Organization (NATO, now the EU) play an even larger role. The implementation of the Dayton Peace Accords clearly envisioned a dual process. The international community, through the Contact Group, oversees the political and civilian administration of Bosnia through the Office of the High Representative (OHR), while the military provisions of the Dayton Peace Accords are enforced by NATO and the EU. The integration of these two international bodies is limited, and their responsibilities and chain of command are separate. This was done purposefully, as the United States, primarily, had little faith in the UN being able to fulfill the military clauses of the Dayton Peace Accords.

The Dayton Peace Accords brought an end to the most horrific warfare and slaughter seen in Europe since World War II. It did not, however, provide a viable concept for building a new state. The process of partition into entities has inexorably drawn the ethnic communities further apart. As such, there has been a renewed call by Bosniak political leadership and some members of the international community for a revision of the Dayton Peace Accords, a call that the Serbs vehemently oppose, as it clearly threatens their entity and perceived security. There has been little reduction in the strength of the wartime nationalist parties, and paltry evidence of local ethnic reconciliation or the elite cooperation necessary to make power-sharing work and avert a return to war in the future.

The fears that Bosnia's dominant group, the Bosniaks, will submerge the Croat and Serb identities through control of the government are real. The friction is based on the unwillingness of the Croats and Serbs to submit to the authority of Muslim-dominated Sarajevo. The inability of the Muslims to have a state that they control—that which is the internationally recognized boundary of Bosnia and Herzegovina—continues to be a source of tension among ethnic groups.

The label Bosnian (or Bosniak) imparts the idea that the state of Bosnia belongs to this group. On the other hand, "Bosnian" Serb or "Bosnian" Croat only indicates their presence in Bosnia. Dropping the adjective "Bosnian" is of no concern as both peoples look to their respective bordering states for support and even identity.

Only through the capacity of the Bosniaks, Croats, or Serbs to "extend or modify" their national ideologies can a successful outcome be achieved. Whether Bosnia succeeds as a sovereign state or one day dissolves depends on whether the national groups can coexist within the current territorial and political framework mandated by the Dayton Peace Accords. Each group's perception of itself and its territory was hardened in the civil war. Although it may be difficult to imagine a state like Canada, the United Kingdom, or Belgium plunging into a civil war over national ideologies, it is sadly a realistic possibility in Bosnia as it struggles to develop as a state. The notion of forging a common Bosnian national identity and territory was not achieved at the Dayton negotiating table. The Bosniaks alone associate their collective identity and interests with the development of a functional unitary Bosnian state. The presence of the High Representative (HR), NATO, and European Union Forces (EUFOR) calms ethnic tensions and compels

View of the famous Old Bridge in Mostar, which was rebuilt after its destruction during the country's 1992–1995 civil war. The bridge was originally constructed in 1566 during the Ottoman Empire rule in Bosnia-Herzegovina and had been designated a UNESCO monument of exceptional artistic and structural value. (iStockPhoto.com)

"good behavior," thereby maintaining the political and territorial integrity of the Bosnian state.

This notion of a Bosnian identity is beset with challenges by the state's citizens. The use of "Bosnian" as a regional label in the pre-1990s Yugoslav period has changed to be understood as a national identity based on Bosnia's independence. A Bosnian state exists, so logically a Bosnian state-centered identity should exist. However, again, this is not the case among the Bosniaks, Croats, and Serbs. Current research suggests that only the Bosniaks are appropriating a Bosnian identity to maintain and, even further, their demographic and political hegemony within Bosnia. National identity simply serves as a centrifugal force in Bosnia. The Serbs wish to preserve their current level of pseudo-statehood of RS within the framework of the Dayton Peace Accords. The Croats increasingly desire a strong level of autonomy within Bosnia by maintaining the concept of cantons. Indeed, today, Croat nationalists are advocating a third entity to safeguard their national and political interests.

The rejection of a Bosnian identity by the Croats and Serbs promoted Bosnian Muslim efforts in assuming it within the label of "Bosniak." Even the international community, such as the UN High Commission for Refugees (UNHCR), has labeled the Muslims as Bosnian in public documents, and by assuming the title of Bosniak, the Bosnian Muslims are stressing their territorial rights.

Historical events and the post-1945 communist political institutions and arrangements have strengthened Croat and Serb national ties to Croatia and Serbia proper such that any aspirations toward a true Bosnian identity will be difficult. The efforts of the Bosniak and Muslim community to demand such allegiance only adds to alienation on the part of the Croats and Serbs and animosity toward Bosnia's Muslims.

The recent civil war radicalized most elements of Bosnian society and enhanced the already strong bond between religion and identity. The current reality in Bosnia today indicates that, at most, both Croats and Serbs may acknowledge some level of a Bosnian civic identity, but not one of national identity. The issuing of uniform Bosnian identity cards, Bosnian automobile license plates, and Bosnian passports helps reinforce this civic identity but provides little counterweight to the national religions, nationalist politics, and the very real and bitter memories of the war. As such, these aspects will provide a source of tension among Bosnia's three major national groups and will actively inhibit the establishment of a Bosnian national identity in the years to come.

Selected Bibliography

Allcock, J. B. 2000. *Explaining Yugoslavia.* New York: Columbia University Press.

Bose, S. 2002. *Bosnia after Dayton: Nationalist Partition and International Intervention.* New York: Oxford University Press.

Bringa, T. 1995. *Being Muslim the Bosnian Way.* Princeton, NJ: Princeton University Press.

Burg, S., and P. Shoup. 2000. *The War in Bosnia and Herzegovina: Ethnic Conflict and International Intervention.* Armonk, NY: M. E. Sharpe.

Ćirković, S. M. 2004. *The Serbs.* Malden, MA: Blackwell Publishing.

Jelavich, B. 1983. *History of the Balkans: Eighteenth and Nineteenth Centuries.* Cambridge: Cambridge University Press.

Malcolm, N. 1994. *Bosnia: A Short History.* London: MacMillan.

Perica, V. 2002. *Balkan Idols: Religion and Nationalism in Yugoslav States.* New York: Oxford University Press.

Shatzmiller, M., ed. 2002. *Islam and Bosnia: Conflict Resolution and Foreign Policy in Multi-Ethnic States.* Montreal: McGill-Queen's University Press.

Sugar, P., and I. Lederer, eds. 1994. *Nationalism in Eastern Europe.* Seattle: University of Washington Press.

Velikonja, M. 2003. *Religious Separation & Political Intolerance in Bosnia-Herzegovina.* College Station: Texas A&M University Press.

White, G. W. 2000. *Nationalism and Territory: Constructing Group Identity in Southeastern Europe.* Lanham, MD: Rowman & Littlefield.

Catalonia

Kathryn Crameri

Chronology

801 Franks begin to capture the land now known as Catalonia from the Muslims.

988 The Catalan counts rebel against Frankish rule.

1137 Catalonia is linked by marriage to the Crown of Aragón.

1469 The Crown of Aragón is linked by marriage to Castile.

1640 A Catalan peasant revolt leads to an 11-year war with Castile, which Catalonia loses, although it retains its former level of autonomy.

1714 Catalonia comes fully under Castilian control after the Wars of Succession and loses its autonomy.

1830s A renaissance (*Renaixença*) of Catalan language and culture begins.

1892 A group of Catalanists produce a document called the *Bases de Manresa*, which sets out a program for Catalan autonomy.

1914 Catalonia is granted a limited territorial authority called the *Mancomunitat*.

1932 Catalonia gains autonomy during Spain's Second Republic.

1939 Franco wins the Spanish Civil War and sets about suppressing regional differences.

1975 Franco dies, and Spain begins to move toward democracy.

1978 The new Spanish constitution paves the way for all regions to have a degree of autonomy.

1980 Jordi Pujol and his party Convergència i Unió (Convergence and Union, CiU) win the first elections to the *Generalitat* (they remain in power until 2003).

1992 The Barcelona Olympics brings Catalonia to the world's attention and starts a tourist boom.

2003 Pasqual Maragall and his party, the Partit dels Socialistes de Catalunya (Socialist Party of Catalonia, PSC), head a left-wing coalition that takes power in the *Generalitat* after the first elections in which the CiU was not led by Pujol.

2006 A new Statute of Autonomy is approved to replace the one in force since 1978. Maragall decides not to stand for reelection, and José Montilla (PSC) becomes president of the *Generalitat*.

Situating the Nation

Catalonia forms part of the Spanish state and is located in the northeastern corner of the Iberian Peninsula, near the French border. When Spain returned to democracy after the rule of the dictator Francisco Franco, who died in 1975, a regional layer of government was put in place that gave regions powers in specific areas, although these varied slightly from region to region. Catalan demands for self-rule had been one of the key factors in the decision to allow the devolution of power to the regions, and Catalonia has remained highly influential as one of the new autonomous communities, using its powers to promote a distinctive Catalan identity. This has happened partly as a way of correcting the suppression of

Catalan culture and identity that formed part of Franco's plan for a unified Spain. However, Catalonia's national identity has deep roots, and its sense of distinctiveness is not simply a product of those particular injustices.

Catalonia traces its origins to the 9th century, when a drive by the Franks to stop the advancing Muslim conquerors, who had already claimed most of Iberia, led to the establishment of Frankish settlements south of the Pyrenees, around Barcelona. These settlements gradually broke away from Frankish rule and established a new relationship with the Crown of Aragón in the 12th century. Catalonia was the more active partner, embarking on forms of trade and conquest that eventually gave them political or financial power over much of the western Mediterranean. One of the most important legacies of this time is the Catalan language itself. Derived from Latin and used first as a vernacular language, then for literature, law, and philosophy, Catalan spread within both eastern Spain and southern France, even reaching outposts such as Alghero in Sardinia. Another notable factor was that, unlike the rest of the Iberian Peninsula, Catalonia developed a fully feudal social system, which has been linked with its subsequent achievements and character. However, this period of expansion and flourishing trade and culture came to an end because of internal conflict and the effect of natural disasters such as outbreaks of plague. The eventual result of this turmoil was the union by marriage of Aragón and Catalonia with the kingdom of Castile in the late 15th century. Although the two elements in this new relationship were supposedly independent from one another, power shifted to Castile, and Catalonia was sidelined. Resentment among the Catalan population grew to such a point that, during the Spanish Wars of Succession, Catalonia decided to back a different candidate from Castile, hoping in this way to regain its status and independence. Unfortunately, they backed the loser, and Catalonia's right to self-government was removed after the conquest of Barcelona by Castilian troops on September 11, 1714.

Despite measures that were designed to bring Catalonia into line with the rest of Spain, the region's differences persisted. Catalan was still the language of the majority of the population, even if formal contexts now required knowledge of Castilian (Spanish). Catalonia's economy also evolved along particular lines, developing a relatively strong bourgeoisie and an industrial infrastructure based on products such as textiles. In the 19th century, Barcelona was one of the key motors of Spain's economy, and it remains so today. This period also saw social changes linked to industrialization and a revival of interest in Catalan culture and identity, which eventually led to the formation of regionalist and nationalist organizations. The fact that this renewed interest in Catalan language and culture was directed by the educated middle classes has given mainstream Catalanism a "bourgeois" tag that it has been unable to shake off, despite the fact that a wide variety of social groups have been involved in Catalanist projects over the last two centuries, especially during the period when Catalonia enjoyed a brief spell of autonomy under Spain's Second Republic (1931–1939).

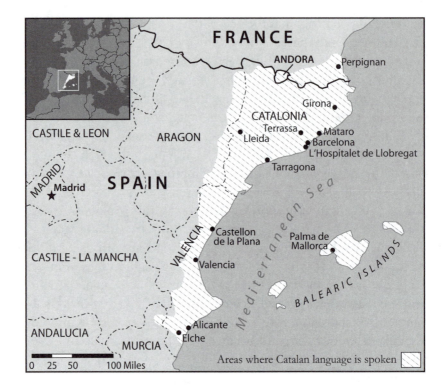

By the mid-20th century, the question of class had taken on a new significance because of the large numbers of people moving to Catalonia from other parts of Spain. The vast majority of the incomers were working-class economic migrants fleeing the harsh conditions of the rural south, which reinforced the perception that the native Catalans were middle class. By 1970, over a third of the population of Catalonia had been born outside the region. During the Franco regime, very little could be done collectively to persuade newcomers to take an interest in Catalan identity, although some individuals certainly did. The large numbers of "new Catalans" posed a particular problem for those working for a revival of the Catalan language and culture after the death of the dictator in 1975.

Instituting the Nation

The Spanish constitution of 1978 made provision for the autonomous communities to have a regional parliament and executive whose exact name, composition, and symbols would be decided by the region itself and laid out in its Statute of Autonomy. Following historical precedent, Catalonia's governing institution is called the *Generalitat de Catalunya,* and the region's flag is the *senyera,* which is composed of four horizontal red stripes on a yellow background. The *Generalitat* has extensive powers and responsibilities in areas such as culture, heritage, education, media and communications, internal transport, financial planning, natural resources, and social welfare. Although Catalonia's institutional framework is that of a regional government within the Spanish state (and *not* a federal arrangement), the *Generalitat* has plenty of scope for designing policies that directly affect the everyday lives of residents. It can also use its powers to "re-Catalanize" society through education, cultural policy, language planning, and promotional activities.

The first formal elections to the *Generalitat* produced a narrow victory for the center-right Catalanist coalition Convergència i Unió (Convergence and Union, CiU), led by Jordi Pujol. Although at this stage CiU was only able to govern with the support of other minority parties, the victory in 1980 was the start of a 23-year period in power during which Pujol became the voice of Catalonia. He was able to appeal to a broad spectrum of Catalans and to convince them that he had a workable vision of a dynamic future for Catalonia and its people. Despite inevitable setbacks in his campaign to wrest more power from the Spanish state, and a few sticky moments involving allegations of corruption, Pujol retired from the presidency in 2003 undefeated. This long term in power meant that Catalonia's development as an autonomous community has been largely controlled by one particular vision—a vision that was passionately nationalist, but not separatist.

The CiU did not have it all its own way, as it was unable to take control of Barcelona City Council, which is an influential institution in its own right. Instead, voters preferred the Partit dels Socialistes de Catalunya (Socialist Party of Catalonia, PSC) for this task, many of them seeing a nationalist party as best suited to the regional arena, while a left-wing party would give them what they wanted at

Catalan Politics

Originally a coalition, now a federation, of two "center" Catalanist parties, from 1978 to 2003 the Convergència i Unió (Convergence and Union, CiU) was led by Jordi Pujol i Soley (born 1930), who had been a Catalanist activist during the Franco regime. Pujol was president of the *Generalitat de Catalunya* from 1980 to 2003. Since then, the CiU (under leader Artur Mas) has been the opposition party, having failed to find coalition partners to allow them back into power in 2003 and 2006.

The Partit dels Socialistes de Catalunya (Socialist Party of Catalonia, PSC) is affiliated with the Spanish Socialist Party. Founded by Joan Reventós in 1978, the PSC has been in power in the Barcelona City Council since 1979 and the main partner in the coalition governing the *Generalitat* since 2003. Pasqual Maragall i Mira (born 1941) was president from 2003 to 2006 and was succeeded by José Montilla Aguilera, the first president of the *Generalitat* in the modern era to have been born outside Catalonia.

the municipal level. Here, too, one man emerged as an emblem of Barcelona's new possibilities: Pasqual Maragall, who was mayor of Barcelona from 1982 to 1997. Maragall presided over the successful Barcelona Olympics of 1992 and the regeneration of the city that surrounded the event. His popularity as mayor meant that many people saw him as the natural challenger to Pujol for the presidency, and although Maragall narrowly failed to oust his rival in the 1999 elections, he did manage to outmaneuver Pujol's successor in 2003. Since then, the PSC has governed in a three-way, left-wing coalition. While this change has meant a redirection in the *Generalitat*'s approach—for example, broadening the definition of Catalan culture to include all culture produced in Catalonia, whether in Spanish or Catalan—the parameters and priorities that were marked out by the CiU still condition the terms of nationalist debate.

It will be clear from this description of the two main political forces in Catalonia that there is a fine line between nationalism and regionalism in contemporary Catalan politics. Although support for independence has grown slightly in the last few years—as seen in the increased vote for Esquerra Republicana de Catalunya (Republican Left of Catalonia, ERC), which believes in gaining independence through democratic means—the majority of Catalans are not in favor of separatism, with only around a quarter seeing independence as a viable option.

Pasqual Maragall, former president of Catalonia, speaks during an election campaign meeting in Barcelona, November 2003. (Cesar Rangel/AFP/Getty Images)

There have been few violent incidents in the name of Catalan nationalism since 1980. As we have noted, members of the CiU are not promoting independence, although they do believe in achieving the highest possible level of autonomy for Catalonia within the Spanish state. Most of their rhetoric has revolved around achieving proper recognition of Catalonia's essential difference from the rest of Spain—the so-called *fet diferencial* or "fact of difference," a term that does not in itself point particularly to nationalism or regionalism. The PSC refer to themselves as "Catalanists" and not "nationalists," again sidestepping the question of regionalism versus nationalism. Furthermore, Catalans themselves are divided on the question of whether Catalonia is a region or a nation, despite the fact that all the rhetoric emerging from the *Generalitat* makes reference to a Catalan nation and urges Spain to recognize it as such. Catalan representatives such as Pujol, Maragall, and the former mayor of Barcelona, Joan Clos, have been very active in European forums and institutions that aim to strengthen the voice of regions, such as the European Union's Committee of the Regions, and they have also taken a variety of opportunities to promote Catalonia further afield. However, they have been wary of appearing too belligerent in international circles, aware that the term "nationalism" often carries negative connotations.

Defining the Nation

Rather than separatist claims, then, most Catalanist ideologies have been based first and foremost on language, culture, and the right of individuals to realize their potential through full recognition of their group identity. Language and culture were the key to the development of Catalanism in the 19th century and remain at the heart of Catalan distinctiveness. Jordi Pujol's own words sum up the feelings of most Catalans: "The identity of Catalonia is mainly linguistic and cultural. . . . There are many components in our identity, a whole bunch of them, but language and culture are its backbone. This means that if the language and culture were badly affected the personality of Catalonia would be too" (Pujol 1995, 6; my translation). Of course, the language and culture of Catalonia were indeed badly affected by their suppression under the Franco dictatorship, and the *Generalitat* made it one of its primary tasks to reverse the damage. This effort meant the introduction of language planning policies designed to "normalize" the position of Catalan by making sure that everyone was able to use it and had every opportunity to do so. Catalan is now the default language of education, and surveys reflect good progress in the acquisition of the language, with 95 percent of the population able to understand Catalan, 75 percent able to speak it, and 50 percent able to write it. Although there have been controversies over some aspects of the *Generalitat*'s language policy, most Catalans agree with the promotion of Catalan to strengthen its position as compared with Spanish, which has fundamental advantages over Catalan. Spanish is the only language that is official in the whole of the Spanish state, although other languages can be co-official in specific autonomous communities.

Catalan nationalism has only rarely been influenced by issues of ethnicity and prefers to see itself as an inclusive phenomenon. In other words, anyone who lives in Catalonia can be regarded as a Catalan, whatever their ethnic origins. However, the process of "becoming Catalan" functions in a more complex way than this pronouncement might suggest. First, there is an expectation that those who want to be Catalan will also want to speak Catalan, hence proficiency in the language is one of the surest ways to acquire a Catalan identity. Second, distinctions are still drawn between "new Catalans," "other Catalans," and "Catalan Catalans" when referring to people, although not usually in a negative way—just as a convenient description. However, stronger terms such as *xarnego*, a more pejorative term for an immigrant to Catalonia, do still circulate. Third, although the newcomers of the 1950s and 1960s had plenty of reference points in common with their Catalan hosts, the same cannot always be said of the immigrants who have made Catalonia their home since the 1980s. With democracy and economic progress have come a new influx of foreign migrants from Latin America, North Africa, and eastern Europe. The challenges posed by their cultural, religious, and linguistic differences have led to an increased awareness of ethnicity as an issue.

As a result, some more controversial elements have found their way into debates on Catalonia's future, including a concern that the low birth rate of the Catalans compared with that of the immigrants will endanger the continuity of the Catalan identity.

Despite these issues, Catalan nationalism remains basically civic in its orientation, although it could be argued that the strong stress on language introduces an ethno-cultural element into an otherwise civic framework. Citizens are urged to participate actively and proudly in the "project" of constructing a successful Catalonia and preserving its distinctive identity.

Narrating the Nation

This call to action is reinforced, as in all nations, by an appeal to historical memory, tradition, and symbols. One of the key moments in Catalan history was their defeat at the hands of the Castilians in 1714; September 11 is thus their national day. Catalans are keen to point out that this is not a "celebration of defeat" but a reminder of the brave fight put up by those who tried to defend Barcelona, of the autonomy Catalonia had enjoyed up to that point, and of the crude attempts to Castilianize Catalonia that followed. In other words, September 11 acts as a call to Catalans to continue to defend their identity.

As has already been mentioned, high culture plays a major role in defining Catalan identity, and it is featured in one of the region's best-loved traditions, the *Dia de Sant Jordi* (St. George's Day, April 23). The event combines the legend of St. George, Catalonia's patron saint, with a celebration of reading. People buy books and roses for loved ones from the many stalls that line the streets during the day. In the mid-1990s, the *Generalitat* joined forces with publishers and others to persuade UNESCO to declare April 23rd "World Book Day," then used this as a pretext for a series of high-profile advertisements in foreign papers explaining the tradition and highlighting Catalonia's economic and cultural achievements. Literature in Catalan is seen as one of the key barometers of the health of the nation and was one way in which Catalans perpetuated their language and cultural heritage during the Franco regime despite censorship and restrictions. Since the 1980s, literature has continued to have a symbolic importance but has encountered a different type of difficulty: free-market conditions are not particularly favorable to minority literatures, and it is a struggle to make publishing in Catalan viable and to persuade people to read in Catalan rather than Spanish, if they read at all. The *Generalitat* has therefore had to put into place a program of subsidies for publishing in Catalan, alongside aid for other cultural forms such as cinema, the performing arts, and the media.

Alongside this emphasis on high culture, Catalans are also proud of their popular traditions, especially the national dance, the *Sardana*, and competitions between towns and villages to build "human towers" or *Castells*. These two pastimes symbolize the ethos of participation and cooperation that characterizes Catalan society. Other character traits that have been identified by writers and commentators over the years as being particularly Catalan are *pactisme*—a willingness to compromise and negotiate—and *seny*, which is hard to translate directly but refers to a particular type of good common sense.

Mobilizing and Building the Nation

Most Catalans are proud of their identity and happy to support the promotion of Catalonia's distinctiveness. However, the extent to which they are willing to be actively involved in nationalist politics varies greatly. Surveys show that the vast majority of Catalans feel a clear affiliation with Spain, even if they describe themselves as Catalan first and Spanish second. Many Catalans see questions of nationalism/regionalism as firmly secondary to worries about employment, health care, immigration, or terrorism. There is even evidence that the younger generations are beginning to feel more ambivalent about questions of language; they have been educated to be bilingual, and they will normally use either language depending on the situation, but this means that they have no particular loyalty to Catalan over Spanish. These groups have been the particular target of nationalist persuasion in recent years, especially through advertising campaigns by the *Generalitat* designed to reinforce a sense of community and the individual's responsibility toward it.

New residents of Catalonia are another group felt to need particular attention because of the challenge to Catalan nationalism posed by immigration. The aim here is to make new arrivals aware of Catalonia's difference from the rest of Spain and to encourage them to learn Catalan (as well as Spanish, if necessary). Strategies have included the production of bilingual guidebooks (in Catalan and the main languages understood by immigrants) that explain Catalonia's cultural and social makeup as well as offering practical advice on work, health care, and so on.

Immigration is also one of the issues driving the current political agenda on Catalan autonomy, as the *Generalitat* has been pushing for more control over how many people settle there and what kinds of skills would be most useful to the region's economy. The beginning of the 21st century saw a campaign to reform the Catalan Statute of Autonomy, with corresponding changes to Spanish institutions, to give Catalonia more powers in a variety of areas. However, while the current Spanish government has allowed every autonomous community to propose a new statute, it is clearly intended that they should all remain fundamentally equal. Unlike the rigidly centralist Conservative government of José María Aznar (1996–2004), the Socialists, in power since 2004, have gone some way toward

People create a human tower, or *castell*, a popular tradition that originated in Catalonia. (iStockPhoto.com)

acknowledging the "multinational" nature of Spain, although it remains to be seen whether this acknowledgment will be enough for the Basques and Catalans. Many Catalan nationalists are pushing for a form of asymmetrical federalism or regionalism in which the "historic nations" of Spain (Catalonia, Galicia, and the Basque country) are given more powers and status than communities with less distinctive identities.

The fact that Catalonia technically exists as a region within the Spanish state has not stopped its political leaders from carrying out forms of nation-building. The institutional framework now in place performs as a kind of quasi-state in many areas directly relevant to citizens' perceptions of their individual and group identity. Catalan is now the language of all public institutions at local or regional levels, and its presence in education and in the media is especially significant for making a direct connection with ordinary people. A wide range of cultural products is available in Catalan that employ specifically Catalan frames of reference. High-profile cultural and sporting events and international trade and political links have also made the rest of the world more aware of Catalonia than ever before.

However, some Catalans worry that the emphasis on "normalization" and institutionalization obscures fundamental weaknesses in Catalonia's position. There are still areas of life that remain situated within a deeply Spanish linguistic, cultural, and social context, including Catalan citizens' formal interactions with the state and the most influential elements of the press, television, and mass culture. Private business has also been reluctant to adopt Catalan as its working language, often for practical reasons since the use of Catalan would complicate business relationships within Spain and abroad. A further problem arises in Catalonia's dealings with the other main areas of Spain where Catalan is spoken: the Valencian community and the Balearic Islands. Some people refer to these areas as part of a territorial entity they call the *Països Catalans* or "Catalan Countries," meaning all the areas where Catalan is spoken, including a small area of France around Perpignan. This entity has no legal existence, and even the areas within it that are located in Spain are expressly forbidden from federating by the Spanish constitution. Furthermore, relationships with Valencia and the Balearics are often strained and even hostile, for complex political reasons that have both historical and contemporary roots. Many Valencians prefer to refer to their language as Valencian and not Catalan, and some have gone as far as to deny any relationship between the two, despite incontrovertible linguistic evidence that Valencian is a variety of Catalan. This lack of solidarity among the Catalan-speaking areas of Spain has a very negative impact on efforts to promote the Catalan language and culture, and it is one reason the Catalans are demanding more powers to safeguard them within their own territory and more active promotion and recognition of them by the Spanish state.

The question of whether the Statute of Autonomy approved in 2006 is nothing but a step toward a demand for outright independence is too difficult to answer at this point. Much will depend on the ongoing process of reforming Spain's relationship with its constituent parts, as well as on external factors such as the eventual shape of the European Union and the effect of cultural globalization on minority languages and identities. The nationalists' ability to mobilize the sectors of the population for whom national identity is no longer a major issue will also prove crucial.

Selected Bibliography

Balcells, Albert. 1996. *Catalan Nationalism: Past and Present.* Edited by Geoffrey J. Walker. London: Macmillan.

Conversi, Daniele. 1997. *The Basques, the Catalans and Spain: Alternative Routes to Nationalist Mobilization.* London: Hurst.

Guibernau, Montserrat. 2004. *Catalan Nationalism: Francoism, Transition and Democracy.* London: Routledge.

Hargreaves, John. 2000. *Freedom for Catalonia: Catalan Nationalism, Spanish Identity and the Barcelona Olympic Games.* Cambridge: Cambridge University Press.

Institut d'Estadística de Catalunya. 2003. *Estadística d'usos lingüístics a Catalunya.* Barcelona: Generalitat de Catalunya.

McRoberts, Kenneth. 2001. *Catalonia: Nation Building without a State.* Oxford: Oxford University Press.

Payne, John. 2004. *Catalonia: History and Culture.* Nottingham, UK: Five Leaves.

Pujol, Jordi. 1995. *Què representa la llengua a Catalunya?* Barcelona: Generalitat de Catalunya.

Sobrer, Josep Miquel. 1992. *Catalonia, a Self-Portrait.* Bloomington: Indiana University Press.

Woolard, Kathryn Ann. 1989. *Double Talk: Bilingualism and the Politics of Ethnicity in Catalonia.* Stanford, CA: Stanford University Press.

Germany

Paul Maddrell

Chronology

1990	(October 3) Accession of the five *Länder* (federal states) of the German Democratic Republic (GDR) to the Federal Republic of Germany (FRG). (December 2) A coalition of the Christlich-Demokratische Union (Christian Democratic Union, CDU), its Bavarian sister party the Christlich-Soziale Union (Christian Social Union, CSU), and the Freie Demokratische Partei (Free Democratic Party, FDP) wins the first parliamentary elections held in the newly united Germany. The CDU's chairman, Helmut Kohl, consequently remains chancellor. These are the first all-German elections since March 1933 and the first fully free ones since November 1932.
1991	(September) Attack by hundreds of local people and right-wing youths from other parts of East Germany on foreigners and asylum-seekers living in Hoyerswerda, Saxony.
1992	(August) Attack by thousands of local people and neo-Nazis, who traveled to the city, on an asylum hostel in Rostock, in Mecklenburg-Vorpommern (eastern Germany). (November) Murder, in a fire-bombing attack, of three Turks in Mölln, Schleswig-Holstein (western Germany).
1993	(July 1) The amendment to Article 16 of the *Grundgesetz* (Basic Law), restricting the right to asylum, comes into force.
1994	(September 1) Withdrawal of the last Russian troops from German soil. Corresponding withdrawal of the last U.S., British, and French troops from West Berlin.
1998	(October 11) Controversial speech by Martin Walser, accepting the Peace Prize of Germany's book publishers. (October) The coalition of the Sozialdemokratische Partei Deutschlands (Social Democratic Party of Germany, SPD) and Bündnis 90/die Grünen (Alliance 90/the Greens) wins a majority of seats in elections to the *Bundestag* (federal parliament).
1999	(September) The *Bundestag*, the federal government, and the most important ministries start work in Berlin, having moved from Bonn.
2000	(January 1) The new law on German citizenship comes into force.
2002	(January 1) Adoption by Germany of the euro, the common currency of the European Union states, as its currency.
2003	(March) Application made to the *Bundesverfassungsgericht* (Federal Constitutional Court) by the federal government, the *Bundestag*, and the *Bundesrat* (Federal Council) to ban the National-demokratische Partei Deutschlands (National Democratic Party of Germany, NPD) is rejected.
2005	(May) Opening of a Holocaust memorial near the Brandenburg Gate in Berlin. (September) In elections to the *Bundestag*, the SPD-Green coalition loses its majority there, leading to a "Grand Coalition" of CDU/CSU and SPD.

Situating the Nation

Most of the German nation was united in one state, the Federal Republic of Germany (FRG), on October 3, 1990, when the German Democratic Republic's (GDR's) five *Länder* acceded to it under Article 23 of the FRG's *Grundgesetz*. The FRG's political structures therefore continued in existence, as did the network of alliances the West German governments had built up over the previous 40 years. Of the latter, the main treaties involved were the North Atlantic Treaty (1949) and the Treaty of Rome (1957). These respectively bound the Federal Republic to a defense pact, the North Atlantic Treaty Organization (NATO), and an economic and political union, the European Union (EU) (known until 1993 as the European Community). West German statesmen had entered into these and other treaties to control German nationalism, prevent Germans from again seeking to dominate Europe, and persuade the other European nations to no longer see Germany as an enemy. Indeed, a sense of being good Europeans has become, in the opinion of most Germans, an element in their national identity. The post-1990 governments have therefore sought to maintain and, indeed, increase the FRG's integration into the West (its *Westbindung*); they have insisted that German reunification be accompanied by European unification. This is an expression of identity; they are European Germans, and the two identities are inseparable. In this respect, German nationalism is very different from that of the British or the French, which have laid much greater stress on national independence.

Many West Germans before reunification, including the main political parties, had seen their country as progressing toward a post-national future. They anticipated that the EU would become a full European federation, of which the FRG would be one state. In fact, reunification has further stabilized the German nation-state, whereas the EU's enlargement to include 27 states, economic difficulties, disagreements over foreign and defense policy, and controversial currency have prevented this expectation from being realized.

German reunification stimulated another wave of European integration. The Treaties of Maastricht, Amsterdam, and Nice came into effect in 1993, 1999, and 2003, respectively. By these treaties, the EU's responsibilities were greatly expanded,

Helmut Kohl (1930–)

Kohl, the sixth and longest-serving chancellor of the Federal Republic, grew up in a conservative, Roman Catholic household in Rheinland-Pfalz. His older brother was killed in World War II while serving in the German Army—an event that helped convince Helmut of the overriding importance of peace in Europe. His political career was marked by a longing for German reunification and by a desire to complete the reconciliation with Germany's neighbors that Konrad Adenauer had begun, above all by creating a European federation. Kohl became chancellor in 1982; his tenure is the longest so far (1982–1998). He exploited the collapse of the German Democratic Republic skillfully, pressing for swift German reunification and winning the consent of the Soviet Union and Germany's allies to this plan. Germany's rush to unification in 1990 represents the greatest achievement of his long and very successful political career. Although his dream of a European federation has not been realized, it was he more than anyone else who ensured that a single European currency, the euro, was introduced in 2002.

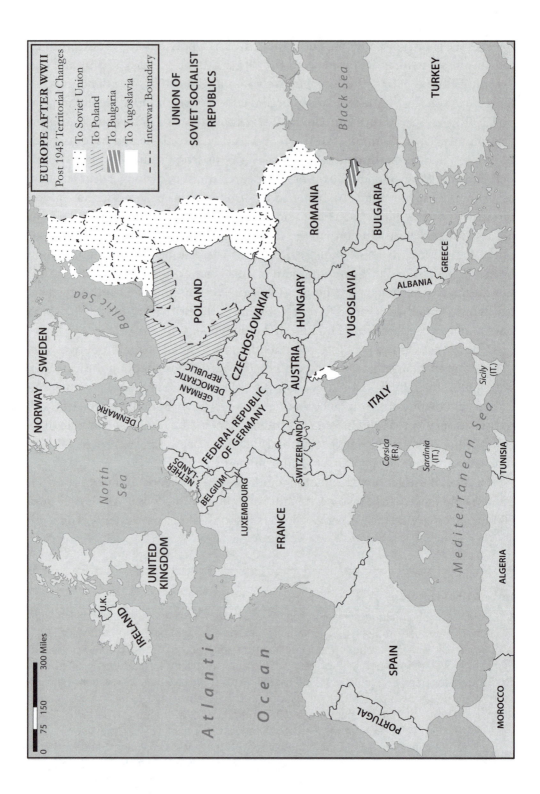

EUROPE AFTER WWII

Post 1945 Territorial Changes

- To Soviet Union
- To Poland
- To Bulgaria
- To Yugoslavia
- Interwar Boundary

UNION OF
SOVIET SOCIALIST
REPUBLICS

TURKEY

Black Sea

ROMANIA

BULGARIA

GREECE

ALBANIA

YUGOSLAVIA

Baltic Sea

POLAND

CZECHOSLOVAKIA

HUNGARY

GERMAN
DEMOCRATIC
REPUBLIC

AUSTRIA

ITALY

NORWAY

SWEDEN

DENMARK

FEDERAL REPUBLIC
OF GERMANY

SWITZERLAND

Mediterranean Sea

NETHER-
LANDS

BELGIUM

Sicily
(IT.)

LUXEMBOURG

Corsica
(FR.)

Sardinia
(IT.)

TUNISIA

FRANCE

*North
Sea*

UNITED
KINGDOM

U.K.

IRELAND

ALGERIA

*Atlantic
Ocean*

SPAIN

PORTUGAL

MOROCCO

0 75 150   300 Miles

THE EUROPEAN UNION

above all to include foreign and defense policy and justice and home affairs. A common currency, the euro, was introduced in 2002, superseding the deutschmark, previously the source of much German national pride. If the EU reform treaty signed by European leaders in Lisbon in December 2007 is ratified, the post of EU high representative for foreign affairs (essentially, the position of EU foreign minister) and an EU diplomatic service will be created. The aims of greater integration are to bind Germany more closely into Europe and to enable Europe to defend its interests in the world. German governments, by entering into the treaties, were deliberately emphasizing that German nationalism was consistent with and would promote internationalism. Contemporary German nationalism is remarkable: Germans are very willing to separate government from the nation-state and transfer it to international bodies, above all those of the EU. This international governmental network greatly reduces German national independence. The problem with it is that it weakens German democracy.

Instituting the Nation

German national identity has been the subject of intense debate in the political arena. The key institutions involved in identity issues are political. The institution that represents the German nation is the *Bundestag*, elected by the German people. The federal states are represented by another institution, the *Bundesrat* (Federal Council), to which their governments send representatives. The other key institutions in the debate over German national identity are the political parties, which divide into four camps. The CDU, CSU, and FDP make up a conservative alliance. Their principal rival for power is the alliance of the SPD, a socialist party, and Bündnis 90/die Grünen, a party of liberal environmentalists. On the extreme right wing are the nationalist parties, the NPD, the Deutsche Volksunion (German People's Union, DVU), and the Republikaner (Republicans). On the extreme left is Die Linke (the Left). Die Linke was known from 1990 until 2005 as the Partei des Demokratischen Sozialismus (Party of Democratic Socialism, PDS); from 2005 to 2007 it was known as Die Linkspartei (PDS). In June 2007 it merged with its western German ally, the Wahlalternative Arbeit & Soziale Gerechtigkeit (Voting Alternative Work and Social Justice, WASG) and became Die Linke. It is the successor party to the GDR's ruling communist party, the Socialist Unity Party (Sozialistische Einheitspartei Deutschlands, SED).

Defining the Nation

One challenge has been to create an all-German national identity in place of West and East German identities. The restoration of a sense of a common nationality has proved to be longer and more difficult than many expected. Common nationality is a sense of solidarity with the other members of a nation. This solidarity has proven to be incomplete. The sense of German nationality derives from the German Reich, which, for practical purposes, ceased to exist in 1945. Living for 45 years in two states with very different political, economic, and social systems created deep-seated differences between East and West Germans that have been difficult to overcome. Economic hardship in the eastern *Länder* has added to these difficulties, since many East Germans feel disadvantaged in the new Germany. Die Linke has been able to win seats in elections at all levels of representation (local, state, federal, and European), in part because it has been able to represent a continuing East German identity. The *Bundestag* election of September 2002 may therefore indicate that this East German identity is being eroded by an all-German one, because it was the first such election since 1990 at which Die Linke (then the PDS) lost votes. The party failed to achieve 5 percent of the national vote, which meant it was not entitled to be proportionately represented in the

Supporters of Germany's right-wing National Democratic Party (NPD) shout slogans and wave anti-foreigner placards as they gather by the Brandenburg Gate in Berlin on March 12, 2000. (Reuters NewMedia Inc./Corbis)

Bundestag. Its share of the vote in the eastern *Länder* fell from about one-quarter in 1998 to approximately one-sixth. However, it returned to the *Bundestag* in the election of September 2005.

Another key debate has been over German national identity. The terms of debate in Germany are hard to express in language familiar to Americans. However, broadly speaking, the debate has been over whether German nationalism should be conservative or liberal in character. The view taken of national identity has reflected the broader political attitudes of the participants, who can be classified as conservatives and liberals (in actual fact, the "liberal" position is that generally taken up by the SPD and Greens and in Germany would be called "left-liberal").

First, conservatives believe that the nation should remain as ethnically homogeneous as possible. By contrast, liberals have maintained that Germany has long been changing owing to mass immigration and should accept that it is now a multicultural country. This division affects attitudes toward both citizenship and immigration. Compromises have been reached on these issues, though how stable they will prove to be is uncertain.

Second, many people, conservatives prominent among them, have argued that Germany should assert its interests more strongly and play a larger international role. There has been much liberal support for this position; consequently, agreement has been easy to reach, and there was much continuity in foreign policy when the SPD and Greens replaced the CDU/CSU and FDP in power in 1998. Germany has proven more willing to assert itself internationally, even to the point of using military force. It continues to seek a permanent seat on the Security Council of the United Nations. Although it refused in 1991 to form part of the UN-backed, American-led alliance that expelled Iraqi forces from Kuwait (Operation Desert Storm), the German air force did participate in the bombing campaign in 1999 that drove Serbian forces out of Kosovo (Operation Allied Force). This was the first time that German armed forces had waged aggressive war on another state since 1945; moreover, they did so without any mandate from the United Nations. However, it is important that they intervened for humanitarian reasons; in Germany, the use of force for other reasons would have encountered fierce public opposition. Germany did not participate in the invasion of Iraq in 2003, public opinion being strongly against this action. However, the country has been the "lead nation" in peacekeeping in Macedonia and gave military support to the U.S. attacks on terrorist targets in Afghanistan late in 2001.

Conservatives and liberals agree on the correctness of anchoring Germany in the West and integrating it into the EU. They argue that this is established by the success of the Federal Republic between 1949 and 1990. Where they differ is in the role they see for the nation-state in the future. The conservatives see the nation-state as normal; reunification represented a German return to normality. This normality should be developed. Germany should behave more like a normal nation-state in its foreign policy by being more willing to use military force abroad and asserting its interests more strongly. A stronger line on "national"

Joschka Fischer (1948–)

Fischer's political career represents one of the most extraordinary journeys in modern European politics. He was born in 1948 in Gerabronn, Baden-Württemberg. He left high school before graduation and did not take a degree at university. As a young man, he settled in Frankfurt-am-Main, where he became involved in the revolutionary student movement of the late 1960s. He was involved in many violent confrontations with the police; among his friends and acquaintances were notorious terrorists. However, in the 1970s he underwent a profound change of mind, abandoning support for revolution in favor of Green politics. He is significant for German politics because he led the Greens toward acceptance of more pragmatic mainstream politics. As foreign minister from 1998 to 2005, he fused their liberalism with a more calculating assessment of German national interest, thus helping a liberal nationalism to develop. As foreign minister, he led the Greens away from their long-standing pacifism to support using military force for humanitarian purposes. He convinced the party to support German involvement in the Kosovo War of 1999, the first time since World War II that the Germans had used military force; he argued that the Serbian policy of "ethnic cleansing" in Kosovo represented a resurgence of European fascism that German antifascists had to resist.

---

issues—such as asylum, citizenship, and immigration—is also justified at home. Encouraged by national reunification, extreme right-wing groups and individuals have gone further and committed acts of violence against foreigners. By contrast, liberals argue that Germany has an abnormal history and therefore cannot assert itself as strongly as other "normal" nation-states. Moreover, they believe that Germany still needs to work to create a post-national world in which the nation-state is superseded. Both are currently strong supporters of European integration, but liberals more unreservedly than conservatives.

Extreme right-wing parties have argued that Germany should abandon its integration into Europe, withdrawing from both the EU and NATO, and seek more independence; this position harkens back to the tradition of the *Sonderweg* ("special path"). They also wish to restore the German borders of 1937. However, there is little popular support for these positions. Most Germans reject an aggressive external nationalism, and Germany's governments have not pursued an aggressive foreign policy. However, domestically Germans are more willing to assert their national identity.

Third, the Germans' relationship with the past has been the subject of much disagreement. Conservatives have argued that Germans should take more pride in being German and assert their identity more strongly. Consequently, they should no longer feel such shame about the Nazis' crimes, which now lie long in the past. However, the Holocaust still weighs heavily on the Germans, and many still feel the need to do penance for it. Indeed, the SPD-Green government in recent years has tried to ensure that the Holocaust continues to shape German national identity. An example is the large memorial to the Holocaust that opened in Berlin in 2005.

Citizenship, immigration, and asylum have been very divisive issues. Strictly speaking, "citizens" is the legal and political term given to those people of full age within a nation-state who exercise political rights within the nation. Some German intellectuals, Jürgen Habermas and Dolf Sternberger chief among them, have sought to fuse the concepts of nation and citizen by putting forward the idea of *Verfassungspatriotismus* ("constitution patriotism"). By this reasoning, a German national identity results from an individual's support for the democratic political order created by the *Grundgesetz*. The citizen's loyalty to Germany is conditional; it lasts only as long as Germany remains a democracy. This is a very liberal construction of national identity and very characteristic of the political development of West Germany since 1945.

By contrast, there is a tendency within European nations to define themselves ethnically. This tendency is particularly strong among the German nation. Since the Germans did not have a national state until 1871, citizenship could not be derived from birth within a specific territory; it had to derive from ethnicity. This was called the *ius sanguinis* ("the law of blood"); the alternative tradition is that of the *ius soli* ("the law of territory").

Reunification brought with it an upsurge in popular nationalism and a huge influx of ethnic Germans, immigrants, and asylum-seekers. In the eastern *Länder*, there was also a severe economic crisis and mass unemployment. The result was a furious outburst of extreme right-wing violence against foreigners, who were seen as threats to the German nation because, purportedly, they undermined its identity and caused economic and social problems. The attacks have been expressions of both nationalism and racism; most of the perpetrators have been youths. The attacks have continued until the present time; in all, there have been many thousands of them. Well-organized gangs of neo-Nazis have played a considerable role in them, though others have been more spontaneous attacks. They have usually been committed by relatively few perpetrators and have taken the form of murder, manslaughter, assault, and arson. There was an increase in such violence in 1991, the first year after reunification; the two weeks surrounding the first anniversary of reunification, on October 3, 1991, were marked by an upsurge in violence. The violence in 1992 was even greater than that of the previous year. It declined following the amendment of Article 16 of the *Grundgesetz* (see below) but has persisted to the present.

The attacks have taken place in the new eastern *Länder* and in the old western ones. However, there have been more attacks in the East than the West. In 2000 there were 2.21 xenophobic attacks per 100,000 population in the East, compared with 0.95 in the West. Moreover, the violence has sometimes taken a different character in the eastern *Länder*. Instead of being attacks by a few criminals, they have been riots involving many people. When neo-Nazi youths attacked a hostel for asylum-seekers in Rostock in August 1992, they were cheered on by

Neo-Nazi

The term neo-Nazi was first coined in April 1945, when Germany was being overrun by the Allied armies, to describe the radio broadcasts of Nazi guerrilla fighters who continued to resist the conquest of their country. It has since come to be used to describe the racist and ultranationalist far right of German politics. The main political parties that unquestionably fall under this label are the NPD and the DVU. People on the far right are considered neo-Nazi because their attitudes, broadly speaking, resemble those of Adolf Hitler's National Socialist (or "Nazi") German Workers' Party in the 1920s and 1930s. Intensely nationalistic, they want to free Germany of foreign influences, which are seen as damaging to the nation. Accordingly, they dislike Germany's membership in powerful international organizations like the European Union and NATO, which limit the country's freedom of action. They also want to see Germany expand its territory again, returning to the borders of 1937. Most of all, they are furiously racist, believing that the German nation should be ethnically homogeneous. In short, they oppose the whole modern course of German national development.

onlookers. There is also significant silent approval for such violence in the East—more so than in the West. These differences point to a difference between East and West Germans; in the FRG violence against outsiders came to be seen as socially unacceptable in a way that it did not in the GDR, where an old-fashioned German nationalism survived more intact. The East German communist regime failed to change traditional German customs, values, and prejudices as profoundly as the democratic, economically and culturally very dynamic West German state changed social customs in the West. Traditional hostility toward Poles also remained stronger in East Germany than in West Germany. This violence against foreigners led, in 1993, to the right to asylum being severely restricted. German conservatives thought that the very generous right of asylum that had existed until then had been the cause of the violence. Liberals disagreed; they considered Germany's excessively restrictive law on citizenship to be at the root of the trouble and pressed for its reform. In their view, it encouraged antagonism toward foreigners by preventing them from becoming Germans.

Narrating the Nation

The choice, in 1991, of Berlin as the new national capital indicated that Germans had pride in their past and wished to assert their identity more strongly. However, the Holocaust, and to a lesser extent World War II, continue to obstruct this assertion. Both loom large in the national memory. German politicians, particularly on the left, continue to insist that Germany commemorate the horrors of the Nazi past and make public acknowledgment of the crimes committed against

Europe's Jews. The reconstruction of Berlin following the dismantling of the Berlin Wall has encouraged this commemoration to take an architectural form. A Jewish Museum opened in Berlin in 2001; a memorial to the Holocaust opened there in 2005. This reflects the belief that only when the Germans have done adequate national penance for this appalling crime will they be comfortable with their identity; penance and national confidence go together. This has attracted criticism from those in Germany who feel that enough penance has been done. The distinguished novelist Martin Walser, accepting Germany's most famous literary prize in 1998, argued that commemoration of the Nazi past was excessive, had been turned into meaningless ritual, and was being used to shape the national conscience. His argument was that the Germans were a normal people now, and each German should be left to reach his own moral verdict on the past. He spoke for many. Walser connected national self-confidence not with penance but with the lack of it—with normality, in other words.

Mobilizing and Building the Nation

The political parties have made great efforts to mobilize support for their contrasting conceptions of national identity. The most striking example is the CDU/CSU's attempt to stop the SPD-Green coalition's reform of citizenship law by mounting a petition campaign against dual citizenship in the federal state of Hessen in January 1999. The campaign did indeed mobilize much popular opposition to dual citizenship and helped the CDU win the state election in Hessen the following month. As Martin Walser's condemnation of "instrumentalization" of the Holocaust indicated, commemoration of the past by means of museums, memorials, and anniversaries has also been used to mobilize opinion in favor of a liberal Germany.

The federal government has tried to turn opinion against neo-Nazi organizations by banning them. Several were banned in 1992. However, the membership of the NPD, DVU, and Republikaner has increased since 1990. Their share of the vote has also increased, giving them significant representation in state (*Landesparlamente*) and local (*Kommunalparlamente*) parliaments. In 2001 the federal government, the *Bundestag*, and the *Bundesrat*, applied to the *Bundesverfassungsgericht* to ban the NPD; however, this application was rejected. In 2004 the NPD achieved 9.2 percent of the vote in elections to the state parliament of Saxony.

Since 1990, the FRG has made profound changes to its law on asylum, immigration, and citizenship. These changes have been the subject of furious debate between conservatives and liberals. At the root of the debate has been disagreement over whom the nation should include. While the right to asylum has been considerably restricted (a victory for conservatives), the law on citizenship has been significantly relaxed (a victory for liberals). Both changes have been, in part, efforts to prevent further extreme right-wing violence.

Article 16 of the *Grundgesetz* conferred the constitutional right to asylum and hence made West Germany, and from 1990, Germany, the European country to which most asylum-seekers flocked. All the extreme right-wing parties are hostile to it. The collapse of the communist regimes of Central and Eastern Europe in 1989 caused a big increase in the number of political refugees claiming asylum in Germany. In 1990, there were 193,063 such applications; in 1991, 256,112; and in 1992, 438,191. The wave of attacks on asylum-seekers and other foreigners in 1991–1992 persuaded the mainstream political parties that the violence would only diminish if the right to asylum were significantly restricted. An amended Article 16, reflecting a compromise between differing positions, came into effect in July 1993. This amendment greatly reduced the number of those applying for asylum. Migration to Germany by ethnic Germans living in eastern Europe and the Commonwealth of Independent States (the successor to the Soviet Union) was also restricted.

German citizenship has traditionally been derived from descent from a German parent (the *ius sanguinis*). Consequently, children of non-Germans born in Germany have not become German citizens. One reason for this restriction is the opposition of German conservatives to dual nationality. If the place of birth determined nationality (the *ius soli*), the children of non-Germans born in Germany would not only become Germans but, very often, would inherit the nationality of their parents as well. Dual nationality, conservatives argue, obstructs full integration into the German nation. Another reason for the resistance to change is an unwillingness to change the ethnic character of the German people. The SPD-Green coalition acted quickly to change Germany's citizenship law when it came to power in October 1998. The new law, which came into force on January 1, 2000, made it easier both for non-Germans to become naturalized and for children of non-Germans who were born in Germany to become German citizens, even if this meant that they had dual nationality. The law incorporated elements of both the *ius soli* and the *ius sanguinis*.

Children of non-Germans born in Germany will become Germans if one parent has lived in Germany for 8 years and has permanent residency status. Any resultant dual nationality may be retained until the person in question reaches the age of 23, when he or she must choose one nationality or the other. Only 8 years' of residency, instead of 15, is required for naturalization. Germans living abroad can only pass German citizenship on to their children and not to later generations. To ensure integration, the law also insisted that the new citizen be competent in German and swear loyalty to the *Grundgesetz*. This latter requirement, like the law itself, moves Germany closer to a political conception of nationality, though it still has a cultural component.

By creating a liberal Germany—nationally inclusive, free, tolerant, democratic, and international—liberals hope to make the national question their own for the first time in almost 150 years. The problem is that the international structures to which the state belongs will weaken German democracy and may stimulate a conservative nationalist backlash in the name of democracy. A key issue for Germans is whether conservative nationalist support for internationalization will continue.

Selected Bibliography

Berger, S. 1997. *The Search for Normality.* Providence, RI: Berghahn.

Conradt, D. 2003. "Political Culture and Identity: The Post-Unification Search for 'Inner Unity.'" In *Developments in German Politics 3*, edited by S. Padgett, W. Paterson, and G. Smith, 269–287. Basingstoke, UK: Palgrave Macmillan.

Finzsch, N., and D. Schirmer, eds. 1998. *Identity and Intolerance: Nationalism, Racism and Xenophobia in Germany and the United States.* Washington DC: German Historical Institute.

Green, S. 2003. "Citizenship and Immigration." In *Developments in German Politics 3*, edited by S. Padgett, W. Paterson, and G. Smith, 227–247. Basingstoke, UK: Palgrave Macmillan.

Langewiesche, D. 2000. *Nation, Nationalismus, Nationalstaat in Deutschland und Europa.* München, Germany: Beck.

Mommsen, W. 1999. "The Renaissance of the Nation-State and the Historians." In *German and American Nationalism: A Comparative Perspective*, edited by H. Lehmann and H. Wellenreuther, 283–300. Oxford: Berg.

Müller, J.-W. 2000. *Another Country: German Intellectuals, Unification and National Identity.* New Haven, CT: Yale University Press.

Panayi, P. 2001. "Racial Exclusionism in the New Germany." In *Germany since Unification*, 2nd ed., edited by K. Larres, 129–148. Basingstoke, UK: Palgrave.

Schulze, H. 1998. *Germany: A New History.* Cambridge, MA: Harvard University Press.

Sternberger, D. 1990. *Schriften, Teil 10: Verfassungspatriotismus.* Frankfurt-am-Main, Germany: Insel-Verlag.

Greenland

Søren Forchhammer

Chronology

8,000 years ago So-called Proto Eskimos—people with a material culture and pattern of adaptation resembling the ones of the historical Inuit—live in the Bering Sea region.

5,000 years ago Small groups of Proto Eskimos migrate along the Arctic Coast from the Bering Strait to Greenland as the ice retracts. Many migrations follow.

ca. AD 800 The immediate forefathers of the modern Inuit begin a migration eastward from the Bering Strait region, settling along the arctic coast.

900–1000 Inuit bands spread to Hudson's Bay and other parts of Canada and cross the Ellesmere Strait between Canada and Greenland.

Before 1000 In southwest Greenland and coastal Labrador, Inuit bands encounter Norse peasants who have migrated from Iceland and Norway.

ca. 1500 Whaling commences in the North Atlantic. In the following centuries, whaling, trapping, and trade intensify in all Inuit territories and strongly influence the way of life of the Inuit.

1721 Colonization proper commences in southwest Greenland, led by private companies with a royal grant. By the end of the century, trading and mission stations, so-called colonies, have been put up all along the west coast of Greenland, and the state has taken over and monopolized the trade.

1800s The quest for a passage to the East via arctic North America, as well as numerous arctic and polar expeditions, prompts contact between Inuit and European explorers. In Greenland the state consolidates its presence, extracting substantial profits from the trade. In the middle of the century, a profitable private mining industry is initiated. All West Greenlanders have converted to Christianity, the old religion having been eradicated; literacy is widespread, and Greenlanders are being educated as catechists. Furthermore, the local population is included in political, administrative, and judicial institutions, which have been formed in all colonial districts, thus introducing the Greenlanders to a form of democracy. By the end of the century, the Danish state finally puts up a colony in the only inhabited region of East Greenland, and in 1910 a private company establishes a trading and mission station in Avanersuaq (Thule), the northernmost part of West Greenland from where numerous American expeditions aiming for the North Pole have departed.

post-1945 Large military bases and warning systems are deployed all over the arctic, and substantial mineral and oil exploration and extraction begin. Southerners migrate to the arctic in an unforeseen scale. Inuit are relocated to permanent villages in a process most local populations are unable to influence.

1977 Natives all over the arctic (except in the Soviet Union) begin to organize in the 1950s and 1960s. In 1977 Inuit from Greenland, Canada, and Alaska found the Inuit Circumpolar Conference (ICC). (The Yupigyt of Chukotka joined the ICC only a few years ago.) The aims of the organization include strengthening the unity of the Inuit, promoting Inuit rights, protecting the environment, and securing Inuit participation in political and developmental processes.

1979 Greenland acquires Home Rule but is still a part of the Danish state.

Situating the Nation

Replacing the allegedly derogatory word Eskimo in the 1970s, the term Inuit became the common designator for a number of arctic and subarctic peoples who
all belong to the Eskimo Aleut language group and most of whom traditionally
had a maritime adaptation pattern. Today approximately 150,000 Inuit are living
in small communities and towns along more than 6,000 miles of arctic and subarctic coastline from Chukotka to East Greenland. Although some of the groups
do not refer to themselves as Inuit and prefer the word Eskimo as a common designation, I will use the word Inuit in this article. Inuit (singular, *inuk*) is the word
for human beings or people in most Eskimo languages from northern Alaska to
Greenland. Variants are Yupiit (southwest Alaska) and Iit (East Greenland).

Two Inuit societies stand out as being potential nation-states: Nunavut and
Greenland. They have comparable geographic, demographic, linguistic, economic,
and ethnic traits, and they both have experienced quite far-reaching self-rule devolved to them by the states of Canada and Denmark, respectively. In Greenland,
the Kalaallit have almost 150 years of history of integration into the political and
administrative system. Since the 1860s, all major disputes between the Kalaallit
and colonizers have taken place inside the formal political framework established
by the Danish colonial authorities. The Inuit of Nunavut have only recently been
integrated into the political system in a similar way.

From the mid-19th century, the West Greenlanders had representatives in
small councils governing local matters such as welfare, hunting, personal disputes, and much more. In 1912 two regional councils were added, which had to
be heard on all matters concerning their region before Danish authorities could
take any action. Since the 1950s Greenland has also had representatives in the
Danish parliament.

Today the Kalaallit, or Greenlanders, are considered a people or nation, not
only by themselves but also by the surrounding world, including the Danish government. However, Greenland is not a sovereign nation but a semi-autonomous
part of the Danish kingdom defined by the Home Rule Act, which the Danish
parliament adopted in 1978, and by subsequent bilateral agreements. The Home
Rule parliament (*Inatsisartut*) and government (*Naalakkersuisut*) are situated in
the capital of Nuuk. There are elections every four years in West Greenland as
well as Avanersuaq (Thule) and East Greenland. The Greenlanders have the right
to pass laws and to self-govern under certain restrictions defined by the Home
Rule Act. The Greenlanders govern industry, environment, health care, schooling,
culture, infrastructure, and much more. However, to this day Greenlandic sovereignty does not include matters as important as mineral and oil exploitation,
defense, or foreign policy. These matters, crucial to any truly sovereign nation,
Greenland has to address in common with the Danish parliament and government. This limitation of Home Rule has, for the entire Home Rule period, been a

point of criticism, particularly to the more nationalistically minded political parties and parts of the population.

Unlike Denmark, Greenland is neither a member of the European Union nor of NATO. However, as a result of an agreement struck between Denmark and the United States during World War II, the United States has had numerous military bases and radar sites in Greenland. Today only one radar site, in Avanersuaq (Thule), remains part of the American nuclear missiles warning system. For a number of years, negotiations regarding American military presence in Greenland have been trilateral, also due to Home Rule.

Economically, Greenland is dependent on fish processing and export. In addition, Greenland also receives a substantial block grant from Denmark as an effect of the Home Rule Act. Though relatively few pursue traditional sea mammal hunting, it contributes to the informal economy all over Greenland, including the modern towns. Until approximately 1950, Greenland was more or less cost free to the Danish treasury, allowing Denmark to profit for long periods from the trade with sea mammal products. Also, both private companies and the state profited well from mining activities beginning in the 1860s. Until the 1950s, Greenland's economy was small but stable due to a system introduced by the state that countered fluctuations on international markets for Greenlandic products. After around 1900, fishing became more and more important in the economy and eventually raised both the private and national economies to a much higher level. The Danish state, holding a trade economic monopoly in Greenland until the 1950s, was crucial in spurring this process. Fishing was a small-scale industry and was only conducted near the coast until the state began investing in a high sea fishing fleet in the 1970s. It was not until the 1980s that substantial private means were invested in the fishing sector. In colonial times, the Danish state completely dominated the economy. Today, Home Rule has taken over the dominant position. Home Rule owns the largest fish catching, processing, and exporting company, as well as the largest retail store chain in Greenland. It also owns the greatest part of Greenland's real estate (housing) sector, which has only recently become a subject for private investment.

Being a discrete island (the world's largest), speckled with archaeological evidence of former Inuit and Proto Eskimo presence, the geographical foundation or framework of the Greenlandic Inuit nation is very clearly defined as encompassing the totality of the island of Greenland and its surrounding waters. A prerequisite to the Greenlandic claim of sovereignty over the whole island, however, is the successful exercise of the sovereignty of the Danish state through the course of history, whether in regard to foreign whaling, bartering, and fishing interests off and on the west coast, Norwegian interests in East Greenland, or American military presence in the Avanersuaq (Thule) region. In any case, it would be a much greater problem in the future to claim Greenlandic sovereignty to the island and sea territory had the Danish state not successfully done so over the past centuries.

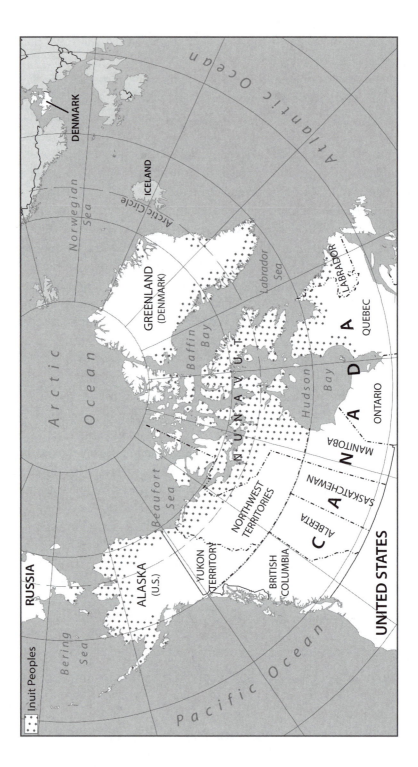

From the earliest times of contact and colonial history, there has been a clear sense of being a separate people. This distinctness is, for instance, expressed in a separate pan-Eskimo word for Southerners (*Qallunaat*) as opposed to *Inuit*. It is also seen in old tales of how the Qallunaat came into being: as the offspring of an Inuk woman and a dog. Numerous written sources from missionaries and trades people also tell about an Inuit identity different from the European one. However, the idea of the Kalaallit being a people or nation in the modern sense of the word only dates back to the mid-1800s, originating in a European context where ideas on the nation and democratic rule were defining the political agenda. Danish missionaries and administrators were instrumental in the dissemination of the idea of the Greenlandic nation, especially the Danish governor of South Greenland who in the mid-1800s instigated what can be seen as a national resurrection campaign. He gathered and published Greenlandic tales and customs, initiated a Greenlandic tradition of painting and drawing, and started a nationwide newspaper still in existence. He also initiated the formation of mixed European and Greenlandic councils vested with formal administrative, political, and judicial authority, which led directly to the Home Rule parliament and the legal institutions of today. In short, what happened in Greenland in the mid-1800s was in many ways similar to what happened in Europe: a national literature, art, newspaper, and national democratic, political, administrative, and judicial structures were created. Albeit the ideas and systems were European, the Greenlandic population soon adopted them and made them their own. There is ample evidence, not least from the Greenlandic contributions to their newspaper, that the ideas of a Greenlandic nation and Greenland as a national home spread rapidly to large parts of the population during this period. Probably leading that process were Greenlandic—or, as they were called, "national"—catechists, educated at the two catechist and teachers' colleges established in the 1840s. In the beginning of the 1900s, national identity was subjected to lively discussions in the national newspaper. To some, the real Greenlander was the seal hunter; to others—such as many catechists—being in good command of the Greenlandic language was the decisive criterion. To many, Greenlanders were modern people in a modern world, with fishermen using motorboats and women processing the fish (the traditional Greenlandic hunter and his wife). From the 1970s, when nationalistic ideas were (again) given much emphasis in the political discourse, the pristine Greenlandic way of life—seal hunting and the small communal settlement—defined Greenlandicness. This idea was primarily disseminated by the educated parts of the population, many of whom had been trained in Denmark.

Although the educated part of the population at times has held a key position, a broad range of the Greenlandic population participated in formulating nationalistic ideas and politics. The latest nationalistic surge, which began in the mid-1990s, has led to the election of monolingual Greenlanders to the highest political positions.

Initially, in the 1800s, nationalistic ideas were introduced in an effort to change colonial politics and to integrate the Greenlandic population into societal processes. Greenlanders were to take on more responsibility, and at the same time they were bestowed with more influence. There was a low life expectancy, and many Greenlanders lived on social welfare. Leading colonial administrators and politicians saw the integration of Greenlanders into political, administrative, and judicial processes as the only option, an idea also in accordance with the dominant political ideologies of the time. Eventually, this involvement also meant empowerment as a nation, on the ideal level as well as on the political and economic ones. In the 1960s, when new nationalistic feelings surged in Greenland, they did so in response to a global nationalistic wave that accompanied the liberation of other former colonies. The renewed focus on the Greenlandic nation, however, also came in response to Greenland's integration as a part of the Danish kingdom "on an even footing with Denmark," as well as to the intensified Danish investments that followed and that led to the immigration of thousands of Danish workers, teachers, and administrators. With the exception of the years between 1950 and 1964, all the important decisions were now being made in Denmark. Many Greenlanders felt they were being put on the sidelines, as mere spectators to what was going on in their country, a new sensation for them. Now leading Greenlanders claimed they were being alienated not only from the development of their country but also from their culture and language, which was being subjected to a pressure due to educational politics that emphasized Danish. Their reaction was to focus on the cultural and historical differences between the Danish way of life and the original Greenlandic one as it was, allegedly, still found in remote parts of the country.

Instituting the Nation

Today the Inuit live inside the framework of four different state structures, namely Russia (Chukotka), the United States (Alaska), Canada (Northwest Territories, Nunavut, Quebec, and Labrador), and Denmark (Greenland). The main groupings of Inuit are as follows: In Greenland, the self-designation Kalaallit applies to West Greenland. The East Greenlanders call themselves Iit, and those in Avanersuaq are Inughuit. Canada contains four main groups: the Nunavummiut of Nunavut in the former northeastern part of the Northwest Territories, the Nunavimmiut of Nunavik in northern Quebec, the Sikumiut of the Labrador coast, and the Inuvialuit of the Inuvialuit Settlement Region in the Northwest Territories near the Alaskan border. Their neighbors across the border to the west are the Iñupiat of the North Slope Borough in northernmost Alaska. Outside the borough, without any formally recognized political self-government, the Inuit, Yupiit, and Alutiit mostly live in settlements surrounded by non-native Alaskans. Across the Bering Strait, the Yupigyt in a similar way constitute a small minority.

Evidently, the Inuit are living under very different political and judicial circumstances resulting from historical processes. Basically there are two models: one based on the devolution of state authority, and one based on private, for-profit corporations. The Kalaallit (including the Inughuit and Iit), Nunavummiut, Nunavimmiut, Inuvialuit, and the Iñupiat of North Slope Borough enjoy varying degrees of political self-rule (including taxation rights) based on the devolution of state authority, which they execute within specified geographical boundaries. Their constituencies include the population living inside the geographical boundary, regardless of ethnicity (the vast majority being Inuit). Their authority, however, does not include subsoil (mineral and oil) rights or foreign or defense policy.

In the rest of North America, all Inuit rights are derived from aboriginal land claims. Land claims have been settled between the Inuit of Alaska and the Inuvialuit of the Northwest Territories and the United States and Canada, respectively. In contrast to the Inuit of Greenland, Nunavut, and Nunavik, most of the Alaskan Inuit have very limited territorial rights (except for the Iñupiat who have borough rights).

Defining the Nation

The national idea of the 1800s and early 1900s was connected to the enhancement of political self-determination. There was very little emphasis on culture and language. The focus was on educating the population—the nation—to enable Greenlanders to take over all the functions of society. This included training in the Danish language and in all other skills necessary, regardless of the Greenlanders' cultural origin. All in all, the national idea was connected to the notion that Greenlandic culture, ethnicity, and language were all very different from the Danish.

There has been, and still is, a conflict between a focus on the specific Greenlandicness on one hand and, on the other, the focus on Greenlanders as a mixed population who have much in common, culturally and historically, with other Nordic countries. In the beginning of the 20th century and in the 1970s, many Greenlanders protested the narrow definition of Greenlandicness as being identical with the way of life of the hunting communities. Many Greenlanders not only felt very little in common with that definition but they also considered it to be derogatory and detrimental to their political goals for Greenland. They considered development and modernity to be necessary for obtaining more national independence.

The spatial dimension of the Greenlandic nation, by today's definition, includes the territory over which the Danish state has sovereignty and that seems "natural"; that is, anything encompassing the whole island of Greenland, including the ice sheet (2,175,600 square kilometers) and the surrounding ocean (2 million square kilometers).

Whereas West Greenland, where the majority of the population lives, has been undivided by natural barriers and is easily accessible from the sea, East Greenland has historically been an isolated place, divided from the rest of the world by 300 kilometers of ice sheet to the west and, to the east, by the sea ice of the East Greenland Current, which wooden sailing ships were unable to penetrate. Avanersuaq (Thule) was separated from West Greenland by the uninhabitable Melville Bay.

Of the three ethnically and linguistically different Inuit groups in Greenland today, the West Greenlanders or Kalaallit is by far the largest one, and their lands have been colonized for the longest time. They number approximately 50,000. The Thule people or Inughuit were not formally colonized until the 1930s and today number about 800. The East Greenlanders, or Iit, who were colonized in 1894, number less than 4,000. The two smaller ethnic groups have been more or less ignored by the West Greenlandic majority in terms of protection and development of their language and culture. The language politics under Home Rule does not acknowledge the fact that there are three different languages in Greenland. For instance, no official orthography or grammar has been developed for the two small languages. The West Greenlandic language is used in the schools all over Greenland. In addition, East Greenland and Avanersuaq are among the least economically developed and poorest regions.

Narrating the Nation

In Greenlandic nationalistic symbolism, the year 1721 is crucial as the year when colonialism and missionary activities commenced. That date stands for the end of independent Greenlandic development, which some have claimed was about to lead to an autonomous Inuit state formation independent of the outside world. According to the nationalism of the 1970s and 1980s, the time before colonization was a happy one, whereas colonization has only led to misery; therefore, the original culture should be restored. Today's nationalism does not look back to pristine times in this manner. Instead it is oriented toward the future. Greenland is viewed as a modern country with its own historic and cultural roots, and it must develop its own modernity.

The most important myth of the nationalism of the 1970s and 1980s involved original commonality, or even original communism. According to this myth, original Greenlandic Inuit culture is characterized by being peaceful, nonaggressive, and in concord with nature. It is thus presented as the opposite to Western culture in what can seem to be a form of modern civilization critique.

Today, Greenlandic identity is expressed in a multitude of ways. Numerous symbols express the Greenlandic Inuit or Kalaallit identity, most of them taken from the material culture of the Inuit. The kayak is probably the most common symbol, but others include tools such as the toggle head of the harpoon, the *tuuk-*

kaq, the semi-circular women's knife, the *ulu*, or clothing such as the parka and skin boots. Sea mammals, fish, and other natural phenomena with a special bearing on the Inuit way of life are also used to symbolize national identity. More modern kinds of national symbols include the national costume, especially women's elaborate skin and pearl embroideries, and the Greenlandic flag, designed in the early 1980s by a well-known Greenlandic artist and prominent politician of the Home Rule government. The contour of the island of Greenland is also commonly used to designate Greenland itself. There also exist symbols derived from colonial times, for example, the polar bear standing upright, a former emblem of the Royal Greenlandic Trade Department. Buildings from colonial times are often used as emblems, such as municipalities, and the Danish flag is almost as popular as its Greenlandic counterpart, even today. The church and symbols related to Christianity also play a role in defining Greenlandicness.

Since the popular and national revival of the mid-1800s, art has been a vehicle for expressing the essential Greenlandicness. From the 1960s and 1970s, artists were expected to use "national" Greenlandic motifs even when they did not match the subject, such as seals and whales on stamps for Christmas instead of motifs related to church, Christmas, and Christianity. There is an old tradition of songwriting that expresses love of the country, and in the 1970s, a new nationalistic tradition grew out of the old based on rock music and the genre of protest

Emblem of the Royal Greenland Trade Company. Today the polar bear on a blue background is the emblem of Home Rule. (Wolfgang Kaehler/Corbis)

The Greenlandic Flag

In 1985 the Home Rule parliament introduced Greenland's national flag. The flag is a geo-metrical composition in red and white, divided horizontally in two squares of equal size, the lower one red and the upper one white. Into the squares is embedded a circle divided into two, the upper red and the lower white. The flag symbolizes the return of the sun, rising over the ice in spring. The colors also symbolize the relation to Denmark, whose flag is a white cross on a red background. The Home Rule parliament as well as the Greenlan-dic population was divided over the flag issue. A majority of the population preferred a flag in green and white with a cross to symbolize the Christian religion as well as the rela-tionship to the Nordic countries. Today some still prefer to fly the Danish flag.

Hunting, the Original Culture

Although traditional Greenlandic marine mammal hunting has been on the wane from the early 1900s as fishing and industrialization took its place, it still has importance as a symbol of Greenlandic national identity. During the nationalistic surge in the 1970s and 1980s, the remote and less-developed parts of rural Greenland were dignified as being a sort of cultural treasure island where the original and pristine Greenland culture based on marine mammal hunting had survived the waves of colonization that had struck urban Greenland, the latter being considered impure and Europeanized. The Greenlandic cul-tural and national resurrection was to begin in the hunting communities. Probably due to this idea, scholars have taken what may seem an unproportional interest in "traditional" hunting, thus backing Greenlandic nationalism.

---

song. The same period experienced a wave of political poetry with obvious na-tionalistic and anticolonialist content. Literature has also dealt with the Green-landic nation since the first Greenlandic novel was published in 1914. Already in the 1800s the newspaper *Atuagagdliutit* was broadly used for discussions of "na-tionalistic" issues, and this tradition continued in the 20th century.

Mobilizing and Building the Nation

From the mid-1800s, the idea of an indigenous Greenlandic nation has been con-veyed broadly to the Greenlandic population as well as to the Danish administra-tion, polity, and Danish citizens in general. From the 1960s both educated and uneducated Danes as well as Greenlanders were regarded as important to the nation, but there was an emphasis on the educated parts of the populations. Ed-ucated Greenlanders were especially criticized for not being sufficiently Green-landic, and Danes were considered to be simply colonialists and oppressors. Today, all inhabitants of Greenland have the same civil rights despite their ethnic back-ground. No laws or bylaws favor one ethnic group over another. However, the Greenlandic language is favored both in schools and elsewhere in society. Greenlandic is the first language of the country, and all children must learn Greenlandic from first grade regardless of their linguistic and ethnic background. But due to the large proportion of Danish speakers and the many Greenlanders who speak Danish as their first language, Danish is still the dominant language in the public and private administration and elsewhere. One of the main goals of the Greenlandic government is to replace Danish with Greenlandic. To this end, Home Rule has put much effort and economic resources into building and strengthening institutions for primary, secondary, and higher education in Greenland. The replacement of Danish with Greenlandic is proceeding steadily but not very rapidly. The trend is to homogenize the society if not ethnically, in the strict sense of the word, then linguistically. Greenland has for many years been a very homogenous society with a great deal of integration between the ethnic groups. Danish-Greenlandic marriages, for instance, are common and have been so ever since the early times of colonization. There is no outspoken hostility between the two groups in everyday life.

The ultimate political goal for Greenlandic nationalism today is sovereignty. At the time of this writing, a joint Danish-Greenlandic government commission is discussing the prospects of enhanced Greenlandic self-rule inside the realm of the Danish kingdom. However, to many nationalists, this goal is not enough. For them, the ultimate goal is an independent nation-state based on the Greenlandic culture and language.

It is not possible to speak about a nationalistic propaganda in the strict sense of the word. Nationalists as well as other political groups address the public by way of the ordinary printed media. Arts, music, and theater, for instance, cannot be said to be vehicles of nationalistic propaganda as such, even though nationalistic ideas are often expressed.

There has always been a broadly shared agreement that the Greenlanders constitute a separate people or nation and that this nation is entitled to the land it inhabits. The Danish state legitimized its presence in Greenland by the Greenlanders' need to be protected until they were able to "stand on their own feet," as it was often phrased. So, in that way, the Greenlanders have never been in need of legitimizing nationalistic aspirations. Rather, the problem has been twofold: to secure finances and to secure independence (as Greenland was evidently inside the American realm as defined by the Monroe Doctrine). Both problems the nation had to meet as a member of the Danish kingdom, securing funds as well as a certain kind of limited independence.

In Greenlandic nation-building, there has from the outset been an influx of ideas from the outside world, especially from Denmark, which the Greenlanders, as well as many Danes, have molded to fit the Greenlandic circumstances.

Today the main goal is a greater degree of national sovereignty. Some envision an independent nation-state; others see merely enhanced self-rule within the realm of the Danish kingdom. To strengthen the nation, one strategy is to homogenize the population linguistically and culturally and to limit the influx of specialists, including teachers and administrators. Education has a high priority, and today more Greenlanders than ever before hold university degrees and high positions in society, replacing the migrant specialists from Denmark. Regarding the formal political and judicial relationship to Denmark, the strategy seems to be a gradual increment of Greenlandic influence over foreign policy and resource development.

Selected Bibliography

Dahl, Jens. 1986. "Greenland: Political Structure of Self-Government." *Arctic Anthropology* 23, nos. 1–2: 315–324.

Dahl, Jens. 1996. "Arctic Peoples, Their Lands and Territories." In *Essays on Indigenous Identity and Rights*, edited by Irja Seurujarvi-Kari and Ulla-Maija Kulonen. Helsinki, Finland: Helsinki University Press.

Danker, Per, ed. 1999. *This Is Greenland.* Copenhagen: Greenland Resources A/S.

Gad, Finn. 1970. *The History of Greenland.* London: C. Hurst and Company.

Gad, Finn. 1984. "History of Colonial Greenland." In *Handbook of North American Indians*, vol. 5, edited by David Damas, 56–77 and 556–577. Washington DC: Smithsonian Institution.

Kjær Sørensen, Axel. 1995. "Greenland: From Colony to Home Rule." In *Ethnicity and Nation Building in the Nordic World*, edited by Sven Tagil, 85–105. London: Hurst and Company.

Kleivan, Helge. 1984. "Contemporary Greenlanders." In *Handbook of North American Indians*, vol. 5, edited by William C. Sturtevant, 700–718. Washington DC: Smithsonian Institution.

Kleivan, Inge. 1991. "Greenland's National Symbols." In *North Atlantic Studies*, edited by Susanne Dybbroe and Poul Brobech Moller, vol. 1, no. 2, 4–16. Aarhus, Denmark: Aarhus University Press.

Langgård, K. 1998. "An Examination of Greenlandic Awareness of Ethnicity and National Self Consciousness through Texts Produced by Greenlanders 1860s–1920s." *Études/Inuit/Studies* 22, no. 1: 83–107.

Nuttall, Mark. 1994. "Greenland: Emergence of an Inuit Homeland." In *Polar Peoples*, 1–28. London: Minority Rights Publications.

Nuttall, Mark. 2005. "Greenland." In *Encyclopedia of the Arctic*, vol. 2, edited by Mark Nuttall, 778–785. New York: Routledge.

Nuttall, Mark. 2005. "Inuit." In *Encyclopedia of the Arctic*, vol. 2, edited by Mark Nuttall, 990–997. New York: Routledge.

Latvia

Kathleen Woodhouse

Chronology

1721	Czarist Russia gains control of the Baltic region.
1850s–1880s	A national awakening takes root.
1905	A revolution against czarist control fails.
1914–1918	The German army controls a large portion of the Baltic region.
1918	Independence is declared, forming the first Republic of Latvia.
1922	The first constitution is drafted.
1920s–early 1930s	A series of parliaments are established and dissolved. Latvia undergoes political instability but benefits from land reforms.
1934	Kārlis Ulmanis overthrows the government and establishes his regime. Latvian enters into the Baltic Entente pact.
1940	"Year of Horror"; Latvia is incorporated into the Soviet Union. The deportation of Latvians begins, including Kārlis Ulmanis, who dies in a Soviet prison in 1942.
1941	(June 13) Soviet authorities deport approximately 15,000 Latvians to far areas of Russia, including professionals, intellectuals, religious figures, and landowners. A total of 35,000 Latvians are resettled over the course of the year. The later occupation by the German military results in some political independence; Jews living in Latvia are killed, sent to Germany, or forced into local camps.
1944	The Soviet army regains control. There is a mass exodus of Latvians to Western Europe, fearing deportation to Siberia. Deportations continue and Russians are relocated into Latvia.
1960s–1970s	Scattered incidence of nationalism results in Soviet clampdown on Latvian cultural life.
1980s	*Glasnost* initiative begins; environmental and cultural movements become openly nationalistic.
1988	Latvian Popular Front initiates independence campaign.
1989	(August) Two million people from Tallinn to Vilnius form a human chain, earning the title "singing revolution" from the global community.
1991	The Popular Front wins majority elections; Latvia declares itself independent from the Soviet Union.
1994	The last Soviet troops leave Latvia.
1999	President Vīķe-Freiberga is elected, then reelected in 2003.
2004	Latvia joins the European Union.

Situating the Nation

Latvian nationalism formed and evolved due to strong kinship ties and a quest for a cohesive national identity. For the last two centuries, this country witnessed perpetual change in its political and social structure. The present-day Republic of Latvia is situated on the Baltic Sea, with Estonia to its north and Lithuania to its

south. A relatively flat country, Latvia boasts a long coastline with beautiful
beaches and wooded lowland. Its mysterious natural scenes and varying amount
of sunlight has inspired a wealth of myths and legends over the generations. The
population hovers around 2.5 million, though the growth rate is in decline.

Outsiders may regard the Baltic trio as one region, but each country has its
own identity. Latvia's fertile land and access to the sea made it appealing to those
involved in early trade. Originally ruled by Germans, Swedes, and Poles, Latvia
came under Russian rule in 1721 as a result of the Swedish defeat in the Great
Northern War (1700–1721). Historically, Latvia was comprised of the following
regions: Kurzeme (Courland), Zemagale (Semigallia), Vidzaeme, and Latgale (Lat-
gallia). Serfdom was abolished in 1819, but Latvians remained on the outskirts of
political life. Russians and Germans dominated the urban areas and the political
positions. Settling of different landowners along with the boundary changes
caused by both world wars drastically influenced Latvia's ethnic composition.

Currently over 57 percent of the population is considered Latvian, though they remain a minority in the capital city, Rīga. The tradition of a strong rural Latvian population continues even today. Russians are the most significant minority both in number (about 30 percent) and in socioeconomic influence. There are also a substantial number of Belarusians, Ukrainians (often lumped together with Russians), Poles, and Lithuanians. During Latvia's incorporation in the Soviet Union, policies of Russification resulted in heavy migration of Russians into its lands. These policies also influenced language and culture, causing great resentment from the Latvian people. Since the country's independence, Russians have had to adapt to policies catering to Latvian language and culture.

Politically, Latvia has undergone enormous change. At the conclusion of World War I, Latvia suddenly formed as its own country. Citizens enjoyed independence during the interwar period, but forcibly became a part of the Soviet Union in 1944. During this time, Latvia provided the interior states of the Soviet Union with a large amount of crops and land for industry. Upon its independence in 1991, Latvia reinstated its original constitution and established a parliamentary democracy. Latvian nationalism closely followed these events and can be examined in different waves. The rise of the peasantry in the beginning of the 19th century marks the true start of Latvian nationalism. As the vast majority lived in rural areas as serfs, their movement was firmly anchored in a sense of land and community. After a brief revolution in 1905, Latvians abandoned their nationalist movements. It was not until the end of World War I that a renewed interest in Latvian independence surfaced. The vacuum caused by the changes in Europe afforded the country a rare opportunity, and Latvia became its own country on November 18, 1918. Never had they been in a position to truly envision independence. Then, after decades of functioning as a Soviet state, nationalism again gained strength among Latvians. From 1988 to 1991 the country made enormous changes, eventually regaining its independence. Since that time, Latvia has enjoyed more stability and economic growth than in past decades.

Instituting the Nation

Several institutions aided nationalist movements within Latvia. The first to explore the ideas of nationalism were the intellectuals seeking to consolidate Latvian identity. These Latvian and German scholars formed groups that examined ways to unite the people. The involvement of intellectuals in strong displays of nationalism continued over the 20th century. In the mid- to late 1980s, literary groups such as the Latvian Writers Union also came forward as active participants in the freedom movement. They became more vocal in their displeasure over the diminishing use of the Latvian language and censorship. Poet Janis Peters emerged as the leader, making speeches and writing about Latvian frustrations. Sometimes grouped with these intellectuals were the environmentalists. Many Latvians began showing their concern for the pollution caused by Soviet industrial initiatives. In the 1980s, Moscow allowed for some discussion between local authorities and those concerned. This opened the door to a nationalistic agenda as the environmentalists could claim that "their Latvia" was being polluted by outsiders.

Earlier, other types of small nationalist groups had been able to voice their displeasure with Russian control. The later years of the 19th century brought about new groups heavily voicing their displeasure over the socioeconomic condition of the rural communities. Groups such as the *jaun stvānieki*, with their newspaper *Dienas Lapa* began protesting Moscow's policies. While Alexander I was previously willing to promote ethnic awareness, he began enforcing Russification policies. These types of policies would emerge during every span of Russian or Soviet control. In 1899, after an impressive protest, 87 Latvians were arrested and tried. In 1905, however, the Latvian people began to change their tactics. Latvians banned together more openly, protesting violently both German and Russian authority. By the year's end, about 2,600 revolutionaries were executed, with thousands more exiled to Russia. This marked the first sweep of Latvians fleeing westward for Europe and North America, which would recur in the decades to follow. Other such groups formed during the Soviet era, including the famous Forest Brothers or Meža Brāli. About 12,000 nationalists took to the forests, hiding and showing signs of resistance whenever possible. By 1956, however, they were disbanded, as the Soviets made it a priority to imprison or kill this threatening group.

Latvian political parties were extremely important to nationalistic movements. On November 18, 1918, leaders of different Latvian parties assembled to create the first national council. The provisional government was led by Kārlis Ulmanis, the leader of the Agrarian Union. Many of these parties, even in the contemporary context, have made rural issues one of their top priorities. This goes beyond helping Latvian farmers maintain their way of life. Latvian identity's roots are in the physical land and the tradition of respecting the earth passed down through the generations. Respecting the land also means believing in hard work and dedication to mother Latvia. Political parties have used these ideas to draw in members. During the Soviet era, the Latvian Communist Party was the only truly recognized group, though others did exist. Currently, nationalism finds a home in many parties including the Latvian National and Conservative Party (LNNK), For the Fatherland and Freedom (FFF), Democratic Centre Party, and the Latvian Peasants' Union.

Strong ties among the three Baltic nations also remained a priority from 1918 to the present. Latvia's foreign policy after World War I retained a sense of neutrality, but a treaty of understanding was signed by Estonia, Latvia, and Lithuania. As all three were experiencing similar trials and successes, a unified front provided some security. During the Soviet era, the countries maintained their rapport and banded together in the fight for independence. While each country dealt with Moscow in their own manner, they looked to one another for support. Today the Baltic trio continues its strong diplomatic ties.

Defining the Nation

Past and present Latvian nationalism relies on a number of ethno-cultural fac-tors to foster a sense of cohesiveness among the people. Latvian identity formed itself around language and the rich art forms of folk songs (particularly the *dainas*), myths, and fairytales. The original four Latvian regions all included tribes with their own variations of language and culture. Originally, these groups were considered "non-Germans," as landowners were unable to label them. Latvian and German intellectuals of the 19th century were the first to seek a manner in which to unite the "non-Germans." Most of these intellectuals were educated in Estonia or Russia and returned to the region with a thirst for understanding the culture. Developing a unifying language became the first priority. This proved dif-ficult as each region drew on Danish, German, Polish, and Russian influences. They needed a method in which to convince Latvians that their language was not a peasant dialect but a steppingstone to create a national consciousness. Fur-thermore, the vast majorities of these "non-Germans" were uneducated and had little hope of a structured education. There were, however, important similarities among these groups. The folk tradition of songs, poetry, and stories surfaced as a strong bridge between the regions. Each group exhibited a wealth of songs de-picting everyday life. Atis Kronvalds and Krišjānis Barons, along with others, began working with songs and poetry to develop the language. The *dainas* folk songs allowed Latvians to relate their experiences with the land, water, and sky. The culture proved to be very rich, with celebrations of daily life and the different deities associated with natural elements.

Once language and a sense of culture developed, Latvians began to see them-selves as a united people. The biggest test came when Latvia found itself on the brink of independence. Although the initial years were chaotic, the people rallied

---

Dainas

Dainas are a type of Latvian folk song or poetry that expresses important aspects of na-tional identity. Themes usually include natural elements important to pre-Christian tribes— showing respect to land, sea, and sky. Unlike other cultures, Latvians did not create heroes but rather developed deities such as *saule* (sun). Songs also examine life journeys, includ-ing birth, marriage, work, and death. Thousands of these songs exist, emerging from all corners of the country. Krišjānis Barons, known as the father of the *dainas*, was the first to consolidate many of these songs into published text. They served as a means of bringing Latvians together during its initial waves of national awakening during the 19th century. This would remain an important manner in which to show nationalism while under Soviet control. Latvians came together in singing protests, demanding their rights to their culture and land. Large communities living outside of the homeland also held song festivals as a means to teach their children and keep their identity alive. Song festivals continue today as touring groups from both within and outside of Latvia celebrate their roots.

---

easily around the notion of a unified nation. This feeling of Latvianness became stronger over the years as events challenged the newfound freedom. The Year of Horror, starting in 1940, provided many events for rallying the national identity. The night of June 13–14, 1941, was the bleakest moment in Latvian history. The Soviet state security, the NKVD, rounded up and deported 15,000 people, sending them to working camps and special settlements in eastern provinces of the Soviet Union, mainly in Siberia. This night became a key event on which nationalism could rest. Russification policies, including the resettlement of Russians, Belarusians, and Ukrainians within Latvia, became increasingly difficult to bear. Language policies made Russian the official language for almost everything including commerce, education, street signs, and law enforcement. Latvian risked disappearing from their lives entirely. Outspoken politicians such as Edvards Berklāus attempted to point out the pitfalls of Russification. He and 2,000 of his supporters were eventually sent into exile. These events created yet another important issue for nationalists to address. In the wake of the Soviet Union, the Latvian government made the reinstitution of the Latvian language its first priority.

Narrating the Nation

Many individuals, nonpolitical and political, have been critical to the survival of Latvian nationalism. Krišjānis Barons worked with other intellectuals during the mid-1800s to develop a basis for Latvian identity. Aside from language, Latvians also had folk songs, specifically the *dainas*, in common. Impressed by their cultural richness, Barons began to compile and publish these songs. This legacy provided Latvians something to claim as their own, apart from any other influence. Barons continues to be revered today as a cornerstone of Latvian nationalism and even has a museum dedicated to his work in Rīga.

The importance of culture grounded Latvian nationalism, but actors were needed to take the cause forward. Prime Minister Kārlis Ulmanis remains the most prominent figure of Latvia during its initial years of independence. Ulmanis fled Latvia after his involvement in the 1905 revolution and studied agriculture in western Europe, eventually moving to the United States. Upon his return to Latvia in 1913, he became active politically and served as a founding member of the Latvian People's Council. Political instability afforded him an opportunity in 1934 to eventually dissolve the government and become president in 1936. Though Ulmanis fashioned a dictatorship, he led his country through difficult times with no violence and little displeasure from the people. His focus on Latvia's rich history and strong values of hard work and connection to the land won him respect. In 1940, the Soviet Union began sending troops to Latvia. President Ulmanis urged the people to avoid violence, realizing their military inferiority. He was deported and died in a Soviet prison in 1942.

Though Latvia regained its independence in the 1990s, many nationalist figures continue to emerge. Current president Vaira Vīķe-Freiberga, elected in 1999 and 2003, has played an enormous role in helping Latvia gain a foothold in Europe. Journalists compare her to Margaret Thatcher—Latvia's Iron Lady. She is noted for her direct approach in dealing with the Kremlin, gaining her both support within her country and enemies within the Russian government. She openly discusses possibilities of Russian military attack and stands firm on issues (such as language) that promote Latvian identity. Having fled Latvia at seven years old in fear of deportation, President Vīķe-Freiberga eventually became a professor of psychology at the University of Montreal. Her life work included studying Latvian identity, particularly folk tradition. After spending 55 years outside of Latvia, she returned to lead a small institute, which surprisingly led her to the presidency. She not only supports policies to strengthen Latvian culture but spearheaded initiatives to build strong ties within the Baltics and pushed to join the European Union in 2004.

Many symbols also help demonstrate Latvian nationalism. Over the years, symbols have hearkened back to the "real" life and have served as ways to keep the people together. Strong ties to the land and nature are expressed in the form of symbols, art, and holidays such as Midsummer's Eve. In the past these have

Mother Latvia stands at the top of the Freedom Monument in Rīga, Latvia. The monument commemorates the fallen soldiers of the Latvian War of Independence (1918–1920). (iStockPhoto.com)

Midsummer's Eve or *Janu Naktis*

Midsummer's Eve is a celebration of the summer solstice. This originally pagan holiday allowed Latvians everywhere to show their appreciation of the sun (*saule*). Rural communities built bonfires, drank, and ate cheese with caraway seeds. This celebration included jumping over the bonfire and singing folk songs all night long. Men sported oak crowns, and young girls wore flower halos. All of these symbols illustrated the devotion of the Latvian people to their land. When the Christian church took its roots in the region, both Catholic and Latvian Lutheran congregations included this holiday, renaming it St. John's Day. Until the annexation by the Soviet Union, *Janu Naktis* was a nationally observed holiday. As part of the Soviet Union, observing the day became difficult because Moscow discouraged this very Latvian display. Those living in the diaspora held their own *Janu Naktis* events, showing their respect to their ancestors. In present-day Latvia, one can still see the flower halos, bonfires, and cheer associated with this day.

helped people remember when the land was their own and life was good. The image of a Latvian woman, dressed in traditional clothing in a nature scene, helped reinforce this idea.

The Freedom Monument is possibly the most important physical site within the capital city. The base shows the struggle of the people, and the top of the column serves as a pedestal for mother Latvia holding three stars. These stars represent the three regions united with the independence of 1918. A restricted area during the Soviet regime, Latvians began placing flowers and Latvian flags there during the 1960s and 1970s. Though some were punished, people continued to show their support, growing bolder. Soviet leaders encouraged a certain amount of cultural freedom, and Latvians celebrated their holidays with folk songs and dances. While ethnic Latvians of the diaspora rallied around the world for global involvement, things in the homeland had to move slowly. Perhaps the most awe-inspiring representation of nationalism during this time was on August 23, 1989, when 2 million people from Tallinn to Vilnius joined hands to create a human chain. This nonviolent act of solidarity and protest earned it the title of the "singing revolution" in the rest of the world. Many protests followed, including a nonviolent protest with 300,000 participants marking the November 18 Independence Day in 1990.

Mobilizing and Building the Nation

The overarching themes of Latvian nationalism have always included the cultural values of dedication to nature and work, belief in a common origin, and a right to land. While nationalist movements surfaced over the decades, it was not until the 1980s that things truly began to change. The once quiet people began to grow restless under the Soviet thumb. Mikhail Gorbachev's ideas of *perestroika* and *glasnost* opened the door to many questions about how willing the government was to loosen its policies. During the mid-1980s, the government began squeezing out any blatant forms of anti-Soviet behavior. This repression, however, opened the door to more subtle nationalist groups. The first to emerge in June 1987 was Rebirth and Renewal founded by the Latvian Lutheran Church. The group's main goal was to examine how life in the Soviet Union hindered the exploration of Christian beliefs. Environmentalist groups also began to surface throughout the Baltic States. Their expressions of nationalism were closely tied to the earth and how industrialization affected its health. Latvians easily sympathized with these groups as their identity closely linked them to nature. The first major triumph ensued after a protest of a planned hydroelectric complex, which the Soviet government then agreed to abandon.

The victory inspired other groups to come forward. In 1987 three different demonstrations showed that Latvian nationalism had not vanished. These protests remembered the June 13 deportations, the signing of the Molotov Ribbentrov Pact, and the November 18 Independence Day. Folk song festivals and other celebrations of Latvian culture remained a delicate and effective manner in which to show resistance. In 1988 Janis Vagris was appointed head of the Communist Party, the first Latvian to hold such an influential role since 1959. LNNK held its first congress in 1989, shortly after that of the Latvian Popular Front. During this time, leaders from the three Baltic nations began meeting to discuss secession from the Soviet Union. Celebrations of Independence Day and the flying of national flags did not appear to affect the Soviet government. Timidly, the Baltic States saw this as their time to act. They joined forces and presented a united front to Moscow, sending leaders to represent their regional concerns.

In March 1990, an election resulted in the Popular Front gaining 134 of the 170 government seats. Lenin's statue was removed from the museum. The Soviet government began to pay closer attention to the Baltic States, threatening to implement economic sanctions. Negotiations ensued, and Gorbachev agreed to grant Latvia special status within the Soviet Union. Yet on May 4, 1990, Latvians and many Russians overwhelmingly voted to reinstate the Republic of Latvia. That year, the folk song festival included choirs consisting of members from the Latvian diaspora, opening the country to the global community. Since the inclusion of Latvia in the Soviet Union, members of the Latvian diaspora had constantly worked toward involving the global community. By the end of World War II, an estimated 1.6 million Latvians had fled their homeland. Many, however, did not forget their roots, keeping the memory alive in their new homes. These communities did a tremendous amount for their homeland and continue to contribute funds and resources to help rebuild Latvia.

In 1991, the Soviet Union threatened Latvia with severe punishment if nationalists did not quiet down. In January of that year, several Lithuanians were killed and 150 were wounded by Soviet Black Berets outside a radio station. In response to this event, 700,000 Latvians left their homes to guard various important buildings in Rīga. Several were killed later that month when the Black Berets raided the Ministry of Internal Affairs. Yet a major crackdown never occurred. In March, Moscow allowed the Latvian Soviet Socialist Republic to once again be called the Republic of Latvia. The leader of the Latvian Communist Party, Alfrēds Rubriks, was one of the few anti-independence supporters who wished to fight the growing majority. His arrest in 1991 marked the political transition of the country as the Latvian nationalists were able to gain a greater foothold in his wake. During his trip to accept the Nobel Peace Prize, Gorbachev threatened to reinstate economic pressures to prevent more separatist nationalism. In response, the Latvian leaders insisted they would charge the Soviet Union real prices for all agriculture exported from their country. The government also began privatizing land, creating a new monetary system, and devising ways in which to define Latvian citizenship. Soviet vice president Gennadii Yanaev was then slated to overrule the Latvians and become acting president. Yet again, these threats never yielded results. Latvia continued its fight for freedom and was eventually recognized by the deteriorating Soviet Union.

Latvia joined the European Union in May 2004, an important step in its journey toward stability. Attempting to regain its footing, the government passed many laws regarding reinstating the Latvian language. One of the biggest issues faced by the Latvian government since 1991 has involved Russia and the local Russian community. Recent border disputes over land have increased the stress in the already tense situation between the two governments. Latvia also demanded an apology for the treatment of Latvia by the Soviet Union. Russia, in turn, has demanded better treatment for Russians living in Latvia. Language policies made Latvian the official language in all realms of Latvian life. Many Russians never felt the need to learn the language and are now suffering the consequences. Protests ensued after the government demanded that all schools teach in Latvian. Many local Russians find life more difficult, though they are adapting by creating their own communities. The future of Latvian nationalism remains uncertain as the tension at home continues. Right-wing groups have emerged, voicing their displeasure of an ethnically "impure" state. Joining the European Union and working toward a more European identity will most likely change how Latvia views itself. Nonetheless, its strong sense of belonging to the Baltic region and celebration of Latvian culture will undoubtedly continue.

Selected Bibliography

Commercio, Michele E. 2004. "Exit in the Near Abroad: The Russian Minorities in Latvia and Kyrgyzstan." *Problems in Post-Communism* 51, no. 6: 23–32.

Dreifelds, Juris. 1996. *Latvia in Transition.* Cambridge: Cambridge University Press.

Eksteins, Modris. 2000. *Walking since Daybreak: A Story of Easter Europe, World War II, and the Heart of Our Century.* New York: Mariner.

Gordon, Frank. 1990. *Latvians and Jews between Germany and Russia.* Stockholm, Sweden: Momento.

Lieven, Anatol. 1994. *The Baltic Revolution: Estonia, Latvia, Lithuania and the Path to Independence.* New Haven, CT: Yale University Press.

Melnika, Iveta. 2003. *Tale of the White Crow: Coming of Age in Post-Soviet Latvia.* Granite Falls, MN: Ellis Press.

Nesaule, Agate. 1997. *A Woman in Amber: Healing the Trauma of War and Exile.* New York: Penguin.

Palmer, Alan. 2006. *The Baltic: A New History of the Region and Its People.* New York: Overlook Press.

Plakans, Andrejs. 1995. *The Latvians, a Short History.* Stanford, CA: Hoover Institution Press.

Rudenshiold, Eric. 1992. "Ethnic Dimensions in Contemporary Latvian Politics: Focusing on Forces of Change." *Soviet Studies* 44, no. 4: 609–639.

Wyman-Moz, Mark. 1998. *DPs: Europe's Displaced Persons, 1945–1951.* Ithaca, NY: Cornell University Press.

Romania

George W. White

Chronology

1945 (March) Petru Groza becomes the leader of a new Communist-dominated government.
1946 (November 19) The Communist Party of Romania wins the national elections. Gheorghe Gheorghiu-Dej becomes general secretary.
1947 (December 27) King Michael abdicates his throne under pressure from the Communists.
1948 (April 13) The Romanian People's Republic is declared and a new constitution is adopted.
1953 Following the death of Soviet leader Joseph Stalin, Gheorghiu-Dej seeks a greater path of autonomy from the Soviet Union.
1957 Gheroghiu-Dej convinces the Moscow government to withdraw the remaining Soviet troops from Romania.
1965 Gheroghiu-Dej dies and is replaced by Nicolae Ceauşescu, who declares Romania a Socialist Republic and oversees the writing of a new constitution. Ceauşescu also creates a cult of personality around himself and builds a highly repressive dictatorship.
1989 (December 25) Nicolae Ceauşescu and his wife Elena are executed by a firing squad after having tried to flee the country amid political unrest, massive demonstrations, and riots.
1990 Following free elections, Ion Iliescu and Petre Roman of the National Salvation Front (FSN), formerly low-ranking Communists, become president and prime minister, respectively.
1991 A new national constitution is adopted.
1992 Ion Iliescu (having formed the Democratic National Salvation Front [FDSN]) is reelected president and Nicolae Văcăroiu (FDSN) becomes prime minister. The coalition government includes three extremist parties: the Romanian National Unity Party (PUNR), Great Romania Party (PRM), and Socialist Labor Party (PSM).
1996 Following dissatisfaction with slow reform and corruption, Ion Iliescu loses the presidential election to Emil Constantinescu of the Romanian Democratic Convention (CDR) Party.
2000 Following the dissatisfaction with the pace of reforms, Ion Iliescu of the Party of Social Democracy of Romania (PDSR) returns for his third term as president, and Adrian Nastase (PDSR) becomes prime minister.
2003 The national constitution is amended.
2004 Traian Băsescu of the Democratic Party (PD), former mayor of Bucharest and former Communist, wins the presidential election. Călin Popescu-Tăriceanu of the National Liberal Party (PNL) becomes prime minister.

Situating the Nation

Prior to 1878, the various Romanian territories were under the control of the Habsburg, Russian, and Ottoman empires. With the Treaty of Berlin in 1878, Romania achieved independence but was primarily comprised of only Wallachia, Moldavia, and part of Dobrogea. Emerging on the victorious side after World

War I, Romania gained Transylvania, Maramureş, eastern Crişana, the eastern two-thirds of the Banat, Bucovina, and Bessarabia.

Following Romania's involvement in World War II, it lost southern Dobrogea to Bulgaria and northern Bucovina and Bessarabia to the Soviet Union in 1945. Northern Bucovina and southeastern Bessarabia became part of the Soviet Republic of Ukraine, and the majority of Bessarabia became the Soviet Republic of Moldova. A thin slice of land on the eastern bank of the Nistru (Dnestr) River in Ukraine was added to the newly created Moldovan Soviet Republic. At the same time, Romania effectively became a Soviet satellite until 1989, when it then became a truly independent country. It joined the North Atlantic Treaty Organization (NATO) in 2004 and the European Union (EU) in 2007, both organizations requiring the Romanian government to launch democratic reforms. The challenge of the Romanian government has been to weld together territories with peoples who have been ruled by differing governments through history.

As possessions of various empires for much of modern history, most Romanian territories languished economically, remaining largely agricultural with little modernization. Industrialization only began at the end of the 19th century and then was inhibited by lack of investment monies, technical expertise, markets, the two world wars, and the intervening economic depression. Romania's economy stabilized after World War II but was operated according to the Soviet model until 1989. The Communist government made all the economic decisions and emphasized heavy industrial production. Romania transformed from a country that primarily exported raw materials such as grain, timber, animal products, and petroleum in 1939 to one producing industrial goods. Despite the requirement to pay the Soviet Union more than $1.7 billion in war damages, Romania's industrial production grew by an average of almost 13 percent between 1950 and 1977. Following an economic downturn in 1976, Romania was in deep economic crisis by 1981, with a huge foreign debt. Determined to repay the national debt, Nicolae Ceauşescu launched a severe austerity program. By 1989, the foreign debt was repaid, but Romania had sunk to one of the lowest standards of living in Europe. Electricity, for example, was not available throughout most of any given day.

Following the ouster of Ceauşescu in 1989, Romania began moving toward a free-market economy. Dilapidated industry, corruption, and a burdensome bureaucracy have inhibited economic growth. However, beginning in 2002, Romania embarked down the pathway of increasing economic growth, recording some of the best growth rates in Europe.

The major territories of Romania are Wallachia, Moldavia, and Transylvania. Wallachia's major city, Bucharest, serves as the country's capital. Moldavia's capital, Iaşi, also serves as a major political, economic, cultural, and educational center for the country. Transylvania's major city is Cluj-Napoca, but other cities like Alba Iulia, Blaj, and Braşov are major cultural centers. For example, the first leader to unite Wallachia, Moldavia, and Transylvania was Michael the Brave in 1599. He had himself crowned in Alba Iulia. The city was chosen again in 1918 by the

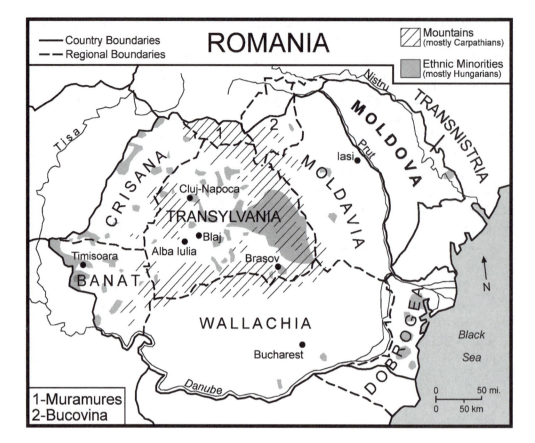

"Nation Assembly of the Romanian Nation" when it proclaimed the unification of all Romanian territories. King Ferdinand built a coronation church there in 1922 and had himself crowned the first king of a united Romania. In 1990, following the end of the Communist regime, the government changed the national holiday from August 23 (the day Romania abandoned Nazi Germany in 1944 and allowed Soviet troops to peacefully occupy its territory) to December 1, the day Romania was proclaimed united in 1918. The ceremonies were held in Alba Iulia. Blaj was an important center of the national movement in the 19th century, particularly the 1848 revolution. Timişoara in the Banat was an important center of the 1989 revolution.

In democratic elections since 1989, definite urban-rural differences exist. The urban areas tend to support the parties advocating greatest reform. The rural areas have been more cautious, supporting such parties as those run by the former Communists. Along with this political geography, Wallachia and Moldavia have supported the former Communists such as Ion Illiescu and the political parties known as the National Salvation Front (FSN) and its successors, the Democratic National Salvation Front (FDSN), the Party of Social Democracy of Romania (PDSR), and the Social Democratic Party of Romania (PSD). As can be gleaned from the above chronology, the people of Wallachia and Moldavia have deter-

Governing Political Parties

The Romanian Communist Party governed from 1946 until 1948 when it merged with one branch of the Social Democratic Party to create the Romanian Workers' Party (PMR). In 1965, the PMR was renamed the Romanian Communist Party (PCR).

Following the end of Communist rule in 1989, more than 200 political parties emerged. The National Salvation Front (FSN), made up of many formerly low-ranking Communists, won the first election in 1990. In 1992, an internal dispute led hard-liner Ion Iliescu to break with FSN and found the Democratic National Salvation Front (FDSN), which was victorious in the 1992 election. In 1993, the party's name was changed again to the Party of Social Democracy in Romania (PDSR). In 2001, the PDSR merged with the Romanian Social Democratic Party (PSDR) and together became the Social Democratic Party of Romania (PSD).

Three extremist parties formed a coalition government with the FDSN in 1992. The Romanian National Unity Party (PUNR) and the Great Romania Party (PRM) were both right-wing Romanian nationalist parties. In 2005, the PRM became more moderate and changed its name to the Great Romania People's Party (PPRM). The other party in the 1992 coalition was the left-wing Socialist Labor Party (PSM). In 2003, the PSM merged with the more moderate PSD. The wing of the party that wanted to stay Marxist formed the Socialist Alliance Party (PAS).

From 1992 to 2000, a coalition of political parties known as the Romanian Democratic Convention (CDR) formed to challenge the FSN. Following the 1996 election, it formed a governing coalition with the Democratic Party (PD) and the Democratic Union of Hungarians in Romania (UDMR). Following the CDR's loss in the 2000 election, the UDMR formed a government with the PDSR.

The FSN changed its name in 1993 to the Democratic Party (PD) and was led by the more reform-minded Petre Roman. In 2003, the PD allied itself with the center-right liberal National Liberal Party (PNL) in a coalition called Justice and Truth (DA) (whose abbreviation also means "yes" in Romanian). Following the 2004 election, the DA formed a coalition government with the UDMR and the Romanian Humanist Party (PUR) (known as the Conservative Party [PC] after May 2005).

---

mined the winners of most of Romania's post-1989 elections. However, beginning with the 1996 election, Transylvania's stronger support for more reform-minded parties put such parties into power. Parties centered in Transylvania have also been part of the governing coalitions, whether liberal or conservative. The Democratic Union of Hungarians in Romania (UDMR) is the most notable example. Involvement of Transylvania's ethnic minorities (the largest in the country) in governing coalitions most likely led to the constitutional reforms of 2003, which broadened the rights of ethnic minorities and others.

Prior to World War II, most Romanians were agricultural peasants. After the war, communist ideology worked not only to industrialize the country but also to create an industrial working class. Communist elites governed the country, promoted the virtues of the industrial working class, and determined the cultural characteristics of Romanians. Though Romania's Communist leaders steered Romania

Constitution

During the Communist period, the constitution of Romania was rewritten three different times: 1948, 1952, and 1965. The 1952 constitution guaranteed all citizens the right to work, and full equality was granted to national minorities. Private ownership was possible, though major industries were nationalized. While the 1952 constitution emphasized Romania's close ties to the Soviet Union, the 1965 constitution omitted all such references. Private ownership was also sharply reduced. In 1974 the constitution was amended to create an office of the president, which became the most powerful office in the country.

A new constitution was adopted in 1991. Of its many features, it declared that Romania was a republic and "the common and indivisible homeland of all its citizens, without any discrimination on account of race, nationality, ethnic origin, language, religion, sex, opinion, political adherence, property or social origin." The right to vote for any political party and the right to privately own land was guaranteed. The term of the president was set at four years.

The constitution was amended in 2003. Many changes were made, including the lowering of the number of citizens able to promote a bill from 250,000 to 100,000, the lowering of the age limit of candidates for the Senate to 33 years of age, and the extension of the term of the president from four to five years. National minorities were given the right to officially use their languages, and private property was protected.

on a course as independent as possible from the Soviet Union, they still had to accept Russian influence. For example, the Soviets put Russian words into the Romanian language and classified the people of the neighboring Soviet Republic of Moldova as Moldovans and not Romanians. In addition, the Soviets only approved histories that depicted Russians as liberators of Romanians and generally as culturally akin to Romanians.

Following the changes in 1989, democracy allowed for a greater expression of Romanian identity, from socialist to ultra-conservative opinions. Despite the range of views, Romanians of most social classes have generally turned westward away from Russia, as exemplified by Romania's new membership in NATO and the EU. Russian influence on the Romanian language has been reversed, and closer ties with Moldova have been pursued.

Instituting the Nation

During the Communist period, no separation existed between executive, legislative, and judicial powers. The main organ of government was the Grand National Assembly (GNA), which met twice a year. The State Council was in permanent session and assumed the powers of the GNA when the GNA was not in session. The Council of Ministers was the supreme body of state administration, overseeing all levels of government. The Communist Party was the dominant political party, meaning that the general secretary of the Communist Party also effectively led the Romanian government. Gheorghe Gheorghiu-Dej was the general secretary from 1946 to 1965, and Nicolae Ceauşescu held the position from 1965 to 1989.

After 1989, Romania became a democratic republic with separate executive, legislative, and judicial branches of government. The head of the executive branch is now the president, who is elected by popular vote every five years (four years until 2005). The president appoints a prime minister, who heads the government and appoints the other members of the executive branch. The legislative branch is divided into two chambers, a 137-member Senate and a 332-member Chamber of Deputies. Members of both chambers are elected every four years.

Since 1989, former Communists generally have been elected president. For example, Ion Iliescu won the 1990, 1992, and 2000 elections, and Traian Băsescu won the 2004 election. Only in 1996 did a more reform-minded candidate win the presidency, in this case, Emil Constantinescu.

During the Communist period, governmental institutions promoted the idea of a fraternal brotherhood of communism, which argued that all Romanians and peoples in other countries were united by their communist ideology. After 1989, numerous political parties have advocated differing concepts of what it is to be Romanian. On the far right is the Great Romania People's Party (PPRM) (simply the Great Romania Party [PRM] until 2005), which has been very nationalistic and likewise very anti-Semitic, anti-Hungarian, and generally xenophobic. However, ethnic political parties such as the Democratic Union of Hungarians in Romania (UDMR) argue for a more multicultural definition of the Romanian nation that would allow ethnic minorities to use their languages officially. Though the PPRM and other nationalist parties receive many votes in elections, Romania has moved in a more multicultural direction. The combination of years of Communist influence that downplayed nationalism and the significance of cultural differences, the political activism of a number of ethnically based political parties such as the UDMR, and the desire to join the EU, which requires respect for multiculturalism, has pushed the Romanian nation to be more inclusive. Ironically, these same three factors have also encouraged a more intolerant, ethnic Romanian nationalism among some segments of Romanian society.

Defining the Nation

Romanian nationalism first emerged in the 19th century under the influence of Romanticism, which stressed ethnicity and language as the basis of nationhood. The Transylvanian School played a major role in defining the characteristics of Romanian nationhood in these terms. With Transylvania in the Austria-Hungarian empire until 1918, members of the Transylvanian School were connected to and

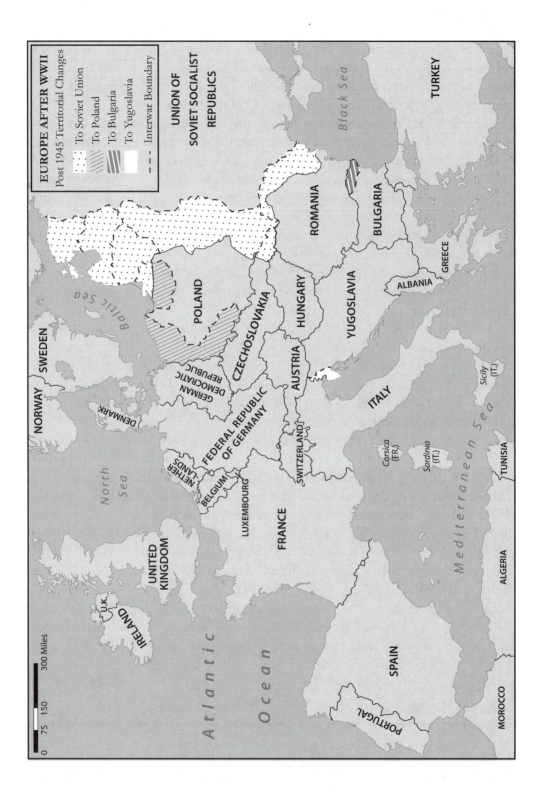

EUROPE AFTER WWII
Post 1945 Territorial Changes

To Soviet Union
To Poland
To Bulgaria
To Yugoslavia
Interwar Boundary

UNION OF
SOVIET SOCIALIST
REPUBLICS

TURKEY

Black Sea

ROMANIA

BULGARIA

POLAND

GREECE

ALBANIA

CZECHOSLOVAKIA

HUNGARY

YUGOSLAVIA

Baltic Sea

SWEDEN

NORWAY

GERMAN
DEMOCRATIC
REPUBLIC

DENMARK

AUSTRIA

ITALY

Sicily
(IT.)

FEDERAL REPUBLIC
OF GERMANY

SWITZERLAND

NETHER-
LANDS

BELGIUM

North
Sea

Corsica
(FR.)

Sardinia
(IT.)

Mediterranean Sea

TUNISIA

LUXEMBOURG

FRANCE

ALGERIA

UNITED
KINGDOM

U.K.

IRELAND

Atlantic

Ocean

SPAIN

PORTUGAL

MOROCCO

300 Miles

0 75 150

influenced by Vienna and Rome. With such influence, the Latin alphabet was adopted for the Romanian language, though Orthodox Christians like the Romanians normally use the Cyrillic alphabet. The Transylvanian School also advocated the use of the term Romanian rather than Wallachian to emphasize their nation's western connections, as the former term, which meant "land of the Romans," implied that the nation's inhabitants were descendents of Romans.

While under the influence of the Soviet Union from 1945 to 1989, the Soviets attempted to reorient the Romanian nation toward the Slavic east. In the Moldovan Soviet Republic, which the Soviet Union annexed from Romania in 1945, Soviet authorities changed the script from Latin to Cyrillic, the alphabet used by Russians, and also encouraged the use of Russian. At one point they even insisted that no Romanians lived in Moldova. In Romania, Soviet policy makers insisted that Romania be spelled Rumania, with the root *rum* meaning Eastern Orthodox Christian, an identity that both Romanians and Russians shared. In 1953, Soviet authorities went a step further and insisted that the letter *â* be replaced with the letter *î*. Consequently, Rumânia was then written Rumînia, further distancing the word from its implied Roman origins. After 1968, Ceauşescu reversed some of the language changes. De-Sovietization of the Romanian language and history continued after 1989. The government of Moldova changed the alphabet of their language back to Latin in 1989.

The spatial dimensions of the Romanian nation are most directly defined by a combination of natural features and ethnic distributions. Numerically, ethnic Romanians clearly dominate all of the territories that comprise the Romanian and Moldovan states. These territories are primarily bounded by natural features. For example, Wallachia is between the Carpathian Mountains on the north and the Danube River in the south. Moldavia is between the Carpathian Mountains and the Prut River, and Moldova lies between the Prut and Nistru (Dnestr) rivers. Transylvania lies within the arc of the Carpathian Mountains. Romanian nationalists have tended to argue that these territories, bounded by such natural features, naturally belong to the Romanian nation; therefore, ethnic minorities are unnaturally present in these regions and have no right to claim these territories.

It could be argued that the Carpathian Mountains are a barrier within the country that inhibits transportation and communication networks within the country, in turn inhibiting Romanian unity. However, Romanian nationalists frequently see the Carpathians as a fortress and a refuge where their ancestors escaped to in times of crises. They also see Romania as ringed by a series of rivers that act as moats for national defense.

Romanian nationhood is subdivided into a number of regional identities with corresponding dialects of the Romanian language: Moldavian, Muntenian (Wallachian), Transylvanian, and Banation, and so on. The regional dialects and cultures are very similar. Transylvanians and Bucovinans have been influenced by Hungarian and Austrian cultures, respectively.

Narrating the Nation

Roman and Dacian history are still very important to modern Romanians who see themselves as a product of these earlier cultures, which were also great civilizations. Replicas of the she-wolf in Rome depicting Romulus (the founder of Rome) and Remus serve as common statues, as do statues of Dacian leaders. Notable medieval leaders who fought for independence were Basarab (Wallachia), Stephen the Great (Moldavia), Vlad the Impaler (aka Dracula), and Iancu de Hunedoara (the latter two of Transylvania). However, Romanian ancestors did not build another great united civilization or completely rule themselves again until Michael the Brave united Wallachia, Moldavia, and Transylvania in 1600. Monuments and place-names associated with Michael the Brave are also common. The national revolutions that swept across Europe in 1848 also occurred in Romanian territories as well. This event is particularly important to modern Romanians, who see this revolution as an expression of their ancestors' desire for national self-determination at a time when no Romanian territory was independent. Avram Iancu was one of the key leaders at the time. Mihai Eminescu is a cherished poet of the late 19th century. December 1, 1918, is celebrated with more spirit because it marked the unification of all Romanian territories into a Greater Romania.

The Romanian flag is comprised of three vertical colors: cobalt blue, chrome yellow, and vermilion red. The royal coat of arms was replaced by socialist symbols (e.g., wheat and a red star) during the Communist period. During the revolution of 1989, people literally cut the socialist emblem out of the flag. "Three Colors," which describes the flag, was the national anthem until 1989. Lyrics were changed from the original version written in the 19th century to reflect communist philosophy. "Awaken Ye, Romanian!" was originally written during the 1848 revolution, banned during Communist times, spontaneously sung during the 1989 revolution, and became the national anthem after 1989. It was also adopted in neighboring Moldova until 1994 when it was replaced with "Our Language."

The Romanian coat of arms consists of a golden eagle on a blue shield holding an Orthodox Christian cross in its beak. On the eagle's chest is another shield with the five symbols of Romania's five territories: the golden eagle of Wallachia, the auroch (ancient ox) of Moldavia, the lion of the Banat, the dolphins of the coastal lands of Dobrogea, and the eagle over the seven fortresses of Transylvania. The neighboring country of Moldova also uses the auroch as its symbol.

Mobilizing and Building the Nation

Romania is about 90 percent ethnic Romanian. Of the remaining 10 percent, Hungarians are the largest ethnic minority, followed by Roma (Gypsies), Ukrainians, Saxon Germans, Russians, Turks, Tatars, and a number of other smaller groups.

Romanian coat of arms. (Vector-Images.com)

During Communist times, ethnicity was seen as irrelevant and was de-emphasized; yet ethnic minorities were seen as having rights and, therefore, protected. For example, the Hungarians of Transylvania were given an autonomous region. However, though Communist philosophy de-emphasized ethnicity, it also advocated the homogenization of the population. Thus the belief in equal protection under the law was often contradicted by other policies that aimed to eliminate difference

among the people. For example, in 1968, Ceaușescu abolished the Hungarian autonomous region in Transylvania that the Soviets had insisted on creating after
the war.

Many ethnic Romanians see ethnic minorities as an internal threat, although
others do not. Jews were heavily persecuted during World War II. During Communist times, Jews were often targeted during purges. Ethnic Hungarians have
been frequently accused of collaborating with the Hungarian government to return Transylvania to Hungary. The strong desire for democracy after 1989 led to a
freer society for ethnic minorities, many of whom have their own political parties.
The participation of the Democratic Union of Hungarians in Romania (UDMR) in
governing coalitions has helped to ensure the rights of minorities. However, the
ethno-nationalist Romanian Great Romania Party (PRM) receives great support
from ethnic Romanians.

Historically, ethnic Romanians have been concerned about gaining and then
preserving their independence. Since 1945, they have seen external forces as the
greatest threat, particularly the Soviet Union, which took away Bessarabia (now
Moldova) and northern Bucovina. Hungary is also seen as a threat because it possessed Transylvania and other western territories before 1918 and annexed northern Transylvania during World War II. After the disintegration of the Soviet Union
in 1991, many Romanians are still wary of the succeeding Russian Federation.
They blame the presence of the 14th Russian army in Moldova and Moscow's med-
dling for preventing Moldova from uniting with Romania and for Moldova's inability to bring ethnic separatists under control. The perceived Russian threat led
Romanians to join NATO and the EU as a means of preserving their independence.

Conclusion

Romania emerged after World War II as a Soviet satellite and with a Communist government. Gheorghe Gheorghiu-Dej (1946–1965) and Nicolae Ceaușescu
(1965–1989) were the two leaders of the country during the Communist period.
After 1989, Romania became a democratic republic holding free elections. Though
former Communists have since won many of the elections, Romania has become
a more pluralistic society where ethnic minorities enjoy greater rights. Discontent
with former Soviet control, which also led to the loss of Bessarabia and northern
Bucovina, Romanians tend to prefer links with western Europe.

Selected Bibliography

Bachman, Ronald D., ed. 1991. *Romania: A Country Study.* 2nd ed. Washington DC: Federal Re-
    search Division, Library of Congress.

Carey, Henry E., ed. 2004. *Romania since 1989: Politics, Economics, and Society.* New York: Lex-
    ington Books.

Constitution of Romania. 1991. (Retrieved June 29, 2005), http://www.cdep.ro/pdfs/constitutie_
    en.pdf.

Deletant, Dennis. 1991. "Rewriting the Past: Trends in Contemporary Romanian Historiography." *Ethnic and Racial Studies* 14 (January): 64–86.

Deletant, Dennis. 1999. *Romania under Communist Rule.* Portland, OR: Center for Romanian Studies, in cooperation with the Civic Academy Foundation.

Fedor, Helen, ed. 1995. *Belarus and Moldova: Country Studies.* Washington DC: Federal Research Division, Library of Congress.

Fischer-Galati, Stephen. 1978. "The Continuation of Nationalism in Romanian Historiography." *Nationalities Papers* 6, no. 2: 179–184.

Gallagher, Tom. 2005. *Modern Romania: The End of Communism, the Failure of Democratic Reform, and the Theft of a Nation.* New York: New York University Press.

"Major Provisions of the Law for the Revision of the Constitution of Romania." 2003. (Retrieved June 29, 2005), http://www.cdep.ro/pls/dic/site.page?id=336.

Matei, Sorin. 2004. "The Emergent Romanian Post-Communist Ethos: From Nationalism to Privatism." *Problems of Post-Communism* 51 (March–April): 40–47.

"National Symbols." 2004. (Retrieved June 29, 2005), http://ue.mae.ro/index.php?lang=en&id=210.

Roper, Steven D. 2003. "Is There an Economic Basis for Post-Communist Voting? Evidence from Romanian Elections, 1992–2000." *East European Quarterly* 37 (March): 85–100.

White, George W. 1998. "Transylvania: Hungarian, Romanian, or Neither?" In *Nested Identities: Nationalism, Territory and Scale*, edited by Guntram Herb and David Kaplan, chap. 12, 267–287. Lanham, MD: Rowman & Littlefield.

White, George W. 2000. *Nationalism and Territory: Constructing Group Identity in Southeastern Europe.* Lanham, MD: Rowman & Littlefield.

Russia

Grigory Ioffe

Chronology

1991	The Soviet Union disintegrates; 15 republics, including the Russian Federation, become independent nations. Boris Yeltsin is elected president.
1992	Yeltsin ends the supremacy of the Communist Party, privatizes state-run enterprises, and guarantees a free press. Mobsters begin to take over the economy.
1993	Standoff between the pro-reform government and the largely Communist Supreme Soviet (parliament) resolves forcibly in favor of the government. The Supreme Soviet is renamed the Duma.
1994–1996	The first war in Chechnya, a breakaway province of Russia. The federal army withdraws with heavy casualties.
1996	Yeltsin is reelected president.
1998	The Russian stock market crashes.
1999	Resumption of economic growth. The beginning of the second Chechen war. Yeltsin resigns, and Vladimir Putin is appointed acting president.
2000	Vladimir Putin is elected president.
2004	Vladimir Putin is reelected president in a landslide.

Situating the Nation

Present-day Russia, officially called the Russian Federation, dates back to the breakup of the Soviet Union (December 1991). The Russian Federation was the Soviet Union's largest republic with three-quarters of the entire Soviet Union's land area and half of its population. The official declaration of Russia's sovereignty (June 12, 1991) predated and facilitated the Soviet Union's disintegration.

Following the 1989 elections to the Russian legislature (at the time called the Supreme Soviet, renamed the Duma in 1993), many in the new Russian political elite sympathized with the Baltic States' quest for independence. They also considered Russia to be the financial donor of most, if not all, union republics, hence getting rid of them was viewed as potentially benefiting Russia's development. This idea coexisted with the short-lived but pronounced prevalence of the Westernizing geopolitical vision of Russia (discussed below) of the intelligentsia and political elite in Moscow and Saint Petersburg. According to this vision, once Russia adopted principles of Western-style democracy and did away with central planning, it would soon become part of the advanced West. The abortive coup of August 19–21, 1991, by which the staunchest Communists planned to undo Gorbachev's reforms, reinforced the Westernizing vision and precipitated the Soviet breakup.

Instituting the Nation

Among the principal actors in Russia's reemergence as a country stripped of much of its long-time empire was Boris Yeltsin, the leader of the Russian legislature and soon to become its first president. Yeltsin co-signed the Belavezh agreement of December 1991 with Leonid Kravchuk of Ukraine and Stanislav Shushkevich of Belarus, the agreement that did away with the Soviet Union. Other prominent figures shaping the post-Soviet future of Russia early on were Acting Prime Minister Yegor Gaidar, Foreign Minister Andrei Kozyrev, and the architect of the privatization schemes that transferred most lucrative industrial assets into the hands of new entrepreneurs, Anatoly Chubais. All of these politicians are now considerably discredited in the eyes of most Russians, and only Chubais retains a high-power position as head of Russia's state electric grid monopoly.

By 1993, the political division within the Russian legislature between the allied forces of communists and ethnic Russian nationalists, on the one hand, and the Westernizing liberals, on the other, became so bitter that it was resolved only through an armed standoff. The Westernizing block won, but it now looks like

---

Boris Yeltsin

The first democratically elected president of Russia (1991–1999), Boris Yeltsin was formerly a regional Communist Party boss. He quit the party in 1990. In December 1991, together with the leaders of Ukraine and Belarus, Yeltsin co-signed the Belovezh agreement, which did away with the Soviet Union and created the Commonwealth of Independent States in its place. As president of an independent Russia, Yeltsin moved to end state control of the economy and privatize most enterprises. However, economic difficulties and political opposition, particularly from the Supreme Soviet, slowed his program and forced compromises. In 1993, Yeltsin suspended the parliament and called for new elections. When the parliament's supporters resorted to arms, they were crushed by the army. In foreign affairs, Yeltsin greatly improved relations with the West and signed the START II nuclear disarmament treaty (1993) with the United States. In 1994, Yeltsin sent forces into Chechnya to suppress a separatist rebellion, forcing Russia into a difficult and unpopular struggle. In 1996, Yeltsin ran for reelection against a number of other candidates and won the first round, garnering 35 percent of the vote to Communist Gennady Zyuganov's 32 percent; Yeltsin then won the runoff election. In the late 1990s, however, a series of economic crises, frequent cabinet reshufflings, and his own deteriorating health cast doubt on his ability to rule; charges of corruption in his family and among members of his inner circle also became prominent. In 1999, Yeltsin survived an impeachment attempt spearheaded by the Communist opposition. A second invasion of Chechnya (1999), prompted by a Chechen invasion of Dagestan and related terrorist bombings in Russia, proved popular with many Russians, and pro-government parties did well in the 1999 parliamentary elections. On December 31, 1999, the long-ailing Yeltsin suddenly announced his resignation; Prime Minister Vladimir Putin succeeded him as acting president.

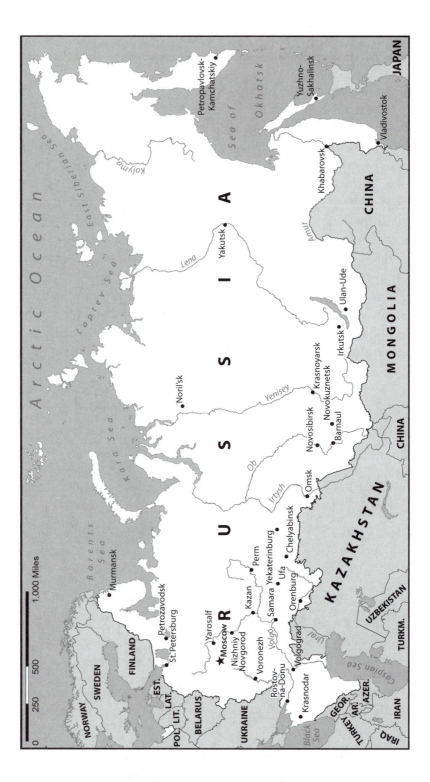

that victory will be its last for quite some time. The pendulum then began to swing in the opposite direction: toward ethnic nationalism of the Eurasian (as opposed to Westernizing) brand and profound disillusionment with the West. The ensuing steep economic decline of 1991–1998, privatization and the development of crony capitalism, loss of a sense of economic security by many, and a far-reaching social stratification discredited the Westernizing vision in the eyes of many Russians, as did the country's loss of superpower status. Nevertheless, the new geopolitical reality of a Russia separated from the rest of its former empire had been irrevocably established. "The new delimitation happened quickly and without deep reflection or real debate" (O'Loughlin and Talbot 2005, 26).

Defining the Nation

As the multifaceted consequences of this new delimitation sank in, Russians had to "re-conceptualize their country within a territory for which there are few historical antecedents" (O'Loughlin and Talbot 2005, 23). To a significant extent, the borders of today's Russia are not associated with established ethno-cultural frontiers. This is especially true of the borders with Ukraine, Belarus, and Kazakhstan. Even borders with Estonia and Latvia, the countries that are not perceived by most Russians as culturally close, cut across the areas currently populated by a Russian-speaking population. Ironically, some of Russia's internal division lines, especially those in the northern Caucasus, are more distinctive in an ethno-cultural sense than much of its external borders.

Throughout much of the Soviet Union's existence, the ethnic nationalism of Great Russians was discouraged, whereas that of other ethnicities was tolerated to a larger extent. (Here, "Great" fits the historic designation practiced in the Russian empire and used to distinguish Russians proper from Little Russians or Ukrainians and White Russians or Belarusians.) The theoretical foundation for such a differential treatment was invariably justified by the article "About the National Pride of Great Russians" by Vladimir I. Lenin, who described Russian nationalism as chauvinism by the colonizer and argued that the ethno-national pride of ethnicities oppressed in the Russian empire deserved sympathy. Thus the Russianness of the Soviet power was to be toned down in exchange for conciliation of the minorities. Indeed, there were Communist parties of Ukraine, Belarus, Latvia, and so on, but there was no Russia-based Communist Party; there, the rank-and-file communists were members of the Communist Party of the USSR. It was quite obvious for all those initiated that, in Moscow, the citywide and all-Union tiers of the Soviet government were more influential than the intermediate Russian Federation tier, whose ministries enjoyed more modest premises than their counterparts in other union republics. Of considerable importance is the fact that the ethnic Russian countryside, a wellspring of folk traditions in all the

Old World countries, became much more neglected and depopulated under the Soviets than the countryside in all the other republics. Designed to compensate for ethnic pride was the promotion of civic identity, whose subject and rallying point was defined as the Soviet people. Ethnic Russians embraced this identity more vigorously than did all other groups, with the exception of Belarusians, residents of eastern Ukraine, and some Russified urban intelligentsia of Central Asia. It has thus been all the more painful for most Russians to reconcile with the new post-Soviet reality. From the perspective of many Russians, their country was dispossessed of its inalienable parts. The formal separation from Ukraine, Belarus, and northern Kazakhstan, which Aleksander Solzhenitsyn calls southern Siberia, has been perceived as particularly unnatural. Some 25 million ethnic Russians living in former Soviet republics sometimes face ethnic and linguistic discrimination, another source of trauma.

Within Russia proper, ethnic Russians account for 82 percent of the entire population. The largest concentration of non-Russian ethnicities is in the North Caucasus, and the second largest is between the Volga River and the Urals, where most Tatars, the second-largest ethnic group of the Russian Federation (4 percent), live. Altogether, there are 21 ethnic homelands known as republics within the Russian Federation. During the Yeltsin presidency (1992–1999), these republics enjoyed some fiscal advantages over ethnically Russian regions, including a lower rate of corporate tax transfers to the federal budget. Just as in the Soviet Union at large, whose breakup was in part conditioned by ethnic nationalism, so in the Russian Federation ethnicity became a rallying point in the 1990s and sparked separatism ranging from armed guerilla movements (Chechnya) to vocal assertion of fiscal autonomy, to requirements that all public officials learn the local language, and so on, as is the case in Tatarstan and some other republics. Even among the more Russified groups that never entertained separatist ideas (e.g., Udmurt, Mordva, or Mari), ethnic pride and ethnically tainted grievances are on the rise.

In the Russian Federation, ethnicity thus provides a crucial identity challenge to civic nationalism, which continues to be weak. Formally, the idea of an all-Russian civic identity is not dead; it is conveyed by the adjective "Rossiisky" as opposed to "Russky." While both adjectives are rendered in English as "Russian," they have a different connotation in Russia, with Rossiisky being statewide and inclusive and Russky being a marker of ethnic Russianness. Russia's civic identity is more vigorously embraced by the intellectual Westernizers, whose leading position in Russian society has been shattered by the traumas of post-communist development. The Westernizers believe that Russia is in essence a European cultural entity, just being vast and having absorbed Asiatic influences. Russia can reclaim its European self by following in the footsteps of West European developments in political, social, and economic areas. The opposite flank of the political spectrum, which commands at least as large a following, is represented by the intellectual heirs to the Slavophils. In the tradition of the eponymous school of

Vladimir Putin

A shadowy KGB agent stationed in East Germany, Vladimir Putin assumed a position with the International Affairs section of Leningrad State University in 1990. He rose through the political ranks and in August 1999 was appointed prime minister of the Russian Federation. Putin benefited from an image of toughness, bolstered by his hard-line approach to the renewed crisis in Chechnya. On December 31, 1999, Boris Yeltsin resigned and appointed Putin the second president of the Russian Federation. Putin won the office in his own right three months later. Upon his election, Putin undertook measures to restore the primacy of the Kremlin in Russia's political life. One of his first acts was to restore a strong central state and to minimize the rejection of the Soviet era. He retained many Soviet-era symbols, including the trademark red military flag, the "Soviet Star" crest, and the Soviet national anthem (although with revised lyrics). He placed most Russian TV stations, newspapers, and other media under Kremlin control. And he reined in some of Russia's leading business tycoons.

thought in the Russian émigré circles of the 1920s and 1930s, those heirs now prefer to call themselves Eurasianists. For them, Russia is neither Europe nor Asia; it is, in the words of Vladimir Lamansky, "the middle world of Eurasia," a unique civilization that should not by any means imitate the West. Rather, it should oppose and challenge it. The Eurasianists draw inspiration from the works of the late Nikolai Gumilev and to some extent from Alexander Solzhenitsyn. Some of the most radical personalities in this movement fan the flames of anti-Americanism. Alexander Dugin, for example, claims that "the desire to see in America a democratic partner would be equivalent to an appeal to collaborate with Hitler after World War Two began. According to this calendar, now is July 1941" (Dugin 2005).

Identities overlap in contemporary Russia. For example, "ethnic Tatars may view the region as homeland to Tatars dispersed throughout the Russian Federation and even beyond, or may see Kazan' [the capital of Tatarstan] as a special historical center not just for ethnic Tatars or residents of Tatarstan but those in the entire Volga-Ural region" (Bradshaw and Prendergrast 2005, 103). Although civic Russian identity remains weak, much has been done to bolster it under President Vladimir Putin, whose second and last (according to the Russian constitution) term expires in 2008.

Narrating the Nation

Because of multiple and competing identities, there is no single brand of national mythology that appeals to all or most citizens of Russia. Even the ethnic Russian majority is torn between several competing brands. Perhaps their sole unifying thread is a feeling of inferiority with respect to the West, particularly to the United States, the sole remaining superpower. Westernizers claim that Russia can successfully bridge the gap with the West by consistently emulating Western economic and political solutions on Russian soil. The inferiority feeling is deeper and more painful, however, for the Eurasianists, who declare that economic and political comparisons with the West are an intellectual taboo of sorts because Russia is a different civilization that "cannot be understood in European terms" ("Rossiya–Yevropeiskaya strana?" 2005). They brand the United States as Russia's principal geopolitical and civilizational rival. Spiritual and averse to egotism, Russians are described as gaining strength exclusively from collective, not individual, mobilization and pursuits. Alexander Block's stanzas from his 1918 verse "Scythians" can be considered a manifesto of the Eurasianists and a message that they believe Russia ought to send to the West:

> You are the millions, we are multitude
> And multitude and multitude.
> Come, fight! Yea, we are Scythians,
> Yea, Asians, a slant-eyed, greedy brood.
> For you the centuries, for us—one hour.
> Like slaves, obeying and abhorred,
> We were the shield between the breeds
> Of Europe and the raging Mongol horde.
> (Translated from the Russian; Yarmolinsky 1949, 167)

The third brand of Russian nationalism, its neo-Soviet brand, is receding but still commands a significant following, hence the long and acrimonious public debate about the Russian anthem. The debate ended in 2000 with the restoration of the Soviet anthem's music, for which Sergei Mikhalkov wrote new lyrics just as he had a couple of times under the Soviets, first preaching up Stalin and then purging him from the anthem's lyrics. From 1992 to 2000, Mikhail Glinka's "Patriotic Song" was the Russian anthem, but the nostalgia of the Soviet glory days embraced by too many Russians prompted President Putin's decision to resuscitate the Soviet anthem despite many protests by Russian Westernizers. However, Russia's current flag and its national emblem are replicas of those of pre-1917, czarist Russia.

Until 2004, November 7 was one of the main national holidays in Russia. Though no longer devoted to celebrating the anniversary of the 1917 Revolution, the holiday remained, as Russians had been used to it. In 2005, the decision was made to move the national holiday to November 4, the day when patriotic Russian militia under the guidance of Kuz'ma Minin and Dmitry Pozharsky expelled Polish-Lithuanian invaders from Moscow in 1612. The Russian Orthodox Church, whose role in Russian society is on the rise, lobbied for this move. Now, it is habitual for Russian authorities, including the president, to attend church and to be pictured in company with its supreme leaders.

The church positions itself as the custodian of Russia as a godly nation averse to Western materialism. The Orthodox Church also cultivates the sense of victimhood in relation to Catholic and other Western missionary invasions of its traditional domain. Although much of the alleged invasion took place in western Ukraine, Russian Orthodox hierarchs still consider these acts treachery and resist the normalization of interdenominational relationships. The late pope John Paul II was unable to visit Russia despite invitations by two Russian presidents because the Orthodox Church did not endorse the invitations.

Since the late 1990s, there has been a steady effort to revert to a glorification of Joseph Stalin. Eurasianists and neo-Communists are behind this effort. Already in some cities and towns, monuments to Stalin have been re-created, and many petition the government to restore Stalingrad as the name of the city (renamed Volgograd in 1961 by Nikita Khrushchev) where the famous battle took place in 1942. Although an ethnic Georgian, Stalin comes across to many in Russia as the leader with whom the most glorious accomplishments and victories of Russia are associated. Most importantly, during his reign Russia inspired awe in her detractors. It is also remembered that in his famous speech of July 3, 1941, following the commencement of the Nazi invasion of the Soviet Union, Stalin openly appealed to the national pride of ethnic Russians and sought support of the Orthodox Church after two decades of its brutal oppression. The Soviet Union lost 25 million lives in that war. Most probably, close to half of all the victims were residents of Russia. The number of casualties from Stalinist purges was even higher. Ironically, this does not prevent quite a few Russians from rallying around the dictator's name.

Joseph Stalin (1879–1953),
Soviet leader from 1922 to 1953.
(Library of Congress)

Mobilizing and Building the Nation

Officially, the goals of post-Soviet Russia are to create a vibrant market economy and democratic forms of governance. For the Westernizers, these goals, as well as elevating living standards, maintaining the human dignity of Russia's citizens, and fostering entrepreneurial initiative, indeed reign supreme. For the Eurasianists and neo-Communists, however, the utmost goal is restoration of Russia's faded glory and its superpower status. They also talk about dignity, but for them it is not the individual but the entire community of Russians that would once again inspire awe and outright fear in its neighbors and potential offenders. The Eurasianists also view the privatization of the 1990s as outright robbery from the state (a stand with which many agree) and demand nationalization, particularly of those assets that accrued to ethnically non-Russian "oligarchs."

Given the multiplicity of national blueprints and visions of Russia, there is no single way to shepherd the nation. Cognizant of this problem, President Putin and his powerful administration send conflicting messages mobilizing different and mutually conflicted sections of the Russian populace in ways attuned to their cherished political and economic goals. On the one hand, the all-too-powerful owner of the most successful Russian company is persecuted for alleged tax violations (committed by the vast majority of those who seized the most lucrative assets in the early 1990s), independent TV channels are muzzled, and interference in close neighbors' (e.g., Ukraine) elections campaigns is financed and orchestrated. On the other hand, close cooperation with the United States and NATO is sought, economic liberals are kept at the helm of executive power, liberal economic reforms continue, and the period during which privatization deals can be legally questioned gets diminished from 10 to 3 years to appease the entrepreneurial class.

One more area of disagreement in Russia conducive to different ways of national mobilization is the ongoing population decline. While all political camps bemoan it, different actions are advocated. The Westernizers claim that, because the excess of deaths over births cannot be undone in the foreseeable future, even under the most favorable scenario for Russia's economic growth, the necessity of large-scale immigration must be openly acknowledged and a foreign labor force ought to be welcomed. Moreover, because much of Europe is going to compete with Russia for the better-skilled immigrants, changes in legislation and in attitude toward immigrants ought to occur without delay, lest it be too late.

In contrast, the Eurasianists believe that banning abortion and fostering fertility are the ways to go and that immigration is a national threat. As of now, immigrants from Asia and Africa to Russia face discrimination from xenophobic skinheads and their sympathizers and often risk their lives. Among the Russian minorities, for a long time Jews were the least welcomed group, but now people from the Caucasus (whether from the North Caucasus region of Russia or from

Armenia, Georgia, or Azerbaijan) and from Central Asia seem to draw more en-
mity. There is also widespread fear of a creeping Chinese invasion of the Russian
Far East. Rumors circulate about millions of Chinese illegally settling in that region, although professional demographers do not believe their number exceeds
400,000 in the sparsely settled and steadily depopulated Russian Siberia.

Given a long tradition of state paternalism and a weak civic society, a tradition that dates back much further than the 1917 Communist Revolution, the
most important nation-building strategies employed are top-down. They derive
from the political initiatives of the top executive, not from grassroots initiatives
and not even from those of the parliament. Under President Putin, who came to
power following the 1999 resignation of Boris Yeltsin and was then popularly
elected in 2000 and 2004, one of the principal slogans became the strengthening
of the entire system of vertical subordination (the so-called *vlastnaya vertikal'*),
from the president to the regional and then local administration. Yeltsin's slogan,
"Grab as much sovereignty as you can digest," directed to the leaders of ethnic republics, is now viewed as undermining the integrity of the Russian nation. Consequently, Putin did away with preferential treatment of those republics in the fiscal
area. He subsequently initiated the end of the short-lived (1992–2004) practice of
electing regional leaders through a popular vote, and the Duma rubber-stamped
this change. Although this was done in the wake of the Chechen terrorist attack
on the school in Beslan (a town in North Ossetia, just one out of 21 ethnic homelands established in the Russian Federation) and was motivated by the necessity
to strengthen public security, most analysts interpreted the move as a long-
cherished element in the top-down nation-building strategy designed to preclude
the potential disintegration of Russia along the lines of the Soviet Union's breakup.
Now, each regional leader is proposed by the president, and the local legislature
—not the citizenry at large—votes for or against the proposed candidate. While
this change faced mixed reactions from the Russian elites and outright censure
by the West, no grassroots protests took place.

A spiritual authority has been reclaimed by the Russian Orthodox Church,
both in Moscow and in the ethnic Russian regions, while mosques have mushroomed in Muslim regions. The role of the Orthodox Church in particular can be
seen as a nation-building factor, integral to czarist Russia's defining triad of autocracy, Orthodoxy, and Russian ethnicity. The rebuilding of the Cathedral of
Jesus Christ the Savior (blown up by the Soviet government in 1931) in Moscow
and its opening for worship services in 1997 was one of the most important steps
in this regard. Efforts are being made to prevent the penetration of the "wrong"
kind of Islamic teachings into the areas with compact Muslim settlement.

The joint effect of ethnic separatism and of highly centralized nation-building
efforts has been the much publicized war in Chechnya and tensions in the adjacent Muslim and non-Muslim regions in the North Caucasus. To a significant
extent, poverty and the accelerated growth of the Muslim population against
the backdrop of the overall population decline in Russia provide a nourishing

The Cathedral of Jesus Christ the Savior in Moscow, Russia, was built over a period of 44 years and was completed in 1882. It was destroyed in 1931 to make way for a socialist monument, but was rebuilt and reopened in 1997. (Vitt Guziy)

environment for these tensions. However, despite much attention to ongoing conflicts, many multiethnic areas remain calm, as available institutions effectively promote an "integrative diversity" (Zuercher 2000) vital for Russia. Russian leaders have been adamant in asserting their sovereign right to maintain the territorial integrity of Russia by all means, including military. The growing and often well-documented aid to Chechen rebels by some foreign Islamic centers legitimizes Russia's claim that it is waging a war with international terrorism, much like the United States does.

Overall, comparisons with America permeate the entire discourse on national and virtually all other issues of public concern. On the one hand, such comparisons are instrumental in unmasking the double standard that the American administration allegedly resorts to when it criticizes Russia's war in Chechnya and Russia's departures from democracy. On the other hand, comparisons with America are called for to pinpoint and rectify Russia's own shortcomings in maintaining public order, responding to citizens' needs, safeguarding private property, and so on. Related to the painful loss of a superpower status, Russia's identity crisis is far from over.

Selected Bibliography

Bradshaw, M., and J. Prendergrast. 2005. "The Russian Heartland Revisited: An Assessment of Russia's Transformation." *Eurasian Geography and Economics* 46, no. 2: 83–123.

Chudodeyev, A. 2005. "Proletarii vsekh stran." Interview with Zhanna Zayonchkovskaya. *Itogi*, no. 14 (April 16).

Dugin, A. 2005. "SSHA pribirayut k rukam postsovetskoye prostranstvo." *Izvestia*, April 13, www.izvestia.ru/comment/article1583000.

Koch, Alfred. "K polemike o yevropeiskosti Rossiii" [Is Russia a European Country?]. (Retrieved December 29, 2007), http://www.polit.ru/lectures/2005/07/11/koh.html.

Lamansky, Vladimir I. 2001. "Tri mira Aziisko-Yevropeiskogo materika" [Three Worlds of the Asian-European Continent]. *Vestnik MGU*, series 12, *Politicheskie Nauki*, no. 1. (Reprinted from the 1892 edition.)

Lenin, V. I. 1914. "O Natsional'noi gordosti velikorossov." *Sotsial Demokrat* (Saint Petersburg). (Retrieved December 12, 2007), http://www.fortunecity.com/victorian/prado/574/works/26-3.htm.

O'Loughlin, J., and P. Talbot. 2005. "Where in the World Is Russia? Geopolitical Perceptions and Preferences of Ordinary Russians." *Eurasian Geography and Economics* 46, no. 1: 23–50.

"Rossiya–Yevropeiskaya strana?" 2005. *Izvestia*, April 22, www.izvestia.ru/comment/article 1662081.

Solzhenitsyn, A. 1990. *Kak nam obustroit' Rossiyu.* Moscow: Komsomolskaya Pravda, http://teljonok.chat.ru/nam/kak.htm.

Yarmolinsky, A., ed. 1949. *A Treasury of Russian Verse.* New York: Macmillan.

Zuercher, C. 2000. "Multiculturalism and the Ethnopolitical Order in Post-Soviet Russia." *Russian Politics and Law* 38, no. 5: 6–24.

Sami

Jouni Häkli

Chronology

1542	Groups of Sami people have inhabited northern Scandinavia since time immemorial. The king of Sweden, Gustav Vasa, decrees that all lands without a formal proprietor belong to the Swedish Crown, causing the Sami to lose most of their land to the state.
1553	Gustav Vasa decides that the Sami must pay taxes directly to the Crown.
1600	The Swedish Evangelic Lutheran Church starts to make inroads into "Lapland."
1613	Russia, Denmark, and Sweden lay claim to the Finnmark area and the northern Norwegian coast. The Sami have to pay taxes to three countries for many years.
1673	The colonization of the Sápmi homeland begins as the Lappmark Proclamation encourages non-Sami settlers to move into the area.
1685	States take oppressive measures toward indigenous Sami religion and culture.
1700	The *siida* system of villages, with boundaries as the basis of the Sami political society, is gradually replaced by administrative bodies and divisions imposed by the Nordic states.
1751	The Swedish-Norwegian border is redrawn. The Lapp Codicil allows the Sami to cross the border with their reindeer regardless of national boundaries.
1809	Finland becomes the autonomous Grand Duchy of Russia, furthering the territorialization of the Scandinavian north.
1826	The border between Russia and Norway is determined.
1852	The border closes between Norway and Finland, causing problems for nomadic Sami who revolt in Norwegian Kautokeino. The revolt is suppressed by the Crown.
1905	The union between Norway and Sweden is dissolved by the Karlstad Convention, pushing the nomadic mountain Sami to choose their country of residence.
1917	First pan-Sami conference in Trondheim.
1918	First national conference for Swedish Sami in Östersund.
1944	Finland's border with the Soviet Union is revised, causing deportations of Skolt Sami to more western and southern areas.
1948	United Nations declaration of human rights.
1952	Radio broadcasting in Sami language starts in Sweden.
1956	The Nordic Sami Council is established as a cooperative body among the Norwegian, Swedish, and Finnish Sami political organizations.
1973	The Sami Delegation is set up in Finland, which later becomes the Finnish Sami Parliament.
1977	The Swedish Parliament recognizes the Sami as an indigenous people in Sweden.
1980	The Alta conflict in Norway over the construction of a hydroelectric power plant on the Alta River; the Sami are mobilized to protect their environment.
1986	The Sami flag is adopted.
1989	A Sami parliament is set up in Norway.
1990	Norway ratifies the ILO 169 decree on rights for indigenous peoples.
1993	A Sami parliament is set up in Sweden.
2000	The Sami Parliamentary Council is established as a Nordic cooperation forum.
2004	Finland passes the Sami Language Act to ensure the rights of the Sami to use their own language before courts and other public authorities.

Situating the Nation

The Sami are a northern European indigenous people with their own history, language, culture, livelihoods, ways of life, and self-reflected identity. They inhabit a homeland that reaches from central Norway through the northernmost parts of Sweden and Finland and into the Kola Peninsula in Russia. The term indigenous people has no fixed definition. A widely accepted formulation includes cultural groups who have a continuous historical connection with a homeland, originating from the time before its colonization or annexation by a nation-state. Furthermore, the group should have maintained some of its distinct linguistic, cultural, and organizational characteristics and must self-identify as an indigenous people. The designation as an indigenous people has played an important role in the emergence and politicization of the modern Sami identity.

The Sami have been living in northern Scandinavia well before it was settled and colonized by Norwegians, Swedes, Finns, and Russians. Over their history, the Sami have faced problems and challenges similar to many other indigenous groups. Among the most critical issues have been the preservation of Sami culture and language, as well as its material foundation—the land title rights. The size of the Sami population can only be estimated because the states' assimilatory and oppressive policies have forced many to hide or reject their Sami identity. In addition, interethnic marriages have blurred boundaries such that many Sami have ancestors from groups other than Sami. According to a recent estimate published by the Finnish Ministry of Justice, there are more than 50,000 Sami in Norway, some 20,000 in Sweden, 8,000 in Finland, and 2,000 in Russia. In total, this amounts to more than 80,000 Sami.

The Sami policies of Norway, Sweden, and Finland officially recognize as Sami those who claim Sami identity and use, or have used, Sami as their home language. Moreover, people with at least one Sami-speaking parent, grandparent, or great-grandparent are considered Sami. This definition is used for voluntary registration for the right to vote in elections for Sami parliaments. No other records of who are Sami exist in Sweden or Norway. In Finland the enfranchisement decision has been partly based on old land or tax registers, hence most Sami have not had to register themselves. Aspiring Sami may apply for registration, but all claims are carefully considered because of a fear that people of Finnish origin will seek individual benefits from participating in Sami politics. In Russia the number of Sami is somewhat uncertain because people with mixed ethnic background have often chosen not to declare Sami as their nationality.

The traditional foundation of the Sami livelihood, based on a hunting culture, was greatly harmed by the exploitation of the most important game animals—beaver and wild reindeer. As game decreased, many Sami resorted to more nomadic sources of livelihood, such as reindeer herding, which demanded mobility according to the reindeer grazing areas. These Sami used their land less intensively,

and their connection to land as property weakened considerably. Consequently, the Sami were removed from the states' land registers, and their land title rights were no longer recorded. The right to own, not merely use, land is one of the most pressing issues in current Sami politics and is a key factor in Sami mobilization.

The revival and politicization of Sami identity are connected to the increased visibility of various ethnic groups in international organizations working to protect the rights of indigenous peoples. Among the most prominent are the United Nations (UN), the International Labour Organization (ILO), the World Bank, and the European Union. These institutions have launched several policies, charters, and forms of economic aid that have enabled the Sami to become politically active, along with other ethnic and indigenous groups all over the world.

Instituting the Nation

As with all nations or ethnic groups, the idea of the Sami as one people with a shared collective identity is a relatively modern phenomenon. However, historical records of "Phinnoi" or "Finns" living in northern Scandinavia predate the Christian period. The emerging Swedish, Norwegian, Finnish, and Russian states used the term Lapp to denote various northern populations with shared characteristics, ones that later have adopted a pan-Sami identity. Between 1251 and 1550, Sweden (including Finland), Norway, and Russia (Novgorod) agreed on borders and taxation rights in the "Lappish" area, which includes the contemporary Sami homeland. The czars of Russia had the right to tax areas all the way to the Norwegian Lapland, known as Finnmark. In return the Sami were granted letters of protection for lands, waters, and taxation on the basis of land registers and land ownership.

Sweden's geopolitical position in northern Scandinavia strengthened in the mid-16th century, and the Sami fell under the rule of the Swedish judicial system, administration, and church. In terms of rights and duties, the Swedish Crown treated the Sami like any other peasants until the late 18th century. The *siida* system of Lapp villages was acknowledged as the basis of Sami land ownership and "Lapp taxes" to the state. *Siidas* were a form of practical cooperation among several family groups, primarily regarding management and sharing of natural resources and game. The individual *siida*, led by a council, had a collective right to hunting and fishing within its area. In 1602 the Sami were even granted representation in the diet, making the Swedish Crown also the king of the "Lapps of Norrland."

A Sami sleigh driver in traditional dress poses with a reindeer in Lapland, Finland. (Jorma Jaemsen/zefa/Corbis)

The *Siida* System

Traditional Sami society was based on a system of Lapp villages, or *siidas*, that covered most of northern Scandinavia. The *siidas* usually had established borders defining both the *siida* community and the area it was entitled to use. Hence, although the Sami were nomadic, they moved only within their own *siida*.

The *siida* had common lands and waters that were divided into usufructuary areas for each clan and family for whom their use was an exclusive right. A village meeting was the central administrative body of the *siida*, defining and controlling its usufructuary rights, justice, and other common affairs. The meeting also sanctioned marriages and admitted new members to the village. Everyone who lived in the village had the right to vote in the meeting.

The Nordic states recognized the *siida* system until the early 1700s. After that point, this traditional Sami structure gradually eroded under the states' colonizing practices. For contemporary Sami politics, the *siida* system is important as a basis for claims to land title rights in the Sápmi.

With the rise of national romantic thought, which emphasized ethnic purity in Sweden, Norway, and Russia, the Sami were subjected to increasingly assimilatory and oppressive policies. From the end of the 18th century until the rise of the Sami movement in the mid-20th century, the Sami had mainly duties but no rights. To start with, they were discharged from the Swedish diet in 1760. Moreover, in 1808 Russia conquered Finland from Sweden, thus pushing the states of Sweden, Norway, Finland, and Russia to demarcate their territorial borders and thus divide the Sami homeland into parts of four states. Finally, in 1917 Finland became independent from Russia, which sealed northern Scandinavia's territorial division.

The period from the mid-19th century to World War II has been called the century of Sami assimilation in Scandinavia. The northern Sami were subjected to governmental assimilation policies aimed at forcing the Sami to relinquish their language and culture. In the more southern areas, the key issue was the threat to reindeer herding caused by non-Sami agricultural expansion. Few explicitly political responses arose from the Sami minorities before the early 20th century, however. Only around 1900 did the Swedish and Norwegian Sami begin to establish organizations for securing their interests during the land use conflicts caused by the Swedish and Norwegian settlers who had moved into the Sami living areas. These conflicts were typically related to differing interests and needs between the permanently settled agriculturalists and the nomadic Sami. The state authorities were reluctant to protect the rights of the Sami, and this recalcitrance activated mobilization based on ethnic identity. Also, the repeated attempts to linguistically and culturally assimilate the Sami eventually provided incentive for organized resistance.

The first organized forms of mobilization had their roots in the Sami newspapers *Sagai Muittalaegje* (1904–1911) and *Waren Sardne* (1910–1913 and 1922–1927) in Norway. Several assemblies were held, and attempts were made by the Sami activists to organize a movement to counter the policies of the authorities. An attempt was also made to establish a nationwide organization in Norway to coordinate the actions of local Sami associations. This attempt failed, however, and by 1930 the first wave of Sami mobilization had dried up.

In Finland, school education was key in the policies of Sami enculturation and ideological assimilation. It was typical to forbid children to use Sami language in the school area, and teachers were strongly encouraged to promote Finnish language throughout. Those Sami teachers who objected were often replaced by non-Sami. The first concrete step toward Sami mobilization was taken in 1932 when Lapin Sivistysseura (Society for the Promotion of Lapp Culture) was formed in Helsinki. A number of Sami participated, but most of the members were non-Sami. The society was active primarily in publishing books and a newspaper in the Sami language, as well as increasing ethnic awareness among the Sami people. Some attention was also directed at concrete social problems of the Sami.

Defining the Nation

Despite awareness of common ethnic origins and the similar problems caused by assimilatory policies by the different Nordic states, the early Sami movement had difficulties formulating common goals that would politically unite the different Sami groups. There are several geographical, economic, and cultural factors that divided the Sami internally. First, the traditional sources of livelihood and the concomitant ways of life among Sami range from reindeer herding and hunting to fishing, agriculture, trade, small-scale industry, and handicrafts. These differences can be seen as functions of the local resources and natural conditions in arctic and subarctic areas. This economic system is exemplified by the changing between agriculture and fishing as sources of livelihood in Sami coastal societies. The Sami have also adapted to the prerequisites for production in specific ecological niches by strongly integrating production, culture, and family. Resources in the Sami areas have seldom given sufficient economic nourishment for single occupations, and therefore combinations of jobs are typical. Over time, however, the Sami sources of livelihood have become closer to those of the majority populations.

Second, some of the dialects of the Sami language have so little in common that they could be considered independent languages. Some 70 percent of Sami speakers use the northern Sami dialect, whereas others use some of the remaining nine dialects. The six main dialects are North Sami, Lule Sami, South Sami, Enare Sami, East Sami, and Kildin Sami. This linguistic diversity is doubled by the fact that most Sami actually speak Norwegian, Swedish, Finnish, or Russian instead of using their native languages. This is the consequence of assimilation policies that encouraged the Sami to relinquish their language in favor of the official language of the respective nation-state. However, since the 1960s teaching in Sami has been allowed in schools located in Sami homelands.

These internal divisions partly explain why Sami mobilization took off slowly during the first half of the 20th century. World War II, and especially the hardships it brought to the Sami, was a crucial watershed for Sami nationalism in Scandinavia, and particularly in Finland. Some of the Sami were forced to fight against other Sami in the war because they lived in different nation-states. Moreover, the Skolt Sami living in Petsamo had to resettle when Finland ceded the area to Russia. The war marked the politicization of the Sami culture and stands out as a period during which Sami identity was first given a discursive form, which was later territorialized in the context of claims for their rights to cultural autonomy and land titles.

For pan-Sami identity to overcome internal differences, the ethno-cultural history of the Sami had to be emphasized. In the definition of Sami identity, two dimensions were important. First, reindeer herding and traditional costumes became uniting symbols, even though they have been part of everyday life only for a diminishing number of the Sami. In addition, the Sami language, despite its various dialects, together with the traditional *yoik* singing, gained importance as "objective" signifiers of Sami identity. The Sami national dress is a uniting symbol even though the types of costumes vary in different parts of the Sami homeland. The national anthem common to all Sami is called "Same soga lavla" ("Song of the Sami Family"). It was written by Isak Saba as early as 1906 but recognized as the official anthem by the 13th pan-Sami conference in Åre, Sweden, in 1986. The official Sami flag was also adopted in the 1986 conference and is now acknowledged in all parts of the Sami homeland. The flag symbolizes the moon and the sun and uses colors of the traditional Sami costumes. Finally, the Sami national day is the 6th of February, which commemorates the first congress for Swedish and Norwegian Sami held in Trondheim in 1917.

The Sami identity was firmly connected to the Sápmi, the territorial homeland inhabited by the Sami since time immemorial and characterized by relatively harsh northern landscape. Stretching across four contemporary nation-states, the Sápmi represents a strong statement about the distinctive and original nature of the Sami as a unified nation. In the Sami language, the term *Sápmi* refers to the Sami homeland but also to the Sami people and their spirit, underlining the historical connection of the Sami with a particular territory and cultural landscape. However, the legal status of the Sami homeland remains vague. From the legal point of view, the Sami live as ethnic minorities in countries exercising sovereignty over Sápmi. Of the Nordic countries, only Finland officially recognizes that the Sami have a particular authority over the Finnish part of the Sápmi, mainly in issues related to cultural autonomy.

Narrating the Nation

The Sami have strong oral traditions that carry an understanding of the people's origin. Storytelling used to be the task of Sami *noaide,* a person with strong mental and spiritual powers. The traditional Sami *yoik* chants have contained beliefs and teachings, tales and stories of the Sami society from the remote past to the present day. *Yoiking* is based on a special vocal technique where the melody, rhythm, and scanty words are used to describe or "sing" a person, an animal, or an event. Since the mid-20th century, these oral narrative forms have been complemented by modern means of communication, such as newspapers, literature, visual arts, handicrafts, music, and theater. The traditional cultural forms have, however, had great importance to the emerging pan-Sami identity.

The written Sami language originates from as early as the 17th century. Sami poems were published in 1673 in Johannes Schefferus's work *Lapponia.* The 20th century saw the birth of indigenous Sami literature. However, a uniform way of writing Sami was not established until 1978. As yet, the amount of Sami literature is small, and only some of it is fiction. Representations of Sami life and history have first concentrated on the hardships the people have been subjected to by the states colonizing the Scandinavian North. This history of oppression has functioned as a significant symbol uniting the different Sami groups.

More positive expressions of Sami identity have been connected with the rise of global concern for indigenous peoples since the 1960s. A new and more global dimension in the narratives on the significance of being a Sami gained foothold in the Sami movement of the 1960s and 1970s. The Sami began to view themselves as part of the movement of indigenous peoples fighting for their rights and cultural survival in the international arena. New narratives of Sami history and identity reflected the Sami involvement in intercultural affairs, such as participation in indigenous peoples' conferences and festivals. Simultaneously, the indigenous people's perspective gained importance at the local level and in the organization of Sami politics. The Sami status as an indigenous people was brought into play in issues such as education, the construction of Sami kindergartens, or encroachments upon the natural environment perceived as harmful to Sami forms of livelihood.

The understanding of Sami as an indigenous people has now become conventionalized among the population. This view has stimulated a new self-understanding that has expanded from the narrow elite in the Sami movement to a number people in more popular arenas. Especially important voices have arisen from amid the producers of contemporary Sami culture, those journalists, authors, actors, and musicians who have contributed to the revitalization of Sami identity. In the space of merely four decades, the Sami have progressively turned away from self-understanding as a subordinate population scattered in four states. Instead they have come to realize that the Sami constitute a people with Sápmi as their homeland, an indigenous people who have much to gain from political visibility and recognition on the global scale.

Mobilizing and Building the Nation

The Sami movement began after World War II. This mobilization was largely a response to the hardships the Sami experienced during and after the war. Still functioning today in Norway, the Sami Reindeer Herders' Association (NRL) was established in 1947. It was followed by the National Association of Norwegian Sami (NSR) established in 1968, and the Norwegian Sami Union (SLF), founded in 1979. These organizations have aimed at improving the living conditions and protecting the rights of the Sami.

In Finland the war caused considerable damage to the Sami as the German army withdrew from Finland through Lapland; many Finnish Sami lost their homes because of the German scorched earth policy. Moreover, some 650 Skolt Sami were displaced from their native homeland in the Petsamo area when Finland ceded the area to the Soviet Union in 1944. The Skolt Sami were resettled by the Finnish government in the northeastern part of Inari. These events served to accentuate the deteriorating situation of the Sami, who began to organize in 1945 when Samii Litto (Sami Union) was founded. The political weight of this organization, however, never reached the level of its Swedish and Norwegian counterparts. More successful in this respect was the Sami Delegation, organized by the Finnish state as a committee for advisory purposes. However, the Delegation was not able to make decisions in matters concerning the Sami people but could only make recommendations, or it could respond to proposals by the Finnish state.

The Norwegian, Swedish, and Finnish Sami wanted to establish Nordic cooperation early on. Important steps in this regard were pan-Sami conferences in

The Sami as Politicians

The growing pan-Sami activism since the 1970s was an international movement led by several prominent Sami politicians in Norway, Sweden, Finland, and Russia. These elites came from a wide range of fields and typically had political experience as leaders and representatives of Sami parliaments, their secretariats, and various Sami associations.

The pan-Sami movement has strong parallels with the politics of ethnic revival and regionalism in other parts of Europe. It has been led by educated protagonists who have worked to fashion a public Sami identity based on symbolic differentiation of the Sami from their respective national majority populations. In the process, reindeer herding has become an essential symbol establishing historical legitimacy for the Sami culture and identity. Many Sami politicians are strongly associated with this "traditional Sami livelihood," even though the majority of the Sami work in other occupations.

This notwithstanding, the Sami politicians are active in spheres ranging from the local to the international. They work in Sami parliaments and participate in the politics of their respective nation-states, but are also an international political force. In their capacity as an indigenous group, the Sami are lobbying for international recognition and rights together with other indigenous peoples.

Jokkmokk, Sweden, in 1953 and in Karasjok, Norway, in 1956. The latter conference voted to launch a Nordic Sami Council as a cooperative body among the national Sami political organizations of Norway, Sweden, and Finland. The Nordic Sami Council proved instrumental in the internationalization of the Sami movement as it provided a platform for Sami participation in the World Council of Indigenous Peoples (WCIP) until its dissolution in 1996.

The most important bodies defining the Sami as a political community have been the Sami parliaments in Norway, Sweden, and Finland. It has been through the national Sami parliaments that the Sami have really been able to voice their demands for recognition as a national minority, as well as for a greater cultural autonomy and, perhaps most importantly, for Sami land title rights. The last of these demands has given the traditional Sami conception of territory a more consciously political tone, while also allowing for nonterritorial solutions to be sought. The three Sami parliaments have had some common meetings and made statements on important common questions for the Sami people. They also made a statement for "Common Objectives and Joint Measures of the Sami Parliaments" as part of the UN international decade of indigenous peoples.

International recognition for the Sami as an indigenous people has been vital for the Sami movement's political visibility. With the support of the international movement of indigenous peoples, the Sami have gained political strength vis-à-vis their respective state governments. The international presence of the Sami has grown significantly since the 1960s. In the last 10 years, this presence has become a major force as the Sami have interacted with other indigenous groups on all national and international levels. The Sami have utilized the international organizations' support perhaps more effectively than any other indigenous nation or ethnic minority.

One watershed in the Sami nation-building was the 1980 Alta movement against the harnessing of the Alta River in northern Norway. This external threat to the Sami sources of livelihood mobilized the Sami across national borders to reassert their identity as an indigenous people. The Alta movement also gave new strength to the demands of the Sami for self-determination and cultural autonomy. Although this pan-Sami movement lost its fight over the dam, it spawned a national awakening, especially among younger Sami and Sami artists. It gave impetus for a collective Sami identity, increasing cultural vitality, and a sense of affiliation with other indigenous peoples of the world.

Currently the Sami participate in and sponsor many transnational conferences and alliances. The Sami have also become increasingly active on the international scene, both at UN meetings and as founder members of the World Council of Indigenous Peoples. The Sami also work closely with the Inuit Circumpolar Conference (ICC), the Russian Association of Indigenous Peoples of the North (RAPON), and other indigenous groups. Moreover, manifesting the rise of pan-Sami activity at the level of international cooperation, the first Sami Parliamentarian Conference gathered in Jokkmokk, Sweden, in February 2005. The conference was an historical event bringing together for the first time representatives from the Sami parliaments of Finland, Norway, and Sweden with representatives for the Sami in Russia. Although a small event as such, the conference is a step toward a more visible unified political agency for controlling and governing issues pertinent to the Sápmi, the Sami homeland area.

The Sami have never been a cohesive ethnic group. As is the case with many dispersed ethnic groups, the pan-Sami movement was created out of an ethnic artificiality. Prior to the 1960s there were only minor indications of a pan-Sami culture. The Sami movements of the early 20th century were attempts at collective action, but they withered because of the internal divisions of the Sami and the negative attitude of the authorities. Hence, the Sami elite found it necessary to create an historical case that would legitimate and authenticate their claims for land, resources, and cultural survival. By creating such an historical narrative, the Sami movement has been able to increase its presence and political elbow room vis-à-vis the Nordic state governments. Especially the realization of the Sami as an indigenous people has emerged as an effective tool for presenting a cohesive front in the struggle for cultural autonomy and political self-determination.

Selected Bibliography

Aikio, Samuli. 1994. "The History of the Sami." In *The Sami Culture in Finland*, edited by Samuli Aikio, Ulla Aikio-Puoskari, and Johannes Helander, 21–47. Helsinki: Lapin Sivistysseura.

Haetta, Odd M. 1996. *The Sami: An Indigenous People of the Arctic.* Karasjok, Norway: Davvi Girji.

Häkli, Jouni. 1999. "Cultures of Demarcation: Territory and National Identity in Finland." In *Nested Identities: Identity, Territory, and Scale*, edited by Guntram H. Herb and David H. Kaplan, 123–149. Lanham, MD: Rowman & Littlefield.

Ingold, Tim. 1976. *The Skolt Lapps Today.* Cambridge: Cambridge University Press.

Jones, Mervyn. 1982. *The Sami of Lapland.* Minority Rights Group, Report 55. London: Minority Rights Group.

Korpijaakko, Kaisa. 1993. *Legal Rights of the Sami in Finland during the Period of Swedish Rule: A Survey of the Past, Thoughts on the Future.* Ottawa: DIAND.

Lehtola, Veli-Pekka. 2002. *The Sámi People: Traditions in Transition.* Inari, Finland: Kustannus-Puntsi.

Pietikäinen, S. 2003. "Indigenous Identity in Print: Representations of the Sami in News Discourse." *Discourse & Society* 14:581–609.

Salvesen, Helge. 1995. "Sami Aednan: Four States—One Nation? Nordic Minority Policy and the History of the Sami." In *Ethnicity and Nation Building in the Nordic World*, edited by Sven Tägil, 106–144. Carbondale and Edwardsville: Southern Illinois University Press.

Ukraine

Taras Kuzio

Chronology

1929 Organization of Ukrainian Nationalists (OUN) is established.

1942 OUN creates the Ukrainian Insurgent Army (UPA) guerrilla force to fight for an independent state. The UPA conducts a decade-long guerrilla struggle against Nazi and Soviet occupations.

1957 and 1959 Émigré leaders of OUN are assassinated by the Soviet KGB secret police.

1960s–1970s Dissident nationalist groups are established in Soviet-occupied Ukraine (i.e., the Ukrainian Nationalist Front, Ukrainian Helsinki Group).

1988 Ukrainian Popular Movement for Restructuring (Rukh) is formed by cultural intelligentsia and former dissidents.

1990 Republican parliamentary elections leads to the entry of Rukh into parliament with 25 percent of seats. Rukh takes control of western Ukrainian councils after local elections. The Ukrainian Helsinki Union adopts a nationalist platform of Ukrainian independence. The Ukrainian parliament declares sovereignty. Rukh adopts a nationalist platform seeking Ukrainian independence.

1991 The Gorbachev all-Soviet referendum on "renewed federation." Ukraine holds two additional polls, one on independence and another seeking a confederation of sovereign republics. A hard-line coup fails. The Ukrainian parliament overwhelmingly votes for a declaration of independence. Independence is supported by 92 percent in a referendum. Leonid Kravchuk is elected president. Rukh leader Vyacheslav Chornovil comes in second with 23 percent of the vote.

1994 Parliamentary and presidential elections are held. Leonid Kuchma is elected president on an "anti-nationalist" platform.

1998 Parliamentary elections are held. Centrist parties enter parliament for the first time.

1999 Rukh leader Chornovil dies in a suspicious car accident. Kuchma is reelected for a second term. Viktor Yushchenko is appointed prime minister.

2001 Yushchenko's government is removed. Yushchenko leads the national democrats in opposition to Kuchma.

2002 Yushchenko's national democratic Our Ukraine bloc wins parliamentary election with 24 percent of the vote. Our Ukraine has the largest faction in parliament.

2004 The presidential election is won by Yushchenko after the Orange Revolution forces authorities to hold a repeat of round two of the elections.

2005 Yushchenko is inaugurated president.

2006 The Anti-Crisis Coalition wins election. Viktor Yanukovych, leader of the left-leaning Party of Regions, assumes the post of prime minister.

2007 Preterm elections won by Orange Revolution parties who create orange coalition and Tymoshenko government. Party of Regions goes into opposition.

Situating the Nation

Ukrainian nationalism began in the 19th century as local non-Russians began to seek their own identity. Language and culture consistently played an important role in the self-definition of this group. Changes to the country's political boundaries during the 20th century incorporated many ethnic Ukrainians as well as other ethnic groups. The country first gained independence in 1918 but suffered during the many attempts to gain control by the Stalinist government. Since gaining independence in 1991, the Ukraine has seen a number of changes among its population, along with changes in local and the national government. Border conflicts with Russia, tension among ethnic groups, and struggles toward finding a voice in Europe all play an important role in current Ukrainian nationalism.

Though referred to as "little Russians" over the last century, Ukraine is a diverse and fascinating country. It is touted as the first Slavic state and serves as the gateway between Europe and Asia. Influences from Scandinavians, Mongols, Tartars, and Turks formed the early tribal identity of Ukrainians. Historically Ukrainians look to the Cossacks as their ancestors. Arising from rural areas in the

15th century, they were known as hard, independent fighters who felt a strong connection to their land. During the Soviet era, many looked to their perceived Cossack roots as nationalist guides.

Since the 17th century, Russia has maintained an interest in Ukraine due to its access to the Black Sea and large amount of fertile land. Currently, it borders seven different eastern European countries, including Russia. The country has a varied landscape, with the Carpathian Mountains in the west and the plains toward the east. As the largest country fully in Europe, Ukraine houses a diverse population. The two largest groups are ethnic Ukrainians who make up about 78 percent of the population (with about 2.5 percent from the Diaspora) and ethnic Russians who number about 17 percent. The Russians are mainly found in the eastern portion of the country, where most of the industry is housed. Many other ethnic groups reside within the country, scattered throughout the landscape. The Tartars, however, are almost exclusively found in the Crimea region.

Instituting the Nation

The national democrats have coexisted in an uneasy alliance with centrists and shared similar views with them on the definition of Ukraine in inclusive, civic terms. This definition has never been a point of discussion. The authorities also delegated educational policies and history teaching to national democrats, who dominated the Academy of Sciences, academia, and cultural institutions. The only major area of disagreement between national democrats and the authorities rested over language policy. National democrats and Communists-Russian nationalists were polar opposites on this issue, with the former supporting rapid Ukrainianization and the prioritization of the Ukrainian language while the latter sought to place Russian on an equal par with Ukrainian.

Under Presidents Leonid Kravchuk and Leonid Kuchma, nation-building policies were divided between centrist political parties (who dominated language policies) and national democrats (who dominated education and history teaching). This division led to moderate language policies but more radical policies in the educational domain, where Ukrainian language usage rapidly advanced. This result contrasted with the Soviet era when Russification policies had been promoted.

In the 2004 elections, the authorities' candidate, Viktor Yanukovych, was seen to be weak on core issues central to nationally conscious Ukrainians. These perceived deficiencies were deepened when he supported making Russian a second state language. Raising the language issue brought Yanukovych more Communist votes, but his support for this policy negatively affected his popularity outside his home base of east Ukraine.

Defining the Nation

Ukraine has two competing national identities and visions of nation-building: a national democratic "ethnic Ukrainian" view and a centrist "eastern Slavic" one. These two visions of nation-building dominated discourse and policy making in independent Ukraine under Presidents Leonid Kravchuk and Leonid Kuchma. The 2004 presidential election brought into the open the competition between these two definitions of the nation, as represented by the two leading candidates, Yushchenko ("ethnic Ukrainian") and Yanukovych ("eastern Slavic").

Kuchma was able to balance Ukraine's ethnic Ukrainian and eastern Slavic identities throughout his decade in office and therefore satisfied both camps at different times. The victory of Yanukovych in the 2004 elections meant the coming into power of a more avowedly eastern Slavic identity, a step too far for many Ukrainian voters and members of the ruling elites. Yanukovych's background in the Donbas and his views on nationality issues also turned nationally conscious Ukrainians against him, further fueling pro-European, civic nationalist mobilization against him. The choice between building Ukraine around an ethnic Ukrainian core or around an eastern Slavic core would influence the country's foreign policy orientation. Yushchenko's ethnic Ukrainian identity was in favor of the coun-

One in five Ukrainians participated in Europe's largest nonviolent protest of election fraud in the 2004 presidential elections. (AP Photo/Alexander Zemlianichenko)

try's rapid integration into NATO and the European Union. Yanukovych's eastern Slavic identity favored a more gradual integration into the European Union, close ties to Russia, and opposition to joining NATO. Yushchenko's ethnic Ukrainian identity is associated with democratic reform and "returning to Europe." Joining NATO and the European Union requires a certain amount of democratic and economic reforms. The Yushchenko administration supported the definition of the nation in inclusive, civic ways that would ensure Ukraine's position within Europe. This position would be accompanied by the greater prioritization for Ukrainian language and culture that existed during the Kuchma era. The ethnic Ukrainian force was far better at mobilizing the population and giving a "fire in the belly" energy, thus creating the Orange Revolution. This pro-Yushchenko, pro-European nationalism was a crucial mobilizing factor in the revolution that followed the election fraud in round two of the 2004 elections. A strong link had always existed in Ukraine between national identity and civil society, and this connection was clearly confirmed in the Orange Revolution.

The two major contending issues of the nation surround language and region. Historical legacies of former czarist Russian, Soviet, or Austro-Hungarian occupations have played a major role in creating strong regional identities. These regional identities, in turn, influence attitudes toward the use of language. Both Ukrainian and Russian ethnic groups maintain that their language is important to the country. In eastern and southern Ukraine, the dominant language is Russian, whereas in western and central regions, the main language used is Ukrainian. These linguistic differences have not only caused divisions on a local level but also inspired changes in policy. Under Yushchenko's presidency, regional councils in eastern Ukraine have adopted resolutions in support of the Russian language. The Party of Regions, which dominates eastern and southern Ukraine, included in its 2006 election program the elevation of Russian to a second state

Viktor Yushchenko (1954–)

Becoming president of Ukraine following the Orange Revolution of November through December 2004, Yushchenko had been chairman of the National Bank throughout the 1990s until he was promoted to become prime minister in December 1999. Yushchenko's term as prime minister lasted 16 months, until a parliamentary vote of no confidence removed him. Yushchenko created the Our Ukraine bloc of political parties for the 2002 elections and transformed it into Ukraine's main opposition force. Our Ukraine united center-right national democratic parties. In the 2004 elections, Yushchenko was the main candidate of the opposition facing the authorities, who sought to impose Viktor Yanukovych as Leonid Kuchma's successor. During the elections, Yushchenko was poisoned in an attempt to remove him from the election race. Yushchenko was elected with 52 percent of the vote following the widespread protests against election fraud that became known as the Orange Revolution.

language (alongside Ukrainian). The Party of Regions, led by defeated presidential candidate Viktor Yanukovych, came first in the 2006 elections with 32 percent of the vote.

Narrating the Nation

Nationalists in the late Soviet era devoted little attention to different elements of nation-building, as their main preoccupation was how to mobilize Ukrainians to support an independent state. All political groups, except the radical right, defined Ukrainians in a territorial, civic manner as all those living in Ukraine, regardless of ethnic origin. This view granted automatic citizenship to all residents upon independence in January 1992, following the "zero option" policy employed by other former Soviet republics.

Ukraine, however, consistently opposed the introduction of dual citizenship. While the idea of dual citizenship was unpopular, only the radical right supported an ethnically exclusive definition of Ukrainian. This ethnic idea more closely followed the Estonian and Latvian models. According to this view, only ethnic Ukrainians would have been eligible for citizenship. Such a view never found broad support, even in the western territory, the Ukrainian heartland. Radical-right ethnic Ukrainian nationalists also never influenced domestic policies. Their views in support of ethnic discrimination, hostility to national minorities, anti-Semitism, and strident anti-Russianism proved to be unpopular among Ukrainian voters.

Organization of Ukrainian Nationalists

The Organization of Ukrainian Nationalists (OUN) was established in 1929 as a radical-right political force aimed at establishing an independent Ukrainian state. OUN's ideology moved close to fascism in the 1930s when it undertook terrorist attacks against Polish and Soviet targets. Ukraine was then divided between Polish and Soviet occupations. In 1940 the OUN split into two groups: a moderate faction led by Colonel Andrei Melnyk and a more radical group led by Stepan Bandera. During World War II, the Bandera wing of OUN created a guerrilla group titled the Ukrainian Insurgent Army (UPA) that fought against Nazi and Soviet occupiers. The UPA continued to fight against the Soviet occupation after World War II, until the early 1950s when it was crushed. The Soviet authorities were concerned about the lingering influence of the OUN and targeted its exiled leaders living in Germany for assassination in 1957 (Lev Rebet) and 1959 (Bandera).The OUN divided into three groups in 1940, between followers of Andrei Melnyk (OUNm) and Stepan Bandera (OUNb), and in 1952 between Bandera (OUNb) and Lev Rebet (OUNz). From the 1960s through the 1980s, dissident groups drew on the OUN nationalist tradition. OUNb was the only wing of the three OUNs that established a political party in Ukraine in 1992: the Congress of Ukrainian Nationalists (KUN). OUNb and KUN were led by Slava Stetsko until her death in 2003.

Their views were also unpopular within academic and media discussions, which were dominated by political groups from the democratic camps.

Ukraine has pursued moderate nationality policies throughout its existence as an independent state. Affirmative action for Ukrainians has been gradual, primarily targeting the educational system by changing the language of teaching from Russian to Ukrainian. Government support has been provided to national and Jewish minorities to pursue cultural and religious revivals. Eastern Ukrainian elites were given the option of a "voice" in the Ukrainian political system that gave them a stake in the newly independent state. The option of "exit" (i.e., separatism) was therefore not considered. The election of Kuchma in 1994 led to an influx of officials from his home region of Dnipropetrovsk in eastern Ukraine.

While the national government battled out the issues of citizenship, each region saw changes in its political structure. The eastern Ukrainian Donbas region was permitted a degree of self-rule through Free Economic Zones, allowing local elites to enrich themselves into oligarchs. Ukraine's wealthiest oligarch, Renat Akhmetov, emerged in Donetsk. The entry of the Donbas into the Ukrainian parliament did not take place until 2002 when Yanukovych was made prime minister. The use of different languages also came into play on local levels. In 1989 the Ukrainian language was made the "state language," while granting Russian the right to be used locally, which was later reinforced in the 1996 constitution. Language policies have always been moderate and applied differently across regions. For instance, in the Donbas (Donetsk and Luhansk oblasts) and in the Crimea there has been little attempt to introduce Ukrainian but, rather, a desire to make Russian the official language.

Since independence in 1992, many have predicted that interethnic and regional conflict was imminent in Ukraine. That no conflict has taken place suggests that these fears were based on incorrect assumptions. Ethnic tension in the Crimea, the only Ukrainian region with an ethnic Russian majority, proved short-lived. In 1994–1995, Russian separatists there briefly took control of the presidency and Supreme Soviet. Since 1996 the Crimea has returned to its 1991–1993 political configuration wherein pro-Ukrainian centrists have remained in control and the Communist Party plays the role of the main opposition force.

Mobilizing and Building the Nation

Nationalism is a multifaceted concept that incorporates many different definitions. Although the tendency among scholars has been to define nationalism in Ukraine as one continuous process from the second half of the 1980s until the present, this approach has serious flaws, for nationalism can manifest itself in various ways during different periods of history. Nationalism prior to independence sought to establish a newly independent state (e.g., Ukraine from the former Soviet Union).

Nationalists after independence seek to build an independent nation-state, and they can differ as to how its cultural component can be structured (e.g., one or two state languages). Several groups have emerged over the years, all playing important roles in how Ukraine defines itself.

The Ukrainian Popular Movement for Restructuring (Rukh) became a key player in Ukrainian politics. After it was established in 1988, Rukh declared its support for self-determination, becoming de facto a nationalist movement at its October 1990 congress. The civic nationalist approach adopted by Rukh was a product of three factors. First, the dissident political prisoner wing of Rukh had a long tradition dating back to the 1960s of support for human rights. Second, the conservative Soviet Ukrainian leader Volodymyr Shcherbytsky ruled the republic from 1972 to 1989, and Rukh only developed into a mass movement after he left office. Finally, the large number of Russian-speaking Ukrainians and ethnic Russians influenced Rukh's adoption of an evolutionary and nonradical program.

Alongside the evolution of Rukh, the Communist Party Ukraine began to divide into three groups. The first group was the Democratic Platform, which included the young, democratic wing of the Communist Party of Ukraine that then broke off and formed the Party of Democratic Revival of Ukraine. Being more inclined to political reform, the Democratic Platform often leaned closer to the democratic opposition. Communists who supported Ukrainian sovereignty and the Democratic Platform wings of the Communist Party of Ukraine both became nationalists after the collapse of the hard-line coup in August 1991, when they moved to a position of supporting Ukraine's independence. The second group was the sovereign communists (often mistakenly dubbed "national communists") led by Leonid Kravchuk, ideological secretary of the Communist Party of Ukraine and parliamentary speaker from 1990 to 1991. The third faction of the Communist Party of Ukraine was the "imperial communists." As the ideological heirs of hard-line Communist Party of Ukraine leader Shcherbytsky, they detested both

---

Rukh and Our Ukraine

The Ukrainian Popular Movement for Restructuring (Rukh) was established in 1988 by former political prisoners and the cultural intelligentsia as a popular front. In 1989–1990 Rukh moved toward support for Ukraine's independence from the USSR. After Ukraine became independent in 1991, Rukh went into decline with some leaders co-opted by the new state structures while others, grouped around Vyachslav Chornovil, went into constructive opposition. Yushchenko's entry into opposition politics in 2001 led to the creation of the Our Ukraine bloc of which Rukh was a central party. Other political parties in Our Ukraine aside from Rukh included national democratic and nationalistic parties. In the 2002 elections Our Ukraine came first with 24 percent of the vote but then declined in support to 14 percent in the 2006 and 2007 elections. Our Ukraine was one of three political groups that supported Yushchenko's candidacy in 2004. Our Ukraine's current leader is Vyacheslav Kyrlylenko.

---

the Democratic Platform (which leaned toward Rukh) and the sovereign communists (led by Kravchuk and Kuchma). After the Communist Party of Ukraine was banned for supporting the August 1991 coup, the hard-line remnants of the Communist Party of Ukraine re-formed, becoming the Communist Party, legalized in October 1993. The Communist Party of Ukraine had the largest faction in the 1994–1998 and 1998–2002 parliaments. Therefore, throughout 8 of Ukraine's 14-year history, the largest party in parliament has been *antinationalist*, opposed to the very concept of an independent Ukrainian state.

Nationalism postindependence has changed aspects of these political groups. National democrats, such as Rukh, occupy a center-right niche and cannot be classified as nationalists in the post-Soviet period, even though Rukh was certainly a nationalist party for self-determination in 1990–1991. National democrat and centrist political parties were allied against internal and external threats to Ukraine's statehood and on most issues pertaining to how to formulate the national idea. Because centrists dominated Ukraine's presidency from 1991 to 2004, their view inevitably moderated the contours of how nation-building was to be implemented and over what timeframe.

Radical-right nationalists grouped in the Ukrainian National Assembly (previously the Inter-Party Assembly) have a less defined view of the state. Ethnic Russian and Soviet nationalists always argued that Ukraine had no right to exist as an independent state but only to abide in a vaguely defined eastern Slavic union or in a revived Soviet Union. The homeland for Russian nationalists in Ukraine is an eastern Slavic union, revived Soviet Union, or czarist empire. Russian nationalists in Ukraine have difficulty accepting Ukraine's right to exist as an independent state. They vacillate between a belief that the three eastern Slavs are merely regional branches of one Russian nation or recognizing that a Soviet Ukrainian republican identity now exists that has harmed the "natural" unification of the three eastern Slavic "Russian" peoples.

Russian nationalism in Ukraine has other defining attributes, many of which are jointly held with Soviet nationalists. These include defining liberal values as "un-Russian." They tend to be anti-Western (especially anti-American), anti-NATO, and often anti-Semitic. Russia is looked up to as the "natural leader" and "big brother" of the eastern Slavs. Finally, they oppose affirmative action for Ukrainian culture and language and accuse the authorities of "discrimination" in policies aimed at upgrading Ukrainian culture and language. The Russian language, they believe, is a "higher" language and should be placed on a par with Ukrainian as a second state language.

Ukrainian ethnic nationalists share one idea with their ethnic Russian counterparts: the rejection of post-Soviet Ukraine as the homeland for Ukrainians. Both groups want to expand the borders of the state to its "ethnographic borders." As with Russian nationalists, Ukrainian nationalists seek to unite all those they define as belonging to one ethnic group within one state (an eastern Slavic union). Ethnic Ukrainian nationalists seek to incorporate territory in Poland, Slovakia,

Moldova, Belarus, and Russia into a "greater Ukraine." Ethnic Russian and Soviet nationalists, however, would like to see Ukraine included within the Russian-Belarusian union or in a revived Soviet Union.

Toward the end of the Kuchma era, the authorities increasingly relied on radical-right groups to undertake policies they themselves did not want to be associated with. These groups included the co-opted Ukrainian National Assembly, which had grown out of the late Soviet Inter-Party Assembly, Bratstvo (Brotherhood) led by the former Ukrainian National Assembly leader Dmytro Korchynsky, Rukh for Unity led by a splinter Rukh faction that had been co-opted, and the Organization of Ukrainian Nationalists (OUN) in Ukraine. These four groups were assigned set tasks during the 2004 elections. The Ukrainian National Assembly provided street parades wherein participants wore Nazi-style uniforms and proclaimed their support for Yushchenko, thus dubbing him in the state-controlled media as a "nationalist extremist." The leaders of the other three parties registered as candidates in the elections; as candidates, they had the right to allocate a certain number of their supporters to the election commissions. These "technical candidates," as they became known, supplied additional election officials who could then assist the authorities in election fraud.

In the 1994 and 1998 parliaments, Rukh and allied national democratic parties had the second largest factions after the Communists. These proportions only changed in the 2002 parliament when Yushchenko's Our Ukraine bloc ensured that national democrats became the largest parliamentary faction, with the Communists in second place. After Kuchma was reelected in 1999, national democrats gradually evolved from "constructive opposition" to the authorities to being in outright opposition. Two factors propelled this evolution. The first factor was the removal of the Yushchenko government in April 2001 following the Kuchmagate scandal. The Kuchmagate scandal erupted on November 28, 2000, when tapes that had been illicitly made in the president's office were released. The tapes revealed the president ordering the journalist Georgiy Gongaze (killed in the fall of 2000) to be "taken care of." The second factor was Kuchma's growing reliance upon, and alliance with, corrupt oligarchs attempting to build an authoritarian state.

The victory of Yushchenko in the 2004 elections and the Orange Revolution transformed nationalism in Ukraine. Soviet nationalists are in a terminal decline from their heyday in the late 1990s. The 20 percent they obtained in the 2002 elections dramatically declined to 3.5 percent for the Communist Party of Ukraine in the 2006 elections. The Communist Party of Ukraine's peak of popularity was 120 seats in the 1998 parliament, a figure that halved in the 2002 parliament. The Communist Party of Ukraine has only 21 deputies in the 2006 parliament.

Yushchenko established a presidential party in 2005 entitled People's Union–Our Ukraine that is more liberal in its orientation than the traditional national-democratic orientation of Rukh, for it is dominated by pro-Western liberal and business groups. The participation of Yushchenko's People's Union–Our Ukraine in the 2006 and 2007 elections has crowned the emergence of a new, liberal civic

Yulia Tymoshenko Bloc

Yulia Tymoshenko became an opposition leader in 2000–2001 after she was arrested on fraudulent corruption charges as deputy prime minister in charge of energy in the Yushchenko government. Her opposition hardened during the 2000–2001 Kuchmagate crisis where her political force called for President Kuchma's impeachment. Tymoshenko was instrumental in establishing the Forum for National Salvation in 2001 and her eponymous bloc entered parliament in 2002 with 7 percent of the vote. Tymoshenko was a key organizer in the 2004 Orange Revolution and was awarded with the position of prime minister in 2005. The Tymoshenko bloc increased its support in the 2006 and 2007 elections where it obtained 23 and 31 percent of the vote respectively, eclipsing Our Ukraine as the largest orange political force and with the second largest parliamentary faction. Tymoshenko returned to government in December 2007 following the creation of an orange coalition when orange forces won the 2007 elections.

nationalism. The traditional romantic nationalism of Rukh that dominated the Ukrainian center-right from the late Soviet era and throughout the 1990s is no longer a political force. The People's Union–Our Ukraine is dominated by liberal, civic nationalists and has a liberal, center-right ideology. In the 2006 elections, the People's Union–Our Ukraine joined with other national democratic parties in an Our Ukraine bloc. In the 2007 preterm elections they established the Our Ukraine–People's Self-Defense bloc with nine center-right parties, including Yushchenko's People's Union–Our Ukraine. In both the 2006 and 2007 elections, Our Ukraine and the Our Ukraine–People's Self-Defense blocs received 14 percent, down 10 percent from the 2002 elections. Most of their support was taken by the Yulia Tymoshenko bloc led by Prime Minister Tymoshenko (from 2007). Pro-Orange Revolution parties won the 2006 and 2007 elections but only managed to create a parliamentary coalition and government following the 2007 elections. The Tymoshenko bloc unites Tymoshenko's Fatherland Party, the Reforms and Order and Social Democratic parties. The People's Union–Our Ukraine and the Tymoshenko bloc are members of the European People's Party, a center-right political group in the European Parliament.

Through all these changes, the Ukraine continues to find a political and social balance within its large territory. Defining itself both geographically and ethnically has raised issues over the years, especially due to regional differences. The country will undoubtedly see further developments both on local and national levels as it strives to find its place in greater Europe.

Selected Bibliography

Arel, Dominique. 2005. "The 'Orange Revolution': Analysis and Implications of the 2004 Presidential Election in Ukraine." Third Annual Stasiuk-Cambridge Lecture on Contemporary Ukraine, University of Cambridge. www.ukrainiancambridge.org/Images/Arel_Cambridge_english.pdf.

Armstrong, John A. 1980. *Ukrainian Nationalism.* Littleton, CO: Ukrainian Academic Press.

Fournier, Anna. 2002. "Mapping Identities: Russian Resistance to Linguistic Ukrainisation in Central and Eastern Ukraine." *Europe-Asia Studies* 54, no. 3: 415–433.

Janmaat, Jan G. 2000. *Nation-Building in Post-Soviet Ukraine: Educational Policy and the Response of the Russian-Speaking Population.* Amsterdam: University of Amsterdam.

Kubicek, Paul. 1996. "Dynamics of Contemporary Ukrainian Nationalism: Empire-Breaking to State Building." *Canadian Review of Studies in Nationalism* 23, nos. 1–2: 39–50.

Kuzio, Taras. 1998. *Ukraine: State and Nation Building.* London: Routledge.

Kuzio, Taras. 2006. "Post-Soviet Ukraine. The Victory of Civic Nationalism." In *Nationalism after Independence: Making and Protecting the Nation in Postcolonial and Postcommunist States*, edited by Lowell Barrington, 187–224. Ann Arbor: University of Michigan Press.

Kuzio, Taras. 2008. *Theoretical and Comparative Perspectives on Nationalism: New Directions in Cross-Cultural and Post-Communist Studies.* Hannover, Germany: Ibidem-Verlag.

Kuzio, Taras, and Paul D'Anieri, eds. 2002. *Dilemmas of State-Led Nation Building in Ukraine.* Westport, CT: Praeger.

Magocsi, Paul R. 1996. *A History of Ukraine:* Toronto, ON: University of Toronto Press.

Magocsi, Paul R. 2002. *The Roots of Ukrainian Nationalism: Galicia as Ukraine's Piedmont.* Toronto: University of Toronto Press.

Molchanov, Mikhail A. 2000. "Post-Communist Nationalism as a Power Resource: A Russia–Ukraine Comparison." *Nationalities Papers* 28, no. 2: 263–288.

Shulman, S. 2002. "Sources of Civic and Ethnic Nationalism in Ukraine." *Journal of Communist Studies and Transition Politics* 18, no. 4: 1–30.

Shulman, Stephen. 2005. "National Identity and Public Support for Political and Economic Reform in Ukraine." *Slavic Review* 64, no. 1: 59–87.

Subtelny, Orest. 2000. *Ukraine: A History.* Toronto, ON: University of Toronto Press.

Yekelchyk, Serhy. 2007. *Ukraine: Birth of a Modern Nation.* Oxford: Oxford University Press.

Wilson, Andrew. 2000. *The Ukrainians: Unexpected Nation.* New Haven, CT: Yale University Press.

Wilson, Andrew. 2005. *Ukraine's Orange Revolution.* New Haven, CT: Yale University Press.

Wales

Rhys Jones

Chronology

1263   Creation of the first Welsh principality by Llywelyn ap Gruffudd, the so-called last prince of Wales.

1282–1283   Edward I's conquest of Wales, which led to the majority of lands within Wales being controlled by the English Crown.

1536–1542   Acts of Union, which formally incorporated the remaining independent areas of Wales into the kingdom of England. The Acts of Union led to the systematic extension of English law into Wales.

1588   Translation of the Bible into Welsh by Bishop William Morgan.

1886   Formation of Cymru Fydd (Young Wales), which argued for Welsh Home Rule.

1925   Formation of Plaid Cymru, the Welsh nationalist party, which sought to defend the Welsh language and promote political independence for Wales.

1962   The broadcast of "Tynged yr Iaith" ("Fate of the Language") by Saunders Lewis, which acted as a source of inspiration for Welsh linguistic nationalism during the 1960s.

1966   The election of Gwynfor Evans as the first Plaid Cymru member of Parliament in a south Wales constituency.

1979   A failed referendum on the devolution of power to Wales.

1982   The first broadcasts by S4C, the Welsh-medium television channel.

1993   The formation of the Welsh Language Board, the statutory board with responsibility for the Welsh language.

1997   The successful referendum on the devolution of power to Wales.

1999   The opening of, and first elections for, the National Assembly for Wales.

Situating the Nation

For much of its history, the fortunes of the Welsh nation have been tied closely with that of England and a broader Britain, forming as it does part of the Celtic fringe discussed by Hechter in his famous account of internal colonialism. Wales, since the Middle Ages, has existed in an ambiguous political, cultural, and economic position with regard to England/Britain. It is this relationship between Wales and a broader British state that has contributed to certain political and cultural tensions within the Welsh nation.

Until the formation of the National Assembly for Wales (NAfW), the Welsh nation did not benefit from the protection that would have been afforded to it by a Welsh state. The political formations that have existed in Wales, especially since the 16th-century Acts of Union between England and Wales, have been based on those of the English state and most notably its shires and legal system. The existence of a powerful neighboring English state has also shaped Welsh cultural identity, which has led to certain tensions within the country. We notice this most clearly with regard to the Welsh language. Although, at certain times, the patronage of the English has played an important role in supporting the Welsh language (e.g., through its support of the translation of the Bible into Welsh), it has also undermined its use within Wales. The so-called "treachery of the Blue Books," for instance, refers to the denunciation of the Welsh language by the British state's education inspectors during the mid-19th century. Although acting as a clarion call for many Welsh nationalists, this episode confirmed in other people's minds the need to jettison the Welsh language in favor of the more cosmopolitan and powerful English language.

Wales has also enjoyed an ambiguous relationship with England/Britain in more economic terms. Wales has been blessed with a variety of natural resources: coal, slate, iron ore, tin, and water in particular. The presence of these raw materials within Wales and their exploitation as part of a British state have contributed to divisions within Welsh nationalist politics. The use of Welsh water by English municipalities, for instance, has acted as a raw nerve within mainstream Welsh nationalism, since it illustrates the exploitation of Welsh resources by external bodies. Welsh coal, on the other hand, was proudly viewed by certain sections of the Welsh population as the raw material that sustained much of Britain's world domination. As well as sustaining many of its indigenous industries, the coal resources of Wales helped tie the country more closely to a British sense of identity, as well as a broader British empire.

National Assembly for Wales

The National Assembly for Wales represents a devolved form of government created to govern Wales in 1999. The Labour Party was elected to power in the United Kingdom in 1997 in a landslide victory. One of the party's stated aims was to modernize the governance of the United Kingdom through concerted governmental devolution of power. Wales, along with Scotland and Northern Ireland, was in the vanguard of this process. A referendum was held in 1997 wherein the opportunity to create a National Assembly for Wales, possessing secondary legislative powers, was offered to the Welsh public. The result of the referendum hung in the balance until the final votes had been counted. The support of nearly 51 percent of the Welsh population on a turnout of approximately 50 percent was not particularly inspiring, but it provided enough legitimacy for the U.K. government to propose a Government for Wales Act, which became law in 1999. The first elections for the National Assembly for Wales were held the same year. The formation of the National Assembly for Wales has opened up a new space for political dialogue in Wales and, furthermore, has led to the promotion of a more civic vision of the Welsh nation, which is said to apply to the whole of the population of the country and not just its Welsh-speaking constituents.

But in addition to this important British political, cultural, and economic context, we also need to focus on the geographic variables that have contributed to the development of Welsh identity. Wales's location next to a politically and economically dominant English/British state has already been noted. Other important geographic themes have impacted the Welsh nation. Certain landscapes, for instance, have been deemed of crucial importance to the Welsh nation. Gruffudd (1995) has shown how Plaid Cymru has traditionally glorified the rural and mountainous areas of Wales as being the true core of the Welsh nation. During the interwar period, for instance, the party argued that the Welsh people would have to "return to the land" if they were to gain their rightful place as a moral nation, since it was here that they could avoid Anglicized metropolitan values. In another context, certain places within Wales have played a crucial role within the development of the Welsh nation. Recent work has shown, for example, that the university town of Aberystwyth has contributed to the development of Welsh nationalist ideology since the 1960s as a result of the mixing of people and ideas that has taken place there.

In terms of its social makeup, the Welsh nation has drawn on a number of different classes and groups of people. The established nationalism of Plaid Cymru, for instance, has traditionally been led by an educated, Welsh-speaking, and largely religious elite. It is thus notable that the party was far more concerned with

---

Plaid Cymru

Formed in 1925, Plaid Cymru is an organization that has been concerned with securing the political, linguistic, and moral future of the Welsh nation. Gruffudd has argued that for much of the early period of its existence Plaid Cymru was more worried about the linguistic and moral well-being of the people of Wales than it was with overtly political or nationalistic issues, and, as a result, its main area of support tended to be the Welsh-speaking rural areas of the west and north. This underlying connection between Plaid Cymru and the Welsh rural landscape is highly symbolic. Even today, Plaid Cymru's motif comprises a Welsh dragon emblazoned across three stylized mountains. By the 1960s, Plaid Cymru's political ambitions had increased, and these were fulfilled in 1966 with the election of its first member of Parliament, Gwynfor Evans, to the seat of Carmarthenshire in south Wales. Further election success followed, with the party, at its peak, supplying four Members of Parliament to the Westminster Parliament. It is significant that this electoral success, however, has been focused solely on the more western parts of Wales, where the highest percentage of Welsh speakers are located. Plaid Cymru's connection with the more rural and Welsh-speaking parts of Wales has given the impression of a party that is centered on ethnic rather than civic concerns. The party sought to address this issue in the late 1990s by re-branding itself as Plaid Cymru, the Party of Wales, and attempting, at the same time, to reach out to the mainly English-speaking south Wales valleys. The re-branding has led to certain internal divisions within the party between traditionalists in the north and west, for whom linguistic issues are paramount, and members and supporters in the south and east, who espouse more socialist ideals.

securing the linguistic and moral future of the Welsh nation than it was with political independence as such during its early years. Plaid Cymru, as similarly done
by a number of other nationalistic movements, also made considerable ideological use of a largely working-class Welsh folk—the *gwerin*—as the repositories of
age-old Welsh customs and traditions.

Instituting the Nation

Within this broad context, it is possible to outline a number of key institutions
that have contributed to the evolution of the Welsh nation. The significance of
Plaid Cymru as the critical driving force behind a politicized Welsh nation for
much of the 20th century has been noted. But other organizations, too, have promoted different visions of the Welsh nation at different points in time. The Welsh
Language Society (Cymdeithas yr Iaith), for instance, was formed during the
1960s as a pressure group especially tasked with promoting the status of the
Welsh language within Wales, although it also contributed to a broader political
project of creating a Welsh nation in which the Welsh language was of equal status to that of English. In more recent years, the pressure group Cymuned (Community) has attracted considerable support, especially among Welsh speakers. Its
aim is to secure the future of Welsh as a community language, since it is only this
living language, they argue, that can testify to Wales's distinctiveness as a nation.
In addition to these political and linguistic groups in civil society, there is no

Cymdeithas yr Iaith Gymraeg

The Welsh Language Society was formed in 1962 as an offshoot of Plaid Cymru. The context for its formation was the perceived collapse in the number of Welsh speakers within Wales and the subsequent impact of that decrease on the distinctiveness of a Welsh cultural and political identity. The immediate impetus for the formation of the society was a BBC radio broadcast by Saunders Lewis, who had been a key figure within Welsh nationalist circles for much of the 20th century. His account of the "Fate of the Language" provided considerable inspiration for the formation of Cymdeithas yr Iaith as well as for a series of acts of civil disobedience carried out throughout Wales during the 1960s. Today the Welsh Language Society still campaigns on linguistic issues and calls for a stronger Welsh Language Act and a Property Act, which would alleviate the lack of affordable housing for Welsh speakers in rural Wales. Some of Cymdeithas yr Iaith's thunder has been stolen in recent years, however, by the new pressure group Cymuned (Community). Formed in 1999, the latter has sought to preserve the use of the Welsh language within the communities of the Welsh "heartland."

doubt that the major institution currently involved in shaping the future of the Welsh is the NAfW. Formed in 1999 under the U.K. Labour government, it has brought issues to do with political representation, democracy, and the Welsh language to the center stage of Welsh politics. The NAfW, for instance, has published a number of documents that outline specific policies and strategies that can enable Wales to remain a bilingual country. It has also promoted broader visions concerning the need for an open, vibrant, and forward-looking Welsh nation. In this respect, there is some tension among the philosophical foundations of these different institutions involved in the reproduction of the Welsh nation. While pressure groups such as Cymdeithas yr Iaith and Cymuned have advocated an ethnic vision of the Welsh nation, Plaid Cymru in more recent years, as well as the NAfW, has emphasized a more inclusive and civic conception of Wales and Welshness. There is no doubt that these different perspectives on Welshness could lead to political debate and divisiveness within Wales over the coming years. Finally, attention should be drawn to the Welsh television channel, S4C, formed in 1982 as a direct result of political agitation in Wales and, most notably, a hunger strike by Gwynfor Evans, long-term president of Plaid Cymru. Part of S4C's output is in the Welsh language, thus ensuring that the language gains a certain credibility through its presence within a key contemporary cultural medium.

Defining the Nation

These alternative visions of the past, present, and future of the Welsh nation have led to certain divisions within Welsh civil society. The Welsh language, in particular, has been viewed by many as a divisive force within the Welsh nation. The established nationalism of Plaid Cymru, Cymdeithas yr Iaith, and Cymuned has, in the past, tended to conflate the ability to speak the Welsh language with membership in the Welsh nation, but this equation of linguistic ability with national identity has been problematic. This conflation of language with national identity is difficult to sustain since only approximately 20 percent of the population of Wales now claim a mastery of the Welsh language. Other dissenting voices have attempted to delineate the Welsh nation in alternative ways and have drawn on broader cultural themes as well as those of social justice. Ethnic minorities and feminist groups in Wales, too, are increasingly trying to articulate different versions of Welshness that take into account the plurality of peoples living within Wales. The formation of the NAfW has further cemented this growing civic and inclusive conception of the Welsh nation, and, indeed, there are increasing signs of a more open definition of the Welsh nation by organizations such as Plaid Cymru. Its recent re-branding as Plaid Cymru, the Party of Wales, for instance, points to a far more inclusive take on Welsh nationalism that appeals to both Welsh speakers and non-Welsh speakers.

In general terms, the process of defining the Welsh nation has proceeded relatively smoothly when compared with a number of other nations. The geographic definition of the Welsh nation, for instance, has been characterized by a relatively high level of agreement. The Acts of Union between England and Wales during the 16th century were highly significant in this respect. Although the acts led to an administrative homogeneity between England and Wales, most clearly with regard to the extension of the shire system throughout the whole of Wales, it also emphasized the boundaries between the two countries through its precise definition of English and Welsh shires. Furthermore, the fact that Wales's other three boundaries are defined by the Irish Sea has, undoubtedly, helped quell any nationalist conflict concerning the definition of the Welsh national territory. In a similar vein, there are few geographic features within Wales that have served to divide the nation. Although traveling between the north and the south of the country can be relatively arduous, there has been little sense of the need to surmount any internal physical divisions. The only geographic debate taking place with regard to the contemporary Welsh nation has revolved around its linguistic geographies. Cymuned—the recently formed political pressure group discussed above—has sought to define a Welsh "heartland" in its political rhetoric in which Welsh is used as a community language. Cymuned's focus on the preservation of this geographically delineated language "heartland" stresses the existence of important internal borders within Wales. Here, a strong link has been forged between the Welsh language and identity and a geographically restricted Welsh territory. This claim has provoked a strong reaction from Cymdeithas yr Iaith and Plaid Cymru. For these latter groups, it is the Welsh territory, considered as a whole, that should form the basis for political action and language policy.

Narrating the Nation

The use of the Welsh nation's past has also been subject to debate. Contemporary Welsh nationalism draws much succor from the struggles of the Welsh people against an English state that took place during the medieval period. Certain heroic figures stand out in this respect, most notably Llywelyn ap Gruffudd and Owain Glyndŵr, who led a major revolt against the English at the beginning of the 15th century. Llywelyn ap Gruffudd's struggle against the English Crown was characterized by considerable highs and an equally ignominious end. Llywelyn's brief success and his subsequent death have acted as a source of inspiration for Welsh nationalists, especially with regard to his efforts to create the first Welsh proto-state. Today, his deeds are remembered in a ceremony that takes place annually in Cilmeri, the remote village where he was killed. The other historic hero for the Welsh nation is Owain Glyndŵr, a nobleman from northeast Wales who led a revolt against English rule between 1400 and 1415. During this period, Glyndŵr was able to carry out a successful guerilla campaign against English forces in Wales and succeeded in capturing many of their castles, boroughs, and military leaders. Once again, Glyndŵr's efforts have cast an important shadow over more recent nationalist ideologies in Wales, most infamously in the form of the extremist organization Meibion Glyndŵr, which carried out a series of fire-bombings of holiday homes located in Wales during the 1980s and 1990s. Despite the importance of these two historic figures for recent Welsh nationalist rhetoric, the actions of Llywelyn ap Gruffudd and Owain Glyndŵr can only be used to a certain extent as an inspiration for the contemporary Welsh nation. After all, the forces arrayed against these two alleged leaders of the Welsh nation were full of Welsh soldiers. Indeed, it has been argued that there were far more Welsh soldiers in the army sent out to subdue Llywelyn ap Gruffudd's bid for independence than were in his own army. There is a clear sense in which the Welsh nation's remembrance of these historic events is highly selective and comprises what Anderson has described as "remembering-forgetting."

In addition to the use of these historic figures as a way of narrating the Welsh nation, other key symbols for expressing the identity of the Welsh nation include the use of the daffodil and the leek as its national symbols; the cultural festival of the Eisteddfod; the strong tradition of choral music; unique musical forms such as Cerdd Dant (in which a vocal melody is dovetailed in complex ways with a countermelody played on a harp); folk dancing, particularly in clogs; the national sport of rugby union; and the landscape art of painters such as Kyffin Williams and Aneurin Jones. Although these symbols are significant reminders of the distinctiveness of the Welsh nation, there is some doubt as to their impact on the totality of the Welsh nation. Far higher numbers of people watch and play soccer in Wales than rugby union, for instance, yet the latter is still considered to be the national sport. Similarly, it is noticeable that some of these symbols of Welsh

Bilingual sign in Wales with information in
both Welsh and English: note the order.
(iStockPhoto.com)

nationalism possess relatively short histories and may well represent what
Hobsbawm and Ranger have termed an "invention of tradition." Some of the traditions associated with the cultural festival of the Eisteddfod, for instance, were
literally invented by a laudanum addict named Edward Williams (more commonly known as Iolo Morgannwg) during the late 18th century. In this respect, it
may be more useful to think of the symbolic significance of banal indicators of
the national distinctiveness of Wales, such as the presence of bilingual road signs
throughout the whole of its territory. As Billig has noted, these banal symbols are
extremely powerful reminders of the distinctiveness of particular nations. There
is no doubt that the physical imprint of the Welsh language on the landscape in
the form of road signs helps reinforce the existence of the Welsh nation in the
minds of inhabitants and visitors alike. The political struggle over bilingual road
signs during the 1970s in particular illustrates the significance of such banal reminders of the distinctiveness of the Welsh nation.

Mobilizing and Building the Nation

These historic and other symbols have helped mobilize different sections of the
Welsh nation over time. But the majority of these symbols have been of more relevance to the traditional middle-class, white, and Welsh-speaking core of the

nation. Efforts have been made in recent years to mobilize different types of social and ethnic groups into being members of the Welsh nation. The driving forces
in the process, as noted above, have been the attempts by Plaid Cymru to re-
brand itself into a nationalist party that is relevant to all sections of Welsh society
and the formation of the NAfW. The latter development, in particular, has been
associated with a sustained attempt to rearticulate the character of Welshness by
extending its relevance to all social, ethnic, and linguistic groups within Wales.
Significantly, as part of this change, the NAfW has drawn on the more neutral language of citizenship rather than the politically loaded language of nationalism.
Despite these attempts to broaden the appeal of the Welsh nation to more varied
social groups within Wales, however, it is clear that the NAfW and other groups
are facing difficulties achieving these aims. There is a general apathy with regard
to the more civic form of nationalism being promoted by the newly devolved organization. Part of the problem is linked to the communication of these new
national ideals to the mass of the population. Wales is perhaps unusual, in this respect, since only a low percentage of people within the country read Welsh newspapers and watch Welsh television programs. This is especially the case when
compared with other U.K. national territories such as Scotland. Only 13 percent
of Welsh households take a daily morning newspaper published and printed in
Wales; in Scotland, the figure is 90 percent. In a similar context, a large number of
households on the eastern border of Wales cannot—or choose not to—receive
television transmissions that emanate from Wales and instead tune into the television transmissions emanating from England.

Despite these difficulties, it is important to emphasize the success stories
within regard to the mobilization of the Welsh nation. Particular attention should
be paid to the efforts to mobilize the young people of Wales into a Welsh nationalism. Urdd Gobaith Cymru, or the Welsh League of Youth, has been an important organization since its formation at the beginning of the 20th century. Its
emphasis on enabling young Welsh people to socialize through the medium of
Welsh and on perpetuating key aspects of Welsh culture, especially the cultural
festival of the Eisteddfod, has been a significant contributor to the reproduction
of a Welsh-speaking nationalism among the youth of Wales. In total, these efforts
to mobilize the Welsh population have centered on a mixture of political and
more cultural goals. Admittedly, certain organizations have been more concerned
with the cultural future of the Welsh nation (e.g., the Urdd's emphasis on the need
to preserve important aspects of Welsh culture), while others have focused on
more political goals (e.g., Plaid Cymru's political campaigning and electioneering).
At the same time, it would be unwise to attempt to distinguish too firmly between
these different goals. Indeed, it would be better to think of the various mobilizers
of the Welsh nation as a kaleidoscopic mix of organizations whose goals are overlapping. Moreover, the exact nature of the proposed political and cultural futures
of the Welsh nation advocated by these various organizations is constantly
evolving. Plaid Cymru in recent years, for instance, has demonstrated a lack of

consistency with regard to its stated aims for the future of the Welsh nation. It has oscillated between full independence and a more extensive devolution of power within a federal United Kingdom.

Two final considerations should be mentioned with regard to efforts to mobilize and build the Welsh nation. The first is that these attempts have progressed along peaceful lines. Apart from some fire-bombings during the 1980s and 1990s, Welsh nationalism has never engaged in the political violence that has been a feature of other insurgent nationalisms. Second, it is possible to discern a trend from more ethnic interpretations of the Welsh nation, which have highlighted linguistic and cultural themes, to a more civic articulation of Welshness. A major contributing factor within this change of emphasis has been the creation of the NAfW. Although dissenting voices—promoting alternative, more ethnic takes on the Welsh nation—continue to exist, there are clear signs of a growing engagement with this Welsh civic nation. This shift has been apparent in both the political structures of the NAfW and in Welsh civil society. Whether this growing engagement with civic notions of Welshness will lead to the creation of a more united Welsh nation or will, alternatively, undermine the distinctiveness of a Welsh identity is uncertain. What is certain is that this shift in the essence of Welshness will be the subject of considerable political debate and study by social scientists of all kinds over the coming years.

Selected Bibliography

Bowie, F. 1993. "Wales from Within: Conflicting Interpretations of Welsh Identity." In *Inside European Identities*, edited by S. MacDonald, 167–193. Oxford: Berg.

Davies, C. A. 1999. "Nationalism, Feminism, and Welsh Women: Conflicts and Accommodations." In *Nation, Identity and Social Theory: Perspectives from Wales*, edited by R. Fevre and A. Thompson, 90–108. Cardiff, UK: University of Wales Press.

Dicks, B., and J. van Loon. 1999. "Territoriality and Heritage in South Wales: Space, Time and Imagined Communities." In *Nation, Identity and Social Theory: Perspectives from Wales*, edited by R. Fevre and A. Thompson, 207–232. Cardiff, UK: University of Wales Press.

Gruffudd, P. 1995. "Remaking Wales: Nation-Building and the Geographical Imagination." *Political Geography* 14:219–239.

Hechter, M. 1975. *Internal Colonialism: The Celtic Fringe in British National Development 1536–1966*. London: Routledge and Kegan Paul.

Jones, R., and C. Fowler. 2007. "Placing and Scaling the Nation." *Environment and Planning D: Society and Space* 25:332–354.

McAllister, L. 2001. *Plaid Cymru: The Emergence of a Political Party*. Bridgend, UK: Seren.

Osmond, J. 2002. "Welsh Civil Identity in the Twenty-First Century." In *Celtic Geographies: Old Culture, New Times*, edited by D. Harvey, R. Jones, N. McInroy, and C. Milligan, 69–88. London: Routledge.

Richter, M. 1978. "The Political and Institutional Background to National Consciousness in Medieval Wales." In *Nationalism and the Pursuit of National Independence*, edited by T. W. Moody, 37–55. Dublin, Ireland: Appletree Press.

Taylor, B., and K. Thomson, eds. 1999. *Scotland and Wales: Nations Again?* Cardiff, UK: University of Wales Press.

Williams, C. 1999. "Passports to Wales? Race, Nation and Identity." In *Nation, Identity and Social Theory: Perspectives from Wales*, edited by R. Fevre and A. Thompson, 90–108. Cardiff, UK: University of Wales Press.

Williams, G. A. 1985. *When Was Wales? A History of the Welsh.* London: Penguin.

Turkey

Aygen Erdentug

Chronology

1923	The proclamation of the Republic of Turkey; Ankara becomes the capital.
1924–1925	The caliphate is abolished, together with religious courts and orders. The international calendar and system of time is officially adopted.
1926	New civil, penal, and commercial codes are adopted. They are based on the Swiss, Italian, and German codes, respectively.
1928	The Latin alphabet is adopted.
1934	Extension of suffrage to women; adoption of family names.
1938	The death of Mustafa Kemal Atatürk.
1942	The Wealth Tax is enacted, which leads to impoverishment or displacement of mainly non-Muslim citizens.
1950	The Democratic Party wins the 1950 general elections, ending the monoparty rule of the Republican People's Party, which had been in power since 1924.
1952	Turkey becomes a full-fledged member in NATO.
1955	Anti-Greek riots take place in three major cities.
1960	Officer coup d'état to stop corruption and unconstitutional acts.
1969	The Nationalist Action Party is formed.
1970–1971	The first pro-Islamic party is formed but is closed down due to antisecular activities. (A religious party eventually becomes a member of the coalition government in 1996 but is also closed down in 1998.)
1971	The Labor Party is closed down for separatist and communist propaganda. (In 1989, the Communist Party is legalized in Turkey.)
1974	Turkish forces enter Cyprus to prevent further massacre and to protect the rights of Turks on the island.
1980	A coup d'état by Turkish armed forces to reestablish law and order.
1987	The Nationalist Action Party is accused of ultranationalist activities; the chairman is imprisoned. A national referendum lifts the ban against former political leaders. Turkey recognizes the right of its citizens to apply to the European Human Rights Commission.
1991	A bill revoking the ban on the spoken use of Kurdish passes in parliament.
1993	Sunni Muslims set fire to a hotel in Sivas; 37 Alevis are burned to death.
1999	The outlawed Kurdistan Workers' Party (Partiya Karkeren Kurdistan—PKK) leader, Abdullah Öcalan, is captured, tried, and convicted of treason. (Capital punishment is abolished; his death sentence is not carried out.)
2000	The Court of Appeals decides in favor of freedom to use Kurdish names.
2001–2002	Economic crisis and recession forces coalition governments to generate new economic programs and reorganize financial institutions.
2003	Suicide bombings, allegedly Al Qaeda attacks, of two synagogues in Istanbul.
2004	In accordance with the integration negotiations with the European Union (EU), Turkish Radio and Television (TRT) begins limited broadcasting in the Kurdish, Bosnian, Arabic, and Circassian languages.

2005   The EU opens accession negotiations with Turkey for full membership.

2006   The court cases of writers charged with "insulting Turkishness" are publicized in the mass media, spurring various forms of aggression from the ultranationalists against the defendants.

2007   (April 14) The Republic Protests—huge, peaceful mass rallies in support of secularism in Turkey—take place successively in Ankara, İstanbul, Manisa, Çanakkale, İzmir, Samsun, and Denizli.

Situating the Nation

Turkey has its roots in the semi-theocratic Ottoman Empire that lasted for 600 years. At its zenith in the 16th century, its borders stretched from central Europe to North Africa and the Arabian Peninsula in the south, and to Persia in the east. İstanbul (Constantinople) became the capital in 1453. The modern Republic of Turkey emerged, with Ankara as its capital, in 1923. It is the only completely secular Muslim nation-state that has a legal system based on codes adopted from European nations.

Ankara was at the core of the Turkish struggle for independence during World War I, when the Ottoman Empire was divided by European powers. Mustafa Kemal was the national hero who led the liberating resistance and became the head of the countergovernment in Ankara. In recognition, the Turkish parliament later awarded him the surname *Atatürk* (the father of the Turks). The nation-building process consisted of a series of sweeping reforms aimed at modernizing the country and transforming Ottoman subjects into Turkish citizens. This process was carried out during the first two decades of the republic by Ankara's political elite, who had emerged from Ottoman bureaucracy and from the military. However, the target of this modernizing, also known as the "revolution from above," was not only the civil bureaucracy but also the illiterate and tradition-bound peasantry, who constituted about 83 percent of the republic in 1927. Atatürk defined this group as "the true masters of the nation" during his opening speech of the Grand National Assembly in 1922 in which he also drew attention to the importance of rural development.

Turkey is in southeast Europe, next to Greece and Bulgaria, and it bridges the continents of Europe and Asia. It is located in the Anatolian peninsula in southwest Asia, with a small portion of its territory (Thrace) stretching into the Balkan region of southeastern Europe. The fertile coastal regions are densely populated, particularly in the northwestern provinces. As one of the countries bordering the south shore of the Black Sea, Turkey is a neighbor to Ukraine, Russia, and Georgia. Its territory is flanked by Azerbaijan, Armenia, and Iran in the east and by Syria and Iraq in the south. Turkey is at the crossroads of politically active and economically viable areas, and its geopolitical importance has invited both alliances and hostilities throughout history.

The Ottoman economic legacy of a weak industrial base, coupled with a decline in agricultural production, had led to an impoverished population. During the Ottoman era, non-Muslim minorities monopolized urban economic life and commerce. In the mid-1920s, when a considerable number of these minorities became victims of war or emigrated, an economic vacuum emerged. Neither economic liberalism nor the succeeding statist era (1930–1950) improved the backward, agriculture-based economy, and the growth of a middle class was postponed until later.

In the 1950s, the introduction of a multiparty system generated another set of political, economic, and social changes in Turkey. Since that time, the regions to the northwest, west, and south of the capital have become more developed and modernized. In contrast, the east and southeast regions remain relatively underdeveloped and conservative; tribal traditions and sectarian ties are still decisive.

It was only in the 1960s—after the first coup d'état in the republic and a new constitution ratified by national referendum in 1961—that planned development with broader economic and social goals was possible. Yet, the confrontations between the Marxist, the ultranationalist, and the Islamic fundamentalist groups led to student unrest and a military coup by memorandum during 1971–1973. The ensuing numerous coalition governments, shortages due to deteriorating economic conditions, and an inflation level reaching the triple digits brought instability to the country by the late 1970s. The 1975–1978 American arms embargo on Turkey, which was imposed as a result of Ankara's Cyprus operation of 1974, also had economic repercussions. Foreign financial/economic institutions moved slowly on aid and credits and refused to reschedule Turkey's debts. The concomitant political instability and clashes between student groups, complemented by nationwide strikes of leftist unions and bloody anti-Alevi reactions in two cities, resulted in another military intervention in 1980–1983. Political parties were dissolved. The backlash was another constitution ratified by national referendum in 1982 that was more restrictive with regard to civil liberties than the previous, liberal one had been.

Between 1983 and 1991, imports were greatly liberalized and an export-oriented economic policy placed a greater emphasis on international competition. Succeeding governments from 1991 to 1999 tried to improve the persistent gap in income distribution and managed to control inflation to some degree. However, in 2001, an unexpected devaluation of the Turkish currency plunged the country into a serious financial crisis. This crisis brought back political bickering, unpunished corruption, rampant inflation, and soaring unemployment. Political stability was possible in 2002, when an Islam-based party that had turned conservative came to power alone with the support of about 35 percent of the electorate. This party was able to initiate the accession negotiations of making Turkey—with a population of 70.5 million in the year 2007—a full member of the EU.

Instituting the Nation

The Young Turk movement in the last decades of the 19th century was a turning point in the Ottoman Empire. It was the voice of opposition dedicated to replacing an absolute monarchy (i.e., the autocracy of Abdulhamid II) with a constitutional one. This movement also laid the foundation of the nationalistic official ideology of the republic. The Young Turks first had the utopian dream of binding all by "Ottomanism"—a patriotism that would disregard religion or ethnicity, contrary to the reality of the Christian-Muslim dichotomy and the multiple ethnicities of the empire. With the secession of the Balkans and Greece (Christian territories) after the Balkan Wars (1912–1913), they turned to Turkish nationalism; they did not want to embrace pan-Islamism, an identity based on religion. Hence another political movement, pan-Turkism, emerged and was aimed at uniting the Turkic-speaking peoples under one state. It was adopted by the younger generation of Turks who had been drawn to the idea of cultural nationalism, an identity and loyalty based on "Turkishness." A concomitant movement was Turanism, or pan-Turanism, that embraced the unity of Ural-Altaic peoples together with those of Finno-Hungarian stock (i.e., the union of Eurasian peoples stretching from Hungary to the Pacific Rim; "Turan" was the region from which these peoples had originated).

With the establishment of the Republic of Turkey, ethnic nationalism gave way to territorial nationalism, a patriotism seeking allegiance only to Turkey. Atatürk expressed this identity transfer with the popularized statement that ended his address to the nation on the 10th anniversary of the foundation of the Turkish republic: "Happy is he who calls himself a Turk!" One crucial component of Atatürk's nation-building strategy was to make citizens of the new nation proud of being Turks. Their self-image had been battered by the demoralizing shrinkage of the grand Ottoman Empire and by Western prejudice. However, Atatürk's quote was to be challenged in later decades by ultranationalists and Kurdish separatist groups who felt his words demonstrated the ethnic hegemony of citizens of Turkic origin.

The campaign to restore self-respect to the Turks embraced their bio-cultural origins and included their language and history, cornerstones of the official agenda. The zeal of some Turkish scholars of the time went to extremes, resulting in research of dubious scientific merit that served political ends; it created the Anatolian movement that, by the 1930s, had become the official ideology. The movement came to an end with the death of Atatürk, in 1938, when its proponents abandoned the cause.

The primary factors in sustaining national identity in Turkey have been Atatürk, a pro-nationalist education policy dating to the 1930s, the Turkish flag (red with a white crescent and star), and the military. The citizens of Turkey and the Turkish diaspora are proud of the fact that Atatürk has become a universally recognized Turk. He remains a unifying figure for all age categories and culturally or politically disparate groups, through an emphasis on or an embracement of

---

Early Ethnocentric Theories (The Anatolian Movement)

During the 1930s in Turkey, research of dubious scientific merit produced theories arguing that all history and languages had a basis in Turkish history and language, since they originated from Central Asia, "the cradle of human civilization." This was the homeland of the Turks, who had migrated in waves to different parts of the world. In this respect, the "Turkish Historical Thesis" maintained that the history of Turkey went beyond the history of the Ottoman Empire to that of Central Asia; for example, the Sumerian, the Hittite, the Chinese, the Roman, and the ancient Greek histories were all derivatives of the Turkish one. Likewise, the "Sun Theory of Languages" claimed that Turkish was the first language spoken, and hence was the foundation for all human languages like Latin and the Romance languages, classical Greek, and even Anglo-Saxon. Though these theories were abandoned in later years, they remained in the national curriculum in schools. They have also affected the configuration of the presidential seal. The radiating sun at the center of this red seal represents the Republic of Turkey, while the circle of 16 stars around this sun signifies the 16 Turkish states in history (the number of these states has been a contentious issue). Recently, a similar theory has linked the Turks—through those who crossed the Bering Strait—to the early American Indians on the basis of their artifacts and language.

Mustafa Kemal Atatürk: The Eternal Leader (1881–1938)

Primary school children begin their day by taking an oath in which they express what it means to be a Turk, their dedication to the Turkish existence, and their allegiance to Atatürk's principles (i.e., republicanism, secularism, nationalism, populism, and revolutionism-reformism). Atatürk rests in his eternal abode at the Atatürk Mausoleum in Ankara. He is omnipresent in Turkey. His busts or statues are seen in the yards of all institutions of education and in at least one square in urban settlements. Practically every city has a main street, if not a stadium or a cultural center, named after him. His portrait hangs on office walls in public buildings, private enterprises, and homes, and it is also seen on postage stamps and bank notes. Law 5816, passed in 1951, states that the defamation of Atatürk or the disfiguring of his images is a criminal offense, the punishment of which is imprisonment up to three and five years, respectively. The sentence can be increased if coercion or the media is involved. To outsiders who are not familiar with the Turkish psyche, Atatürk may be seen as a cult figure. There is a lucrative market in Atatürk memorabilia, similar to the one for the icons of the Western world.

different facets of his identity and accomplishments, such as "a national hero," "a secularist and republican," "a nationalist," "a father figure."

The military is the only institution that enjoys the complete faith of the majority of Turks, whether during war or in peace. In retrospect, the military has taken on three roles. One of these roles has been as the self-proclaimed guardian of secularism, persistently vigilant against Islamist retrogression. In its second role, as the protector of an idealized version of democracy, the military has intervened in Turkish politics when the governments were incapacitated or when extreme political activities threatened the regime. Its third role has been an assimilative one; mandatory military service for men has served as a catalyst, enhancing patriotism and emotional attachment to the Turkish flag. Martyrdom, dying in military action for Turkey, is an exceedingly honorable status, and slighting the Turkish flag is a criminal offense that can provoke outbreaks of violence against perpetrators and trigger the nation to rally around it.

Defining the Nation

In 1923, the Treaty of Lausanne determined the initial territory of Turkey. In 1926, the border with the new state of Iraq was redrawn to create the present southeastern frontier. By 1939 the province of Hatay was ceded from Syria to join Turkey, finalizing the boundaries of the country. The official doctrine at the time was to create a homogenous Turkish-speaking nation, as stated in the successive constitutions of the republic. This meant that any threat to national unity and

"Turkishness" was suppressed, persecuted, or prosecuted. At present, article 301 of the Turkish penal code, which limits freedom of speech and prosecutes anyone insulting the Turkish state or its citizens, has become a stronghold for ultranationalists. It is also a matter of contention between Turkey and the EU.

The only minorities that were officially recognized were the preexisting non-Muslim communities (usually understood as Jews, Greeks, and Armenians, although there were other groups), whose protection and rights had been determined by the Treaty of Lausanne. In practice, governments violated these rights through restrictions on their education and curriculum, free expression, and charitable institutions. Particularly in the 1930s, the Greeks in İstanbul were barred from entering a large number of professions. The population of non-Muslims in Anatolia decreased with World War I as a result of forcible relocation, repatriation, or population exchange, followed by emigration to Western nations in later decades. A considerable number of those remaining have penetrated the affluent professional groups or established businesses in Turkey.

Following World War I, with the Armistice of Mudros (1918) that marked the defeat and commenced the partitioning of the Ottoman Empire, İzmir (Smyrna) was occupied by Greek forces. What the Greeks referred to afterward as the "Asia Minor Catastrophe" was set in motion when the Greeks left İzmir, after the city was taken back by Turkish forces in 1922. An agreement between Turkey and Greece to exchange populations took effect in 1924, leading to the deportation of Greeks from Anatolia (i.e., Asia Minor) and Muslims from Greece. Only the Muslims in western Thrace and the ethnic Greek communities in İstanbul and on the Aegean islands of Bozcaada (Tenedos) and Gökçeada (Imbroz) were exempt from this reciprocal expulsion. Some of the ethnic Greeks in İstanbul emigrated after a violent incident in 1955. The distorted reports in Turkey on a glass-shattering bomb attack on the Turkish consulate in Salonika (Greece), near the house where Atatürk was born, triggered wholesale anti-Greek riots in İstanbul, Ankara, and İzmir and ended with the destruction of commercial property belonging to ethnic Greeks and the desecration of Greek religious sanctuaries. Yet another evacuation of thousands, and the confiscation of their property, occurred in the mid-1960s. This time, it was in retaliation to the stalemate in discussions on the rights of the systematically intimidated and murdered ethnic Turks in Cyprus. The agreements in 1960, which created the Republic of Cyprus, made Turkey and Greece (together with the United Kingdom) guarantor powers of the constitutional rights of their respective communities in Cyprus.

During the Caucasus Campaign (1914–1918), the loyalty of the Ottoman Empire's Armenian subjects became unclear; Armenian nationalists collaborated with the Russian armies, and separatists staged rebellions and raided Turkish villages. The Young Turk government decided to relocate the Armenians outside of the war zones with the objective of dispersing them; however, many Armenians—artisans and civil servants, families whose men were serving in the Ottoman armies, Catholic and Protestant Armenians—were exempt from this resettlement. Nevertheless, the Armenian experience during World War I, referred to as the "Great Calamity," has led to the most controversial and highly politicized issue in Turkish history. Some historians and the Armenian diaspora claim that the Great Calamity was genocidal, considering the thousands who became victims of atrocities during this forced relocation in 1915. Their opponents argue that it was not annihilation and that the death toll was an unfortunate consequence of the mismanagement of resources and the austere conditions that prevailed during the war. Some of the groups being transferred contracted contagious diseases or were attacked and murdered by marauders along the way—a common risk for travelers at the time. Today, historians continue to search the Ottoman archives in an effort to find the truth. It is considered offensive to speak or write in support of the claim of the Armenian diaspora, since that viewpoint is seen as "insulting Turkishness." Many scholars and authors, including Orhan Pamuk, the 2006 Nobel Laureate for literature, were taken to court and faced imprisonment for this offense; however, all were acquitted.

Relationships with the Jews in Turkey—the majority of which are Sephardic—have comparatively been more peaceful. Jews expelled from Spain in the 15th century took refuge in the Ottoman Empire. This was followed by waves of Jewish refugees during the 19th century, who were escaping the harassment, oppression, or ethnic cleansing in Europe and the Balkans. Jews fleeing Nazi Germany again found sanctuary in Turkey. In 1933, Atatürk invited professors of Jewish origin to contribute to intellectual progress in the country; the German school they represented had an impact on the development of the university system, scientific institutions, fine arts, and performing arts in Turkey. Between 1940 and 1950, many Turkish Jews migrated to Palestine, which became the State of Israel as of 1948, out of a desire to return to their millennia-old homeland. Anti-Semitic activity in Turkey has been restricted mainly to news in the mass media; Islamists or ultra-nationalists have demonized Israel and the Jews in their reports to produce a negative image. Most of these have ended up at court. Recent instances of violence have included tomb desecrations by Islamic fundamentalists and suicide bombings (allegedly by Al Qaeda) of two synagogues in İstanbul.

Anthropologically, outside the non-Muslim communities, there are innumerable subcultures in Turkey—as reflected in the variations of local traditions, folklore, and costumes—all contributing to the greater national culture. Though the influx of migrants from villages to metropolises and the ensuing acculturation has somewhat homogenized this cultural diversity in the urban environment, the new urbanites still identify more with their native villages or hometowns than with their city of residence. Regionalism or hometown-based social networks are important frames of reference in supporting or eroding nationalistic sentiments. There are hundreds of hometown associations in metropolises that maintain economic and emotional ties with an Anatolian town or its administrative unit. Each association aims to sustain its culture among its emigrants by organizing picnics and annual outings, and by providing events and courses for the younger generation that promote their ethnic characteristics such as local food, folklore, crafts, and even dialect or language.

The definition of a Turk has come to mean one who is Sunni Muslim and speaks Turkish as the native tongue. Factions within Turkish society claim that this definition places others in a secondary position. New terms like "citizen of Turkey" and *Türkiyeli* (someone originating from and/or a resident of Turkey)— as opposed to "Turkish citizen," which had overtones of ethnicity—were recently coined to unify the citizens of the republic. These terms generated further discussions but failed to produce a consensus.

In Turkey, historical and environmental circumstances have produced different cultural groups within the population identified as "true Turks" (ethnic Turks). The Anatolian Turks are the most widely dispersed and most numerous, showing significant variations in cultural patterns; they were the group targeted for the republican reforms. Another entity, known as the "Balkan immigrants," are ethnic Turks (Sunni Muslims) and their descendants from the Balkans, who resettled primarily in the Thrace and Marmara regions starting in the 1870s and continued in sporadic waves until the early 1990s. Other Turkic-speaking immigrants and their descendants from southern Russia (e.g., Crimean Tatars) and Central Asia (e.g., Turkomans), along with groups from the Caucasus (e.g., the Laz, the Circassians, the Muslim Georgians), can be lumped together into a third group. Their communities have been scattered all over the country due to settlement policies at the time of their immigration. Muslim refugees, such as the Bosnians and the Afghans, are a more recent addition to the population.

Due to the liberal atmosphere of the 1961 constitution, the 1965 census registered population details according to ethnic, linguistic, or religious distinctions; however, since then it has not been possible to correctly enumerate the citizens according to this information. The Kurds have been the biggest and most significant group to challenge the image of a homogenous nation. In fact, like the ethnic Turks, they show regional and sectarian differences (most are Sunni Muslims, the rest are Alevis of the Shiite sect), as well as class distinctions. They are estimated to constitute at least 10 percent of the population and live predominantly in the southeast, with some groups in the eastern provinces. Within the last two decades, many Kurds have migrated to cities in the west. Governments first labeled them "mountain Turks," then "eastern Turks," not only rejecting the existence of a Kurdish language, but also failing to distinguish between the different Kurdish groups. However, since the 1990s, and particularly as of the turn of the 21st century, most of their cultural and political rights—with some assistance from the EU—have been granted.

Arab-speaking communities are not uncommon along the Syrian border of Turkey. Most are Alevi (Alewite) though there are also Assyrian (Christian) communities among them. Discriminatory administrative practices, along with the terrorism of the late 1980s, forced the village-based Christian population to immigrate to nearby cities or even seek refuge in Western countries. Though the border of 1939 divided Arab Alewite lineages, their members in Turkey have maintained their ties with kin and with Syria.

Narrating the Nation

In spite of projects to educate and develop peasant communities, the republican reforms created a two-tiered Turkish society: a Western-oriented and secular elite contemptuous of the masses that are heavily under the influence of traditions and religion. The political affiliations in later decades perpetuated this polarization, setting off political and economic turmoil. The nation is still haunted by the unwarranted leveling mechanisms that took place in the 1970s; long queues for staple goods, shortages of industrial and intermediary goods that led to facility failures, and the regional PKK terrorism of the 1980s that spread nationwide in the 1990s.

Atatürk frequently bolstered the self-respect of his citizens—as he did in his address on the 10th anniversary of the foundation of the Turkish republic—with statements such as, "The Turks, as a nation, are intelligent!" and "The Turks, as a nation, are industrious!" The achievements of his period made the public proud, as summarized in the lyrics of the "10th Year March." For each year after his death, until the 1990s, the nation was in a state of mourning on November 10. Since then, the commemoration of Atatürk during this occasion has stretched to a week of various activities that are named after him. The goal of these activities is to help the nation better understand his reforms.

Turkish ethnocentrism became somewhat eroded due to the crippled economy, the corruption, and the political unrest of later decades, causing some Turks to question their self-esteem. This state of morale was reflected in the popular expression, "We will never grow up." However, their pride in Turkish hospitality and communal traits, such as solidarity in the face of adversity, was persistent and remained. Public protests during this period included blowing tin whistles, hitting pans, and turning out the lights at home for one minute each evening. One of the popular mass media cartoons of this pessimistic period depicted the republic as a young woman draped in the Turkish flag, prey to the sinister intentions of men surrounding her.

A chain of events occurred that began to restore confidence and kindle nationalist sentiments. In 2001, the gratifying performance of Turkish soccer teams and the national basketball team's participation in international matches created euphoria and triggered an upsurge in Turkish flag sales. "Turkey is the greatest / There is none other greater!" was chanted for almost every following occasion.

Another development was the anxiety over increasing threats to secularism. This concern incited droves of prosecular citizens to organize demonstrations of national unity during which hundreds waved the national flag and chanted in support of secularism. They wore Atatürk badges or carried his portrait. Even preschool children wore red headbands with the words *ATAM İZİNDEYİZ* ("We walk your path *Atam*"; *Atam* is a popular possessive form of address and reference to Atatürk) in white letters. The headbands were in response to the green headbands with Arabic inscriptions observed during the demonstrations of the Islamists. Since the 75th anniversary of the republic in 1998, the republican spirit has been revived with a popularized version of the "10th Year March" that is now sung spontaneously by prosecular citizens of all ages and classes when they are in a jubilant mood.

Ethno-political confrontations also created a surge in nationalism. The twists and turns of foreign intervention on nationally sensitive issues—such as the Cyprus issue, the PKK, the Armenian question, U.S. policy in the Middle East and Iraq, and EU accession—infuriated the nation, causing it to close ranks.

Turks are predisposed to react promptly, even aggressively, to any provocation involving an insult to their national icons, to their pride, or to Islam. They mount nationwide protests with hate demonstrations or campaigns boycotting the commodities of the foreign countries concerned, sometimes publicly destroying these goods. At the very least, they will protest by placing a black wreath at the gate of the embassy of the country involved.

Mobilizing and Building the Nation

Standard Turkish, taught and maintained through state channels, was essential in the establishment of a national identity and central to the assimilative strategy. Mandatory military service and intercultural marriages have been other channels of integration and assimilation. The adoption of the Latin alphabet, a secular national curriculum, and compulsory, free, primary school education have increased access to schooling. These measures have proven to be effective: children of immigrant groups have assimilated into the national culture, partially maintaining parental traditions yet ignorant of their parents' native tongue.

In the years 1925 and 1940, another assimilative strategy involved giving Turkish names to villages with non-Turkish names. Though this renaming process covered all of Turkey, the percentage of renamed villages has been particularly high in the eastern Black Sea region and east and southeast of Turkey. These were villages originally inhabited by Christian groups or people of Tatar (Crimean), Circassian, Laz, Arabic, Persian, and Kurdish origin. Over time, the older generations —who communicated in the local dialect or tongue—have ignored and left the usage of these imposed names to the younger generations attending school.

Apart from the proclamation of the republic—which has become a national holiday attracting increased participation since its 75th anniversary when it was unofficially claimed by civil society to activate solidarity against antisecular movements—official public holidays are dedicated to certain groups. The anniversary of the first opening of the Turkish parliament honors the children. On that day, designated children sit in the seats of power and act like the incumbents of those posts. The anniversary of the beginning of the national liberation movement is set apart for youth and for commemorating Atatürk (in addition to November 10, the day he died), and the day celebrating the victory of the War of Independence is dedicated to the armed forces.

National celebrations used to be instigated by the state and consisted of gymnastics, marching bands in stadiums, and military parades in the streets. Since the late 1980s, local administrations have taken the initiative to also organize street parties, including pop concerts and fireworks. The Turkish flag and images of Atatürk are an integral aspect of these celebrations.

In spite of the equality of citizens decreed by the constitution of the republic, there is still a Muslim–non-Muslim cleavage that overrides national citizenship and impinges upon the psyche of the ethnic Turks with provincial roots. More often than not, the non-Muslim citizens of Turkey are uneasy about the prejudice and interpersonal (and sometimes institutional) discrimination of fanatical Turkish nationalists and Islamists. This apprehension has been justified with the 2007 assassination of a prominent Armenian-Turkish citizen and journalist who had been conciliatory in the Armenian question of whether there was an Armenian genocide in 1915, during the Ottoman period; those who misconstrued his views made him a victim of article 301 and an open target.

New or amended legislation has somewhat relaxed the tensions caused by factions, but three cultural fault lines have emerged: secularists versus Islamists, Sunni versus Alevi, and Turks versus Kurds. Each group is adamant in its stance and ready to look for ulterior motives in any steps taken by its opponent; they usually disagree over major issues.

Since the proclamation of the republic, the city-based political elite, and later the middle class, have become secularists and die-hard proponents of the tenets and reforms of Atatürk, practicing a form of ancestor worship. However, religion is no longer a matter solely of private conscience. The provincially based Islamists, proud of Turkey's Islamic heritage, were traditionally confined to the lower strata of Turkish society. They have gained ground in the past decade and infiltrated the cultural mainstream through upward mobility; some entrepreneurs have penetrated into the upper economic class. They accept Atatürk as a national hero for "saving the country from the infidels [the Christians]," but they reject his antireligion and pro-Western stance. Some fanatics, when not in quest of an Islamic state, have sporadically defaced Atatürk busts or statues. Women in clothes that conceal all but their face and hands are perceived as a symbol of the rejected Islamic traditionalism. This has become a divisive issue because covered women are banned from institutions of education and from working in public office, and they are overlooked in some state functions—all of which are bastions of prosecular women in Western clothes.

The tug-of-war between prosecular citizens and political Islam came out into the open in April 2007, prior to the election of a new president by parliament. There were mass rallies against the Islamic-rooted government to prevent its candidate from taking the post. The protestors flooded streets and squares, creating a sea of red Turkish flags and chanting, "Turkey is secular and secular it will remain." The "Republic Protests" of the prosecular were a show of strength that had previously not been seen in the republic; the Western press reported the protests as an indicator of the cultural and political cleavage in the country. The main concern of those who participated—the majority being women from every region of Turkey and from various backgrounds—was the possible concentration of power in the hands of the Justice and Development Party, the Islam-based party that had turned conservative and already controlled parliament. Subsequent parliamentary tinkering with the legislation in question ended in an early general election in 2007. However, the same party again came to power— the electorate proved to be also concerned about prolonging political and economic stability— and their candidate was elected as president.

Alevi is a blanket term referring to the heterodox religious communities of Anatolia, which are estimated to make up 15–20 percent of the total population. Some of these groups are also Kurds. The directorate of religious affairs, looking

Turkish people shout slogans in support of secularism as they hold a huge Turkish flag at the Mausoleum of Ataturk, founder of modern Turkey, during the "Republic Protests" in Ankara in April 2007. (Tolga Bozoglu/epa/Corbis)

upon the Alevi communities as Shiite (Shia) Muslims, has always imposed Sunni practices on them; for example, undertaking the building of mosques in their villages and paying the salary of the Sunni *imam* (Muslim cleric) appointed there, and requiring their children to attend Sunni religious and ethics courses at school. This offensive attitude toward the Alevis has increased their alienation from the state and forced them ultimately to contest this religious discrimination in court. Until recently, they were not allowed to open a house of gathering or communal building (*cemevi*), which is a place of fundamental importance for their rituals.

Starting in the 1950s, Alevis gradually left their isolated villages in the highlands to immigrate to urban centers, usually creating distinctly Alevi quarters and refusing to mix with Sunnis through marriage. Their integration into the cultural mainstream by practicing the profession of their choice brought them into direct contact and competition with the Sunnis and fueled the overt and covert antagonism between them. Because Alevis have identified more with the left in Turkey, extremist right-wing Sunni citizens have fallen easily into bloody Sunni-Alevi clashes. During the politically and economically unstable period of the 1970s, anti-Alevi activities in some cities resulted in violent incidents and mass murders.

For decades, official policy undermined Kurdish identity, but in the 1970s, Kurdish nationalism began to challenge this view. The measures taken during the military regime of 1980–1983 to repress this movement backfired and alienated even more Kurds; they became sympathizers or supporters of the PKK, a separatist group fighting with brutal violence for the liberation of the Kurds. The PKK leader, Abdullah Öcalan, was captured, tried, and convicted of treason in 1999. The PKK took on another name, opting to defend its cause politically. Empathy for the PKK still lingers today, and some of the Kurds in southeast Turkey are known to take offense when PKK is categorized as a terrorist group.

The first half of the 1990s witnessed a bill that lifted the ban on speaking in Kurdish. Later, Kurds were free to celebrate the Kurdish New Year (*Newroz*), though displaying the Kurdish tri-colors (green, red, and yellow) of independence was considered suspect. The 1990s was also the period for ill-fated Kurdish-backed political parties. They were closed down due to separatist activity, and some Kurdish members of parliament were imprisoned for backing the PKK. As of 2000, however, people were permitted to give Kurdish names to their children and, more recently, Kurdish was among the courses offered at private language schools.

Nonetheless, PKK terrorism—which lasted from 1987 to 2000 and still continues sporadically—did take a toll both in the high number of casualties and in the nonstop out-migration that left some towns and villages depopulated. These developments made the Turks in western locations more conscious and anxious about the Kurdish presence in their midst. At the same time, the Kurdish pockets in the metropolises developed a heightened ethnic consciousness that had previously been confined to their rural brethren.

In spite of a ravaging earthquake in 1999 that hit an industrial belt in the northwest and a crippling economic crisis, Turkey has been experiencing an economic progression since the turn of the 21st century. Though its geopolitical importance is an asset in the accession negotiations for the EU, the same is not true for the majority of Turkey's young population. In spite of some highly qualified bilingual or multilingual university graduates in demand by high tech industries, the inadequate and overcrowded state education system continues to neglect vocational training; the system generally fails to equip youth with the range of skills required in the secondary and tertiary sectors. There have been radical legal reforms prompted by the EU, but the human factor in Turkey's judicial and administrative systems is in need of urgent attention. A new mentality must be adopted and internalized for the democratic implementation of this legislation that will sustain a tolerant and culturally diverse society.

Selected Bibliography

Andrews, P. A. 1989. *The Ethnic Groups in the Republic of Turkey.* Wiesbaden, Germany: L. Reichert.

Grigoriadis, I. N. 2006. "Upsurge amidst Political Uncertainty: Nationalism in Post-2004 Turkey." SWP Research Paper 11, Berlin.

Heper, M. 2002. *Historical Dictionary of Turkey.* 2nd ed. Lanham, MD: The Scarecrow Press.

Kazancıgil, A., and E. Özbudun, eds. 1997. *Atatürk: Founder of a Modern State.* 2nd ed. London: C. Hurst & Co.

Landau, J. M. 1994. "Ethnonationalism and Pan-nationalism in Turkey and the Ex-Soviet Republics." *Migration* 28:67–84.

Lewis, B. 2002. *The Emergence of Modern Turkey.* 3rd ed. New York: Oxford University Press.

Mango, A. 2004. *The Turks Today.* London: John Murray.

Poulton, H. 1997. *The Top Hat, the Grey Wolf, and the Crescent: Turkish Nationalism and the Turkish Republic.* London: Hurst.

Tocci, N. 2001. "21st Century Kemalism: Redefining Turkey-EU Relations in the Post-Helsinki Era." Working Document No. 170, Brussels, Belgium: Centre for European Policy Studies.

van Bruinessen, M. "Kurds, Turks and the Alevi Revival in Turkey." (Retrieved August 30, 2006), http://www.uga.edu/islam/alevivanb.html.

Zürcher, E. J. 2004. *Turkey: A Modern History.* 3rd ed. London: I. B. Taurus.

Angola

Norrie MacQueen

Chronology

1575 Port and settlement of Luanda is founded by the Portuguese.

1600s and 1700s Angola provides a major source of slaves for Portuguese plantations in Brazil. Luanda becomes a major point of embarkation.

1891 Borders of colonial and postindependence Angola are defined. The territory includes the coastal enclave of Cabinda between the French Congo and the Belgian Congo.

1915 Effective Portuguese control of Angola is established in all but the remote southeast and mountain areas in the north.

1926 The authoritarian corporatist "New State" (*Estado Novo*) is established in Portugal.

1955 The Union of the Peoples of Northern Angola (União dos Povos do Norte de Angola, UPNA) is formed and later becomes the National Front for the Liberation of Angola (Frente Nacional de Libertação de Angola, FNLA).

1956 The leftist Popular Movement for the Liberation of Angola (Movimento Popular de Libertação de Angola, MPLA) is established.

1961 (February–March) MPLA attacks prisons and police posts in Luanda. UPNA uprising takes place in northern Angola. This is followed by brutal suppression by the Portuguese.

1966 The National Union for the Total Independence of Angola (União Nacional para a Independência Total de Angola, UNITA) is formed.

1972–1973 Struggles occur within MPLA factions.

1974 (April) A military coup takes place in Lisbon, and Portuguese withdrawal from Africa becomes inevitable.

1975 (January) The Alvor Agreement is signed between Portugal, MPLA, FNLA, and UNITA, and the three nationalist factions agree to share power after Angola is granted independence. (April–July) Civil war breaks out between the three movements; FNLA and UNITA enter into alliance against the MPLA. (November) Portugal transfers sovereignty to "the Angolan people." MPLA holds control of Luanda.

1979 President Agostinho Neto dies and is succeeded as head of state and party by José Eduardo dos Santos.

1985 U.S. military aid for UNITA begins to arrive through Zaire.

1991 (April) MPLA formally abandons its Marxist ideology.

1992 United Nations (UN) certifies that elections are free and fair, but in September UNITA resumes civil war.

1994 Government and UNITA sign peace accord. A large-scale UN peacekeeping operation is deployed, but the war continues.

2002 (February) UNITA leader Jonas Savimbi is killed by government troops.

Situating the Nation

Angola's five centuries as the *joia da coroa do imperio portugues* ("jewel in the Portuguese imperial crown") has been the dominant element shaping Angolan nationalism in the 20th and 21st centuries. Nationalism has thus principally surrounded the anticolonial struggle, though this struggle has been fragmented by different regional, ethnic, and ideological interests. At the time of independence from Portugal in 1975, the Marxist-oriented MPLA victory over competing nationalist factions marked the beginning of a long period of one-party rule. MPLA dominance was fiercely opposed by the rival nationalist movement, UNITA, which was supported by various external interests—mainly from the Western side in the Cold War. Meanwhile, the MPLA regime relied on the presence of about 50,000 Cuban troops to help maintain its position of power. In the early 1990s, with the end of the Cold War and the transition to majority rule in South Africa, external involvement ended, and the war became almost entirely internal for Angola. There was a widespread view held even by expert commentators abroad that this outside interference was the reason for the war lasting so long, so there was hope that the war would end with the withdrawal of external support. However, by this point the struggle had become deeply rooted in Angola's

MPLA recruits training in Cabinda enclave in the closing phase of the liberation war. (Keystone Features/Getty Images)

regional and ethnic divisions and despite continuous diplomatic efforts to find a solution, it was not until 2002—with the death of UNITA leader Jonas Savimbi—that the war finally came to an end.

Angola's international identity is expressed through its active membership in a range of international organizations that reflect both its geographical location (e.g., the African Union and the Southern African Development Community) and its history (e.g., Lusophone African Countries and the Community of Portuguese Speaking Countries).

Up until the 19th century, the colonial economy in Angola was based on the trading of slaves, particularly with (Portuguese) Brazil. Later, a plantation economy developed that produced rubber, followed by—particularly in the northern part of the country—more profitable produce like cotton and coffee. Also, Angola's railway system and its location on the Atlantic seaboard made it a major transport route for the export of the produce of bordering countries, in particular copper from the Belgian Congo (later called Zaire). During the 20th century, Angola developed its own extractive industries. Iron was important for a time, although this product was overshadowed by the discovery of large-scale offshore oil deposits. Diamond mining also developed in the northeast section of the

The Nationalist Movements

MPLA (Movimento Popular de Libertação de Angola, or the Popular Movement for the Liberation of Angola): a leftist group formed in 1956. It drew its support from the Mbundu people of the Luanda area and from the industrial workers of the coastal cities.

FNLA (Frente Nacional de Libertação de Angola, or the National Front for the Liberation of Angola): a northern-based movement that was popular among the Bakongo ethnic group.

UNITA (União Nacional para a Independência Total de Angola, or the National Union for the Total Independence of Angola): a breakaway faction from the FNLA formed in 1966. Its power base was among the Ovimbundu people of the central plateau.

FLEC (Frente de Libertação do Enclave de Cabinda, or the Front for the Liberation of the Cabinda Enclave): formed in 1963 to press for the independence of the fragment of Angolan territory on the coast between the Republic of Congo and the Democratic Republic of Congo.

---

country. Oil and diamonds continued to fund the postindependence civil war long after external supporters lost interest. Government control of oil concessions allowed it to equip and re-equip the national army throughout the struggle, while UNITA's control of much of the diamond mining areas bankrolled its apparently endless rebellion.

The three main nationalist movements that emerged to resist the Portuguese —and which then fought among themselves for "possession" of the postindependence state—drew their support in broad terms from distinct geographical regions. The MPLA had its primary power base among the Mbundu of the Luanda area, the urbanized *mestiço* (mixed race) and white radicals of the central coastal cities. The FNLA drew its main support from the Bakongo of the north. The Bakongo people, who make up about 15 percent of Angola's population, straddle the border with the modern-day Democratic Republic of Congo, where it is the largest single ethnic group. The geographical base of UNITA was among the Ovimbundu people of Angola's central plateau. All three movements, however, claimed to have a "national" following.

No such claim was/is made by the nationalist movement in the Cabinda enclave, a small fragment of Angolan territory that lies between the Democratic Republic of Congo and the separate (former French) Congo Republic. Cabinda was "given" to Portugal by agreement among the European imperialists in the 1880s. Since 1963, a separatist movement there—the Front for the Liberation of the Cabinda Enclave (*Frente de Libertação do Enclave de Cabinda*, FLEC)—has fought for the separation of the territory from the rest of Angola.

The geographic bases of the three main Angolan nationalist movements reflected different social conditions, which in turn shaped their respective "national visions." The Marxist orientation of the MPLA was largely determined by the fact that its support lay among the urban working class and the "non-tribal" mixed race population of the coastal cities. This *mestiço* element was a distinctive feature of nationalism in Angola (as well as in Mozambique, Portugal's other large African territory). So, too, was the presence of European activists, attracted by the MPLA's commitment to Marxism and the prospect of a revolutionary project in Africa grounded in non-racial "internationalist" ideals.

In contrast, the mainly Bakongo plantation workers who provided the power base of the UPA/FNLA represented a quite different "style" of nationalism. The Bakongo's cross-border presence qualified its "Angolan" nationalism, while both the MPLA and UNITA were wholly "internal" in terms of their ethnic and regional bases. Small farmers and traders were prominent among the Ovimbundu of the central plateau, who were the basis of UNITA's support. The Ovimbundu are Angola's largest single ethnic group—constituting about 37 percent of the total population—and had a reputation for both a strong work ethic and obedience to traditional authority. These qualities may have contributed to the persistence of UNITA through the many troughs and setbacks it faced from the time of its formation.

The internal "culture" or "personality" that developed within the FNLA and UNITA was influenced by a long history of local resistance to the Portuguese in the areas from which the parties drew their support. Angola was not "pacified" by the colonial power until well after World War I. In contrast, the MPLA's "modernism" and its declared commitment to revolutionary internationalism meant that its historical reference points were more diverse. Its heroes and models for action came from beyond Angola. Indeed, they frequently came from beyond Africa. The MPLA saw itself as a component of the global resistance to imperialism and neo-imperialism; however, the MPLA was also happy to point to the historic role of the Mbundu (from the Luanda area)—from the earliest days of the colonial presence in the 16th and 17th centuries—in the forefront of resistance to the Portuguese.

Instituting the Nation

The character and personalities of the leadership of the three movements were critical elements in their individual development and political fortunes. Agostinho Neto, who emerged as leader of the MPLA in 1962 and who was president of Angola from independence in 1975 until his death in 1979, was a poet and physician. Like the leaders of the nationalist movements in other parts of Portuguese Africa—such as Amílcar Cabral of Guinea-Bissau and Eduardo Mondlane of Mozambique—he had studied in Lisbon and had close contacts with both fellow nationalists from the other colonies and with the Portuguese resistance to the authoritarian regime. Neto's Marxism (and more generally that of the MPLA) was therefore shaped by the political culture of continental Europe. This may have contributed to the MPLA's tendency to ideological factionalism, an ailment typical of the European left. Both before and after independence, Neto's leadership was challenged by other factions within the MPLA that were led by such figures as Mário de Andrade and Daniel Chipenda.

Holden Roberto of the FNLA was in many ways an unlikely "nationalist" leader, having spent most of his life outside of Angola. He had lived almost all of his life in the Congo to the north; first when it was a Belgian colony, and then when it became the independent state of Congo after 1960. As a result, he spoke better French than Portuguese. This cross-border identity was underlined by his relationship through marriage with the Congo/Zairean dictator, Mobutu Sese Seko. These transboundary politics in northern Angola were intensified by the fact that about a half million Bakongo had fled across Angola's northern border after the 1961 uprising to escape Portuguese reprisals. Roberto commanded considerable loyalty from the Bakongo who looked to him to defend their traditional interests against those of the central coastal "elite."

Jonas Savimbi, the founder and leader of UNITA, was a charismatic leader who commanded an almost religious devotion from his Ovimbundi supporters. In the later phase of his life, however, he proved to be an unpredictable, brutal, and despotic figure. In the years before his death at the hands of government forces in 2002, he had come to dominate his movement as much through fear as through positive support. Nevertheless, in an earlier period, the extent of his leadership powers was evident in his capacity to repeatedly lead UNITA back to war. He succeeded in reigniting the national conflict when the temptations of peace

---

The Nationalist Leaders

Agostinho Neto (1922–1979): Leader of the MPLA from 1962 and president of Angola from 1975 until his death in 1979.

Jonas Savimbi (1934–2002): Founder and leader of UNITA until he was killed by MPLA government forces in 2002. Of Ovimbundu parentage, he was educated in Portugal and Switzerland.

Holden Roberto (1923–): Leader of the FNLA who, though born in Angola, spent most of his life across the border in Congo/Zaire.

Mário de Andrade (1928–1990): A founding leader of the MPLA and one of its dominant intellectuals. He split with the movement in 1973 to form the "Active Revolt" (Revolta Activa) faction.

Daniel Chipenda (1932–1996): Once a famous national soccer player, he led the "Eastern Revolt" (Revolta do Leste) from the MPLA in 1973.

José Eduardo dos Santos (1942–): Soviet-educated MPLA leader who became head of state in 1979.

---

must have been all but irresistible to the rank and file of the movement. If nothing else, the collapse of UNITA's war effort after Savimbi's death can be considered a measure of his personal power, regardless of how it was exerted.

The MPLA's "capture" of postindependence Angola initially meant that the country became a one-party state with a typically communist institutional structure. The MPLA ceased to be a "liberation movement" and became a "vanguard party." Party and state were largely indistinguishable from each other. The "political bureau" of the MPLA overlapped with the government and its ministries. The legislature was "elected" from MPLA candidate lists. Constitutional changes in the early 1990s—driven partly by local attempts to settle the war with UNITA and partly by broader transformations throughout the African continent as a whole—created the necessary conditions for multiparty democracy. However, continuing civil war meant that the new structures' effectiveness was yet to be tested by postconflict elections, which did not take place until the first decade of the 21st century.

Defining the Nation

The MPLA's Marxist internationalism led postindependence Angola into a close relationship with the Soviet Union and more directly with Cuba. Depending on the perspective, this relationship either caused the catastrophe of the first phase of Angolan statehood, or it was the sheet anchor that permitted a vulnerable, independent Angola to establish itself. The "national idea" of the MPLA was one based on concentric circles of internationalism. Beyond Angola lay the other Afro-Marxist states of Portuguese-speaking Africa: Mozambique, Guinea-Bissau, São Tomé e Príncipe, and Cabo Verde. Beyond Africa were the revolutionary countries of the Third World more generally. Cuba had a central place here, but the communist states and revolutionary movements of Latin America and Southeast Asia were also included. Finally, there were the Soviet Union and "socialist" states of Eastern Europe.

In the 1990s, this revolutionary socialist vision evaporated with the collapse of the Soviet Union and the abandonment of Marxism in Angola. Since that time, particularly after the civil war ended in 2002, Angola (under the post-Marxist MPLA) has tried to define itself as a key player in the southern region of Africa. Its claims to this status, despite the many problems of postwar reconstruction it confronts, are based on its military and economic power (the first actual and the second potential).

The FNLA's view of the Angolan nation was never coherently expressed. The FNLA was essentially an ethno-nationalist movement, whose appeal was based on Bakongo identity rather than on a truly pan-Angolan vision. An FNLA-dominated Angolan state—which seemed to be a possible outcome in the chaos immediately prior to independence—would have been subject to extensive Zairean influence.

The Ethnic Dimension

Ovimbundu: the largest of Angola's ethno-linguistic groups, constituting about 37 percent of the country's total population. Its main concentration is on the country's central plateau.

Mbundu: the second largest national ethnic group, constituting about 25 percent of the population. The Mbundu dominate the Luanda area and the adjacent interior.

Bakongo: the dominant ethnic group in the north of Angola and the third largest in the country as a whole, constituting about 15 percent of the national population.

Mestiços: Angola's mixed-race (Euro-African) population. Large by African standards, it comprises about 2 percent of the population.

White Europeans: Large settler population that was unusual in 20th-century colonial Africa in its commitment as an active minority to the nationalist cause.

UNITA was more successful than the FNLA in extending its appeal beyond its immediate ethnic base. In the preindependence period, UNITA had flirted with Maoism, though more as a means of acquiring Chinese aid (as Beijing sought to counter Moscow's influence over the MPLA) than as a genuine ideological commitment. Later, UNITA positioned itself as an anticommunist, pro-Western movement that was ready to challenge the pro-Soviet MPLA regime. UNITA's reliance on the support of apartheid South Africa, however, fatally compromised it (in the eyes of most African states) and also undermined its nationalist credentials. To other Africans, UNITA's Angola would have provided a Trojan horse for South African interests and a base for neocolonial interference in the continent as a whole.

Narrating the Nation

Angola's national "narrative" takes on different forms depending on the varying political ideologies and ethnicities that have competed in recent times. In the north, for example, the tradition of Kongo kingship—dating back to before the first Portuguese incursions—remain immensely important. Also important is the tradition of anti-Portuguese resistance in the 19th and early 20th centuries.

However, the divisions in the anticolonial struggle during the second half of the 20th century show that there was no unifying narrative in the guerrilla war leading up to independence. Although for outsiders an armed struggle began in 1961, from the Angolan perspective two separate uprisings took place that year and subsequently followed different trajectories. For the Bakongo and the FNLA, the key event, which took place in March, was the major rebellion on the northern plantations. For the MPLA, the true armed struggle began in February with its attacks on prisons and police posts in Luanda. The MPLA's domination of government since independence has given this partial view an official status; however, it is questionable how much of the nation shares this same viewpoint.

In the postindependence period, the officially celebrated national milestones are also partite; for example, the defeat of the northern advance against the MPLA by South African forces at the beginning of 1976 and their expulsion from Angola. The complicating factors here are that the feat was only performed with the assistance of other foreign forces (i.e., Cuban forces), and that South Africa was in Angola in support of UNITA.

With the arrival of long-term peace, however, and with the evident consolidation of MPLA power, it is likely that the MPLA narrative will gradually become the nationally accepted one. Moreover, Angola's dominant cultural, literary, and intellectual traditions are associated much more with the MPLA traditions than with those of its rivals. This linkage is perhaps to be expected given the MPLA's urban, cosmopolitan, and leftist foundations. Almost exclusively, it is the work of pro-MPLA authors such as a Luandino Vieira (president of the Angolan Writers' Union) that has won a wider international readership.

Mobilizing and Building the Nation

In the years immediately following independence, the MPLA regime tried actively to downplay, if not suppress, ethnic and regional differences. It sought to do so while still celebrating the "African" identity of the state. Inevitably, this agenda led to some contradictions. While cultural activities—usually in the form of music and dance—were to be celebrated as markers of postcolonial identity, emphasis on their specific local origins risked encouraging antinational regionalism. The official objective was the construction of a new national consciousness based on the concept of the *homen novo* ("new man"), an idea borrowed from the Cuban revolution. This new Angolan would be free of the inferiority complex engendered by colonialism, aware and proud of the nation's cultural heritage but not trapped by its divisive and obscurantist aspects.

Initially, Bakongo, Ovimbundo, and Cabindan supporters of the MPLA benefited from a kind of unofficial affirmative action within the party and state; however, the continuing pressures of war and a natural reassertion of traditional patron-client forms of rule against "imported" Marxism changed the situation. The dominance of an urban Mbundu and *mestiço* elite in party and government became increasingly obvious. This situation was brutally underlined after the bloody suppression of a leftist coup attempt within the MPLA in May 1977. By the late 1990s, due to this imbalance, Angola had established a reputation as one of the most corrupt countries in the world.

The means by which the MPLA state asserted its national vision were typical of other communist states in the 1970s. Political propaganda was strongly influenced by Soviet-style socialist realism. In contrast to other African states, Angola inherited a relatively sophisticated communications infrastructure at the time of decolonization (a product of the large preindependence white settler population). For example, Angola had a functioning television network. With foreign help, the state proved to be adept at exploiting this medium for propaganda purposes.

Despite this, the MPLA, and therefore its distinctive national idea, faced real difficulties in legitimizing itself. In the early phase of independence, the MPLA struggled both internally and externally to validate its right to rule. At the time of decolonization, the doctrine of "revolutionary legitimacy" defined the transfer of power from Portugal to the new regimes in its former possessions. In essence this doctrine stated that the very fact of protracted armed struggle bestowed the "right" for nationalist movements and their objectives to rule. It was a philosophically questionable stance, but one which served the interests of all sides. It permitted the liberation movements to dodge questions about the real level of their popular support. It also provided Portugal with an exit strategy without the requirement to organize and then implement democratic settlements; however, while the doctrine addressed the circumstances of Portugal's other African territories, the Angolan situation was more complicated. Here, three separate movements claimed revolutionary legitimacy. Faced with a civil war that had spun out of control by the date fixed for independence (November 1975), Portugal produced a pragmatic constitutional formula to cover its withdrawal. Power was transferred not to a particular regime or government—which would have involved Lisbon in anointing a successor from among the competing movements—but rather to the Angolan people. Both the MPLA and a quickly arranged FNLA-UNITA alliance claimed legitimacy, but it was the MPLA that controlled the capital (due to the location of its power base). Although diplomatic recognition quickly followed from the communist bloc and from the majority of African states, Western acceptance of the MPLA regime's legitimacy was withheld for some time (e.g., the United States did not recognize its legitimacy until the 1990s).

Since the end of the war in 2002, reconstruction has been the main focus of national consolidation. This focus is viewed by Angolan leaders as both a vehicle and a prerequisite for nation-building. Of course, the expansive, ideology-driven programs of the late 1970s have long been abandoned, but one characteristic of the Marxist project still remains: a high degree of centralization. Although there are signs that the regime is willing to accommodate its former enemies in new political structures (mostly the result of abortive peace plans from the 1990s), real political authority resides in Luanda, and power remains in the hands of the successors (often family members) of the previous MPLA elite.

The economic base for nation-building certainly exists in Angola with its extensive oil reserves and additional mineral wealth. Direct foreign investment has flown freely since the end of the war. A major constraint, however, is Angola's now deeply rooted corruption. This delivers a double blow to the nation-building process: it deprives the country of the proper return for its trade in oil and other natural resources and engenders a culture of cynicism.

Today, nation-building on the basis of its external standing and image is less of a problem for Angola. Its size and wealth make it a major participant in its own southern African region and beyond. Angola is one of Africa's leading military powers. This status, of course, is a consequence of the years of civil war; but although military capacity has been sharply reduced since 2002, it still remains considerable. Angola was one of a number of regional states that intervened in the chaos of the Democratic Republic of Congo in 1998. The previous year it had sent troops to support the government of the Congo Republic (i.e., the "other Congo" on its borders). In the late 1970s, an invited Angolan intervention had stabilized a dangerous situation in the fellow Portuguese-speaking island state of São Tomé e Príncipe. All of these actions helped Angola develop a reputation as a strong nation capable of regionally projecting its power. The military, moreover, acts as a unique agent of nation-building in contemporary Angola. Under successive peace plans, it is committed to integrating former antigovernment fighters into its ranks. In this way, the military could potentially become a model for the larger national project.

Selected Bibliography

Anstee, M. 1996. *Orphan of the Cold War: The Inside Story of the Collapse of the Angola Peace Process, 1992-93.* London: Macmillan.

Birmingham, D. 1992. *Frontline Nationalism in Angola and Mozambique.* Oxford: James Currey.

Bridgland, F. 1986. *Jonas Savimbi: A Key to Africa.* Edinburgh: Mainstream.

Guimarães, F. A. 1998. *The Origins of the Angolan Civil War: Foreign Intervention and Domestic Political Conflict.* London: Macmillan.

Heimer, F.-W. 1979. *The Decolonization Conflict in Angola: An Essay in Political Sociology.* Geneva: Institut Universitaire de Hautes Etudes Internationales.

Henderson, L. 1979. *Angola: Five Centuries of Conflict.* Ithaca, NY: Cornell University Press.

Heywood, L. 2000. *Contested Power in Angola, 1840s to the Present.* Rochester, NY: University of Rochester Press.

Library of Congress Federal Research Division. 1989. "Angola: A Country Study." Edited by Thomas Collelo. (Retrieved January 3, 2008), http://lcweb2.loc.gov/cgi-bin/query/r?frd/cstdy:@field(DOCID+ao0000).

MacQueen, N. 1997. *The Decolonization of Portuguese Africa: Metropolitan Revolution and the Dissolution of Empire.* London: Longman.

Marcum, J. 1969–1978. *The Angolan Revolution.* 2 vols. Cambridge, MA: MIT Press.

Somerville, K. 1986. *Angola: Politics, Economics and Society.* London: Pinter.

Wright, G. 1997. *The Destruction of a Nation: United States Policy towards Angola since 1975.* London: Pluto.

Rwanda and Burundi

Helen Hintjens

Chronology

1350s–1500	Dates of first kingdoms in regions now known as Rwanda and Burundi, based on oral traditions.
1894	First Germans set foot in Rwanda and speak with the king. Coffee becomes the first cash crop some 20 years later.
1923	Belgium becomes responsible for Ruanda-Urundi under the League of Nations (Trusteeship).
1933	Belgians introduce administrative reforms, including identity cards with fixed, paternally inherited markers according to "ethnicity" (i.e., Hutu, Tutsi, Twa).
1945	Ruanda-Urundi becomes a United Nations (UN) Trust Territory under Belgian control.
1957	The Hutu manifesto is published in Ruanda.
1958	The rise of anti-Belgian sentiment in Burundi.
1959	Rwandan King Rudahigwa dies under suspicious circumstances. Tutsi are killed and others flee.
1961	The monarchy is abolished in Rwanda. More Tutsi flee Rwanda for Uganda, Burundi, and Tanzania.
1962	Independence of Rwanda and of Burundi.
1972	An estimated 100,000–200,000 Hutu are massacred in Burundi. There is a retaliatory purge of Tutsi in Rwanda.
1973	Following his involvement in purges of Tutsi, Major Juvenal Habyarimana ousts Gregoire Kayibanda and declares a new Republic.
1975	Rwanda becomes a one-party state.
1986	The world price of coffee plummets, damaging the economies of Rwanda and Burundi.
1988	The Rwandan Patriotic Army (RPA) is created in Uganda. (October) After the massacres in Burundi in August, President Buyoya creates the National Commission to Study the Question of National Unity.
1990	Reforms for multiparty elections in Rwanda. In Burundi, President Buyoya rejects multipartyism. (October) The RPA invades Rwanda. At the same time, structural adjustment starts in Rwanda. (November) President Habyarimana promises elections in Rwanda. (December) Military rule in Burundi ends; democratization begins under the National Unity Charter.
1991	(February) Habyarimana agrees that Rwandan exiles in Uganda have the right to return. The National Unity Charter is supported by over 89 percent of Burundi voters in a referendum. (August) New Rwandan political parties are created: MDR (Mouvement Démocratique Republicain), PSD (Parti Social Démocrate), and PL (Parti Libéral). (November) There are antigovernment demonstrations in Kigali.
1992	(February) "Practice" massacres of Tutsi in Bugesera, Rwanda. (July) A cease-fire with the RPA is negotiated under the Arusha Accords, with Tanzanian mediation. (August) Violent demonstrations by militias start in Kigali. (April) A new cabinet is nominated in Burundi; half the seats are for Hutu.

1993   (February) The RPA is at the outskirts of Kigali. (April) The ICRC (International Committee of the Red Cross) warns of famine in Rwanda. (June) There are elections in Burundi. Melchior Ndadaye, the Hutu leader of the Front for Democracy in Burundi (Front pour la Démocratie au Burundi, or FRODEBU), wins two-thirds of the vote and becomes president. (June–October) UNAMIR (United Nations Assistance Mission for Rwanda) is created in Rwanda; General Dallaire is appointed as commander. (October) Ndadaye is killed by soldiers in Bujumbura barracks. Mass refugee flight from Burundi to Rwanda. (December) Diplomats in Kigali learn of genocide plans.

1994   (January) The United Nations is warned of genocide plans; Dallaire is not allowed to seize weapons. (February) Opposition (southern) politicians are being assassinated in Rwanda. Willy Claes, Belgian foreign minister, visits Rwanda and warns of the need to respect the Arusha Accords. (April 5) The Security Council threatens to pull out the UNAMIR if the Arusha Accords are not implemented. (April 6) President Habyarimana of Rwanda and President Ntaiyamira of Burundi are killed when their plane is shot down above Kigali. Genocide starts within the hour, with Tutsi blamed for killing the president. Prominent Tutsi and opposition Hutu leaders are the first to be killed. (April 7) Ten Belgian peacekeepers are killed; four days later, foreign nationals leave Rwanda; Belgian troops and 90 percent of the UNAMIR troops withdraw; it takes the United States until July 15 to acknowledge the genocide as reality. (July 5) The French establish a "safe zone" in the southwest of Rwanda, and 1 million people flee toward Zaire, including 13 members of the Interim Government. On August 16, Dallaire leaves Rwanda. (November) The UN Security Council creates an International Criminal Tribunal for Rwanda to try crimes of genocide.

Situating the Nations

The present borders of Rwanda closely resemble those of the precolonial kingdom of the *mwamis* ("kings"), except in the northwest, where Hutu kingdoms were annexed in the early 20th century. Burundi has never been centralized in the same way as Rwanda, and in the precolonial era, it was made up of many princely kingdoms. They feuded, paid tribute, and rebelled against the *Ganwa*, a royal caste that oversaw this messy, shifting assemblage. Rwanda, by contrast, was a unitary system of obligation, allegiance, and tribute, with an overarching and complex system of chiefdoms, stratified into regions, localities, and hillsides.

The Burundian capital, Bujumbura, located on Lake Tanganyika, became the major urban, administrative, and commercial city of Ruanda-Urundi under Belgian Trusteeship from the 1920s onward. Here, the East African trading language, Kiswahili, started to be spoken alongside French and Kirundi, which is the sister language of Kinyarwanda, spoken in Rwanda alongside French and, since 1994, alongside English as well.

The main regional connections of Rwanda and Burundi are with the Democratic Republic of Congo, the Kivu region in particular, and there are road links with Tanzania and Uganda. Principal international air links are with Nairobi, Brussels, and Paris. In both countries, Tutsi are estimated at around 14 percent of the population, Hutu at 85 percent, and the minority Twa at just 1 percent. Mixed

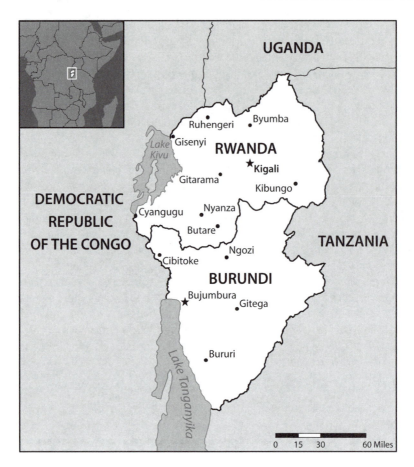

marriages, particularly common in northern Burundi and southern Rwanda prior to the genocide, are less common now, at least according to anecdotal accounts. They hardly ever happened in the Rwandan northwest.

In 1959 a popular "revolution" against the Rwandan aristocracy was supported by Belgium, and many Tutsi were killed, especially those associated with the monarchy and the colonial administration. When Prince Rwagasore was assassinated in Burundi shortly before independence in 1962, his death ended hopes of a cross-communal democracy in that country. In both countries, independence followed in an atmosphere of fear and distrust, because the process of "national self-determination" involved killings and pogroms that were almost always one-sided. The Catholic Church did nothing to reduce Hutu and Tutsi divisions, and it took different sides at various times. Rather than reconciling Hutu and Tutsi among themselves, the church and its offshoot, the schools, and the colonial administration tended to feed a highly divisive version of history.

In both Rwanda and Burundi, economic life is now in deep crisis. The main reasons are long-term structural poverty, physical violence, and growing insecurity. Pockets of affluence exist in Bujumbura and Kigali, but the benefits fail to "trickle down" to most ordinary Rwandans and Burundians. This was not always the case; from independence onward, there was a period of relative economic stability, if not exactly prosperity. Now, however, things are getting steadily worse. Since prices for coffee slumped in the mid-1980s, the main source of state revenue and cash income for farmers has evaporated. Farmers have been sucked dry, and Rwanda and Burundi became heavily indebted at the same time, coming to resemble their neighbors Tanzania and Uganda in this respect. Prior to the late 1980s, Rwanda in particular was known in aid circles as well managed, a model developing country, relatively free of graft and highly organized. It was the mid-1980s' coffee price collapse that started the process of economic decline. Steady growth in the 1970s and 1980s gave way to a negative growth rate, minus 6 percent for Rwanda in 1989, and zero growth in Burundi in the same year. Economic conditions have improved slightly for Rwanda since the disaster of the genocide, but things have deteriorated further for Burundi. By 2000, the growth rate (a pretty crude indicator of success) was 3.1 percent in Rwanda and −1.6 percent in Burundi.

In this intensively farmed part of the world, complex and sophisticated crop-rotation systems are needed to maintain soil fertility and prevent erosion. Such systems have all but collapsed under the combined pressures of war, insecurity, refugee departures and returns, and growing poverty among the rural population. Soil is cultivated right up to the summits of the hills. Terracing, which extends acreage and reduces erosion, was abandoned for some time in the late 1980s and early 1990s. State extension services have been cut because of privatization. The result is that food crops, including beans, bananas, rice, and other grains, are in decline, and more and more basic foodstuffs now have to be imported from Uganda and further afield simply to ensure food self-sufficiency. Meanwhile, coffee and tea are not viable for small farmers to grow. Around 90 percent of the population in each country is still engaged in subsistence farming, and famine has become a recurrent threat.

Both Rwanda and Burundi are small, landlocked, and densely populated; people live cheek by jowl. As social bonds have been split through war, genocide, retribution, and mistrust, it has become more and more difficult to mobilize people for voluntary public works. Apathy is a new problem, especially in Rwanda since the genocide, which has left a society traumatized and many socially excluded. With more than 200 people per square kilometer in Burundi, and 250 in Rwanda, even the flora and fauna of the region have proven difficult to protect. Constant movements of internally displaced people and refugees have all but destroyed what little game or natural reserves there were in this area, undermining the potential for long-haul tourism.

After 1998, the Democratic Republic of Congo (DRC) became a major focus for both Bujumbura and Kigali because of continued warfare and refugee movements into and out of the Congo, a situation to which both regimes have contributed, especially Rwanda (and also Uganda), through interventions and documented pillage of mineral and other resources. Retaliatory raiding parties follow cross-border incursions from forces hostile to both the Burundi and Rwanda governments, confirming this as the "wild west" of the Great Lakes region. The lure of mineral wealth, lawlessness, and impunity go hand in hand, with DRC being one of the "softest" states anywhere in the world.

Instituting the Nations

After independence, the relationship between nationalism and the state in Burundi and Rwanda were like mirror images of one another. Official Burundi nationalism claimed to be blind to ethnicity and race; Rwandan nationalism was explicitly racialized in favor of the "majority population," who were presumed to be entitled to rule from the time of independence. The Tutsi, 14–15 percent of the population in both countries, were dominant in Burundi, including in the administration and especially in the army (where a subclan known as the Bahima were heavily overrepresented). In Rwanda, the Tutsi were suppressed by quotas in higher education and largely kept out of the top ranks of the army and civil service. Many were exiled, and their main routes for social promotion were in business, law, and the professions rather than in government. Forming a marginalized and beleaguered minority, the Twa in both countries were treated as an underclass and were occupationally confined to pottery and related activities. They were all but invisible and voiceless in public debate.

The task of state leaders in Rwanda and Burundi since the early 1990s has been to rework the sense of nationalism inherited from the postindependence era. After the 1994 genocide, state-led nationalism in Rwanda has officially removed ethnic and race labels, like Hutu, Tutsi, and Twa, from Rwandan political identity (and also from identity cards). It is noteworthy that the backbone of the post-1994 regime is formed by returnees from Uganda, many of whom speak English. They have elaborated a form of what Robin Cohen terms "victim diasporic" nationalism, akin to that of Israel, where genocide is similarly central to national identity formation. This type of nationalism was born out of the experience of exile and the long-lived hope of eventual return to Rwanda. To ensure that their own conception of the Rwandan nation is the dominant one, the new political elite of Rwanda has introduced a raft of institutional changes since 1994. These include new laws against divisive language, special *gacaca* ("village") courts to try genocide crimes, solidarity camps where an authorized version of national history is taught to young and old alike, and a National Reconciliation Council and Genocide Survivors' Fund. In the brave new Rwanda, shared national Rwandan identity is supposed to override all other forms of political identity. This Herculean task is far from being achieved. Instead of Tutsi, Hutu, and Twa, new terms have emerged: survivor (i.e., surviving Tutsi), suspected *genocidaire* (assumed to be Hutu), old caseload (Tutsi), and new caseload (Hutu) refugees (returnees).

These terms are now more widely used that the overt race labels of the past; in a sense, politically correct terms have replaced the "tribal" labels of the past. The genocide of 1994 has become the point of origin of official nationalist ideology in postgenocide Rwanda.

Official Rwandan nationalism has also come into line with the official nationalist line in Burundi since independence, namely, that all citizens are equal, and that any remaining conflicts among them are just the psychological projection of divisive attitudes inherited from the colonial past. Race divisions are seen not as a reality, or as based on unequal living conditions, but as a hangover and evidence that decolonization is still incomplete. So when the first popularly elected Hutu president of Burundi, Melchior Ndadaye, was swept to power in early 1993, it seemed the prospects for peace were greatly enhanced for the entire region. Just four months later, he was murdered by the army, in the Bujumbura barracks. Tragically, this event ended "Burundi's gradual but brave and determined progress towards democracy and power sharing" (Melvern 2004, 71–72). Ndadaye's killing ended hopes for peaceful coexistence in both countries and immediately prompted mass retaliatory purges of Tutsi in many parts of Burundi. As an estimated 350,000 Burundian refugees fled to Rwanda in a heightened state of tension and fear, their presence helped fuel intergroup tensions inside Rwanda. Meanwhile, the Rwandan Patriotic Army (RPA) crossed the Ugandan border into

Refugees wait for water at a distribution center on their way back to Rwanda after the Rwandan genocide in 1994. (U.S. Department of Defense)

Rwanda in October 1990. The rebels did not seek compromise, nor did the Rwandan government. The RPA invasion fueled militarization in Rwanda and prompted the diversion of resources into arms spending. Inside Rwanda, politicians advocating *Hutu Pawa* ("Hutu power") used the killing of Ndadaye as they would later use the killing of Habyarimana, to convince Hutu Rwandans that Tutsi planned not only to rule over them once more, but even to massacre them en masse, starting with their leaders.

Political democratization in Rwanda and Burundi has had a bumpy ride over the past two decades. In Rwanda's case, political opposition has barely been tolerated during any period. Each successive regime acts with impunity where its perceived enemies are concerned. Since 1994, RPA soldiers have committed atrocities both inside Rwanda and in neighboring countries, especially in the DRC, and hardly anyone has been prosecuted. Paul Kagame and the Rwandan Patriotic Front (RPF) were elected in 2001 and 2002, in part by intimidating, and even imprisoning, opposition politicians. The key institution in both countries today seems to be the intelligence services, with which Kagame has been closely associated. The army and intelligence services are able to operate throughout Burundi, for though the country's administrative, judicial, and criminal justice systems have come to a virtual standstill.

In terms of international relations, Rwanda does marginally better than Burundi. During the postgenocide era, as prior to 1994, the Rwandan government

---

Hotel Rwanda

This 2005 film depicts the true story of Rwandan assistant hotel manager Paul Rusesabagina, who sheltered more than 1,500 people fleeing the genocide outside the hotel walls. The director, Terry George, worked with Paul on the film, which was shot in South Africa rather than Rwanda. The hero now lives in quiet exile in Brussels and denies he is a hero at all. Don Cheadle stars in the lead, and Paul's wife is played by Sophie Okonedo. When it was released in February 2005, the film was shown at film festivals internationally, winning several awards and Oscar nominations. Shown in Kigali in April, on the 11th anniversary of the genocide, the film was criticized for not depicting the real horror of the genocide. However, the director defended his decision to leave the scale of the slaughter implicit, as he wanted *Hotel Rwanda* to be accessible to high school audiences, especially in the United States, as an educational device. Since then Rusesabagina has published his own version of the story. The official film Web site (http://www.hotelrwanda.com/main.html) has many clips and commentaries. *Sometimes in April*, a film directed by Raoul Peck, was also released in early 2005 and was much more explicit in its depiction of the genocide, and much more direct in accusing Westerners of indifference to the genocide, indicting the media's excessive attention to more trivial matters. Unlike *Hotel Rwanda*, which was filmed in South Africa, *Sometimes in April* was shot inside Rwanda. More recently, there have been efforts by Rwandans themselves to create a Rwandan film industry that can produce films in Kinyarwanda, moving beyond genocide themes to produce comedies and dramas.

---

managed to mobilize considerable international support for its policies from Western donors. Postgenocide reconstruction and justice systems have been partly underwritten by foreign aid budgets. The danger is that the country's "genocide credit" may inadvertently lead to the continuance of impunity, with the covering up of human rights violations by the current regime, both inside Rwanda and in the DRC. By contrast, Burundi's government has been almost abandoned by the international community as civil war has raged on and on. Postconflict systems of criminal justice in Rwanda are managing to end certain kinds of impunity related to the genocide itself, but the war crimes of those in power are still being ignored or denied. Rwanda's genocide has acquired a high profile through the media, and has even been converted into a successful Hollywood movie, *Hotel Rwanda*.

As political repression continues in both countries, more and more refugees leave to seek safety elsewhere. According to Filip Reyntjens (a leading Belgian expert on the region), increasing numbers of these exiles are Tutsi rather than Hutu.

Defining the Nations

Since independence, Rwandan and Burundian nationalists have been divided into three kinds: (1) those who think the majority has the right to determine what happens to the minority; (2) those who think a minority has the right to rule over the majority; (3) and those who believe in inclusive, cross-cutting Rwandan and Burundian political identities. For all three categories, the state is the main center of power, with the means either to undermine or to shore up separate ethnic and racial identities. Forget tropical images of chaotic filing systems, lazy fans, flies, and large-bellied corrupt officials snoozing while secretaries file their nails; these do not work in Rwanda or Burundi. Bureaucratic structures, when they work, give an impression of precision and machine-like precision, especially in Rwanda.

Far from having collapsed during or after the genocide, the Rwandan state has proven to be a remarkably resilient and formidable structure, able to gain the passive, as well as active, consent of most ordinary Rwandans. In Rwanda, channels of state power are everywhere present and obvious; officials monitor and control the people through a whole host of complex regulatory mechanisms. Tight top-down political control is a tradition; prior to 1994, every Rwandan needed official permission from the local authorities before being allowed to move to another village or town. Record keeping at the local level has generally been immaculate, something that greatly facilitated genocide in 1994. The importance of authority was clear in the way Tutsi victims fled to municipality buildings, schools, and churches during the early days of the genocide itself, seeking safety. They sought protection. But these three major institutional sites of state power—the church the more informal, the state the most formal, and the education system a meeting point between the two—delivered the fleeing citizens into the hands of killers, and many teachers, priests, and local officials also took part in the killings themselves.

Although the army and state employment are also important in Burundi, the control of the state over its citizens is less clear-cut than in Rwanda. The consent of ordinary Burundians is harder to obtain, and so is control over their movements. The counterpart of this growing distance between states and citizens is that Burundians are largely being left to their own devices in terms of their daily life and survival. Public services like transport, health, and education are either costly, chaotic, or largely unavailable outside major towns and settlements.

A few years after independence, in what remains the major comparative work on Rwanda and Burundi, Rene Lemarchand noted major differences between social structures in the two countries. What he says is worth quoting in full:

> In Rwanda one notices an almost perfect coincidence of social stratification and ethnic divisions; in Burundi, on the other hand, social stratification and cultural or ethnic pluralism were anything but "consistent" in the sense that one automatically replicated the other. (Lemarchand 1970, 474)

The relative *complexity* of social stratification in Burundi has been used to explain why national and ethnic identities in that country have been more localized, less systematic, than in Rwanda. In Rwanda, the relative *simplicity* of the fabric of social differentiation has proven highly dangerous; it both integrates and includes Rwandans into a single, centralized system of controls and provisions and can fatally divide them, as during the era of preparation and implementation of the genocide. But systematic, state-directed genocide is not confined to Rwanda. Both Stephen Weissman, the Holocaust historian, and the British philosopher Bertrand Russell termed the killing of 100,000 to 200,000 Hutu people in Burundi in 1972 a "genocide" at the time.

After independence, official Burundi nationalism claimed not to see ethnic or racial differences among Burundian citizens. Meanwhile, the army periodically massacred any educated Hutu who might aspire to transform the dominant political order at local or national levels. Official Rwandan nationalism was more ambiguous, since it explicitly or implicitly rested on the notion of a Hutu majority. In Burundi, violence was more sporadic, less controllable, and eventually involved violent conflict between two sides. It resembled a festering sore, a "nightmarish sequence of terrorism and counter-terrorism," involving an "ever larger segment of the peasantry" in violence (Lemarchand 1970, 483). In Rwanda, by contrast, until the RPA invasion of 1990, violence was almost entirely in one direction, was clearly targeted, and was quite carefully managed by the state; it could almost be switched on and off. The Rwandan Revolution involved violence that resulted in one set of officials being replaced with another—Tutsi with a new class of Hutu leaders. For the ordinary Rwandans, there was no escape from their utter reliance on authority in their everyday lives, and they remained locked into complex, and occasionally deadly, ties of dependency and subordination with dominant local elites.

Rwanda's national unity has been disputed from the start. In the northwest, as already noted, a distinctive system of Hutu kingdoms survived well into the 20th century that was fiercely resistant to encroachment by Rwandan structures. The elites of this region retained a certain distance from the rest of Rwanda, from Hutu southerners and from Tutsi elites. This region provided the base for President Habyarimana, who ousted President Gregoire Kayibanda, a southerner, in a coup in the early 1970s, after himself being involved in massacres of Tutsi civilians, ostensibly as "reprisals" for killings of Hutu by the army under Micombero in Burundi. Most of those who propagated the *Hutu Pawa* ideology of the early 1990s, which facilitated genocide in 1994, also came from the northwestern region of Rwanda, the first to be affected when the RPA invaded from Uganda in 1990. Their reaction was to mobilize resistance to the Arusha Accords that sought to bring about peace and integrate the RPA into national military structures. Instead, the northwestern elite worked hard to avoid peace, and indeed decided that the killing of Tutsi on a massive scale should be organized and implemented.

The efficacy of state structures is less obvious in Burundi, where unity and order have broken down under the pressure of prolonged civil war, massacres, and political stalemate. Here political violence initially took the form of periodic cycles of repression of educated Hutu, often on a regional basis. The Tutsi elite are increasingly living like internal exiles within Bujumbura, and many have left the country. Educated Hutu are attacked periodically because they are seen as potential leaders of a political opposition. Educational institutions, church missions, and other institutions that have sought to protect Hutu have also been targeted by the army during these massacres, the worst being in 1972 and 1988. Until 1993, massacres in Burundi were a means of defending the status quo, by eliminating leadership among the Hutu majority population. Tutsi were completely dominant in Burundian politics and the army. Since 1993, however, the situation has changed, as the opposition Palipehutu movement has been able to mobilize and arm large numbers of Hutu to retaliate, with widespread anti-Tutsi massacres. A full-blown civil war has been the result, and the army no longer sees itself as restoring or maintaining social order but now claims to be fighting "terrorism." Throughout its history, there has arguably been little sense of shared Burundian national identity. Yet successive governments have all claimed to be in favor of one, inclusive Burundian identity. This is not unreasonably regarded by many Hutu as propaganda, and now persuades almost nobody.

Narrating the Nations

The histories of Rwanda and Burundi are still deeply debated today. Not only are different versions of the past used to justify present policies, but recent history is also understood through the images of the more distant, and even mythical, past.

These different versions of history need to be part of the picture to explain why recurrent political violence has marred national life in both countries over the past few decades. Colonial ideas of race were constructed along scientific lines, taking height and facial features into account. The Belgians allied themselves with the Tutsi elite, strengthening their dominance and making it something new, something colonial. The inequalities inside Burundian and Rwandan society, which were inherited from the precolonial era, were thus remolded to suit the colonizers' purposes and interests. Since independence, recurrent political violence and persecution have become tied in with different stories about the past. Generally speaking, where one chooses to "start" the massacres and cycles of killings will reveal where one's sympathies lie. Deep-seated psychological tensions among Rwandans and Burundians themselves persist in relation to the past and its relationship with the present. Complex religious and cultural notions of the self and the other can to some extent explain how killings proceed, but only to some extent. There were also local variations, and one single commune even escaped genocide (Giti). More than 10 years after the genocide, more complex understandings of its causes and dynamics started to emerge.

Both in Rwanda and Burundi, precolonial myths of origin combined with European ideas of race to create a strange offspring: the Hamitic hypothesis. This ideology of racial difference between Hutu and Tutsi is still important today. According to this story, Tutsi were interlopers from the Nilotic North, and Hutu were the indigenous Bantu people who already lived in the Great Lakes region (the Twa do not figure in this story, as they would have to be even more indigenous than the Hutu). This particular reading of the past was echoed in church teachings and in mission schools, ad nauseam. Initially, such ideas sanctioned the control of the Tutsi elite over Rwandan society. Later, the Hamitic hypothesis became, particularly in Rwanda, an excuse for denying Tutsi the status of authentic Rwandans, true sons of the soil. History is still spoken about in lively terms by Rwandans and Burundians alike, and stories about the past affect people's daily perceptions profoundly. Race can seem to come into everything. When foreign tourists were killed by Rwandan Hutu *interahamwe* militia (genocide militia) in Camp Buhoma in southern Uganda in 1999, Anglo-Saxons were specifically targeted racially for having betrayed their Bantu (i.e., Hutu) brothers by allying themselves with the Tutsi.

With ideas of race so prominent in people's minds, democratization has proved very difficult in Rwanda and Burundi and remains all but blocked. Moves toward more democratic forms of politics have been accompanied by genocide and massacre, in Burundi's case, and by full-blown genocide in Rwanda. It is hard to be hopeful in such a context. The years 1989–1991 marked the start of an experiment in democratization in both countries, largely at the behest of Western donors, who sought democratic reform after the end of the Cold War. Unfortunately, the push for democratic political reforms coincided with the hardened resolve of the armed forces to retain tight control over the population as a whole. With the shattering of the old economic order, the 1990s became a time of "state collapse, ethnic conflict, economic disintegration, ecological destruction, health crises and political turmoil" (Rugumamu 2004, 157). This applies not only in Rwanda and Burundi but also in other economically devastated and war-torn regions.

Democracy has had its enemies in both countries. In Rwanda, both the RPA, invading from Uganda, and the northwestern elites, dominant in the army, were determined that peace and free and fair elections would not prevail. In Burundi, the army prepared to override the decision of the majority, and massacred Ndadaye. In Rwanda, the genocide plan was also intended to put an end to any hopes of democratic politics, and the war with the RPA was used as a cover for making plans to target civilians through militias of armed killers. Real reforms were taking place at the same time, and there were mass demonstrations against the Rwandan government in early 1992. This frightened the military, who feared power-sharing with the RPF (the political wing of the RPA). In Burundi, race politics and militarization have played a large part in delaying the long-awaited return to democratic politics. In the Great Lakes region generally, in the past decade, refugee politics, and the forces that displace people, especially serious human rights abuses and the fear of massacres, undermine local and international moves to consolidate peace and a transition to power-sharing. In such a climate, fear has become endemic, and massacres have become a form of "preventative" political action, intended to avert massacres of one's own group.

It seems strange to define whole countries by the violence that has taken place there rather than by their language, history, and cultural attitudes, but something like this has happened for national identity in both Rwanda and Burundi. Historical memories of political disaster, whether of genocide or massacres, can create a strong sense of cohesion among an ethnic group but result in a fragmented sense of national identity when divisions of race cut across the citizenry, as they are thought to in Rwanda and Burundi. The genocide of 1994 is for some the culmination of a legacy of persecution in Rwanda that dates from the fall of the monarchy and the chasing of tens of thousands of Tutsi refugees out of the country in the early 1960s. Several studies have recently looked at the stories Rwandans and Burundians tell themselves about the past, and how these help one understand what has happened in both countries since independence, and how Burundi and Rwandan identity could have become synonymous with violence and killing.

Building and Mobilizing the Nations

It is important to remember that the mobilization of the national populace in Rwanda and Burundi has not always been lethal—far from it. National mobilization for the purposes of peaceful "development" was prevalent during the first few decades after independence. This mainly involved Rwandans and Burundians in unpaid work on public infrastructure projects, including road building, terracing, weed clearing, and construction of public buildings. For some critics, like Peter Uvin, this kind of involuntary mobilization had its history in the colonial era, in forced labor and compulsory taxation, all operated through tight central controls.

The mechanisms of mobilization periodically worked in different, more lethal ways, by the time of the genocide. Where the postindependence regimes, especially in Rwanda, mobilized peasants for collective works, during the 1990s, the population was increasingly mobilized through arms and militarization. The development era of the 1970s and 1980s involved mobilizing people to build schools, clinics, roads, and terrace fields, often through ostensibly community-based labor. Mutuality on the local level could involve weed clearing and preparing fields and harvesting. But collective work mobilized through official state structures was generally compulsory, as it had been during the colonial years. At times of violence, including the 1994 genocide, terms normally associated with collective development work came to be used to mean something different, namely preparation for the killing of Tutsi. Organized slaughter of Hutu also took place in Burundi, albeit in different, more secretive, ways than in Rwanda.

What is remarkable about nation-building in both Rwanda and Burundi is the way it has not happened, in spite of promising beginnings in both cases. Burundi seemed to have the advantage of a complex social structure, as identified by Lemarchand. Rwanda seemed to have the advantage over many other African nations of postindependence state borders that almost matched the precolonial Rwandan kingdom. Yet today in Burundi and Rwanda, the nation and the state are as mismatched as they were at the time of independence; perhaps more so.

The main reason for the disintegration is a history of violent conflict and genocide in both countries since independence in 1962. These two countries are now almost defined by the lack of any continuous peace, since this is a marked feature of their recent national history. For Rwanda, the role of the genocide of 1994 is now akin to that of the Holocaust for Israel. It is a collective national tragedy and also a divisive wound used as an excuse for continuing repression of any opposition. In neighboring Burundi, the role of past massacres and the 1972 genocide in particular is more akin to the Armenian genocide in Turkey; it is a festering, officially unacknowledged sore, and its denial continues to destroy trust and prevent national reconciliation.

Of course, the genocides of the past will never happen again, in the sense that history will not be repeated. But neither Rwanda nor Burundi has overcome the roots of the problem of violence. Government impunity, a lack of political dialogue, and the imposition of a market economy on subsistence economies are among the problems that continue to undermine the prospects for long-term peace in the future. As long as conflict continues, and as long as human rights violations remain a daily reality, the movement of the population in cycle after cycle of refugees throughout the Great Lakes region will continue. Resource scarcity will be exacerbated, and the fruits of past growth and development squandered on fighting and weapons. The only hope of a safer future for Rwandans and Burundians lies in their own efforts to overcome the roots of conflict. They must rely on themselves, because there is little chance that the international community's indifference to events in the Great Lakes will change in the foreseeable future.

Selected Bibliography

Adelman, H., and A. Suhrke, eds. 2000. *The Path of a Genocide: The Rwandan Crisis from Uganda to Zaire*. New Brunswick, NJ: Transaction Publishers.

Bloomfield, S. 2007. "Welcome to Hillywood: How Rwanda's Film Industry Emerged from Genocide's Shadow." *The Independent* (London), August 30.

Eltringham, N. 2004. *Accounting for Horror. Post-Genocide Debates in Rwanda*. Sterling, VA: Pluto Press.

Goyvaerts, D. 2000. "About Bantu and Nilotes." In *Conflict and Ethnicity in Central Africa*, edited by D. Goyvaerts, 301–304. Tokyo: Institute for the Study of Languages and Cultures of Asia and Africa.

Jose, A. M. 2004. "Sustainable Agricultural Development and Environment: Conflicts and Contradictions in the Context of Rwandan Agriculture." In *The Quest for Peace in Africa. Transformations, Democracy and Public Policy*, edited by A. Nhema, 379–402. Addis Ababa, Ethiopia: International Books/Ossrea.

Lemarchand, R. 1970. *Rwanda and Burundi*. New York: Praeger.

Lemarchand, R. 1994. *Burundi: Ethnocide as Discourse and Practice*. Cambridge: Cambridge University Press.

Mamdani, M. 2001. *When Victims Become Killers: Colonialism, Nativism and the Genocide in Rwanda*. Princeton, NJ: Princeton University Press.

Melvern, L. 2004. *Conspiracy to Murder. The Rwandan Genocide*. London: Verso.

Reyntjens, F. 2004. "Rwanda Ten Years On: From Genocide to Dictatorship." In *African Affairs* 103:177–201.

Reyntjens, F., and C. Legum. 1998a. "Burundi towards Power Sharing: A Brave Experiment in Democracy." In *Africa Contemporary Record 1990–92*, B272–275. New York: Africana.

Reyntjens, F., and C. Legum. 1998b. "Rwanda: The Roots of Genocide." In *Africa Contemporary Record 1990–92*, B357–362. New York: Africana.

Rugumamu, W. 2004. "Understanding the Link between Post-Conflict Environmental Management and Peace in the African Great Lakes Region." In *The Quest for Peace in Africa: Transformations, Democracy and Public Policy*, edited by A. G. Nhema, 157–171. Addis Ababa, Ethiopia: International Books/Ossrea.

Rusesabagina, P. (with Tom Zoellner). 2006. *An Ordinary Man: The True Story behind "Hotel Rwanda."* London: Bloomsbury.

Straus, S. 2006. *The Order of Genocide: Race, Power and War in Rwanda*. Ithaca, NY: Cornell University Press.

Taylor, C. 1999. *Sacrifice as Terror: The Rwandan Genocide of 1994*. Oxford: Berg.

Third World Institute. 2003. *The World Guide 2003/2004: An Alternative Reference to the Countries of the Planet*. Oxford: New Internationalist.

United Nations. 2002. *Report of the Panel of Experts on the Illegal Extraction of Natural Resources and Other Forms of Wealth of the Democratic Republic of Congo.* UN Reference No. S/2002/1146, submitted October 16. (Retrieved December 21, 2007), http://www.security councilreport.org/atf/cf/{65BFCF9B-6D27-4E9C-8CD3-CF6E4FF96FF9}/DRC%20S% 202002%201146.pdf.

Uvin, P. 1998. *Aiding Violence: The Development Enterprise in Rwanda.* Bloomfield, CT: Kumarian Press.

Vlassenroot, K. 2000. "Identity and Insecurity. The Building of Ethnic Agendas in South Kivu." In *Politics of Identity and Economics of Conflict in the Great Lakes Region*, edited by R. Doom and J. Gorus, 263–288. Brussels: VUB University Press.

Burundi Government. Burundi : site portail des institutions République du Burundi [in French]. (Retrieved December 21, 2007), http://www.burundi.gov.bi/.

Rwandan Government. Official Website of the Government of Rwanda [in English, French, Kinyarwanda]. (Retrieved December 21, 2007), http://www.gov.rw/.

[The best Web site for current news is AllAfrica.com, as it uses African and international media sources and digests them, updating daily. News bulletins for Burundi and Rwanda can be found at http://allafrica.com/burundi/ and http://allafrica. com/rwanda/.]

Afghanistan

Conrad Schetter

Chronology

1747–1773	Ahmad Shah of the Pashtun Durrani (Abdali) tribal federation establishes the Durrani empire.
1879	(May 26) Treaty of Gandomak. Afghanistan becomes a half-autonomous protectorate of British India.
1888–1893	Abdur Rahman subdues the Shiite Hazaras in atrocious wars.
1893	(January 12) The Durand Treaty determines the border between Afghanistan and British India.
1919	(August 8) A provisional treaty regulates the independence of Afghanistan.
1923	(April 10) Amanullah proclaims a constitution.
1929	(January 16) Habibullah II overthrows Amanullah. (October) Nadir Shah terminates the rule of Habibullah II.
1934	Afghanistan joins the League of Nations.
1948–1975	The Pashtunistan claim is raised by Afghanistan.
1964	(September) A constitution that contains the first signs of Western parliamentarianism is adopted.
1973	(July 17) Mohammad Daud Khan carries out a coup d'état and proclaims the "Republic."
1978	(April 27) In the April Revolution (*inqilab-i sawr*), the People's Democratic Party of Afghanistan (PDPA) overthrows Mohammad Daud. Mohammad Taraki is appointed president and Afghanistan becomes a "Democratic Republic."
1979	(December 24–27) Soviet intervention in Afghanistan. Beginning of the Afghan war.
1989	Withdrawal of Soviet troops from Afghanistan.
1992	(April) Overthrow of Najibullah by the Mujahideen. Afghanistan becomes an "Islamic Republic."
1996	(September) The Taliban capture Kabul. The other parties merge into the Northern Alliance.
2001	Fall of the Taliban and the appointment of the interim government under Hamid Karzai.
2002	(mid-June) A *loya jirga* (large tribal assembly) confirms Karzai as president of the Afghan interim government.
2004	(January 4) Adoption of the new Afghan constitution by a *loya jirga*.
2005	(October 9) Hamid Karzai is elected president in democratic elections.

Situating the Nation

In the historiography, Afghanistan is often described as the "Highway of Conquest" or the "Crossroad of the Conquerors." Indeed, the region has served as a bridge for migrations, conquests, and the dispersion of religions (e.g., Buddhism, Islam) among Persia, Central Asia, and the Indian subcontinent for a long time.

Although Afghanistan is often traced back to early ancient times, the Afghan nation-state can be considered a product of modernity, since it was created artificially after the long-running colonial confrontations between British India and Russia in the 19th century, which went down in history as the "Great Game." At the same time, the geographical term "Afghanistan" underwent a spatial metamorphosis: whereas in the 18th century, "Afghanistan" had been a very loose term used by the Persian-speaking population to refer to the area settled by Pashtun tribes, the colonial powers demarcated the entire area between Persia and their empires as Afghanistan, an area characterized by an opaque and changeable distribution of power. Advances by British Indian troops into the eastern Pashtun tribal areas had made tribal or ethnic borders with neighboring Afghanistan obsolete. Afghanistan was no longer understood to refer "ethnographically" to the Pashtun tribal areas but rather to refer "politically" to the ungoverned buffer zone between Russia, British India, and Persia. Between 1887 and 1893, British India and Russia delineated Afghanistan with precisely defined territorial boundaries (Durand Treaty) and created a kingdom under the rule of Abdur Rahman called Afghanistan within this territory. It remained a semiautonomous protectorate of British India until its independence was achieved by King Amanullah after a short war in 1919. Interestingly, this newborn state was located much further north of the area that had been termed Afghanistan at the beginning of the 19th century.

Abdur Rahman (1844–1901)

Abdur Rahman can be regarded as the founder of the modern Afghan nation-state. In 1879, when the British government decided to create the state of Afghanistan, it placed Abdur Rahman, who lived for about 10 years in exile in Bukhara, on the Afghan throne. Abdur Rahman ruled Afghanistan from 1879 to 1900. Abdur Rahman's most impressive, but also most questionable, effort was establishing a monopoly of violence and ending tribal and regional autonomies. This is why he earned the nickname "the Iron Amir." In numerous wars, he subjugated a myriad of sovereign regional and tribal leaders. The Shiite Hazaras, especially, were subjected to a protracted and extremely brutal war. The submission of the Kafiris (unbelievers) of the Hindu Kush was conveyed by their conversion to Islam and renaming to Nuristani. Abdur Rahman's rule was based on a dense network of police spies, and he answered any moderate resistance with rigorous repression. The traditional elites, especially, including Islamic dignitaries and tribal leaders, lost power under his rule. Abdur Rahman also laid the groundwork for the development of a modern state. Thus, he reformed the army and the tax system. However, his reform agenda remained limited. Therefore, he maintained the isolation of the country and rejected any technical modernization (e.g., building a railway or telegraph system). Abdur Rahman was, furthermore, the first Afghan ruler who used the term "nation," although his concept of "nation" was blurred. He used the term "nation" for the Afghans as well as for particular ethnic groups, such as the Kafiris or the Pashtun Durrani tribe. Despite, or because of, his iron rule, Abdur Rahman is one of very few Afghan rulers who died a natural death.

Perhaps the most striking feature of this artificial character of the Afghan state is its geographical surface. The Afghan landscape is dominated by the Hindu Kush, a high mountain range stretching from the Pamir Mountains in the east of the country to the deserts in the west, and thus subdividing the country into several parts. This rough terrain was not only a severe obstacle for the building of an infrastructure but also for the creation of an overarching national identity. In addition, this delineation of borders took no account of cultural or ethnic homogeneity. Afghanistan is characterized by a high diversity of cultural patterns, ethnicities, languages (Pashtu, Dari [Persian], Uzbek, etc.), and ways of life and economy (e.g., pastoral nomadism, farming). Even Islam, which is followed by about 99 percent of the approximately 30 million (2005) Afghans, is marked by heterogeneous trends (Sufism, Islamism) and sects (Sunna, Shia, Ismailia). It is equally difficult to distinguish the multiple ethnicities. According to different scientific sources, the number of ethnicities ranges from 50 to 200. Likewise, figures on the members of the respective ethnicities are highly contested. The most important ethnic categories are the Pashtuns (40–60 percent), the Tajik (20–35 percent), the Hazaras (7–20 percent), and the Uzbeks (8–15 percent). Furthermore, patronage networks constitute important references of identity and action that are based on local, tribal, or religious bounds. Accordingly, even today, the elite of the country is made up of clan chiefs, tribal leaders, and religious dignitaries who hold power, especially in the rural regions.

Instituting the Nation

Even though Afghanistan was only founded at the end of the 19th century, its roots lie in the 18th century. At the time, Ahmad Shah merged the Pashtun tribal federation of the Durrani and formed a great empire, including today's Afghanistan. Although the royal dynasty devolved from the Popalzai to the Barokzai tribe in the mid-19th century, the Pashtun Durrani ruled the royal house from 1747 to 1973, which is one of the few fundamental national continuities. The only interruption was caused by the politics of Amanullah in the 1920s, who attempted to lead Afghanistan to modernity. This modernization provoked the objection of the population, culminating in the eviction of Amanullah by the Tajik Habibullah II in 1921. He only held power for a few months before being overthrown the same year by Nadir Shah, who belonged to a branch of the royal family.

In the 20th century, Afghanistan first was a kingdom with a rudimentarily developed state apparatus. The majority of Afghans perceived the state as an alien, even hostile entity. A fundamental reason for this perception was the fact that Abdur Rahman subdued all local potentates, clans, and local communities at the end of the 19th century in countless wars. Particularly, the Shiite Hazaras living in central Afghanistan underwent a brutal subjugation. The national politics of

Loya Jirga

The *loya jirga* can be seen as the only national political institution that is accepted by all inhabitants of Afghanistan without any reservations. The term *jirga* is of Mongolian origin and is used in Pashtu for tribal gatherings. Usually, a *jirga* is a temporary body that is created for solving disputes among tribes, subtribes, clans, families, or individuals. *Loya* is Pashtu and means "big" or "grand." Thus the *loya jirga* is the national assembly, which decides about national affairs of great interest. Afghans tend to understand the *loya jirga* as a democratic forum, where the representatives of the Afghan people decide upon the future of country. Furthermore the *loya jirga* is seen as an ancient institution that was introduced by the Aryans in ancient times. However, historical research shows that the *loya jirga* is a relatively young phenomenon and was established during the 20th-century state-building project. A first *loya jirga* took place in 1915. Also, the *loya jirga* never worked in a democratic way. Most *loya jirgas* solely served the enforcement of the rulers' interests. Under the Bonn Agreement of 2001, the *loya jirga* experienced a revival to legitimate the political process: the emergency *loya jirga* in June 2002 decided on the transitional administration; the constitutional *loya jirga* in December 2003/2004 approved the new Afghan constitution. However for both *loya jirgas*, it turned out that the general rules of how these gatherings should function were nonexistent: while in the emergency *loya jirga*, an election about the head of the transitional administration took place, in the constitutional *loya jirga*, Hamid Karzai solely proclaimed the new constitution without any voting. Although traditional *loya jirgas* were all male, women have progressively made their way into this decision-making body, often with special seats reserved for them.

Rahman's successors were marked by the strategy of equilibrating the relations between the local potentates and the bureaucratic elite of Kabul by distributing benefits in a clientelistic manner. The sole national institution that could develop as an integrating force was the *loya jirga*, the large tribal assembly, which was summoned for important political decisions.

In 1963, King Zahir Shah (1933–1973) established a constitutional monarchy with a modern constitution and a bicameral parliament. The political parties that mushroomed in Kabul in the 1960s mostly had a communist or an Islamic background; only very few ethno-nationalist parties were founded (e.g., the Pashtun *afghan mellat*). Parliamentary elections were held in 1965 and 1969 but hardly found any resonance within the population. In 1973, Zahir Shah was expelled in a coup d'état by his cousin Mohammad Daud Khan (1973–1978). The Communist Democratic Party of Afghanistan (PDPA) finally seized power in 1978 under the leadership of Hafizullah Amin and Mohammad Taraki. When the party was increasingly confronted with rebellions in the country, due to drastic and overhasty implementation of reforms, and on the verge of collapsing, Soviet troops marched into Afghanistan on December 25, 1979, to maintain the Communist rule, leading to a further intensification of the conflict. During the Soviet occupation, Afghanistan was subject to a radical destruction caused by the fighting between the Soviet occupants and the Mujahideen resistance fighters operating from Pakistan and Iran. Approximately 6.5 million Afghans fled to Pakistan and Iran, leading to the largest mass exodus worldwide since World War II. The action radius of the Communist government of Babrak Karmal (1979–1986) and Najibullah (1986–1992) was confined to Kabul and a few provincial cities.

With the withdrawal of the Soviet troops, which was completed in 1989, and the Mujahideen seizing power in 1992, Afghanistan collapsed into petty empires that were ruled by a myriad of warlords and local rulers. Even national borders lost their function as barriers for political and economic actors: while cross-border trade and smuggling (e.g., drugs) to and from neighboring countries flourished, internal trade almost came to a standstill. After seizing power in 1996, the Taliban succeeded in bringing around 90 percent of the country under their control and driving away the specter of Afghan fragmentation.

The ouster of the Taliban by the military intervention of the Coalition against Terrorism in autumn 2001 led to the reconstruction of the country. In this regard, the national institution *loya jirga* played a decisive role in the establishment of an interim government and the approval of a constitution.

Defining the Nation

Since the founding of Afghanistan, every ruler has tried to pin down certain power and interest groups through the alignment of the Afghan national ideology. Among these interest groups are the Sunni clergy (*ulama*), the Pashtun tribes, and the urban elite. According to these three power groups, the Afghan national ideology was based on religious, ethnic, and demotic references. In most cases, rulers strove for hybrid forms.

Until the beginning of the 20th century, the national self-perception was grounded in a religious interpretation. Sunni-Hanafite Islam was suitable as a national force since it not only enabled the dissociation from the colonial powers of British India and Russia but also from the Shiite Iran, even though this meant factoring out about 20 percent of the Shiites living in Afghanistan. This religious notion of *millat* ("nation") provided a clear understanding of the state with which the population could easily identify. Nonetheless, the significance of the state was restricted to its function as guardian of the religion in the eyes of the Afghans. So the compliance with the Islamic system of values was the sole leveling rule for state activities. The right to exist of both state and ruler was always questioned whenever doubts were cast on their ability to fulfill their function as defender of the religion. This was clarified in particular by the expulsion of Amanullah (1929), whose reforms were denounced as un-Islamic, as well as by the uprisings against the Communist Amin-Taraki regime (1978–1979). During the 20th century, the Islamic alignment continuously lost significance due to the increasing modernization of the urban intellectuals and the creation of the state of Pakistan, which also legitimized its existence by referring to Islam. It was only after the capture of Kabul by the Mujahideen (1992) and in particular since the rule of the Taliban that Islam regained its role as the constitutive interpretation of the national ideology.

The Afghan national ideology was also grounded ethnically. Already the state labeling of "Afghanistan" implies a Pashtun reference, as Afghan is the Persian term for Pashtun. The nine-month-long rule of the Tajik Habibullah II, who subdued Amanullah in 1929, marked the signal for a Pashtun interpretation of the national ideology, as the Pashtuns saw their "natural" supremacy jeopardized for the first time. The Pashtun definition of the Afghan nation gained significance after the reestablishment of Pashtun supremacy under Nadir Shah and advanced as the political guideline until the outbreak of the Afghanistan war in 1979. The idea of a nation-state—that the borders of the national territory should conform precisely to ethnic boundaries—was the ideological starting point for the explosive Pashtunistan dispute.

Similarly, the Pashtun perception of the nation, in line with the zeitgeist of a racial interpretation of the Afghan nation, gained ground among Afghan intellectuals during the 1930s until the 1950s. The notion of Afghans being Aryans was supported by a scientific substantiation ranging back to early history. Even more, the spatial location of the antique Aryans was equated with that of the young nation-state of Afghanistan. The artificial geopolitical product Afghanistan was in fact elevated to an imagined Aryan homeland. By emphasizing the common Aryan descent, the discrepancies among some ethnic categories, such as the

Pashtunistan Claim

The Pashtunistan claim emerged after the displacement of British India by India and Pakistan. Since 1948, the Afghan government had challenged the legal validity of the Durand line, once established as the border between Afghanistan and British India, and wanted to turn Pashtunistan into reality. Hereby, the Afghan government perceived the state of Afghanistan as encompassing the imagined homeland of the Pashtuns. Despite the demarcation of the entire region, which lay on both sides of the Afghan-Pakistani border, up to the Indus is regarded as part of Pashtunistan, the Pashtun territory of dominion. The Afghan government—especially under Mohammad Daud Khan (1953–1963 and 1973–1978) —attempted to organize a national mobilization on this issue from the early 1950s until the 1970s. Moreover, the Afghan government endeavored to incite tribal unrest in the uncontrollable Pakistan border area. Subsequently, the Pashtunistan claim defined much of the relations between Afghanistan and Pakistan from the 1950s to the 1970s and brought both countries several times to the brink of war. However, in Afghanistan, the interest in this topic remained restricted to the urban elite, and it failed even to produce a lasting echo in the Pashtun tribal areas.

Pashtuns, Tajiks, and Nuristanis, could be revoked. The Aryan notion was so popular among the Pashtuns that the old belief in the derivation from the lost tribes of Israel became less and less significant.

After the Soviet invasion, the ethnic interpretation of the national ideology underwent a paradigm shift at the beginning of the 1980s, as the nationality politics were based on the Soviet model. The fundamental goal of these politics was to win over ethnic minorities (in particular Uzbeks, Turkmen, Hazaras, Baluchis, Nuristanis) to the Communist regime by producing positive self-perceptions of these minorities and promoting them on the cultural as well as political level. Ultimately, the nationality politics negated the existence of a unified nation "Afghanistan" and tinkered with the idea of dissolving the state due to a lack of national integration. The largely anti-Pashtun alignment of these politics was mirrored in the calls to rename Afghanistan to Khorasan, Bactria, or Azadistan. During the Afghanistan war in the 1990s, the ethnic heterogeneity of the country was particularly highly explosive in nature, since the different parties used ethnicity as a means of political and military mobilization.

A demotic perception of the nation was already propagated by Amanullah in the 1923 constitution, defining every citizen of the country as Afghan. This interpretation, however, was rejected by the majority of the Afghan population, as it was diametrically opposed to the religious *millat* perception. Only in the middle of the 20th century did the urban elite emerge as a decisive power factor that had to be taken into account for a demotic interpretation of the national ideology. With the consent of Zahir Shah, the constitution of 1964 extended the term Afghan to every citizen of the country, albeit emphasizing the "exceptional position" of the Pashtuns. Likewise, democratic and parliamentary elements were strengthened, including minority provisions for non-Muslims. The demotic moments witnessed a verbal up-valuation under Daud and later under the Communists' rule—for example, the renaming to the "Democratic People's Republic"—but the respective governments neglected to acknowledge democratic aspects in their political action.

After the fall of the Taliban, the nation-building project experienced another boom. The current government follows an integrative approach in which the different perceptions of the nation are taken into account. This approach, however, has led to a set of serious contradictions. For example, Afghanistan has become an "Islamic Republic" since the constitution adopted by a constitutional *loya jirga* on January 4, 2004, states that "no law can be contrary to the beliefs and provisions of the sacred religion of Islam" (Article 3). Likewise, the constitution attempts to meet a demotic approach by determining that "the word Afghan applies to every citizen of Afghanistan" (Article 4, Sentence 4). The same article (Sentence 3) also acknowledges the ethnic diversity of the country and provides a number of privileges to religious and ethnic minorities (e.g., freedom of religions and language). There is no explicit Pashtun reference. It remains equally contested just how Islamic the Republic of Afghanistan is. Thus ethnic and religious minorities as well as women are still subject to discriminations in everyday life.

Narrating the Nation

According to the different notions of the Afghan nation, there are different historical points of reference and personalities for narrating the nation. A fundamental myth that plays a role in all of the aforementioned nation concepts is the styling of Afghanistan as a "freedom-loving country"—an idea that is omnipresent. It is argued that none of the great powers—whether the Moguls and Safavids in the early new age, British India and Russia in the 19th century, or the Soviet Union in the 1980s—was able to control Afghanistan for a long period. Even the military operations of the Coalition against Terrorism in autumn 2001 were influenced to a large extent by a tremendous respect for the Afghans' "love of freedom." As a result, the United States and its allies preferred to leave the fighting of the Taliban to their Afghan allies rather than deploy their own troops and thus risk offending the sentiments of the Afghan population. However, it has to be stressed that it was not the national unity of Afghans, but their diverging particular interests that rendered an external conquest difficult. Well-known heroes of this freedom myth, for example, are Khan Khushal Khan Khattak in the struggle against the Moguls, Mir Wais in the struggle against the Safavids, or Abdul Haq and Ahmad Shah Masood in the struggle against the Soviets. Maiwand, where the Afghans defeated the Britons on July 27, 1880, advanced as the topographical symbol for this resistance, while Gandomak, where the Afghan ruler Yaqub Khan agreed on the

Afghan protectorate status on May 26, 1879, marked the negative counterpart of this myth.

Moreover, Gandomak was the starting point of a trauma that most notably played a role in the Pashtun definition of the nation. The Treaty of Gandomak set the seal on the loss of the eastern Pashtun tribal areas and the royal summer residence Peshawar, which laid the ground for the Pashtunistan issue. Historically, these territorial claims were substantiated with the expansion of the empire of Ahmad Shah, who Afghans often titled as father of the Afghan nation, in the middle of the 18th century. The myth of the *loya jirga* is also closely connected with Ahmad Shah. He was the first ruler to convene a *loya jirga* for his own legitimacy. Kandahar, where this assembly was held, is thus regarded as the birthplace of Afghanistan by many Afghans and as the secret capital of the country by many Pashtuns.

Yet there also are two historical points of reference that question the Pashtun interpretation of the Afghan nation. On the one hand, the brutal subjugation of the Shiite Hazaras in central Afghanistan by Abdur Rahman at the end of the 19th century marked a trauma for the Hazaras, which advanced as a basis of a collective identity and explains the often surfacing animosities against the Pashtuns. On the other hand, the takeover by Habibullah II in 1929 challenged the Pashtun dominance. Accordingly, there are two coexisting myths regarding Habibullah II: the first insists on the legitimacy of his rule, while the second considers him a bandit of low descent and derogatively calls him *Bacha-ye Saqqao* ("son of the water carrier").

Finally, the reference to former empires plays a crucial role for the narration of the nation; for example, the glamorous Islamic empires of the Ghaznavids with Ghazni as the capital in the 10th century, and the Timurids with Herat as the center in the 15th century. Bactria and the Kushan empire are two important examples for the pre-Islamic epoch. The destruction of the 2,500-year-old Buddha statues of Bamyan by the Taliban is an example of the incommensurateness of diverging notions of the nation. In the traditional Afghan historiography, Bamyan exemplarily stands for the deep historical roots of Afghanistan, while the Taliban were keen to eradicate all reminders of the pre-Islamic time because of their religious concept of the nation. Even though the Pashtun narration of the nation was dominant throughout, non-Pashtun symbols also influenced the national ideology: the *loya jirga* and the east Pashtun dance *atan*, the Uzbek equestrian game *buzkashi*, and the statues of Bamyan evolved into constitutive symbols of the Afghan nation.

Mobilizing and Building the Nation

Until the outbreak of the Afghan war in 1979, nearly all Afghan rulers regarded the cultural heterogeneity of Afghanistan's territory as an annoyance from the outset and considered it an obstacle for the development of a national ideology. For this reason, the state policy was marked throughout this time period by efforts to homogenize the population through forced resettlement and the redistribution of land. This policy was primarily characterized by Pashtun-tinted nationalism, which meant that in general Pashtuns profited from it most: Pashtun settlers received the irrigated land originally possessed by Uzbek landlords in the oases of northern Afghanistan, and the pastures in central Afghanistan were handed over from Hazara farmers to Pashtun nomads. This process was accompanied by a religious nationalism that was reflected in a number of proselytizations. Under Abdur Rahman, for example, the animistic Kafiri ("Unbelievers") were Islamized at the end of the 19th century and renamed the Nuristani ("inhabitants of the country of light"). Conversion of the Shiite Hazaras yielded little success. Thus, the victims of religiously or ethnically legitimized national mobilization attempts were population groups differing from the national norm. Hindus and Sikhs, who together made up less than 1 percent of the Afghan population, underwent social exclusion time and again and were barred—for example, under the Taliban—from practicing their religion. Particularly, the Shiite Hazaras were subject to discriminations and persecutions. The Shia is considered heresy by the Sunni majority of the population. The Shiite Hazaras experienced a racially motivated exclusion due to their predominantly Mongolian physiognomy. As the alleged descendants of the Mongolian troops of Genghis Khan, the Hazaras are at times even made responsible for the destruction caused by the Mongolians and the backwardness of the country.

To level out the ethnic heterogeneity of Afghanistan's territory, and to thwart any attempts at secession, a redefinition of spatial units took place during the course of the 20th century. Geographical terms that carried any ethnic or particularistic perceptions, such as Kafiristan/Nuristan, Khorasan, Turkistan, Qataghan, or Hazarajat, were replaced by administrative terms that often referred to provincial towns (e.g., Herat, Kunduz, Bamyan) or rivers (e.g., Kunar, Hilmand) and did not imply any ethnic connotations. The administrative reorganization that took place in the course of the introduction of the constitution in 1964 also gerrymandered territorial administrative units with the intention that they should be dominated by a Pashtun majority wherever possible. Another moment of this Pashtunization was the promotion of Pashtu as the sole national language in 1936, which had previously been on an equal footing with Dari. The Pashtunization of the state apparatus failed due to the refusal of the predominantly Persian-speaking civil servants to attend Pashtu language courses. It was only in 1964 that Persian was put on par with Pashtu again.

Moreover, the ruling politics regulated the access to state goods and posts by means of an ethno-religious horizontal stratification of the Afghan society. While both the Pashtuns, as such, as well as prestigious spiritual families (e.g., Mojadiddi, Gilani) were favored and controlled key positions within the state and the military, the Tajiks made up the bulk of the middle class, which dominated the economy, the state administration, and the education apparatus. The Uzbeks had very little influence altogether and were largely confined to their settlement area in northern Afghanistan. Due to their alleged Turko-Mongolian looks and their Shiite confession, the Hazaras were marginalized and by and large excluded from participation in social resources. The members of smaller ethno-religious categories (e.g., Qizilbash, Nuristanis) occupied either economic or administrative niches. This ethno-religious stratification experienced major changes during the course of the Afghanistan war. For example, today the Tajiks dominate the military, while many entrepreneurs are Pashtuns.

Overall, in Afghanistan, national ideologies played an inferior role. This was largely the result of a lacking infrastructure; most Afghans paid attention solely to their village, their tribe, or their valley community but seldom to the incidents in distant Kabul. This changed with the outbreak of the Afghan war. Thus, the war accounted for a national mobilization by the Mujahideen under the banner of Islam against the Soviet occupying forces. Hereby, the religious interpretation was essential for the understanding of the nation by the Mujahideen. Nonetheless, during the war, there were considerable differences between the various and often contrary currents within Islam that were concealed by the proclamation of the jihad against the infidel Communists. It also has to be emphasized that many Mujahideen were not primarily interested in religious matters, but rather in the protection of the traditional local independence that had been impaired by the Communists. This religious mobilization was contrasted by the nationality politics of the Communists that aimed to promote ethnic groups as sociopolitical points of reference and thus to base the Afghanistan conflict on ethnicity. With the fall of the Communist regime in 1992, the Mujahideen got the upper hand, but at this stage, the "ethnicization" of the war had already come to light. Although the Mujahideen established an "Islamic Republic" in 1992, the religious interpretation of the war lost significance and fights broke out within the Mujahideen (e.g., between Gulbuddin Hikmatyar and Ahmad Shah Masood) along ethnic fractures. However, it has to be mentioned that the ethnicization of the war did not lead to an ethnicization of the masses.

Interestingly, it was precisely in parallel with the ethnicization of the war, the erosion of state structures, and the appearance of countless petty empires that a national self-confidence emerged within the population in the 1990s, whose only goal was the integrity of the national territory of Afghanistan. However, this Afghan identity could hardly be anchored to any common values, traditions, or experiences, since any definition of national values inevitably failed against the cultural heterogeneity of Afghanistan and the various existing models of ethnic origin or religious community. This tremendous significance of the national territory as a frame of reference for the Afghan identity is the main key to an understanding of the initial sympathies and also the subsequent growing dissatisfaction the population had with the Taliban. At first, a large part of the population hoped the Taliban would bring about a territorial reintegration of the country, which

Ahmed Wali Karzai (left), the brother of Afghan president Hamid Karzai, meets with tribal leaders on August 28, 2002. Though centralized government is a goal for Afghanistan, local problems are still resolved by traditional tribal leaders, and violence between ethnic groups is on the rise. (AP/Wide World Photos)

was in a process of disintegration. Their aspiration was that the once fixed territorial delineation of Afghanistan should endure. The Taliban came close to fulfilling this desire, as they brought around 90 percent of the country under their control and drove away the specter of Afghan fragmentation. However, the Taliban rule also made it clear that spatial integrity did not necessarily bring about social integration. The erecting of a Sunni orthodox order named "Islamic Emirat of Afghanistan," in which the *sharia* (or Islamic law) formed the legal basis for the entire population and in which every deviation from the norm was punished draconically, led to an exclusion and suffering of large parts of the population. This in turn caused disappointment within the population with the Taliban's radical policies and in particular their treatment of women and minorities.

After the collapse of the Taliban, the international community followed the strategy to create a broad-based government, which included members of the largest ethnic groups as well as religious dignitaries, technocrats, and warlords. Despite the constitution of 2004, which attempted to balance ethnic and religious, as well as demotic perceptions of the Afghan nation-state, ethnicity, played an especially important role in everyday politics. In the first years of the new government (December 2001–January 2003), Tajiks had an above average representation in the government. Tajiks controlled core ministries, such as the Interior, Foreign, and Defense ministries, and staffed them with their own clientele.

The ethnic awareness also caused the mushrooming of new provinces and districts: Day Kundi (formerly part of the province Uruzgan), mainly inhabited by Hazaras, was the first province to be established. The Panjshir Valley, the stronghold of Tajik Panjshiris, also received the status of a province. Furthermore, in nearly every province, disputes about the creation of new districts arose, mostly stipulated by ethnic antagonisms.

The presidential elections in October 2004 were tinged by ethnicity. Hamid Karzai (with 55.4 percent) won the ballots in the Pashtun belt; Mohammad Mohaqeq (with 11.7 percent) in the Hazarajat; Rashid Dostum (with 10 percent) in the Uzbek settlements in Northern Afghanistan; and Yunus Qanuni (with 16.3 percent) in the Tajik settlements of Northeastern Afghanistan. Thus, the results of the presidential elections coincided roughly with the ethnic identities of the country. With his reelection, Hamid Karzai has brought about a rebound that aims for participation of ethnic elites under a Pashtun claim to leadership, similar to Zahir Shah.

Selected Bibliography

Anderson, E. W., and N. H. Dupree, eds. 1990. *The Cultural Basis of Afghan Nationalism.* Oxford: Pinter.

Fröhlich, D. 1969. "Nationalismus und Nationalstaat in Entwicklungsländern. Probleme der Integration ethnischer Gruppen in Afghanistan." PhD diss., Cologne.

Grevemeyer, J.-H. 1988. "Ethnicity and National Liberation: The Afghan Hazara between Resistance and Civil War." In *Le fait ethnique en Iran et en Afghanistan*, edited by J.-P. Digard, 211–218. Paris: Ed. du Centre National de la Recherche Scientifique.

Hyman, A. 2002. "Nationalism in Afghanistan." In *International Journal of Middle East Studies* 34:299–315.

Nölle-Karimi, C., C. Schetter, and R. Schlagintweit, eds. 2002. *Afghanistan—A Country without a State?* Frankfurt: IKO Verlag.

Orywal, E. 1986. *Die ethnischen Gruppen Afghanistans.* Wiesbaden, Germany: Reichert.

Pstrusinska, J. 1990. *Afghanistan 1989 in Sociolinguistic Perspective.* London: Central Asian Survey Incidental Paper Series 7.

Roy, O. 1986. *Islam and Resistance in Afghanistan.* Cambridge: Cambridge University Press.

Rubin, B. R. 1995. *The Fragmentation of Afghanistan.* New Haven, CT: Yale University Press.

Schetter, C. 2003. *Ethnizität und ethnische Konflikte in Afghanistan.* Berlin: Dietrich Reimer Verlag.

Schetter, C. 2005. "Ethnoscapes, National Territorialisation, and the Afghan War." *Geopolitics* 10, no. 1: 50–75.

Shahrani, M. N. 1986. "State Building and Social Fragmentation in Afghanistan: A Historical Perspective." In *The State, Religion, and Ethnic Politics: Afghanistan, Iran, and Pakistan*, edited by A. Banuazzi and M. Weiner, 23–74. Syracuse, NY: Syracuse University Press.

Armenia

Razmik Panossian

Chronology

ca. 860 BC	Urartu emerges as a powerful state around Lake Van.
ca. 782 BC	The Fortress of Erebuni is built by Urartians (currently in Yerevan, capital of Armenia).
ca. 585–200 BC	The Yervanduni Dynasty rules over Armenia, either as vassals or as independent kings.
ca. 520 BC	First mention of Armenia and Armenians in history, on Behistun Rock, by King Darius I of Persia.
188 BC–AD 10	Artashesian Dynasty.
95–55 BC	King Tigran II "The Great" establishes a short-lived Armenian empire, stretching from the Caspian to Mediterranean seas.
ca. AD 66–428	Arshakuni Dynasty.
ca. 301–315	Armenia adopts Christianity as the state religion; the population is converted to the new religion.
387	Armenia is partitioned between Byzantine and Persian (Sassanid) empires.
405	The Armenian alphabet is invented by Mesrop Mashtots; beginning of the "golden era" of Armenian literature.
451	Armenian rebellion against Persia and the Battle of Avarayr. Armenians lose the battle but maintain Christianity as the state religion. Also, the Council of Chalcedon, the decisions of which the Armenian Church eventually rejects to maintain its independence from the Byzantine church.
484	Treaty of Nevarsak between Persia and Armenia, granting Armenians certain rights, and allowing them to remain Christian.
640	Beginning of the Arab invasions of Armenia.
884–1045	Bagratuni Dynasty.
1045	Ani, the capital of the Bagratuni Dynasty, falls to the Byzantines (followed by the fall of Kars in 1064).
1071	Battle of Manzikert. The Seljuks defeat the Byzantines after conquering Armenia.
1080s	The establishment of Rubenian and Hetumid principalities in Cilicia, on the Mediterranean coast. A kingdom is eventually established in 1199.
1236	Mongol invasions of Armenia begin, leading to century-long domination.
1375	The last Armenian kingdom, in Cilicia, falls to the Mamluks of Egypt.
1386	Timur (Tamerlane) invades Armenia.
1400s	Consolidation of Ottoman rule over Armenia.
1453	Ottoman conquest of Constantinople.
1512	The publication of the first Armenian book (in Venice), and the beginning of Armenian printing. The Bible is published in Armenian in 1666 (in Amsterdam). The first comprehensive dictionary is published in 1749 (in Venice). Father Mikayel Chamchian's *History of the Armenians* is published in 1784 (in Venice). And in the 1770s, the first political tracts calling for the liberation of Armenia are published (in Madras, India).

1514–1639	Ottoman-Safavid (Iran) wars over Armenia.
1722–1728	Rebellion led by Davit Bek (in Eastern Armenia) against local Muslim rulers and Ottoman conquest.
1722–1828	Frequent wars in or around Armenia among Russian, Persian, and Ottoman empires. Russia advances into South Caucasus and gains control over eastern Armenia. The borders delineated by the Treaty of Turkmenchai (1828) between the Russian and Persian empires eventually become the borders between present-day Iran, Armenia, and Turkey.
1839–1876	Tanzimat (reform) era in the Ottoman Empire. Armenian *millet* constitution is adopted in 1863.
1877–1878	Russian-Ottoman war, and expansion of Russian control of Armenian provinces.
1840s–1890s	Height of the Armenian national "renaissance," particularly in culture.
1885	The establishment of the first Armenian revolutionary political party in the Ottoman Empire, followed by revolutionary activities.
1915	The genocide of the Armenians from Ottoman lands.
1918–1920	Establishment of an independent Armenian republic in the territories of Eastern (Russian) Armenia.
1920–1921	Sovietization of the Armenian Republic.
1988	The beginning of the popular national movement in Armenia, demanding the unification of Gharabagh with Armenian SSR (Soviet Socialist Republic). Major earthquake in northern Armenia.
1991	Independence of Armenia, as the Union of Soviet Socialist Republics collapses.
1994	Cease-fire agreement in the war with Azerbaijan (but no peace agreement).
1998	Forced resignation of first post-Soviet president, Levon Ter-Petrossian, through a "constitutional coup." Robert Kocharian, the prime minister of Armenia (originally from Gharabagh) becomes president.
2007	The U.S. House Committee on Foreign Affairs approves a bill (HR 106) that recognizes the Armenian genocide, bringing a total of 25 countries that have passed resolutions or laws on the Armenian genocide in the preceding decade as a result of diaspora advocacy.

Situating the Nation

The first recorded reference to the Armenians and their country dates back to ca. 520 BC when the king of Persia, Darius I, etched his victories over conquered peoples on the Behistun Rock (presently Bisitun in western Iran). Armenians had already emerged as a distinct people from the Urartian tribal confederation, a dynastic state (ca. 870 to ca. 590 BC) centered around Lake Van. Greek author Xenophon wrote about the Armenians when the Greek army, retreating from Persia, passed through Armenia in 401–400 BC. In the *Anabasis*, he recorded his observations about the social habits and economic life of a people known as Armenians.

The historic territory of the Armenians is often referred to as the "Armenian Plateau" and more recently as the "Anatolian Plateau," largely in eastern Turkey. Until 1915, most Armenians lived in these historic territories: between the Kur River to the east, the Pontic mountain range to the north, the Euphrates River to the west, and the Taurus Mountains to the south.

This vast land was composed of mountain ranges, valleys, and rivers. Such geographical features had political consequences: the physical composition of the territory mitigated against the emergence of a strong central political power throughout much of Armenian history. Consequently, various regions and enclaves, at different times, could maintain a degree of autonomy from the centralizing tendencies of both domestic and external (imperial) sources of political power. In addition to the geographic divides, Armenia was often partitioned between rival empires, being the scene of long and bitter wars involving the Persians, Romans, Arabs, Byzantines, Ottomans, and Russians.

Such divisions had profound impacts on Armenian ethno-national identity. While an overarching sense of "Armenianness" always remained, deep divisions emerged within this identity and were—and still are—manifested through politics, culture, and language. Armenian identity has evolved in a multilocal manner, with the diaspora often playing an important (and at times even central) role in its formulation, particularly in the modern period.

The boundaries of the contemporary Armenian Republic reflect these geographic and imperial divisions and are roughly the same as the boundaries among the Persian, Russian, and Ottoman empires of the 19th century. The republic is situated in what used to be Eastern Armenia; its southern border with Iran and the western border with Turkey follow the Arax and Akhurian rivers. To the east is Azerbaijan, and to the southwest is the Azerbaijani exclave of Nakhichevan. To the north is Georgia. The republic constitutes a small portion of historic Armenia, with a population of approximately 3 million people. There are another 5 million or so Armenians living in the diaspora, with particularly large communities in Russia, the United States, and France.

Western Armenia no longer exists as a separate political, social, and demographic entity, having been integrated into eastern Turkey. The 1915 genocide eliminated Armenians from these territories and destroyed Armenian culture.

Instituting the Nation

Three sets of institutions have been the "backbones" of the Armenian people: dynastic kingdoms (until AD 1375), the Armenian Apostolic Church (since the fourth century) and, in the modern period, diasporan organizations, including merchant communities.

Five major dynasties ruled over Armenia:

1. Yervandunis (a.k.a., Orontids), ca. 585 to 200 BC
2. Artashesians (a.k.a., Artaxiads), 188 BC to AD 10
3. Arshakunis (a.k.a., Arsacids), ca. first century AD to AD 428
4. Bagratunis, 884 to 1045
5. Rubenians and Hetumids in the "diasporan" kingdom of Cilicia, on the Mediterranean coast, 1199 to 1375.

The fortunes of these dynasties were closely tied to geopolitical dynamics, imperial rivalries, and conflicts among various Armenian ruling families based in specific regions of the country. The borders of Armenia expanded or retracted accordingly (reaching their greatest extent in the first century BC). During periods of relative peace, Armenia prospered. Medieval kings and princes (*nakharars*) supported the arts, culture, and the construction of churches, strengthening the foundations of a unique identity. The 4th and 5th centuries AD, as well as the 10th and early 11th centuries, were periods of particular innovation.

Maintaining state unity under one ruler has been a persistent challenge for Armenians, as evidenced by the gaps in the succession of dynastic kingdoms. In such periods, Armenia was ruled through various fiefdoms or direct imperial rule through "governors." However, leading families continued to provide the institutional basis of collective identity. As the Mongol invasions ravished Armenia in mid-13th century, and as the last kingdom fell in 1375, dynastic rule came to an end; the leading families eventually disappeared. They were either eliminated, fled to exile, or assimilated into the imperial elites. Armenians refer to the period between the 1400s and the 1800s as the "dark centuries."

The one institution that played a central role in maintaining an ethno-religious collective identity during these difficult centuries was the Armenian Apostolic

Church. Partly because of its internal administrative independence, and the Ottoman *millet* system (based on the Muslim tradition of granting limited communal autonomy to "peoples of the Book"), the "national" church came to play a decisive role in maintaining a unique Armenian identity.

The formal adoption of Christianity as the state religion of Armenia took place sometime between AD 301 and 315 (the oft-cited date is 301), making Armenia the first state to formally become Christian. The new religion cemented the distinctiveness of Armenian identity in the classical period and remained the anchor of collective identity until the 20th century.

The conversion to Christianity by Armenians was a response to Sassanid Persian pressure to accept Zoroastrianism as part of the Persian empire's drive to centralize and assert its control over neighboring territories. The Armenian elite wanted to maintain local religious-cultural traditions and the political control of its territory. In this context, King Trdat III "The Great," who was educated in Rome, embraced the Christian faith as the official religion of his kingdom, as did many of the other Armenian noble families. Trdat, along with St. Gregory "The Illuminator" (the first patriarch of the Armenian Church), set out to convert all subjects under his domain.

In a period when religion was a central element of identity, such a conscious decision to convert en masse to a new faith so different from that of their neighbors already indicates a sense of distinctiveness that Armenians sought to maintain through institutional mechanisms that were available to them at that point. Later, when the Roman Empire itself embraced Christianity, Armenians held on to tenets of the faith that were different from the other major churches. They rejected the decisions of the Council of Chalcedon (451) on the nature of Christ and subsequently seceded from the "Universal Church"—i.e., the Byzantine branch of Orthodoxy.

As such, despite the loss of statehood, wars, and much political turmoil after the fall of the last Armenian kingdom, the church remained a bedrock institution preserving and enhancing collective identity. Its head, the Catholicos, was recognized as the "leader" of all Armenians.

In addition to the Apostolic Church, the small Armenian Catholic brotherhood of Mekhitarians, founded in the early 18th century and based in Venice, played a crucial role in the modernization of Armenian identity through the preparation and publication of dictionaries, national histories, philosophical treatises, and translations of European religious and secular texts.

The third set of actors who were instrumental in instituting the nation was diaspora-based Armenian merchants, particularly from the 17th century onward. In the absence of a state and a secular political elite, merchants and other wealthy Armenians (e.g., *amiras*) played a key role in financing the spiritual, cultural, and social needs of the community.

Never a very large group, merchant families were nevertheless spread throughout the world with nodal centers in Persia, India, and Constantinople.

They traded from the Far East to Moscow and Amsterdam. These merchants and *amiras* contributed large sums of money toward the running of the Armenian Church (in addition to building churches in their far-flung communities), they commissioned the writing of manuscripts and later set up or sponsored printing presses and published books and journals, they financed schools and hospitals and provided scholarships to young Armenians to study in Europe, and they engaged in other community support activities. In short, they played a role similar to that of an Armenian state in the absence of one. However, most of the Armenian "business" elite remained steadfastly outside of formal politics and, moreover, were almost exclusively situated in diasporan communities, including Constantinople/Istanbul, Tiflis/Tbilisi, and Moscow.

As will be outlined below, the institutionalization of the nation continued into the 20th century with the Soviet and post-Soviet Armenian states, as well as with diasporan mobilization. In both cases, the institutional foundations of the Armenian nation were strengthened through governmental and communal actions (e.g., the establishment of schools, printing presses, community structures, etc.).

Defining the Nation

The Armenian nation can be defined through nine main characteristics. Four of these are from the classical period, and five are from the modern period.

The Classical Period

A national church. From its very inception, the church focused on the Armenian people. After the initial proselytizing zeal in the fourth and fifth centuries within Armenia, the church turned inward to protect its flock rather than convert others. This was particularly the case after the emergence of Islam in the region. Hence, church and ethno-national identity came to be infused, and remained so until the modern era. To this day, to be Armenian means to be (at least nominally) Christian. The Armenian Apostolic Church belongs to the Orthodox branch of Christianity, being closer to the Monophysite doctrine, but it is completely independent of external authority, that is to say, it is autocephalous; it rejected the authority of the patriarchate of Constantinople in 554. The church service was—and still is—conducted in Armenian.

A distinct language and alphabet. Armenian is a separate branch of Indo-European languages, with its own literary tradition dating back to the fifth century AD. There is evidence that it was the spoken language of the region in the fifth century BC. Around AD 405, a distinct alphabet was invented specifically for the language by clergyman-scholar Mesrop Mashtots, under the auspices of the King Vramshapuh and Catholicos Sahak of Armenia (it was subsequently propagated as a God-given revelation). Soon after, the Bible and other texts were translated into—and original works written in—Armenian, beginning in the fifth century, the "golden age" of Armenian literature.

A deep sense of history. As an ancient people, Armenians have a very deep sense of history. They began writing their own history in the fifth century AD. The most significant author is Movses Khorenatsi, who was purported to write in the second half of the 400s, although some scholars place him a few centuries later. Despite arguments about his dating and errors in some of the factual basis of his history, Khorenatsi was instrumental in giving Armenians a sense of belonging that stretches back over two millennia or more. He was the first to write the entire history of the Armenians—from the beginning to his purported present time—in a systematic manner, with a long and continuous sense of history that was integrated into world civilization and into the biblical narrative. What is fascinating is that he did this *consciously* a thousand years before the "age of nationalism." Khorenatsi's work was read and reread, used and abused, by national historians from the 18th to 20th centuries, and it was internalized by Armenians. In addition to history, Armenians also wrote texts on law, philosophy, the sciences, and religion.

A connection to territory. The Armenians' connection to the land is ingrained in the national myth of origin (as written down by Movses Khorenatsi). It asserts that Armenians are direct descendants of Noah, through his son Japheth. Haik, the father of Armenians, comes from this lineage. He rebelled against Bel, the evil leader of Babylon. Haik, a righteous man, moved from Babylon back to the land of the Ark, where he settled along with his family and followers. But Bel pursued Haik to subjugate him. In the subsequent battle, good won over evil, and Bel was slain. The roots of the Armenian nation were thus established in the same location as where Noah's Ark landed, on Mount Ararat, the national symbol of Armenians. Of course, in addition to the myth, Armenians had also very tangible connections to the land, as peasants, as landowners, and as builders who had

---

Mount Ararat

The twin peaks of Mount Ararat (or *Massis* in Armenian) is one of the "core" symbols of Armenians, situated at the heart of historic Armenia. The majestic sight of the mountain (5,165 meters or 16,945 feet) is clearly visible from the Armenian capital, Yerevan.

According to the biblical narrative, Noah's Ark landed on Mount Ararat, making the region the "cradle of civilization" and Armenia a "chosen land." The image of the mountain is a national symbol, appearing on everything from the republic's coat of arms to the living rooms of many diaspora Armenians.

Mount Ararat also has a special place in Armenian nationalism. It is a daily remainder of Armenian irredentism and claims against Turkey. Clearly visible from Armenia, it is nevertheless on the Turkish side of the border and therefore inaccessible to Armenians.

---

continually constructed innumerable churches, cathedrals, and forts on the Armenian Plateau.

The Modern Period

The characteristics from the classical period remained but were augmented or transformed by other features that came to define what it meant to be Armenian in the modern period. Between the 18th and 20th centuries, Armenian collective identity changed profoundly, from a traditional ethno-religious sense of belonging to a modern national identity based on ethnic roots. This transformation is referred to as the *zartonk* by the Armenians (i.e., the awakening or renaissance).

National rights. The demand for national rights became an important part of Armenian identity. The cultural and political movement that emerged had two overall objectives: the modernization of the nation (along the lines of European enlightenment), and its emancipation from Ottoman and Russian rule (i.e., political rights, the betterment of social conditions, land and tax reform, etc.). The ethno-national collective was a "given"—Armenians were a distinct people—but they now demanded modern rights. This process of liberation became an important defining moment for modern Armenians. Some of its constituent elements were the adoption of the *Polozhenie* law (decree) by the Russian empire in 1836 that gave the Armenian Church certain autonomy and rights, the establishment of schools with modern curricula, the writing of vernacular literature, the enactment of some church reforms, the establishment of political and revolutionary parties, the dissemination of nationalist and progressive ideologies, and so forth. In short, the demand and mobilization for national rights transformed an ethno-religious community into a modern nation.

A divided nation. The Armenian renaissance was a pan-national process, but there was a schism within the nation because the nation was divided between empires. The east-west division of Armenia (between Russian and Ottoman empires) affected the evolution of modern national identity. For example, two vernaculars emerged (eastern and western Armenian), two literary traditions (romantic and realist), two sets of political ideologies (radical and liberal). This pattern of duality has come to define "Armenianness" in the modern period, and some of its elements are currently manifested in Armenia-diaspora differences.

The formation of a vernacular language. By the beginning of the modern era, classical Armenian was not used as a daily language. It was the language of the church, and known by a few intellectuals. Ordinary people mostly spoke their local dialect or Turkish in the Ottoman Empire. The establishment of a common vernacular thus became an important objective of intellectuals. By the end of the 19th century, a modern vernacular Armenian had emerged and was being taught in schools and used in publications. However, this vernacular had two branches, eastern and western. They were mutually comprehensible and used the same alphabet, but certain grammar rules, declinations, and pronunciations were different, and remain so to this day.

The central role of the diaspora. As one of the "paradigmatic" diasporas, Armenians outside of the homeland played a central role in the reformulation of modern national identity. Be it the merchants in India or the Catholic monks in Venice, diasporans not only contributed to but shaped the definition of the nation. Diasporan communities acted (and still act) as filters through which new ideas entered national consciousness, as "representatives" of the nation, and as nonstate actors who defined nationality in ways that were community or culture centered as opposed to state centered. Currently, more Armenians live in the diaspora than in the homeland.

The genocide. The 1915 extermination of practically all Armenians from their historic homeland in the Ottoman Empire constitutes the most important defining characteristic of modern Armenian identity. Armenians had fled into exile for centuries at moments of severe persecution (e.g., at the fall of kingdoms in AD 1045 and 1375), but the 1915 genocide was the total elimination of the nation from most of its land. Some 1 to 1.5 million Armenians were killed, and the few hundred thousand survivors became refugees with no possibility of return. A deep sense of loss, of being uprooted, of injustice, and of anti-Turkishness entered Armenian collective identity. Moreover, the genocide became a paradigm through which politics was and is understood, conflict analyzed (especially over Gharabagh), and identity shaped. Most Armenians today would define their nation as a "genocided" people.

The Genocide

There were some 2 million Armenians in the Ottoman Empire in 1914. By 1923, only some 70,000 remained in what became the Turkish Republic. The Young Turk regime of the empire had decided to eliminate the Armenians from their historic territories. The result was the murder of 1–1.5 million Armenians. The few hundred thousand that survived in the deserts of Syria eventually became the backbone of the modern Armenian diaspora in the Middle East, Europe, and North America. The genocide itself became a central marker of Armenian national identity.

Armenians were eliminated for various reasons: the Young Turk ideology of creating a homogenous empire, fear of Armenian separatism, resistance to Ottoman (mis)rule, usurpation of Armenian lands and wealth, wartime contingencies, and so forth. Experts continue to debate these and related issues, but the genocide is an accepted fact in mainstream historiography. However, successive Turkish governments and a small group of Western academic sympathizers deny that the elimination of the Armenians constituted a genocide.

Currently, the recognition of the Armenian genocide and its denial have become a political issue. The Armenian diaspora advocates for its recognition by various governments —and some 25 countries have formally recognized it—while the Turkish government and its supporters abroad counter these efforts. Genocide recognition will remain an important issue for both Armenian and Turkish nationalism in the foreseeable future, especially in light of negotiations on Turkey's accession to the European Union.

Armenian orphans board barges bound for Greece at Constantinople, ca. 1915. The genocide of Armenians under Ottoman rule during World War I left thousands of orphans,
many of whom eventually left Turkey through international humanitarian aid programs.
(Library of Congress)

These 9 characteristics define the Armenian nation at the beginning of the
21st century. For part of the 20th century, a 10th characteristic was notable as
well: being a Soviet nation (from 1921 to 1991). With the emergence of the nationalist movement in the late 1980s and the subsequent collapse of the Union of
Soviet Socialist Republics, this characteristic is no longer prominent, although
the effects of Soviet rule persist in Armenia.

A nation of some 8 million people, about 3 million of whom live in the newly
independent post-Soviet state, Armenians are constantly battling not to lose
their distinct culture, identity, and the newly established independent statehood.
A powerful sense of ethnic identity permeates most Armenians, giving them a
clear overarching sense of nationality despite many internal divisions.

Narrating the Nation

The Armenian nation is "narrated" through a rich web of historical and contemporary "stories." These can be divided into four categories.

First, the historical narration evolves around key moments in Armenian history and the geographical locations associated with them (mountains, valleys,
ancient towns, etc.). The mythical founding moment of the nation is the story of

The Gharabagh Conflict

Nagorno-Karabakh (NK), Gharabagh, or Artsakh, in Armenian, is an Armenian-populated region (4,400 square kilometers) that was put under the authority of Azerbaijan in 1923 (as an autonomous oblast) by the Soviet regime. Beginning in the late 1920s, Armenians demanded that the region be transferred to the Armenian SSR (Soviet Socialist Republic). Their arguments were based on historical considerations, population figures (Armenians were an overwhelming majority in the region), economic maldevelopment, and cultural persecution (lack of Armenian schools, newspapers, and churches in NK). Moscow and Baku rejected all such claims.

In the context of Gorbachev's *perestroika* and *glasnost*, Armenians in the republic—and subsequently in the diaspora—mobilized en masse to support the transfer. The spark that ignited the movement was the NK Soviet's vote in February 1988 to join the Armenian SSR. Within days there were million-strong demonstrations in Yerevan, the capital of Armenia, in support of NK, and counterdemonstrations and riots in Azerbaijan. Soon violence erupted between the two communities, leading to the expulsion of Armenians from Azerbaijan (except in NK where there was resistance) and Azerbaijanis from Armenia. The violence became a full-scale war after the two republics became independent in 1991 upon the collapse of the Union of Soviet Socialist Republics.

A cease-fire was signed in 1994, which still holds. However, there is no peace agreement despite various attempts and international mediation (mostly by the Organisation for Security and Co-operation in Europe, OSCE). Armenians won the war as they took complete control of NK and territories around it, including the Lachin corridor that links NK to Armenia. Armenian forces have expelled all Azerbaijanis from these lands, displacing hundreds of thousands of people. The current population of Gharabagh is estimated to be around 100,000, nearly 100 percent Armenian.

The Gharabagh movement heightened both Armenian and Azerbaijani nationalism and swept from power the Communist leadership in both countries. The leaders of the Gharabagh movement became the leaders of post-Soviet Armenia.

Haik and Bel, as told above. Some people go as far as dating the story as a historical fact (2492 BC). This is followed by the conversion to Christianity in the early 4th century. "Being the first Christian nation"—a fact proudly asserted by most Armenians —gave Armenians a powerful claim to be a "chosen people" (the textual basis of this notion was already set in the 5th century by the Armenian historian Agathangelos, who wrote that Armenia was "where God's grace has been manifested"). The "revelation" of the Armenian alphabet in the 5th century is another important narrative. More recently, the narrative included the works of the radical intellectuals of the 18th and especially the 19th centuries who advocated liberation (e.g., Raffi), and revolutionary heroes who fought and died for the nation. Armenian political parties founded in the 19th century have their respective "pool" of heroes whom they celebrate and whose deeds they commemorate. Finally, the most important narrative since 1915 is the genocide itself—more specifically, the injustice suffered, the losses endured, and the will to survive.

The second category of narration is the Soviet one, emanating from the Soviet Republic. In this case, the overarching story is one of building the nation, materially and culturally. Modernization and industrialization were an intricate part of this narrative, as well as the cultural heights attained by Soviet Armenian intellectuals and artists, especially after Stalin's death. These included the musician Aram Khachaturian, the painter Martiros Saryan, the poets Yeghishe Charents, Paruir Sevak, and others. This "nation-building" narrative articulated by the Soviets was eventually accepted by almost all Armenians by the 1970s. The former first secretary of Soviet Armenia, Karen Demirchian put it thus (in an interview with the author):

> The Communists first saved Armenia from guaranteed destruction in 1920. They took it out of the mouth of the lion or the crocodile and saved it. . . . We [i.e., the Communists] prepared the country for independence, to be a strong republic. Hence, we did two things: (a) kept national identity unique and developed it further, and (b) built a strong economic base; we developed the country.

This had become a widely held view, part of the national narrative, by the 1980s, and still persists.

The third category is the narrative within the postgenocide diaspora. It oscillated between the narrative of exile, persecution, and assimilation, on the one hand, and defiance, the will to survive, and a vague conception of "return," on the other. It included the notion of "building up" communities—churches, community centers, and schools—and the necessary mobilization for this. The diasporan narrative celebrated past greatness, the inalienability of the "lost lands" in Turkey, and the drive to seek justice for the genocide (which even included certain terrorist acts against Turkish diplomats and interests between 1975 and 1985). It also included pride in the success of Armenians around the world, particularly emphasizing the Armenian heritage of famous individuals (e.g., Charles Aznavour in France, Kirk Kerkorian in the United States).

Finally, the post-Soviet narrative has been one of survival in the face of hardship. The 1988 earthquake, which killed at least 25,000 Armenians, the 1990–1994 war against Azerbaijan over Gharabagh (an Armenian-populated enclave—formally known as Nagorno-Karabakh—within the Azerbaijani SSR (Soviet Socialist Republic) that voted to secede from Azerbaijan in 1988), the economic collapse, and the political turmoil fed into the Armenians-as-victims narrative. But this coexisted with a new narrative that emerged, one of Armenians-as-victors. The military triumph in the Gharabagh war, sustaining and then building up the country despite economic blockades, and maintaining a relatively stable and a semi-democratic political system contributed to this narrative of success.

Historians, intellectuals, public figures, and cultural workers play a key role in the articulation of narratives. They tie the various "stories," ideas, and belief systems into a "coherent" whole. What is incredible in the Armenian case is the historical depth of this process and the remarkable stability of many aspects of the "master narrative." Some 1,500 years ago, Movses Khorenatsi wrote, "Even though we are a small people, limited in numbers and weak in power, frequently subjugated by others, nevertheless great acts of courage have taken place in our land that are worthy to be recorded in writing and remembered." This thinking still guides the narrative of Armenians and gives them the impetus to remain distinct and to survive as a nation.

The section below further explains the historical bases of these narratives.

Mobilizing and Building the Nation

In the modern period, there have been four distinct episodes of mobilizing the Armenian nation. These mobilization efforts provided new foundations for instituting the nation, in line with modern conceptions of nationhood.

The first is the mobilization efforts of the 18th and 19th centuries. The aim of these efforts was to transform a traditional ethno-religious identity into a modern nationality, free to rule itself. It included much intellectual and organizational work, as well as limited revolutionary activities. In the latter part of the 19th century, Armenians started to establish political parties and various other secular institutions to advance and protect national rights and identity. For example, three important national political parties were established in this period: the Armenian Revolutionary Federation (*Dashnaks*), the Democratic Liberal Party (*Ramkavars*), and the Social Democrat Hnchakian Party (*Hnchaks*). After Armenia's Sovietization in the early 1920s, these parties became exclusively diasporan bodies, playing an active role in the institutionalization of Armenian communities in many parts of the world. They are still active in the diaspora and "returned" to post-Soviet Armenia in 1990–1991 (*Dashnaks* being the most influential among them).

The second episode is the Soviet mobilization to create a Soviet society in what used to be Russian Armenia. It entailed forced modernization and industrialization, ideological indoctrination, but also—ironically—the strengthening of national identity through the reinforcement of Armenian culture. The Soviet federal constitution formally institutionalized republics based on nationality, Armenia being one of the 15 SSRs. This meant that the Armenian SSR could develop "national" institutions within the confines of the Soviet system, particularly after Stalin. Hence, the usual Soviet mobilization instruments (mass media, propaganda drives, education, youth engagement, historiography, cultural production, political debate, policy making, etc.) took place within a specific national context, and mostly in the Armenian language. Importantly, in the mid-1960s, Soviet Armenia also established a distinct institution to manage relations with the diaspora—the Committee for Cultural Relations with Diaspora Armenians. Needless to say, instituting national identity had to be done within the overall dynamics of the Union of Soviet Socialist Republics.

Third, a parallel process of mobilization was taking place in the diaspora throughout the 20th century, except, in this case, instead of creating a Soviet society, a diasporan nation was being forged with its own institutions and intellectuals, mostly cut off from the Sovietized "homeland." The diasporan stateless nation-building emphasized the maintenance of identity and the strengthening of community structures—and it produced some very tangible institutions: churches and schools in cities where there were sizable Armenian communities, media outlets (newspapers, radio, TV programs), and more recently, significant Web-based virtual "communities." These formal institutions, along with informal networks, were both the result of diasporan mobilization and contributions to it, further strengthening national identity (of course, this is only one side of the equation; modern diasporas by their very nature are also malleable entities, constantly in flux, subject to the policies of host states, and prone to assimilation). In terms of politics, once some diasporan communities reached a certain level of political stability internally, they began to mobilize—on the whole successfully—for the recognition of the Armenian genocide by the world community. After 1988, the diaspora also mobilized significantly in support of Armenia and Gharabagh.

The final mobilization episode is that of the nationalist movement in the Armenian SSR and the post-Soviet politics it led to, including the massive mobilization to win the Gharabagh war. This episode began in earnest in February 1988, when close to a million Armenians protested in the streets of Yerevan in support of Gharabagh's unification with Armenia. In the ensuing turmoil, the Communists were swept from office, and power was assumed by nationalist leaders. When the conflict became a full-fledged war (fought within Azerbaijan, Gharabagh, and some border regions of Armenia), practically the entire population in Armenia, and a good part of the diaspora, mobilized to support the military defense of the enclave. The aim of this mobilization was to unite Gharabagh with Armenia. Armenians defeated Azerbaijan and took control of Gharabagh, as well as land around it. Gharabagh has become part of Armenia de facto, but not de jure; it is a self-declared (but internationally unrecognized) independent republic of some 100,000 people. One of the important consequences of the 1990s mobilization was the expulsion of all Azerbaijanis from Armenia and the further homogenization of the republic—from being 90 percent Armenian in the late 1980s to 98 percent Armenian by the mid-1990s.

The 1988 mobilization refocused Armenian nationalism from the "lost lands" of historic Armenia (in eastern Turkey) to the Gharabagh conflict. Genocide recognition and claims against Turkey remained important—particularly in the diaspora —but the more pressing problem of Gharabagh's security and the strengthening of Armenia's statehood took center stage. Real, immediate, and even grave military, political, and economic problems had to be addressed, and Armenians everywhere rallied to overcome these difficulties.

Armenia acquired independence in 1991 when the Union of Soviet Socialist Republics collapsed due to its internal contradictions, most notably the tensions emanating from its "nationalities problem," including the Armenian-Azerbaijani conflict. The republics that emerged from the defunct Soviet Union inherited institutions that were far from perfect, nearly bankrupt, and fraught with inefficiencies if not dysfunctional. Nevertheless, these Soviet state structures did provide some sort of an institutional framework around which the post-Soviet nation and state could be built (or at least sustained): the Armenian Supreme Soviet became the parliament, the function of the first secretary was assumed by a presidency, communist institutions were transformed into national ones, and the military was built relatively easily with the assets left behind by the Soviet Army. The Academy of Sciences, universities, and schools all went through transformations but continued to function within Armenia, retaining their nation-building roles (minus the communist ideology).

However, in addition to the "normal" problems of post-Soviet societies, Armenia faced serious additional challenges associated with war, blockades, severe energy shortages, and near-total economic collapse. Post-Soviet challenges had to do more with survival than with nation- or state-building, at least in the early 1990s. But once the Gharabagh war came to an end in 1994, collective efforts could be directed toward nation-building goals: maintaining a strong military to defend the security of Gharabagh, economic growth based on market-oriented policies and foreign investment (much of it from or through diaspora Armenians), a political system based on democratic principles, the reinforcement of national culture, and a balanced foreign policy. Of course, important challenges remain: a structurally weak economy, prevalent corruption, and a political elite whose legitimacy is questioned due to election fraud and informal power relations.

As an independent state, Armenia has managed to maintain very good relations with Russia; the two countries are particularly close in their military cooperation (Russia has military bases and border guards in Armenia). Similarly, good relations are maintained with Iran (in the early 1990s, Armenia's only open land border was with Iran), and there is brisk trade between the two countries. Relations with Georgia, in the north, are friendly and cordial despite certain differences in the strategic visions of the two countries—relations between Russia and Georgia are often tense—and despite the occasional flare-up of tensions between the Armenians of the Javakh (a region in southern Georgia on the Armenian border) and Georgian authorities.

Armenia has also maintained very good relations with the United States, particularly in the domain of foreign aid and economic ties; the role of the Armenian diaspora in the United States has been particularly important in the evolution and maintenance of this relationship. Relations are antagonistic with Azerbaijan, and their improvement is not very likely in the short term; in fact, the resumption of hostilities remains a possibility in the absence of a peace agreement. Relations with Turkey are frosty—formally nonexistent. Armenia's borders with these two countries are closed, even though Armenia has made it clear that it would like to have an open border and normal relations with Turkey. Because of Armenia's closed eastern and western borders, South Caucasian economic integration has been difficult. Important economic initiatives, such as the oil pipeline between Azerbaijan and Turkey, have consequently bypassed Armenia.

Armenia-diaspora relations have been generally positive since independence (with the exception of a few years in the mid-1990s due to political tensions). As mentioned, the diaspora has played a crucial role—formally and informally (e.g., foreign investment and family-to-family transfer of funds)—in the sustenance of Armenia's economy; in some communities (e.g., the United States and France), it has also been a critical factor in the political mobilization in favor of the republic.

In conclusion, the Armenian nation has been in the making for millennia. The roots of the modern nation go back at least 2,500 years, when Armenians were first mentioned. Major "moments" of nation-building have occurred in the 4th and 5th centuries, in the 18th and 19th centuries, as well as at other key junctures throughout history. Nation-building continued in the 20th century, and still continues—both in Armenia and in the diaspora.

After Armenia's independence in 1991 and the cease-fire in the Gharabagh war in 1994, the intensity of Armenian nationalism somewhat dissipated, as Armenian politics entered a period of "normalcy" with predictable dynamics and patterns. Three important elements constitute contemporary Armenian nationalism. The first is the strengthening of the statehood of the Armenian Republic and Gharabagh (i.e., their institutions, economic development, military capacity, and political impact). The second is the maintenance and strengthening of national identity in the diaspora, and building up diasporan institutions where these are weak (e.g., in Russia). The third is the continuing advocacy for the recognition of the Armenian genocide by the world community, and ultimately by the Turkish government. These three overall elements encapsulate the dynamics of Armenian nationalism in the first decade of the 21st century. Of course, the balance between the three elements shifts based on circumstance and need.

Finally, it should be noted that the above nation-building processes and dynamics are taking place outside of historic Western Armenia, where the bulk of the Armenian population lived up to 1915. On those lands, the nation has died.

Selected Bibliography

Bakalian, A. 1993. *Armenian-Americans: From Being to Feeling Armenian.* New Brunswick, NJ: Transaction Publishers.

Bournoutian, G. 2006. *Concise History of the Armenian People: From Ancient Times to the Present.* 5th and rev. ed. Costa Mesa, CA: Mazda Press.

Chorbajian, L., ed. 2001. *The Making of Nagorno-Karabagh: From Secession to Republic.* Basingstoke, UK: Palgrave.

Dadrian, V. 1995. *The History of the Armenian Genocide: Ethnic Conflict from the Balkans to Anatolia to the Caucasus.* Oxford/Providence, RI: Berghahn Books.

Hovannisian, R., ed. 1997. *The Armenian People from Ancient to Modern Times.* 2 vols. New York: St. Martin's Press.

Kévorkian, R., and P. Paboudjian. 1992. *Les Arméniens dans l'empire ottoman à la veille du génocide.* Paris: Les Editions d'Art et d'Histoire ARHIS.

Libaridian. G. J. 2004. *Modern Armenia: People, Nation, State.* New Brunswick, NJ: Transaction Publishers.

Malkasian, M. 1996. *"Gha-ra-bagh!" The Emergence of the National Democratic Movement in Armenia.* Detroit: Wayne State University Press.

Mouradian, C. 1990. *De Staline à Gorbatchev. Histoire d'une république soviétique: l'Arménie.* Paris: Editions Ramsay.

Panossian, R. 2006. *The Armenians: From Kings and Priests to Merchants and Commissars.* New York/London: Columbia University Press/Hurst.

Redgate, A. E. 1998. *The Armenians.* Oxford: Blackwell.

Suny, R. G. 1993. *Looking toward Ararat. Armenia in Modern History.* Bloomington: Indiana University Press.

Walker, C. 1990. *Armenia: The Survival of a Nation.* 2nd ed. New York: St. Martin's Press.

Azerbaijan

Shannon O'Lear

Chronology

1918 The independent state of the Azerbaijan Democratic Republic is established following the collapse of an independent Transcaucasian democratic federative republic.

1920 The Soviet authority is established; Azerbaijan becomes a member of the Soviet Union in 1922.

1988 Karabakh Armenians seek to have authority over their autonomous region shifted from Azerbaijan to Armenia. When that effort fails, they vote by a majority to secede from Azerbaijan as an independent region altogether. Tensions between Karabakh Armenians and Azerbaijan increase.

1990 Tensions between Azeris and Armenians in several locations in Azerbaijan increase to the point that Gorbachev declares a state of emergency and sends troops in to the area. These events become known as Black January.

1991 Azerbaijan regains independence when the Soviet Union collapses.

1992 Abulfaz Elchibey is elected as Azerbaijan's first new, post-Soviet president and focuses on his ambition of creating a single, unified state for the Azerbaijani people. Several hundred Azerbaijani civilians are killed during a one-night massacre in the town of Khojali, where Armenians took over the only airport in the region and thereby gained a stronghold in the Nagorno-Karabakh region.

1993 Heidar Aliyev, the deputy speaker of the parliament and Communist leader of Azerbaijan during the Brezhnev era, is elected president.

1994 President Aliyev signs the "Contract of the Century," creating opportunities for international investment in Azerbaijan's oil sector and allowing the long-established oil industry to expand.

2003 Ilham Aliyev, Heidar Aliyev's son, becomes president in elections that international observers declare as flawed; public protest and violence erupt following these elections.

2005 The Baku-Tbilisi-Ceyhan oil pipeline, constructed by an international consortium and supported by the United States, officially opens. There is speculation that this pipeline is likely to influence geopolitics by shaping relationships among different countries and interests in the region.

Situating the Nation

Since its independence in 1991, Azerbaijan has maintained a secular Muslim identity, expanded international links in its oil industry, and fostered a national identity that reflects multiple layers of history in a complex place.

Azerbaijan is located along the Caucasus Mountains that form an east-west bridge between the Black Sea and the Caspian Sea. Previously a southernmost border area of the Soviet Union, Azerbaijan and its Caucasus neighbors, Georgia

and Armenia, now look westward toward such European organizations as the Council of Europe while adjusting relationships with still-powerful Russia. Azerbaijan is also one of five countries that border the Caspian Sea. The Caspian Sea basin area has proven to be rich in petroleum and natural gas. Azerbaijan's situation could allow Azerbaijan to take advantage of this resource wealth as long as it is able to export oil. Despite this potential resource wealth, Azerbaijan's future is far from settled.

The notion of an Azerbaijani national identity first emerged during a brief period of independent statehood for Azerbaijan in 1918. In less than two years, the Soviets overtook Azerbaijan and, with some adjustments to its territorial borders, incorporated the land of Azerbaijan into the Soviet Union as one of 15 nationality-based republics. Azerbaijan became an independent state once again when the Soviet Union disintegrated.

Geopolitically, Azerbaijan has been at the heart of the historical "Great Game" of territorial rivalry among Russia, Turkey, and Iran. Within the Caucasus land bridge, Azerbaijan is part of a crossroads between north and south, and between east and west. Azerbaijan is on the periphery—both geographic and figurative—of Russia's realm of influence and is at the edge of post-Soviet identification as a superpower. Although there is not a large population of ethnic Russians in the Caucasus, economic and geopolitical factors continue to attract Russia's attention to this region. Azerbaijan's oil wealth, Azerbaijan's possible role as an entry way for radical Islam in the region, and Azerbaijan's ongoing territorial conflict with Armenians who themselves are fellow ex-Soviet citizens, place Azerbaijan squarely on Russia's geopolitical map. Although Azerbaijan returned to the Commonwealth of Independent States (CIS) following a brief withdrawal, Azerbaijan strives to assert a distinct national identity from its former colonizer.

Instituting the Nation

Legacy and Leadership

Even before the disintegration of the Soviet Union, the threat of territorial loss to an Armenian population in the Nagorno-Karabakh conflict inspired nationalistic cohesion among Azerbaijanis, particularly in the late 1980s. Responding to such nationalist sentiment, the first elected president in Azerbaijan following the Soviet collapse, Abulfaz Elchibey, promoted a political platform that included a refusal to join the Russian-led CIS and a refusal to surrender any of Azerbaijan's sovereignty over the Armenian-declared Nagorno-Karabakh Autonomous Region.

Although Elchibey's government did not last very long, territorial integrity in regard to Nagorno-Karabakh remained a priority for Heidar Aliyev's administration, which came to power in 1993 and lasted for 10 years. Aliyev had experience as a former KGB officer and as the Communist Party head of the Azerbaijan Soviet Socialist Republic (SSR) under Brezhnev. Aliyev and his New Azerbaijan Party (Yeni Azerbaycan) wielded strong control over the government, the oil industry, and other key sectors of the economy. President Aliyev's strategy for building stability and independence centered on forging strong links with the West. Most significantly, in 1994, President Aliyev enacted the "Contract of the Century," which opened up opportunities for international investment in Azerbaijan's oil sector. Under Aliyev's presidency, Azerbaijan boosted its presence in the international oil industry, privatized its economy, and joined organizations, including the CIS, the Council of Europe, and the North Atlantic Treaty Organization's (NATO) Partnership for Peace Program. Yet Aliyev's centralization of personal power put in place a simultaneous obstacle to democracy-building. The enduring legacy of Aliyev's concentration of power raises questions about how much progress Azerbaijan is making toward becoming a democratic state.

In October of 2003, amid election-day riots that captured world media attention, Heidar Aliyev's son, Ilham, became president of Azerbaijan. Although it is too early to assess how much this administration will alter the course of the country, there is yet little evidence that Ilham Aliyev is challenging the regime that his father established, and there remains some concern about how much the material and political lives of the Azerbaijani population will change under the current leadership.

Current Social Issues in Azerbaijan

Internally Displaced Persons

Internally displaced persons from the Gharabagh conflict with Armenia are a concern for Azerbaijan, as well as for the international community, since they depend directly on state and donor assistance. A result of the ongoing territorial dispute between Azerbaijanis and Armenians is that one in seven Azerbaijani citizens is an internally displaced person. Most of these people are surviving in makeshift camps, railroad cars, and other difficult conditions. A serious issue for Azerbaijan's future is the fact that many of these people are children who have no access to regular schooling and education.

Islam in Azerbaijan

Over 90 percent of the population of Azerbaijan is Muslim (Shia), and there is a growing number of mosques. Azerbaijan's approach to Islam, however, is predominantly secular.

United Nations Educational, Scientific and Cultural Organization (UNESCO) World Heritage Site: Walled City of Baku with the Shirvanshah's Palace and Maiden Tower

Recognized as treasures of a part of present-day Baku, inhabited continuously since the Paleolithic period, the ancient Walled City shows evidence of successive Zoroastrian, Sasanian, Arabic, Persian, Shirvani, Ottoman, and Russian cultures. At risk from the effects of an earthquake in 2000, urban development, and limited conservation policies, the Walled City and the Maiden Tower represent a rare representation of multiple urban architectural styles (http://whc.unesco.org/pg.cfm?cid=31&id_site=958).

Defining the Nation

Language and Identity

Before 1918, the place currently referred to as Azerbaijan was called Caspia-Albania by the Romans and Arran in Persian. Other names that people have called the area include Caucasian Albania and Shirvan. The people of Azerbaijan represent several ethnic groups, including Airums, Karapapakhs, Padars, Shahsevens, Karadags and Afshars. Turkic immigrations into the area contributed to present-day Azeri identity, and Mongol and Indo-European influences shaped Azeri language and culture.

When the Soviet Union annexed Azerbaijan's territory, Soviet leaders took a dual approach to Azerbaijan's identity. On the one hand, Soviet ideology promoted internationalist education and the virtues of socialism in their construction of the "Soviet man" identity. On the other hand, the Soviets claimed that their government comprised a voluntary union of independent, nationality-based states. For this reason, the Soviet leadership needed to create specific national identities to fill the republics that it was establishing. Additionally, Soviet leaders aimed to distinguish and distance the subjugated peoples from each other while increasing their dependence on a centralized Soviet state.

One author has argued that Soviets generated national "myths" as a foundation for several national groups identified within the Soviet Union, and that such myths have played an essential role in shaping Azerbaijan's view of its history (Hunter 1994). One such idea is that Azerbaijan, the birthplace of Zoraster, is a 5,000-year-old country rooted in the ancient kingdom of Albania. Another key ingredient of Azeri identity, according to Hunter, is that between 1813 and 1828, negotiations between czarist Russia and Iran (a Persian empire at the time) led to a joint conspiracy to divide Azerbaijan into two parts to prevent Azerbaijan's Turkic culture from flourishing. Hunter argues that this is an artificial myth created by the Soviets to serve their political agenda. However, other scholars offer alternative perspectives. One view is that a shared Azerbaijani identity gained momentum in the early 1900s as a result of economic cohesion and the rise of an intelligentsia that was brought about by Russian influence. Simultaneously, Islamic, Persian, and Turkic aspects of the shared identity reinforced a desire for political autonomy. Another view suggests that common, albeit differentiated, Azeri identity on both sides of the Azerbaijan-Iran border provides strong evidence supporting the reality of an ethnic identity shared by people in both countries. Whether or not national "myths" are rooted in historical fact, interpretation, or invention is a question that has led to much academic debate. However, various strands of stories and belief that weave together the fabric of identity and the relationship of that identity to a particular place are important and valuable in their own right for any national identity. The strength of a national identity lies most significantly in its very persistence, maintenance, and promotion by various interests.

Language, usually a key element of a nation, is particularly complex in the case of Azerbaijan. The Azeri language is of Turkic origin and, together with other Turkic languages, is part of the Altaic branch of languages. Persian remained the common language in the countryside, whereas people in urban areas spoke in Russian and Azeri prior to Soviet incorporation of the area. Following Soviet-era Russification and the dominant use of the Russian language in education and official business throughout the Soviet era, Russian remains a common language in Azerbaijan, particularly in urban areas. In recent years, the government of Azerbaijan declared that Azeri, and not Russian, is the official language of the government, thus challenging many government officials to enhance their Azeri language skills. However, Azerbaijan blends its Soviet past with its own national identity in other ways. For example, official state holidays include such Soviet-era holidays as Women's Day (March 8) and Victory in World War II Day (May 9), along with holidays specific to Azerbaijan identity: *Novruz Bayrami* (Holiday of Spring) (March 21), Republic Day (May 28), and Day of Solidarity of Azerbaijanis throughout the World (December 31).

Language is often a cohesive feature of national identity, so it is important to recognize that the alphabet of Azerbaijan has changed four times in the last 100 years. At the beginning of the 20th century, people used the Arabic alphabet to write the Azeri language. Then, in 1929, the government of the Azerbaijani SSR introduced a Latin alphabet. Within 10 years, the Soviets forced the use of the Cyrillic alphabet, bringing about another alphabet change. Following the collapse of the Soviet Union and Azerbaijani's independence in the early 1990s, the government of Azerbaijan reintroduced a Latin alphabet for the Azeri language. These frequent and dramatic changes in alphabet effectively rendered large groups of people illiterate at particular times and limited the potential for communication through mainstream newspapers, books, government forms, and public signs on the landscape. The discontinuity of alphabet usage in Azerbaijan has challenged a sense of shared identity and distinctive culture among generations. However, the government's current promotion of the Azeri language suggests a renewed sense of identity and a sense of place.

Narrating the Nation

The Role of Nagorno-Karabakh

It would be remiss to assess present-day Azerbaijani nationalism without recognizing the role of the Nagorno-Karabakh conflict. This dispute between Armenians and Azerbaijanis, similar to other conflicts throughout the newly independent republics of the former Soviet Union, involves several contentious factors, including religion, ethnicity, and a legacy of Soviet borders and institutions. Azerbaijanis and Armenians construct and communicate public narratives of the conflict based on different elements. The predominant Armenian view emphasizes a struggle for national survival justified by a claim to a shared history of genocide during World War I. The Armenian focus tends to be centered on the Armenian people. The mainstream Azerbaijani perspective of the conflict centers, instead, on the importance of abiding by international standards of territorial integrity. The scale of focus for Azerbaijanis is the state. Azeris claim that Armenians in the Nagorno-Karabakh region and in surrounding areas are occupying between 14 and 20 percent of Azerbaijani territory, depending on the source. From the Azerbaijani standpoint, Nagorno-Karabakh is a matter framed in terms of sovereignty, the inviolability of borders, and territorial integrity.

There are differing accounts of when Armenians came to be in the region known as Nagorno-Karabakh, but the Soviets drew the borders of present-day Armenia and Azerbaijan in the 1920s, when they forcibly annexed both independent states into the Soviet Union. The Soviet Union drew the boundaries of the Armenian and Azerbaijani SSRs such that Armenians in Nagorno-Karabakh, officially part of the Azerbaijani SSR, were separate from the main population in the Armenian SSR. Similarly, the Azeris of Nakhchivan, also officially part of the Azerbaijani SSR, were separate from the main population in the Azerbaijani SSR. This interlaced demarcation of boundaries and division of peoples gave the Soviets leverage as the central authority over both groups.

The Soviets granted the area of Nagorno-Karabakh the special status of Autonomous Oblast (region) within the Soviet Union to recognize the Armenian majority there. The Karabakh Armenians' declarations, first of their desire to be united with Armenia and then of their move toward independent government in 1988, are generally recognized as the first of several events, including violence in Sumgait, Baku, and elsewhere, that led to the disintegration of relative stability. At no point during this conflict has Armenia formally been at war with Azerbaijan, but the involvement of Armenian troops renders the Nagorno-Karabakh situation an international armed conflict by the standards of the Geneva Convention.

Viewed by some as a third party to the conflict, Nagorno-Karabakh identifies itself as an independent state, has an elected president, and claims that it should be included in the resolution negotiation process. The international community, including Armenia, has not recognized Nagorno-Karabakh as an independent state. Azerbaijan's leadership is reluctant to bestow any legitimacy on Nagorno-Karabakh's claim to Azerbaijan's internationally recognized territory by accepting Nagorno-Karabakh as a viable player in the negotiation process.

Since the 1994 cease-fire, the death toll from this conflict has declined significantly, but the conflict remains unresolved. The conflict has led to negative economic impacts, displaced persons, and troops killed on all sides. The critical obstacle to resolving the Nagorno-Karabakh conflict is that each side views the problem in absolute, territorial terms, yet territory does not hold a universal meaning. Each party to the conflict values the physical territory differently through associations with political, historical, and even future meaning. For Azerbaijan, the conflict represents a challenge to sovereign control over territory and, as such, is a threat to the well-being of the Azerbaijani state. The frozen Karabakh conflict maintains a presence in mainstream media, and the presence of internally displaced persons (IDP) in cities, towns, villages, and IDP camps sustains public awareness of the unresolved situation. One faction favors reclaiming Karabakh militarily. These different forms of attention paid to IDPs and to the frozen conflict serve to unify a sense among Azerbaijanis that one of the most significant issues they face as a nation is overcoming the threat to their national territorial integrity.

Mobilizing and Building the Nation

Oil in Azerbaijan

Since its independence following the Soviet collapse in 1991, Azerbaijan has rapidly expanded its oil industry and is poised to continue to do so. However, the simultaneous unfolding of oil development and modern state-building pose a particular challenge for this young state. Although its oil wealth has allowed Azerbaijan to make some significant political headway in strengthening contact

View of the port of Baku in Azerbaijan, 1998. (Remi Benali/Corbis)

with other countries, the domestic emphasis on oil development has been detrimental to other parts of the economy, since the oil sector does not appear to draw from, build on, or spill over to most other economic sectors.

On September 20, 1994, President Heidar Aliyev signed the "Contract of the Century," which welcomed the investment and technology of major oil companies from other countries to help exploit Azerbaijani oil. This arrangement was a symbolic recognition of Baku as the historical birthplace of the international oil industry and suggested the possibility of post-Soviet political and economic reform in Azerbaijan. President Aliyev himself referred to oil as "the main and richest national wealth of the Azerbaijan Republic and Azerbaijani people."

A significant aspect of Azerbaijan's "Contract of the Century" is that non-Azerbaijani signatories of the contract, many of which are in western Europe and the United States, are to divide 20 percent of the profits among themselves. It was important to President Aliyev that strong links be established with other countries as a way of legitimizing Azerbaijan's sovereignty. A second significant point of the contract is that, at the time the contract was enacted, all five states surrounding the Caspian Sea had not yet come to agreement about how aspects of the resource, such as offshore oilfields, would be shared or divided. By welcoming contracts for exploration and development of oil reserves, most of which are offshore, Aliyev was establishing a claim to those offshore fields as part of Azerbaijan's sovereign territory. Since then, Azerbaijan's oil exports have increased in value and have led to increased income for the country, but the long-term benefits that this income may have for the people of Azerbaijan are not yet certain.

Selected Bibliography

Altstadt, A. L. 1997. "Azerbaijan's Struggle toward Democracy." In *Conflict, Cleavage and Change in Central Asia and the Caucasus*, edited by K. Dawisha and B. Parrot, 110–155. New York: Cambridge University Press.

Croissant, M. P. 1998. *The Armenia-Azerbaijan Conflict: Causes and Implications.* Westport, CT: Praeger.

de Waal, T. 2003. *Black Garden: Armenia and Azerbaijan through Peace and War.* New York: New York University Press.

Helsinki Watch. 1992 (September). *Bloodshed in the Caucasus: Escalation of the Armed Conflict in Nagorno-Karabakh.* New York: Human Rights Watch.

Herzig, E. 1999. *The New Caucasus: Armenia, Azerbaijan and Georgia.* London: The Royal Institute of International Affairs, Chatham House Papers.

Hunter, S. T. 1994. *The Transcaucasus in Transition: Nation-Building and Conflict.* Washington DC: The Center for Strategic and International Studies.

Minahan, J. 1998. *Miniature Empires: A Historical Dictionary of the Newly Independent States.* Westport, CT: Greenwood Press.

O'Lear, S. 2001. "Azerbaijan: Territorial Issues and Internal Challenges in mid-2001." *Post Soviet Geography and Economics* 42:305–312.

Shaffer, B. 2002. *Borders and Brethren: Iran and the Challenge of Azerbaijani Identity.* Cambridge, MA: The MIT Press.

Smith, G. 1999. *The Post-Soviet States: Mapping the Politics of Transition.* London: Arnold.

Swietochowski, T. 1985. *Russian Azerbaijan, 1905–1920: The Shaping of National Identity in a Muslim Community.* Cambridge: Cambridge University Press.

Van der Leeuw, C. 2000. *Azerbaijan: A Quest for Identity.* New York: St. Martin's Press.

Indonesia

Michael Wood

Chronology

1800	The Dutch government takes over the Dutch East India Company's colonial possessions.
1910	Sarekat Islam, the first mass nationalist organization, is formed.
1926–1927	Communist-inspired uprisings in West Java and Sumatra fail.
1928	(October 28) Youth Pledge calls for "one people, one language, one nation."
1930	Sukarno gives a famous speech defining Indonesian nationalism and history.
1933	Sukarno is exiled to Flores and subsequently to Bengkulu, Sumatra.
1942	Japan invades the Dutch East Indies.
1945	(June) Pancasila is formulated. (August 17) Indonesian independence is declared by Sukarno and Mohammad Hatta. (November 11) The Battle of Surabaya starts.
1945–1949	The Indonesian Revolution is waged against Dutch rule.
1950	Indonesia becomes a unitary state.
1955	The first general elections are held.
1957–1959	Rebellions break out in Sumatra and Sulawesi.
1957–1965	Guided Democracy period. Sukarno rules as semi-dictator and engages in a struggle for power with the army and the Communist Party of Indonesia (PKI).
1962–1963	Campaign by Indonesia for Irian Jaya, which becomes part of Indonesia in 1969.
1963–1965	*Konfrontasi* ("Confrontation") aimed at the newly formed state of Malaysia, part of a larger anti-Western campaign.
1965	An attempted coup associated with the "September 30 Movement" leads to the destruction of the PKI, large-scale massacres, and the removal of Sukarno from power.
1968–1998	Suharto is president of Indonesia; he emphasizes economic development and political control. East Timor is invaded and eventually annexed by Indonesia.
1998	The fall of Suharto; B. J. Habibie becomes president.
1999	Referendum leads to violence and eventual independence for East Timor. Abdurrahman Wahid becomes Indonesia's fourth president.
2001	Wahid is replaced as president by Megawati Sukarnoputri.
2002	The Bali bombing, the work of Islamic militants, kills over 200 people.
2004	Susilo Bambang Yudhoyono is elected president of Indonesia in a direct vote.

Situating the Nation

On August 17, 1945, Indonesia was declared independent of Dutch colonial control. This proclamation was the culmination of the work of a group of Indonesians who had been developing the concept of the nation and agitating for independence for decades. Indonesians had the common experience of colonial rule, but this was not a uniform experience. Some peoples and territories were taken over by the Dutch East Indies Company 350 years earlier, while such areas as Bali and Aceh had only been conquered at the turn of the 20th century. The Dutch did not relinquish control of their colony without a struggle; they tried to regain authority over the archipelago through a variety of means, including negotiation and armed intervention. They also tried to co-opt nationalist sentiment through setting up a series of nominally independent Indonesian states that would in fact be beholden to the Dutch Crown. The federal United States of Indonesia, granted sovereignty in December 1949, would in under a year become the unitary Republic of Indonesia. Since that time, federalism has been viewed with suspicion. Indonesia as a unified entity remains perhaps the central element of Indonesian nationalism.

The new nation operated under severe economic constraints. Indonesia was subjected to the successive blows of the Great Depression, the Japanese occupation, and the Indonesian Revolution. In addition, the colonial system itself had not been run for the benefit of Indonesia's native population. The Dutch had exploited the colony's great natural resources but had left little behind in the way of infrastructure. Economic problems remained a constant throughout Indonesia's years of independence. One could in fact argue that Indonesia's biggest challenges were in fact economic. Two were of particular note: the absolute poverty of much of the population and the fact that, while natural resources were concentrated in the Outer Islands, political power and population were concentrated in Java. It could be argued that the political disputes of succeeding decades were basically over how to reform a deeply troubled economy. The Communist Party of Indonesia (PKI) offered a radical Marxist solution. Indonesia's first president, Sukarno, saw a continuous nationalist revolution as a solution, while the New Order regime of President Suharto tried market-oriented development coupled with political repression. Currently Indonesia continues to try to attract foreign investment in a competitive globalized world while trying to foster a democratic society based on respect for individual rights and the rule of law.

Beyond economic challenges and opportunities, keeping the Indonesian nation together has been a difficult task. By population, Indonesia is the fourth largest country in the world (currently around 220 million). Indonesia is a huge archipelago with many ethnic groups, religions, and languages. The nationalist movement developed in the cities of colonial Java and the independent Republic of Indonesia clearly has had Jakarta as its focus. This has caused a great deal of resentment in other regions. At the same time, the movement was not one of Javanese nationalism. Nationalist participants included many from other islands, in particular the Minangkabau from Sumatra. The leadership of independent Indonesia has tended to be Javanese and Muslim, but other groups have not been totally shut out from positions of authority. The nation's motto, *bhinneka tunggal ika,* translates as "unity through diversity." It is assumed that all of the many ethnic groups that inhabit the archipelago contribute to the nation. The Javanese language itself is not dominant in Indonesia. In fact, it has little presence in the media even though it is the first language of about 60 percent of the population.

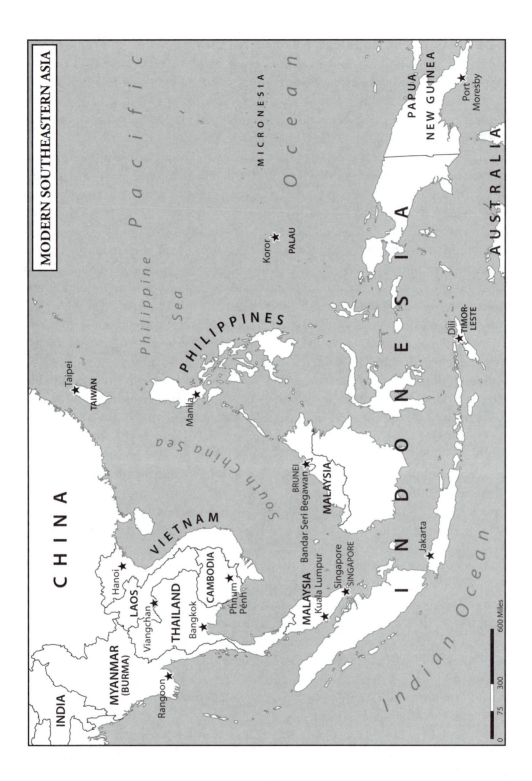

MODERN SOUTHEASTERN ASIA

CHINA

INDIA

MYANMAR
(BURMA)

Rangoon

LAOS

Viangchan

THAILAND

Bangkok

VIETNAM

Hanoi

CAMBODIA

Phnum
Pénh

TAIWAN

Taipei

South China Sea

Philippine
Sea

PHILIPPINES

Manila

Pacific
Ocean

MICRONESIA

Koror
PALAU

MALAYSIA

Kuala Lumpur

Singapore
SINGAPORE

BRUNEI
Bandar Seri Begawan

MALAYSIA

INDONESIA

Jakarta

Indian Ocean

PAPUA
NEW GUINEA

Port
Moresby

AUSTRALIA

Dili
TIMOR-
LESTE

0   75   300   600 Miles

Instead, Indonesian (a dialect of Malay) has become the common language of the population. This again points to Indonesian nationalism being distinct from Javanese nationalism. The Indonesian nation is held to encompass all other ethnic groups; during the New Order, celebration of such identities was restricted to selected nonpolitical spheres, such as dance and the visual arts.

Various social classes were involved in developing Indonesian nationalism. The nationalist movement was dominated by "new type nationalists" who looked for inspiration to Western methods of political organization and hoped in the future to build a viable independent society. This approach stood in contrast to that employed by earlier resistance figures who had aimed to overturn Dutch rule and resurrect traditional kingdoms. Indonesian nationalists tended to be educated, the sons of minor aristocrats, and trained as lawyers, doctors, economists, engineers, and journalists. Because of the nature of Dutch colonial society, they seldom achieved positions of power and prosperity. Aristocratic rulers tended to work with the Dutch, and those few Indonesians who had found employment in the government of the Dutch East Indies advanced the nationalist project in only a minor way. The social composition of the nationalist movement changed after independence was declared. Political activists, such as Sukarno, remained prominent. They formed and led political parties and took over the bureaucratic machinery inherited from the Dutch. But the armed struggle to expel the Dutch brought forth new actors, who would contribute not just to the development of the newly independent Republic of Indonesia but would also help to define the content of Indonesian nationalism. Military officers trained by either the Dutch or the Japanese rose to prominence. The military remains an important institution in Indonesia to this day. Suharto, who served as Indonesia's president for over three decades, was a career officer, as is Indonesia's current president, Susilo Bambang Yudhoyono. Religious figures and youth also gained some authority. The latter in particular would be long identified as the embodiment of the importance of self-sacrifice on behalf of the nation, whether in confronting the Dutch or in 1998 helping to end the rule of Suharto.

Postindependence nationalism is a clear extension of the nationalist movement that emerged in Indonesia at the beginning of the 20th century. It is difficult to really note an Indonesian identity earlier, although nationalists make frequent references to the 14th-century Majapahit empire, seen by some as a "proto-Indonesia," and to the activities of a pantheon of national heroes who battled the Dutch. The nationalist movement initially focused on winning political independence. Postindependence leaders took up the task of defining a national identity and fostering national unity through the powers of government and through the mobilization of Indonesia's citizens.

Instituting the Nation

A key institution in the history of nationalism was the Investigating Committee for Preparatory Work for Indonesian Independence, which in 1945 drafted a provisional constitution. The body ultimately rejected the Jakarta Charter, a supplementary clause that proposed to make it obligatory for Indonesian Muslims to follow Islamic law. Instead the nation was to be run according to the state ideology of Pancasila, a set of five broad principles that have been at the core of Indonesian nationalism to the present day. Throughout the postindependence period, Indonesian nationalism dominated politics, in parliament and at the party level. Leaders, such as Sukarno and Suharto, presented themselves as the embodiment of the nation's destiny. The Indonesian military, which played a key role in Indonesian political life, also saw itself as the main protector of the Indonesian nation. However, Indonesian nationalism has never been simply a political project. Political goals included independence, unity, stability, prosperity, justice, and development. But many of these goals are connected to and were achieved through the creation of an Indonesian identity. Indonesian nationalism was transmitted to the people through whatever media were available. Before the revolution, it

Pancasila

The Pancasila forms the centerpiece of Indonesian state (and nationalist) ideology as follows:

1. Belief in one God
2. A just and civilized humanitarian
3. Indonesian unity
4. Popular democratic sovereignty
5. Social justice

The "five principles" were formulated by Sukarno during preparations for independence in 1945 (there is still some controversy over whether he was the sole author). They were subsequently incorporated into Indonesia's 1945, 1949, and 1950 constitutions. During the Guided Democracy period, Pancasila was identified with Sukarno's radical plans for the nation. The interpretation of the ideology was even more restricted during the New Order. An official take on Pancasila was propagated as a specific component of the school curriculum and in mandatory workshops for state employees. The requirement to believe in one God, originally intended to placate Muslim opinion, was used against alleged supporters of the "atheistic" Indonesian Communist Party. All organizations had to agree that Pancasila was the "sole basis" of their groups' thinking and actions. Government opponents were labeled "un-Pancasila." This heavy-handed approach has to some extent discredited Pancasila during the post-Suharto period. But most Indonesians still see the basic ideas as integral to their sense of nation and a good example of their tolerance for diversity.

was spread through mass rallies and speeches. Nationalist leaders showed their love of the nation through the example of courting arrest and exile. During the Japanese occupation, Indonesian leaders conducted radio propaganda under the sponsorship of the Japanese to advance the ultimate goal of national independence. Independent Indonesia employed the full tools of the state, such as official pronouncements and the education system. During the Guided Democracy and New Order periods, debate was severely curtailed. Indonesian nationalism was defined by the state, and the population was expected to follow the official interpretation. Since the fall of Suharto, debate has continued over the nature of Indonesian nationalism and over how it is to be understood and implemented.

Appeals to nationalism have generally been to the historic unity of Indonesia and to the heroism of the Indonesian people in resisting foreign occupation. To a lesser extent appeals were to a modern, progressive future, which could be built if Indonesians succeeded in achieving and preserving their independence. Indonesian nationalism was not noted for an extensive group of writers who dealt with the implications of nationalism on a philosophical level. Pancasila, for example, was clearly a functional tool designed to achieve the unity of the nation, rather than a means to explore the definition of Indonesian and what an independent Indonesia should actually look like. A few figures did examine the basic tenants of Indonesian nationalism. They tended, however, not to delve too deeply. Sukarno synthesized perhaps incompatible elements—*nasionalisme, agama, komunisme* (nationalism, religion, and communism)—into the single concept of NASAKOM. Muhammad Yamin, a journalist and politician, was a key figure in the

National History

There is a great reverence among many Indonesians for the 14th-century Majapahit empire. Such writers as Muhammad Yamin (1903–1962) looked on Majapahit as a "proto-Indonesia" and celebrated Majapahit's great statesman, Gajah Mada, as the nation's great unifier. The New Order in particular looked to Majapahit for inspiration; the Suharto regime, with its fondness for central political control, hierarchical structures, and Javanese mannerisms, could be seen as a "new Majapahit." Majapahit was Hindu in orientation. This did not sit well with some in a majority Muslim country.

Indonesian nationalists also venerate various *pahlawan nasional* ("national heroes") who fought the Dutch. These men and women were representative of all of Indonesia's regions, religions, and ethnic groups. Although they fought long ago for their own kingdoms, religions, and ambitions, they have been viewed as fighting for the Indonesian nation.

Current history also provides a powerful set of images. The Indonesian Revolution represents triumph over foreign domination. The involvement of the Indonesian Communist Party in the September 30, 1965, coup attempt and the subsequent violent suppression of the party can be seen as the "founding myth" of the New Order. The collapse of the Suharto regime in the face of student protest may provide Indonesia with a new set of heroes.

construction of a "national history." He tended to assume that a Javanese identity was also an Indonesian one. This line of thought was to some extent also followed by the New Order regime of President Suharto. Others believed that local traditions would simply recede into the background as Indonesia developed as a modern country.

Defining the Nation

Indonesia was not really defined in ethnic terms, although there were some historical elements that could form a basis for an Indonesian nation. These include the Malay language, spoken across the archipelago. Majapahit provided a precedent for a unified though Javanese-dominated Indonesia. But the objective argument for the validity of Indonesia was that a modern state could be built to replace the Dutch East Indies. The colony was to be seized by Indonesians through political action and an act of will. The act of will involved the realization that they had a common history and identity. There was some conflict between different cultural orientations within nationalism. Some looked to the West, some to China or Japan, some to a wider Islamic world.

Around 85 percent of Indonesians are nominally Muslim. Islam apparently arrived in Indonesia around the end of the 13th century, spread through trade and missionary activity rather than through outside invasion. Muslim institutions and individuals have all contributed to Indonesia's development; the republic's fourth president was both an Islamic scholar and the head of Indonesia's largest Muslim organization. There is a great deal of variety among Islamic practice in Indonesia today, ranging from the integration of pre-Islamic customs to a militant fundamentalist approach. Indonesians have largely resisted the urge to equate an Indonesian identity with an Islamic one. Recent attempts to adopt Islamic law have failed, although some provinces and municipalities have moved in that direction. Indonesians are proud of their relative tolerance toward religious minorities. However, recent attacks on churches, sectarian violence, and terrorist attacks indicate that some Indonesians are sympathetic to a radical Islamic message, perhaps questioning the whole concept of Indonesia as a separate nation. However, militants generally have had limited success in interesting Indonesians in their agenda.

Indonesian nationalism did not really favor one ethnic group, although the Javanese dominated its development and implementation. Indonesian nationalism is also not specifically identified with Indonesia's dominant religion, Islam. Instead, there have been attempts to "tame" Islam through Pancasila. Indonesian nationalism has not, however, been totally inclusive. Not all inhabitants of the archipelago are automatically Indonesian. There have historically been two problematic minorities. The first of these consisted of Eurasians, who had mixed

European and indigenous heritage. Some members of this group were very involved in the early nationalist movement, while others were very much opposed to Indonesian independence. Most Eurasians either left Indonesia after independence or have been assimilated into the larger population. The second group consists of ethnic Chinese, many of whom in fact speak no Chinese and have roots in Indonesia that go back centuries. Nevertheless, many Indonesians identified the Chinese with the colonial authorities, with whom they were seen as working closely. The apparent reluctance of many Chinese to fully engage with the nationalist project led many to question their loyalty. The perceptions were also held that many Chinese were sympathetic to Communist China and unfairly dominated the economy. The Chinese minority was subject to various legal disabilities. The status of Chinese-Indonesians probably hit its lowest point during the final years of the New Order. A few wealthy Chinese businessmen were allowed access to President Suharto, while the majority of Chinese were subject to petty indignities, discrimination in terms of employment and education, and the real threat of communal attacks. The situation has certainly improved in recent years, with some members of the community achieving positions of authority in the government, for example. Chinese customs and culture are now more or less openly celebrated and there has been some attempt to see the community's history as integral to that of the Indonesian nation as a whole. Steps in this latter direction are still, however, rather tentative.

Immigrants to Indonesia, beyond a few Dutch military deserters and artists, have until recently been quite few in number. In the last couple of decades, however, some foreigners have moved to Indonesia, particularly to Bali. While in general these newcomers have been well received by local people, the government has not facilitated this form of immigration, nor has it helped the Indonesian spouses of such foreign residents. Overseas, the Indonesian population has earned a reputation for friendliness toward foreign visitors. Indonesia receives millions of visitors a year, both tourists and businesspeople. Indonesian nationalism is not seen as something intrinsically xenophobic. However, not all Indonesians share this, perhaps stereotypical, attitude toward outsiders. The government has on occasion hampered visits by foreign journalists. Terrorist attacks, such as the October 2002 Bali bombing, point to a few Indonesians being very uncomfortable with a foreign presence on their soil.

The boundaries of Indonesia were held to be both natural and political. Indonesia was to include most of island Southeast Asia, but only those areas that had been under Dutch control. Some attempts were made to include parts of Malaysia within an independent Indonesia, but these were dropped at an early date. Indonesian nationalism was also in some sense ethnic, in that only those who had the common experience of fighting for the independence of the Dutch East Indies were part of the nation. East Timor, never part of the struggle against Dutch colonialism, could not be successfully integrated into an independent Indonesia. Schemes to unite all of island Southeast Asia were doomed to fail, despite common culture motifs across the region. Indonesia has no revisionist attitudes toward national borders, and disputes with neighbors, while often heated, involve specific political problems.

Narrating the Nation

In narrating the nation, Sukarno employed a model using three stages of history. Indonesia had experienced an ancient "golden age." The coming of the Dutch initiated the current "dark age," despite heroic Indonesian resistance when the colonial authorities consolidated their power. In doing so, the Dutch both exploited Indonesia and pushed it off its ordained path of development. Sukarno felt that once the Dutch were expelled, Indonesia would enter a bright future of progress, prosperity, and justice. This historical analysis was embraced by subsequent Indonesian nationalists. Debate was restricted to at what point the bright future was to begin. Postindependence Indonesia was beset by a myriad of problems; many, including Sukarno himself, felt that the revolution and the construction of Indonesia were still very much a "work in progress." For the New Order, the dark ages had in fact continued for the country until the communists were suppressed during 1965–1966. The sustaining myth of Indonesian nationalism involved that of a unified nation resisting colonialism and building a bright future. The related concept, that the Dutch in fact "created Indonesia" through bringing disparate regions and peoples together, was definitely rejected. Independent Indonesia is a very centralized country. Both Sukarno and Suharto constructed political structures where power was concentrated in the capital. Post-Suharto governments have begun to devolve some powers to the provinces and municipalities, but a national identity remains paramount to most Indonesians.

Indonesian nationalism can be described as having definite and limited goals involving national independence and internal development. An exception involved the Sukarno period, during which Indonesian nationalism presented itself as in the vanguard of a larger revolution of the Third World against Western powers led by the United States. Sukarno rejected Western-style democracy as being incompatible with Indonesian norms. Instead he was in favor of new authoritarian structures that he felt were necessary to protect the Indonesian Revolution against internal and external enemies. Sukarno gave lengthy, impassioned speeches and built grand monuments to remind the population that they were all part of a continuous revolutionary struggle that was leading the nation forward. This course of action was tied in with a sharp move toward the political left involving open sympathy toward Communist China. The PKI gained a great deal of political influence, and many of its ideas and even its slogans were incorporated into the accepted interpretation of Indonesian nationalism.

This approach stood in sharp contrast to that of Sukarno's successor. Suharto's Indonesia was a military-dominated and hierarchical society with a deeply conservative worldview. A particular version of Indonesian nationalism that included a reverence for the ancient Majapahit empire and the incorporation of many Javanese cultural elements was presented as the norm. The government's interpretation of Pancasila was the only accepted one. Communism was seen as a latent threat to Indonesia's stability, prosperity, and even existence. Communism was portrayed as intrinsically "un-Indonesian."

Although the New Order regime was interested in attracting foreign investment and was involved in such groupings as the Non-Aligned Movement, the Association of Southeast Asian Nations, and the Organization of the Islamic Conference, it was basically inward looking. An exception may have involved the 1975 invasion of East Timor. The occupation of the former Portuguese colony, like the previous Sukarno-era campaign to annex Irian Jaya, could be viewed as a nationalist project intended to fully integrate Indonesia within its "natural borders." However, other factors, such as the fear of a power vacuum in a neighboring state

Sukarno addresses a crowd, September 1950. An anticolonial activist and the first president of Indonesia, the controversial Sukarno contributed to the country's political development and to building its national identity. (Bettmann/Corbis)

in an environment of "spreading communism" in mainland Southeast Asia may have been seen as a more important motive. Certainly, East Timor was never seen as historically part of Indonesia. Post-Suharto Indonesia has taken a rather cautious approach to the nation's identity and its place in the world. Political liberalization has led to an abandonment of a rigid interpretation of Pancasila and even to the questioning of whether the state ideology is still relevant. Some Indonesians have pushed for the nation to adopt a more Islamic identity, a move rejected by many other Indonesians. For many Indonesians, issues of national identity retain little interest as the country tries to recover from dictatorship, economic crisis, and a series of natural disasters. Certainly no current Indonesian leaders have put forward a coherent, passionately felt national vision in the manner of Sukarno and Suharto.

Indonesian identity has been expressed through a variety of media, such as the national anthem, the flag, and various symbols. The latter include the Garuda, the magical steed of the Hindu god Vishnu, now the name of the Indonesian national airline and an element of the nation's coat of arms, and the 8th-century Buddhist shrine of Borobudur. Some symbols were given a very long pedigree (Yamin refers to the Indonesian flag having been used for a full 6,000 years). The territory of Indonesia itself is seen as a symbol, embodied in the phrase *tanah air kita*, "our land and water." Other powerful images for Indonesian nationalism involve those connected to the revolution. The city of Surabaya was the site of a battle between Indonesian youth and British forces. Indonesians believed that the British were facilitating the return of Dutch authorities. The start of this battle on November 10, 1945, the embodiment of the Indonesian will to resist, is still celebrated as Heroes' Day.

Sukarno put up numerous monuments to the national struggle, including a notable one in Jakarta to celebrate the return of the western half of New Guinea to Indonesian control. The slogan "Sabang to Merauke" was common during the Sukarno era and reflected a firm commitment to a united Indonesia, stretching from Sabang in Sumatra to Merauke in (then) Dutch New Guinea. The national cemetery at Kalibata, Jakarta, is a reminder to the population that independence was won at a considerable price in lives lost. The New Order regime of Suharto was able to transform the latter site into a monument with its own take on the Indonesian Revolution through the burial at the cemetary of the military officers slain during the September 30, 1965, incident. These reported victims of the radical PKI were made into "Heroes of the Revolution." The Indonesian Revolution was thus not just against the Dutch but also against those who would hijack it for their own selfish purposes. Lubang Buaya, a disued well on the outskirts of Jakarta where the generals were slain, became for the New Order the embodiment of Indonesian nationalism. A lavish monument and museum at the site presented the New Order as the main defender of the Indonesian nation. In the wake of the death of the generals, hundreds of thousands of suspected communists were also killed. There are no monuments or memorials to these deaths, and the massacres of 1965–1966 still remain a taboo subject. They are not part of the official, or even popular, national narrative. National symbols for post-Suharto Indonesia have yet to really emerge. One potential symbol might involve the self-sacrifice of students on behalf of the nation. This symbol, however, is still treated rather tentatively, despite the clear parallels with politically active youth in the earlier national struggle. Only a modest monument has been erected to the students slain in May 1998 at Trisakti University, Jakarta, while demonstrating against the Suharto regime.

Mobilizing and Building the Nation

The mobilization of the people of Indonesia to construct the Indonesian nation was facilitated by a variety of catalysts. Such external events as the Japanese occupation, the Cold War, the rise of the "Asian model of development" of the 1970s to 1990s, and serious problems with this model at the end of the 1990s all caused Indonesian nationalism to take on certain characteristics. It is unlikely that Indonesia would have gained its independence when it did if it were not for the fact that the Dutch were defeated militarily in 1942. They were forced to, in a sense, "reconquer" their colonial possessions after the Japanese surrender in August 1945. Indonesia won its independence and maintained its unity in a Cold War context. Matters were complicated by the existence of a large, powerful, indigenous Communist Party and the armed conflict in nearby Indochina. After the suppression of the PKI during 1965–1966, the Suharto regime tried a local variant of the Asian model of export-oriented development. This approach to the economy and politics was judged less nationalistic by many outside commentators. Certainly it was more interested in attracting foreign investment than the previous regime, which had actively courted conflict with outside powers, at least on a rhetorical level. But perhaps the single-minded pursuit of economic progress could itself be seen as a nationalist project. One sees similar strategies, coupling economic growth with the strengthening of a unified national identity, in Singapore and Malaysia. The Asian economic crisis during 1997–1998 destroyed much of the economic advancement made by the New Order regime and may thus have removed its nationalist credentials, leaving it simply a tired, corrupt dictatorship.

The political goal of Indonesian nationalists was originally the obtainment of independence from the Dutch. During the Indonesian Revolution, the debate was over whether the struggle should be simply a political fight for independence or a true social revolution involving the total transformation of the nation, perhaps on radical or populist lines. Later, the argument was over whether the revolution was indeed finished or was in fact still an ongoing process. Sukarno favored the latter interpretation, seeing the granting of independence as simply the first step in a larger Indonesian, if not world, revolution. Suharto and his New Order, concentrating on economic development, definitely saw the revolution as over, although it continued to employ revolutionary symbols and language. Many Indonesians apparently felt that such terminology was still important; some of the popularity of Megawati Sukarnoputri (Indonesia's fifth president) may have stemmed from nostalgia for her father as a revolutionary figure.

To obtain the goal of independence, the Indonesian nationalist movement employed a diversity of tactics, including mass mobilization and noncooperation with Dutch authorities. Interestingly, much more effort seems to have been expended in the early days on creating Indonesians than on expelling the Dutch (although after the failure of the 1926–1927 armed rebellions and subsequent Dutch repression, this latter approach may have simply been unrealistic). The Youth Pledge taken by a gathering of Indonesian nationalists in Jakarta in 1928 called for "one nation, one people and one language." Violence was only resorted to after it showed some hope of success in the wake of the Japanese defeat. Even then, it was always tempered by attempts to negotiate and to gain international support. The debate is still open as to whether it was negotiation or armed struggle that was decisive and over the relative importance of outside diplomatic pressure in winning independence.

After independence, the government employed such tools as textbooks and monuments to solidify the identification of the citizenry with the Indonesian nation and to foster loyalty to the Indonesian state. During Sukarno's time as president, force was used to keep the national territory intact (although regional rebellions were more concerned with defining power at the center than with actual independence from Indonesia). Force was also used during the New Order in Irian Jaya, East Timor, and Aceh, but these were all regions that possessed unique histories. All had come into Indonesia under different circumstances. East Timor was originally a Portuguese colony, Irian Jaya was brought into Indonesia through diplomatic maneuvers in the context of the Cold War, and Aceh was voluntarily part of Indonesia but fiercely proud of its resistance to any outside attempts at domination. Propaganda tended to refer to an agreed upon "national history." The national ideal was legitimized by the struggle for independence. After the latter had been achieved, a variety of threats were identified, including neocolonialism during the Guided Democracy period and the possibility of a resurgent PKI or at times an "un-Indonesian" militant Islam during the New Order. Finally, appeals were made to success: economic development meant that Indonesia was a viable and legitimate nation.

With the end of Suharto's authoritarian regime in May 1998, some predicted the "breakup" of Indonesia; comparisons were made to the Soviet Union and Yugoslavia. Such sentiments seem now to be misplaced. Indonesia's unity, based on a common Indonesian nationalism, seems quite strong. The winning of independence from the Dutch was followed by the construction of a common national identity acceptable to a very diverse population. Possible divisive issues involving the place of Islam in Indonesian society, the dominance of Java, and regional disparities have been downplayed. Instead, Indonesians are held to have a common history and, through cooperation, a bright future. The central feature of Indonesian nationalism, of a common national identity based on the unity of the diverse peoples of the Archipelago, has remained remarkably resilient despite the many political, social, and economic changes of recent decades.

Selected Bibliography

Anderson, B. 1990. *Language and Power: Exploring Political Cultures in Indonesia.* Ithaca, NY: Cornell University Press.

Bourchier, D., and V. R. Hadiz, ed. 2003. *Indonesian Politics and Society: A Reader.* New York: RoutledgeCurzon.

Feith, H. 1962. *The Decline of Constitutional Democracy in Indonesia.* Ithaca, NY: Cornell University Press.

Feith, H., and L. Castles, eds. 1970. *Indonesia Political Thinking, 1945–1965.* Ithaca, NY: Cornell University Press.

Friend, T. 2003. *Indonesian Destinies.* Cambridge, MA: Harvard University Press.

Kahin, G. M. 1952. *Nationalism and Revolution in Indonesia.* Ithaca, NY: Cornell University Press.

Legge, J. D. 2003. *Sukarno: A Political Biography.* 3rd ed. Singapore: Archipelago Press.

Ramage, D. E. 1995. *Politics in Indonesia: Democracy, Islam and the Ideology of Tolerance.* New York: Routledge.

Ricklefs, M. C. 2001. *A History of Modern Indonesia since c. 1200.* 3rd ed. Stanford, CA: Stanford University Press.

Sukarno. 1970. *Nationalism, Islam and Marxism.* Introduction by R. McVey. Ithaca, NY: Cornell University Modern Indonesia Project.

Sukarno. 1975. *Indonesia Accuses! Soekarno's Defence Oration in the Political Trial of 1930,* edited, translated, annotated, and introduced by R. K. Paget. Kuala Lumpur, Malaysia: Oxford University Press.

Weatherbee, D. E. 1966. *Ideology in Indonesia: Sukarno's Indonesian Revolution.* New Haven, CT: Yale University Southeast Asian Studies.

Wood, M. 2005. *Official History in Modern Indonesia: New Order Perceptions and Counterviews.* Leiden, The Netherlands: E. J. Brill.

Iraq

Tareq Y. Ismael

Chronology

1915	Britain invades Iraq to safeguard Iranian oil during World War I.
1916	The Arab revolt against the Ottoman Empire begins under the leadership of Sharif Hussein.
1917	Britain consolidates its rule over Iraq, proclaiming itself a liberator.
1919	At the Paris Peace Conference, as per Article 22 of the League of Nations, the Iraq mandate is given to the British; the modern borders of Iraq are created.
1920	Iraqis revolt against British mandatory rule, encompassing the Sunnis, Shiites, and Kurds; the revolt is largely quashed by the end of the year.
1921	(August) To create a façade of an independent state, Faisal bin Hussein (Faisal I) is proclaimed king of Iraq by the British.
1930	The Anglo-Iraqi Treaty is signed, giving the British both military and commercial rights in Iraq; this treaty is particularly important given the discovery of oil in 1927.
1932	The British mandate officially ends in Iraq, and Iraq is nominated to the League of Nations.
1933	(September 8) King Faisal I dies and is succeeded by his son Ghazi (d. 1939), a pan-Arab nationalist.
1940–1941	Nationalist Rashid Ali al-Kaylani gains power and tilts toward the Axis powers.
1941	(April 18) British forces put down the Rashid Ali coup. (May 31) A pro-British government is reinstalled.
1948	(January) *Al-Wathba*—the Leap—is the most formidable mass insurrection in the history of the monarchy; it forces the monarchy to shelf the proposed Portsmouth Treaty of 1948, a revised version of the 1930 treaty.
1952	(November) The *Al-Wathba* of 1948 continues in the form of an intifada, in which the social, economic, and political policies of the monarchy are challenged.
1954	(April 21) "Military Assistance" understanding between Iraq and the United States.
1955	Iraq joins the "Baghdad Pact," an anti-Soviet security bloc.
1958	The "Free Officer" coup brings Brigadier General Qasim to power; he initiates a progressive program and withdraws Iraq from the Baghdad Pact.
1963	The first Ba'ath coup, with U.S. backing; the Ba'ath (Arab Socialist) Party and its army allies take over the reins of the state; an army countercoup replaces the regime nine months later under the leadership of Abd al-Salam Arif, who is proclaimed president of the country.
1968	The second Ba'ath coup, again with the support of the United States and army allies, declares Ahmed Hasan al-Bakr president of the republic.
1973	Iraq nationalizes its oil industry.
1979	al-Bakr resigns, and Saddam Hussein assumes power as president.
1980	Iran-Iraq war; an immensely costly war, it drags on for eight and a half years.
1990	(August 2) Iraq invades Kuwait; four days later, the United Nations imposes economic sanctions on Iraq.

1991   (January 17) Operation Desert Storm begins; it ends six months later with devastating effect to Iraq. The UN-sanctioned regime continues and erodes Iraqi infrastructure and society over the next decade.

1992   The United Kingdom and the United States impose a "no-fly zone" over northern Iraq (Kurdish region).

2001   (September 11) Terrorist attacks against the United States in New York, Washington, and Pennsylvania; these attacks provide a political pretext to the invasion of Iraq.

2003   (March) Anglo-American forces invade Iraq. (April) The invading forces complete the occupation of Iraq.

Situating the Nation

Iraq, the ancient Sumerian name meaning "country of the sun," is a relatively modern state—admitted to the League of Nations as an independent state in 1932—that is situated on a historically ancient land, largely contiguous to the ancient borders of Mesopotamia. Iraq, centered between the Tigris and Euphrates, has a preeminent place in Arab and Islamic history and has long functioned as a coherent cultural and economic entity. Modern Iraq is marked by cultural plurality, with Arab Shiites, the majority, living alongside substantial Arab and Kurdish Sunni populations, as well as smaller groupings of Turkmen, Chaldean Catholics, Mandaeans, and more esoteric sects. Notwithstanding this diverse population, modern Iraq is largely defined by a shared cultural and political experience that has impressed itself on all its peoples.

In the history of Islam, Iraq served as a backdrop for early religious drama, notably in the events that gave rise to Shiism; the shrines of Najaf and Karbala leave a lingering testament to the country's preeminence in Islam. Baghdad, under the Abbasid Dynasty from AD 750 to 1258, was the seat of Islamic power and presided over the resurrection of neo-Platonic thought and various innovations in philosophy and the sciences.

Historically, the Shiite Twelvers denomination was concentrated in southern Iraq, from Basra to the middle Euphrates. In Baghdad and its outlying areas, Sunni Muslims have historically made up the majority. In Mosul and farther north, the Kurds have inhabited the rugged mountainous terrain for centuries. By the process of urbanization in the 20th century, these populations have become increasingly mixed, particularly in the capital Baghdad.

With the Ottoman conquest of the Arab-Muslim lands in the 16th century until the collapse of the Ottoman caliphate after World War I, the Iraqi provinces of Baghdad, Basra, and Mosul were administered from Baghdad as a periphery of the Ottoman Empire.

The incorporation of Iraq into the world capitalist system occurred in the 19th century. Private property in the late 18th century was almost nonexistent in Iraq; it could be easily confiscated, and where it existed, it existed in rudimentary form and did not acquire political overtones. The incorporation of Iraq into the world capitalist system brought on highly disruptive changes. Communal property was expropriated by a relatively powerful few, leading to concentrations of private property. Expanding monetary transactions, real estate speculation, and the introduction of land laws between 1858 and 1932 resulted in an increase in state power. In parallel, there was a spread of modern communication technologies, a diffusion of European ideas and techniques, and a breakdown in the self-sufficiency of the traditional tribes. River steamships were introduced in 1859, the electric telegraph in 1861, state schools in 1868, and, critically, the public press in 1908.

It is important to note that the territory of Iraq, as it was constituted following World War I under British rule and later as it became independent, was not an invention of Western statesmen. The boundaries adopted, though modeled upon Ottoman design, were remarkably similar to those that have been in existence since the time of the Early Dynastic Period, which originated during the reign of the Sumerian king, Sargon. Archaeologists and historians now trace the line of Sumerian kings further into antiquity than 2700 BC and entertain the legend of Gilgamesh, King of Uruk, taking that date as a provisional starting point

for the history of ancient Iraq. Its boundaries, through bonds of culture and the administrative allure of Baghdad, and despite the various disruptions of succeeding invaders, has remained largely intact until the present day.

Instituting the Nation

A historical sense of "Arabness" was a natural attribute of both Sunni and Shiite populations of Iraq, and Islamic heritage forged social and psychological ties among Sunni and Shiite Arabs as well as the Muslim Kurds. Hence, this cultural plurality in Iraq has historically been a dynamic rather than divisive force. In the formative and early periods of Iraqi history, there existed a complex hierarchy that involved several principles: a pyramid structure of religion, of sect, of ethnicity, and of power. In parallel, there existed a hierarchy of status that compromised the Ottoman ruling Pasha, military officers, and civil servants, descendents from the Prophet's lineage (*Sadah*), Sufi orders, public religious scholars (*Ulama*), and wealth-based groups. Submission to structure and hierarchy did not bring, however, practices of strident racism or systemic discrimination.

Nascent notions of Arab nationhood began to take substantive form in the period starting in 1908 and into World War I. In 1908, the Young Turks seized power in Turkey, initiating a program to create a modern nation-state along European lines; the modernization program of the Young Turks was accompanied by a Turkish ultranationalism that inevitably alienated Arab populations. Consequently, many Arab nationalists joined opposition movements, including the Ottoman Decentralization Party and the Young Arab Society (*al-Fatat*), and aspired to institute an independent Arab nation-state.

In World War I, this Arab nationalism erupted in the "Arab Revolt" of 1916. The leader of the revolt, Sharif Hussein, entered into alliance with the British and the French, anticipating that the end of the war would see these powers recognize an independent and unified Arab state. The British and French meanwhile, as per the secret Sykes-Picot Agreement, had instead designated themselves, not the Arab nationalist, as heirs to the liberated Arab provinces. In 1920, the League of Nations granted the British mandatory rule over the new state of Iraq.

Following the imposition of British mandatory rule in Iraq from 1920 onward, diverse social actors and institutions converged to express an Iraqi nationalism. This expression of Iraqi nationhood suppressed religious and social divisions, bringing Arab nationalists, the Shia clerical leaders, and even the Kurds together in revolt against British rule in Iraq; notable in this nationalist revolt was the *Haras al-Istiqlal* (Independence Guard), which was a Shiite-led anticolonial group. The British would reestablish control by early 1921 and retain mandatory rule until 1932, when Iraq became nominally independent.

Defining the Nation

Iraq's collective identity emerged historically in relatively isolated communities over a large geographical expanse despite poor or inadequate transportation. Increased Iraqi attendance at Ottoman institutions of higher learning and a spread of Arab clubs and societies, as well as newspapers, coalesced to raise interest in Arab history and formulated early theories of Iraqi nationhood. The collective identities of Iraqis underwent further refinement as intensive interaction within and among communities softened traditional kinship ties (tribe, religion, etc.) and encouraged the emergence of new identities and national interest.

Noted histories of the late 19th century show that the collective identities of Iraqis were tolerant of diversity; the reader discovers, for instance, correspondences of warm relations between a Shiite Muslim and a Catholic trader in premodern Iraq and Greater Syria, respectively. Social distinctions, such as sectarian backgrounds or ethnic origins, were in constant flux; the literature of this period shows no rigid racial, social, or even economic biases. In other words, the sectarian and ethnic divisions have not been natural or inherent facets of the Iraqi historical experience. Furthermore, some of the writings of the late 19th century show proto-nationalist references indicating that a sense of an Iraqi nation existed even in preindustrial and pre-mass-literacy Iraq. There were frequent references to the "Iraqi" frontier, delimiting tribes and towns within Iraq.

Life events in early Iraq show that, at the individual level, a person can depart from his/her communal or ethnic roots through interaction with the larger community. Such was the documented case of an Iraqi Jewish physician, Dr. Naji, who felt more integrated into the life of provincial, Muslim functionaries and was detached from his Jewish communal connections and networks. Mohammad Mahdi al-Jawahiri, an Iraqi poet known as "the greatest Arab poet," who was from a well-known Shiite family from Najaf, would likewise become known for his emphasis on nation not defined by sect or ethnicity.

By the turn of the 20th century, these fluid relationships among Iraq's diverse populations set in motion a process of national transformation, which was witnessed in the 1920 revolt, as the diverse Iraqi communities united under the banner of Iraqi nationalism and anticolonialism. And while Iraqi nationhood proved to be uneven, and occasionally contradictory, it coalesced as a genuine phenomenon. In the monarchical period, a deliberate process of state-building sought to inculcate an Iraqi identity, incorporating Sunni and Shiites alike. This process found its climax under the short-lived Qasim regime, where the regime worked to contain Arab chauvinism and formulate a multicultural Iraq by way of a progressive program. This process met its end with the Ba'athi coup of 1963, after which the repressive regime worked to redefine Iraq in official party terms.

The secular ideology of Ba'ath pan-Arabism was conceived and written by non-Iraqi intellectuals like Michel Aflaq; on a theoretical level, it is foreign to

Iraq's collective and shared experience. Consequently, pre-Ba'ath civil society was brutally suppressed during 1963–1964. Civil society was re-created in the following years when all cultural forms of expression were put under Ba'ath control. The chauvinistic core of Ba'ath ideology is regional leadership of the Arabs.

Given Iraq's material resources, human infrastructure, and rich civilizational history, the Iraqi Ba'ath regime pressed hard for its candidacy to Arab leadership after 1979, when Egypt made peace with Israel and, thus, relinquished its leadership position. But pan-Arabism did not resonate with the historical memory of modern Iraq. This contradiction gave rise to the two-pronged policy of authoritarian statism and the Ba'ath Project of Rewriting History, both textually and culturally.

Social and cultural associations were subject to state apparatus control, and the education system became a tool for propagating pan-Arabism. For this goal, the Ba'ath regime sought to co-opt, through intimidation and rewards, the prominent intellectuals among the intelligentsia to rewrite Iraqi history from the vantage point of pan-Arabism. Some agreed for the tempting rewards, like Dr. Nuri Ali Hammudi al-Qaysi and his book *al-Shir wa al-Tarikh* (*Poetry and History*). He became the regime's spokesman in Arab intellectual forums from early 1980 to mid-1990. Others, like Kamal Mazhar Ahmad, cooperated out of fear but challenged the regime's project by inserting subtle messages that undermined the regime's ideology, as in his book, *al-Tabaqa al-'Amila al-Iraqiya: al-Takkawun wa Badiyat al-Taharruk* (*The Iraqi Working Class: Its Formation and Early Activities*). The regime's apparatus of kinship ties culminated with the political dominance of Saddam Hussein's Tikriti clan, which severely undermined the rhetoric of pan-Arab Iraqi identity. To compensate for this apparent contradiction, the Ba'ath regime resorted to more measures of repression. The staff of Saddam's security apparatus was chosen on the basis of loyalty; therefore, almost equal numbers of Sunni and Shiites were in service to Saddam's cultic politics.

The loyalty-driven rule of Saddam Hussein exacerbated latent subnational tendencies. Shortly before the end of the Iraq-Iran war, and following the imposition of economic sanctions, Saddam's regime transformed into a cultic-based political system as the social sector collapsed, and power, thereafter, was increasingly leased to traditional groupings. Among the Shia, traditional bonds reasserted strength and gave rise to religious revival, a notable case in point being the rise of the Sadr movement, which exploded in prominence following the Anglo-American invasion of 2003. Likewise, ethnic minorities within Iraq, such as the Assyrians and Turkmen, have countered the Arab particularism of late Ba'athist state-building with their own ethnic particularism. The Kurdish population, since the early times of modern Iraq, have demanded cultural recognition and a degree of administrative autonomy within the Iraqi nation. Successive governments have contemplated redressing policies. Under the repressive Ba'ath, however, the Kurds took up arms and rebelled against the central Baghdad government. As contemporary history has sent Kurdistan on a sociopolitical trajectory apart from larger

Iraq, further alienating it from the Arab majority, national reconciliation now seems unlikely.

Narrating the Nation

The modern history of Iraq begins with the British invasion of Iraq. British forces began by taking Basra, in the south, in 1915, to safeguard Iranian oil during World War I. The British forces expanded progressively northward through Iraq until they occupied Baghdad in 1917, and Mosul a few months later. On conquering Baghdad, the British commander, Sir Stanley Maude, announced the advent of his army as a liberator of the Iraqi people from Ottoman rule. The intention of the British administration, in any event, was to establish British direct rule through a hierarchy of councils under British control. The British project was intended to squeeze maximum revenue from the Iraqi resources to boost the war-exhausted British Exchequer. For the Iraqis, even those who were considered pro-British, this restructuring meant an assault on their lives and their social practice. Consequently, nationalist sentiment exploded. On July 2, 1920, British administrator A. T. Wilson met with 14 nationalist delegates and 40 invited community leaders, including Jews and Christians who were known to be pro-British to water down the nationalist claims for independence. Nevertheless, both the nationalists and some of the 40 chosen members demanded the election of a national assembly. The continued British military presence, and a failure to respond to nationalist demands, drove the Iraqi people into armed resistance. Both Shiite and Sunni took up arms in the revolt, and even Kurds rose up against the British.

Unsurprisingly, the superior British firepower quelled the revolt in a few months. But Iraqi nationalism became a political nightmare for the British, who attempted to pacify it by installing a Hashemite monarchy in Iraq, under King Faisal I, as a façade of a process toward Iraqi independence.

Following the reign of Faisal I, the Iraqi monarchy staggered and sputtered, hopelessly attempting to mitigate the rising current of Iraqi nationalism while maintaining its pro-British posture. The failure of the monarchy to build a genuine national constituency brought about its demise, culminating with the "Free Officer" coup of Brig. Gen. Abd al-Karim Qasim. With the coup of 1958, a new constitution was proclaimed, declaring the equality of Iraqi citizens, regardless of race, language, or religion. Qasim—of mixed Sunni-Shia parentage and part Kurd —established a progressive political compact that limited the power of traditional pan-Arabism, instead emphasizing a multiethnic and ecumenical Iraq; a significant portion of his ruling council would in fact be Kurdish and Shia.

Qasim's organizing efforts for the Organization of Petroleum Exporting Countries (OPEC) in 1960 and the nationalization of 99.5 percent of the oil concessions precipitated the doom of his regime, when the United States saw present and real danger to its hegemonic role in the Middle East. A Ba'ath coup ended Qasim's regime in 1963 and reversed the nationalist policies. A high-ranking Ba'athist, Salih al-Sa'di, repeatedly said, "We came to power on the CIA train." The prospects for state-building on nationalist principles of equality, unity, and equal opportunity thus ended.

Iraqi society, following the Ba'athist coup of 1968, though having seen initial gains in education and wealth, developed painful fissures as the regime's cynical rule subjugated all social organization to the prerogatives of the party. Because the regime was loyalty-driven, it proved to be indiscriminately brutal, and in its rule, bloodied the hands of each of Iraq's communities. The megalomaniac mind-set that defined Saddam Hussein and suffused his era was exemplified with the invasion of Iran in 1980.

The eight-year war with Iran, which cost billions of dollars and hundreds of thousands in human lives, was succeeded by a catastrophic war with Kuwait. Following its defeat in Kuwait, Iraq suffered under the dual burden of Saddam Hussein's cruel dictatorship plus the suffocating measures of United Nations Resolution 687, the economic sanctions regime. This sanctions regime not only impoverished the Iraqi people but also shepherded in a return of traditional social associations (sect, ethnicity) and weakened the coherence of the Iraqi national idea. These difficulties were exposed and made raw with the U.S. invasion of Iraq in 2003 and the subsequent dismantling of the state.

Mobilizing and Building the Nation

Following independence, and throughout modern Iraqi history, the institution of the state acted as a preeminent force for shaping Iraqi political culture, an inculcator of Iraqi national identity. The institutions of the education system and the military, in particular, have served throughout Iraqi history as "schools for the nation." Early in Iraq's modern history, education was used to integrate the Shia population into Iraq's national vision. During the latter part of the monarchical regime, Shia enrollment in secular schools saw a dramatic rise, as did enrollment in teacher colleges. This process continued even into the Ba'ath era, though in perverted form.

In the formative period of the modern Iraqi state, King Faisal I faced three emergent visions of the country. One centered on pan-Arabism, which traced the origins of Iraq to the pre-Islamic era and the greatness of the Islamic civilization when Arabs were united; in other words, Arab unity was a prima facie condition for the greatness of modern Iraq. The second vision proposed Iraqi nationalism as a celebration of Iraq's ancient civilization, which predated Arabs and Islam without renouncing its Arab-Islamic heritage. In this vision, Sunnis, Shiites, and other minority groups could partake of the historical memory of Iraq. The third was a

Iraqi soldiers patrol Baghdad following a coup by the Arab Ba'ath Socialist Party in 1963. Abd al-Karim Qasim, the founding leader of the Iraqi Republic and deposed prime minister, was executed. (AFP/Getty Images)

Shiite vision of unconditional independence, with a clergy-based Islamic government. The Shiite demand alarmed Britain, which along with the king rejected such a vision. The various nationalist visions were eventually institutionalized in political parties, different professional organizations, and social clubs, as well as a proliferating press that disseminated nationalist and anti-British discourse. Between 1920 and 1929, no less than 109 newspapers were in circulation, and Shiites and Sunnis worked along with non-Muslims in journalism, propagating national sentiments. Among Iraqi nationalists, ethnic divisions and religious differences were less pronounced than among the higher rungs of Iraqi society, which local elites and Britain manipulated to their own advantage. Prominent among the Iraqi nationalists were the Iraqi Communist Party and the National Democratic Party, which called in their program for social justice and cultural pluralism. The political community envisioned by pan-Arabism had many parties and organizations, including the quasi-fascist, like al-Muthanna Club and its youth wing, al-Futuwwa; the most important political party was, however, the Arab Socialist Ba'ath Party, founded in Iraq in 1952.

King Faisal (1921–1933) sided with the Iraqi nationalist vision to counterbalance Britain's heavy weight. Thus, the king, or for that matter the state, became a social agency for building a nation-state, and Britain, the foreign factor, was a catalyst accelerating the process. The king was aware of the importance of the Shiite constituency in domestic politics, but British constraints left very little room for maneuvering, which resulted in underrepresentation for the Shiites in the cabinet. Conscious of the complexity of the situation, King Faisal began building schools and state-sponsored education to nurture national sentiments, common feelings, and common purpose, thus adding to the middle-class intelligentsia, the carrier of national ethos. Between 1921 and 1940, elementary students increased from 8,001 to 89,482, and secondary students, from 110 to 13,959. Toward the project of building a nation-state, Faisal placed the promising youths among the Shiites into an accelerated training program to afford Shiites high positions in the government; he gave the Kurds an appropriate quota of public positions; and by 1933, he had raised the number of the military from 7,500 to 11,500 men, because he considered the army to be the backbone of nation-state building. In 1934 the army became based on conscription, thus weakening tribal/urban divisions through intermingling. Faisal's sociopolitical projects aimed at containing the power of the tribal chiefs by building a responsive state with a strong army and neutralizing the Shiite religious leadership by building modern education. Successors to Faisal were, however, less politically astute. The monarchy, as a social agency for integration, changed with the coming of Abd-ul-Ilah in 1939 until the outbreak of the Qasim Revolution in 1958. Power was distributed narrowly within family and kin, the army became highly politicized, and the monarchy alienated Iraqi nationalists by identifying more closely with the British; hence, the urban uprisings of the *Wathba* in 1948, the two intifada in 1952 and 1956, and finally, the July 1958 Revolution of General Qasim.

The regime that General Qasim instituted was secular-progressive and aimed to counterpoise reemerging reactionary and traditional forces. Toward that goal, Qasim initiated progressive policies, such as land reforms, cutting rent rates, raising the minimum wage, raising taxes on the rich, raising tariffs, and building housing, schools, and medical centers for the poor, as well as legal reforms that introduced the Personal Status Law 188/1959, which emphasized the unity of the Iraqi people under the fairness of one law. Qasim's ideological politics eliminated recruitment on sectarian bases. Recruitment into the government machinery and the army emphasized "Iraqiness," not religion or ethnicity. The sociopolitical landscape at the time witnessed a thriving civil society of journalists, educators, artists, businesspeople, traders, and others. Qasim's nationalist progressive policies and his anti-imperialist platform led Iraq to withdraw from the Baghdad Pact, posing a threat to Western interests in the region. Consequently, Qasim's regime would be toppled by the Ba'ath, with strong indications of Central Intelligence Agency (CIA) backing.

The rule of the Ba'ath, particularly following the ascension of Saddam Hussein, was tyrannical and parasitic. Whereas previous state-building had progressively strengthened the organic bonds among Iraq's communities, under the national logic of Saddam Hussein, Iraq became one of unflinching loyalty to the party, enforced by violence. And with the huge wealth that accrued from the skyrocketing prices of oil revenue after 1973, the Ba'ath state was able to incorporate different classes and professions into state-sponsored projects in industrial, financial, and service sectors. By the end of 1977, about one-fourth of the Iraqi people became dependent on the Ba'ath government for their livelihood. In Iraqi towns, the government employed more than one-third of employable people.

In spite of the repressive rule of the Ba'ath, the Iraqi impulse largely remained, and in the Iran-Iraq war, Iraqi Shiites fought against their Iranian coreligionists under the Iraqi flag. As a consequence of this war, there was reallocation of much of the peasant-human resource to the battlefield, which jeopardized agricultural production. Peasants from Arab countries, particularly Egypt, were offered lucrative incentives to fill the widening gap of human input. Near the end of the war, many Iraqi conscripts returned home to find their plots and dwellings occupied by fellow Arabs. The Iraqis, on many occasions, killed the Arab peasants, whom they considered foreign usurpers, and the Ba'ath government did not intervene.

Subsequent to the 1990–1991 Gulf War, Iraq was placed under a crippling sanctions regime that impoverished its people and encouraged the reemergence of traditional bonds. This process of national unraveling was solidified with the U.S. invasion of Iraq in 2003, and its dismantling of Iraqi society.

In conclusion, the United States, in its invasion of Iraq in 2003, proclaimed itself, much like the earlier British, as a liberator bringing freedom and democracy to the people of Iraq. The progressively escalating resistance was a response to U.S. dismantling of the state, the de-Ba'athification of government employees, and the disbanding of the large Iraqi army, which deprived about 500,000 families of their livelihoods overnight. The disappearance of the state created a socio-political vacuum that was necessarily filled by remnants of traditional forces; the tribe replaced the state in providing services and security, and Shiite religious authority occupied the moral-legal domain. The constitution of 2005, drafted under the oversight of the occupation, sanctified religioethnic communities in articles 39 and 41; the present government is constituted along the same divisive segmentation, and the Iraqi cabinet cannot make a decision without consulting the Shiite religious establishment.

It is ironic that it was a Western military action in the 1920s that first propelled Iraqi nationalism, and it is now another Western military action that designs to vanquish Iraqi nationalism and its modern nation-state. Contemporary Iraq is a social incinerator plagued by party militias, rampant criminality, and foreign occupation. Furthermore, the nucleus of what could form a national movement—the educated, the technically trained, and the middle class—have all but been destroyed or expelled. Iraq was once not only viable but forward-looking; now, however, the future of Iraq and Iraqi nationhood looks immensely bleak.

Selected Bibliography

Abdullah, T. A. J. 2006. *Dictatorship, Imperialism and Chaos: Iraq since 1989.* London: Zed Books.

Batatu, H. 2000. *The Old Social Classes and New Revolutionary Movements of Iraq.* London: Saqi Books.

Davis, E. 2005. *Memories of State: Politics, History, and Collective Identity in Modern Iraq.* Berkeley: University of California Press.

Herring, E., and G. Rangwala. 2006. *Iraq in Fragments: The Occupation and Its Legacy.* London: C. Hurst & Company.

Ismael, J., and W. H. Haddad, eds. 2007. *Barriers to Reconciliation: Case Studies on Iraq and the Palestine-Israel Conflict.* Lanham, MD: University Press of America.

Ismael, T., and J. Ismael. 2004. *The Iraqi Predicament: People in the Quagmire of Power Politics.* London: Pluto Press.

Khalidi, R. 2004. *Resurrecting Empire: Western Footprints and America's Perilous Path in the Middle East.* Boston: Beacon Press Books.

Jabar, F. A., and H. Dawod. 2007. *The Kurds: Nationalism and Politics.* London: Saqi Books.

Jwaiden, W. 2006. *The Kurdish National Movement: Its Origins and Development.* Syracuse, NY: Syracuse National Press.

Marr, P. 2004. *The Modern History of Iraq.* 2nd ed. Boulder, CO: Westview Press.

Nakash, Y. 1994. *The Shi'is of Iraq.* Princeton, NJ: Princeton University Press.

Shahid, A. 2005. *Night Draws Near: Iraq's People in the Shadow of America's War.* New York: Henry Holt.

Japan

Takashi Yamazaki

Chronology

1868	The Meiji Restoration.
1894–1895	The Sino-Japanese War. Japan colonizes Taiwan.
1904–1905	The Russo-Japanese War.
1910	Japan colonizes Korea.
1914–1918	Japan enters World War I.
1931	Japan's military invasion into China begins.
1941–1945	Japan enters World War II (defeated).
1945–1952	Japan is occupied by the Allied Powers (U.S. military forces).
1946	The new constitution of Japan is proclaimed.
1949	The Chinese Revolution initiates the Cold War in Asia.
1952	Japan's sovereignty is restored; the Japan-U.S. Security Treaty becomes effective.
1955–1974	High economic growth.
1964	The Olympic Games are held in Asia for the first time, in Tokyo.
1972	U.S. administrative rights over Okinawa revert to Japan.
1985	The patriarchal Nationality Law is revised so that children with a Japanese mother are given Japanese citizenship.
1986–1991	There is a drastic increase in stock and land prices (the Bubble Economy).
1989	The Showa emperor dies (the end of the Showa era).
1991	The demise of the Soviet Union.
1999	The National Flag and Anthem Law is legislated.
2001	Japan's Self Defense Forces (SDF) provide logistic support for the U.S. military campaign in Afghanistan.
2003–present	SDF supports the rehabilitation of Iraq following the U.S.-U.K. attack on the country.
2006	The Fundamental Law of Education is revised.

Situating the Nation

The sociocultural uniformity of the Japanese is high, with two factors promoting it. Geographically, Japan is an island country surrounded by ocean. Historically, it adopted an isolation policy from the 17th to 19th centuries. The basis of the uniformity was established in near-modern times. However, the expansion of Western imperial powers into Asia during the 19th century forced Japan to open itself to the world. The Meiji Restoration in 1868 was a kind of coup d'état in which the feudal Tokugawa shogunate was replaced by a new government aiming to reconstruct Japan as a modern nation-state ruled by the emperor (*Tenno*). The restoration was the beginning of Japan's industrialization and military build-up, to make an underdeveloped state comparable to the West. The new government promoted the drastic centralization of the country, which had been divided into various feudal domains. As Japan was incorporated into the competitive modern world, the construction of the Japanese nation through public education and the print media was also initiated.

From the late 19th to the mid-20th centuries, Japan colonized Taiwan, Korea, and part of China through repeated wars. Such colonization made the "new" Japanese nation multinational. However, resistant movements by colonized people, such as Koreans and Chinese, took place. An imperialist attempt to integrate East Asians against the West was an utter failure, leading to Japan's defeat by the Allied powers in World War II. As a result, Japan lost its colonies and accepted occupation by U.S. military forces until it restored sovereignty in 1952. Due to the loss of its colonies and the suspension of nationality for the colonized peoples, the Japanese became socioculturally uniform once again.

The new constitution of Japan, which was drafted by the U.S. occupation force and proclaimed in 1946, declares that Japan is a pacifist state and has prevented the rise of aggressive nationalism. After the Chinese Revolution in 1949, the Cold War developed in East Asia between such capitalist countries as Japan, South Korea, and the United States and such socialist countries as China, North Korea, and the Soviet Union. For this reason, U.S. military forces continued to be stationed in Japan. These conditions enabled Japan to focus on economic recovery without significant defense spending. The resulting economic growth from the late 1950s to the early 1970s succeeded in narrowing the income and information gaps among Japan's localities. Unlike Europe and the United States, Japan achieved high economic growth in part by absorbing not foreign immigrants but the rural population within Japan. Although the number of foreign nationals has been increasing since the late 1980s, Japan's strict immigration policy contributed to postwar national uniformity. Due to an absence of international conflicts and the maintenance of national uniformity, large-scale nationalistic movements have rarely taken place in postwar Japan. A few exceptions include leftist resistance to the U.S. military presence within Japan from the 1960s to 1970s and rightist historical revisionism for the reconstruction of national identity since the 1990s.

Article 9 of the new constitution stipulates that Japan must forever renounce war as a sovereign right of the state and the threat or use of force as the means of settling international disputes. Instead, the Japan-U.S. Security Treaty (effective in 1952, revised in 1960) provides that U.S. military forces be stationed within Japan to protect the country. Along with the postwar democratization, led also by the U.S. occupation force, antiwar pacifism embodied in the constitution was favorably accepted by the Japanese public. Leftist intellectuals and workers, who had been oppressed by the prewar government, first welcomed the U.S. occupation. However, realizing that Japan would be incorporated into the U.S. military strategy against the Communist bloc, they organized protests against the Japan-U.S.

Security Treaty. Although anti-U.S. movements such as this did not necessarily address the socio-historical contents of the Japanese nation, they regarded the antiwar pacifism, based on the common memory of the war, as a new element of Japanese national identity.

After Japan achieved high economic growth in the 1960s, the positive reevaluation of the Japanese nation repeatedly appeared in the domestic and international media. Japan's success story tended to be ascribed to several attributes believed to be socioculturally unique, such as its cultural uniformity, group orientation, diligence, consensus building, and so forth. Until the second peak of economic growth in the late 1980s, Japanese national identity was not so threatened as in the following decades. One of the reasons for this is that, under the Cold War and the U.S. nuclear umbrella (i.e., protection) over Japan, Japan's international role was easily defined as a capitalist growth pole in Asia.

However, the demise of the Soviet Union in 1991 and the increasing economic globalization elsewhere in Asia necessitated the redefinition of Japan's relationship to the United States and Asia. This structural change over Japan's political economy in the region gave rise to the rightist historical revisionism that attempts to positively reevaluate Japan's imperialist past so that the Japanese can be proud of themselves. This nationalistic movement was first organized by a group of university professors who aimed at revising school history textbooks. It not only promoted broader public debates over the future of Japan but also attracted governmental and public criticism from South Korea and China. The reestablishment of Japan's subjectivity in the increasingly competitive international arena has now become one of the crucial agendas in Japan's foreign and domestic policies. The Japanese prime minister's visit to the Yasukuni (War) Shrine, which enshrines class-A war criminals from World War II, may be accepted in Japan as an action to redefine the collective memory of the war. However, such an action has induced strong opposition in South Korea and China, since their postwar nationalisms have been formed as resistance against Japan's imperialism. The (re)construction of national identities in East Asian countries does not stand alone but can be closely related to others' memories and interpretations of the war. Thus, how to situate the Japanese nation in Asia is not limited to the matter of Japan itself.

Instituting the Nation

The institutional core of the Japanese nation has been the emperor (*Tenno*) since the Meiji Restoration. The historical roots of the imperial family trace back to 585 BC. The emperor/empress ruled Japan until the 12th century when the shogun came to power. Upon the Meiji Restoration, modernist politicians reinstalled the emperor system into the new regime to transform Japan into a unitary nation-state. The deification of the emperor contributed to national integration and the rise of aggressive nationalism until the end of World War II. Dying for the emperor constituted part of Japanese attitudes toward wars. The idea of the Japanese nation under the emperor, therefore, was a political project promoted by elites. However, the concept of the Japanese nation-state sometimes appeared in premodern textual materials, and the imperial family has its origin in the ancient period. From the late 19th to early 20th centuries, Japan attempted to create a multinational empire consisting of Japanese and colonized people, which was a serious failure. The slogan of fighting against Western colonial powers did not generate any shared values between colonizing Japan and colonized Asia.

After World War II, the Allied powers questioned the status of the emperor as one of the sources of Japanese militarism. However, General MacArthur, who led the U.S. occupation force, considered the survival of the emperor system as the means for a smooth occupation and postwar reform. The emperor was finally exempted from his responsibility for the war, and the new constitution was drafted to limit the roles of the emperor to symbolic (nonpolitical) ones, such as participation in national ceremonies. In this sense, the emperor system has worked to

The Postwar Emperor System

Unlike the emperor before World War II, the current emperor is neither a sovereign of Japan nor the living God of the divine nation. According to the new constitution, the emperor is the symbolic figure representing Japanese citizens, and the sovereign power of Japan exists in Japanese citizens. The roles of the emperor are regulated by the constitution. It limits the official functions of the emperor to 12 national ceremonies, such as the formal appointment of the prime minister selected by the National Diet. However, when the Showa emperor died in 1989, most Japanese, whether positively or passively, went into mourning for him. The media report on the lives of the imperial family on a daily basis. They gain public attention and popularity. The birthday of the emperor has been designated as a national holiday.

---

help integrate the Japanese. As mentioned above, the loss of former colonies also contributed to the reintegration of the Japanese. It pushed back the boundaries of the Japanese nation to those in the precolonial periods, which promoted a public sense of national uniformity at the existential level and discrimination against foreign nationals within Japan.

Political parties have promoted politics over nationalism. The new constitution drafted by the U.S. occupation force regulates the rebirth of aggressive nationalism by protecting individual rights and prohibiting the possession of aggressive military forces. However, dissatisfied with the contents of the constitution, two major conservative parties united themselves into the Liberal Democratic Party (LDP) in 1955. The objective of this union was to occupy more than two-thirds of the seats in the National Diet so that the constitution could be amended. Since then, the LDP has been a dominant party potentially in favor of the promotion of nationalism and the amendment of the constitution. Leftist parties, such as the Japan Socialist Party (currently the Social Democratic Party of Japan) and the Japan Communist Party, support the constitution and its pacifist contents. As the leftist parties declined after the 1990s, the conservative politics supported by the LDP came to the fore. The legislation of the National Flag and Anthem Law in 1999 and the revision of the Fundamental Law of Education in 2006 aimed to cultivate patriotism among younger Japanese. In addition, Japan's Self-Defense Forces (SDF) were dispatched to provide logistic support for the U.S.-led military campaigns after 9/11.

Defining the Nation

It is not easy to define "the Japanese nation" objectively. Its commonsensical definition may be ethnic Japanese that share a common language, culture, and history. Currently, all children born to a Japanese parent are given Japanese citizenship.

The nation may be called *Yamato minzoku* (Yamato nation), which is distinguished from minority ethnic groups, such as *Ryukyu minzoku* (mainly Okinawans) and *Ainu minzoku* (Ainu). These ethnic groups were included into Japan as it expanded beyond its three original islands (Honshu, Shikoku, and Kyushu). Near the end of the 19th century, the current territorial and ethnic boundaries of the nation were settled.

As mentioned above, however, prewar Japan was a multinational empire in which Japan ruled the Asia-Pacific region. After World War II, the loss of the former colonies and the denial of Japanese citizenship for colonized people (even those living in Japan) helped the Japanese define themselves as a uniform nation. Due to such postwar national uniformity, mainland Japanese (i.e., native Japanese in Japan proper) tend to believe that the boundary of their nation is self-evident and neglect that there have been ethnic minorities in Japan. Foreign nationals living in Japan total not more than 2 percent of the total population. Almost three-quarters of them are Asian nationals, such as Koreans and Chinese. Both the strict immigration law and the blood-based nationality law have also contributed to the exclusion of foreign nationals from the range of the Japanese nation.

On the other hand, postwar intellectuals have tended to describe Japanese sociocultural uniqueness in comparison to the West, not necessarily to Asia. Since the Meiji Restoration, one of Japan's political economic goals has been Westernization as modernization. The postwar occupation, democratization, and economic rehabilitation of Japan were led by the United States. The relationship to the United States promoted, rather than hindered, the goal of Westernization.

The Ethnic Composition of Postwar Japanese Society

The boundaries of the Japanese nation are difficult to determine. Because the national census excludes any questions about ethnic origin (it is argued that the existence of any would promote ethnic/racial discrimination), the actual ethnic composition of Japan cannot be known. The blood-based nationality law and the strict immigration law contribute to the reproduction of a racially uniform society. The rough numbers of ethnic Okinawans and Ainu are 1 million and 25,000, respectively. Approximately 15,000 foreign nationals (two-thirds of whom are Koreans) are naturalized every year. Since naturalization is the result of long-term residence and/or international marriage, applicants tend to assimilate themselves into Japanese society. The ratio of international marriage was over 5 percent of the total marriages in 2004, which means a racial/ethnic mix is very gradually underway in Japan. The rate of foreign nationals has been increasing and exceeded 1.5 percent of the total population in 2004 but is still significantly low. The biggest group of foreign nationals living in Japan in 2004 was Koreans (30.8 percent) followed by Chinese (24.7 percent). Many of those Koreans are second and third generations fully integrated into Japanese society but excluded from citizenship due to the strong feeling of a mono-ethnic society. Statistical data on foreign nationals can be obtained from the Immigration Bureau of Japan.

Therefore, the postwar self-definition of the Japanese nation has still been wandering between the West (or the United States) and Asia.

After the war, the northern and southern fringes of Japan's precolonial territory were occupied: the Northern Territories by the Soviet Union, and the Amami and Ryukyu islands by the United States. The movements aimed at the return of the territories have continued but have not grown nationwide. Unlike the territories from which Japanese were evacuated during and after the war, Japanese (mainly Okinawans) remained in the southern islands. Before the islands reverted to Japan proper, there were a series of irredentist (reversion) movements for national reunion in the islands, despite the fact that people in these islands are ethnically different from mainland Japanese. The rise of such irredentist nationalism was caused by the U.S. (foreign) control over the islands.

The same can be said with Japan proper. The occupation of Japan by U.S. military forces ended in 1952, but Japan has since been dependent on U.S. forces for territorial security. This has become one of the reasons for anti-U.S. sentiments among Japanese. Such sentiments have been constructed against the new constitution drafted by the U.S. occupation force. Leftists regard the constitution as a basis of postwar pacifism against U.S. military hegemony. Rightists consider it a hindrance to Japan's complete independence with its own constitution and military power. However, generally speaking, anti-U.S. sentiments as a form of Japanese nationalism have not been strong among the Japanese public. This is probably because many Japanese still believe that the U.S. nuclear umbrella is necessary for Japan. Instead of historical revisionism or disputed territories (i.e., Takeshima Island and the Senkaku Islands), Japanese nationalism might be stimulated by anti-Japanese sentiments among South Koreans and Chinese.

Narrating the Nation

Japan's defeat in World War II had a tremendous impact on the nation's memory. Most notably, the atomic bombings of Hiroshima and Nagasaki have been referred to as fatal lessons of a totalitarian militarist state. The ground zeros of the bombed cities have been preserved as memorial sites for Japanese antiwar pacifism. Due to the postwar complete transformation of the Japanese value systems, the prewar achievements by victories and heroes in wars are not necessarily admired. Instead, a number of war monuments and memorial sites are dedicated to victims of the war. For many Japanese, Hiroshima and Nagasaki represent not only the lessons of the war but the possible outcomes of future nuclear wars. The memory of the war has constituted a basis of postwar pacifism that swears not to repeat the disasters.

Yasukuni (War) Shrine in Tokyo has played an opposite role. The shrine used to be the national center of state *Shinto* (the native religion of Japan) and enshrines

Prewar Japanese military officers visit the Yasukuni Shrine, a war memorial in Tokyo, Japan, in this undated photo. (Library of Congress)

not only fallen soldiers since the Meiji period but also class-A war criminals during the war. The ideology represented by the shrine is a positive evaluation of Japan's imperial past, which contradicts the international consensus condemning it. Former prime minister Koizumi justified his visits to the shrine as a way to express respect for war victims for the state. His statements brought up diplomatic issues with South Korea and China, both of which consider his conduct insulting to their nations.

Before the end of the war, the emperor attended religious ceremonies at the shrine. According to the old constitution, he was to be respected as a sovereign of the Japanese empire and to be treated as a living God. Even after the war, the new constitution maintains his symbolic role and leaves room for him to act for national unity. For rightists, his ideological role for the Japanese nation is not negligible. Even though the modern status of the emperor is an invention by political elites, the ancient origin of the imperial family, which traces back more than 2,000 years, strengthened the emperor's political legitimacy as a national sovereign. Discourses regarding the historicity of the imperial family have contributed to the creation of a patriarchic state and affected the Japanese people's popular consciousness about their national origin.

Japan's postwar economic success has added group orientation and diligence to the resisters of Japanese national traits that used to be recognized by

Flag of Japan. (Corel)

Westerners through Zen, Bushido, Noh, or Ukiyoe. However, as mentioned above, Japanese intellectuals have tended to describe Japanese sociocultural uniqueness in comparison with the West. Western intellectuals have also represented the uniqueness as something absent in their own cultures. Such a mutual recognition actually constitutes part of Japanese cultural identity. At the symbolic level, the national flag (*Hinomaru* or "rising sun") and anthem (*Kimigayo* or "your era") are most frequently used to express Japanese national identity at public ceremonies and international events today. However, the reflection on the war has long suppressed the overt expression of national identity or nationalism among the Japanese public. On the other hand, ethnic minorities, such as Okinawans and Ainu, are actively attempting to express their ethnic identities through unique cultural activities.

Mobilizing and Building the Nation

Under the U.S. nuclear umbrella during the Cold War, Japan faced few dangers of military conflicts and felt little necessity to mobilize the nation. Thus, there have been no large-scale national movements. Rather, antiwar pacifism and antinationalistic sentiments themselves constituted part of the postwar Japanese col-

Hinomaru and Kimigayo

Although the Japanese national flag (*Hinomaru* or "rising sun") and anthem (*Kimigayo* or "your era") was not officially institutionalized until 1999, the official use of them began in the Meiji period. They have also been widely used for ceremonies and international events, such as the Olympic Games. However, since the flag and anthem became the symbols of Japan's militarism before World War II, there has been strong opposition (mainly by leftists) to their use in such public spaces as schools since the end of the war. The Ministry of Education attempted to obligate public schools to use them for ceremonies in 1996. This caused heated public debates and serious conflicts between school principals and opposing teachers, students, and parents. To settle this issue, the Liberal Democratic Party (LDP)-led cabinet presented to the National Diet the bill of the National Flag and Anthem Law in 1999. The bill passed by more than a two-thirds majority. The law does not obligate their use but actually legitimizes it. The emperor himself commented in 2004 that it was better not to impose their use.

lective identity. Through the media and public education critical of World War II, the Japanese had been socialized as such. However, the Japan-U.S. security arrangements caused nationwide anti-U.S. movements in the 1960s and 1970s. These movements can be categorized as national protest against U.S. military hegemony over Japan and Asia. In relation to them, the irredentist movements were initiated locally in Okinawa. The movements were also nationalistic protests against the U.S. military presence (Okinawan movements later shifted toward the preservation of their ethnic identity).

After the demise of the Soviet Union, some rightists began to argue that a lack of national consciousness among Japanese politicians and citizens could become a serious problem, and others suggested that school education attempted to weaken the national pride of children by overemphasizing the negative aspects of prewar (and wartime) Japan. Since the late 1990s, grassroots movements to revise school history textbooks have prevailed nationwide and promoted historical revisionism aimed at reconstructing Japanese national identity. The rise of such revisionism was in parallel with the decline of leftist parties and has seemingly contributed to the formation of a series of LDP-led coalition cabinets. These cabinets have promoted neoliberalism (market economy) and neoconservatism (national unity and active diplomacy). During the 1990s, the Japanese economy experienced a serious recession and faced increasing competition with emerging economies in Asia. Under such circumstances, the Japanese nation may need to be mobilized for national interests.

Neoconservative politics promoted by the cabinets included the overseas dispatch of SDF to logistically support the U.S. military campaigns after 9/11 and tougher diplomacy toward China and South/North Korea. Military cooperation with the United States against terrorism, nuclear tensions with North Korea, and territorial disputes with South Korea and China are all new political agendas for Japan in the 21st century. Given that sociocultural uniformity has been kept high in Japan, external threats such as these may mobilize the Japanese nation against them. In light of the deepening human and economic interaction among Asian countries, including Japan, a more multicultural or civic sense of nation needs to be cultivated within Japan.

This chapter begins with the statement, "The sociocultural uniformity of the Japanese is high." As shown above, however, such uniformity must be understood in relation to its geo-historical contexts. The uniformity of the Japanese nation is socially constructed and tends to conceal the reality that Japanese society has included various minority ethnic groups. As the international environment surrounding Japan becomes increasingly competitive, the myth of mono-ethnic Japan is reconstructed and tends to be reinforced. As shown in the case of the former prime minister's visits to Yasukuni Shrine, an attempt to reconstruct Japanese national identity through historical revisionism may have serious conflicts with identities of other nations in Asia. Such conflicts may not be contained within the realm of national identities but may develop further into political economic issues in Asia. An attempt to know the origin of a nation can become an opportunity to realize that the geo-historical construction of the nation's nationality cannot be separated from the existence of other nations.

Selected Bibliography

Constitution of Japan. (Retrieved January 4, 2007), http://list.room.ne.jp/~lawtext/1946C-English.html.

Dower, J. W. 1999. *Embracing Defeat: Japan in the Wake of World War II.* New York/London: Norton.

Field, N. 1991. *In the Realm of a Dying Emperor.* New York: Pantheon Books.

Immigration Bureau of Japan. (Retrieved January 4, 2007), http://www.immi-moj.go.jp/english/index.html.

Ishihara, S. 1991. *The Japan That Can Say No.* New York: Simon and Schuster.

Prime Minister of Japan and His Cabinet. (Retrieved January 4, 2007), http://www.kantei.go.jp/foreign/index-e.html.

Sakai, N., B. de Bary, and T. Iyotani, eds. 2005. *Deconstructing Nationality.* Ithaca, NY: Cornell University East Asia Program.

Shimazu, N., ed. 2006. *Nationalisms in Japan.* New York/London: Routledge.

Yoshino, K. 1992. *Cultural Nationalism in Contemporary Japan: A Sociological Enquiry.* New York/London: Routledge.

Jammu and Kashmir

Vernon Hewitt

Chronology

1846	Treaty of Amritsa.
1931	Riots in Srinagar highlight the plight of Muslims in state-run factories dominated by the Dogra Rapjut Hindus.
1932	The Glancy Report calls for educational reform and setting up some form of representative government inside the Princely State.
1932–1933	Sheikh Abdullah forms the Muslim Conference (MC).
1942	Split occurs between the MC and Abdullah, who forms the National Conference.
1944	Abdullah publishes *The New Kashmir*, in which the concept of *Kashmiriyat* figures prominently, and he calls for a socialist Kashmiri identity free from narrow religious identities.
1946	Abdullah calls upon the Dogra Rajput ruling house and its maharaja, Hari Singh, to "Quit Kashmir."
1947	(August) The British grant independence to the dominions of India and Pakistan. (September–October) Muslim tenants involved in a long-standing rent strike against the Dogra Rajputs in the Poonch Jagir resist the maharaja and begin a rebellion. (October 27) Sheikh Abdullah is released from prison. The maharaja signs the Instrument of Accession joining India. Correspondence from the governor general and from Indian prime minister Nehru conclude that, once the state settles down, the maharaja's decision to join India will be ratified by a plebiscite asking the people of the former Dogra Kingdom whether they wish to stay with India or join Pakistan. (October–November) Afridi Muslim tribal members begin to cross from the North West Frontier Province (NWFP) in the newly constituted state of Pakistan to help "liberate" their fellow Muslims in Kashmir. This "invasion"—perceived as a Pakistani ruse to force Kashmir to join with Pakistan—leads to chaos in the summer capital of Srinagar.
1948	(December) A cease-fire is mediated in Kashmir by the United Nations.
1952	The Delhi Agreement between Nehru and Abdullah limits Indian and Union state rights versus the state over communications, foreign policy, and economic taxation.
1953	Sheikh Abdullah is arrested by the Indian authorities for "entering into a treasonable correspondence" with foreign powers. Allegations of communalism are also made against him.
1956	The Srinagar state government ratifies Jammu and Kashmir as an integral part of the Indian state subject to the provisions of Article 370. The Sino-Pakistan Border Treaty alters the status of the territory in the former Dogra state.
1962	The Indochina War leads to fighting in the vicinity of Ladakh.
1964	Theft of the Holic Relic in the Hazratbal Mosque in Srinagar leads to Muslim riots and agitations throughout the Vale.
1965	Pakistan launches Operation Gibraltar in which Kashmiri operatives from Pakistan infiltrate the cease-fire line. Second Indo-Pakistani War.
1968	Sheikh Abdullah is released from jail. He has formed the Plebiscite Front while in prison.

1971   Sheikh Abdullah is rearrested after giving an "inflammatory" speech in Srinagar. (October) Pakistan makes a preemptive strike in the western sector as India prepares to invade east Pakistan. Heavy fighting in Kashmir.

1972   The Shimla Conference produces an apparent settlement in which the cease-fire line is moderated into a line of control. Pakistan and India agree to resolve their differences "bilaterally and in accordance with the UN charter." India sees this agreement as taking the Kashmir issue outside the orbit of the United Nations and of replacing New Delhi's earlier commitment to a plebiscite.

1975   Mrs. Gandhi declares a national state of emergency. Abdullah is released from prison and signs an agreement with Indira Gandhi. Abdullah is "inducted" as the chief minister of a Congress-run state party.

1977   Mrs. Gandhi declares national elections and is defeated by a coalition of parties at the political center. Sheikh Abdullah wins a state election as head of a National Conference government, having spurred a congressional offer of a coalition.

1982   Sheikh Abdullah dies. His son, Farooq Abdullah, is sworn in as chief minister. Protests in Srinagar occur over the nepotism and corruption of the National Conference government.

1984   Mrs. Gandhi dismisses the Farooq government under Article 356 of the Indian constitution. (October) Mrs. Gandhi is assassinated by her Sikh bodyguard. Farooq is reinstalled as chief minister.

1985   Rajiv Gandhi undermines Farooq Abdullah's control of the National Conference and installs G. M. Shah as chief minister. Widespread unrest spreads throughout the valley. Formation of the Muslim United Front.

1987   Rajiv Gandhi announces an electoral pact with Farooq Abdullah for the forthcoming Jammu and Kashmir state elections. They face a coalition of Muslim parties. The electoral victory of the Congress/National Conference coalition is greeted with widespread cynicism in Kashmir.

1988–1989   Widespread unrest, including bomb explosions and the targeting of National Conference politicians and Hindus in the Vale itself.

1989   The Kashmiri state government is dismissed. Widespread violence occurs. The Jammu and Kashmir Liberation Front (JKLF) kidnap the daughter of the home minister of the new non-Congress national coalition government of V. P. Singh, the daughter of the prominent Kashmiri politician Mufti Sayed.

1990–1994   These years witness widespread insurgency with a sudden growth in militant organizations with various political wings and fronts, including the formation of Hurriyat. The Indians deploy large numbers of security forces and military personnel.

1994   State elections are held, but there is a low turnout. Farooq Abdullah is returned to power but is increasingly confronted by Bharitya Janata Party (BJP) (Hindu)-led coalitions at the center of Indian politics.

1996–1997   The Farooq government responds to various initiatives by the center to engage in talks over Article 370.

1999   (May) Pakistan assists and supervises an attack by Afghan militants from the Kashmiri town of Kargil, 12 miles inside the Line of Control. Heavy fighting ensues.

2000   State autonomy bill is presented, which seeks a revamping of Article 370. It is criticized by the center and is seemingly unable to convince people in the Vale that it will be able to deliver the goods.

2002   State elections; Faroog Abdullah is defeated by Munsi's Muslim Popular Front.

2003   An Indo-Pakistan peace process is initiated.

Situating the Nation

There are three main variants of Kashmir national identity. The first emphasizes a territorial "language of belonging" that charts Kashmir across shared cultural and linguistic understandings, regardless of religion. This view stresses the similarities and familiarities among ostensibly differing faiths that have, over the *longue duree*, contributed through conversion and coexistence to a so-called *Kashmiriyat*, a form of nationalism associated with Sheikh Abdullah and wider concepts of secularism and socialist emancipation. The second is a shared conception of Kashmiri identity and culture premised on Sunni interpretations of the Muslim faith but that does not seek to be a theocratic stance. The third emphasizes the importance of religion, expressed through the language of Urdu, and potentially excludes other religious minorities by imagining and narrating an Islamic state.

Within the territorial rivalries of South Asia, these differing routes to nationalism have been mostly demonstrated by the standoff between India and Pakistani nationalism that has shaped the subcontinent since independence in 1947. The ideas of the *Kashmiriyat* support a secular project that lies close to official Indian nationalism, as well as the idea of a separate but secular Kashmiri state. The centrality of Muslim Sunni identity for the second supports in theory the inclusion of the Muslims of Kashmir into the state project envisaged by the Muslim League and Pakistan, whereas the third demands a separate Islamic state, or the incorporation of the state into a "properly" theocratic Pakistan. This latter version leaves unanswered the difficulties of integrating Hindus and Buddhists and "tribal" Kashmiris, as well as the considerable variation within and between Kashmiri Muslims themselves given the small Shia population situated around Kargil.

Sheikh Muhammad Abdullah (1905–1982)

Abdullah was one of the principal Kashmiri nationalists and instigator of the Quit Kashmir campaign in 1946. Cofounder of the Muslim Conference and then the National Conference, Abdullah was profoundly impressed by his experiences at Aligarh, in the United Provinces of India, where he studied chemistry. Upon his return to the valley, he came to believe that the most successful way of opposing the maharaja's rule was not through a narrow appeal to Muslim religious grievances but through a socialist and secular agenda that targeted land reform and promised employment. His vision of Kashmir was close to Nehru's project of a secular and progressive India, but he never abandoned the idea of an independent Kashmir, "the Switzerland of Asia," a bridge between India and Pakistan. Known as the Lion of Kashmir, he spent 1953–1968 imprisoned by his old friend and ally, emerging in the 1970s as a key ally of Mrs. Gandhi. Toward the end of his life, however, he was criticized for presiding over an increasingly moribund and authoritarian party that ignored a new generation of Muslims and failed to accommodate the growing ethnic differences within Kashmir itself.

The territory at the heart of the present dispute is historicized as the former Dogra Kingdom of Jammu and Kashmir. This area consists of approximately 223,000 kilometers of land situated in the northeast region of the South Asian subcontinent. Since December 1947, the former Dogra state has been divided between India, Pakistan, and China, 78,000 square kilometers in Pakistan, 101,000 square kilometers in India, and 44,000 in China; 45 percent of the former Princely State is administered by India and contains a majority of the population. The area has seen several wars (1948–1949, 1965, and 1971), with a serious Indo-Pakistani incident in 1999.

Kashmir was integrated into Hindu and Muslim kingdoms emanating from India and with Buddhist kingdoms linking the Vale into Tibet and across into northern China. Kashmir remained within the Moghul empire until incursions by the Afghans cut off and surrounded the Vale toward the middle of the 18th century. Eventually the Afghans were driven out by the emergent Sikh empire in 1819, until eventually the area was ceded to the British in the wake of the Anglo-Sikh wars under the Treaty of Amritsa in 1846.

Defining and Instituting the Nation

Kashmiri nationalism is a "modern force" emerging from British colonial reforms made in the middle of the 19th century, especially in the realm of education. The British administered the South Asian peninsula through direct annexation and by coopting existing Princely States through treaties, a general principle known as paramountcy. The legacy of education reform was crucial for later nationalism. In part it created the first generation of Muslim leaders, people such as Sheikh Abdullah, Gulam Abbas, Mirza Beg, and G. M. Sadiq, who were exposed to the idea of mass-based politics and, through ideas such as the Khalifat Movement, saw Muslims as a "community" regardless of their territorial location. It allowed Muslims in Kashmir to see themselves as both part of and, later, different from their brethren throughout the British empire. Yet Western ideas of education brought concerns about the role of Islam and the need to ensure religious identity separate as much from "other" Muslim practices as from "other" religious groupings.

The ruling house of Kashmir, the Dogra Rajputs, were Hindus closely aligned with the Sikhs and were of ethnic Punjabi stock. While still submitting to the Sikh empire, Maharaja Gulab Singh had pressed on with a policy of annexation and conquest that had brought Ladakh and parts of Baltistan into his *jagir*, increasing the multiethnic, multicultural dimensions of his state. However, a majority of the maharaja's subjects were Sunni Muslim and, in comparison with the Pandit Hindus who worked closely with the Dogras, were desperately poor. Mass education encouraged political thought, which shifted toward ideas of mass representation and a demand for jobs. By the late 19th and early 20th centuries, these ideas began to consolidate into religious, communal identities as well as exposing differences in language, script, and social practice within these apparently homogenous groupings.

Khalifat Movement (1919–1924)

A campaign organized by Indian Muslims, the Khalifat Movement was founded in the provinces of British India to protest British war aims against Turkey and the abolition of the sultan, who was recognized as the caliph of Islam. Muslims then worked alongside the Gandhian-run Quit India Movement, which involved a large majority of Hindus and was successful in bringing together India's two main communities as well as the Congress and the Muslim League, which had been formed in 1906. In retrospect, the Khalifat Movement is significant because it shows the complex positioning of Islamic "pan-national" symbolism alongside political parties aiming to capture a share of national power. Although Congress supported the movement, it was unhappy at the degree of Islamic activism it encouraged in support of the sultan. In Kashmir, the Khalifat Movement was an important reminder for how close the language of nationalism comes to the language of religious revivalism.

Sheikh Abdullah, an educated Muslim, returned to Srinagar in 1930 from Aligarh, where he had been deeply influenced by the political ferment throughout India led by the Indian National Congress Party and the Muslim League. In 1931, riots broke out in the state jail over apparent slurs against Islam by officers of the Dogra police force (a Hindu in this case), and strikes and agitations aimed at improving the conditions of Muslim workers occurred. Sheikh Abdullah used these incidents to launch the All Jammu and Kashmir Muslim Conference (the Muslim Conference) in 1932 to open the Dogra state to political reform. The British assisted in this process by recommending, through the Glancy Commission, that the maharaja introduce a legislative assembly—the Praja Sabha—containing 75 members, 35 of which would be voted for from communally defined constituents on a limited franchise (about 3 percent of the population). In 1932, Abdullah's party took 11 of the 35 elected seats.

These early participatory politics revealed divisions within the Muslim elite and among Kashmiris of differing religious belief, class, and language. Abdullah soon felt that his political ambitions were constrained by what he saw as the narrow communal platform of the traditional Urdu-speaking Sunni Muslims who, he felt, due to their religious conservatism, were reluctant to embrace reform. They, in turn, were concerned about Abdullah's populism and his attempts to propagate ideas of the *Kashmiriyat*, as well as his commitment to socialism. Eventually the differences between Abdullah and his former ally, Mirwaiz Yusuf Shah, led to a split within the Muslim Conference and the formation of a rival party in 1939, significantly known as the *National* Conference.

Abdullah's use of the *Kashmiriyat* to stress his secular credentials attracted the attention of Jawaharlal Nehru and the Indian National Congress, but *Kashmiriyat* disguised the extent to which Abdullah was careful to articulate in his political speeches concepts of the homeland that were profoundly Muslim and potentially independent of India. In 1946, as the pace of colonial reform quickened in New Delhi on its way to independence, Sheikh Abdullah called upon the Dogra Rajputs, the maharaja, and the flunkies of the Princely State to "Quit Kashmir." He was immediately imprisoned for challenging the maharaja.

By early 1947, Britain's attempt to retain a weakly federated, three-tiered system of government for a united India had failed. In June of that year, the British committed themselves to partition and insisted that the Princely States join either India or Pakistan, premised mainly on geographical location and several other ill-defined factors. Because of its position, Kashmir could join either state, and it signed temporary treaties with both. By August 15, 1947, the maharaja Hari Singh had not signed the Instrument of Accession—the legally binding document—and was complaining of Pakistani pressure. Matters became immensely more complex by two interrelated events: a rebellion in the Poonch district by Punjabi Muslims, who had long-standing grievances of their own, and a tribal incursion from the North West Frontier Province along the Jhelum Valley, which, by October 1947, threatened the capital of Srinagar. Both pressured the maharaja to join Pakistan.

Jawaharlal Nehru (1889–1964) (years in office, 1950–1964)

One of India's leading politicians, and closely associated with Mahatma Gandhi, Jawaharlal Nehru was one of the leading congressmen from the 1920s to the 1960s. Imprisoned by the British on and off between 1921 and 1944 (for 18 years in total), Nehru intellectualized and articulated a version of Indian nationalism that was both multicultural and secular. He took the territorial outlines of the former British Indian empire and sought, through parliamentary government, to construct a federal system premised on liberal democracy in a society that was profoundly hierarchical and communalized through British colonial practice. In 1947 he reluctantly conceded to the partitioning of South Asia and the creation of Pakistan as a state for the Muslims of South Asia, but he categorically rejected that Congress was a Hindu organization and that Muslims would face systematic discrimination in a united India. His friendship with Sheikh Abdullah was critical in ensuring that India's initial policy toward Kashmir was popular in the valley. He was himself of Kashmiri descent.

Punjabi Muslims had long-standing ethnic and kinship ties with Muslims in Poonch, and the widespread communal killings in British India had incited feelings against the maharaja and the Hindus. The Muslim Conference, by supporting the Muslim League and Pakistan, aligned itself with the Poonch rebels as well as the tribal groups, although again they were seen as "outsiders" by Muslims as much as by other non-Muslim Kashmiris. By October 1947, the maharaja was forced to flee Srinagar, and he signed the Instrument of Accession on October 27 en route to Jammu, committing his state to join with India. Correspondence in the public domain reveals that the imminent fear of a Pakistani attack forced the maharaja's hand such that he joined with India to obtain Indian forces to take on the rebels. The documents also reveal that, at the suggestion of the governor general (the former viceroy, Lord Louis Mountbatten), the Indian government committed itself to holding a plebiscite "once normality had been restored" to ascertain whether the peoples of Kashmir wished to join India or Pakistan.

Narrating the Nation

The Indian authorities ensured that Sheikh Abdullah was freed and made de facto chief minister of the Praja Sabha. Members of the Muslim Conference, however, now situated outside the valley in the town of Muzaffarabad, favored the Pakistani demand to include the former Dogra Kingdom within the new state created for the Muslims in South Asia. By November and December, Pakistani regular troops were fighting the Indians, and on the last day of December 1947, the matter was referred to the United Nations by India under Article 35. At the signing of a cease-fire in late 1948, the former Dogra Kingdom was itself partitioned.

Although given their own constitution, Azad Kashmir remained administered by the central Pakistani government, with the Northern Territories being hived off from Muzzaffarabad. Like Abdullah, leaders of the Muslim Conference continued to hold a vision of an independent state along the lines of the former Dogra territory. From the mid-1970s onward, this vision of a "third way"—the call for a separate Kashmiri identity and nationalism free of both Delhi and Islamabad—was to emerge as an explicit option. Ultimately, the remaining territory—Jammu and Kashmir—became part of the Indian union.

Beginning with the Delhi Agreement of 1952, Abdullah sought to preserve Kashmir as a "unique" state within India's federal setup. A detailed federal constitution for India devolved some financial and legislative powers to a Kashmir assembly, elected through a noncommunal, universal franchise, and Kashmir was given seats in the national parliament (six as of 2004). For its part, the Muslim Conference sought to establish Azad Kashmir as an autonomous zone within Pakistan. In this regard, in part because of the greater institutional capacities of the Indian state, Abdullah seemed to be more successful, and yet by 1953 he had been arrested under Nehru's orders. The sudden deterioration in the relationship between Nehru and the leader of the National Conference probably resulted from India's growing cold feet over the thought of a plebiscite, as well as due to disagreements over the eventual status of Kashmir within Indian federalism.

Following Abdullah's removal, New Delhi imposed Gulam Mohammad Bakshi as state leader, and in 1956, he led the National Conference in a vote for the inclusion of Jammu and Kashmir into the Indian constitution under the ambit of Article 370, which granted Jammu and Kashmir extraordinary rights—among them the ability to prevent Hindu immigration into their territories, to show and display the Kashmiri flag, and to refer to its leader as prime minister. Yet Nehru saw Article 370 as temporary, as marking a process of transition, whereas Abdullah and others saw it as a permanent recognition of Kashmiri difference. However special, Article 370 sat uneasily within the Indian constitution, which was in many senses covertly centralist. The constitution retained a series of emergency clauses that would enable central intervention into the workings of a state government (including nomination of powerful governors). Despite specific rights laid down in the agreement, state governments in Srinagar could be—and frequently were—dismissed by a Congress-run center. India's financial structures gave all vested powers to the center.

In prison, Abdullah formed a new party—the Plebiscite Front—and corresponded further with former colleagues in Azad Kashmir, who were growing disenchanted with their own relationship with Pakistan. His new party was banned in 1953. In 1968, Abdullah was released but was rearrested in 1971 by Indira Gandhi, the daughter of Nehru. The cause of the arrest was a provocative speech given by Abdullah in Srinagar in which he seemed to question the long-term future of Jammu and Kashmir as an integral part of India. He implied not so much a shift of loyalties to Pakistan but an assertion of the idea of an independent nation.

From 1953 onward, Kashmir was ruled through the local Congress state party in close coordination with New Delhi, or through manipulating the factions within the National Conference. In 1965, during the second Indo-Pakistan War, Kashmir was directly involved in an attempt by Pakistan to infiltrate the cease-fire line with Kashmiri operatives. In 1975, ironically during the Internal Emergency (which saw the collapse of Indian democracy for a time under Mrs. Gandhi), Sheikh Abdullah was released and led a Congress state government, a move seen by many former allies as a betrayal. Then, in 1977 following the restoration of Indian democratic rule, Sheikh Abdullah emerged as the leader of a National Conference administration for the first time since 1953. This period, until his death in 1982, was marked by growing corruption within the state government and a shift toward populist authoritarianism within the party. Social and cultural differences within the former Dogra Kingdom had also began to emerge, with Buddhist demands in Leh for greater regional autonomy within the state and from the Jammu region, which desired autonomy within the state of Jammu and Kashmir. On his death in 1983, his son, Farooq Abdullah, inherited the National Conference.

Mobilizing and Building the Nation

Following India's unilateral cease-fire in the wake of Bangladeshi independence, New Delhi moved to make good some territorial gains in the west, and at the former British summer residence in India—Shimla—Mrs. Gandhi and Zufika Ali Bhutto for Pakistan concluded a treaty. There were no Kashmiri representatives present, and this treaty converted the cease-fire line into an apparently "soft" Line of Control (LoC). This was, on the whole, a novel move that would eventually "merge" the former Dogra Kingdom into India and Pakistan but allow Kashmiris to travel relatively easily within their former kingdom. The attempt to convert the LoC into the new international border failed because of general Kashmiri outrage over not being directly consulted and a lack of clarity within the Shimla Accord itself over the status of the "soft border." Still in jail at that point, Abdullah opposed the Shimla Accord, believing that it undermined the wider Kashmiri cause; he insisted on the commitment to a plebiscite and the treatment of the former Princely State as a whole. India saw Shimla as removing, once and for all, the Kashmir dispute from the remit of the United Nations by committing Pakistan to treating the matter bilaterally, and as burying its earlier commitment to holding a plebiscite. The United Nations had, despite a series of resolutions and reports, long ceased to be an effective vehicle through which to arrive at a settlement.

Between 1972 and 1983, relative peace reigned in Kashmir. Yet, in the wake of Mrs. Gandhi's assassination in 1984 and the rise of Rajiv Gandhi's Congress, New Delhi reverted to directly and shamelessly intervening in the state. In 1985, Rajiv Gandhi orchestrated a "coup" within the National Conference Party that replaced

Farooq Abdullah by installing his brother-in-law, G. M. Shah, as chief minister. Such moves alienated popular opinion from a belief in the viability and desirability of Indian democratic practice. Marred with growing corruption, the political institutions of the state and their ability to provide for the expectations of a new generation of Kashmiris declined. There was a growing sense that Kashmir had been ill served both by its own elite and by Article 370.

Cultural and religious identities were also changing. These changes were partly a consequence of poor governance and partly in response to changes throughout the Islamic world in the wake of the Iranian revolution, occurring throughout the Gulf states generally and in India itself. They were also due to influences emanating from Azad Kashmir. In the early 1980s, the Farooq Abdullah government allowed up to 20,000 Azadi Kashmiris to resettle in the Vale before the process was delayed by the intervention of the Indian Supreme Court. These refugees were religiously orthodox, reflecting the experience of Pakistan's own growing Islamic identity. Generational changes and a wider dissemination of religious tracts and ideas led to a growth in religious foundations and seminaries. Linked to local issues such as low levels of employment and corruption, these institutions deepened social and cultural change. India itself witnessed the growth and emergence of Hindu nationalism, which quickened its pace during the Rajiv Gandhi years. It enhanced the concerns of Kashmiri Muslims, as the ideology of Hindutva sought to influence Indian ideas of secularism through Hindu cultural revivalism.

The growth of overt religious symbolism from 1985 onward alarmed Delhi as well as the National Conference at a time when the old party structures were in decline. Once again, the old opportunist tendencies between Kashmiri leaders and the center created a spectacular show of cynicism. Despite the 1985 coup, Rajiv Gandhi formed an electoral pact with Farooq Abdullah for the forthcoming state elections. They confronted a coalition of Muslim politicians—the Muslim United Front—that were closer in their use of Muslim identity to the old Muslim Conference. The Gandhi-Abdullah pact sought to manipulate Islamic imagery to capture political power—especially in the Vale—but ended up merely consolidating the power of Islamist groups as legitimate vehicles of concern and anger against years of misrule. Such blatant opportunism by Congress also alienated other religious identities, especially the Hindus, and Jammu and Ladakh became concerned about potential domination by Muslims. In the years that followed, the increase in Islamic identity within the valley further differentiated religious and cultural identities.

The 1987 elections produced a Congress/National Conference victory amid widespread allegations of rigging and corruption. The defeat of the Muslim United Front was widely (if inaccurately) believed to have been the result of a conspiracy. Into this growing controversy sprang other parties and other social movements—the Jammu and Kashmir Liberation Front, Islamic student organizations, and several Islamic parties and movements, most principally the Jamaat, linked to Pakistan (although increasingly critical of Pakistan's own social and religious policies). Other groups were home-grown militant outfits or entirely foreign and increasingly linked not so much with Kashmiri politics but with international Islamic revivalist movements. By 1989, the JKLF—a separatist, secular movement —had gained popular support in the Vale and had, in combination (and competition) with other organizations, brought law and order to its knees. Political violence and assassination had escalated rapidly by 1989; prominent National Conference politicians and businesspeople—especially Hindus—were being targeted. In 1989, the state government resigned. This resignation took place against the background of a weak national coalition government in India as a whole.

By 1989–1990, Muslim demands had breached the willingness of India to tolerate concessions for fear of encouraging Pakistani intervention or outright separatism. The release of four JKLF militants by the then Indian government of V. P. Singh (in response to the kidnapping of the new Indian home minister's, Mufti Sayeed's, daughter in Kashmir) sealed the fate of the Kashmiri Pandits, who believed they were no longer safe. They fled to Jammu where, well over a decade later (2004), they remained, having fled on the apparent advice of the state governor, Jagmohan. Only in 2003–2004 did a newly elected government in the state try to persuade them to return.

From 1989 until 1994–1995, the political process of Indian-administered Kashmir was suspended. The political structures of the National Conference and the Congress, and many other regional parties, disintegrated as the area was directly administered from Delhi, and the territory became the scene of a large-scale deployment of Indian security forces and the widespread use of preventive detention ordinances. Contributing to, but not initially creating, the insurrection, the Pakistani state covertly supported the activities of various Islamic militant outfits, especially the Jamaat and its militant wing, Hizbullah. Pro-Pakistan outfits, allegedly trained inside Azad Kashmir, fought with the JKLF to gain popular support, while a loose coalition of parties formed the All Party Hurriyat Conference (APHC) to pressure India into allowing Kashmiris to choose their future as a part of India, part of Pakistan, or an independent state (either secular or Islamist, an issue the Hurriyat left open). By 2002, the APHC consisted of over 26 political organizations and parties of a bewildering variety of views.

Between 1989 and 2003, over 40,000 Kashmiris died in the violence, and the Indians have deployed up to 60,000 troops and paramilitary outfits in the state. A majority of the deaths have been civilian. Hindu organizations in Jammu, in part invigorated by the rise of Hindu nationalism throughout India in the 1990s, became determined to press on with the "integration" of Jammu and Kashmir into the mainstream political fabric of India, believing that Article 370 had been to blame for fanning Muslim aspirations. Amid alleged human rights violations by Indian security forces and militant outfits, and allegations of Pakistani infiltrations over the LoC, the 1990s became the vortex of a separately articulated Kashmir nationalism, a result that ironically neither India nor Pakistan was prepared to accept.

A Pakistani soldier stands along the Line of Control near Chakoti in Pakistani-held Kashmir in August 2002. (AP/Wide World Photos)

In 1996, the Indian state normalized the political situation and held state elections under the Indian constitution. The APHC boycotted these elections, in which Farooq Abdullah returned to power after a low turnout amid widespread intimidation of voters. The National Conference was committed to reworking and reinvigorating Article 370 as a basis to calm the Kashmiri situation and restore it to India under its special status. Yet Farooq found himself paradoxically sharing power at the center with a Hindu, nationalist-led coalition government, hostile to the continuation of Article 370 and, by the late 1990s, apparently contemplating talks with the APHC and even the reorganization or partition of the state. In 2000, aware of his failing popularity, Farooq Abdullah sponsored an autonomy bill that sought to entrench Kashmir's status while restoring it to the outlines of the Delhi Declaration of 1952, afraid that New Delhi would actually make an overture to the APHC.

The sticking point appeared to be the insistence by the APHC that any talks with Delhi include trilateral talks with Pakistan. Eventually the APHC was to split over this issue in 2003, with the pro-Pakistani elements being purged, but this happened only after the National Conference itself was widely discredited. In state elections in 2002, Farooq Abdullah was defeated and replaced by a Muslim-based party known as the People's Democratic Party and led by the former home minister, Mufti Sayeed (whose daughter had been kidnapped in 1989). This government shared power with a revitalized Indian National Congress. This change in regional government was matched with a later defeat of the BJP-led National Democratic Alliance in New Delhi and the return to power of the Indian National Congress. The Sayeed government remains committed to protecting Kashmiri interests within the Indian constitution.

The crisis is less acute than in the 1980s but is still evident. Recent peace overtures between India and Pakistan (August 2005) appear to be gathering momentum, but it is too early to tell whether this latest round of initiatives will break the regional deadlock and open a space for some form of settlement. Profound differences still exist between India's answer of making the LoC the permanent but porous border between the two parts of the former Dogra Kingdom and Pakistan's hope that the borders will be redrawn, giving it a significant stake in the valley itself. Many Kashmiris now want an independent state but are exhausted by over a decade of violence. The political and institutional renewal of state and national parties may, however, prove adequate for maintaining the current peace process and leading to some sort of solution.

Selected Bibliography

Ganguly, S. 2001. *Conflict Unending: India-Pakistan Tensions since 1947.* New York: Columbia University Press.

Hewitt, V. M. 1995. *Reclaiming the Past? The Search for Political and Cultural Unity in Contemporary Jammu and Kashmir.* London: Portland.

Lamb, Alastair. 1991. *Kashmir: A Disputed Legacy, 1846–1990.* Hertingfordbury, UK: Roxford.

Schofield, V. 2003. *Kashmir in Conflict: India, Pakistan and the Unending War.* London: I. B. Tauris.

Wirsing, R. G. 1994. *India, Pakistan and the Kashmir Dispute: On Regional Conflict and Its Resolution.* Basingstoke, UK: Macmillan.

Zutshi, C. 2004. *Languages of Belonging: Islam, Regional Identity and the Making of Kashmir/ Chitralekha Zutshi.* London: Hurst.

Korea

Dennis Hart

Chronology

First millennium BC   Old Choson Period. The oldest recorded period on the Korean peninsula.
57 BC–AD 668   Three Kingdoms Period. Control of kingdoms that extends throughout the peninsula and includes almost all of modern-day Manchuria.
668–935   Unified Silla. Cited by South Korea as the "start" of a unified Korea.
935–1392   Koryo Dynasty. Cited by North Korea as the "start" of a unified Korea.
1392–1910   Choson Dynasty. The final Korean dynasty, destroyed by foreign imperialism.
1894–1895   Sino-Japanese War. Japan defeats China in Korea to become the dominant Asian power.
1910   Korea is colonized by Japan. Japan begins to destroy Korean society and culture.
1919   March First Movement. Koreans display modern national identity and stage a nationwide protest against Japanese colonialism.
1945   Korea is liberated from Japan and divided at the 38th parallel into North and South by the United States and the Soviet Union.
1948   The Republic of Korea (South) and Democratic People's Republic of Korea (North) is established. The division of the peninsula continues through today.
1950–1953   Korean Civil War. More than 2.8 million Koreans are killed as the United States, China, and the United Nations (UN) wage war on the peninsula.
1961–1979   General Park Chung Hee stages a coup; he becomes president of the Republic of Korea (ROK). The ROK undergoes capitalist industrialization.
1987   Civil Democratic Movement in the ROK. Dictatorship in the ROK ends and formal democracy arises.
Mid-1990s   The Democratic People's Republic of Korea's (DPRK) economy collapses. Kim Il Song dies in 1994 after leading the DPRK since 1946. Leadership is assumed by his son Kim Jong Il.

Situating the Nation

Korea is a divided nation and has been for over half a century. This division is more than a line on a map. It is a division made by rival regimes, opposing ideologies, and global politics. Korea is also a nation divided by rival forms of nationalism. There have been, and are, a variety of nationalisms. These nationalisms are varied and complex, reflecting the various histories, polities, ideologies, classes, and genders experienced by Koreans. That Korea is one nation with two rival political systems is a result of the global struggle between superpowers from 1945 to 1948 during the Cold War. During this time, the global and ideological aspirations of the United States and Soviet Union clashed in a Korea that itself had social and political divisions. This set the stage for the rise of two different polities, the division of the nation, and the beginning of rival national identities.

The people on the Korean peninsula have a recorded history of over 2,000 years. During this time, they were largely independent from foreign rule. However, from 1910 until 1945, Korea suffered under a brutal and repressive colonial rule by the Japanese. Much of the land and wealth of Korea was put under Japanese control, and the Japanese attempted to eradicate the Korean people's national identity by a series of harsh policies. Most Korean political movements were banned, and patriots were put into prison, tortured, and often killed. It was a dark and terrible time for the Koreans, as the Japanese worked hard to remove all traces of Korean national identity from existence.

When Japan surrendered to the Allied forces at the end of World War II, the American and Russian military forces occupied the Korean peninsula, divided it at the 38th parallel, and accepted the surrender of Japanese forces located there. Though this division was originally designed to be temporary, by 1948, the politics of the Cold War gave birth to a civil war and more than a half century of division.

In the southern part of Korea, the Americans viewed the actors and events in Korea through the lens of the Cold War. They believed that, unless strong action was taken, communism might emerge victorious in Korea. The Americans worked with a collection of right-wing groups, which included well-to-do landlords, Koreans who had collaborated with Japan, and Koreans who had lived outside the peninsula during the colonial period. An American occupation, headed by General John R. Hodge, ruled over Korea in the late 1940s and was determined to maintain order and control during a time of great change. As part of their policy of control, the American military actively helped suppress indigenous popular movements, such as people's committees who did not support the right-wing groups favored by the United States. A series of widespread rebellions and strikes occurred during 1946–1950, which the American military helped South Korean president Rhee Syngman put down. Koreans clashed with American soldiers as well as South Korean police forces, and tens of thousands of Koreans died while hundreds of thousands were imprisoned.

In the North, very different events took place under the Soviet occupation from 1945 until 1948. Similar to the Americans in the South, the Russians eventually came to see events in Korea in terms of the ideological rivalry of the Cold War. Early on, the Soviet forces lacked a coherent policy, other than disarming the surrendering Japanese forces in Korea. They quickly discovered that a coalition of nationalists led by Cho Man Sik, indigenous leftists, and returning communists lead by Kim Il Sung, who became leader of the provisional government in February 1946, desired a social and political revolution that would rid Korea of Japanese influences. An interim government approved by the Soviets and headed by Kim Il Sung began a series of radical reforms that included a land reform program, equal pay for women, an eight-hour workday, and social security insurance.

South Korea (Republic of Korea, ROK) was officially established on August 15, 1948, and North Korea (Democratic People's Republic of Korea, DPRK) on September 9, 1948. This formalized the divisions already put in place by global superpowers.

Instituting the Nation

One early form of nationalism occurred in Korea from 1894 to 1895, during the Tonghak Rebellion. It was perhaps the first organized step by Koreans in a movement that simultaneously questioned the traditional polity and ideas and was a form of resistance to foreigners. This movement appealed to many Koreans suffering under heavy taxation, government corruption, and economic troubles brought on by foreign merchants. The Tonghak did not envision the creation of a modern nation-state and was more a reaction to the Korean government's inability to deal successfully with foreigners. Ironically, one result of the rebellion was to spark the Sino-Japanese War (1894–1895) and set the stage for the Japanese takeover of Korea in 1910.

The next major event that helped Koreans define their nation was the March First Movement in 1919. Seen within the context of the Japanese seizure and colonization of Korea from 1910 to 1945, it is an event that is generally considered by most Koreans as being the "true" beginning of Korean national identity. For the people in both Korean states, this movement is considered the first time when all Koreans had to confront their identity both within and through the context of modern nationalism. Oppressed by the Japanese, who served as the national Other, contemporary Koreans used this movement to reify a widespread sense of being Korean that was born of the ideals and constructions of the 20th century.

In the wake of the protest, Japan briefly granted considerable latitude to Koreans during the 1920s. In the 1930s, however, hypermilitarization in Japan and the outbreak of war between China and Japan resulted in a reversal of these policies. The Japanese government began an extensive top-down mobilization of the Korean people to serve in the war effort. More insidious was a series of oppressive policies aimed at eliminating Korean identity. These policies forbade the use of the Korean language, compelled Koreans to adopt Japanese names, and forced them to worship in Shinto shrines. The desired end, for the Japanese government, was the total assimilation of Koreans into Japanese culture.

During this period, some Koreans collaborated with the Japanese. Other Koreans resisted both outside and inside the peninsula. This ultimately helped set the stage for the rise of rival ideological groups among the Korean resistance. The Japanese set up such an extensive and effective police state that many Koreans were forced to flee the country to escape capture. Those Koreans who fought for Korean independence from abroad fell into two basic groups—the Korean Provisional Government, which operated out of Shanghai, and Communists who fought a guerilla war in Manchuria during the1930s and 1940s. From these two groups would eventually come the leaders of the South and North Korean states, respectively. During these hard times, to simply be a "Korean" was a form of resistance toward Japanese imperialism.

Defining the Nation

Nationalism in Korea is best defined as resistance. Since the intrusion by foreign powers in the late 19th century, Koreans have had to confront their identity in ways that contrasted them against foreigners, against tradition, and even against themselves. The result has not been a single or simple form of nationalism. Koreans have witnessed and participated in a wide range of nationalist actions; but all have been some form of resistance.

Nationalisms in Korea should also be classified as Third World nationalism. Third World nationalisms are fundamentally different from First World nationalisms, seen in such nations as the Unites States, England, France, and other former colonial powers. First World nationalism by its nature carries with it assumptions of privilege and entitlement, and often is imperialist. Third World nationalisms, by contrast, rise in the nations that have been colonized and exploited. The nationalisms of these nations were forged in a furnace that required resistance to (neo)colonial domination in order to survive. Korea is among these nations.

Narrating the Nation

If Koreans share a single past, then why do North and South Koreans today have differing narratives on national identity? Within the twin social and political settings since national division, a challenge for each regime has been to win the hearts, minds, and memories of its own people while simultaneously creating fear and loathing for their rival across the 38th parallel. That is, making citizens into good North or South Koreans became more important than making them into Koreans.

The problem for each state has not been to generate nationalism out of thin air. Instead, the challenge has been to first create narratives that support the claim of being the only legitimate government and, second, to delegitimize the rival attempting to do the same thing. For nationalism in the North and the South, it is not enough to teach citizens how fortunate they are to live in their respective nation-states; it is also necessary to make a national Other out of their rival. Each regime's vision of nationalism assumes that each system is mutually exclusive. To be a follower of one regime, a person cannot be part of the other. If a Korean claims allegiance to North, he or she is automatically seen as an enemy of the South, and vice versa. At the same time, each Korean state commonly uses its rival as an enemy to generate fear and insecurity among its own citizens so that they will seek the protection and safety offered by their own state. Interestingly, the North and South Korean governments often speak of unification, but they need each other as a key source of their own legitimacy.

To this paradoxical end, each state narrates a history that reconstructs the national memory in a way that serves its own needs and interests. These memories are communicated through the media, campaigns of mass mobilization, legal systems, and education, to name a few. Among these, perhaps none is as widespread or effective as public education in ensuring that young children eventually become old patriots. Each state has created a centralized, universal, uniform educational system and pays close attention to the lessons contained in the schools and textbooks. This provides a uniform set of narratives on the nation.

Starting in the 1950s for South Korea, the control of education was concentrated in the Ministry of Education. By the late 1980s, the ministry was responsible for administration of schools, allocation of funds, certification of schools and teachers, and curriculum development, including the textbook guidelines. In North Korea by 1959, state-funded universal education was established and centralized instruction, educational facilities, textbooks, and uniforms were provided to students without charge.

Students in each country receive assurances that their own state is the natural product of Korean historical forces. For the South Korean state, the history provided through the national education system justifies the existence of the South Korean polity, as well as economic and social systems. For example, textbooks teach that its export-led capitalist economy is natural. School lessons laud the existence of many foreign influences and praise capitalist growth. Lessons teach southern school children how to properly greet foreign tourists, who bring both money and "progress." The textbooks repeatedly demonstrate how Korea, for centuries, engaged in commercial activities with a wide variety of other countries, and how such exchanges have helped Korea become modern.

In the North, where a belief in *juche* (self-reliance) is firmly in place, foreigners are shown as threats to national independence and that the Korean people have long resisted any foreign intrusion. Foreigners do not serve as equals or as friendly bearers of material improvements. Korea's march to modernity is not, therefore, a cooperative effort with foreigners; instead, it is an indigenous movement conducted by Koreans for Koreans. The textbooks also show how the ordinary people actively resisted foreign invasion; however, say the school lessons, without the brilliant leadership of Kim Il Sung, they would not have been able to succeed.

For decades, the school lessons in the both Koreas have taught children to loath the rival regime, but feel sorry for Koreans living there. In the South, the northern state and its agents are shown as a monolithic threat to the lives and to the safety of the South. The textbooks contain many stories of northern spies and guerrillas who follow a foreign ideology (communism) and routinely kill South Korean children and their families. Yet, in other stories, southern children learn how their northern cousins are poor, starving, and suffering under communism. This prompts the children to feel pity and superiority at the same time. At one level, southern students learn to feel unity and sympathy for their northern brethren. Yet, at another level, fear is used to help secure the power of the southern regime since it offers protection from the northern regime.

In the North, similar narratives appear. Students learn to feel sympathy for southern children who are starving, in rags, and even "sell their eyes" to get food. At the same time, foreigners are held up as a constant danger, and only continued allegiance to the state and the ideology of *juche* can save the children. The North's ideology voices a need to exorcise the demons of foreign influence while working toward completing liberation of the people in the South and establishing socialism throughout the Korean peninsula.

Mobilizing and Building the Nation

The question addressed here is how the rival states of North and South Korea mobilize their people in support of their respective different national and ideological visions of Korea in the world. To answer this, we need to see how Koreans live their daily lives, since that is where nationalism is manifested. The South envisions the nation in competition with the North and its people as tied to export-led capitalist industrialization that requires them to be "citizens of the world." The need for foreign trade requires the South to invite in foreign influences and products and to live life in a way that supports a market economy. The North adheres to *juche*, which teaches economics and political self-reliance as a nation and as a people. The basis for national identity and strength is seen as emanating from the Korean people, and foreign intrusion is regarded as a threat. The North's desire to defend against foreign aggression has combined with the *juche* ideology to produce a militarized society. Thus, at the fundamental level of how Korea is to be located within the larger global community, the two regimes are at odds. However, both regimes also feel the need to mobilize their people in the name of the nation.

Following Park Chung Hee's 1961 coup d'état, South Korean state policies orchestrated a march toward capitalist industrialization that eclipsed traditional society and gave rise to urbanization, new forms of labor, and a consumer culture. The goal of the authoritarian rulers was to create a society that was socially disciplined and economically advanced so as to be able to defend against the Communist North. One famous mobilization campaign was the Saemaul Movement, instituted in the fall of 1971. The movement was an intensively administered campaign to improve the quality of rural life, and it eventually reached into 36,000 villages. Emblematic of larger policies, this movement evolved into an extensive ideological campaign that mobilized the entire country in support of "nation-building." It also helped mark the end of a rural Korea and ushered in widespread industrialization, which in turn changed the nature of life in South Korea.

By the 1980s, these policies brought a number of unexpected social changes that have promoted the emergence of a more materialist, consumer society. They also redefined everyday life and generated a need for production and consumption to bolster economic development, which resulted in the creation of the middle-class family. As a result, the activity of consumption is central to everyday life today and, for most South Koreans, is part of a national identity that separates them from tradition. The typical Korean in Seoul might feel more comfortable in New York City, Tokyo, or London than in rural Korea of 200 years ago. These changes have not been easy, nor have they been peaceful; but for many Koreans, they have raised the key question of "Who are we?" There have been contesting answers to this question by a variety of groups within South Korean society, and no consensus has emerged.

The democracy movements and events surrounding the June 1987 protests serve as one example of how modern identity has been highly contested. Economic growth and consumerism eroded traditional sources of political legitimacy —Confucian morality and hierarchy. Instead, political legitimacy became linked more to economic performance and an abundance of material goods. Prior to the 1980s, the focus of dissenting discourses addressed (1) the end of authoritarian state oppression, and (2) how to stop capitalism's erosion of Korean society. By the late 1980s, protesters still waged a battle against the authoritarian state; however, instead of seeking to end the effects of capitalism, protests argued over the best ways to continue capitalist growth. This shift marked a de-radicalization of political demands as popular discourses accepted the aims of capitalism. Having grown up within a capitalist society, people's identity as Koreans and their vision for the nation diverged sharply from that of the Korean Civil War generation.

As an example, in 1985, opposition leader Kim Dae Jung revised his decades-long opposition to capitalism and agreed with the government to end his ties with radical leftist forces. He later remained silent in 1986 during a government crackdown on radical university students, a group who theretofore he had counted as political allies. For South Koreans, the nation increasingly meant a capitalist nation capable of satisfying the consumer demands of its people.

North Koreans define the nation quite differently. *Juche* mandates self-reliance from foreign powers and requires extreme and disciplined unity throughout society. One part of this was a level of hero worship rarely seen. Kim Il Sung was

Student demonstrators wear police riot gear as they walk with a banner during a protest in Seoul, South Korea, on June 23, 1987. Resistance and protest are integral parts of Korean national identity, and rallies all over South Korea eventually brought the authoritarian regime of President Chun Doo Hwan to an end. (Patrick Robert/Sygma/Corbis)

Leaders, Parties, and Political Tension

Kim Il Sung (1912–1994)
Kim Il Sung was the ruler of North Korea from 1946 until his death in 1994. He was born near Pyongyang, and he joined the Korean Communist Party in 1931. He was a legendary leader of the anti-Japanese guerilla army in Manchuria, and he became the center of an extensive and lavish personality cult.

Kim Jong Il (1942–)
Kim Jong Il is the son of Kim Il Sung. He succeeded his father as president of North Korea in 1994.

Korean Civil War (1950–1953)
In 1945, the United States and the Soviet Union divided Korea. In 1949, both powers withdrew, leaving behind two separate and opposing Korean regimes. On June 25, after a series of border clashes, the North Korean military moved south to unify the peninsula. The United States and the United Nations soon intervened in the civil war, which later drew in China.

Japanese Occupation of Korea (1910–1945)
Following the imperialist lessons learned from European nations, Japan colonized Korea officially in 1910. During this time, Japan attempted to replace Korea's national identity with Japanese nationalism.

Juche
Socialist North Korea's guiding ideology is *juche*, which means self-reliance, literally. It has two main principles: (1) a person is the master of his or her destiny, and (2) he or she should remain free from outside influences. This ideology was used to legitimize the rule of Kim Il Sung and later Kim Jong Il.

March First Movement
On March 1, 1919, Koreans rose up and protested Japanese colonial rule and oppression while proclaiming independence for Korea as a nation. The events were widespread and peaceful. The responses of the Japanese were severe and violent. More than 2 million Koreans took part in the movement. The Japanese killed over 7,500 of the participants, tortured thousands of others, and imprisoned another 46,000 men, women, and children.

Park Chung Hee (1917–1979)
President of South Korea from 1962 until his assassination in 1979. Park Chung Hee served in the Japanese military during World War II. Later, as a general in the South Korean military, he led a coup over a democratic government. He oversaw the industrialization of South Korea.

Rhee Syngman (1875–1965)
Rhee Syngman was the first president of South Korea, from 1948 until 1960. He was an early member of the Korean independence movement. In 1960, he was forced to flee the country due to corruption and an election-rigging scandal.

The Tonghak Rebellion (1894–1895)
The Tonghak Rebellion was a religious peasant uprising based on ideals drawn from different traditional thoughts, including Confucianism, Buddhism, and Taoism. It opposed foreign intrusion into Korea and preached social egalitarianism.

not merely the "iron-willed, ever-victorious commander" or the "respected and beloved Great Leader," he was "the supreme brain of the nation."

From 1946 to 1958, North Korea faced national division, removed the legacy of colonial exploitation, overturned a traditional class system, conducted the most successful land reform program in history, repelled invasion by the United States and the United Nations, and rebuilt its economy after a devastating civil war. Until 1975, its standard of living was second in Asia only to that of Japan. Without "iron-willed" discipline and national unity, it is doubtful if the North would exist today, let alone have accomplished any of these. Regardless of how they are viewed by outsiders, North Koreans believe themselves members of a nation that is the envy of the world.

During those halcyon days, North Koreans enjoyed modest material wealth and a safe society. They participated in state and local political meetings on a daily basis, and enthusiastic participation was mandatory. Public parades of nationalist pride, private rituals honoring Kim Il Sung, workplace meetings on the brilliance of *juche*, schoolyard assemblies lauding the nation, and media broadcasts soaked in state-approved propaganda permeated every facet of life. Never before has a nation so mobilized and orchestrated the daily lives of its citizens. By all accounts, the vast majority of North Koreans, if not fully convinced of the "Great Leader's" brilliance, at least were comfortable enough to give him the benefit of the doubt.

In the mid-1990s, life got worse in a hurry. The internal limitations of *juche* combined with years of natural disasters to push the economy and the socialist paradise into virtual collapse. Since then, nearly 200,000 North Koreans have fled their homeland to China in hopes of food and survival; though once there, they often suffer discrimination, abuse, violence, torture, human trafficking, and rape. However, interviews show that the North Korean refugees still deeply support the North's current political and ideological system and hope to return in the future. They are food refugees and not political refugees. In North Korea, a generation is virtually wasted by malnutrition and lack of medical care. Yet, its citizens remain loyal to their ideology and nation.

Selected Bibliography

Armstrong, C. 2004. *The North Korean Revolution: 1945–1950.* New York: Columbia University Press.

Cumings, B. 1997. *Korea's Place in the Sun.* New York: W. W. Norton.

Cumings, B. 2004. *North Korea: Another Country.* New York: W. W. Norton.

Eckart, C. 1991. *Offspring of Empire.* Seattle: University of Washington Press.

Hart, D. 2003. *From Tradition to Consumption: Constructing a Capitalist Culture in South Korea.* 2nd ed. Edison, NJ: Jimoondang Press.

Lee, C.-S. 1965. *The Politics of Korean Nationalism.* Los Angeles: University of California Press.

Lee, K.-B. 1988. *A New History of Korea.* Cambridge, MA: Harvard University Press.

Nelson, L. C. 2000. *Measured Excess: Status, Gender, and Consumer Nationalism in South Korea.* New York: Columbia University Press.

North Korea. Library of Congress. (Retrieved 1/15/08), http://countrystudies.us/north-korea.

Pratt, K., and R. Rutt. 1999. *Korea: A Historical and Cultural Dictionary.* Richmond, UK: Curzon Press.

Schmidt, A. 2002. *Korea between Empires.* New York: Columbia University Press.

South Korea. Library of Congress. (Retrieved 1/15/08), http://countrystudies.us/south-korea.

Mongolia

Christopher P. Atwood

Chronology

1206	Premodern Mongol *ethnie* (ethnic group) unified by Chinggis (Genghis) Khan. The traditional Mongolian script is adopted.
1871	Injannashi's *Köke Sudur* ("Blue Chronicle") envisions a more secular Chinggis Khan and laments the degraded state of the Mongol people.
1892–1901	Russian and Chinese officials begin abolishing traditional Mongol autonomy and encourage peasant colonization of Mongol grazing land. Widespread resistance by aristocrats, herders, intellectuals, and bandits follows.
1911–1913	Khalkha Mongolia declares independence from China and establishes a theocratic regime; unsuccessfully tries to free Inner Mongolia from Chinese control.
1919	Chinese troops reenter Mongolia, officials and soldiers of the theocratic regime organize revolutionary cells.
1920–1921	The revolutionary cells merge, forming the Mongolian People's Party (later the Mongolian People's Revolutionary Party); they appeal to Soviet Russia and help the Soviet army establish a revolutionary government. Mongolia becomes a magnet for pan-Mongolists in Russia and China.
1924	Mongolia declares a people's republic; the first Inner Mongolian nationalist party is organized.
1931–1945	The Japanese occupy Inner Mongolia.
1932	D. Natsugdorji pens Mongolia's most famous patriotic poem, "My Homeland" ("Minii nutag").
1937–1940	Stalinist purges in Mongolia nativize the elite and destroy Buddhist institutions, as border clashes with Japanese stimulate xenophobia.
1945–1946	Mongolia joins the Soviet attack on Japan and is formally recognized as independent by China.
1947	Inner Mongolian Autonomous Government is formed by the Communists in China's civil war.
1962	The commemoration of Chinggis Khan is criticized by Mongolia's pro-Soviet ruler, Yumjaagiin Tsedenbal, as a nationalist.
1968–1969	Tens of thousands of Inner Mongols are killed in China's Cultural Revolution for allegedly supporting a secret pro-independence organization.
1981–1982	Large-scale Mongol nationalist demonstrations by students in Inner Mongolia, demanding justice and reparations.
1989–1990	Demonstrators criticizing the ruling party's subservience to Russia force out the ruling Mongolian People's Revolutionary Party.

Situating the Nation

The Mongolian people today exist in a divided state. In one sense, this division is between three contiguous states: people of Mongol ancestry are found not only in the independent state of Mongolia (*Mongol uls*), in the center of the Mongolian plateau, but also in the People's Republic of China to the south and the Russian Federation to the north. In another sense, this division is over the definition of the Mongol nation: Are those people of Mongol ancestry in China and Russia truly Mongols? Or are they independent, albeit related, peoples with their own destiny? Or are they people losing their Mongolian identity entirely, as they are assimilated with the Chinese or Russians?

The State of Mongolia (before 1992, the Mongolian People's Republic) is a relatively homogenous nation-state of about 2.75 million people. Of these, about 95 percent are of Mongol ancestry, broadly speaking, and 81.5 percent are of the Khalkha Mongol people, the dominant subgroup within the Mongolian nation. Once the Soviet Union's most loyal satellite state, Mongolia today is a multiparty democracy with a strongly nationalist political climate.

To the south of Mongolia is the Inner Mongolian Autonomous Region in the People's Republic of China. This autonomous region is tightly integrated into China, politically and economically, but has an official policy of multiculturalism, including preferential policies for Mongol students and cadres, subsidized Mongolian-language education, and an increasingly commodified Mongolian "tradition." While Mongols make up only 17 percent of the autonomous region's population, they total 3.4 million, and about 65 percent live in compact communities in the autonomous region's drier areas. The Inner Mongols see themselves as part of the core of the Mongol nation and harbor considerable separatist sentiment, despite strict repression. China also has a number of smaller autonomous prefectures and counties for isolated Mongol populations in Manchuria, the Tibetan plateau, and Xinjiang (Eastern Turkestan).

Within the Russian Federation, the Buriat Republic of southern Siberia and the Kalmyk Republic far to the west along the Caspian Sea both have their origin in Soviet-era autonomous republics. Until recently, there were also two small Buriat autonomous areas near the Buriat Republic. The Buriat and Kalmyk areas were incorporated into the Russian empire in the 17th and 18th centuries and today use Cyrillic-script versions of the local language (Buriat and Kalmyk). The Buriats (421,000 persons) and Kalmyks (174,000 persons) have strong local identities but also see themselves as part of a larger transnational Mongolian cultural sphere.

Traditionally the Mongol peoples have identified their lifestyle with nomadic pastoralism. In the center of the Mongolian plateau, this was the overwhelmingly dominant way of life in premodern Mongolia, although in southeastern Inner Mongolia and in northwestern Buriatia a semi-sedentary or sedentary agropastoral economy has been practiced for centuries. The settlement and colonization by Chinese farmers from the 18th century on, and Russian peasants from the late 19th century, provoked both local rebellions and nationalist movements among the intelligentsia, who in the early 20th century frequently extolled the Mongols' tradition of public ownership of pasture as a precursor of socialism. In Mongolia proper, Khüriye (today Mongolia's capital Ulaanbaatar) was an important urban settlement, but the Mongol people became involved in significant industrialization only after the success of the various revolutions, first in Russia in 1920, then in Mongolia proper in 1921, and then in Inner Mongolia in 1949. Thus, Mongolian nationalism took its first steps in an overwhelmingly rural economy with only a tiny class of officials and teachers.

Geographically, Mongolian nationalism developed in two basic areas: first along the periphery of Chinese or Russian settlement and then in the traditional capital Khüriye (Russian Urga; modern Ulaanbaatar) in the Mongolian heartland. Along the frontier of Chinese settlement—the Kharachin, Kheshigten, and Khorchin districts of southeastern Inner Mongolia, the Daur Mongols of northeastern Inner Mongolia, and the Chakhar area of south central Inner Mongolia —all became early cradle areas of modernizing, often anticlerical, nationalism. In Buriat lands, Russian education created a similar modernizing nationalist intelligentsia.

In Mongolia proper, however, isolated from direct Chinese colonization, the high lamas and aristocracy based in Khüriye broke away from Qing Chinese rule in 1911 and established a theocratic state, devoted to preserving the traditional culture, religion, and social order. The bureaucracy and schools of this new state nurtured a small urban and commoner-based intelligentsia that resisted the reimposition of Chinese rule in 1919 and with Soviet support formed a new revolutionary government in 1921. Throughout the 1910s and 1920s, Khüriye, renamed Ulaanbaatar ("Red Hero") in 1924, attracted expatriate Buriat and Inner Mongolian nationalists. Increasing international tensions from 1929 on, and the Stalinist Great Purges from 1937 to 1940, annihilated this cosmopolitan, expatriate nationalist intelligentsia, as a new generation of purely native-born, mostly Khalkha, intelligentsia was trained to take its place.

Up to 1950, the Inner Mongolian nationalist movement drew in Chinese-educated sons of wealthy rural herders and farmers (often landlords of immigrant Chinese tenant farmers), and the petty nobility (the *taiji* class). The Buriat nationalist movement before 1920 similarly drew on wealthy Buriat ranchers, junior members of the nobility (*taisha*), and those enrolled in Cossack regiments. In reaction against official czarist pressure for Christianization, Buddhist lamas played a significant role in early Kalmyk and Buriat Mongolian nationalism.

In Mongolia proper, nationalist resentment of Soviet domination from the 1950s on grew among younger urban Mongolians, even within the party apparatus, and played a major role in the 1990 democratic revolution that established a multiparty democracy. Today in Inner Mongolia and Buriatia, the Mongol population has rates of education as high or higher than the local Chinese or Russian population. The Mongol peoples of China and Russia also have a similar occupational profile: overrepresented in agriculture (herding and farming), government service, education, and culture and arts, but underrepresented in commerce, industry, and manufacturing occupations. Since the local economies are still dominated by state-owned enterprises with Russian or Chinese staff, the source and

Chinggis (Genghis) Khan and Mongolian Nationalism

Central to Mongolian identity is Chinggis (Genghis) Khan. While known outside Mongolia primarily as an empire builder, his Mongolian image was much more as a ruler, culture founder, ancestor, and tutelary spirit, traditionally worshiped in a number of shrines throughout Mongolia and Inner Mongolia. In the 20th century, increasing knowledge of 13th-century Islamic, European, and Chinese sources on Chinggis Khan secularize and democratize his image. From being the literal ancestor of the Mongol nobility, Chinggis Khan has become the symbolic ancestor of the nation as a whole and proof that at least once in its past Mongolia has been in the forefront of world history.

In the 19th and 20th centuries, European, Chinese, and Mongolian philologists rediscovered the *Secret History of the Mongols*, a Mongolian-language biography of Chinggis Khan written ca. AD 1252. The *Secret History of the Mongols* created a third image of Chinggis Khan, as a unifier of the Mongols with human failings but a divine destiny and a compelling and charismatic personality. The *Secret History of the Mongols* (whose language is about as archaic as that of Chaucer in English) is now one of the foundations of Mongol identity, paraphrased several times into modern Mongolian. It has been translated into the related Buriat and Kalmyk languages spoken by Mongol peoples in Russia as well.

---

audience for Mongol nationalist dissidents is the white-collar intelligentsia, often Chinese or Russian speaking.

The origins of the modern Mongol nation (or nations) lie in the premodern *ethnie* (ethnic group) unified by Chinggis (Genghis) Khan in AD 1206. The ensuing world conquests dispersed much of the Mongol people, however. In the 16th century, Dayan Khan (1480?–1517?), a descendant of Chinggis Khan, and his empress Mandukhai reunited the Mongols and enfeoffed their sons and grandsons. The nomadic shrine and relics of Chinggis Khan (now placed in southwestern Inner Mongolia) became a powerful talisman of Mongol unity and military success. By 1700, most of Mongolia was divided between literally thousands of descendants of Dayan Khan and, through him, of Chinggis Khan. The traditional Uighur-Mongolian script and chronicles focusing on the legendary tales of Chinggis Khan and how Dayan Khan reunified the Mongols solidified an aristocratic national consciousness. The conversion of the Mongols in 1581 to an unusually militant and intolerant form of Buddhism, the *Gelugba* ("Yellow Hat") order presided over by the Dalai Lama in Tibet and China's Manchu emperors, further unified the Mongol *ethnie*. Yet the Buddhist *sangha* (clergy) in Mongolia was not placed under any centralized administration. The central or Khalkha Mongols saw themselves as the *shabi* (disciples) of the great incarnate lama lineage of the Jibzundamba Khutugtus, residing in Khüriye, but his prestige was not nearly so great in Inner Mongolia or Buriatia.

In the course of the 17th and 18th centuries, the Mongols of today's Mongolia and China fell under control of China's Qing (Ch'ing) Dynasty, ruled by a Manchu emperor. The Qing, however, left the Mongol areas under a number of autonomous

Scene depicting the capture of a Chinese town by Genghis (Chinggis) Khan, from a 14th-century manuscript of the Persian history of the Mongols, *Jami al-Tavarikh*. Known in the West, Middle East, and China as a ruthless conqueror, Genghis Khan is honored by the Mongols as their unifier and national founder. (Corel)

The Manchu Yoke

The Mongols were ruled by China's last dynasty, the Manchu Qing Dynasty, from the 17th century to 1911. Under the Manchus, the traditional old regime of a Chinggisid aristocracy and a vast and wealthy Buddhist *sangha* (monastic community) reached its height. Despite the considerable artistic and cultural efflorescence, clerical and aristocratic privilege came under criticism by the Inner Mongolian writer Injannashi in the later 19th century. After the fall of the Manchu Dynasty, Mongolian nationalists in both independent Mongolia and Inner Mongolia (still part of China) excoriated the "Manchu yoke" as the nadir of their history. Mongol nationalists accuse the Qing of pursuing "divide and rule" strategies, deliberately isolating the Mongols from world progress, propping up the corrupt nobility, allowing Chinese commercial exploitation, and artificially promoting an out-of-control monasticism that led to a declining population and rampant venereal diseases. This distorted negative picture is still common in school textbooks. The 20th century is thus seen as a revival from benighted ignorance and foreign oppression.

banners (or fiefdoms) each ruled by a hereditary nobleman who was a descendant of Chinggis Khan or one of his brothers. There were 86 such banners in Khalkha (Outer) Mongolia, 49 in Inner Mongolia, and scores more of Oirat or Western Mongols scattered through western Mongolia, Xinjiang, and Qinghai. Although movement between banners was strictly limited, the Qing did enforce a uniform administrative culture over all the Mongols that promoted cultural homogeneity. At the same time, in the 19th century, Mongol writers often conceived of their people as part of a multinational pan-Buddhist commonwealth, loyally serving the Manchu Qing emperor.

Only with the reversal of Mongolian autonomy and the imposition of aggressive Sinicizing policies in 1901 did the Mongolian clergy and aristocracy turn and abandon their Qing loyalism. When the Eighth Jibzundamba Khutugtu (1870–1924) declared Mongolia independent of the Qing in 1911, he sought to rally all of the rulers of the Mongol banners in Mongolia, Inner Mongolia, and points west. Despite considerable support—a number of Mongol noblemen outside Mongolia proper led their subjects to migrate to Outer Mongolia—Russo-Chinese diplomatic moves prevented the formation of a pan-Mongolian state and ratified the separation of Outer Mongolia, under Russian protection, from Inner Mongolia, part of the new Chinese republic.

Those Mongol people in southern Siberia fell under Russian rule from the mid-17th century. Called Buriats by the Russians, they differed significantly in dialect from the Mongols of Mongolia, lacked the Chinggisid aristocracy, and were only partially converted to Buddhism. The western Buriats remained shamanist or else converted to Russian Orthodoxy and never used the traditional Uighur-Mongolian script, being literate only in Russian. The border between the Qing and Russian empires was tightly policed, allowing little interaction with Mongolia. By the mid-19th century, Buriat chronicle writers expressed czarist loyalism,

Mongol ancestry, and a growing sense of the Buriats being one people, closely related to but distinct from the Mongols.

Instituting the Nation

Suiting its dispersed state, no one institution or person has defined modern Mongolian nationalism. In Mongolia proper, the 20th century's chief nationalist institution was the Mongolian People's Revolutionary Party. Founded in 1920 as the Mongolian People's Party by merging two circles of young dissident officials, translators, and army officers, who had served Mongolia's theocratic government from 1911 to 1919, the group opposed renewed Chinese rule and sought Soviet Russian intervention. During the course of the 1921 revolution, this party turned against the old aristocracy and much of the high clergy, while adopting many modernizing and populist reforms. The party also received an influx of Buriat members, who sharpened its radical edge and strengthened its original pan-Mongolian goals. In 1925, however, the party, renamed the Mongolian People's Revolutionary Party, was forced by Soviet pressure to abandon the pan-Mongolist plank in its program. The Soviet Union found certain forms of nationalism in Mongolia to be a useful ally in excluding Chinese or Japanese influence, but at the same time, they began to develop a suspicion, which turned into a raging paranoid fear in the 1930s, of "pan-Mongolist Japanese spies."

The Mongolian revolutionaries early began to purge their own ranks. By 1924, all the original leadership troika were dead, two executed by their former comrades. The third member, General Sükhebaatur (1893–1923), had been popular among his troops and slowly became the posthumous icon of the Mongolian revolution. After 1936, when Marshal Choibalsang (1895–1952) rose to unchallenged power as Stalin's man in Mongolia, the portraits of Choibalsang and Sükhebaatur became ubiquitous images of the 1921 revolution and hence of Mongolia's independence.

In Inner Mongolia, the nationalist movement traces its origin to the iconoclastic writings of the southeastern Inner Mongolian poet and romance writer, Injannashi (1837–1892). His work, especially the *Köke Sudur* or "Blue History," exposed for generations of young intellectuals the Chinese stifling of Mongol talent, the corruption of the nobility, the obscurantism of the Buddhist lamas, and the shining value of Mongolia's ancient accomplishments under Chinggis Khan. In the 20th century, leading icons of Inner Mongolian nationalism included the multi-talented Daur intellectual Merse (1894–1934?), the banner official Gada Meiren (1893–1931), who led a doomed revolt against a Chinese colonization scheme in Khorchin in 1929, and especially, Prince Demchugdongrub (1902–1966). The Chinggisid nobleman Prince De (as his name was respectfully abbreviated) led a Mongol autonomous movement in central Inner Mongolia and eventually headed an autonomous government of Mongolia under Japanese protection from 1937 to 1945 and again on his own in 1949. His betrayal by the government of the Mongolian People's Republic and his imprisonment in China from 1950 to 1963 has made him a martyr for dissident Inner Mongolian nationalists.

More ambivalent is the role of Ulanfu (also known as Ulanhu, Wulanfu, and Ulaankhüü; 1906–1988). A loyal member of the Chinese Communist Party, Ulanfu helped co-opt left-wing nationalist governments in Inner Mongolia during 1945–1947 and became the head of the Inner Mongolian Autonomous Region from 1949 to 1966. During this time, he was criticized for toning down class struggle in Mongol regions and staffing the region's government with his own landsmen. Attacked, demoted, and forced to recant during the Cultural Revolution, he was rehabilitated in 1979 and made China's vice president until his death. While rejected as a model by dissident nationalists, he is seen as an honest defender of ethnic Mongol interests in China by moderate nationalists.

Defining the Nation

Under the Qing dynasty, the Mongol bannermen were defined by language (Mongolian was the local administrative language of the banners), religion (all banners had an official Buddhist temple and local cults), dress (court dress was regulated by sumptuary laws), and endogamy (Chinese men were forbidden to marry Mongol women). The nobility were almost all descendants of Chinggis Khan or his brothers. Local resources were collectively owned by these banners.

In the 20th century, this ethno-cultural definition became the basis for arguments of self-determination. In 1911, the Jibzundamba Khutugtu argued for Mongolian independence both in public and in private letters to foreign governments on the basis of Mongolian ancestry, language, religion, and customs, all of which differed from the Chinese. In 1919, as Mongolian autonomy was threatened by Chinese warlords and Buriats were caught in the Russian Civil War, a pan-Mongolian independence movement was organized at Dauriia Station. Composed of Inner Mongolian and Buriat representatives, the movement sent an appeal to the Paris Peace Conference explicitly demanding a pan-Mongolian state on the basis of American president Woodrow Wilson's principle of self-determination.

This focus on objective factors defining the Mongolian nation continued into the 1940s. As Communist influence increased, however, the Buddhist religion was eliminated as part of the national culture, while the descent from Chinggis Khan, previously a marker of class status (only the *taiji* aristocracy were really descendants of the national founder), was generalized to include all the Mongols. The establishment of official nationality identifications first in Russia and then in China at first reinforced the tendency to treat ethnicity as purely objective, while creating additional complications. In Russia, the Kalmyks and Buriats were clearly

Ambiguous Heroes: Lamas and Legends

The heroes of the Buddhist conversion of the Mongols in the 16th and 17th centuries have had a somewhat divisive effect on Mongol nationalism, since none are honored by all the Mongols. After the 1911 restoration of independence, Mongolia's theocratic government instituted regular offerings at the relics of Abatai Khan (1544–1588), the khan of the Khalkha Mongols who first accepted the new strict form of Buddhism. The great Buddhist incarnate lama Zanabazar (1635–1723), the first of the Khalkhas' Jibzundamba Khutug-tus, was a revered religious leader, artist, designer of the *soyombo* symbol now on the Mongolian flag, and an astute political leader. Although he is still revered as a Khalkha Mongolian national hero, his decision to lead the Khalkha into submission to the Qing Dynasty is viewed ambivalently. For the Kalmyk Mongols, the great Buddhist cleric Zaya Pandita (1599–1662), who designed a new script for the Oirat or western Mongolian dialect, has been seen as a patron saint of cultural revival and learning.

From the late 17th century to 1755, the Zunghars, a branch of the Oirats or western Mongols, led a resistance against the Qing Dynasty based in Xinjiang (East Turkistan). The Zunghar rulers are naturally seen as heroes by the Oirats in western Mongolia and Xinjiang. For the Khalkha, they are more ambiguous figures, since they also made war on the Khalkha. In Inner Mongolia, the Zunghars are seen by Chinese historians as "rebels" conspiring with czarist Russia to attack Qing China, yet Inner Mongolian historians writing in Mongolian often treat them as nationality heroes fighting against the Qing Dynasty's "feudal nationality oppression."

Fictional heroes of epics have been particularly important for Buriat and Kalmyk national feeling. Geser, the main Buriat epic hero, is the only figure shared by all the Buriats, Buddhist and shamanist alike. Jangghar, the only Kalmyk epic hero, has likewise been a noncontroversial unifying figure.

Buriat history lacks a direct association with the great figures of Chinggis Khan and other Mongol rulers. In recent decades, the memory of previous figures who led the doomed Buriat resistance to Cossack incursions in the 17th century have been cultivated as important historical figures in the Buriat past. The most revered heroes of Buriat nationalism today are the brilliant and multitalented nationalists of the early 20th century who were slaughtered in Stalin's purges during 1937–1940.

---

defined not only as separate from each other but also from the Mongols of Mongolia. In Inner Mongolia, the Mongols were still termed Mongols, but the separation of the Daurs, a small but highly educated and influential ethnic group of 121,000 (1990 figure) in northeast Inner Mongolia, was controversial. In 1982, the Chinese government allowed anyone with one Mongol grandparent to switch their ethnic registration to Mongol. At present, almost 15 percent of those officially designated as Mongols are such newcomers to the ethnic group that they have little or no affiliation with the Mongol community. Meanwhile in independent Mongolia, the awareness of such state-controlled manipulation of identities in Russia and China has strengthened their consciousness of themselves as being the only "pure" (*tsewer*) Mongols left in the world.

In China and Russia, widespread loss of Mongolian language in the cities created the ironic situation of cadres and intellectuals, who benefited most from official multicultural policies, finding their children unable to speak their ancestral language. Such acculturated urban youth were important leaders in the ethnic revivals that swept Inner Mongolia, Buriatia, and Kalmykia from the 1980s on. As a result, many urban, educated Buriats, Kalmyks, and Inner Mongols view their identity not in objective ethno-cultural terms, but rather as having a heart for their people, political activism on their behalf, and a love for their ancestry. In Russia, the obvious racial difference between Buriats and Kalmyks and the Slavic population has kept race and ancestry at the foreground of national definition. Similarly, religion (Buddhism in Kalmykia, Buddhism and shamanism in Buriatia) remains a major aspect of national identity for Mongol peoples in Russia. It is much less salient in Inner Mongolia, where nationalism has a long anticlerical tradition and where the majority of Chinese are also Buddhist (albeit of a different tradition). Many Mongols in Mongolia and Inner Mongolia believe Buddhism was harmful to the Mongols' national development, by encouraging celibacy and pacifism.

Given the territorial divisions among the Mongols and the competing empire-building of China, Russia, and Japan, the spatial dimensions of the Mongolian nation have always been a divisive issue. When the Eighth Jibzundamba Khutugtu declared independence in 1911, it was at first his own 86 banners of the Khalkha whom he called on to support him. From the beginning, however, he hoped to rally all of the Qing Dynasty's Mongol banners, whether in Inner Mongolia, Qinghai (Kökenuur), or Xinjiang (East Turkistan) to his new state. In 1913, he invaded Inner Mongolia to vindicate this claim, but was defeated when the Russians, wary of conflict with other powers, threatened to cut off support. Likewise, the Mongolian People's Party, in its first program of 1921, included pan-Mongolian unification as its ultimate aim. One area of conflict was the Turkic-speaking Tuvan Republic, northwest of Mongolia. Traditionally under the Khalkha nobles and with a heavily Mongolian religion and high culture, Tuva had been carved out as a separate puppet state by Russia. In 1925, the Mongolians were forced by Soviet pressure to delete their party's pan-Mongolian plank and recognize Tuva as independent. Mongolian financial support to Inner Mongolian nationalists continued, however, until 1933.

In 1945, Mongolia's dictator Marshal Choibalsang again tried to rally Inner Mongolia for pan-Mongolian unification in the wake of the fall of the Japanese empire. He was, however, blocked by the Sino-Soviet treaty of that year. Forced to sacrifice his pan-Mongolian ambitions, Choibalsang turned instead to securing China's formal recognition of Mongolian independence, which he achieved in 1946 and confirmed in 1949 with Mao Zedong's new Communist government of China. Since then, Mongolia's government has rigorously renounced any support for pan-Mongolism.

Although Inner Mongolians supported Mongolia's pan-Mongolian ventures in the 1910s, the 1920s, and in 1945, outside patrons and allies of Inner Mongolia's nationalists, whether Soviet, Japanese, or Chinese revolutionaries, always blocked the realization of these pan-Mongolian plans. After these defeats, the unification of Inner Mongolia, which was divided among seven Chinese provinces, as a single autonomous region in China gradually became a kind of substitute for pan-Mongolian unification. Inner Mongolia's East Mongols—populous, well-educated, partially agricultural, and significantly influenced by Manchu culture—and the sparsely settled western Mongols—partly deeply conservative nomads and partly almost completely Sinicized Mongol farmers—were finally unified in 1954 when the People's Republic of China's Inner Mongolian Autonomous Region under Ulanfu was extended west. The resulting sprawling autonomous region is, however, overwhelmingly Chinese in population, which has led contemporary dissident nationalists to propose abandoning either the eastern or western half in any projected independent Inner Mongolia or pan-Mongolian state.

In the early 20th century, Buriat nationalists, such as the lama Agwang Dorzhiev (1853–1937) and the Buddhist socialist folklorist and intellectual Tsyben Zhamtsarano (1881–1942) proposed either a pan-Mongolian state or else a pan-Buddhist state including Tibet. Since this state was to be created under Russian patronage, the Buriat nationalists generally saw their role not as a nucleus or "Piedmont" for a new Mongolian state, but as outside mentors. Only in the 1919 Dauriia Station movement, led by the Buriat secular nationalist Elbek-Dorzhi Rinchino in the middle of the Russian Civil War, did Buriat nationalists seriously consider joining a pan-Mongolian state separate from Russia. Buriat nationalists have generally rejected secession. Rather their focus is on overcoming the differences between the shamanist, semi-agricultural, Cyrillic-script-using west and the more Buddhist, nomadic, and Mongolian-script-using east. Buriatia was unified as an autonomous republic in 1923 and was later strengthened by the imposition of a single Cyrillic script, but Buriatia was dismembered again in 1937 at the height of the Stalin purges. The 1923 name of the Buriat-Mongolian Autonomous Soviet Socialist Republic expressed the Buriats' ambivalent relationship to their Mongolian identity. In 1958, the word "Mongolian" was removed from the republic's name. Today, pan-Mongolism has little if any constituency in Buriatia, unlike in Inner Mongolia. Even the reunification of the Buriat areas sundered in 1937 is seen as impractical by most Buriat nationalists.

Narrating the Nation

The most important national myth of the Mongolian peoples is the steppe and the nomadic pastoral lifestyle. The steppe is the source of the classic images of Mongolian life: the yurt, the horse and rider, the vast herds of horses, sheep, cattle, and camels, and the big blue sky. It is also seen as the repository of Mongolian values of straightforward honesty, lack of guile, reverence for tradition, physical hardiness and manly skills, kindness to domestic animals, and contact with nature.

Finally it is the ideal site for ritual activities, such as the complex and beautiful wedding ceremonies, the "three manly games" of wrestling, horse racing, and archery, and worship of local spirits at *oboo* (cairns), all of which are still widely practiced. For city Mongols and students abroad, the thought of one's old mother and father left behind on the steppe embodies nostalgic patriotism. Even Mongols from eastern Inner Mongolia, western Buriatia, or the cities of Mongolia proper feel that the steppe Mongols are the most truly Mongol Mongols. This national feeling is expressed in poetry, painting, and sculpture, in which traditional and steppe themes are particularly common. Traditional songs also express the ambiance of the steppe.

Patriotism has been a major theme in Mongolian poetry and music. The 1932 poem "My Homeland" by D. Natsugdorji (also spelled Natsagdorj, 1906–1937) became a classic of Mongolian patriotism, as did the poem "Born in Mongolia" by Kh. Perlee (1911–1982). Later, in the 1950s and 1960s, intellectual dissidents, such as the scholar B. Rinchen (1905–1979) and poet R. Choinom (1936–1979), became the voices of nationalist resentment of the compulsory kowtowing to Russian culture. In narrative forms, especially novels and movies, the most popular theme is historical romance about figures and episodes when Mongolian independence was under threat. Modern pop and rock music have incorporated traditional Mongolian poetry and throat singing (a rare form of singing originating in northwest Mongolia and now popular in world music). In the 1989–1990 democracy movement, the folk-rock band Soyol Erdene (Culture Jewel) and the lyrics of D. Jargalsaikhan expressed the Mongolians' feeling of their culture being neglected and suppressed. This role of challenging the conformist and pragmatic adaption to foreign pressures has been continued in the new market-oriented democracy by such figures as the radical traditionalist poet O. Dashbalbar (1957–1999) and the rock band Hurd (Speed).

In the 20th century, memory of political persecution has played a crucial role in nurturing nationalism among the Mongol peoples in China and Russia. During the Chinese Cultural Revolution (1966–1976) when Chinese anti-Soviet xenophobia reached its height, Mongols and their Han sympathizers were tortured into confessing membership in the fictional "New Inner Mongolian People's Revolutionary Party," supposedly controlled by the "revisionist" (i.e., pro-Soviet Communist) Ulanfu. From 1968 to 1969, 20,000 or more were killed and hundreds of thousands arrested. Although the case was pronounced completely groundless in 1978, only one of the leading perpetrators has been punished, and justice and restitution for the victims remains a major cause for Inner Mongolian nationalists, both dissident and mainstream.

The Kalmyks on the Volga were too geographically isolated from the larger body of Mongols to nurture pan-Mongolist movements. The Russian Civil War (1918–1920) led to thousands of Kalmyk Cossacks fleeing to Europe, where they maintained a strong anti-Communist, Kalmyk revivalist movement. In 1943, the remaining Kalmyks were exiled to Siberia and Central Asia by the Soviet government in 1943 for supposedly supporting the Nazi German invasion. Even though they were allowed to return in 1957 and had their autonomous republic restored, full exoneration and even partial restitution only came after the fall of the Soviet Union in 1991. The experience of flight and exile still defines Kalmyk identity today. The Buriat Mongols of Siberia also nourish the memory of great Buriat thinkers killed in the Stalinist purges.

Mobilizing and Building the Nation

In independent Mongolia, the mobilization of the Mongolian nation began in the center, Khüriye, soon to be renamed Ulaanbaatar, and proceeded outward from there. The 1911 restoration treated only the titled nobility and the high Buddhist clergy as part of the political nation, but created a new class of officials, teachers, and army officers. In the 1921 revolution, the Soviet Red Army placed the People's Party in charge of Khüriye, forming a new government representing an intelligentsia numbering a few hundred at most. The challenge for this government was to gain secure guarantees of Mongolia's independence abroad and at home to mobilize the entire Mongolian nation around their new vision of a secular, progressive nation.

Recognition of Mongolia's independence was long stymied by international refusal to recognize any changes in China's pre-1911 borders inherited from the Qing empire. The czarist government reduced Outer Mongolia's status to that of autonomy under a kind of Sino-Russian condominium in the Kiakhta Trilateral Treaty of 1915, and even the Soviet Union conceded a theoretical Chinese sovereignty over Mongolia. In 1946, however, the Chinese Nationalist government recognized Mongolia's independence, a recognition confirmed by the People's Republic of China in 1949. At first, only Communist bloc countries recognized Mongolia, but Mongolia joined the United Nations in 1961, and recognition by non-Communist powers followed.

Without Russian patronage, the Khalkha Mongolian national movements of 1911 and 1921 could not have succeeded. Russian desires to expand their influence also led to an off-again-on-again Soviet Russian sponsorship of Inner Mongolian nationalism from 1925 on. Due to this Russian patronage of Mongol nationalism in the 20th century, the Mongol peoples of Russia—the Buriats and Kalmyks—never seriously considered secession. Instead, Buriat and Kalmyk intellectuals advocated autonomy for themselves and a forward Russian policy of liberation for China's Mongols.

Throughout the 20th century, Mongolia's traditional Russian-allied nationalism has most often seen the Asian powers to the south—Japan or China—as the main danger. From 1931 to 1945, the Japanese threat led to the bloody border battles of Khalkhyn Gol (1939). Despite Nationalist China's 1946 recognition of

Mongolia, border clashes broke out in 1947. After 1949, the Sino-Soviet alliance pacified Mongolian hostility to China until the Sino-Soviet rift in 1960. From 1966 to 1984, movies, articles, academic books, and speeches focused on the dangers of Maoism to Mongolia's borders and the oppression of minorities (including ethnic Mongols) in Mao's China. Since 1984, state-to-state relations with China have been normalized, but there is still widespread anxiety about excessive openness and foreign investment possibly causing Mongolia to lose its hard-won independence and become a Chinese satellite.

From 1921 to 1990, overbearing Soviet control sometimes also generated resentment, even among basically pro-Russian Mongolians. A number of political figures were dismissed from party leadership from 1924 to 1936 for their resistance to Soviet tutelage. By contrast, the young Soviet-educated apparatchiks that took power after the purges in 1940 were at first so pro-Russian they proposed on several occasions to join the Soviet Union as a 16th republic. In the 1970s and 1980s, a massive Soviet presence in Mongolia and the continued servility of this aging post-purge cohort again generated resentment among youth. With the democratic revolution of 1989–1990, Russian control disappeared, and the rather shallow current anti-Russian nationalism soon evaporated. Today, Russia is the country most often chosen by Mongolians as their most reliable friend, with the United States second.

The restoration of the Mongolian state in 1921 opened the way for new government strategies of nation-building. From 1921 to 1925, the new regime was largely occupied with basic legislation involving elimination of clerical and aristocratic privilege, step-by-step secularization, and the reform of administration. After 1923, an economic upswing increased government revenues, generating funds to implement conscription in 1925, rapid expansion of party and youth league membership, and a slow but steady expansion of public schooling. The developing public education system was solely in Mongolian, based on standard Khalkha, and did not use Russian or Chinese language as the medium of education. Citizenship was only slowly extended to non-Mongols, or even to expatriate Buriats and Inner Mongolians from outside Mongolia proper.

From 1929 to 1940, the Mongolian government, under pressure from the Soviet Union, pursued a number of radical campaigns that, while ostensibly focused on class struggle, had a profound effect on national integration. The destruction of the aristocracy solidified the idea of the Mongols as a single, egalitarian national community in which all, not just the favored few, were descendants of Chinggis Khan. The immensely violent campaign against the Buddhist *sangha* (monks) removed what many radicals feared as a state within a state and imparted a secular, strongly statist cast to Mongolian nationalism. Border clashes with imperial Japan, culminating in the Khalkhyn Gol battle of 1939 and massive purges of thousands upon thousands of supposed "pan-Mongolist Japanese spies," nurtured both xenophobia toward Asian powers and dependence on Soviet aid and advice. It also stimulated a deep suspicion toward ethnic Mongols beyond the frontiers as potential stooges of foreign ambitions. The Khalkha Mongols' ethnic identity became closely fused with the Mongolian People's Republic's national culture and historical identity. This fusion was only amplified by the tendency of the purges to hit highly educated Buriat and Inner Mongolian expatriates particularly hard.

Programs of cultural and educational construction proceeded during this period as well, but were hobbled by the shortage of funds (amplified by the economic isolation brought on by xenophobic policies) and personnel (amplified by the wholesale murder of much of the educated class during 1937–1940.) After World War II, education for the booming population was gradually made universal. The curriculum was based on a new view of history that replaced the pre-revolutionary focus on the Chinggisid aristocracy and the spread of Buddhist doctrine. This viewpoint was epitomized by the first edition of the *History of the Mongolian People's Republic* (1954), produced by a team of Soviet and Mongolian scholars. Mongolia, roughly within its modern frontiers, was treated as a self-evident national community passing through the requisite stages of Marxist social evolution. Perhaps as a reflection of the old genealogical focus of the nobility and the common ownership of pasture in the banners, folk conceptions of the Mongolian nation revolved very much around the ideas of purity of blood and national ownership of natural resources. The national heroes of Choibalsang and Sükhebaatur were celebrated in poetry, song, and rewritten folklore. The games at the old Buddhist *danshug* ceremony offered to the Jibzundamba Khutugtu each summer were recast as the national games (*naadam*), timed to commemorate the July 11 entry of the revolutionaries into Khüriye (Ulaanbaatar). The completion of a national ceremonial space shortly after 1945, in the form of Sükhebaatur Square in front of the government palace and the tombs of Sükhebaatur and Choibalsang, created a public stage and symbolic center for the nation.

These nation-building efforts successfully assimilated the urban Chinese and Russian immigrants and the far-western Oirat Mongols. The non-Mongol Kazakh immigrant community in the far west has not been assimilated, however.

In the 1920s, about 20,000 Chinese and Russian urban immigrants in Ulaanbaatar and a few other cities formed most of Mongolia's few proletarian or at least semi-proletarian elements. Due to the ideological and economic importance of this proletariat, Chinese and Russian workers' clubs were allowed through the 1940s, although social pressure for assimilation was strong. Due to xenophobia, the Great Purges devastated the Chinese communities, and urban development in the 1940s broke up Ulaanbaatar's "Chinatown." Since children of intermarriage almost always identified as Khalkha Mongols, by the mid-1950s, Russian and Chinese communities had virtually disappeared. A new population of Chinese guest workers, numbering in the several thousands, settled in Mongolia in the late 1950s and early 1960s, but their numbers were only a tiny percentage of Mongolia's then vastly larger urban population.

The Oirat Mongols of the far west were native Mongols, but had a somewhat more egalitarian social structure and a less specialized pastoral economy than the more feudal Khalkhas, along with a separate history rooted in the 18th-century Zunghar confederation. While generally supportive of the independent Mongolian state, the Oirats occasionally pursued separatist agendas, such as during the radical attack on Buddhism in 1932. At times, even party leaders supported the Oirat demands for separation from the Khalkha. After World War II, however, when an Oirat, Yu. Tsedenbal (1916–1991), became Mongolia's supreme dictator, many Oirats relied on his patronage to achieve high positions in government. This development, along with subsequent linguistic, economic, and social integration and mobility, has made Oirat separatism obsolete.

The Turkic-speaking Muslim Kazakhs are Mongolia's only major remaining unintegrated ethnic minority. Numbering 103,000 or 4.3 percent of Mongolia's population (2000 figure), the Kazakhs began migrating from northern Xinjiang (eastern Turkistan) into current Mongolian territory in the 1880s. In 1912, Mongolia's theocratic government granted citizenship to many Kazakhs. The border between Mongolia and Xinjiang (under loose Chinese administration) remained undefined until 1949, with Kazakhs moving in both directions and numerous frontier clashes between Mongolia and the Chinese authorities.

Mongolian government policy toward the Kazakhs followed the model of Soviet nationality policy. In 1940, the Mongolian government created a majority Kazakh province, Bayan-Ölgii. Education was allowed in the Cyrillic Kazakh script, based on that used in Kazakhstan. Kazakhs were also imported into a number of mining towns in the Mongolian heartland. Despite the considerable integration of Kazakhs into national life, the independence of Kazakhstan sparked an emigration of up to 60,000 Kazakhs from Bayan-Ölgii back to Kazakhstan. More than half have moved back to Mongolia, however, unable to adapt to the Russified life of Kazakhstan. Education in Bayan-Ölgii continues to use Kazakh.

Despite the democratic revolution of 1990, the basic features of Mongolian nationalism in Mongolia proper have remained remarkably constant. The largest change has been the reembrace of Buddhism as a vital aspect of national identity, particularly as a bulwark against evangelical Christianity mission activity that flourished in the 1990s. The state and the concept of nation remain, however, highly secular. The basic perception of safety from the north and danger from the south remains, although the concept of the "third neighbor" (a collective term for powerful countries apart from China and Russia), abortively proposed in the 1920s, has returned to favor as a key plank of foreign policy. Chinggis Khan has been returned to his position as the great progenitor of the Mongol state, but the statues and monuments to Sükhebaatur and Choibalsang are still honored. Figures purged in 1937 have been returned to the national pantheon, but no significant figure has been subtracted. Privatization has weakened the link of national unity to common resource ownership, but continuing anxiety over foreign control of natural resources testifies that this link has not disappeared. Finally, despite the renewed people-to-people connections among Mongolians, Inner Mongolians, and Buriats, Mongolian nationalism in the state of Mongolia remains deeply suspicious of the purity and authenticity of ethnic Mongols outside the Mongolian state. As a result, the thawing of international tensions has exposed not only the strength of the new secular and commoner-based nationalism in Mongolia proper, but also the persistent divisions within the ethnic Mongol family of nationalities.

Selected Bibliography

Atwood, C. P. 1999. "A Romantic Vision of National Regeneration: Some Unpublished Works of the Inner Mongolian Poet and Essayist Saichungga." *Inner Asia* 1, no. 1: 3–43.

Atwood, C. P. 2002. *Young Mongols and Vigilantes in Inner Mongolia's Interregnum Decades.* 2 vols. Leiden, The Netherlands: Brill.

Bulag, U. E. 2002. *The Mongols at China's Edge: History and the Politics of National Unity.* Lanham, MD: Rowman & Littlefield.

Ginsburg, T. 1999. "Nationalism, Elites, and Mongolia's Rapid Transformation." In *Mongolia in the Twentieth Century*, edited by S. Kotkin and B. A. Elleman. Armonk, NY: M. E. Sharpe.

Hangin, J. G. 1973. *Köke Sudur (The Blue Chronicle): A Study of the First Mongolian Historical Novel by Injannasi.* Wiesbaden, Germany: Otto Harrassowitz.

Jagchid, S. 1999. *The Last Mongol Prince: The Life and Times of Demchugdongrob, 1902–1966.* Bellingham: Center for East Asian Studies, Western Washington University.

Jankowiak, W. 1988. "The Last Hurrah? Political Protest in Inner Mongolia." *Australian Journal of Chinese Affairs* 19, no. 20: 269–288.

Kaplonski, C. 2004. *Truth, History, and Politics: The Memory of Heroes.* London: Routledge/ Curzon.

Lattimore, O. 1955. *Nationalism and Revolution in Mongolia.* Oxford: Oxford University Press.

Marsh, P. K. 2005. *The Horse-Head Fiddle and the Cosmopolitan Reimagination of Mongolia.* London: Routledge/Curzon.

Rupen, R. A. 1964. *Mongols of the Twentieth Century.* 2 vols. Bloomington: Indiana University.

Zen-Sun, E-tu. 1952. "Results of Culture Contact in Two Mongol-Chinese Communities." *Southwestern Journal of Anthropology* 8:182–210.

Nepal

Nanda R. Shrestha and Dev Raj Dahal

Chronology

1769	In 1768, Gorkha ruler Prithvi Narayan conquers Kathmandu, one of the three mini states in the Kathmandu Valley; by 1969 he completes the conquest of the entire Kathmandu Valley, thus laying foundation for unified kingdom and Nepali nationalism.
1814–1816	Anglo-Nepal War; political boundaries are established; Nepal becomes a semicolony of Britain.
1846	*Kot Parba* ("courtyard massacre"); the rise of Jang Bahadur Kunwar (Rana) as prime minister.
1923	A treaty with Britain affirms Nepal's sovereignty, but does not change its semicolonial status.
1950	Anti-Rana forces based in India form an alliance with the monarch and launch attacks to overthrow the Rana regime.
1951	End of Rana rule; the sovereignty of the Crown is restored and anti-Rana rebels in the Nepali Congress Party (NCP) form a government.
1955	Nepal joins the United Nations.
1959	A multiparty constitution is adopted; the NCP wins the national elections; B. P. Koirala becomes Nepal's first elected premier.
1960	King Mahendra's coup suspends the democratically elected parliament, constitution, and party politics, and imprisons party leaders, including Prime Minister Koirala.
1962	A multitiered nonparty system known as "Panchayat" instills sole power to the king.
1980	Agitation for reform; the king agrees to allow direct elections to the national assembly (Rashtriya Panchayat), but on a nonparty basis.
1990	Agitation inspired by NCP and leftist groups, resulting in deaths and mass arrests; King Birendra forms a coalition government and a new democratic constitution.
1991	NCP wins the first democratic elections since 1960; Girija Prasad Koirala becomes prime minister.
1994	Koirala's government is defeated; new elections lead to first popularly elected communist Asian government, which is dissolved months later.
1996	Maoists begin an insurrection (Maoist Movement or People's War) in rural areas that is aimed at abolishing the monarchy.
1997–2000	Instability and frequent government changes.
2001	Maoist strikes bring life to a virtual standstill in much of the country; King Birendra, Queen Aishwarya, and other close relatives are killed in a shooting spree by drunken Crown Prince Dipendra, who then shoots himself; Prince Gyanendra is crowned king of Nepal; a state of emergency is declared due to Maoist violence; there are more than 100 deaths.
2002	Parliament is dissolved in May, fresh elections called amid political confrontation over extending the state of emergency. Sher Bahadur Deuba heads interim government, renews emergency; in October, King Gyanendra dismisses Deuba and indefinitely puts off elections set for November. Lokendra Bahadur Chand appointed as prime minister.

2003   (January) Maoist rebels and the government declare a cease-fire. (August) Rebels end a seven-month truce; there is a resurgence of violence.

2004   Nepal joins the World Trade Organization (WTO). Maoist rebels blockade Kathmandu for a week.

2005   Rebels announce a three-month, unilateral cease-fire, the first truce since peace talks in 2003.

2006   The opposition alliance ends strikes and protests after the monarch agrees to reinstate parliament; Maoist rebel leader Prachanda and Prime Minister Koirala participate in talks, agree that Maoists belong in the interim government. Parliament strips the king of his command over the army; the government and Maoists sign a peace accord ending a 10-year rebel insurgency.

2007   In January, Maoist leaders enter parliament under the terms of a temporary constitution. In April, they join the interim government . Violent and deadly protests erupt in southeastern Tarai; demonstrators demand autonomy for the region and greater representation in parliament. In September, Maoists quit the interim government to press their demand for abolishing the monarchy. As a result, November's constituent assembly elections are postponed. In December, parliament approves the abolition of the monarchy, and Maoists agree to re-join the interim government.

Situating the Nation

The ancient history of Nepal is largely based on literary chronicles going back to the origin of the Kathmandu Valley. These chronicles inform us that the valley was once a lake that was later drained by goddess Manjusri for human habitation by cutting a deep gorge in the mountain. Then a *muni* (Hindu sage) named Ne (Nemuni) appeared on the scene as the *pala* (protector) of the valley. So, in early times, the country or state, if it could be defined as such, was called *Ne-pala*, the land protected by Ne. Subsequently, the name was vernacularly shortened to *Nepal*. In other words, Nepal and the Kathmandu Valley are synonymous.

Today's Nepal is much larger in its geographical size than the valley named after Nemuni. It constitutes three major ecological regions. More than 4,800 meters above sea level, the Mountain (Himalayan) region lies to the south of the trans-Himalayan zone of Tibet. It is relatively sparsely populated, and its economic activities are limited because of its harsh climate and topography. Pastoralism and seasonal trade are two important economic activities. Historically, its arduous mountainous topography has served as a natural barrier against large-scale military advances from the north. From a nationalistic perspective, it is plausible to argue that the sense of nationalism in this region and among its population has historically been a lot more subdued than in other regions, with the possible exception of the Rai and Limbu ethnic groups in the east. Culturally, Tibetan influence is noticeable.

The Tarai region represents a sharp contrast to the Mountain region; it is an extension of the Gangetic Plain in north India. It is a subtropical area along the Nepal-India border, occupying more than 60 percent of the total farmland. The

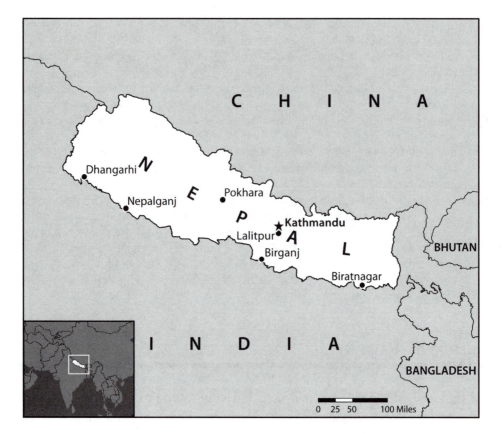

Tarai was subjected to land resettlement to enhance the national treasury and has always been heavily influenced by India. As a result, the Tarai residents of north Indian origin were suspected of being more loyal to India than to the Crown, historically the principal symbol of Nepali nationalism. Not surprisingly, therefore, systematic attempts were made in the 1950s and 1960s to populate the Tarai with hill migrants through land resettlements to establish a hill population majority and ensure the dominance of Nepali nationalism.

Situated between the two extremes, personified by the Mountain and Tarai regions, is the Hill region that includes the Kathmandu Valley, the hub of Nepali art, culture, and civilization. The valley is the most urbanized area in the country, featuring three adjacent cities: Kathmandu (national capital), Patan (Lalitpur), and Bhaktapur (Bhadgaun). The region demonstrates centuries of human impact on its physical environment with its terrace farming and dense population. Despite its relative isolation, inaccessibility, and limited economic potential, the region has always been the political and cultural hearth of the country. To talk about Nepali nationalism is to talk about how the hills and hill-based or hill-focused rulers managed to assume political centrality despite the region's geographical drawbacks in terms of natural resources, transportation, communication, or industrial base.

Instituting the Nation

National unification of Nepal required the conquest of the city-states of the Kathmandu Valley, a valley rich in agriculture, trade and commerce, and other civilizational achievements. It was, after all, the embodiment of Nepal. In addition, its geographical centrality gave an advantage of economic strength and military might. Prithvi Narayan, of the Gorkha raj, wasted no time. After several unsuccessful attacks, his ambition was finally fructified. A surprise attack in September 1768 resulted in his victory over the city-state of Kathmandu, his biggest rival. Soon after that, he managed to seize adjoining Patan unopposed and then moved against Bhaktapur, subjugating it the following year. The conquest of the entire valley and its indigenous inhabitants, the Newars, was completed by 1769, thus unleashing the dynastic Shah rule as a rallying cry and symbol of Nepali unification.

In essence, the year 1769 signified the birth of a new nation. Prithvi Narayan moved his capital to Kathmandu. Not only did the country come under a new ruler, it also acquired a new identity. It was transmorphed into a Nepal increasingly distanced from its original valley identity as the hearth of its indigenous Newars. Prior to the Gorkha conquest, the identity of the Newars and Nepal was one and the same. But the new Nepal emerged as the central domain of the Parbatiya (hill) ruling class, from which Prithvi Narayan was to project his imperial

Nationalist Leaders

Prithvi Narayan Shah (1722–1775) embarked on the path of national unification through territorial annexation and expansion. His campaign continued even after his death, until Nepal surrendered to British India in 1816 and signed a treaty reducing the country's territorial boundary to its present size. He can be seen as the father of Nepali nationalism, for it was his campaign that led to its birth in 1769.

Mahendra Bir Bikram Shah (1920–1972) was perhaps the most cunning of the Shah rulers. He is not only best known for his infamous palace coup against the B. P. Koirala government in December 1960 but also for establishing the Panchayat system that lasted until 1990. He elevated Nepali nationalism to a greater height in terms of scripting its most coherent narrative and socializing it at the mass level. However, this nationalism was mostly carried out under a monarchical dictatorship that regarded any form of opposition to his rule and regime as antinational.

B. P. Koirala (1914–1982) was a prominent founder of the Nepali Congress Party, a party described as the voice of democratic nationalism that is more inclusive of various cultural and ethnic identities in the country. Although Koirala can hardly be viewed as a typical nationalist—and he was an ardent advocate of democratic socialism—he was committed to Nepal's sovereignty and identity in the international arena. In addition, his successful leadership role in bringing down the house of the Ranas laid the foundation for King Mahendra to fashion the narrative of Nepali nationalism in his own image.

Nationalist Movements

The successful territorial annexation and expansion campaign that Prithvi Narayan Shah set in motion in 1769 can be characterized as a nationalist movement that led to the creation of a unified Nepal. The campaign that was carried on by Prithvi Narayan's successors even after his death in 1775 came to an unceremonious end in 1816, but Nepal's territorial boundary/sovereignty was clearly defined. By then, Nepali nationalism was firmly grounded as a national identity.

In late 1950, the Nepali Congress Party launched armed attacks against Rana autocracy with the aim to establish democracy in the country, ultimately dismantling the regime. Although the revolution against the Ranas was not a typical nationalist movement in a traditional sense, it led to the restoration of the Shah rule.

Since the fall of the Panchayat system in 1990 and the subsequent realignment of monarchical rule from *absolute* to *constitutional*, the current of what is known as the *janajati* (ethnic, minority) movement has been swelling. The most notable incident within this movement occurred in early 2007 when the Tarai residents of north Indian origin (commonly identified as *Madhesi*) undertook mass protests demanding regional autonomy and numerically greater political representation in parliament. Those protests, which are now described as the Madhesi movement in some quarters, resulted in violence, claiming many lives.

vision of territorial expansion. Even after Prithvi Narayan's death in 1775, his successors stayed the course, reaching far beyond the nation's current boundaries.

Initially, however, Nepal was not the preferred name for the new nation. In fact, the Gorkhali nobles and soldiers despised it, perhaps because it was synonymous with the Newars whom they had defeated but who were perceived to be culturally far more advanced than the Parbatiyas in all areas of production technology. In their eyes, retaining Nepal as the name of the new nation would symbolically mean that the victors were assimilating into the culture of the vanquished, thus tacitly legitimizing the Newar "cultural superiority." Prithvi Narayan himself openly expressed his racist or ethnic sentiment and contempt toward Nepal and its Newar residents, stating: "This three-citied Nepal is a cold stone. It is great only in intrigue. With one who drinks water from cisterns there is no wisdom; nor is there courage" (quoted in Burghart 1984, 111).

In the victory quarters, the name of choice apparently was Gorkha, which personified the glory of Gorkha as well as the Shah roots and, hence, was a most fitting tribute to the Shah dynasty and its Parbatiya heritage. In short, a distinct nationalist ideology, firmly grounded in the Parbatiya superiority and supremacy, was already being hatched. Although they eventually chose Nepal as the official name, there is no denying that Nepali nationalism at once exudes a great sense of pride in some quarters and apprehension in others, born from the womb of Gorkha conquest and molded in accordance with the Parbatiya ideology and Hindu polity.

Defining the Nation

It is argued that the monarchy, Hinduism, and the Nepali language form Nepali nationalism. Missing from this triad is the role of *territoriality*. The issue of territoriality goes much deeper than its key role as a boundary marker. To be specific, the Gorkhali imperial ambition did not cease with the death of Prithvi Narayan. By 1814, Nepali army forces had marched as far as the Satlej River to the west and the Tista River to the east, covering a total land area about twice as big as today's Nepal.

But the Gorkha raj's very territorial success proved to be its greatest military liability, as it eventually drew the ire of the British raj. Like all imperialist powers, Gorkhalis were foolishly blinded by their own success, paying little attention to the question of when and where to draw the line of their ambition vis-à-vis the British. However, the Anglo-Nepal war broke out in 1814, and Nepal was forced to sign the Treaty of Sagauli after their 1816 defeat. Consequently, the country lost virtually all of its hard-won territorial gains, thus confining it to its current boundary. Ironically, the humiliating defeat pushed the ruling class to consolidate its national power, and authority centered on the narrative of Nepali nationalism rather than territorial expansion.

The British-imposed territorial boundaries ended Nepal's outward ambitions and caused the nation to develop an inward-looking orientation. The ruling circle became intently focused on protecting national sovereignty and Parbatiya cultural heritage from external forces (British), on the one hand, and consolidating disparate territories (*rajyas*) within the national boundary, on the other. However, the two went hand in hand, for protecting the national sovereignty required internal consolidation of diverse groups, whether defined geographically or ethnically. After all, during the march of imperial expansion and unification, it was not easy to bring those *rajyas* under one flag. To appease them, the Gorkhali rulers granted them a substantial measure of local autonomy. Given the conquered *rajyas'* relatively relaxed ties to the central authority, unification looked vague rather than like a Gorkha nation with a dominant national identity. It was a rather unsettling scenario for the Gorkha rulers, particularly at a time when their power and authority had been greatly shaken (weakened) in the wake of their defeat. The grandeur of the Gorkha army's invincibility was gone. Any miscalculation on their part could readily trigger a wave of cessation from the loose federation, reverting the country back to its preunification days.

So, from the Gorkhali rulers' vantage point, protecting the sovereignty of the newly demarcated territory was the demand of the postwar time: (1) to safeguard the national sovereignty and integrity from further erosion, and (2) to preserve their political interest and authority from becoming disintegrated. Achieving these entwined goals required creating one nation with one national identity, a prerequisite to constructing a metanarrative of Nepali nationalism. Obviously,

the *externally* oriented national identity formation and nationhood of Prithvi Narayan was defunct under the realities of the British imperialism of the Indian subcontinent. The only viable and most logical alternative open to them was to become
internally focused, turning Gorkha federation into one Nepali nation through systematic consolidation of the previous *rajyas* and their diverse ethnic groups.

It was at this juncture that Nepali nationalism gradually grew into a larger
narrative. Although Prithvi Narayan was long gone, his historical role was central
to all of this. Heralded as a great, far-sighted leader and nation-builder, he was
the ultimate epitome of the Crown. Ever since his rise, the Crown was projected
as the axis of national unity and *bir* (heroic, brave) history (lore). In addition, regarded as the reincarnation of the Hindu God Vishnu, the king was a religious
symbol with his authority divinely ordained and, hence, just and beyond public
reproach. So at the core of such emerging nationalist narrative was the message
that only under the Crown's stewardship could the country remain unified and
defend its national sovereignty against the ever-present British imperial shadow.

Narrating the Nation

As history informs us, few issues light the nationalist fire among the general populace faster than the existence of an external enemy, whether real or perceived.
Projection of British India as a bogey man, an external enemy, went beyond national sovereignty. It was also a matter of preserving the national (religious) *purity* of Nepal, the last preserve of what King Prithvi Narayan Shah had proudly
pronounced *asal Hindusthan* ("the pure land of Hindus"). In other words, the sanc-
tity of national sovereignty was also fundamental to maintaining Nepal as a pure
domain of Hinduism, free of any ritualistic pollution caused by the cow-killing,
beef-eating British and *Mussalmans* (Muslims) whom the Hindus called *mlakshas*
or the polluted. Subjected to the Mughal (Muslim) and British (Christian) empires as well as their cultures and religions, India was, by implication, no longer
pure and sacred. In fact, so strict was the policy of national purity that those who
returned from Mughal and British India were required to undergo purification,
for they were considered contaminated.

In all likelihood, such a Hindu orthodoxy found wide reception across the
new Nepal territory, clearly demarcated from "impure" British India. After all, the
Hindu social order was quite prevalent in the country. First, heritage Hindusthan
was already present dating back to ancient Nepal, and, later, Hindu immigrants
who fled Mughal India to find safety and shelter in the Nepal hills acted as active
agents of its diffusion in the country. While the Crown-centered, Hinduized narrative of nationalism was still on the rise, the country underwent a tectonic shift
in its political landscape. In 1846, some 10 years after the political demise of
Prime Minister Bhimsen Thapa, who had controlled the country's political ma-

chinery for 31 years, Nepal witnessed an epochal event: the *Kot Parba* (a massacre at the palace courtyard). In its aftermath, one *bhardar* (courtier) from one of the Parbatiya clans named Jang Bahadur Kunwar (Rana) orchestrated his appointment as prime minister and, subsequently, inaugurated his dynastic Rana premiership for the next 104 years.

Despite its strong foundation, Nepal's fledgling nationalism still faced some issues. First, regionally, the southern Tarai and northern trans-Himalayan borderlands, both inhabited by non-Parbatiya people, remained largely out of its reach and influence, thus confining it to the hills and making it an exclusionary narrative from the very outset. Second, Nepali nationalism had yet to mature, with all of its preconditions in place, and diffuse down to the mass level and become socialized among the masses as a cultural identity and patriotic ideology. Two critical barriers were the lack of transportation/communication infrastructure and underdevelopment of a literary foundation. The Rana regime's policy of isolation as a means to protect national sovereignty prohibited Nepal from advancing technologically. The first time Nepal saw mechanical transportation was in 1928. In essence, Nepal was merely a composite of localized pocket economies with practically no interactions with others. Opportunities or the diffusion of nationalist ideology and culture from the center to peripheries was naturally limited.

Another obvious and critical anchor of Nepali nationalism missing from the scene was a national language with a well-developed literary foundation to provide nationalists with a voice. Language is a necessary vehicle of nationalism in terms of its literary formation, cultural development, and demographic socialization through mass education. It was only after the rise of Bhanubhakta Acharya, a Parbatiya *Bahun* (a commonly used Nepali term for Brahman) from the central hills, in the mid-19th century that Nepal set the early foundation of its national language—Nepali—along with its literary tradition. Later, through the determined and diligent efforts of the Nepali diaspora, specifically in different parts of India, the language and its literary foundation became strengthened, thus allowing the narrative of Nepali nationalism to find a wider voice and appeal in the form of Nepal's national identity at home and abroad.

However, Nepali nationalism experienced its great leap forward after the downfall of the Rana regime in 1951, particularly during the Panchayat raj (1960–1990). In December 1960, King Mahendra launched a palace coup against the first democratic government of Prime Minister B. P. Koirala, elected in 1959. After jailing Koirala and decapitating democracy, the king instituted the Panchayat system. Although sold to the public as a home-grown partyless system, Panchayat was basically a one-party system: the king's party, as he directly controlled it and guided all of its apparatus. The king actively pushed Crown-centric nationalism to the forefront of his national agenda to deflect any criticism for his antidemocracy coup, on the one hand, and to legitimize his Panchayat raj, on the other.

In terms of its triumvirate configuration, Nepali nationalism under the Panchayat raj was little different from its previous manifestations. What was different, however, was that unlike in the past its public production and propagation was now openly directed by the king himself. Activist King Mahendra was in full gear. Some of the public mechanisms that Mahendra unleashed and that his son King Birendra later pursued to spread the fire of nationalism across the nation included their omnipresent visibility, both physically and through various media outlets.

In addition, public education was made universal with a royal twist and bias. It received a great deal of push, at least in the media, as being fundamental to social progress and economic development. Textbooks were produced in Nepali for all grades, and the king's pictures were included in virtually every textbook, along with his glorification and that of Nepali nationalism. Their pictures and posters were also produced commercially for wider distribution. In every sense, everything that was done had his stamp and his deification.

Mahendra also pushed for literary advancements, but again, the official direction was Crown-centric. He made efforts to entice writers to use their skills to promote Panchayat utopia and Nepali nationalism centered on the Crown. The king set topics for the poetry competition organized by the Royal Nepal Academy. Themes, such as "honesty and patriotism" and "be a native, sing of the nation, and save the nation," to mention a few of the 25 or so topics given to the poets, are significant indications of the direction that the poets were expected to take. Not surprisingly, nationalistic/patriotic themes became quite common in Nepali literature, and the king himself wrote poems and songs along these lines.

Nationalism was overflowing everywhere. But the nationalism that the king promoted had a kaleidoscopic effect. While it looked like civic nationalism, inclusive and participatory, it was all monarchical in its makeup. Empty slogans go only so far to keep the public pacified. With each passing year, the veneer of the Panchayat raj that King Mahendra had carefully crafted as a symbol of Nepali nationalism and as a foundation of national development unraveled. As poverty grew and the socioeconomic disparity between the rich and poor magnified, the nakedness of Nepal's failed development was openly exposed. The monarch's promise of progress and prosperity for the people increasingly came into question, and opposition to his Panchayat raj escalated, eventually leading to its collapse in 1990. With the collapse of the Panchayat raj and simmering but growing doubts about the efficacy of the monarchical institution as a unifying symbol, Nepali nationalism as a metanarrative has increasingly come under a new microscope, as ethnic and regional forms of nationalism (i.e., ethno-nationalism) are demanding their own voices and spaces in the national discourse. For example, in the Tarai region, ethnic inhabitants commonly known as the Madhesis—who are of north Indian origin and who constitute roughly a third of Nepal's total population—are now demanding rights and autonomy after years of neglect. In essence, they are rejecting Nepali nationalism as a metanarrative that is designed to subsume all other narratives of nationalism that have their roots in Nepal's diverse ethnic or regional identities.

Mobilizing and Building the Nation

Since 1990, Nepali nationalism has arrived at a critical crossroads in its historical evolution. Specifically, the democratic movement of early 1990 succeeded in restoring parliamentary democracy, which King Mahendra had suffocated 30 years ago in 1960. Subsequently, the new constitution rendered the institution of monarchy into a constitutional form. The institution suffered a severe blow in 2001 when King Birendra and his immediate family were gunned down in the palace by his own son, the crown prince who later shot himself and died. As the whole family was wiped out, the royal lineage was passed on to Birendra's brother Gyanendra with a severely stained public reputation. As a result, the deified view of the Nepali monarchy and its image of benevolence were damaged; the king as a divine entity was neither invincible nor benevolent. The aura of the monarchy as the central axis of Nepali nationalism was, therefore, visibly clouded in the public eyes. In fact, the interim government (parliament) has recently approved a bill to abolish the country's monarchical institution. In essence, Nepal will soon be declared a republic.

The point is that restoration of democracy, combined with the diminished stature of the monarchy, opened up a brand-new space for suppressed voices and views to be expressed openly and loudly. In a way, what is transpiring in contemporary Nepal is not much different from the drama of identity (cultural) politics being staged in many Western countries, sometimes with a deep racist undertone. Ethnic identity tends to peak in times of crisis, such as political uncertainties and economic downturns, a scenario that typifies contemporary Nepal.

Not surprisingly, Nepal has witnessed a rising tide of what is commonly known as the *janajati* (ethnic, minority) movement, a form of ethnic nationalism that is increasingly cutting into the heart of the national political and cultural alignments and the structure of governance, including civil society. As a result, the question of Nepali nationalism has surfaced as a hot topic of debate. The issue has gained momentum because of the global awareness and emphasis on minority rights and adverse consequences of globalization, which generally tend to fall disproportionately on the lower sociodemographic layers of society. The ongoing crisis of political authority has proven to be an opportune time for the "suppressed" voices to rise and appropriate their own spaces in the national arena, the outcome being the *janajati* countercurrent to the *modernist* state; nationalism has come face to face with the *postmodern* politics of culture, identity, and ethnicity.

Because the *janajati* advocates regard prevailing Nepali nationalism as a hegemonic ideology, rooted in the Bahun-Chhetri axis of power and authority (i.e., almost absolute control of Nepal's political power structure and leverage by Bahuns and Chhetris [*kshatriyas*]), they accuse its proponents (primarily Bahuns and Chhetris) of relegating *janajati* cultures and identities to the margin with little

Nepalese prodemocracy demonstrators celebrate in the streets of Kathmandu after King Gyanendra announced the reinstatement of the nation's parliament on April 24, 2006. The king succumbed to pressure from a coalition of prodemocracy groups and Maoist rebels demanding a return to democratic rule. (Paula Bronstein/Getty Images)

space to grow. For instance, ever since the Shah dynastic rule began in Nepal in 1769, the Parbatiya Bahuns and Chhetris have enjoyed an absolute monopoly over the country's prime ministerial post, with one aberration in the late 1980s when it went to a Newar. In addition, they enjoy a huge share of civil service (bureaucratic) employment, although they constitute only about 30 percent of the total population of the country. In the meantime, there is little doubt that the *janajati* rhetoric is at times filled more with doses of sweeping polemics than with evidentiary documentation. The proponents of prevailing Nepali nationalism seem almost paranoid or at least deeply disturbed by the *janajati* movement, as they see it as a direct threat to their privileged position.

Irrespective of how this raging debate ends, if it ever does reach that point, the political and cultural landscape of Nepali nationalism is destined to undergo significant transformation. Recently, Nepali nationalism has suddenly become further compounded. The intense power struggle involving the king, political parties, and the Maoist movement has basically come to an end. Specifically, two history-making developments have dramatically transformed Nepal's political landscape. First, in 2006, the interim parliament stripped the king of his command of the Nepal army. In 2007, the Maoists officially joined the current interim coalition government, becoming a player in mainstream democratic politics. In addition, the present parliament eliminated any "Royal" and "His Majesty" designation that previously existed. For instance, it is now the "government of Nepal," not "His Majesty's Government of Nepal." And, as noted above, the parliament has now passed a bill to abolish the whole institution of monarchy, which means it will soon be history.

The *janajati* movement is on the rise, the Bahun-Chhetri nexus is on the defensive, the national economy is coming apart at its seams, and globalization is causing many a rupture in Nepal's sociocultural fabric and political governance, and, therefore, Nepali nationalism finds itself surrounded by internal and external forces that are beyond its control. Now that the Maoist threat has subsided, there is now, as indicated above, a new regional nationalism threat surfacing in Nepal to challenge its Parbatiya narrative of nationalism. This threat comes from the Tarai residents of north Indian origin (with close cultural and family ties to India), who claim to have been peripheralized by the central government and now demand regional autonomy. If the Tarai goes, Nepal will be left with a hollow sense of nationalism, with its economic base severely undermined. For the foreseeable future, the Parbatiya dominance of politics and bureaucracy will continue, the Hindu polity will still carry its clout—although the caste rigidity may wither away—and the Nepali language will remain as the lingua franca. But these are less likely to define and determine the future course of Nepali nationalism and its core identity, at least not to the natives. Whatever transpires in the near future, there will be a new narrative of Nepali nationalism, one that is noticeably different from the current version.

Selected Bibliography

Bista, D. B. 1987. *The People of Nepal*. 5th ed. Kathmandu, Nepal: Ratna Pustak Bhandar.

Burghart, R. 1984. "The Formation of the Concept of Nation-State in Nepal." *Journal of Asian Studies* 44:101–125.

Dahal, D. R. 2004. "Nepal: Conflict Dynamics and Choices for Peace" (unpublished manuscript), 14–31. Kathmandu, Nepal: FES-Nepal.

Gellner, D., J. Pfaff-Czarnecka, and J. Whelpton. 1997. *Nationalism and Ethnicity in a Hindu Kingdom: The Politics of Culture in Contemporary Nepal*. Amsterdam: Harwood.

Gurung, H. 2003. "Nepali Nationalism." In *Nepal Tomorrow: Voices and Visions*, edited by D. B. Gurung, 1–13. Kathmandu, Nepal: Koselee Prakashan.

Joshi, B. L., and L. E. Rose. 1966. *Democratic Innovations in Nepal*. Berkeley: University of California Press.

Onta, P. 1996. "Creating a Brave Nepali Nation in British India: The Rhetoric of *Jati* Improvement, Rediscovery of Bhanubhakta, and the Writing of *Bir* History." *Studies in Nepali History and Society* 1:37–76.

Panday, D. R. 1999. *Nepal's Failed Development: Reflections on the Mission and the Maladies*. Kathmandu, Nepal: Nepal South Asia Centre.

Regmi, M. C. 1978. *Thatched Huts and Stucco Palaces: Peasants and Landlords in 19th-Century Nepal*. New Delhi: Vikas Publishing House.

Shrestha, N. R. 1997. *In the Name of Development: A Reflection on Nepal.* Lanham, MD: University Press of America. Reprint with a new preface and foreword by Devendra Raj Panday, Kathmandu, Nepal: Educational Enterprise, 1999.

Shrestha, N. R., and K. Bhattarai. 2003. *Historical Dictionary of Nepal.* Lanham, MD: Scarecrow Press.

Stiller, L. 1973. *The Silent Cry: The People of Nepal 1816–1839.* Kathmandu, Nepal: Sahayogi Prakashan.

Tibet

P. Christiaan Klieger

Chronology

1000 BC	Ch'iang tribes settle in Tibetan river valleys.
560 BC	Siddhartha Gautama Buddha is born in Nepal.
AD 604–650	King Songtsen Gampo introduces Buddhism to Tibet.
1247	Sakya Pandita becomes the first monk ruler of Tibet under Mongol sponsorship.
1357	Tsongkhapa, founder of the Gelugpa sect, is born.
1578	Altan Khan invites Sonam Gyatso to Mongolia, proclaiming him "Dalai Lama."
1642	The Great Fifth Dalai Lama unifies Tibet.
1644	The Manchus capture Beijing and establish rule over China.
1652	The Fifth Dalai Lama visits the Shunzhi emperor in Beijing.
1909	Thubden Gyatso, 13th Dalai Lama, flees to exile in India due to the Manchu invasion.
1911	The last Manchu emperor abdicates in Beijing.
1913	The 13th Dalai Lama declares Tibetan independence.
1940	The 14th Dalai Lama is enthroned in Lhasa.
1947	The Communists defeat the Nationalists in China.
1950–1951	China invades Tibet.
1959–present	The 14th Dalai Lama goes into exile in India.
1980	Hu Yaobang introduces reforms in Tibet.
1989	Major Tibetan uprising in Lhasa.
1989	The Dalai Lama receives the Nobel Peace Prize.

Situating the Nation

The Tibetan nation, for the last seven centuries, has been constrained by the Chinese empire and its successors, the Republic of China and the People's Republic of China (PRC). These bonds, whenever weakened, allow a measurable amount of Tibetan independence, the last appearing after the fall of the Manchu Qing Dynasty (1911) and extending to the occupation of the region in 1951 by the People's Liberation Army of the PRC. Since this occupation, Tibetan nationalism has primarily been enabled by the action of thousands of Tibetan refugees that live in the West, Japan, India, and Nepal. Transnational organizations articulate the message of Tibetan self-determination, often in conjunction with the widespread establishment of Tibetan Buddhist centers throughout the West.

The Qinghai-Tibet plateau is an extremely isolated geographic form, a fact that had undoubtedly contributed to the development of an independent national consciousness. It is an area of roughly 1.2 million square kilometers, bordered by the world's tallest mountains: to the west the Karakorum, to the north the Kunlun Range, and to the south the Himalaya, whose highest peak, Mt. Everest (*Chomolungma* in Tibetan), straddles the border of Nepal and Tibet and reaches to 29,011 feet (8,848 meters). Tibet is two-thirds the territory of the Indian subcontinent, or about twice the size of the state of Texas, and the average altitude of the plateau is 14,000 feet above sea level. Erosional processes have carved out deep valleys and gorges in the rock of the highlands, allowing for human habitation in one of the most extreme environments in the world. These river valleys are the core of Tibetan civilization.

Because of the great height of the Himalaya, most of the moisture-laden, South Asian monsoon rains fall on the southern slopes of the mountains in India and Nepal, leaving Tibet a high, cold desert. Thus, contrary to popular belief, Tibet is not a land of great snowfall. Nevertheless, Tibet contains over 15,000 natural lakes, which like the Great Salt Lake of Utah, are features left over from the wetter Pleistocene period. The plateau is also the headwaters of most of the continent's greatest rivers: the Indus, Sutlej, Brahmaputra (*Yarlung Tsangpo*), Salween, Mekong, Yellow (*Huang Ho*), and the Yangtze. The waters flowing from Tibet nourish 85 percent of Asia's population—47 percent of the world's total population. Therefore, environmental issues in Tibet are not inconsequential, as they affect much of the earth. Were it not for the great lack of infrastructural development (roads, railroads, etc.), the strategic location of Tibet would have been a great asset in Asian affairs.

Archaeologists and Tibetan historians surmise that people have lived in Tibet for at least 3,000 years. According to legend, about 2,000 years ago, a sacred monkey (an incarnation of the God of Compassion) mated with a rock demon. Their offspring were the progenitors of the six tribes of Tibet. These tribal groups, known as the Ch'iang, slowly expanded their territory, at one time reaching as far south as central Nepal and as far west as Pakistan. Early settlement centered along the broad Tsangpo River Valley, particularly the Yarlung Valley branch, or "Valley of the Kings," named after the early Tibetan kings (300–400 BC), who built fortress-palaces (*dzong*) atop small peaks along the river flood plain.

Most people in Tibet have historically resided in the southern valleys of the Tsangpo and Indus rivers. The higher rainfall and lower elevations allowed for intensive agricultural and urban development in these areas. Lhasa and Shigatse are the two largest cities. The Changtang plateau, a high, arid desert plain that occupies half of Tibet, is home to a half million sparsely distributed seminomadic herders. Amdo, in the northeast, is by far the most developed and urbanized portion of the plateau.

Tibet was historically divided into three provinces: U-tsang, Kham, and Amdo. Today, U-tsang—the central part of the plateau in which the Tibetan capital of Lhasa lies—has been designated the Tibetan Autonomous Region (TAR) by the PRC. It may also be referred to as Xizang (XAR). Both Kham and Amdo are considered separate jurisdictional units encompassed within four distinct Chinese provinces: Gansu, Qinghai, Sichuan, and Yunnan. The TAR itself is home to roughly

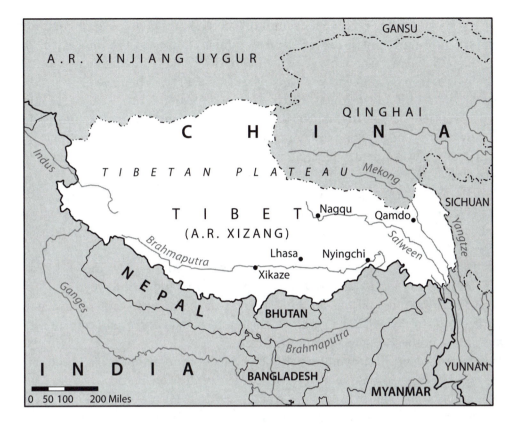

2 million ethnic Tibetans. The Tibetan people in general have a strong sense of national and cultural identity apart from China, but much of this has developed during the occupation. Prior to 1950, the Tibetan state was greatly decentralized, with individuals often identifying themselves with the three large provinces, semi-sovereign principalities, and feudal monastic estates associated with the various sects of Tibetan Buddhism.

The Tibetan language belongs to the Tibeto-Burman family, its script developed from a North Indian Sanskrit script during the seventh century AD, under the direction of King Songsten Gampo—undoubtedly the most famous of the early Tibetan kings. Not surprisingly, Tibetan and Burmese languages are somewhat mutually intelligible.

Instituting the Nation

For over a millennium, Tibet organized its governmental institutions around the idea of the Buddhist state, which was originally established by the Indian emperor Ashoka about 250 years after the death of the Buddha (ca. 250 BC). Ashoka was a "religious king" who used the popular new religion as an attractive force in the conquest of a vast South Asian empire. Tibetan kings of the seventh- to ninth-century Yarlung Dynasty converted to Buddhism and used the imagery of the Ashokan model of sovereignty to consolidate their rule. These religious kings, of whom Songtsen Gampo was perhaps the most celebrated, became great secular patrons of the Buddhist priests who maintained religion for the sake of the state and all sentient beings. In this role as protector, the kings of Tibet became associated with the God of Compassion, Chenrezi (*Avalokiteshvara* in Sanskrit). This dual form of government, with secular and religious arms, became the ideal structure for Tibetan society for over 1,000 years, until the Dalai Lama went into exile in 1959. The system of government can be conveniently referred to as a "patron-priest" form of rule, where a secular patron provides military protection and material aid to the monastic class, who in turn legitimize and sanctify the rule of the patron.

The system existing in old Tibet was quite similar to the early days of the Holy Roman Empire in the West, where the pope and the emperor formed the "twin swords of Christendom" to lead the Western world. And as in the West, with the pope often at odds with the emperor, the grand patron and high priest of Tibet were often not working harmoniously together.

Over the centuries, Buddhism developed to such an extent in Tibet that religious officials eventually became the government. Monasteries, temples, and hermitages were built in every village and town, and every home had its altar for prayer. In the 13th century, envoys of the Mongol ruler Chinggis (Genghis) Khan demanded the submission of Tibet to their empire. Under this threat, the abbot of Sakya Monastery in central Tibet was offered the rule of the entire country, under

---

Tenzin Gyatso, 14th Dalai Lama

Perhaps the most popular Tibetan of all time is the current Dalai Lama, Tenzin Gyatso. He is considered the reincarnation of all 13 of his predecessors, plus the founding religious king of Tibet, Sontsen Gyatso. This lineage is also considered the reincarnations of Chenrezig, the God of Compassion, who additionally was the legendary father of all Tibetan peoples, the Tibetan godhead, represented in the first human, the line of Tibetan kings, and all the Dalai Lamas—all incarnations of Chenrezig. The current Dalai Lama was born in Amdo province in eastern Tibet in 1935. The previous Dalai Lama had died in 1933, and Tibet was under the regency of Reting Rinpoche until the little boy was brought with his parents to Lhasa. There he was enthroned with great pomp. When Tibet was annexed by China in 1951, the teenaged Dalai Lama attempted to negotiate with Mao Zedong and Zhou Enlai for greater freedoms for his people. This was ultimately unsuccessful, and the Dalai Lama and his government went into exile in India in 1959. In 1989, in recognition of his nonviolent quest for respecting the self-determination of the Tibetan people, he was awarded the Nobel Peace Prize. The Dalai Lama remains in exile in Dharamsala, India—and is now a very revered world leader.

Mongol patronage. He accepted, turning Tibet into a feudal theocracy ruled by a high priest within the Mongol empire.

Whereas the Sakya high priest lineage was hereditary (uncle to nephew succession), the celibate Gelugpa sect reproduced their authoritative lineages through the system of reincarnation. This so-called Yellow Hat sect was founded by the reforming saint Tsongkhapa (1357–1419). Through this system, a young child would be discovered, in the country, that bore a strong resemblance, in personality or in physical characteristics, to his predecessor. This was proof of his reincarnation. He would be raised to assume the position of the departed monastic head or governmental official. The system reached its zenith with the monastic lineage of the Dalai Lamas, who beginning in the 17th century, held the highest position in both the secular and priestly realms. This is the core institution upon which modern Tibetan nationalism is based. The Dalai Lamas, ruling from Lhasa, became the kings and high priests of Tibet under the patronage of the Mongols. Altan Khan of the Tumet Mongols proclaimed the lama Sonam Gyatso and his two predecessors the "Ocean of Wisdom Teacher" (*dalai lama* in Mongolian). Each succeeding Dalai Lama, as reincarnation of his predecessor, was considered an emanation or reincarnation of Chenrezig, the God of Compassion and father-guardian spirit of Tibet.

Defining the Nation

Being generally a profoundly Buddhist people, the profession of the faith has long been a defining feature in the establishment and maintenance of Tibetan national identity. In fact, the term *nang mi* or "interior people" simultaneously refers to Buddhist practitioners as well as Tibetans, in opposition to foreigners. Showing affinity on the basis of common language, physical/genealogical heritage, and ties to the local soil are also important, but not as significant as the practice of Buddhism. Within Lhasa is a sizable community of Muslim Tibetans, and throughout are significant numbers of Bonpos, adherents of Bon, the pre-Buddhist shamanistic religion of Tibet. All are, nevertheless, Tibetan.

While Tibetans generally respect other forms of Buddhism, the land of Tibet is seen as a special place of revelation, pilgrimage, and sacredness. As a holy land, Tibet is seen as the holder of the complete tradition of Buddhism, whereas India, where the doctrine was first developed, has lost it. This divine aspect of the landscape and the holders of the Buddhist traditions strongly contribute to the raison d'état of Tibet.

The state of Tibet, as defined by the recent Dalai Lamas (13th and 14th), is essentially coextensive with ethnic Tibet and is perhaps one-third larger than the current Tibet Autonomous Region. References are sometimes made to the larger Tibetan empire of the first millennium AD that included the tributary states of

Ladakh, Sikkim, Bhutan, Assam, and parts of Nepal, the people of which generally no longer identify with the Tibetan state. The Sherpa people of Nepal, for example, speak a dialect of the Tibetan language and adhere to Tibetan Buddhism but generally do not consider themselves ethnically Tibetan.

Concomitant to the nation-building activities of the state in the early 20th century was the uneasy relationship among the imperial powers of China, Russia, and Britain. In the last incidence, Tibet was envisioned or programmed to become a border state separating perceived Russian and Chinese adventurism from British interests in India. Britain forced the dialogue of an "Outer Tibet" that remained radically different from Chinese claims of sovereignty and Russian designs, and was also at odds with homegrown concepts of national development.

Narrating the Nation

The Great Fifth Dalai Lama, Ngawang Lobsang Gyatso, unified the three provinces of Tibet and moved the capital city to Lhasa. In 1645, he began construction of the magnificent Potala Palace in Lhasa atop the ruined fortress of King Songtsen Gampo, the everlasting symbol of the Tibetan nation, now given the poetic name of the Land of the Snow Lion.

Also in the mid-17th century, another nomadic society to the north, the Manchus, had developed imperial ambitions in Asia. As they conquered China and established the Qing Dynasty, they found the old patron-priest relationship expedient to establish their rule in Tibet and Mongolia. The Manchus favored the new sect of Dalai Lamas. In 1652 the Fifth Dalai Lama was welcomed by the imperial court in great state at Beijing, with each leader granting titles to the other.

For the next 260 years, the emperor in Beijing looked to the Dalai Lama as the high priest of Buddhism but viewed the country as a protectorate of the Chinese empire. The Dalai Lama and the government of Tibet, however, considered Tibet to be an independent country. This is the core of the Tibetan issue today. The abdication of Emperor Xuāntŏng (Hsuan-tung; Pu Yi) in 1911 brought an end to the patron-priest relationship between the Manchu empire and Tibet. It was fitting, then, that the 13th Dalai Lama, Thubden Gyatso, took the occasion to proclaim Tibetan independence. Mongolia similarly left the empire. Currency, stamps, passports, and other symbols of the Tibetan nation were circulated during this era. A Tibetan flag was designed, depicting a Himalayan mountain peak, a rising sun with alternating blue and red rays, and the royal seal of two snow lions holding a Buddhist emblem. Coins were minted in Lhasa of silver and copper, and paper currency and stamps were printed from woodblocks. All depicted the two snow lions and Buddhism symbols. The image of the Dalai Lama was never used until the period of exile (post-1959), when a series of commemorative "stamps" was issued by the government-in-exile in the early 1970s that depicted the 14th Dalai Lama.

The Potala, one of the largest palaces ever built, is the traditional home of the Dalai Lama. It was spared the widespread destruction that followed the invasion of Tibet by China in the 1950s. (PhotoDisc, Inc.)

However, from 1912 to the present, the Chinese Republic, both the Nationalist (Guomingdang) and Communist (People's Republic), has viewed Tibet as a renegade province that needs to be brought back into a reconstituted "Chinese" motherland. Tibet, backed by the powerful British empire to the south in India, resisted until the end of the Indian raj in 1947. (Mongolia was supported by the Soviet Union, and remains independent today.) China itself remained weak until after World War II, when Mao unified China under the communist banner in the late 1940s. Considering it a part of China since the days of the Yuan Mongol Dynasty, China invaded Tibet during 1950–1951, forcing the government of the Dalai Lama to sign a 17-point agreement for the "liberation" of the region from "feudal monastic rulers" and foreign "imperialist" influence. To Chairman Mao, Tibet had finally been returned to the Chinese motherland.

The teenaged 14th Dalai Lama lived uneasily under this arrangement in Lhasa until 1959. On March 10, suspecting that the Chinese were planning to kidnap the Tibetan ruler, the people of Lhasa rose up and encircled the Norbulingka Summer Palace, where the youth was living. On advice from his ministers and the

State Oracle shaman, the Dalai Lama escaped under cover of darkness. After several grueling weeks on the road, the Dalai Lama and his party arrived at the Indian border. Here he repudiated the 17-point agreement and went into exile in India. They were given asylum by Prime Minister Nehru. Over the next months and years, over 85,000 Tibetans followed the Dalai Lama into exile. Many died en route. Thousands in Tibet were killed by the People's Liberation Army of China.

After the 1959 Lhasa uprising, Tibetan culture and nationalism were actively suppressed. Buddhism was prohibited, and the Tibetan language was no longer taught in schools. Further assaults on ethnic Tibetans raged during Chairman Mao's Cultural Revolution (1966–1976), a time throughout China when all old traditions and conservative ways were attacked. During this period, hundreds of thousands of Han Chinese also perished.

The Cultural Revolution is one of the most brutal periods in China's history—for Tibetans and Chinese alike. In Tibet, religious persecution was the most brutal aspect of this period. Hundreds of monasteries were razed; monks and nuns killed, jailed, and tortured. Evidence of these ruined temples dot the hillsides throughout Tibet today. The government banned the private practice of religion and used its military to enforce it. A policy known as "destroying the four olds" —culture, ideas, customs, and habits—prevailed.

It is estimated that over 87,000 Tibetans were killed in the first 18 months following the 1959 uprising and up to 1.2 million Tibetans have perished since the occupation—perhaps one-sixth of the total population. Tibetan culture, representing one of the last ancient civilizations still extant, was being destroyed. Most of Tibet's 6,000 temples and monasteries were completely ruined. Golden statues were melted, and sacred books were burned. Items associated with Buddhism—but most especially with the Dalai Lama, who the Chinese labeled a "splittist"—were prohibited. It is not uncommon today for private homes to be searched for photos of the Dalai Lama; it is still illegal for anyone in Tibet to possess such photographs.

Mobilizing and Building the Nation

The 14th Dalai Lama was not the first ruler of Tibet to flee into exile and ask for assistance in securing complete independence from China. In the early 20th century, the 13th Dalai Lama, Thubden Gyatso, went to India to seek asylum from the excesses of the tottering Manchu Dynasty in China. He also sought recognition from the British empire that Tibet was an independent country, not just an amorphous buffer state that the raj projected. After a time in exile, he was urged to return to his country. Following the fall of the Manchu Dynasty in 1911, the Dalai Lama declared independence in 1913. The country was left unoccupied by China until 1950.

When Chinese troops arrived in Tibet in 1950, the young Dalai Lama and his government tried to work out a compromise with Mao that would preserve considerable local autonomy for Tibet within the framework of the PRC. This was known as the "17-Point Agreement." The Dalai Lama and Panchen Lama (second ranking lama in Tibet) even flew to Beijing to hold meetings with Mao, Zhou Enlai, and other Communist leaders. Initially, Beijing agreed to keep Buddhism and the monastic ruling order together. Eventually, however, it became clear that the object of the Chinese occupation was to make Tibet a province of China and to dismiss its unique system of governance. The populace was greatly bereaved when the Dalai Lama fled into exile to India in March 1959. Many thousands of Tibetans gave up everything to follow him, and many died on the perilous journey over the high Himalayan passes. About 10,000–15,000 Tibetans settled in the kingdoms of Nepal and Bhutan. Several additional thousands were settled in Switzerland and other Western countries.

In the first few weeks and months of exile, the Indian government generously provided land for transit camps for the thousands of Tibetan refugees streaming over the border. The most immediate need was for simple housing, food, and medical care. Foreign aid helped provide Tibetans with these necessities. Nevertheless, many immigrants died from diseases not often found on the high Tibetan plateau (such as tuberculosis), but common in the tropical environment of India. During the 1960s, armed resistance to the Chinese occupation was met by Khampa tribesmen from eastern Tibet, who were covertly sponsored by the Central Intelligence Agency (CIA) in the United States as part of its Cold War foreign policy.

But what the Dalai Lama and his many followers found in India was a chance to reestablish their Tibetan identities and engage in a public discourse about the Tibetan cause to an international audience. Once some of the basic needs were attended to, the Dalai Lama was settled in the old hill station of Dharamsala, about 200 miles north of New Delhi and about 60 miles southwest of the Tibetan border. Here, the Dalai Lama was given the freedom to erect a government-in-exile—the *Ganden Phodrang*—which is now responsible for establishing schools to teach Tibetan language, music, and the fine arts. Perhaps most importantly, the Dalai Lama and his subjects were allowed to practice Buddhism freely. Within a few years, Tibetans had reestablished many temples, monasteries, and nunneries in India, the original homeland of Buddhism.

Key to the formation of a Tibetan identity is the acceptance of the Dalai Lama as Tibet's spiritual and political leader. To the Tibetan people, he has a special significance. The 14th Dalai Lama is not only considered the reincarnation of his previous 13 predecessors—as Bodhisattva of Compassion, he is the guardian of the Tibetan people—he is considered a reincarnation of King Songsten Gampo, the founder of the Buddhist kingdom of Tibet. It is not difficult to understand why, despite many attempts by the Chinese to denounce the Dalai Lama and remove him from rule, the Tibetan people both in the homeland and in exile generally refuse to relinquish him. The Dalai Lama forms the link between the secular and the religious. The importance of this dual role is magnified as those still living in Tibet are forbidden to learn of their history and are prohibited political freedom to support the *Ganden Phodrang*; those living in exile cling to the Dalai Lama as the embodiment of the homeland they were forced to leave.

The exile community has been hugely successful in establishing a tie with their unattainable homeland, outside the political boundaries of Tibet. The agricultural settlements in the Himalayan foothills of India are generally prosperous in comparison to their Indian neighbors, and Tibetans have succeeded in promoting crafts, industry and education, hospitals, and other institutions. The system of monasteries survives as it had in Tibet. Indeed, the Indian government, while not officially accepting the Dalai Lama as head of a government-in-exile, has recognized him as the leader of Tibetan communities within India and other refugee areas.

The present government in Dharamsala includes a council of ministers, an elected assembly of legislators, a supreme justice commission, and departments of information and international relations, religion and culture, health, home, finance, education, and security. Notable cultural and educational institutions in Dharamsala include the Tibetan Institute of Performing Arts, Tibetan Children's Village, the Library of Tibetan Works & Archives, and even an accredited college, the Norbulingka Institute. Through the assistance of the Indian government and generous aid from foreign organizations in Europe, the United States, and elsewhere, refugees have thrived. In Nepal and northern India, Tibetans have been active weaving woolen rugs for the export market and leading thousands of people on treks throughout the Himalayas. In the southern parts of India, many Tibetans are productive farmers. In New Delhi and other cities, many Tibetans have now earned a college education and are active in business, health care, and engineering.

To represent the Dalai Lama and the exiled Tibetan people, Dharamsala has established several offices around the world, including Tibet House in Delhi and offices in Kathmandu, New York, London, Taipei, Tokyo, Moscow, and others. These centers serve as unofficial "embassies" representing the independent government of the Dalai Lama that existed in the homeland prior to the Chinese invasion in 1950.

It has been nearly 50 years since Tibetans left their homeland with the Dalai Lama. Throughout the exile communities, Tibetan national identity remains strong. All along, the 14th Dalai Lama has maintained that the struggle for Tibetan freedom must be nonviolent. Like Martin Luther King Jr., the Dalai Lama was strongly influenced by the nonviolent political actions of Mahatma Gandhi, the architect of Indian independence. Nonviolence is also a major religious precept in Buddhism. In 1989, in recognition of his nonviolent campaign for the human rights of his people, the Dalai Lama was awarded the Nobel Peace Prize.

While Tibetans within the occupied TAR lack access to international media, education, and economic development, they engage in resistance to the PRC occupation in more subtle ways. Of course, the more direct means of protest—street demonstrations—do occur, both in large cities and in the hinterlands. The most notable of these protests occurred in 1987, when an uprising of monks, nuns, and students led to massive demonstrations in the streets of Lhasa. In the late summer of 1987, with the city of Lhasa full of Western tourists and journalists, a small group of monks and others were arrested by the police for demonstrating for Tibetan independence. The Dalai Lama had just presented a Five-Point Peace Plan to the U.S. Congress, and the world's attention was currently on Tibet. The demonstration in the streets of Lhasa quickly escalated, and the crowd set fire to the police station. Journalists took photographs of horrifying scenes of people being shot and arrested. Many people died, and many more were taken to prison. Tourists were told to leave immediately. Over the next two years, several other demonstrations were held in Tibet. The revolt, the first major one since 1959, was brutally suppressed by the Chinese. As a result, tourism was halted, and local Tibetans were forbidden from displaying photographs of their exiled leader. Even today, tourism is only permitted in groups under careful supervision by Chinese authorities. And the Dalai Lama remains China's most embarrassing persona.

Aside from direct protest, many Tibetans engage in a quieter form of passive resistance to Chinese rule, simply by continuing to engage in Buddhist ritual. The simple act of burning incense or displaying a photo of the Dalai Lama can be seen as an assertion of Tibetanness and as a way of retaining their rights to religious freedoms.

In addition, religious acts, such as pilgrimage, are also a way of maintaining autonomy under the watchful eye of the PRC. Often the pilgrims' journeys are related to the cycle of mountain agriculture and pastoral activities and reflect a plurality of traditions in the most marginal of geographic areas. Pilgrimages are seen as a means to link concrete geographic places with the world of the gods.

Whether in exile or living in the homeland, whether Bonpo, Muslim, or Buddhist, Tibetans maintain a strong notion of nation. The Tibetans in exile have continued to reproduce their key institutions and maintain a powerful notion of Tibetanness, whether living in Europe, the United States, or India. With history on their side, the cycles of change may again favor a free people living in the Land of the Snow Lion.

Selected Bibliography

Goldstein, M. C. 1989. *A History of Modern Tibet, 1913–1951.* Berkeley: University of California Press.

Grunfeld, A. 1987. *The Making of Modern Tibet.* Armonk, NY: M. E. Sharpe.

Klieger, P. C. 1992. *Tibetan Nationalism.* Meerut, India: Archana Press.

Klieger, P. C. 2006. *Tibetan Borderlands.* Leiden, The Netherlands: Brill Academic Press.

Lehman, S. 1998. *The Tibetans.* New York: Umbridge Editions.

Lopez, D. S., Jr. 1998. *Prisoners of Shangri-la.* Chicago: University of Chicago Press.

Brazil

Anne Marie Todd

Chronology

1822   Brazil proclaims independence from Portugal; King Pedro I begins his reign.
1831   Pedro I abdicates the throne as a result of violent protests, leaving the crown to his five-year-old son, Pedro II.
1888   Slavery is abolished. There is an influx of European immigrants over the next decade.
1889   The monarchy is overthrown; a federal republic is established.
1902   Brazil produces 65 percent of the world's coffee.
1930   Revolts bring Getulio Vargas to power.
1937   Vargas leads a coup, then rules as a military dictator. There is state control of the economy.
1945   Vargas is ousted in a military coup.
1951   Vargas is reelected president, but faces stiff opposition.
1954   Vargas commits suicide after the armed forces and cabinet demand his resignation.
1956   Juscelino Kubitschek is elected president. Development and openness to the world economy create an economic boom over the next five years.
1961   Janio Quadros assumes the presidency, then resigns; he is replaced by Vice President Joao Goulart.
1964   Goulart is ousted in a bloodless coup. Castelo Branco is elected president.
1967   General Costa e Silva is inaugurated president.
1974   General Ernesto Geisel becomes president; he introduces political reforms.
1977   Brazil renounces a military alliance with the United States.
1982   Brazil halts payment of its main foreign debt, which is among the world's biggest.
1985   The military steps down from political power. Tancredo Neves is the first civilian president elected in 21 years, with inflation at 300 percent.
1988   The "citizen constitution" reduces presidential powers. Chico Mendes, rubber tapper, union leader, and environmental activist, is murdered.
1989   The first direct presidential election since 1960 is held. Fernando Collor de Mello is elected president and introduces radical economic reform, including importations and privatization. His efforts fail to improve the economy. By 1991, inflation reaches 1,500 percent. Foreign debt payments are suspended.
1992   The UN Conference on the Environment and Development (UNCED), known as the Earth Summit, is held in Rio de Janeiro. Collor resigns over corruption charges; he is later cleared.
1994   Fernando Henrique Cardoso is elected. A new currency, the *real*, is introduced. Brazil signs the Treaty of Tlatelolco, declaring itself free of nuclear weapons.
1995   Brazil joins the Southern Cone Common Market (MERCOSUR). Cardoso redistributes 250,000 private acres to more than 3,600 poor families.
1996   Cardoso decrees that governments, companies, and individuals can challenge indigenous land claims in the Amazon. The National Defense Policy (PDN) is announced. Police kill 19 Amazon peasants in the town of Eldorado dos Carajas.
1998   Cardoso is reelected. The International Monetary Fund (IMF) provides a rescue package for the Brazilian economy.
1999   Foreign investment in Brazil reaches $30 billion.

2000   Indigenous Indians protest Brazil's 500th anniversary celebration.
2001   The government expects to spend $40 billion on development in the Amazon.
2002   Brazil wins the World Cup. Currency hits an all-time low. Lula da Silva is elected president, promising political and economic reforms; it is the first leftist government in over 40 years.
2004   Brazil applies for a permanent seat on the UN Security Council. Brazil successfully launches its first space rocket.
2005   (February) Missionary campaigner for Amazon peasant farmers, Dorothy Stang, is murdered. (March) A death squad kills at least 30 people on the outskirts of Rio de Janeiro.

Situating the Nation

The largest and most populous country in South America, Brazil borders every national state in South America except Chile and Ecuador. Brazil established independence from Portugal in 1822. In 1889, the monarchy was overthrown and a federal republic established. For nearly a century, Brazil was largely run by military dictators with varying degrees of political reforms. The military regime peacefully ceded power to civilian rulers in 1985. A mostly tropical region, deforestation in the Amazon basin destroys the habitat and endangers a multitude of plant and animal species indigenous to the area. The Amazon jungle is a center of national politics, as the government attempts to compromise between environmental protection and the economic needs of the fifth largest population in the world.

Brazil's economy outweighs that of all other South American countries and is expanding its presence in world markets. Like many in the region, in the 1970s and 1980s, Brazil's economy suffered greatly from runaway inflation and the global collapse in oil prices. In the 1990s, Brazil's foreign debt was $100 billion and grew to more than $200 billion by 2003. While economic management has been good, there remain important economic vulnerabilities. The government is challenged to maintain economic growth over a period of time to generate employment and make the government debt burden more manageable. With a large labor pool and vast natural resources, Brazil pursues industrial and agricultural growth and development and is an emerging economic powerhouse. Considering the dues of a multiyear International Monetary Fund (IMF) loan, $30 billion in foreign investment, and a grossly unequal income distribution, Brazil's economic interests influence the country's politics and national identity.

Instituting the Nation

The vast majority of Brazilians speak Portuguese, which differentiates them from their Spanish-speaking neighbors. Most Brazilians are Roman Catholic, which

provides a general set of ideologies and beliefs held by Brazilian citizens. Brazil is a multicultural nation: a product of the very first wave of globalization, which was prompted by Europe's expanding trade. Brazilian national identity is even more "mixed" than is commonly understood. Notions of Brazilianness are continuously contested and negotiated. Brazil remains a country where hyphenated ethnicity is predominant yet unacknowledged. Since the colonial period, racial and ethnic groups have intermingled and intermarried creating a large mixed-race population. Since many individuals are therefore difficult to classify in racial terms, color, rather than ancestry, largely determines racial identity. Most of the population is considered ethnically "Brazilian." The country's population exhibits various racial backgrounds but resists ethnic subdivisions. In the 2000 census, 55 percent of Brazilians self-reported as white, 38 percent self-reported as mixed or brown, and 6 percent self-reported as black. Indigenous tribes comprise less than 1 percent of the population.

Brazilian national identity remains highly problematic. While official Brazilian culture emphasizes Afro-Brazilian cultural forms like samba music and *capoeira* (martial arts), Brazilian mass media frequently portray Brazilian society as largely white. Furthermore, while Brazil has been touted as a racial democracy, there is a strong correlation between lighter skin color and higher socioeconomic status. Ideas of difference threaten universalist ideas of Brazilian nationalism, particularly in an international economy, where the government emphasizes development as the means to boost Brazil's global standing.

Today, Brazilian nationalism is centered on economic issues, which have political, environmental, and cultural effects. Development efforts tend to privilege industrial and corporate interests at the expense of impoverished or indigenous communities. The expanding gap between rich and poor exacerbates such problems as homelessness, hunger, and environmental destruction. Economic instability breeds insecurity as Brazil's territorial borders and natural resources are perceived as vulnerable. These discussions are not new. Debates about to what degree Brazil's markets should be open to the global economy have characterized presidential, state, and municipal elections for decades.

Defining the Nation

Generally understood as a deep love for one's country, nationalism is "a group consciousness that attributes great value to the nation-state, to which unswerving devotion is tendered. The individual closely identifies with the state and feels that [his or her] well-being depends to a large extent, if not completely on its well-being" (Burns 1968, 3). Contemporary nationalism is generally thought of as an agreement of a nation's citizens "to maintain their unity, independence, and sovereignty and to pursue certain broad and mutually acceptable goals" (Burns 1968, 3). From 1935 to 1980, Brazilian nationalism took the form of military activity and expansion. With developing economic crises and domestic and international pressure for global trade, contemporary Brazilian nationalism stems from the widely held view that Brazil's size and potential mean that it should not relay on foreign money but can compete on equal terms. Nationalism is the result of converging factors: security, economics, and resources. A leading producer of minerals, coffee, oranges, sugar, and beef, Brazil's nationalism is tied to its resources. Nationalism takes the form of reluctance to relinquish domestic control of the country's resources by opening up the country to foreign trade. This extends to protection of the country's greatest natural resource: the Amazon rain forest. International human rights and environmental groups have protested Brazil's development of the Amazon basin and have led the call for international protection of the Amazon. Nationalist tendencies in Brazil have responded by pushing for Brazil's sovereignty rights over the Amazon. Fear of the internationalization of the Amazon has emerged as a security concern, so the military has been deployed to protect Brazil's borders of the Amazon.

Deforestation in the Amazon rain forest of Brazil. (iStockPhoto.com)

Environmental nationalism has led to the establishment of national parks to protect the country's resources. Ethnic tensions have emerged because indigenous peoples are implicated in the plight of the Amazon as they make sovereignty claims to land that is of interest to loggers, ranchers, and urban developers. Economic nationalism has responded to the liberalization of trade barriers by pushing to protect national interests. Environmental nationalism has manifested in indigenous sovereignty claims over environmental resources to protect against ranching and logging. While there are similarities in these types of nationalism (for example, the military wants to protect Amazonia as a key area of national interest), there are often competing claims of nationalism. Tensions emerge over how to best exploit natural resources; indigenous tribes, such as the Yanomami and Seringueros, fight the development of land for logging and ranching purposes.

Narrating the Nation

Brazil's military and economic nationalism was demonstrated from 1930 to 1980. From the mid-20th century, Brazilian and international environmental organizations have pressured the national government to curb damage to the Amazon rain forest. Brazil's economic policy in the 1970s and 1980s aimed to pay off foreign debt, which was the impetus for Brazil to increase exports. The military government, which held power until 1985, used foreign loans to build new industries and improve the country's infrastructure. Although Brazil made economic gains under the military, the country's economy stagnated during the "lost decade" of the 1980s, with a burgeoning foreign debt and runaway inflation. Brazil turned to the IMF following Mexico's banking crisis to establish economic stability. This meant liberalization: opening up to foreign trade. Such IMF demands were seen as loss of sovereignty because privatization and foreign investment meant the government's control over the economy declined, which fueled economic nationalism. President Fernando Henrique Cardoso's economic stabilization policies of the 1990s and the deepening integration of Brazil into the world economy poised the country to assume a greater role in the world economy and in international affairs. After the Rio Earth Summit in 1992, Brazil and other countries issued a joint plan for protection of the rain forest. The

---

Chico Mendes

Born in Brazil on December 15, 1944, Chico Mendes grew up in a family of rubber tappers (*seringueiros*). Rubber tapping is a sustainable agricultural system that impedes profits of cattle ranchers and miners. Mendes organized *seringueiros* to resist development of the forest through political nonviolent protests. He encountered a great deal of opposition and in 1988 was murdered at the order of a rancher, an act that increased the power of his grassroots movement.

Lula da Silva

Born in 1945, Lula da Silva won Brazil's 2002 presidential election on his fourth attempt, leading a coalition of parties behind the Partidos Trabalhadores (PT, the Labor Party). A former shoeshine boy, Lula had a long history with Brazilian labor unions and was a co-founder of the PT. After he was elected president, Lula vowed to end hunger in Brazil.

Amazon Rain Forest

The size of the United States, the Amazon rain forest is the largest remaining tropical forest in the world. Most of the Amazon rain forest is in Brazil, but it also reaches into eight other countries. The Amazon rain forest supports 60,000 plant, 2,000 fish, 1,000 bird, and 300 mammal species. In Brazil, the Amazon is home to 20 million people who rely on this ancient forest for food, shelter, tools, and medicines in addition to playing a crucial role in people's spiritual and cultural lives. Scientists predict planned developments will lead to the damage or loss of between 33 to 42 percent of Brazil's remaining Amazon forest. The forest continues to attract ranchers, miners, and loggers who want to profit from this natural resource.

International Monetary Fund

The International Monetary Fund (IMF) is an organization of 184 countries, working to foster global monetary cooperation, secure financial stability, facilitate international trade, promote high employment and sustainable economic growth, and reduce poverty.

---

recent presidential electoral victory of "Lula" da Silva, raises questions of how the election of a working-class leader to the presidency will affect the balance of power between Brazil's classes, the role of the military, and the fate of the Amazon resources.

Mobilizing and Building the Nation

The need to preserve Brazil's identity and viability is inextricably linked to control over its economy. Intellectuals, politicians, and military commanders formulate nationalist doctrine. For this reason, Brazil's nationalist discourse is found in economic treatises, military policy, and environmental advocacy. Nationalism has become an ideological response to globalization pressures, which are perceived to undermine state security. Economic globalization threatens the traditional core values of the Brazilian military and is thus unpopular among military officers. Nationalism is central to the Brazilian military's desires for greater Brazilian autonomy in the international environment. Civilian government attempts to liberalize the economy are at odds with Brazilian military goals. The Brazilian military largely supports developing the Amazon. Environmental pressures to protect the Amazon basin are seen as strategies to internationalize the Amazon, which is seen as a threat to national resources.

Nationalism is framed as the politics of the national interest. It is an ideology that affirms that Brazil's national interests may coincide with other countries, but are often contradictory. Socially liberal Brazilian economists argue that Brazil's economy is key to maintaining national strength so that it may compete with richer, more developed countries. Economic nationalists perceive an asymmetry of economic power as responsible for regional disparities and insecurity. Brazilian military officers tend to express nationalistic views. Military commanders emphasize territorial sovereignty as essential to maintaining Brazil's integrity and power. Statements by military officials suggest that environmental nongovernmental organizations are perceived as little more than lightly disguised instruments of richer countries seeking to undermine the sovereignty of developing countries without damaging international relations. Military officials argue that due to the region's rich natural resources, other countries instinctively covet Brazil and Amazonia. In this way, Brazilian military nationalism is tied to environmental sovereignty, which is tied to economic growth and development. Nationalist discourse is found in economic and military texts, which are used to persuade citizens and policy makers to protect the country's natural resources and territorial sovereignty.

The concept of national security that prevailed during the Cold War has given way to growing preoccupation with sovereignty and the integrity of national territory. As environmental issues prompt the international community to seek protection of the Amazon as a source of global biodiversity, the threat of internationalizing the Amazon region will likely represent the central Brazilian military concern of the next century. In this way, the development of Brazil's foreign policy is based on national autonomy. Brazil's gradual transition to democracy has made the country's foreign policy vulnerable to pressure and negotiation. In 1985, the first civilian president saw democracy and economic reforms tied together. The nonauthoritarian regime had to implement reforms to maintain economic vitality. In this way, as the national bureaucracy responds to economic challenges, political and economic nationalism is inextricably linked. As economic decisions are made regarding Brazil's resources, environmental and economic sovereignty are the two emerging forms of contemporary Brazilian nationalism.

Brazilians, regardless of their educational background, overwhelmingly list the natural environment as their greatest source of national pride. Natural conservation has been deemed the charge of the state and a matter of national defense. Natural parks and preserves symbolize the power and strength of the state to control its own lands and important biological treasures. Environmental and military concerns converge on the Amazon, an area of international importance. The perceived threat to the Amazon comes from industrialized countries and environmentalists. The sovereignty and integrity of territorial Amazonia have become strategic concerns in the view of the Brazilian military and national developing interests. In 2005, Brazilian president Lula da Silva highlighted his support for the Brazilian military. Lula's socialist roots dovetail with traditional Brazilian nationalism, which is particularly strong in the armed forces. Brazil's politicians and military officials perceive the country's borders with nine neighboring countries as potentially vulnerable in the face of continental competition for resources and international environmental pressures. Brazil's environmental protections reflect the ongoing recognition of the economic and nationalist importance of environmentalism.

As Brazilians emphasize their nation's territorial sovereignty, such social issues as poverty and hunger remain problems within the country's borders. While estimates vary, poverty affects at least one-third of Brazil's population (almost 60 million people), while another 30 million are considered at risk. In the poorest parts of the country, nearly half of all families live on a dollar a day. In Brazil, wealth is concentrated in the hands of a few. The country's income distribution is one of the most unequal in the world and remains at the heart of Brazil's poverty problem. The expanding rich-poor gap ensures that the majority of Brazilians continue to completely lack or have inadequate access to food, healthcare, and education. Hunger is the most extreme manifestation of Brazil's poverty problem. Widespread malnutrition and chronic food insecurity perpetuate a cycle of violence and crime, particularly in industrial areas, such as São Paulo, and in urban slums, such as those in Rio de Janeiro. Brazil's nationalist pursuit of economic growth has not addressed the poverty problem. For example, Brazil's industrial agriculture economy has grown in the last two decades, but has not translated into a strong subsistence-farming sector. Brazil's small farmers have suffered, remaining on small plots of land with which they cannot compete with large-scale industrial farms or migrating to cities in an effort to escape rural destitution, only to remain chronically food insecure. As the world's 10th-largest economy, Brazil's inequality inhibits the country's domestic economy and its international standing.

Social democrats in Brazil evoke the disparity between Brazil and countries like the United States, which set high standards for developing countries but, in the eyes of Brazilians, do not do enough to aid development. Such economists see Brazil pursuing global interests to the detriment of national economic interests. Economic nationalists see multinational, supranational, or international governing bodies as responsible for the loss of Brazilian autonomy. In this view, the global economy is replaying Brazil's colonial history through foreign investments. Such nationalists take care to note that Brazil cannot live in total isolation of the world markets. While globalization is a threat, it is also a chance and a challenge for developing countries.

How Brazil engages the global economy is at the center of contemporary nationalist trends. This is the new nationalism that economists and politicians support. Frustrated that the world thinks of Brazil as only a country of soccer and carnival, new nationalism represents the chance to recoup Brazil's standing in the world through economic prosperity. This new nationalism responds to runaway globalization and is a call for Brazil to defend its values and respect its national identity. New nationalism sees globalization as a threat to the national interest, and the only way for Brazil to meet the superiority of the rich countries is to protect national interest and not open up too much to international pressures. To accomplish this in the coming decades, Brazil will need to perform a balancing act to stimulate investment while maintaining competitiveness.

Contemporary Brazilian nationalism is about a vision of the country whose interests are protected by territorial sovereignty and strengthened by economic growth. Brazilian nationalism has emerged as a military doctrine supported by economic interests based on environmental resources. The convergence of these often-conflicting interests in the nationalist doctrine reveals Brazil's rich history of pride in its territory and the hope in its future as an economic powerhouse. An economically and militarily strong Brazil is the cornerstone of contemporary Brazilian nationalism, which recognizes such natural resources as the Amazon basin and is committed to protecting such interests with economic and military policy.

Selected Bibliography

"Brazil's Backlash." 2000. *The Economist*, February 24.

Bresser-Pereira, L. C. 2000. "New Nationalism." *Folha de S.Paulo* [Leaf of S.Paulo], May 3. (Retrieved January 9, 2007), http://www.bresserpereira.org.br/ver_file.asp?id=460. Translation by Babel Fish, http://world.altavista.com.

Burns, E. B. 1968. *Nationalism in Brazil: A Historical Survey.* New York: Frederick A. Praeger.

Castañeda, J. 2005. "New Arms Race Taking Shape in Latin America. *Miami Herald*, March 27. (Retrieved January 9, 2008), http://blythe-systems.com/pipermail/nytr/Week-of-Mon-2005 0328/014895.html.

Desch, M. C. 1998. "The Changing International Environmental and Civil-Military Relations in Post-Cold War Southern Latin America." In *Fault Lines of Democracy in Post-Transition Latin America*, edited by F. Agüero and J. Stark, 323–344. Coral Gables, FL: North-South Center Press.

Faria, V., and E. Graeff. 2001. *Progressive Governance for the 21st Century: The Brazilian Experience.* Paper no. 1. University of California at Berkeley Center for Latin American Studies. (Retrieved February 20, 2008), http://repositories.edlib.org/clas/wp/1/.

Filho, J. R. M., and D. Zirker. 2000. "Nationalism, National Security, and Amazônia: Military Perceptions and Attitudes in Contemporary Brazil." *Armed Forces and Society* 27 no. 1: 105–129.

Garfield, S. 2004. "A Nationalist Environment: Indians, Nature, and the Construction of the Xingu National Park in Brazil." *Luso-Brazilian Review* 41, no. 1: 139–168.

Gordon, L. 2001. *Brazil's Second Chance: En Route toward the First World.* Washington DC: Brookings Institution Press.

Green, J. N. 2003. "Top Brass and State Power in Twentieth-Century Brazilian Politics, Economics and Culture." *Latin American Research Review* 38, no. 3 (October): 250–260.

Hirst, M. 1996. "The Foreign Policy of Brazil: From the Democratic Transition to Its Consolidation." In *Latin American Nations in World Politics*, 2nd edition, edited by H. Muñoz and J. S. Tulchin, 197–223. Boulder, CO: Westview Press.

Lesser, J. 1999. *Negotiating National Identity: Immigrants, Minorities, and the Struggle for Ethnicity in Brazil.* Durham, NC: Duke University Press.

Canada

Jeffrey J. Cormier

Chronology

1605   Port Royal is settled by Samuel de Champlain and Pierre du Gua de Monts.

1608   Québec City is settled and is largely French, Catholic, and rural.

1759   New France falls to the British in the Battle of the Plains of Abraham, as part of the Seven Years' War (1756–1763).

1763   A royal proclamation provides the "province of Québec" with a formal constitution and establishes a variety of political institutions, all modeled after British ones.

1774   Close to 11 years later, the Québec Act replaces the Proclamation of 1763, in the process increasing the territory of the province of Québec to include the Great Lakes Region, Labrador, the Magdalen Islands, and the Ohio Valley. The Québec Act was also generous politically, returning to the French-speaking colony French civil law, official recognition of the French language, and the Catholic religion. It also allowed for the participation of Canadians of French origin in colonial administration.

1776   The 13 American colonies declare independence from Britain, which ends in the Treaty of Paris of 1783 and the official recognition of the United States of America. As a result, a huge influx of former American colonists heads north to join the now-established British colonies of Nova Scotia, New Brunswick, and the province of Québec. The United Empire Loyalists settle along the Upper St. Lawrence and along the northern banks of Lake Ontario and Lake Erie.

1791   The Constitutional Act divides the former province of Québec into two parts: Upper Canada (Ontario) and Lower Canada (Québec).

1837   A contentious year of insurrectionary activity in both Lower and Upper Canada. In Upper Canada, the rebellion is lead by William Lyon Mackenzie, in Lower Canada, by Louis-Joseph Papineau. Both rebellions are unsuccessful.

1841   The result is the Act of Union that brings the Canadas together as the Province of Canada.

1867   The United Province of Canada (Canada West and Canada East) and the Maritime colonies compose a loose-knit amalgamation of British settlements spread across British North America until the 1860s. Between 1861 and 1865, the United States is involved in violent civil war. As well, a group of Fenians, Irish Catholics who want to free Ireland by attacking British colonies and who fought for the North in the Civil War, threaten to attack many of the British North American colonies. Between September 1864 and July 1, 1867, a series of conferences takes place between the Maritime colonies and the Province of Canada. Eventually an alliance is struck, and Queen Victoria signs the British North America Act (BNA Act) that unites New Brunswick, Nova Scotia, Québec, and Ontario into the Dominion of Canada, with John A. Macdonald as the first prime minister.

1870–1999   Westward expansion later includes Manitoba (1870), British Columbia (1871), and Prince Edward Island (1873) into Confederation. The vast expanse of what was then the Northwest Territories is eventually divided into the provinces of Saskatchewan and Alberta (1905). Finally, after a bitter battle and an almost evenly divided referendum result, the British colony of Newfoundland joins Confederation in 1949. Canada also has three territories, the Northwest Territories (1870), the Yukon Territory (1898), and Nunavut (1999).

Situating the Nation

A unique combination of history and geography has conspired against Canadians having a clear understanding of themselves as constituting "a nation" in the classical sense. If by a nation one means a homogeneous entity composed of individuals sharing a common culture, language, history, and traditions, then clearly the realities of Canadian history are evidence enough against the notion of a single Canadian nation. Nor would it be completely correct to speak about "Canadian nationalism," at least in the sense in which Ernest Gellner defines it: namely, one nation striving for one state. Since the formal signing of the British North America (BNA) Act in 1867, and more recently, Pierre Trudeau's repatriation of the Canadian Constitution in 1982, Canada has had a relatively stable political state system, composed of a central federal government and relatively autonomous provinces, working together in a context of conflict and compromise. Rather than being a nation without a state—which is the case with Québec—one could best describe Canada as a state without a nation. It is a modern democratic multi-national state.

Most would agree that the idea of a Canadian national identity is at best a fragile one. In its efforts to develop a coherent sense of national identity, Canada has had to struggle with—and sometimes against—a variety of very powerful influences. Externally, it has been caught between its colonial past with close enduring attachments to the British empire and, certainly after 1945, its geographically closer (proudly proclaimed "the longest undefended border in the world" by Canadians) and extremely powerful southern neighbor, the United States. The extent of Canada's pre-1945 colonial ties to Britain is easy to demonstrate. Canadians fought in defense of the British empire in World War I and again in 1939, during World War II, even before the arrival of the United States into the conflict. It must be recalled as well that before the Canadian Citizenship Act of 1947, Canadians were British subjects and not Canadian citizens. It was not until 1965 that the red maple leaf flag became Canada's national flag, replacing first the Union Jack, then the Red Ensign (with the Union Jack a prominent symbol). Plus, the majority of the population of Canada was of British, and historically Loyalist, Scottish, English, and Irish extraction, who had strong sentimental attachments to the idea of the British empire.

After 1945, the Canadian struggle for a national identity was largely in opposition to the United States. Canada and the United States share so much in common: geography and a border that stretches from the Atlantic to the Pacific, language (both are majority English speakers), history as colonies of the British empire, and religion (both are majority Christian). The political, economic, social, and cultural links that have developed as a result threaten, many Canadians believe, any uniquely independent Canadian identity from emerging. There is little dispute that the United States is a political, economic, and military powerhouse

that therefore dominates not just North America but the world. Prime Minister Trudeau's metaphor of the mouse sleeping next to an elephant aptly describes the U.S.-Canada relationship. Consider just one point of comparison: Canada's population in 2001 was roughly 31 million, while in 2000, the U.S. population was 281 million, more than nine times in size. Consider also the fact that California's population was over 33 million at the time, and therefore greater than the whole Canadian population. Clearly a key element to understanding any form of Canadian identity is to be found in this struggle against the colossus to its south.

The search to define a Canadian national identity has also had to confront enormous internal diversity. Three dynamics are worthy of special note. The first is between English-speaking Canadians, French-speaking Canadians concentrated in Québec, and the First Nations. The history of French-English relations in Canada is a long and complex one. While historically there had always been tensions, from the 1960s on, a nationalist movement grew in strength in Québec, threatening in 1980 (40.5 percent of Québecers voting "Yes" to proceeding with sovereignty negotiations) and 1995 (49.4 percent of Québecers voting "Yes") to break up the country. The place of the Québécois nation and its relationship to

Canada is a perennial open question. Added to this has been the strength of First Nations' claims for self-government, also an important challenge to the development of the ideal of a homogenous Canadian national identity.

Finally, immigration and regional diversity have plagued the formation of a clear Canadian identity. Continuous waves of immigration, beginning with early colonization, including the expansion of the West after Confederation to the postwar boom during the 1950s and, more recently, with the influx of peoples coming from Asia, Canada has been and continues to be a society of immigrants. The United Nations has declared Toronto the most ethnically diverse city in the world, with 41 percent of its population born outside Canada and composed of more than 80 different ethnic groups and speaking more than 100 languages. In addition, the enormous historic and geographic differences that exist among the provinces in Canada have acted as a centrifugal force against any efforts by the federal government to impose a homogeneous national identity. Regionalism has always been and continues to be strong in Canada, with individual provinces having distinct histories, identities, and economies and being extremely protective of them.

Yet despite these many obstacles, there have been and continue to be attempts to define a Canadian national identity. Many of these attempts have occurred since the 1960s and contain institutional as well as elite efforts to set out what it means to be "Canadian."

Instituting the Nation

The Canadian federal government has historically taken the lead in instituting and implementing nationwide economic and cultural policy. Outside the initial act of union in 1867, Prime Minister Macdonald's "National Policy" stands out as one of the first comprehensive efforts to draw up and realize a national policy for Canada as a whole. The twin pillars of this policy were economic tariffs and aggressive westward expansion. In 1879, Macdonald's Conservatives implemented a tariff on many goods produced in the United States. The idea was that a tax on foreign goods would force Canadians to purchase Canadian-produced goods and thereby strengthen Canadian industries. The completion of the Canadian Pacific Railway in November 1885 first encouraged colonization of the prairies and, second, linked Halifax to Vancouver, encouraging an east-west trade orientation rather than a north-south one. Another example was Pierre Trudeau's introduction in 1980 of the National Energy Program. The program forced western provinces, Alberta in particular, to sell their oil to eastern provinces for less than what they would have received on the open market. The idea is that this would strengthen east-west links and make Canada self-sufficient.

Perhaps a more important element in the development of a Canadian national identity has been the federal government's involvement in culture. This

Multiculturalism

On March 15, 1990, the federal government lifted the ban on Canadian Sikhs wearing turbans while on duty for the Royal Canadian Mounted Police (RCMP). This was a crucial ruling for two reasons. First, it demonstrated the Canadian government's commitment to an inclusive multiculturalism, and second, it challenged one of the most traditional symbols of Canada: the RCMP officers' trademark flat-rimmed Stetson hat.

George Parkin Grant (1918–1988)

In 1965, Canadian philosopher George Grant published what instantly became a classic: *Lament for a Nation: The Defeat of Canadian Nationalism.* Three years earlier, John Diefenbaker's Conservatives were defeated by Pearson's Liberals. Grant admired Diefenbaker's form of Canadian nationalism and his ability to withstand encroaching U.S. imperialism. With the election of the Liberals, Grant believed Canada's independence would be eventually sacrificed to greater political and cultural control from Washington. Ironically, Grant's lament for Canada served to rally nationalists to fight harder for Canadian sovereignty in the late 1960s and 1970s.

Pierre Elliot Trudeau (1919–2000)

Much could and has been said about Canada's enigmatic and charismatic 20th-century prime minister (1968–1979, 1980–1984). Perhaps his greatest legacy was the 1982 repatriation of the Canadian Constitution and a new Canadian Charter of Rights and Freedoms. All provinces except for Québec were signatories to these documents. Trudeau was a firm believer in a strong central federal state, was no fan of Québec nationalism, and therefore spent much of his political career battling Québec separatists. He held to this vision of the Canadian political system even after the near breakup of the country after the Québec Referendum in 1995. Whether or not this vision will hold in the future is an open question.

involvement has usually taken one or a combination of three forms: subsidy, regulation, and protection. In 1948, Prime Minister Louis St. Laurent was informed that he might lose the upcoming election if he did not do something to strengthen a "national culture" in Canada. His response was to establish a Royal Commission on National Development in the Arts, Letters, and Sciences, headed by Vincent Massey, to develop a national cultural policy for Canada. Massey's final report was one of the first to recognize the influence and impact of U.S. popular and mass culture on Canada. It suggested that the government establish a national television service, controlled by the Canadian Broadcasting Corporation (CBC), before granting licenses to private broadcasting companies. The Commission also encouraged the government to strengthen national cultural institutions with subsidies and grants, while creating new ones as well. Although not all of Massey's recommendations were immediately implemented, over the years, new cultural institutions were established in Canada with an overarching agenda to develop Canadian culture.

The Massey Commission established that the federal government had a strategic role to play in developing Canadian culture. In 1955, a second Royal Commission was established, this time to look into the problems associated with the rapid shift from radio to television. The Fowler Commission found the majority of primetime television programs watched by Canadians were from the United States. Fowler wondered if a Canadian national identity could withstand such a powerful cultural influence. From Fowler's recommendations, Prime Minister John Diefenbaker enacted the Broadcasting Act of 1958, which sought to "regulate" the content of both public (the CBC) and private broadcasters by establishing a Board of Broadcast Governors (BBG). Ten years later, this regulating body was changed to the Canadian Radio-Television Commission (CRTC), which began setting Canadian-content quotas on programming. The CRTC in 1970 set out content rules stating that 60 percent of television programming had to be Canadian and 30 percent of music played had to have some Canadian involvement. The CRTC still acts to regulate radio and television programming in Canada.

Finally, the Canadian government has also threatened outright protectionism when it came to U.S. magazines and Canadian advertising in those magazines. Originally brought to the attention of Diefenbaker by the O'Leary Commission in 1961, the government attempted to ban such imports as *Time* and *Readers Digest* and disallow tax exemptions to those Canadian advertisers advertising in such magazines. Diefenbaker's strategy was largely unsuccessful. During the late 1990s, Liberal Heritage minister Sheila Copps attempted a similar strategy, trying to limit the number of "split-run" U.S. magazines on the Canada market. The implementation of the 1988 Canada-U.S. Free Trade Agreement made such protectionism almost impossible to implement, however, especially with certain cultural products, such as magazines.

Defining the Nation

In 2004, the CBC ran a television series modeled after a British contest that had people vote for the greatest Briton. Canadians voted Tommy C. Douglas the greatest Canadian, over Canadian politicians with arguably greater international presence like Pierre E. Trudeau and Lester B. Pearson. Why would Canadians consider a once provincial premier (of Saskatchewan of all provinces), who, even though he was the leader of the national New Democratic Party (NDP), was never prime minister? Part of the reason is the fact that many of the values Douglas held are integral to what Canadians now understand to be essential to their identity. Heading that list would be progressive social values. In 1944, Douglas and the Co-operative Commonwealth Party (CCF) in Saskatchewan became the first socialist government in North America. For 18 years, he and his government introduced some of the most progressive legislation at the time: public sewage and electricity, paved roads and labor reform, and, perhaps his most important achievement, universal public health care. Pearson's Liberals would later introduce a national system called Medicare, a universal or socialized system of health care, but it was Douglas who began the process provincially. Today, national programs like Medicare are what Canadians point to as embodying key Canadian values: universal public access to essential social services.

A 1963 Royal Commission on Bilingualism and Biculturalism (the B&B Commission) provided the impetus for two other defining features of the Canadian nation. The B&B Commission was mandated to examine the situation of "the two founding peoples" of Canada, narrowly defined as the French and the English. The commission discovered that French speakers in Canada were basically "second-class citizens," unable to receive essential services in their first language. The commission's finding eventually led to the 1969 Official Languages Act, recognizing French and English as Canada's two official languages. All federal services were to be provided and all government business was to be conducted in French and English. A second and perhaps unintended consequence of the B&B Commission was the realization that the notion of "two founding peoples" of Canada was inadequate. Aboriginal groups, who were clearly present at the founding of Canada, as well as "other ethnic groups" claimed they were excluded from the original mandate of the B&B Commission. The result was that in 1971, Prime Minister Trudeau encouraged a policy of multiculturalism, the encouragement and development of ethnic pluralism in Canada. In 1982, it became law, and six years later Bill-C-94, the Multicultural Act, was passed.

Other than holding progressive social values, multicultural and bilingual, Canadians tend to define their role internationally as peacekeepers. In 1957, then External Affairs minister Lester Pearson was awarded the Nobel Peace Prize for his proposal to establish a UN Emergency Force to help end the hostilities during the Suez crisis in 1956. During the Cold War, Canada sought to define itself as a "middle power" working toward compromise and conciliation when international tensions like the Vietnam War broke out. While Canada has gone to war and may well do so in the future, Canadians commonly see themselves largely as a peacekeeping nation.

Narrating the Nation

Truly national myths are difficult to construct in Canada given the diversity of Canada's history and population. Constructing a national myth around the 1759 Battle of Québec, for instance, and the victory and ultimate death of the English general James Wolfe, would serve only to exclude the French contribution to the founding of Canada and reinforce the idea that Québecers were a conquered people. The mythologizing of James Wolfe as "the great conqueror of New France" would expose deep rifts in the Canadian national psyche. Perhaps it is for this reason that many of the national myths that Canadian artists—whether painters or writers—have constructed revolve around nature (i.e., The North) and sports (i.e., hockey). The landscape and hockey are by and large neutral arenas that tend to transcend ethnic and linguistic differences.

No group of artists managed to break free of older European styles of landscape painting to create a clearly unique "Canadian style" more than the Group of Seven. Officially formed in 1920, the Group of Seven included founders J. E. H. MacDonald (1873–1932) and Lawren Harris (1885–1970), Franklin Carmichel (1890–1945), A. Y. Jackson (1882–1974), Frank Johnston (1888–1949), Arthur Lismer (1885–1969), and F. H. Varley (1881–1969). Tom Thompson (1877–1917) and Emily Carr (1871–1945) were also important members of this style of painting and contributed to the general myth of the Canadian North. The Group of Seven painters intentionally left the urban centers of Canada—ironic, since the majority of Canadians live in large urban centers clustered along the U.S.-Canada border—to seek and capture the isolation, wildness, majesty, and grandeur of the Great North. Their paintings have come to represent the Canadian myth of the North. In 1972, a young Canadian author named Margaret Atwood completed a similar task by distilling the patterns of Canadian writing. Her reading of Canadian literature (called CanLit) revealed an overwhelming struggle for survival; survival against a hostile natural environment and survival against oneself.

Members of the original Group of Seven, a collection of renowned Canadian landscape painters, in Toronto, 1920. Clockwise from left front: A. Y. Jackson, Fred Varley, Lawren Harris, Barker Firley (not a member), Frank Johnston, Arthur Lismer, and J. E. H. MacDonald. (Arthur Goss)

Most Canadians over the age of 10 in 1972 remember where they were when Paul Henderson scored the game- and series-winning goal in game eight of the Canada-Russia hockey series. In the heart of the Cold War, this sporting event, understood by most as more than just a hockey game, has become embedded in the Canadian imagination like no other event. Hockey is considered "Canada's game" by most Canadians. Every loss by a Canadian team at the international level leads to several months of accusations and recriminations of the "state of our game." Many Canadian national heroes—Maurice "Rocket" Richard, Mario "The Magnificent" Lemieux, and Wayne "The Great One" Gretzky—are hockey players, known internationally. In a sense, hockey transcends many of the divisions that exist in Canada. Roch Carrier's classic short story, "The Hockey Sweater/ Le chandail de hockey," exploits the hockey rivalry between the Montreal Canadiens and the Toronto Maple Leaf but also the French and the English. Ultimately the love of the game of hockey unites both sides in mutual respect that transcends linguistic differences.

Mobilizing and Building the Nation

Nationalism in Canada has never been a mass movement. Other than political scientist Philip Resnick's 1977 Marxian analysis of the links between social class and Canadian nationalism, most commentators agree that Canadian nationalism has largely been elite driven. In his book *Canada, Quebec and the Uses of Nationalism*, historian Ramsay Cook argues that it is usually the intelligentsia —individuals who produce and disseminate ideas, including journalists, university professors, writers, and artists—who have been at the forefront in promoting various forms and manifestations of Canadian nationalism. Similarly, historian Jack Granatstein makes an argument in his classic *Yankee Go Home?* (the question mark at the end intended to express irony) that Canadian elites, politicians as well as professors, have used an integral component of Canadian nationalism, namely "anti-Americanism" to further their careers. The fact that the two most influential expressions of Canadian nationalism in the 20th century, one cultural and the other economic, were led by political and cultural elites demonstrates the truth of this claim.

During the 1960s and early 1970s, U.S. economic and cultural power became a concern to many in Canada, especially those working in universities. Political scientists Kari Levitt and Melvin Watkins began documenting the devastating impact that U.S. direct investment was having on the Canadian economy. Especially in areas such as natural resources, U.S. companies were setting up branch plants in Canada to extract and exploit Canada's resource wealth. Led by federal Liberal finance minister Walter Gordon, a movement to protect Canada's economic independence from the United States grew during this time. On the culture end, the rapid growth of universities, as a result of the baby boom generation's entrance into postsecondary institutions, led to the hiring of many U.S. professors. While not exclusive to the university, a cultural nationalist movement developed around Robin Mathews and James Steele in 1968, two professors of English at Carleton University in Ottawa, to increase the employment opportunities of Canadians in culturally sensitive institutions. It is clear with these two examples, however, that Canadian nationalism was confined to a relatively elite group of individuals, even though the debates and discussions of Canadian culture and economy often spilled out into the public.

Canada is a growing, modern multinational democracy that continues to redefine itself and its place in an increasingly global world. One of its greatest internal threats has been, and continues to be, successive waves of Québec nationalism and its struggle for sovereignty. Much depends on the ability of the Canadian federal system of government to address ever-increasing demands for provincial autonomy. Culturally, the metaphor of the mosaic is used to describe Canada. With a population composed of immigrants, and where population growth comprises waves of new immigrants, this will most likely not change. Canada has been a place that allows a variety of ethnicities and cultural groups to flourish. Diversity, whether ethnic, sexual, religious, or cultural is key to how Canadians see themselves. Whether or not diversity can be balanced with some indefinable quality that unites is not just a Canadian question, it is also a global question.

Selected Bibliography

Atwood, M. 1972. *Survival: A Thematic Guide to Canadian Literature*. Toronto: Anansi Press.

Azzi, S. 1999. *Walter Gordon and the Rise of Canadian Nationalism*. Montreal: Queen's-McGill Press.

Bumsted, J. M. 1992. *The Peoples of Canada: A Post-Confederation History*. Toronto: Oxford University Press.

Cook, R. 1995. *Canada, Quebec and the Uses of Nationalism*. 2nd ed. Toronto: McClelland and Stewart.

Cormier, J. 2004. *The Canadianization Movement: Emergence, Survival and Success*. Toronto: University of Toronto Press.

Gellner, E. 1983. *Nations and Nationalism*. Ithaca, NY: University of Cornell Press.

Gillmor, D., and P. Turgeon. 2000. *Canada: A People's History*, vol. 1. Toronto: McClelland and Stewart.

Gillmor, D. 2000. *Canada: A People's History*, vol. 2. Toronto: McClelland and Stewart.

Granatstein, J. 1996. *Yankee Go Home? Canadians and Anti-Americanism*. Toronto: Harper-Collins.

Grant, G. 2000. *Lament for a Nation: The Defeat of Canadian Nationalism*. Quebec City: McGill-Queen's University Press.

Levitt, K. 1970. *Silent Surrender: The Multinational Corporation in Canada*. Toronto: Macmillian.

Morton, W. L. 1973. *The Canadian Identity*. 2nd ed. Toronto: University of Toronto Press.

Resnick, P. 1977. *The Land of Cain: Class and Nationalism in English Canada, 1945–1975*. Vancouver, BC: New Star Books.

Pan-Aboriginalism in Australia

John Maynard

Chronology

1788   British invasion and occupation of the Australian continent.
1837   British Select Committee recommends Aboriginal protection.
1860   Victorian Central Board for the Protection of Aborigines is appointed.
1883   Aborigines Protection Board (New South Wales [NSW]) is established.
1897   Aboriginal Protection and Restriction of the Sale of Opium Act (Qld).
1905   Aborigines Act (Western Australia [WA]).
1909   Aborigines Protection Act (NSW).
1911   Aborigines Act (South Australia [SA]).
1924   The Australian Aboriginal Progressive Association (AAPA) is formed in Sydney.
1937   NSW Parliament holds a "Select Committee Inquiry" into administration of the Aborigines Protection Board.
1938   Aboriginal activists hold the symbolic "Day of Mourning Protest" to coincide with the 150 years of settlement celebration.
1962   Aboriginal people are given the unrestricted right to vote in federal elections.
1965   Charles Perkins and university students emulate the U.S. civil rights movement's "Freedom Rides."
1966   Gurindji walk-off at Wave Hill.
1967   Referendum grants Aboriginal people citizenship in their own country.
1969   The Aborigines Welfare Board's abolished responsibilities are transferred to the Department of Child Welfare and Social Welfare.
1971   Aboriginal Legal Service is formed.
1972   The Whitlam government introduces a policy of self-determination. Aboriginal Medical Service is established at Redfern in Sydney. Aboriginal "Tent Embassy" in Canberra.
1975   The Racial Discrimination Act is passed. Prime Minister Gough Whitlam hands back Gurindji land in a symbolic gesture.
1977   The Anti-Discrimination Act is passed.
1980   Link Up (NSW) Aboriginal Corporation is established.
1985   Uluru is handed back to the traditional owners.
1987   Royal Commission into Aboriginal Deaths in Custody begins.
1988   Aboriginal people in a great show of unity converge on Sydney to protest the 200 years of Australian settlement bicentennial celebration.
1990   The Aboriginal and Torres Strait Islander Commission (ATSIC) is formed.
1992   The Mabo decision. Prime Minister Paul Keating delivers the "Redfern Address."
1993   Native Title Act is passed by the Commonwealth government for determining Aboriginal land right claims.
1995   A national inquiry into the Stolen Generations is undertaken. This heart-rending inquiry explores the consequences of generations of Aboriginal children being separated from their families.
1998   Wik Decision.
2000   Corroboree Reconciliation Walk across Sydney Harbour Bridge.
2004   The federal government abolishes the ATSIC.

Situating the Nation

To understand the aspirations and tensions of Aboriginal nationalism, one must recognize that Aboriginal people are a nation trapped within a nation—a minority group without genuine representation or recognition—and that the continued impact of invasion and dispossession ensures that colonial oppression has not been lifted. There is no real indigenous governing body, no council of elders, and no recognition in law of prior Aboriginal sovereignty.

The single most important issue for indigenous nationalistic endeavor is self-determination. As a concept, this is central to indigenous people reclaiming control of their lives and directives. Evidence indicates that where indigenous people have been placed in control of their own directives the most positive and beneficial results have been achieved. Examples include the establishment of Aboriginal Medical Services (AMS), Aboriginal Legal Services, and Aboriginal and Islander child care. There is a misconception that the concept of self-determination for Aboriginal Australia was introduced by the Gough Whitlam–led Labour Party during the 1970s. In fact, it was first promoted by an all-Aboriginal political organization, the Australian Aboriginal Progressive Association (AAPA), in Sydney in 1924.

Self-determination is firmly tied to the ongoing struggle for a signed treaty that recognizes both indigenous sovereignty and the past injustices inflicted upon the Aboriginal population. However, such a treaty remains a remote, perhaps unattainable dream. The Australian government is not prepared to negotiate over a treaty through fear of imagined repercussions associated with recognizing prior indigenous sovereignty. Since 1788, Australian history and legal understanding has ignored, obscured, or erased any concept of prior indigenous sovereignty, unlike the United States, where the signing of treaties was insisted on for the recognition of indigenous nation-states (although in most cases these were blatantly abused). An earlier attempt to establish a treaty in Victoria in 1835 by John Batman, who exchanged blankets, tomahawks, and various other items for the acquisition of some 243,000 hectares of land, was not recognized by the colonial authorities, and the purchase was declared void.

Since the invasion and occupation of the Australian continent in 1788, the indigenous population has buckled under the weight of dispossession, disease, violence, and cultural destruction. After the initial impact, Aboriginal people were subjected to generations of imprisonment on government-controlled reserves and institutions. In these concentration camps, they suffered decades of oppressive incarceration. They were forcibly removed out of towns and onto reserves and were under the control of managers who oversaw every aspect of Aboriginal life. During this period, measures were taken to not only restrict the movement of Aborigines but also to prevent general contact with the white populace. The reserve managers had the right to search Aborigines, their dwellings, and their belongings at any time; they could confiscate property, read their personal mail, order medical inspections, confine children to dormitories, and exert control over mobility of movement. They held power over food and food distribution, clothing, education, employment, and even the right of people to marry. They could expel Aboriginal people from reserves or remove them to another altogether and break up families. Therefore, they had absolute control over the children. Such unabated power took on an increasingly sinister nature.

Both off and on reserves, Aboriginal people, until recent times, were not entitled to paid employment and were largely exploited in areas like the stock industry and domestic service. The era of blanket, sugar, and clothing handouts was followed by a benefits and welfare system, which did not encourage or inspire Aboriginal people to endeavor. A previously independent and self-sufficient hunter-gatherer society, the Aboriginal people were driven to a state of welfare-dependent imprisonment. No genuine or uniform policy to escape the enforced tentacles of despair and hopelessness had been implemented.

Until the 1960s, the push for indigenous national identity and political mobilization was largely led by southeastern Aboriginal activists located in urban and rural centers. The 1966 Gurindji Central Australian revolt against severe employment inequalities established a broadened agenda for land rights. This moment signaled a major shift in focus away from urban to remote Aboriginal political activism and the establishment of the Northern Territory Land Rights movement. This relocation of political thrust can be viewed as both a positive and a negative shift because the federal government now largely directs all of its political consul-

---

Charles Perkins (1936–2000)

Arguably the most charismatic and recognized Aboriginal leader of the 20th century, Charles Perkins was born at the Aboriginal reserve near Alice Springs in the Northern Territory. His parents were Arrente and Kalkadoon people. He was taken from his mother at the age of 10 and placed in a home for Aboriginal boys in Adelaide, South Australia.

Perkins enrolled as a student with the University of Sydney and was only the second Aboriginal person to graduate from an Australian university. In 1965, he led a group of students, emulating the U.S. civil rights movement's "Freedom Rides." The Australian "Freedom Rides" will remain forever one of the pivotal moments in Aboriginal history, and it provided the perfect political and public launching pad for Charles Perkins. The students, in visiting outback towns in New South Wales, used the media to draw attention to the deeply segregated inequality of Aboriginal existence. Aboriginal people were denied access to hotels, swimming pools, and in some cases even the streets of these towns.

From that point and for the remainder of his life, Perkins was at the forefront of Aboriginal political activism. He played a role through the Foundation of Aboriginal Affairs in the campaign that led to the overwhelming "yes" vote in the 1967 referendum that resulted in the federal government taking power over Aboriginal affairs from the states. Throughout his dynamic and often turbulent political career, Perkins was compared to such individuals as Martin Luther King Jr. and Nelson Mandela. He died in 2000, leaving a space that is impossible to fill.

---

tation and impetus toward a remote (and preferred) vision of Aboriginal Australian authority.

Instituting the Nation

Prior to the last century, the concept of an indigenous sense of nationalism residing across the Australian continent was nonexistent. The indigenous population of Australia before 1788 consisted of over 500 differing language or tribal groups with their own spiritual ties to well-established areas of country. Although diverse, the indigenous groups operated universally under an intricate egalitarian system that was bound and governed by tight social and environmental controls. Kinship is the central core of the egalitarian Aboriginal extended-family system. There are no chiefs, kings, or headmen. In traditional Aboriginal society, all Aboriginal adults have ongoing commitments to one another.

However, the past century has witnessed a dramatic change of understanding, particularly in the shared experiences of dispossession, frontier violence, cultural destruction, children taken away, confinement on debilitating reserves, and neglect of governments at all levels. The combined impact of these events has affected the well-being of Aboriginal Australians, who hold the worst health statistics within the country—with a general life expectancy that is 20 years shorter than nonindigenous Australians. This is combined with the highest rates of incarceration and the worst employment, housing, and education opportunities. These horrific statistics are embedded in past neglect, but indigenous people have fought politically to alter these appalling numbers, and on those occasions when a general sense of unity and strength evolves, a significant impact is achieved.

Nationalism in its most basic form has close ties to the indigenous "tribal" kinship and extended-family structure of belonging and connection. The concept of belonging to place and family was and remains the core belief within Aboriginal

The Aboriginal Tent Embassy (1972–Present)

In 1972, the establishment of an Aboriginal Tent Embassy was a powerful symbol in the fight for social and political change. Frustration with the lack of progress following the 1967 referendum was the catalyst for young Aboriginal activists establishing the Aboriginal Tent Embassy on the lawn of Parliament House in Canberra. These activists unknowingly followed the path of the 1920s activists before them in seeking influence and inspiration from African Americans, particularly Malcolm X and the Black Panther movement.

These young activists were supported by a large base of nonindigenous student supporters. Eventually the police were called in to dismantle the protest. The violent response by the police led to international media exposure. To this day, the embassy remains a beacon of inspiration and protest for Aboriginal people.

Charles Frederick Maynard (1879–1946)

Fred Maynard was one of the great Aboriginal patriots and organizers of political activism. He was instrumental in forming the first unified and long-lasting politically motivated and organized Aboriginal movement, the Australian Aboriginal Progressive Association (AAPA). Maynard's mother was a Worimi Aboriginal woman from northern New South Wales; his father, an English laborer. After his mother died, giving birth to twins who also died, his father deserted the family, and the six children were all placed with people in the local community. Fred and his brother Arthur were taken in by a Presbyterian minister at Dungog. The boys were cruelly treated and lived in the minister's stable.

As a young man who held a variety of jobs, Maynard was well traveled and witnessed firsthand the hardship and conditions his people had to endure. These early experiences were of major significance in shaping his later political agenda and beliefs. He was a drover and at one time operated a nursery in Sydney. He remained an avid and skilled gardener throughout his life. He spent time as a photographer, worked as a timber-getter on the north coast of New South Wales, and he finally gained work as a wharf laborer on the Sydney docks, where the trade union movement made an important impact on his political beliefs.

It was through his work on the docks that Maynard came into contact with African American influences that had such an impact on the political rhetoric of the Australian Aboriginal Progressive Association (AAPA). For white Australians, the most unsettling aspect of the AAPA was the fact that it was led by a self-educated and indeed well-educated Aboriginal man with a great command of both the spoken and written word. Maynard spoke and wrote passionately and insightfully about the injustices and atrocities committed against Aboriginal people. He spoke of things that either many white people did not know or were not aware of or simply did not want to know. The power of the message that Maynard so defiantly expressed some eight decades ago has not been diminished with time, nor can his grasp of the realities of the Aboriginal situation be at all underestimated. Today his letters and petitions are, in every sense, strangely modern in tone and still as relevant as when they were written.

---

culture and society and, prior to 1788, was the one upon which survival depended. It is therefore understandable that the galvanizing concept of connectedness has on several important occasions been at the forefront of Aboriginal political mobilization against colonialism. So the modern move to Aboriginal nationalism is arguably an organic development.

Recent decades have produced such notable Aboriginal leaders as Charles Perkins, Pat and Mick Dodson, Michael Mansell, Lowitja O'Donoghue, and Noel Pearson, to name but a few, who have in their own way forged a strong sense of indigenous identity and nationalist directive. There have been a number of indigenous national bodies that have attempted to speak on behalf of all Aboriginal people. These groups include the Aboriginal Torres Strait Islander Commission (ATSIC), various state departments of Aboriginal Affairs, the Council for Aboriginal Affairs, the National Aboriginal Consultative Group, and the Aboriginal Provisional Government. Significantly, all of these groups (apart from the Aboriginal

Provisional Government) have been government initiatives and have suffered because the decision-making process has required a rubber stamp by the Australian government.

Nevertheless, the establishment of the ATSIC as an elected indigenous body overseen by the government was a brave step and supported by the majority of indigenous Australians. The ATSIC Act of 1989 established the ATSIC, and operations commenced on March 5, 1990. Eighteen elected indigenous commissioners sat on the ATSIC Board, which until June 30, 2004, was the Australian Government's principal policy-making and advisory body for indigenous affairs. ATSIC and its elected indigenous commissioners were constantly targeted by the media for any perceived wrongdoing in indigenous affairs. Over the years, there have been some problems with ATSIC at the national, regional, and community levels, and the problems inherent with ATSIC and many other Aboriginal organizations have constrained the hopes of Aboriginal nationalism and unity.

Nevertheless, ATSIC was performing well in the majority of Aboriginal communities, assisting in the improvement of their social conditions. Despite an inquiry into the operations of ATSIC instigated by the federal government and to include a report to be conducted by Bob Collins (a parliamentarian) and Jackie Huggins (an Aboriginal spokesperson), the government did not wait for the findings of its own report. In March 2005, the Australian Parliament passed the ATSIC Amendment Bill repealing provisions of the ATSIC Act, in effect abolishing ATSIC. The legislation was proclaimed, and the government transferred responsibility for ATSIC programs and services to mainstream agencies from July 1, 2004. The federal government then sought to install an indigenous advisory committee of hand-picked Aboriginal members. The success or failure of this body remains to be seen, but it does not have the support of the wider Aboriginal community.

Defining the Nation

Aboriginality does not impose specific barriers to inclusion as part of its national fabric. It does not matter what region you come from, urban, rural, or remote. The Torres Strait Islanders are very much a part of this indigenous national cultural identity and commonality of experience. There is no specific cultural insistence: you can be Aboriginal and not speak your language, you do not have to continue with your cultural practices and spiritual beliefs and may well be a practicing Christian or Muslim, you can be dark, or you can be light with blonde hair and blue eyes. The single most important commonality is that all Aboriginal people have suffered the family experience and impact of dispossession. The "Stolen Generations" experience is another crucial area of shared suffering. It has been expressed that nearly all Aboriginal groups or families can trace to a family member that was removed or taken away at some point. This shared grief in the national tragedy exposes the central core to belonging as an Aboriginal person to this Aboriginal nation.

One very important Aboriginal nationalistic moment occurred in 1974 when Harold Thomas designed the Aboriginal flag. Its colors of red, black, and yellow (black for the people, yellow for the sun and life giver, and red for the earth and blood of Aboriginal people spilt since 1788) have become the single most important symbol of Aboriginal unity and strength. Two important days also signify national Aboriginal unity. National Aboriginal and Islander Observance Committee (NAIDOC) Week is celebrated each July and reflects the long history of Aboriginal and Torres Strait Islander efforts to force change upon government policy and wider public thinking. Similarly, Aboriginal people on January 26 each year do not celebrate Australia Day, which commemorates the raising of the British flag on Australian soil, but have since 1988 mobilized their own anniversary, "Invasion Day" or "Survival Day," marking both a point of great sadness and loss with the resilience of people to survive. The first "Survival Day" concert was staged at La Perouse in 1992.

Narrating the Nation

Aboriginal attempts to invoke a sense of Aboriginal nationalism as a source of empowerment dates at least to the 1920s. The AAPA (the all-Aboriginal political organization) was inspired by Marcus Garvey and the Universal Negro Improvement Association (UNIA). Garveyism was universal in its message and appealed to an astonishing variety of nationalities and groups. The Aboriginal activists shaped and remodeled Garveyism to their own needs. They based their platform on Aboriginal rights to land, protecting their children, claiming citizenship in their own country, and defending a distinct indigenous cultural identity; it "was an association, which suggested that they must pull together for the good of all."

The AAPA demanded that the New South Wales (NSW) state government Aborigines Protection Board be abolished and replaced by an Aboriginal Board of Management. It would be a further several decades before such an indigenous body, ATSIC, would be established by the federal government to oversee and advise on indigenous issues.

It has been said that the AAPA emblem, an image of an Aboriginal man encircled by the words "Australia for Australians," was a distinct reference to Aboriginal nationalism. The memory of success and the hope that both the UNIA and AAPA instilled in their people was recognized as a dangerous threat by the United States and Australian governments, and was therefore systematically obliterated. There is no shame from an Aboriginal perspective in that acknowledgment; it reflects the power devices that the government and its agencies had used with great deliberation to silence and break down the resolve of the Aboriginal population in both its actions and also its memories. The erasure from memory was so complete that notable and high-profile Aboriginal activists of the 1960s were unaware of the existence of the 1920s movement.

Aboriginal political mobilization again came to the fore in the late 1930s, but inexplicably, none of the earlier activists from the 1920s were visible. The most notable activists of this era were William Cooper, William Ferguson, Pearl Gibbs, and Jack Patten. This new generation of activists established alliances between Victoria and NSW and made representations in their platform for more remote Aboriginal people, including the Northern Territory. Their most significant achievement was the highly symbolic "Day of Mourning Protest" held in Sydney in 1938. The protest attempted to tarnish the sesquicentennial celebrations of British settlement and highlight the impoverished and neglected state of Aboriginal Australia. The beginning of World War II was responsible for the Aboriginal political movement and agitation disappearing from wider public consciousness for nearly two decades.

Recent decades have witnessed a number of significant moments in Aboriginal unity and sense of nationalistic pursuit. In 1965, Charles Perkins led a group of white university students in emulating the U.S. civil rights movement's "Freedom Ride." The exposure this radical approach achieved was far-reaching in both the indigenous and nonindigenous communities. Perkins, for his part, would achieve legendary status as one of the great Aboriginal leaders of the 20th century. In the campaign to grant Aboriginal people citizenship in their own country, the 1967 referendum on amending the Australian Constitution united indigenous peoples from an astonishing number of areas. In 1972, young Aboriginal activists established the Aboriginal Tent Embassy on the lawn of Parliament House in Canberra. These activists unknowingly followed the path of the 1920s activists before them in seeking influence and inspiration from African Americans, particularly Malcolm X and the Black Panther movement. The sense of growing or rebirth of Aboriginal nationalism was firmly underway.

The 1988 bicentennial again witnessed a surge in Aboriginal unity and protest. Thousands of Aboriginal people from across the continent converged on Sydney to demonstrate and highlight the injustices forced upon Aboriginal Australia since first settlement and draw international media attention to the inequality of Aboriginal life. On January 26, over 40,000 Aboriginal people from all parts of the country, and their supporters, marched from Redfern Park to a public rally in Hyde Park and from there to Sydney Harbour.

The High Court Mabo decision recognized prior indigenous ownership of the Australian continent, acknowledging that Native Title continued to exist over particular kinds of land: unalienated Crown land, national parks, and reserves. Importantly, the concept that Australia never was terra nullius or "empty land" was overthrown. However, despite the decision bringing widespread joy to many, it opened wide fissures of media-fueled division and ignorance in the wider community.

Crowds fill the Sydney Harbour Bridge as part of the "Corroboree 2000" Reconciliation March in support of Aboriginal Australia on May 28, 2000. (John Van Hasselt/Corbis Sygma)

Since the 1980s, there has been an increased rise in adopting Aboriginal culture as a major signifier of wider Australian nationalism. Aboriginal art has achieved worldwide attention and has been vigorously incorporated into the sense of Australian nationhood. Arguably, Aboriginal art has become one of the nation's most powerful symbols. In 2000, more than a half million Australians chose to walk in support of Aboriginal Australia in the Corroboree Reconciliation Walk across Sydney Harbour Bridge. It must be understood, however, that many Aboriginal people chose to boycott the event, seeing it as nothing more than a staged propaganda exercise to demonstrate to the gathering international media contingent in Sydney for the up-coming Olympic Games that Australians were all reconciled with the past.

Mobilizing and Building the Nation

Aboriginal political activists across several decades have demonstrated great initiative and understanding for the importance of mobilizing a nationalistic platform. The movements of the 1920s and 1960s successfully infused a sense of Black nationalism and cultural pride into their agenda. Aboriginal activists have become skilled and articulate operators within the media and employ it for their own propaganda agenda, within both the wider Aboriginal and white communities. During the past decade, there have been several significant developments, including the Mabo decision, Aboriginal Deaths in Custody Inquiry, Corroboree 2000 Reconciliation Walk across Sydney Harbour Bridge, Bringing Them Home Inquiry, and Native Title. However, of these developments, only the Aboriginal Deaths in Custody and Bringing Them Home inquiries have had the majority support among the wider Aboriginal community. Intense individual trauma (such as the death of Joe Pat in a Western Australian jail in 1976) galvanized public Aboriginal protest and anger and is widely recognized for the Aboriginal Deaths in Custody Inquiry.

Despite a widespread belief that indigenous Australians are a united people with a shared history of culture and survival, Aboriginal nationalism is now at a crossroads. Recognition does need to be made, despite many significant moments, that Aboriginal people have not achieved a true sense of nationalism and unity. Inequality and suffering remain a large part of Aboriginal life. Major issues like domestic violence and alcohol and substance abuse continue to fester within Aboriginal communities. Aboriginal nationalism is still very much in the struggle stage of development. The current indigenous leadership is divided and remains largely headless, with varying groups and leaders vying for center stage without any genuine cohesion, collaboration, or consultation. This in effect maintains the status quo and inequality of Aboriginal suffering and experience. The abolition of ATSIC has taken away the one national body with which indigenous Australia identified. The Corroboree 2000 Reconciliation Walk across Sydney Harbour Bridge did demonstrate that Aboriginal Australia can depend on a large nonindigenous body of support, but this support needs to be further nurtured and inspired by committed and united indigenous leaders. Knowledge that continues to be revealed from the past, particularly instances from the 1920s' Aboriginal political movement, can be a platform for the future—challenging the encouraged divisions and factions within the wider Aboriginal community by promoting the rights of a united people. Only when indigenous people acknowledge the legacy of the past can they truly become "one voice."

Selected Bibliography

Attwood, B., and A. Markus. 1999. *The Struggle for Aboriginal Rights.* Sydney, Australia: Allan & Unwin.

Broome, R. 1982. *Aboriginal Australians—Black Response to White Dominance 1788/1980.* Sydney, Australia: Allan & Unwin.

Gilbert, K. 1994. *Because a White Man'll Never Do It.* Sydney, Australia: Angus & Robertson.

Goodall, H. 1996. *Invasion to Embassy—Land in Aboriginal Politics in NSW, 1770–1972.* St Leonards, Australia: Allan & Unwin.

Horner, J. 1994. *Bill Ferguson: Fighter for Aboriginal Freedom.* Canberra, Australia: privately published.

Maynard, J. 2002. "The 1920s' Aboriginal Political Defence of the Sacred 'Ancient Code.'" *Cultural Survival Quarterly* 26, no. 2: 34–36.

Maynard, J. 2003. "Vision, Voice and Influence: The Rise of the Australian Aboriginal Progressive Association." *Australian Historical Studies* 34, no. 121 (April): 91–105.

Maynard, J. 2005. "'In the Interests of Our People': The Influence of Garveyism on the Rise of Australian Aboriginal Political Activism." *Aboriginal History* 25: 1–22.

Reynolds, H. 1996. *Aboriginal Sovereignty: Reflections on Race, State and Nation.* St. Leonards, Australia: Allen & Unwin.

Reynolds, H. 2003. *The Law of the Land.* Camberwell, Australia: Penguin.

Maori Nationalism

Toon van Meijl

Chronology

1642	Discovery of New Zealand by Dutch explorer Abel Tasman.
1769	The British discoverer James Cook establishes the first European contacts with the indigenous population, the Maori.
1814	Arrival of the first missionary, Samuel Marsden. The beginning of European settlement.
1840	Signing of the Treaty of Waitangi, in which Maori people cede "sovereignty" in exchange for the possession of their lands, forests, and fisheries.
1858	Crowning of the first Maori king and set up of a Maori monarchy, the first nationalist movement in Maori history.
1860–1864	Wars between several Maori tribes and the New Zealand government over the access to land and control of the country.
1864	Confiscation of large tracts of Maori land.
1892–1902	A Maori Parliament is set up to present Maori grievances to the New Zealand government.
1897	Founding of the Te Aute College Students' Association, in 1906 renamed the Young Maori Party, advocating pride in *Maoritanga* or Maori culture during the first decades of the 20th century.
1930	Beginning of large-scale Maori urbanization.
1970	The emergence of modern Maori protest movements in cities.
1975	Passing of the Treaty of Waitangi Act, instituting the Waitangi Tribunal for the examination of violations of the historic covenant. The Maori renaissance is partly inspired by cultural campaigns initiated by the Young Maori Party.
1985	The passing of the Treaty of Waitangi Amendment Act, backdating the jurisdiction of the Waitangi Tribunal to 1840. More than 1,200 Maori claims are submitted to the Waitangi Tribunal in the following years.
1987	Recognition of the Treaty of Waitangi by the Court of Appeal, which opens an avenue for the settlement of Maori grievances about violations of the treaty. Reorganization of many Maori tribes in light of their negotiations with the government about their claims.
1995	First major compensation agreement signed between the New Zealand government and the Waikato-Tainui Maori tribes, still supporting the Maori monarchy set up in 1858. The Waikato-Tainui tribes receive a formal apology, some land, and some money.

Situating the Nation

Maori society was made up of independent tribes when the British explorer James Cook established the first European contacts with the indigenous population of New Zealand in 1769. Maori nationalism did not emerge until the Maori people were beginning to lose control of the economic and political situation as a result of increasing numbers of settlers arriving in New Zealand from the 1820s.

From the outset, the discourse on Maori nationalism has been centered around the concept of sovereignty and its implications for contemporary political circumstances in New Zealand. This discussion follows the principal position of the notion of sovereignty in the Treaty of Waitangi, a covenant between the British Crown and numerous Maori chiefs that was signed in 1840. The interpretation of this treaty, however, is hampered by the existence of two different versions in English and Maori, which also explains why both signing parties have different understandings of key aspects.

Under the English version of the Treaty of Waitangi, the Maori chiefs ceded "all the rights and powers of Sovereignty" over their respective territories to the queen of England. The Maori version does not use the nearest equivalent of sovereignty, which is probably *mana*, but uses the term *kawanatanga*, a transliteration of "governorship" improvised by the missionaries. Moreover, the second article of the treaty guaranteed to the indigenous population "the full exclusive and undisturbed possession of their Lands and Estates Forests Fisheries and other properties."

For the British, the agreement signed at Waitangi legitimized the migration of massive numbers of Europeans to New Zealand, which, in turn, accelerated the disastrous transfer of vast tracts of Maori land to European settlers. The dispossession of Maori land given the impact of the Treaty of Waitangi caused Maori tribes to disavow intertribal rivalries and discuss their common interests. A desire for intertribal unity thus emerged in defense of Maori sovereignty. It marks the beginning of a discourse on Maori nationalism, which historically has been characterized by a continuous search for intertribal unity.

Instituting the Nation

The first nationalist movement that had an impact beyond its regional origin was the Maori King Movement. In the 1850s, several Maori tribes began tracing out a common strategy to protect themselves from European interference and to make a ban on land sales effective. At first, the meetings of what became known as the movement for *kotahitanga* or "oneness" were aimed at developing a more coherent political organization, but soon the idea of a Maori king came up. Ultimately, this movement for intertribal unity eventuated in the crowning of the Waikato chief Potatau Te Wherowhero as the first Maori king in 1858.

Initially Potatau was supported by 23 tribes, but the unfurling of the flag of the *Kingitanga* or kingship could only reduce, rather than resolve, traditional tribal rivalries. Nevertheless, the Maori king provided a focus for Maori discontent regarding the government's land purchase policies, which had been implemented to appease disenchanted settlers. The dispute between the government and the Maori about access to land degenerated into a series of wars in 1860.

Kingitanga

The Maori King Movement or *Kingitanga* is still very active in contemporary New Zealand. Over the years the monarchy may have lost support from other tribes, but in the Tainui confederation of tribes, from which the first king was elected, the current head of the movement still holds royal status. From 1966 until 2006 the *Kingitanga* was led by the charismatic Maori queen, Dame Te Atairangikaahu. Her funeral was attended by more than 100,000 people, which illustrates the important role of the Maori monarchy in Maori attempts to achieve unity and to reestablish Maori sovereignty in contemporary New Zealand. On the day of her funeral the Maori queen was succeeded by her oldest son Tuheitia, who is of the sixth generation descending from the first king.

Nowadays, *Kingitanga* activities are mainly characterized by two types of ceremonial gatherings, the *poukai* or loyalty gatherings, and the coronation anniversary celebrations. Every year, 28 *poukai* are held at traditional ceremonial centers or *marae* within the monarchy. *Poukai* primarily provide a communication platform at which old people reestablish links among Tainui tribes in ceremonial speeches. The coronation celebrations, in contrast, attract many visitors from beyond Tainui. Groups from around New Zealand take part in the sports and cultural competitions organized during this gathering, which is important for maintaining unity within Maori society.

These lasted until the end of 1864, after which the government moved to confiscate 3 million acres of Maori land, most of which belonged to the tribal confederation of the Maori king.

After the wars, the then Maori king concentrated his activities on seeking redress for the confiscations, but, as a corollary, his own tribal interests soon became identified with the goal of the *Kingitanga*. This impression confronted the Maori king with great difficulties in acquiring support for his attempt to make the kingship a politically effective institution. Many tribes could not accept his self-constituted claim to rule over the entire North Island of New Zealand. Toward the end of the 19th century, the dissension among Maori tribes regarding the Maori King Movement sparked off a new movement to achieve Maori unity.

In the 1890s, the size of the Maori population reached an absolute low, and some form of cooperation among Maori tribes was deemed necessary to offset the threat of total assimilation. The Maori members of Parliament therefore revived the *kotahitanga* movement of the 1850s and set up a Maori Parliament in June 1892 to present tribal and intertribal grievances to the government.

The story of the Maori Parliament, however, does not amount to one of the most successful episodes in Maori history. European society was by now so well established that it could afford to neglect what it considered a separatist movement, and, even more problematic, many Maori people were scarcely interested in the Maori Parliament. Most people were looking for other avenues to solve their problems of poverty rather than the protest meetings of the Maori Parliament, which often stalled in bickering about tribal differences. The Maori Parliament was finally disbanded in 1902.

The lack of motivation to participate in intertribal protest movements against European domination in the 1890s is intertwined with the emergence of a desire to transcend tribal differences. Throughout New Zealand, massive numbers of Maori people had entered paid employment after they lost their land. Many Maori people were thus meeting fellow Maori people from other tribal districts at work. This situation contributed to the emergence of an unprecedented strain of Maori nationalism, not in intertribal but in pan-tribal form.

Defining the Nation

In the beginning of the 20th century, Maori political aspirations shifted from desires for the return of sovereignty toward equal rights for the Maori people as New Zealand citizens. The great advocators of the new political strategy were members of a students' association from a Maori Anglican Boys College, the Te Aute College Students' Association. The organization is commonly referred to as the Young Maori Party, although it never formed a political party. It was rather a group of educated individuals who operated politically, although some of them took up parliamentary seats.

The Young Maori Party pleaded, first and foremost, for socioeconomic equality. At the same time, however, it aspired to retain a distinctive culture and identity within the boundaries of a society in which Maori and Europeans were to hold an equivalent status. The latter aim has become known as the policy of biculturalism. It involves a complementary—cultural—distinction between different nations within the same state. Thus, the Young Maori Party rephrased the previously political desire for a sovereign Maori nation in which each tribe was to

Sir Apirana Ngata

Sir Apirana Ngata was arguably the first Maori leader who showed statesmanlike qualities. He was born in 1874 and became the first Maori to complete a university degree in 1893 and the youngest Maori to be admitted to the bar. In 1897 he was the most prominent speaker at the inaugural conference of the Te Aute College Students' Association. Soon he entered the national scene, where he helped prepare the act that provided for the establishment of local Maori councils. In 1905 he became a member of parliament. He maintained his seat for 38 years. In 1908 he was elevated to the cabinet, and in 1928 he became "Native Minister." As such, he became known for the introduction of land development schemes that set up incorporations, consolidated fragmented land titles, and developed unused land. These schemes gave a tremendous impetus to Maori farming. Ngata was also behind the establishment of a Maori School of Arts and Crafts at Rotorua, and he encouraged the construction of carved meetinghouses. This interest initiated a widespread revival of respect for traditional culture, for which he is probably best remembered.

retain its own autonomy into an aspiration for a pan-tribal, predominantly cultural nation with a relatively autonomous status within the overarching European society. The new vision of Maoridom is most clearly exemplified by the innovative concept of *Maoritanga*.

The term *Maoritanga*, or "Maoriness," was coined to express the new creation of a Maori identity in the modern world. Initially the term *Maoritanga* was interpreted as a call for separatism, but it was meant to be applied in a context of "biculturalism." The leader of the Young Maori Party, Apirana Ngata defined the term as

> an emphasis on the continuing individuality of the Maori people, the maintenance of such Maori characteristics and such features of Maori culture as present day circumstances will permit, the inculcation of pride in Maori history and traditions, the retention so far as possible of old-time ceremonial, the continuous attempt to interpret the Maori point of view to the *pakeha* [Europeans] in power. (1940, 176–177)

Maoritanga thus underpins a form of Maori nationalism that differs from 19th-century tribal and intertribal initiatives to reacquire Maori sovereignty in that it appeals exclusively to pan-tribal sentiments. In the 20th century, it dominated Maori discourses of nationalism until the 1980s.

Narrating the Nation

Understanding the meaning of *Maoritanga* is important for comprehending Maori nationalism in the 20th century. It should be realized that the very idea of the "Maori" as one people is of postcolonial origin. Before the arrival of European explorers and traders, the Maori had no name for themselves as a people, only a multiplicity of tribal names. Colonial interaction brought about the abstraction known as the Maori. Around 1800 the word *maaori* was first recorded as an adjective of *taangata*, meaning "usual," "ordinary," or "normal" people. Only after the 1850s did the word Maori become commonly used as a noun. From then on, Europeans were referred to as *Pakeha*, derived from the adjective *paakehaa*, meaning "foreign."

During the course of the 19th century, the concepts of Maori and *Pakeha* became gradually accepted, although as a political category Maori was not adopted until after the Young Maori Party had advocated pride in *Maoritanga*. For that reason, too, it is not surprising that the members of the Te Aute College Students' Association were referred to as the *Young* Maori Party. Benedict Anderson (1983, 109) has commented that in nationalist discourses concepts of "young" and "youth" do not necessarily refer to age but signify instead "dynamism, progress, self-sacrificing idealism and revolutionary will." In (post-)colonial circumstances, young and youth invariably refer to "the *first* generation in any significant numbers to have acquired a European education, marking them off linguistically and culturally from their parents' generation" (ibid., author's emphasis). In New

Zealand, too, the Young Maori Party consisted of individuals who without exception had been educated at a European school, which also explains why their campaigns for the improvement of Maori welfare were initially far from successful.

The impact of European education on the political objectives of the Young Maori Party was controversial, and their innovations for promoting a pan-tribal concept of *Maoritanga* raised suspicions among tribal leaders. Forty years later, a well-known Tuhoe leader, the late John Rangihau expressed this widespread feeling as follows:

> There is no such thing as Maoritanga because Maoritanga is an all-inclusive term which embraces all Maoris. And there are so many different aspects about every tribal person. Each tribe has its own history. And it's not a history that can be shared among others.... I have a faint suspicion that Maoritanga is a term coined by the Pakeha to bring the tribes together. Because if you cannot divide and rule, then for tribal people all you can do is unite them and rule. (1977, 174–175)

Thus, an influential tribal leader criticized the ideal of a pan-tribal nation as situated within a nation-state that aims at assimilating Maori nationalist thought. Indeed, the aspiration toward a pan-tribal Maori nation is inherently contradictory. However, the very contradiction in the pan-tribal conception of Maori nationalism also creates the possibility for divergent interpretations and representations of nationalist paradigms.

This also explains why tribal conceptions of nationalism emerged again in the 1980s, when once again Maori protests against the subordinated position of the indigenous population within the liberal-democratic nation-state of New Zealand became more vocal. At the same time, however, the reemergence of tribal organizations at the vanguard of Maori struggles to regain sovereignty was paralleled by a renaissance of "traditional" Maori culture and language, partly inspired by the campaigns of the Young Maori Party. Many educational programs were introduced to revitalize the Maori language, and currently the language is being taught again in many schools and can be studied at all New Zealand universities. This new interest has also led to a growing corpus of Maori literature and a revival of the traditional arts. The performing arts, in particular, have resurged in many areas of New Zealand society, and Maori ceremonial protocol often plays an important role in public events in the country. Indeed, the Maori people have recently become very proud again of their culture, which enhances their nationalist aspirations.

Mobilizing and Building the Nation

Whereas the 19th century in New Zealand might be characterized as the period during which the Maori were dispossessed of their land, the 20th century could be characterized as the era of urbanization. The proportion of Maori people living in cities and boroughs increased from 10 percent in the 1930s to more than

80 percent in the 1970s. Maori began moving to urban environments in search of employment during the Great Depression, but they only qualified for the lower-skilled jobs. Maori therefore became an urban proletariat, which was hit the hardest when New Zealand moved into a long-term recession in the early 1970s. For that reason, too, a protest movement emerged in the cities calling for the recognition of the Treaty of Waitangi. The government responded in 1975 with the Treaty of Waitangi Act, which established the Waitangi Tribunal. This act enabled Maori to submit claims on the grounds of being "prejudicially affected" by any policy or practice of the Crown that was "inconsistent with the principles of the Treaty," although "anything done or omitted before the commencement of [the] Act" was excluded from the tribunal's jurisdiction. In spite of this limitation, the act vindicated Maori faith in the treaty and encouraged them to reinforce their protests. In 1985 the jurisdiction of the Waitangi Tribunal was eventually back-dated from 1975 to 1840 when the treaty was signed. This amendment opened up an important avenue for Maori people to seek redress for past grievances.

Soon after the expansion of its jurisdiction, the Waitangi Tribunal received some 1,200 Maori claims, most of which were submitted by tribal organizations. Although it is possible for any Maori, tribal or nontribal, to submit a claim to the Waitangi Tribunal, most claims concern lands, forests, and fisheries, the ownership

Maori protestors are still demanding the recognition of the Treaty of Waitangi, which was signed between the British and the Maori in 1840. The treaty is crucial for Maori people since it protects their proprietary and civil rights, but it has been continuously violated by the New Zealand government. (Phil Walter/Getty Images)

of which is claimed exclusively by tribes. In consequence, tribes dominate the debate on redressing violations of the treaty. And since this issue has become more topical over the past 20 years, it may be argued that the pan-tribal protest movement that emerged in the cities in the 1960s and 1970s sparked the reemergence of tribes in contemporary New Zealand.

Most claims were triggered by the government's move to transfer lands held in Crown ownership to semiprivate state-owned enterprises in the mid-1980s. Several tribes argued that this action prejudiced their possibilities to resolve long-standing grievances about their dispossession. The New Zealand Maori Council therefore filed an injunction to stop such transfers. This resulted in a judgment by the Court of Appeal, which on June 29, 1987, declared that the transfer of assets to state-owned enterprises would be unlawful without considering the policy in light of the Treaty of Waitangi. It was the first time in New Zealand history that the legality of the treaty was recognized. This judgment made it possible for Maori tribes to seek redress of their long-standing grievances and thus to regain sovereignty, at least to some extent.

After years of negotiations between different Maori tribes and the New Zealand government, the settlement process was finally started in the mid-1990s and has made great progress since. In 1995 the first major compensation agreement was signed with the Waikato-Tainui tribes, the groups upholding the Maori monarchy since the crowning of Potatau in 1858. The deal included a formal apology from the Crown, acknowledging that it acted unjustly in dealing with the Kingites (supporters of the Maori monarchy) in the 1860s, and it provided for the return of 3 percent of the lands originally confiscated and a significant sum for compensation.

Since the mid-1990s, several other compensation agreements have also been signed, notably with the Ngai Tahu on the South Island. All settlements have so far been reached with tribes. The returned lands, forests, and other natural re-

Foreshore and Seabed Controversy

In recent history, Maoridom was most united in its opposition to legislation about the foreshore and the seabed. The saga began with a Court of Appeal ruling in June 2003 that enabled Maori to submit claims to the foreshore and seabed to the Maori Land Court. This decision raised the possibility that private titles might be issued, prompting fears that New Zealanders could be denied access to some beaches. Within a few days, the government announced its intention to remove the Maori Land Court's jurisdiction to investigate Maori customary title over such areas and to legislate Crown ownership of the foreshore and seabed. In December 2004, the government passed an act into law in accordance with this policy. Maori people were united in their stance against this act, and a historic protest march was held. A professor of Maori studies from Auckland even suggested that the controversy could lead to a civil war. The Maori minister Tariana Turia resigned from the government and set up a new political party, the Maori Party. The future will tell whether this party may prove successful in surmounting Maori tribal differences.

sources are used for tribal development programs that aim at restoring sovereignty in rural areas. The ultimate aim is to persuade urban Maori to return to their tribal homes. Notwithstanding the progress being made with redressing long-standing Maori grievances, the settlement process remains controversial since the government negotiates settlements only with tribal organizations, whereas 80 percent of the Maori population is currently living in urban environments in which tribal connections have lost a great deal of meaning.

The debate about the settlement process for tribes versus pan-tribal organizations in the cities reflects the differences in the meaning of Maori nationalism for different sections of the population. Maori tribes are currently seeking redress for their loss of sovereignty in the 19th century, and when they manage to negotiate a satisfactory compensation agreement with the government, their aspirations to achieve Maori nationalism may be partly fulfilled. Maori people in cities, however, have been shaping their pan-tribal identities since the beginning of the 20th century, and they continue their demand for participation in the negotiations over grievances on the history of Maori dispossession and the associated loss of sovereignty. Their struggle for a Maori nation within the state of New Zealand is reinforced by the cultural renaissance initiated by the Young Maori Party.

Selected Bibliography

Anderson, Benedict. 1983. *Imagined Communities: Reflections on the Origin and Spread of Nationalism.* London/New York: Verso.

Awatere, Donna. 1984. *Maori Sovereignty.* Auckland, New Zealand: Broadsheet Publications.

Cox, Lindsay. 1993. *Kotahitanga: The Search for Maaori Political Unity.* Auckland, New Zealand: Oxford University Press.

Fitzgerald, Thomas K. 1977. *Education and Identity: A Study of the New Zealand Maori Graduate.* Wellington, New Zealand: New Zealand Council for Educational Research.

Kawharu, I. H., ed. 1989. *Waitangi: Maaori and Paakehaa Perspectives of the Treaty of Waitangi.* Auckland, New Zealand: Oxford University Press.

King, Michael. 2003. *The Penguin History of New Zealand.* Auckland, New Zealand: Penguin.

Meijl, Toon van. 1993. "The Maori King Movement: Unity and Diversity in Past and Present." *Bijdragen tot de taal-, land- en volkenkunde* 149: 673–689.

Melbourne, Hineani, ed. 1995. *Maori Sovereignty: The Maori Perspective.* Auckland, New Zealand: Hodder Moa Beckett.

Ngata, Apirana. 1940. "Tribal Organization." In *The Maori People Today: A General Survey*, edited by I. L. G. Sutherland, 155–181. Wellington, New Zealand: Whitcombe & Tombs.

Orange, Claudia. 1987. *The Treaty of Waitangi.* Wellington, New Zealand: Allen & Unwin/Port Nicholson.

Rangihau, John. 1977. "Being Maori." In *"Te Ao Hurihuri," The World Moves On: Aspects of Maoritanga*, 2nd ed., edited by Michael King, 165–175. Auckland, New Zealand: Longman Paul.

Walker, Ranginui. 1990. *Ka Whaiwhai Tonu Matou: Struggle without End.* Auckland, New Zealand: Penguin.

Williams, John A. 1969. *Politics of the New Zealand Maori: Protest and Cooperation, 1891–1909.* Auckland, New Zealand: Auckland University Press.

Index

Note: Page numbers in **bold** indicate a main entry for that subject, and numbers in *italic* refer to the sidebar text on that page.

Aasen, Ivar, 226
Abacha, Sani, 1188
Abayomi, Kofo, 1180
Abbas, Ferhat, 1099
Abbas, Gulam, 1763
Abbas, Mahmoud, 1142
Abbas II (Egypt), 261
Abbas the Great, Shah, 1108, 1113
Abd-ul-Ilah, 1745
Abdallah, King (Transjordan), 728, 729
Abdelkader, Emir, 1098, *1099*, 1102
Abduh, Muhammad, 731
Abdülhamid II (Ottoman Empire), 764, 765
Abdullah, Farooq, 1767, 1768, 1770
Abdullah, King (Jordan), 1142
Abdullah, Sheikh Muhammad, 1761, *1761*, 1763,
    1764, 1765, 1766–1767
Abiola, Moshood, 1188
Aboriginal Tent Embassy, *1847*, 1851
Aborigines, Australian, 932. *See also*
    Pan-Aboriginalism
Abrams, Lynn, 53
Abyssinia, 736–737, 739
Aceh, 954, 1468, 1734
Achebe, Chinua, 913, 914, 917, 920, 921, 925
Acton, Lord, 687
Adams, Abigail, 50
Adenauer, Konrad, 947, 973–974, *1549*
Adivar, Halide Edib, 770
Afghanistan, **1683–1695**, 1684 (map)
    and education, 1388–1389
    Germany and terrorists in, 1554
    invasion of, 1497
    and music, 1440
    and new social movements, 1452
    and Pakistan, 1232–1233
    and the Soviet Union, 954
    and terrorism, 1488
    and women, 904, 1457
Aflaq, Michel, 731, 732, 733, 981, 1740
Africa
    and colonialism, 890
    education in, 39–40, 420–421, 424–425, 428, 431
    ethnic cleansing and genocide in, 435, 442
    independence/separatist movements in, 1461,
        1464, 1468–1469

literature/language in, 919–920, 925–927
and music, 1440
and religion, 108
and socialism, 980–981
supranational organizations and, 962, 965
    See also specific African nations
African Americans, 493–494
Afrikaner nationalism, 1144–1153
Afzelius, Arvid August, 73
Agathangelos, 1706
Aghulon, Maurice, 49
Agoncillo, Teodoro, 1245
Aguirre, José Antonio, 1515–1516
Ahmad, Kamal Mazhar, 1741
Ahmad Shah, 1686, 1691
Ahmadinejad, Mahmmoud, 1117
Ahmed, Imam, 739, 743
Aho, Juhani, 605
Aidoo, Ama Ata, 927
Aizawa Seishisai, 810–811, 813–814, *814*, 815
Akbar, 802
Akçura, Yusuf, 766, 770, *771*, 773
Akhmatova, Anna, 1074
Akhmetov, Renat, 1625
Aksakov, K. S., 692
al-Afghani, Jamal al-Din, 261
al-Alayili, Shaykh Abdallah, 732, 733
al-Azmah, Yusuf, *728*
al-Azmeh, Aziz, 725
al-Bakr, Ahmed Hasan, 756
al-Banna, Hassan, 984, 985
al-Bitar, Salah al-Din, 731, 981
al-Bustani, Butrus, 731
al-Husayni, Hajj Amin, 1135, 1136, 1138, 1139
al-Husayni, Musa Kazim, 1136
al-Husri, Sati, 730, 732–733, 751
al-Jawahiri, Mohammad Mahdi, 1740
al-Jazairi, Amir Abd al-Qadir, 727
al-Kailani, Rashid Ali, 753
al-Kawakibi, Abd al-Rahman, 727
al-Miqdadi, Darwish, 734
al-Nashshashibi, Raghib, 1136
Al Qaeda, 986–987, 1484, 1488, 1492
    and Pakistan, 1232
al-Qaysi, Nuri Ali Hammudi, 1741
Al-Sadat, Mohamed Anwar, 1488–1489

Ethnic cleansing, **435–442**, 522–523
    and Afghanistan, 1692
    and Alsace, 1507
    and Bosnia/Herzegovina, 1530, 1531, *1532*
    and Czechoslovakia, *595*, 596, 1020
    and Germany, 617, 622
    and Hungary, 645
    and Jews in Iraq, 756
    and Poland, 681
    and Turkey, 1648–1649
    in Ukraine, 722
    See also Conflict/violence; Genocide
Ethnic conflict. *See* Conflict/violence
Ethnicity, 931, 1354
    and Afghanistan, 1685, 1688–1689, 1693,
      1694–1695
    and Angola, 1660, *1664*
    and Argentina, 276, 277
    and Armenia, 1703, 1709
    and Austria, 543–544
    and Azerbaijan, 1716, 1718
    and the Baltic states, 558
    and Bosnia/Herzegovina, 1528–1530,
      1533–1535
    and Brazil, 1826–1827
    and Bulgaria, 580
    and Burma, 781
    and Canada, 1836
    and Catalonia, 1542–1543
    and Central America, 311, 314
    and China, 1193–1197, *1196*, 1199
    and Czechoslovakia, 590, 1017, 1020–1021
    and education, 35, 36, 39, 40, 1379
    and Eritrea, 1169
    and Ethiopia, 741, 742–743
    and Fiji, 1314
    and Germany, 1554, 1556
    and globalization, 1412–1413, 1415, 1416
    and Greece, 633
    and Greenland, 1570–1571
    and Hungary, 644
    and immigrants, 1424
    and Indonesia, 1723, 1728
    and Iran, 1118
    and Iraq, 1737, 1739, 1740, 1746
    and Italy, 672, 673
    and Japan, *1753*
    and Latvia, 1574–1575
    and Malaysia and Singapore, 1213–1215,
      1225
    and Mongolia, 1790–1791, 1797–1798,
      1798–1799
    and music, 1431–1432
    and nationalist movements, 10, 11, 27, 46,
      1460, 1464, 1465, 1468, 1469–1470
    and Nepal, 1808, 1809–1810
    and the Netherlands, 199
    and new social movements, 1450
    and New Zealand, 868
    and Nigeria, 967, 1178, 1185, 1186

    and Northern Ireland, 1063
    and the Ottoman Empire, 101–102
    and Pakistan, 1231–1232, 1236
    and Paraguay, 362
    and the Philippines, 1243–1244
    and Poland, 209, 212, 213, 214, 216
    in political philosophy, 88–90, 95, 461, 464
    and Québec, 1296–1297
    and religion, 103–105, 107–109
    and Romania, 1592–1594
    and Russia, 1079–1080, 1599–1601
    and Rwanda and Burundi, 1669–1670
    and Scotland, 236–237
    and South Africa, 1144, 1145
    and the Soviet Union, 1076
    and Taiwan, 1254, 1257–1258
    and Turkey, 1650
    and Ukraine, 712–713, 1621
    and the United States, 1309
    See also Minorities; Religion
Eto Shin'pei, 820
Eurasianism, 466
Europe
    borders after World War II, 581 (map), 591
      (map), 616 (map), 668 (map), 684 (map),
      1018 (map), 1550 (map), 1590 (map)
    borders from 1914 to 1938, 170 (map), 184
      (map), 540 (map), 556 (map), 579 (map),
      586 (map), 612 (map), 624 (map), 636
      (map), 656 (map), 666 (map), 680 (map),
      762 (map)
    borders in 1815, 139 (map), 148 (map), 182
      (map), 208 (map), 246 (map), 610 (map),
      664 (map)
    colonialism and, 420–421
    and cultural identity in, 445
    development of nationalism in, 26, 31
    education and, 33–36, 38–39, 422, 427
    ethnic cleansing and genocide in, 435, 437,
      441–442
    and gender/sexuality, 44, 908
    and immigration, 1418, 1421, 1424, 1425
    imperative and imaginary forms of
      nationalism in, 501–503
    and landscape art, 64
    and language, 472, 477
    and music, 73–75, 1432
    nationalism and class in, 4, 11
    nationalism and conflict in, 16, 23–26
    and new social movements, 1447
    perversions of nationalism in, 512–525
    revolutions of 1848 in, 24–25, 47, 52
    supranational bodies in, 948–949, 974
    systems of governance in, 419
    and terrorism, 1494, 1495, 1497
    and transnationalism, 1509–1510
    women's suffrage in, 453
    and xenophobia, 1412
    See also European institutions; *specific*
      European countries and organizations

About the Editors

Guntram H. Herb, Ph.D., is associate professor of geography at Middlebury College, Middlebury, Vermont. In addition to peer-reviewed articles and book chapters, his published works on nationalism include *Under the Map of Germany: Nationalism and Propaganda, 1918–1945* and the collection of essays co-edited with David H. Kaplan, *Nested Identities: Nationalism, Territory, and Scale.*

David H. Kaplan, Ph.D., is professor of geography at Kent State University in Ohio. He is an editor of the journal *National Identities*. His six books include *Boundaries and Place* (with Jouni Häkli) and *Nested Identities* (with Guntram Herb). He has also published over 30 peer-reviewed articles and chapters, many of them in the field of nationalism.